Australia and the World: A Festschrift for Neville Meaney

Edited by Joan Beaumont and Matthew Jordan

SYDNEY UNIVERSITY PRESS

Published 2013 by SYDNEY UNIVERSITY PRESS

© Joan Beaumont, Matthew Jordan, individual contributors 2013
© Sydney University Press 2013

Reproduction and Communication for other purposes
Except as permitted under the Act, no part of this edition may be reproduced, stored in a retrieval system, or communicated in any form or by any means without prior written permission. All requests for reproduction or communication should be made to Sydney University Press at the address below:

Sydney University Press
Fisher Library F03, University of Sydney NSW 2006 AUSTRALIA
Email: sup.info@sydney.edu.au

National Library of Australia Cataloguing-in-Publication entry
Title: Australia and the world: a festschrift for Neville Meaney edited by Joan Beaumont and Matthew Jordan
ISBN: 9781743320006 (paperback)
         9781743320150 (hardback)
Notes: Includes bibliographical references and index
Subjects: Meaney, N. K. (Neville Kingsley)
         Festschriften--Australia
         Historians--Australia
         Historiography--Australia
         International relations--Australia
Other Authors/Contributors:
         Beaumont, Joan, editor.
         Jordan, Matthew, editor.
Dewey Number: 907.2094

Cover design by Miguel Yamin.

Cover image 'Chart of the world on Mercators projection', pub. London. ca 1907, reproduced with permission from Mitchell Library, State Library of NSW – M4 100/1907/1.

Photograph of Neville Meaney by Rhonda Myers.

Contents

Acknowledgements	v
Foreword *Dennis Richardson AO*	vii
AUSTRALIA AND THE WORLD: NEVILLE MEANEY AND THE MAKING OF FOREIGN RELATIONS HISTORY IN AUSTRALIA	1
1. Not the Cinderella it Once Seemed: The Historiography of Australian Foreign Policy *Joan Beaumont*	3
2. Australia and Japan in Focus: From Image to Comparative History *Hugh Clarke*	15
3. Pondering Australia's World: Neville Meaney on the Role of Culture, Ideology and Geopolitics in American and Australian Foreign Policy History *Matthew Jordan*	25
RACE, NATIONALISM AND WHITE AUSTRALIA	55
4. The Chinese Immigration Crisis of 1888 and the Coming of White Australia *Matthew Jordan*	57
5. 'He No Doubt Felt Insulted': The White Australia Policy and Australia's Relations with India, 1944–1964 *Eric Meadows*	81
SENTIMENT AND SELF-INTEREST IN AUSTRALIAN PUBLIC AND INTELLECTUAL LIFE	99
6. A Military Mission for Greater Britain: Edward Hutton's 'A Co-operative System for Defence of the Empire' *Richard Lehane*	101
7. Robert Randolph Garran and the Creation of the Australian Commonwealth *Colin Milner*	121
8. A. C. V. Melbourne in Australian International Thought: Nationalism and Appeasement Between the World Wars *James Cotton*	145
THE BRITISH WORLD COMPARED	167
9. The Political Cultures of Australia and Britain: How Alike Were They? *Ross McKibbin*	169

10. The 'New Nationalism' in Australia, Canada and New Zealand: Civic Culture in the Wake of the British World 191
Stuart Ward

Dependent Ally? Australian–American Relations 215

11. Cold War 'Love Feast': The First US Presidential Visit to Australia, October 1966 217
James Curran

12. Too Much Memory: Writing the History of Australian–American Relations During the Howard Years 237
David McLean

The Making and Unmaking of American Nationalism 259

13. Becoming Wilsonian: Woodrow Wilson's Conversion to the American National Myth 261
David T. Rowlands

14. Recovering the Roots of Reinhold Niebuhr's Critique of American Nationalism 281
Michael G. Thompson

15. An Ideological Odyssey: Nixon, China and the Decline of American Nationalism 301
Tom Switzer

Select List of Publications by Neville Meaney 323

Contributors 327

Index 329

Acknowledgements

This festschrift consists of a collection of essays that celebrate the contribution of Neville Meaney to the study and promotion of foreign relations history in Australia. Taking their cue from the ideas and themes that have dominated the work of this important scholar, the essays that follow focus on several key issues, most notably nationalism and its peculiar manifestation in Australia as 'British race patriotism', the problems this created for Australia's political and strategic identity in the Asia-Pacific region, the role of culture and geopolitics in shaping the 'American national myth' and the impact that the decline of classical nationalism in the Western world in the 1960s and 1970s had on both countries. For their effort the editors wish to thank the various contributors.

The editors would also like to thank those who attended and presented papers at the inaugural forum of Historians of Australia's Foreign Relations on 10–11 November 2011. This forum was specifically convened to celebrate Neville Meaney's long and distinguished career and was made possible by financial assistance from the College of Arts and Social Sciences at the Australian National University, which was also generous in providing a venue and accommodation for contributors. Thanks also to the Department of Foreign Affairs and Trade for contributing to the cost of a formal conference dinner.

The publication of this festschrift, together with its partner volume, *Australia and the Wider World: Selected Essays of Neville Meaney*, edited by James Curran and Stuart Ward, was helped enormously by a subsidy from a committed patron of the Arts in John Feenie. John takes a keen interest in international affairs and brings voracious reading habits and a thirst for knowledge to his understanding of Australia's role in the world. His support has been critical to the completion of this project for which the editors are deeply grateful.

Finally, thanks to the staff of Sydney University Press, in particular Susan Murray-Smith, Agata Mrva-Montoya and Bronwyn O'Reilly for their production, design and editing of this fine volume.

Joan Beaumont and Matthew Jordan

Foreword

It gives me great pleasure to welcome the publication of *Australia and the World: A Festschrift for Neville Meaney*, which recognises the major contribution of Neville Meaney to the development and evolution of Australian and American foreign relations history in this country.

This book emerged from a two-day conference, 'Australia and the World: A Conference Celebrating the Contribution of Neville Meaney', hosted by Historians of Australia's Foreign Relations and held at the Australian National University from 10–11 November 2011.

I attended and chaired one of the sessions at the conference and on the night of 10 November enjoyed a dinner in Neville's honour, which I felt privileged to attend and where I was able to observe the profound effect that Neville's scholarship and qualities as a teacher have had on a variety of colleagues, former students, friends and admirers.

My association with Neville began over forty years ago, when I was studying at the University of Sydney on a country teacher's scholarship. It was Neville who supervised my honours studies for three years and who suggested that I apply for a position in the then Department of External Affairs. But he did the same thing for many others, so there is a whole group of former students now in government who owe him so much. Indeed, I recall being in the Department of Immigration and Multicultural Affairs in the mid-1990s when he gave me a ring to ask if I could help with a particular student who was from 'the wrong side of the street'. Neville's influence covers that timespan and more. Indeed, there will be people in government thirty years from now who owe as much to Neville Meaney as I do today.

I commend *Australia and the World* and its celebration of this great Australian scholar to you.

Dennis Richardson AO
Secretary, Department of Foreign Affairs and Trade
October 2012

I

Australia and the World: Neville Meaney and the Making of Foreign Relations History in Australia

1

Not the Cinderella it Once Seemed: The Historiography of Australian Foreign Policy

Joan Beaumont

In the past half century the academic discipline of history has been transformed into a remarkably broad church. Even before postmodernism and critical theory undermined the confidence of historians that they could aspire to writing an objective authoritative narrative, the primacy of empirical, archival research had been challenged in the 1960s by a growing interest in social and labour history. Since the less literate classes failed to leave an equivalent to the voluminous written records of elites and governments, historians of necessity turned to tapping oral history and data analysis. Subsequently feminist critiques, postmodernism, interdisciplinarity and, most recently, memory studies transformed not only empirical historical methodologies but the definition of what was worthy of study. Whereas in the 1970s a distinguished scholar could ask without embarrassment, 'Why study the poor and the obscure?', by the turn of the twenty-first century the traditional fields of political and economic history had been overtaken by a more eclectic field of subjects including race, grief, commemoration, rape, gender, masculinity, fear, domestic space and violence.

With this broadening of the discipline came fashions and, as any aspirant for a nationally competitive research grant knows, national priorities. The latter were driven by governments intent on applying the hard metrics of neo-liberal performance indicators to curiosity-driven research and by a functionalist search for the relevance of the past to the present.

In this changing environment the history of Australian foreign policy seemed something of a Cinderella. As the historical profession expanded with the growth of Australian universities from the late 1960s on, the number of authors in this field remained small, particularly relative to other areas of historical research. This was in some ways surprising. The cry for 'relevance' and 'national benefit' seemingly gave a salience to the study of Australia's relationships with the world and the region over the past two centuries. Even those who might caution against a simplistic application of the lessons of the past to the present could not deny the value of contemporary policymaking being informed by an understanding of historical precedents. Even more intriguing is the fact that, while tertiary students flocked in ever growing numbers to study political science and international relations, the history of foreign policy was marginalised within most universities.

We can only speculate why this is so. Perhaps the neglect of the history of Australian foreign policy reflects the pervasive 'present-ism' of much of twenty-first century public debate. Often, it seems that meaning can be found only within contemporary memory. Or if societies do turn to the past, as Australians did when they embraced anew the foundational narrative of the Anzac legend in the late twentieth century, the memory is not so much historical as a sentimentalised and mythologised version of events which again invests the present with meaning.

Perhaps too the historiography of Australia's foreign relations has been sidelined because, while much of the historical discipline has been energised by critical theory and interdisciplinary insights, its methodologies have remained generally traditional. Other genres within the discipline have staked (sometimes laboured) claims to being innovative and cutting edge, but the scholars of foreign policy and diplomacy have remained proudly—almost defiantly—wedded to empiricism and documentary evidence. Typically the flagship of the Historical Publications and Information Section of the Australian Department of Foreign Affairs and Trade (DFAT) is called *Documents on Australian Foreign Policy*. Hence the genre of foreign policy history has laid itself open to the charge of being theoretically unsophisticated and naively empiricist.

Finally—and probably most significantly—the history of Australia's foreign policy has lived in what might be called the shadow of the national record of foreign policymaking. In those countries where the history of diplomacy has a long and proud tradition, such as the United Kingdom and the United States, there has also been a history of great-power politics. In contrast, for much of the last two centuries the foreign and defence policies of Australia have been those of a small to middle power. Who, it might be asked, rejoices in recalling the experience of being 'small'? Moreover, Australian foreign policy for many decades was positioned within a paradigm of alliance with Great Britain and the United States, the countries whom Prime Minister Robert Menzies famously called Australia's 'great and powerful friends'. In fact, there was ample scope within these alliance relationships for Australians to feel a strong sense of distinctive national interests and national pride, notably in the performance of Australian troops during wartime. Moreover, this loyalty to Britain and the United States had a strong pragmatic rationale, as the vulnerability of Australia to attack when British imperial power in the Asia-Pacific region collapsed in 1942 seemed to demonstrate. But given that this pragmatism was anchored in values and discourses which are now anachronistic—White Australia, race patriotism and anti-communism—Australian foreign policymakers in the early- and mid-twentieth century were open to representation as dependent and, at worst, subservient to the interests of more powerful partners.

This was particularly the case in the aftermath of Australia's participation in the Vietnam War (1962–72). This foreign policy disaster, significantly, coincided with the expansion of Australian universities and the consequent growth of employment opportunities for historians. Hence there was a generation of academics who gained continuing tenure from the late 1960s on—and who have only just begun to retire in significant numbers—for whom Vietnam and conscription spawned a dominant narrative about Australian foreign policy. It ran something like this: Australians, always anxious about the tensions of being a European outpost in a threatening Asian environment, resorted to an uncritical reliance on British imperial power and ceded to London the control of foreign and defence policy. Even when other dominions pressed for greater autonomy in the inter-war years, and Britain proffered this through the Statute of Westminster (1931), Australians remained diffident about exercising a more independent international role. When the crisis of the Second World War occurred governments on both the right and left of politics had no option but to reassess their strategic and diplomatic options. In December 1941 Prime Minister John Curtin declared that Australia 'looks to America, free of any pangs as to our traditional links or kinship with the United Kingdom' and in the next eight years the Labor external affairs minister, Dr H. V. Evatt, engaged in an exhilarating international activism including a new multilateralism through the agency of the United Nations. But this 'golden age' was soon over. With the coming of the Cold War, the regional instability consequent upon decolonisation and the long period of conservative rule under Menzies, foreign policy reverted to the paradigm of dependence. Since Britain's global and regional power was progressively declining the default protector became the United States whose policies Australians slavishly followed. As one of the more strident radical nationalists wrote in 1988, Australian foreign policy became little more than 'bland subservience to the US' typified by 'fawning rhetoric at the White House [that] would have made even the worst "potato poet" of Boer War jingoism blush with embarrassment'.[1]

This was of course a simplistic interpretation, not universally endorsed. It ignored the degree to which alliance diplomacy was conceived by Australian politicians—from Alfred Deakin and W. M. (Billy) Hughes in the early twentieth century to Menzies and Harold Holt in the post-1945 era—to be a means of promoting rather than subordinating Australian interests. It also overlooked the conflicts about regional and global priorities which could be bitterly contested behind the public face of alliance harmony. Moreover, this narrative with its trope of dependence on allies did little to inform an understanding of the more sophisticated Australian foreign policy of the latter half of the twentieth century. This was not only a period in which Australia, with its own professional diplomatic elite, had the capacity to project its foreign policy globally but bilateral diplomacy gave ground to a more multi-faceted engagement with multilateral forums and regional institution-building.

Yet narratives spawned from personal experience die hard and there are few history or political science departments in Australian universities today where the history of Australian foreign policy is part of the core curriculum. As one participant in a graduate professional development program at DFAT commented in 2012, she had studied other nations' foreign policies at university, but not her own!

However, at the University of Sydney, Neville Meaney consistently swam against this tide, publishing deeply researched accounts of Australian foreign and defence policy history and imbuing successive cohorts of students with a passion for the subject which they carried into their own professional lives. This applies equally to the academic

---

[1] Stephen Alomes, *A Nation at Last? The Changing Character of Australian Nationalism 1880–1988* (Sydney: Angus & Robertson, 1988), 170–71. For examples of this interpretation, especially in terms of the US alliance, see L. G. Churchward, *Australia and America 1788–1972: An Alternative History* (Sydney: Alternative Publishing, 1979); J. A. Camilleri, *Australian–American Relations: The Web of Dependence* (Melbourne: Macmillan, 1980); Dennis Phillips, *Ambivalent Allies: Myth and Reality in the Australian–American Relationship* (Ringwood, Vic.: Penguin, 1988); Alison Broinowski, *Howard's War* (Melbourne: Scribe, 2003); Erik Paul, *Little America: Australia, the 51st State* (London: Pluto, 2006); and Broinowski, *Allied and Addicted* (Melbourne: Scribe, 2007). For critiques of this interpretation, see David McLean, 'Australia in the Cold War: A Historiographical Review', *International History Review*, XXIII (2), 2001, 299–321; and McLean, 'From British Colony to American Satellite? Australia and the USA During the Cold War', *Australian Journal of Politics & History* (hereafter *AJPH*), 52 (1), 2006, 64–79.

historians he taught—amongst them David McLean, Peter Bastian, Roger Bell, Stuart Ward, James Curran and Matthew Jordan—and to the group of foreign policy practitioners that emerged from the Meaney stable. The most notable of the latter include Matthew Neuhaus, high commissioner in Harare (2011–); Alice Cawte, who not only published a pioneering study of Australian nuclear policies[2] but is currently consul-general in Shanghai, China (2011–); John Dauth, former permanent representative to the United Nations (2001–06) and high commissioner to the United Kingdom (2008–12); and Dennis Richardson, ambassador to the United States (2005–10), secretary of DFAT (2010–12) and since October 2012 secretary of the Department of Defence. Recognition of Meaney's significant influence on both the history and practice of Australian foreign and defence policy is the raison d'être for this festschrift.

The Evolution of an Australian Foreign Policy Historiography[3]

As Meaney's record indicates, the lament about the state of Australian foreign policy historiography should not be overstated. While its profile within universities may be low, over the past four decades there has been ongoing scholarship and research of the highest quality. This is largely attributable to the fact that the relatively few academics in the field have engaged productively and systematically in a scholarly dialogue with two other key stakeholders: namely, those practising the diplomatic profession; and the Australian Institute of International Affairs (AIIA), a longstanding advocate of public debate about Australia's foreign relations.

The AIIA can be credited with being first into the field. In the late 1940s the institute, which had been established in the flurry of liberal internationalism after the First World War as a chapter of the Royal Institute of International Affairs (Chatham House), initiated two publications which continue to this day. The first was the journal *Australian Outlook* which sought to distance itself from the narrow focus of its predecessor, the *Austral-Asiatic Bulletin*, by assuming the more wideranging title. (It now sports the blander, if further internationalised, title the *Australian Journal of International Affairs*.) The second was the *Australia in World Affairs* series, which provides authoritative five-yearly reviews of Australian foreign policy in the context of regional politics, global developments and events of special contemporary importance.[4]

The first four volumes of *Australia in World Affairs*[5] were edited by two academics who also made their own major contributions to the field—Gordon Greenwood (University

---

[2] Cawte, *Atomic Australia, 1944–1990* (Sydney: University of New South Wales Press, 1992).

[3] In a historiographical survey such as that which follows it is impossible to list every author or scholarly contribution to the field. The focus has been on acknowledging historians, rather than political scientists, who have made a consistent and significant contribution to the field and to list some of their major works.

[4] See John D. Legge, *Australian Outlook: A History of the Australian Institute of International Affairs* (Sydney: Allen & Unwin with AIIA and ANU Department of International Relations, 1999), 89, 152.

[5] See ibid., 153–54; and Gordon Greenwood and Norman Harper, eds, *Australia in World Affairs*, the first four volumes of which covered the years 1950–70 (Melbourne: F. W. Cheshire for AIIA, 1957, 1963, 1968 and 1974).

of Queensland) and Norman Harper (University of Melbourne).[6] In later years their role was assumed by other academics, including W. J. Hudson,[7] Peter Boyce and J. R. Angel,[8] and James Cotton and John Ravenhill.[9] Like the *Australian Journal of International Affairs*, the *Australia in World Affairs* series had a largely contemporary focus, but it also often carried important historical research. With the passing of time the older volumes became historical resources in their own right capturing, as they did, the best of contemporary thinking by scholars and officials.

Practitioners of Australian foreign policy—ministers, career public servants and diplomats—also played a role in the AIIA and creating the literature of Australian foreign policy.[10] Most notable among the early memoirists were Percy Spender, whose tenure as minister for external affairs (1949–51), though short, was remarkable for the signing of the ANZUS Treaty and the initiation of the Colombo Plan; Walter Crocker, whose eighteen years as a diplomat included being Australian high commissioner to India twice (1952–55, 1958–62); and Howard Beale, Australian ambassador to the United States from 1958 to 1964.[11] Alan Watt, a career diplomat and secretary of the Department of External Affairs (1950–54), provided in 1967 the first survey of the history of Australian foreign policy, *The Evolution of Australian Foreign Policy 1938–1965* and, in 1972, his own memoir of diplomacy.[12]

From such accounts emerged a tradition of diplomatic memoirs and vignettes that, despite the inevitable subjectivity and partiality of this genre, continues to enrich the field. No scholar today can appreciate the amateurism of the early days of the Department

---

[6] For example, see Gordon Greenwood, ed., *Approaches to Asia: Australian Postwar Policies and Attitudes* (Sydney: McGraw-Hill Book Company, 1974); Greenwood and Charles Grimshaw, eds, *Documents on Australian International Affairs 1901–1918* (Melbourne: Nelson in association with AIIA and Royal Institute of International Relations, 1977); and Norman Harper, *A Great and Powerful Friend: A Study of Australian American Relations between 1900 and 1975* (St Lucia, Qld: University of Queensland Press, 1987).

[7] W. J. Hudson, ed., *Australia in World Affairs, 1971–75* (Sydney: George Allen & Unwin for AIIA, 1980).

[8] P. J. Boyce and J. R. Angel, eds, *Independence and Alliance: Australia in World Affairs, 1976–80* (Sydney: George Allen and Unwin for AIIA, 1983); and Boyce and Angel, eds, *Diplomacy in the Marketplace: Australia in World Affairs, 1981–90* (Melbourne: Longman Cheshire for AIIA, 1992).

[9] Cotton and Ravenhill have edited the last four instalments of *Australia in World Affairs*, which together cover the years 1991–2010 (Melbourne: Oxford University Press, 1997, 2001, 2007 and 2012).

[10] Directors of the AIIA have included Sir Alan Watt (1963–69), Sir Laurence McIntyre (1976–79), Ralph Harry (1979–81), James Ingram (1992–93) and Ross Cottrill (1998–2004). Garry Woodard was national president (1991–93), a position which is currently held by former diplomat John McCarthy.

[11] Percy Spender, *Exercises in Diplomacy: The ANZUS Treaty and the Colombo Plan* (Sydney: Sydney University Press, 1969); W. R. Crocker, *Australian Ambassador: International Relations at First Hand* (Melbourne: Melbourne University Press, 1971); Howard Beale, *This Inch in Time: Memoirs of Politics and Diplomacy* (Melbourne: Melbourne University Press, 1977).

[12] Alan Watt, *The Evolution of Australian Foreign Policy 1938–1965* (London: Cambridge University Press, 1967); and Watt, *Australian Diplomat: Memoirs of Sir Alan Watt* (Sydney: Angus & Robertson with AIIA, 1972).

of External Affairs without reading Paul Hasluck's entertaining and incisive *Diplomatic Witness*—intriguingly the only account that this giant of Australian public life published of the portfolio that was his most controversial.[13] Nor can they understand the practice of Australian diplomacy in the 1950s and beyond without consulting the recollections of diplomats captured by the National Library of Australia and the *Australia in Asia* series of the Centre for the Study of Australia–Asia Relations (CSAAR) at Griffith University (the latter series itself edited by a retired diplomat, Hugh Dunn).[14]

With the 1960s and 1970s academic historians began to enter the field in growing numbers. Among them was not only the young Meaney, whose major contribution to the discipline through teaching and research is analysed in chapter 3 by Matthew Jordan,[15] but also T. B. Millar and J. D. B. Miller[16] at the Australian National University, Eric Andrews at the University of Newcastle and W. J. Hudson at the University of New South Wales. These might claim to be the academic 'fathers' of professional Australian foreign and defence policy history (they were, as it happened, all male). Millar's and Andrews' overview histories of Australian foreign policy[17] remained, remarkably, the only successors to Watt's monograph until David Lee published, in 2006, a major study that incorporated much of the recent archives-based scholarship.[18] Andrews' work on inter-war diplomacy,

---

[13] Paul Hasluck, *Diplomatic Witness: Australian Foreign Affairs, 1941–1947* (Melbourne: Melbourne University Press, 1980). For further discussion of Hasluck's silence on his time as external affairs minister, despite having published extensively on all other periods of his life, see Joan Beaumont and Garry Woodard, 'Paul Hasluck as Minister for External Affairs: Towards a Reappraisal', *Australian Journal of International Affairs*, 2 (1), 1998, 63–75.

[14] The CSAAR papers include Francis Stuart, *Towards Coming of Age: A Foreign Service Odyssey* (1989); R. W. L. Austin, *The Narrow Road to a Far Country: Intimations of Things Japanese* (1991); John Rowland, *Two Transitions: Indo-China 1952–1955, Malaysia 1969–1972* (1992); Ralph Harry, *The North was Always Near* (1994); Richard Gate, *From Coup to Coup: Diplomatic Experiences in Five Asian Countries* (1996); David Anderson, *Indo-Chinese Days* (1996); and Pierre Hutton, *After the Heroic Age: And Before Australia's Discovery of Southeast Asia* (1997). A list of official and ministerial memoirs can be found in Joan Beaumont, Christopher Waters, David Lowe, with Gary Woodard, *Ministers, Mandarins and Diplomats: Australian Foreign Policy Making, 1941–1969* (Melbourne: Melbourne University Press, 2003), 213–14.

[15] It is nevertheless worth noting several of Meaney's most important publications: *A History of Australian Defence and Foreign Policy, 1901–23*, vol. 1, *The Search for Security in the Pacific, 1901–14* (Sydney: Sydney University Press, 1976); 'Australia and the World', in *Under New Heavens: Cultural Transmission and the Making of Australia*, ed. Meaney (Port Melbourne: Heinemann, 1989), 379–450; *Towards a New Vision: Australia and Japan Across Time* (Sydney: University of New South Wales Press, 2007); and *A History of Australian Defence and Foreign Policy, 1914–23*, vol. 2, *Australia and World Crisis, 1901–23* (Sydney: Sydney University Press, 2009).

[16] See, for example, J. D. B. Miller, *The EEC and Australia* (Melbourne: Nelson, 1976); and Miller, ed., *Australians & British: Social and Political Connections* (Sydney: Methuen, 1987).

[17] T. B. Millar, *Australia in Peace and War: External Relations 1788–1977* (Canberra: Australian National University Press, 1987); E. M. Andrews, *A History of Australian Foreign Policy: From Dependence to Independence* (Melbourne: Longman Cheshire, 1979).

[18] David Lee, *Australia and the World in the Twentieth Century: International Relations since Federation* (Melbourne: Circa, 2006).

appeasement and relations with China also dominated the field until relatively recently when a new generation of scholars revisited these topics.[19]

Bill Hudson's many books, meanwhile, were exemplars of meticulous research and writing elegance.[20] From each of his studies—including Australia and the colonial question in the League of Nations, Billy Hughes' strident and insensitive 'diplomacy' at the chaotic Paris Peace Conference of 1919 and Stanley Bruce's leadership in the League of Nations during the 1930s—a far more nuanced image of Australian diplomacy emerged. Much of it refuted the stereotypical image of Australians as passive recipients of foreign policy directives from London and Washington. Yet ironically Hudson's later dissection of Australia's reluctance to embrace constitutional change in imperial relations in the interwar years and his brilliant demolition of Menzies' 'blind loyalty' to Britain during the Suez Crisis of 1956 also had the effect of affirming the narrative of dependence.[21] That this was due to a persistence of the Anglo-Australian cultural identification at least on the part of Menzies, who dominated foreign policymaking as did many other Australian prime ministers, was affirmed in Hudson's fine biography of Richard Casey, one of Australia's earliest career diplomats and minister for external affairs between 1951–60.[22]

Hudson left academic life in 1976 to join the Department of Foreign Affairs' Historical Documents Section. Created by cabinet decision in 1970, the mission of the section, initially under historian R. G. Neale, was to publish a series of documents on Australian foreign policy that would be:

> a national project; the documents chosen must reveal what Australian foreign policy was as a whole and how it came to be decided upon. There must be no risk of the series being condemned as a mere justification of government policy or as a partial coverage only.[23]

---

[19] E. M. Andrews, *Isolationism and Appeasement in Australia: Reactions to the European Crises, 1935–1939* (Canberra: Australian National University Press, 1970); Andrews, *Australia and China: The Ambiguous Relationship* (Melbourne: Melbourne University Press, 1985); and Andrews, *The Writing on the Wall: The British Commonwealth and Aggression in the East 1931–1935* (Sydney: Allen & Unwin, 1987). For later scholarship in these fields, see Lachlan Strahan, *Australia's China: Changing Perceptions from the 1930s to the 1990s* (Melbourne: Cambridge University Press, 1996); Carl Bridge and Bernard Attard, eds, *Between Empire and Nation: Australia's External Relations from Federation to the Second World War* (Melbourne: Australian Scholarly Publishing, 2000); Christopher Waters, *Australia and Appeasement: Imperial Foreign Policy and the Origins of World War II* (London: I. B. Tauris, 2012).

[20] See Hudson, *Australia and the Colonial Question at the United Nations* (Sydney: Sydney University Press, 1970); Hudson, *Billy Hughes in Paris: The Birth of Australian Diplomacy* (Melbourne: Nelson with AIIA, 1978); Hudson, *Australia and the League of Nations* (Sydney: Sydney University Press with AIIA, 1980).

[21] Hudson and M. P. Sharp, *Australian Independence: Colony to Reluctant Kingdom* (Melbourne: Melbourne University Press, 1988); Hudson, *Blind Loyalty: Australia and the Suez Crisis* (Melbourne: Melbourne University Press, 1989).

[22] Hudson, *Casey* (Melbourne: Oxford University Press, 1986). See also R. G. Casey, *Australian Foreign Minister: The Diaries of R. G. Casey, 1951–60*, ed. T. B. Millar (London: Collins, 1972).

[23] See cabinet submission 350, 'Publication of Documents on Australian Foreign Policy',

Under the guidance of an editorial advisory board consisting mostly of academics and experts in the field,[24] the section set about producing a comprehensive documentary record of Australian foreign policy covering the years 1937–49 and then chronicling the post-1950 period in a thematic series.[25] Over the years DFAT's Historical Publications and Information Section (as it is now called) became something of a 'nursery' for future historians as employment opportunities in universities froze. Among those who published their own research while working on the *Documents on Australian Foreign Policy* series have been P. G. (Peter) Edwards, Wendy Way, David Lee[26], David Dutton[27] and Matthew Jordan.[28]

Of these, Edwards has (thus far) made the most diverse and monumental contribution, ranging from his seminal work on the making of foreign policy in the first half of the twentieth century[29] to his magisterial official histories of Australian diplomacy during the South-East Asian conflicts of the 1950s and 1960s[30] and his fine biography of perhaps the

---

November 1971, NAA: A5908, 350.

[24] Members of the Board have included: Sir Keith Hancock, J. D. B. Miller, Gordon Greenwood, Norman Harper, Robert O'Neill, Sir Keith Waller, P. J. Boyce, Joan Beaumont, Peter Edwards, Ian Hancock, David Lowe and Kim Jones.

[25] The first series, published between 1975 and 2001, spanned sixteen chronological volumes and two specialist volumes, namely, W. J. Hudson and Jane North, eds, *My Dear P. M.: R. G. Casey's Letters to S. M. Bruce, 1924–1929* (Canberra: Australian Government Publishing Service, 1980) and Hudson and Wendy Way, eds, *Letters from a 'Secret Service Agent': F. L. McDougall to S. M. Bruce, 1924–1929* (Canberra: Australian Government Publishing Service, 1986). The thematic series began with a volume on *The Australia–Japan Agreement on Commerce, 1957*, ed. Wendy Way (Canberra: Australian Government Publishing Service, 1997). Other volumes in this series include Way, ed., *Australia and the Indonesian Incorporation of Portuguese Timor, 1974–1976* (Melbourne: Melbourne University Press, 2000); Stuart Doran and David Lee, eds, *Australia and Recognition of the People's Republic of China, 1949–1972* (Canberra: DFAT, 2002); Moreen Dee, ed., *Australia and the Formation of Malaysia* (Canberra: DFAT, 2005); and S. R. Ashton, Carl Bridge and Stuart Ward, eds, *Australia and the United Kingdom, 1960–1975* (Canberra: DFAT, 2010).

[26] David Lee, *Search for Security: The Political Economy of Australia's Postwar Foreign and Defence Policy* (Sydney: Allen & Unwin and ANU Research School of Pacific and Asian Studies, 1995); Lee and Christopher Waters, eds, *Evatt to Evans: The Labor Tradition in Australian Foreign Policy* (Sydney: Allen & Unwin and ANU Research School of Pacific and Asian Studies, 1997); Lee, *Stanley Melbourne Bruce: Australian Internationalist* (London: Continuum, 2010).

[27] David Dutton, *One of Us? A Century of Australian Citizenship* (Sydney: University of New South Wales Press, 2002).

[28] Matthew Jordan, 'Rewriting Australia's Racist Past: How Historians (Mis)Interpret the White Australia Policy', *History Compass*, 3 (1), 2005, 1–32; Jordan, 'The Reappraisal of the "White Australia" Policy Against the Background of a Changing Asia, 1945–67', *AJPH*, 52 (2), 2006, 224–43; Jordan, 'Decolonisation' and 'Arms Control and Disarmament', both in *Australia and the United Nations*, eds James Cotton and David Lee (Sydney: Longueville Media, 2012), 105–46, 265–309 (respectively).

[29] Peter Edwards, *Prime Ministers and Diplomats: The Making of Australian Foreign Policy, 1901–1949* (Melbourne: Oxford University Press with AIIA, 1983).

[30] Edwards with Gregory Pemberton, *Crises and Commitments: The Politics and Diplomacy of Australia's Involvement in Southeast Asian Conflicts, 1948–65* (Sydney: Allen & Unwin with

most accomplished 'mandarin' of the foreign and defence policymaking bureaucracy, Sir Arthur Tange (external affairs secretary, 1954–65; defence secretary, 1970–75).[31]

Notwithstanding the adverse environment in the academy, historical scholarship on Australian foreign policy continued in the last quarter of the twentieth century and is now thriving, with the three-legged tripod of DFAT, the academy and the AIIA continuing to support its development. Not only does this partnership continue to produce the *Australia in World Affairs* series, the *Australian Journal of International Affairs* and other publications, but DFAT's Historical Publications and Information Section has reached out to the academy in recent years to produce a rich array of original monographs. Notable among these have been the two-volume history of Australia's engagement with Asia published on the centenary of federation in 2001.[32] Meanwhile younger scholars—some but not all protégés of Meaney—who completed doctoral studies in the 1980s and 1990s have joined the ranks of academics, even though their passion for foreign-policy history has sometimes had to be more of a research interest than a core teaching area.

While Meaney, Hudson, Andrews and (to a lesser extent) Edwards largely established the corpus of scholarship on the history of Australian foreign policy in the first half of the twentieth century, it is this new generation of historians who have often focused on the post-war period. Following the release of archival documents under the thirty-year rule, they are creating a rich literature on Australian responses to the transformation of international and regional order after 1945: in particular, the challenges posed by decolonisation, the Cold War and the decline of British imperial power in the Asia-Pacific; the persistence, despite this transformed world, of the Australian sense of Britishness; and the efforts to come to terms with a new identity in the post-imperial world.[33] Considerable attention has also

---

Australian War Memorial, 1992); Edwards, *A Nation at War: Australian Politics, Society and Diplomacy during the Vietnam War, 1965–1975* (Sydney: Allen & Unwin with Australian War Memorial, 1997).

[31] Edwards, *Arthur Tange: Last of the Mandarins* (Sydney: Allen & Unwin, 2006).

[32] David Goldsworthy, ed., *Facing North: A Century of Australian Engagement with Asia*, vol. 1, *1901–1970s* (Melbourne: Melbourne University Press, 2001); and Goldsworthy and Peter Edwards, eds, *Facing North: A Century of Australian Engagement with Asia*, vol. 2, *1970s to 2000* (Melbourne: Melbourne University Press, 2003). Other examples include Don Kenyon and David Lee, *The Struggle for Trade Liberalisation in Agriculture: Australia and the Cairns Group in the Uruguay Round* (Canberra: DFAT, 2006); Boris Schedvin, *Emissaries of Trade: A History of the Australian Trade Commissioner Service* (Canberra: Austrade and DFAT, 2008); Cotton and Lee, eds, *Australia and the United Nations*.

[33] Christopher Waters, *The Empire Fractures: Anglo-Australian Conflict in the 1940s* (Melbourne: Australian Scholarly Publishing, 1995); David Lowe, *Menzies and the 'Great World Struggle': Australia's Cold War, 1948–1954* (Sydney: University of New South Wales Press, 1999); Frank Bongiorno, 'Commonwealthmen and Republicans: Dr. H. V. Evatt, the Monarchy and India', *AJPH*, 46 (1), 2000, 33–50; Stuart Ward, *Australia and the British Embrace: The Demise of the Imperial Ideal* (Melbourne: Melbourne University Press, 2001); David Goldsworthy, *Losing the Blanket: Australia and the End of Britain's Empire* (Melbourne: Melbourne University Press, 2002); James Curran, *The Power of Speech: Australian Prime Ministers Defining the National Image* (Melbourne: Melbourne University Press, 2004); Curran and Ward, *The Unknown Nation: Australia After Empire* (Melbourne: Melbourne University Press, 2010).

been paid in the last two decades to the evolution of Australia's relationship with its most important post-war ally, the United States[34]—although Australian diplomacy during the Second World War, when that relationship began to move to centre stage, remains relatively unexplored.[35] Concurrently there has been a growing body of research on changing attitudes to and engagement with the Asia-Pacific region, especially in terms of bilateral relations,[36] trade[37] and cultural exchange;[38] biographies of ministers and key officials;[39] and studies of the bureaucratic and gendered politics within which they worked.[40]

---

[34] Glen St J. Barclay, *Friends in High Places: Australian Diplomatic Relations since 1945* (Melbourne: Oxford University Press, 1985); Gregory Pemberton, *All the Way: Australia's Road to Vietnam* (Sydney: Allen & Unwin, 1987); David McLean, 'Anzus Origins: A Reassessment', *Australian Historical Studies*, 24 (94), 1990, 64–82; Carl Bridge, ed., *Munich to Vietnam: Australia's Relations with Britain and the United States since the 1930s* (Melbourne: Melbourne University Press, 1991); Phillip and Roger Bell, *Implicated: The United States in Australia* (Melbourne: Oxford University Press, 1993); W. David McIntyre, *Background to the ANZUS Pact: Policy-Making, Strategy and Diplomacy, 1945–55* (London: Macmillan, 1995); Russell Parkin and David Lee, *Great White Fleet to Coral Sea: Naval Strategy and the Development of Australia–United States Relations, 1900–1945* (Canberra: DFAT, 2008).

[35] Important exceptions are Roger J. Bell, *Unequal Allies: Australian–American Relations and the Pacific War* (Melbourne: Melbourne University Press, 1977) and Meaney, *Primary Risks and Primary Responsibilities in the Pacific: The Problem of Japan and the Changing Role of Australia in the British Commonwealth, 1945–1952* (London: Suntory Centre, LSE, 2000). See also David Day, *Reluctant Nation: Australia and the Allied Defeat of Japan, 1942–45* (Melbourne: Oxford University Press, 1992); and Day, *The Politics of War* (Sydney: Harper Collins, 2003).

[36] See generally Edwards and Goldsworthy, *Facing North*, vol. 2 and David Lowe, ed., *Australia and the End of Empires: The Impact of Decolonisation in Australia's Near North, 1945–65* (Geelong, Vic.: Deakin University Press, 1996). More specifically, see Margaret George, *Australia and the Indonesian Revolution* (Melbourne: Melbourne University Press, 1980); Meg Gurry, *India: Australia's Neglected Neighbour? 1947–1996* (Griffith University: Centre for the Study of Australia–Asia Relations, 1996); and Alan Rix, *The Australia–Japan Political Alignment: 1952 to the Present* (New York: Routledge, 1999).

[37] Rix, *Coming to Terms: The Politics of Australia's Trade with Japan, 1945–1957* (Sydney: Allen & Unwin, 1986); Sandra Tweedie, *Trading Partners: Australia and Asia, 1790–1993* (Sydney: University of New South Wales Press, 1994); and Ann Capling, *All the Way with the USA: Australia, the US and Free Trade* (Sydney: University of New South Wales Press, 2005).

[38] Alison Broinowski, *The Yellow Lady: Australian Impressions of Asia* (Melbourne: Oxford University Press, 1992); David Walker, *Anxious Nation: Australia and the Rise of Asia, 1850–1939* (St Lucia, Qld: University of Queensland Press, 1999); Daniel Oakman, *Facing Asia: A History of the Colombo Plan* (Canberra: Pandanus Books, 2004).

[39] Carl Bridge, Frank Bongiorno and David Lee, eds, *The High Commissioners: Australia's Representatives in the United Kingdom, 1910–2010* (Canberra: DFAT, 2010); Allan Fewster, *Trusty and Well Beloved: A Life of Keith Officer, Australia's First Diplomat* (Melbourne: Miegunyah Press, 2009); David Lowe, *Australian Between Empires: The Life of Percy Spender* (London: Pickering & Chatto, 2010). An earlier example in this genre was Warren G. Osmond, *Frederic Eggleston: An Intellectual in Australian Politics* (Sydney: Allen & Unwin, 1986).

[40] My 2003 book with David Lowe, Chris Waters and Garry Woodard has brought Edwards' *Prime Ministers and Diplomats* up to 1969. A final volume in the sequence is needed. For the changing role of women in DFAT, see Moreen Dee and Felicity Volk, eds, *Women with a Mission: Personal*

Given that this research is largely the work of historians who tend to eschew the theory so beloved of their international relations colleagues, this burgeoning literature has not spawned distinctive schools or even approaches. Somewhat oddly there has been little passionate debate, at least comparable to that which was triggered in Britain by A. J. P. Taylor's *The Origins of the Second World War* (1961) or in Germany by the 1980s *Historikerstreit* about the singularity of the Holocaust and its place in German national history. Does this reflect, one is tempted to ask, the lack of urgency that the limited influence and agency of small- to middle-power status brings?

Yet what the new depth and sophistication of Australian foreign policy history has confirmed is that any binary opposition between dependence and independence—if it were ever useful—is now completely anachronistic. However much the US alliance remains a keystone of Australian foreign and defence policy, and however uncritical the attitude to that alliance may sometimes be, Australia's foreign policy is now characterised as much by its engagement with multilateral organisations and a plethora of global and regional forums as by bilateral relationships.

Then and Now

Debate, however, is the lifeblood of historical research and in recognition of this the editors of this volume and some of its contributors took steps in 2011 to revive a network of scholars which three decades earlier had been created to foster discussion and research into the history of Australian foreign and defence policy. The Historians of Australian Foreign and Defence Policy (HAFDP), as the association was called, was again an initiative of Meaney who convened the inaugural meeting in Sydney in the early 1970s. It soon boasted a national membership which at its height included academics,[41] officials[42] and former politicians.[43] Its chapter in Canberra was particularly active, thanks to its executive being based there and its having easy access to the expertise of the Australian National University, the Australian Defence Force Academy and the (then) Department of Foreign Affairs.[44] The association's activities included occasional conferences, workshops piggybacking on other professional meetings and the publication of an annual newsletter detailing research in progress, publications and planned activities.[45]

Perspectives (Canberra: DFAT, 2007). For decisionmaking processes, especially in the 1960s, see Garry Woodard, *Asian Alternatives* (Melbourne: Melbourne Universty Press, 2004).

[41] Among them Fred Alexander, Desmond Ball, Brian Beddie, Geoffrey Bolton, Carl Bridge, Frank Cain, F. K. Crowley, Peter Dennis, Kevin Fewster, Jeffrey Grey, David Horner, L. F. Fitzhardinge, David Goldsworthy, John McCarthy, Neville Meaney, John McCarthy, T. B. Millar, J. D. B. Miller, R. J. O'Neill, A. C. Palfreeman, John Robertson, Roger Thompson and Hugh Smith.

[42] Former officials included Tom Critchley, W. D. Forsyth and Sir Keith Waller.

[43] Former ministers were Howard Beale, Paul Hasluck and Percy Spender.

[44] There were presentations in Canberra from David Horner, L. F. Fitzhardinge, T. B. Millar, Alan Watt and Alan Renouf, secretary of the Department of Foreign Affairs (1974–77).

[45] Copies of the newsletter are held in the National Library of Australia. Editors included Joan Beaumont (then at Deakin University, Victoria), John McCarthy and Jeffrey Grey (ADFA) and Peter Edwards.

Though never grand, the association served a valuable networking purpose in the age before social media and digital communications. However, after more than a decade of active years, other priorities took precedence. These included, in the case of one of its early distinguished members, John R. Poynter, senior university management. With academic workloads also becoming generally more onerous and the space for voluntary work contracting, HAFDP meetings became infrequent and eventually stopped.

The revived Historians of Australian Foreign Relations network was launched in mid-2011 complete, as is appropriate in the digital age, with a website.[46] Its first activity was a conference in honour of Neville Meaney, at the Australian National University in November 2011, which resulted in this volume. All peer-reviewed chapters are contributed by those who had the privilege of being students or colleagues of this influential scholar and teacher. Not all of them are academics but this dialogue between scholars and practitioners, as we have shown, is part of an established tradition and one which Neville Meaney himself has done much to encourage and nurture.

---

[46] Historians of Australia's Foreign Relations, available at www.australiaforeignrelations.org.au/.

2

Australia and Japan in Focus: From Image to Comparative History

Hugh Clarke

I am delighted that I am able to contribute this impressionistic piece to Neville Meaney's festschrift volume. It is a particular honour for me, a specialist in Japanese language and literature, to join the group of Neville Meaney's students and associates, all trained in Australian history and Australian international relations, to celebrate his lifelong contribution to our understanding of Australia's place in the world. I am indebted to Neville for alerting me to the importance of Australia–Japan relations and for introducing me to the concept of comparative history. Thanks to his influence I was able to spend a period of time in 2005 in Kyoto, researching aspects of Australia–Japan relations at the International Research Center for Japanese Studies in Kyoto and to take up a post-retirement position as a visiting professor at Waseda University in Tokyo, teaching, of all things, postcolonial studies. In this endeavour, I made ample use of Neville Meaney's research on the Australia–Japan relationship and the principles of comparative history he espouses so elegantly. I found it a little disconcerting that most of my Japanese students were unaware of the fact that Australians had fought against Japanese in the Pacific War. I had some trouble convincing them that this was indeed so, until I showed them photographs of the Japanese bombing of Darwin, the midget submarine attack on Sydney harbour, and the Cowra breakout.[1] I was also able to demonstrate that European imperialism in Asia and the Pacific was indirectly responsible for the introduction of the White Australia policy on the one hand and the rise of Japanese ultranationalism on the other. But that is putting the cart before the horse somewhat. Let us go back to the beginning.

In the mid-1990s Australia–Japan relations were going through a dull patch. After the euphoria of the boom years, the bubble had burst and Japan was deep in the economic woes of what was later to be called Japan's Lost Decade. That is, before it blew out to become the two Lost Decades. The number of Japanese tourists had dropped alarmingly and Japanese banks had stopped funding extravagant property development projects in Australia. Both parties were beginning to take one another for granted. Something was needed to celebrate and revitalise the Australia–Japan relationship.

Towards a Commemorative History

The centenary of the founding of the Japanese Consulate in Sydney in 1897 afforded an opportune occasion for a celebration and the incumbent consul general lost no time in

---

[1] Neville Meaney, *Towards a New Vision: Australia and Japan Across Time* (Sydney: University of New South Wales Press, 2007), 131–33, 135–38 and 147 (respectively).

calling upon Neville Meaney to chair a committee to come up with ideas. I was lucky enough to be invited to join the committee. We suggested that an appropriate project might be an exhibition of photographs illustrating the history of Australian–Japanese relations. It was also agreed that the celebrations should be extended to include the fortieth anniversary of the 1957 Australia–Japan Agreement on Commerce and the twentieth anniversary of the Basic Treaty of Friendship and Co-operation of 1976, under the banner of 'Australia–Japan Anniversaries, 1996–1998'. The earlier date, 1996, also coincided with the centenary of the establishment of a Japanese Consulate in Townsville.

It is a great credit to the staff of the Japanese consul general in Sydney, the Japanese Ministry of Foreign Affairs and the Japanese government as a whole that they decided to choose an historian and not an advertising company to orchestrate the celebration of one hundred years of the Japanese diplomatic presence in Australia. As the photographs to be considered for inclusion in the exhibition started coming in, it became very clear to the committee that much of the Australia–Japan relationship was not a pretty picture at all. This must have come as a shock and disappointment to some of the members of the committee, particularly the Japanese members, but with Neville Meaney at the helm we were not about to cook the books for the sake of decorum. On the whole, the images—not only photographs in the strictest sense, but documents, cartoons and illustrations—were chosen for their historical significance, photographic quality and general interest, in that order. There was considerable discussion on the committee whether some of the rawer images of the war years should or should not be included, but, at least to my knowledge, there was no suggestion of censorship by the Japanese members of the committee. There may have been some pressure put on our chairman behind the scenes, but if there was, we shall have to wait for the publication of Neville Meaney's memoirs to find out.

There is an element of truth in the old adage that one picture is worth a thousand words. On the other hand, apart from those images that speak for themselves as works of art, a picture is of limited use until it is given a context. This soon became clear to all of us involved with the exhibition. The contextualisation of the photographic record took the form of Neville Meaney's book, the first comprehensive illustrated history of Australia's relationship with Japan, *Towards a New Vision: Australia and Japan Through 100 Years*, published in 1999.[2] In 2006 the exhibition of photographs was updated as part of the celebrations commemorating thirty years since the signing of the Australia–Japan Basic Treaty of Friendship and Co-operation, and an expanded, hardcover edition of the book, *Towards a New Vision: Australia and Japan Across Time*, appeared in 2007.[3]

Visions Old and New

Meaney put a great deal of thought into the choice of a title. 'Towards a New Vision', the title chosen for the exhibition and the two books that stemmed from the initial collection

---

[2] In his preface to the first edition, Meaney said it was significant that the first illustrated history of Australia's relationship with another country should be with an Asian country, in particular, with Japan. See Meaney, *Towards a New Vision: Australia and Japan Through 100 Years* (Sydney: Kangaroo Press, 1999), 8.

[3] Unless otherwise stated, all subsequent citations of *Towards a New Vision* refer to the 2007 edition.

of photographs, can be taken in a variety of ways. As Meaney pointed out in his preface to the first edition of *Towards a New Vision*, the book may be seen firstly to speak to a new perspective on the past, a new picture of the history of the relationship; secondly, to refer to Australia and Japan's shared views, as they have emerged in recent times, about the future of the Asia Pacific region; and thirdly to point to the contemporary redefining of the Australian–Japanese relationship, a redefinition which has the potential to break down the barriers between East and West and provide a new model for cross-cultural understanding.[4]

The story of Australia–Japan relations opens with the swashbuckling exploits of Bourn Russell, Captain of the whaling ship *Lady Rowena* out of Sydney who landed at Hamanaka Bay in Hokkaido in 1831. His journal, preserved in the Mitchell Library in Sydney, records how he and his men opened fire on a group of Ainu and a few Japanese soldiers, before driving them off, robbing their huts and burning down their village. Russell had managed to capture a Japanese who, in flight, had fallen from his horse and broken his leg. Russell later released his captive with orders to carry a letter that Russell had written to the emperor of Japan, calling upon him to open his country to foreign ships and trade. This episode had been described in a book in Japanese by Masako Endō, *Nazo no ikokusen*, published in 1981, and Noreen Jones has given us a fuller account of Bourn Russell's whaling voyage to Japan in her *North to Matsumae: Australian Whalers to Japan*, published in 2008.[5] Both Endō and Jones include another early example of an Australian–Japanese encounter that is not included in *Towards a New Vision*. In 1850 the whaling ship *Eamont* out of Hobart, en route to the rich whaling grounds in the Sea of Okhotsk, north of Hokkaido, was caught in a thick fog and blown onto a reef off the village of Akkeshi, not twenty kilometres from the spot where the *Lady Rowena* had come to grief two decades earlier. Fortunately, as the men of the Eamont were soon to discover, the Shogunate's laws governing the treatment of shipwrecked foreigners had eased considerably since the time of the *Lady Rowena* incident.[6]

The captain, William Lovitt, and the crew of thirty-one men were apprehended by the Japanese garrison posted in the village of Akkeshi. One member of the crew, the twenty-four year old cooper, James Higgins, was drowned when the boat in which the prisoners from the *Eamont* were being escorted to the Japanese authorities in Matsumae was wrecked in a storm. From Matsumae they were transported to Nagasaki where they were tried, acquitted and held in custody at the Dutch station on Dejima until they could be embarked on the Dutch ship *Delft* bound for Batavia. From there Captain Lovitt and two of his ship's officers returned to Australia. The other members of the crew are thought to have joined other ships in Batavia. As the ship's log appears to have been lost, the story of the wreck of the *Eamont* has been pieced together from Japanese sources—entries in the archives of the Kokutaiji temple in Akkeshi and the record of interrogation of the prisoners by the Nagasaki magistrate—together with Captain Lovitt's account which appeared in the

---

[4] Meaney, *Australia and Japan Through 100 Years*, 8.

[5] Endō Masako, *Nazo no ikokusen: Nichigō kōryū no rūtsu o motomete* (Tokyo: Sanshūsha, 1985); and Noreen Jones, *North to Matsumae: Australian Whalers to Japan* (Perth: University of Western Australia Press, 2008), 72–74.

[6] Meaney notes that the draconian expulsion order had been modified in 1842, probably because of foreign pressure, which possibly included Russell's letter. Meaney, *Towards a New Vision*, 74.

Hobart Town Courier on 12 March 1851, shortly after his return. In 1982 a sister city agreement was signed between the city of Clarence across the Derwent River from Hobart and the city of Akkeshi in Hokkaido. The mayor of Akkeshi travelled the 12 000 kilometres to Clarence for the occasion. Coincidentally, both Akkeshi and Clarence are fishing and farming communities situated on the forty-third parallel. The creation of the sister-city relationship between Clarence and Akkeshi effectively commemorated the first Australian to die on Japanese soil, and the kindness and compassion of the people of Akkeshi who cared for the shipwrecked sailors of the *Eamont*. Higgins' grave can still be seen in the old Dutch cemetery in Nagasaki.[7]

Bringing a new vision to the history of Australia–Japan relations, Meaney imaginatively employed the frame of comparative history. He likened, for example, the Australian colonies' push for local autonomy in the 1850s to Japanese reformers, liberals and intellectuals' moves to overthrow the military dictatorship of the Tokugawa shoguns in the 1860s. With his characteristic choice of an apposite metaphor Meaney described how in the struggle for independence of the Australian colonies, the free and freed settlers 'rebelled against the autocratic rule of the military governors, the colonial shogunate'.[8]

In addition to his own substantial research and impressive list of publications on Japan's place in Australia's foreign relations, Meaney has made an enormous contribution in bringing to a general readership a wealth of research on Australia–Japan relations, much of which has lain dormant, unpublished and unread in the archives of the National Library in Canberra. Here I refer in particular to the pioneering work of David Sissons, formerly an historian in the Research School of Pacific Studies at the Australian National University, whose untimely death in 2006 deprived the field of Australia–Japan relations of its most avid researcher. His collection of papers, in sixty boxes comprising 8.4 metres of shelf space, remains a treasure trove for future research.[9]

Of the many appealing and inspiring characters who have contributed to the relationship between Australia and Japan, I have a special respect for E. L. Piesse, director of military intelligence, 1916–19, and head of the Pacific branch of the Prime Minister's Department, 1919–23. Before the photographic display, I had come to know of Piesse indirectly through my interest in James Murdoch, the founding appointment in oriental studies at the University of Sydney. It was, however, only after reading Neville Meaney's book *Fears and Phobias: E. L. Piesse and the Problem of Japan 1909–1939* that I came to understand Piesse's new vision for Australia's relations with Japan, which, had it been fulfilled, might have changed the course of history.[10] Piesse, who initially shared the Australian government's fears of Japanese imperialist ambitions in the Pacific, realised that claims that Japanese expansion posed a danger to Australia were based on scant evidence. He set out to learn as

---

[7] For a full account of the Eamont shipwreck incident see Noreen Jones, *North to Matsumae*, 167–79. The Japanese account is in Endō Masako, *Nazo no ikokusen*, 97–206.

[8] Meaney, *Towards a New Vision*, 11.

[9] Papers of DCS Sissons, National Library of Australia: MS 3092, listed at nla.gov.au/nla.ms-ms3092.

[10] Meaney, *Fears and Phobias: E. L. Piesse and the Problem of Japan 1909–39* (Canberra: National Library of Australia, 1996).

much as he could about Japan and even began to study Japanese. In this task he was fortunate to have the close support of James Murdoch, who had returned to Australia in 1917 after a long career teaching in Japan, to take up a lectureship in Japanese at the University of Sydney. In the following year Murdoch was appointed to the University's inaugural Chair of Oriental Studies. Under Murdoch's tutelage, Piesse progressed in his study of the Japanese language to the point where he was able to read not only Japanese newspapers,[11] but also works on diplomatic history and international relations.[12] His research had led him to the conclusion that in the early years after the First World War, Japan, having seen the error of German aggression in Europe, had renounced any ambitions it might have had to expand southward and that it harboured no desires to occupy Australia. On the other hand, he was convinced that Australia's racist immigration policy, epitomised by Prime Minister Billy Hughes' vehement opposition to Japanese demands at the Paris Peace Conference, was an impediment to friendly relations between the two countries. In the peace settlement, to borrow Meaney's apt description, 'Hughes urged terms that would confine and constrain Australia's enemy ally'. Hughes' refusal to accept a Japanese proposal for a racial equality clause in the Covenant of the League of Nations was seen in Japan as an affront to national pride and had the undesired effect of driving public opinion into the militarist camp. Piesse's calls for a relaxation of the policy restricting immigration on the grounds of race so angered Billy Hughes that he thereafter refused to listen to Piesse's advice.[13] Piesse may, however, have played a part in the conversion of George Pearce, who had been a Japanophobe since at least 1905.[14] In 1922 Piesse had accompanied Pearce, when, as minister of defence, he led the Australian delegation to the Washington Conference on security in the Asia-Pacific. In a speech to parliament on his return from Washington, Pearce reported that he had been impressed by the genuine attitude of cooperation shown by the Japanese delegation and declared that he no longer felt that Japan posed any threat to Australia.[15]

In his preface to the second edition of *Towards a New Vision*, Meaney mentioned that he had brought the text up to date with an additional chapter, 'A New Time: A New World' and expanded his comparative introduction to incorporate more recent research and 'more reflection'. As I was not involved with the 2006 exhibition of photographs, I was curious to see what effect this greater reflection may have had on the important introductory chapter. A cursory comparison of the two volumes revealed that the second edition had more and longer footnotes. Well, not exactly footnotes, because in the attractive hard-covered second edition, the notes in the historical overview chapter are on the side, along the inside margin of each page. The citation of works published after 1997 provided evidence of an enormous

---

[11] Ibid., 16.

[12] Ibid., 21.

[13] Ibid., 30.

[14] For an example of Pearce's earlier Japanophobe views, see Meaney, *A History of Australian Defence and Foreign Policy, 1901–23*, vol. 1, *The Search for Security in the Pacific, 1901–14* (Sydney: Sydney University Press, 1976), 127.

[15] See *Commonwealth Parliamentary Debates*, 1922 Session, vol. XCIX, 27 July 1922, reproduced in *Australia and the World: A Documentary History from the 1870s to the 1970s*, ed. Meaney (Melbourne: Longman Cheshire, 1985), 326–29.

amount of additional reading that had gone into the production of the second edition. In several places Meaney, with characteristic modesty and a desire to encourage his students, had replaced a reference to one of his own works with a more recent publication, or an unpublished PhD thesis by one of his students. It was also clear from the footnotes that there had been an upsurge in publishing on Japanese and Australian foreign relations and several books and articles on the Australia–Japan relationship itself.

The major additions to the introductory overview chapter, however, revolved around the idea of comparative history, where broad geopolitical, economic and cultural factors were invoked to explain the rise of similar phenomena in Australia and Japan. Take monarchy, for example. In his discussion of race and nationalism in Australia and Japan, Meaney wrote, 'the monarch was reinvented as the symbol of British history and heritage and, like the Japanese emperor, became the personal embodiment of the race'.[16] Further, he took up the theme of war and national cohesion, recounting the sense of national pride in the exploits of those who had fought and died on the battlefield aroused in Japan after the Russo-Japanese War and in Australia after the First World War. Meaney then proceeded to show how this pride was harnessed to the task of nation building, taking concrete shape in the form of the Yasukuni Shrine in Tokyo and its equivalent, the Australian War Memorial, in Canberra.[17]

Meaney carried the comparison further in the discussion of both nations' desire for economic security in the Pacific with the observation that 'British empire autarky was in some ways the Australian equivalent of Japan's Greater East Asia Co-prosperity Sphere'—the main difference between the two being that the latter did not enjoy the consent of all the parties involved.[18]

Perhaps Meaney's most perceptive use of the comparative approach was in his identification of the symptoms of similar identity crises in Japan and Australia. He pointed out that recent debates in Japan over the need to become 'a normal country'—by rewriting the Japanese constitution, revising high-school history textbooks and honouring the war dead at Yasukuni shrine—are revisionist measures aimed at quelling the malaise over identity that emerged in Japan after the US defeat in Vietnam, the fall of the Soviet bloc and the end of the Cold War. Similarly in Australia the so-called history wars—instigated by John Howard's 'court historian' Geoffrey Blainey, over what the conservative camp saw as a damaging 'black armband' view of Australian history—together with a watering down of the rhetoric of multiculturalism and the call for a return to pride in the country's British heritage, can be seen as a reaction to the crisis of identity in Australia, a crisis kindled by feelings of guilt over the past treatment of Indigenous Australians, the destruction of the natural environment, and shame over the White Australia policy.

In the new chapter, 'A New Time: A New World', covering the years since the publication of the first edition of *Towards a New Vision*, Meaney focused on exchanges in popular culture and the arts, using as an example the impact that Japanese manga and anime have had on Australian youth. The 2005 Sydney Animania Festival, for example, attracted

---

[16] Meaney, *Towards a New Vision*, 21.

[17] Ibid., 32.

[18] Ibid., 34.

almost 8000 fans, or *otaku*. In the other direction, Australian surf culture and the outdoor lifestyle have exerted an enormous appeal on young Japanese. This trend was depicted in the film *Bondi Tsunami* produced by the Australian filmmakers Anthony Lucas-Smith and Rachael Lucas. Meaney also dealt with Ian Thorpe's contribution to the Australia–Japan relationship from the time he received a rock-star welcome from fans at the 2002 world swimming championship in Fukuoka, to his appointment as Australia's honorary ambassador for tourism in Japan at the 2005 Aichi World Expo.[19] Meaney also showed how close cooperation between Australia and Japan in the areas of regional security—the prime example being that of the leading role both countries played in the restoration of Cambodia—has begun to take the form of a genuine partnership, stemming from both countries' common vision for the future of the Asia-Pacific region.[20] Though Japan's position as Australia's major trading partner may have been usurped by China, Japan's anxiety over Chinese territorial claims and uncertainty regarding the intentions of North Korea has encouraged Japan to strengthen its security ties with Australia and other democratic states in Asia and the Pacific.

In documenting the full gamut of Australia–Japan relations both in the photographic exhibition commissioned by the Japanese government and in the books that followed, Neville Meaney has made a major contribution towards strengthening the bonds between Australia and Japan. His scrupulously fair and balanced accounts make it abundantly clear that for over half of the one hundred and fifty years of contact between Australians and Japanese, the relationship was anything but a happy one. It is really only the past three or four decades that have seen the blossoming of a multi-faceted web of relationships from individuals and grassroots organisations to the highest levels of business and government. Gradually these links, originally forged through economic necessity or self-interest, are developing into genuine friendships based on mutual trust and understanding. In many areas it is appropriate now to speak of an Australia–Japan partnership. We should remember that the relationship is not one of equals, but one between an economic superpower and a middling democracy. Understanding how relationships change over time reminds us how easily things can turn sour and how important the virtues of tact and diplomacy are. The lesson from comparative history is that the destinies of countries are strongly influenced by the geopolitical, economic and security concerns of the regions in which they are situated. Australia and Japan have responded to these factors, sometimes in similar ways, sometimes quite differently. Anybody with an interest in Australia–Japan relations would benefit from reading Neville Meaney's *Towards a New Vision: Australia and Japan Across Time*. I am sure the Japanese translation, which I believe is now in preparation, will contribute greatly to Japanese understanding of Australia and reaffirm the importance of the relationship for both Japan and Australia.

Postscript

I recently returned to Sydney after five years living in Tokyo. During my stay in Japan I was frequently struck by the lack of reporting on Australian affairs in the Japanese vernacular

---

[19] Ibid., 204–07.

[20] Ibid., 232–33.

press. The exception to this was the negative reporting of the Australian government's opposition to Japanese whaling. In 2009, after the release of the documentary film *The Cove*, which depicted the annual dolphin cull at Taiji in Wakayama prefecture, anti-whaling groups persuaded the Broome City Council in Western Australia to sever its sister city ties with Taiji. I understand that it was only after some frantic diplomatic activity behind the scenes that the sister city relationship was eventually reinstated. This was a desirable outcome, given that Taiji had been associated with the pearling industry in Broome since the mid-1880s, and the vast majority of the 800 graves in Broome's Japanese cemetery hold the remains of young men from Wakayama.

Apart from the whaling issue and the occasional article about bushfires, floods or cyclones, news from Australia seems to be given very low priority in Japanese media. I found this puzzling and somewhat disappointing, given the importance of the Australia–Japan relationship and the relatively high profile Japanese affairs enjoy in the Australian media. It gave me the clear impression that Japan is more important to Australia than Australia is to Japan. As Meaney points out, the Australia–Japan relationship is so diverse and far-reaching that it is very difficult to see the big picture, with the result that its great importance remains hidden from the public view.[21] I was surprised, therefore, to read in the online edition of the *Japan Times* of 14 January 2013 an important article about Australia and Japan that drew only very cursory attention in the Australian press.[22]

The article in question was a Kyodo news service report on a press conference following the meeting, held in Sydney on 13 January, of the Japanese foreign minister in the newly appointed Abe cabinet, Fumio Kishida, and his Australian counterpart, Bob Carr. The gist of the meeting was that there should be greater security cooperation between Australia and Japan, in concert with their common ally the United States, in response to China's 'growing maritime assertiveness'. The foreign ministers also agreed that the United Nations Security Council needed to take a stronger stand against North Korea. Increased cooperation, to be implemented as early as 2013, will take the form of an Acquisition and Cross Servicing Agreement between Australia and Japan, under which the Japanese defence forces and the Australian military will be able to share fuel, food and other military supplies during joint security operations. Other topics discussed were China's territorial disputes with Japan and several South-East Asian nations, and proposed bilateral and multi-lateral free-trade agreements. Testing the strength of the Australia–Japan friendship, Carr also called on Kishida to use his influence to prevent any modification of a 1993 Japanese government statement acknowledging the Imperial Japanese Army's involvement in sex slavery. Carr was obviously aware of the rumour that Shirzō Abe's new Liberal Democratic Party government is planning to revisit the issue of *ianfu* (comfort women) and possibly recant the government apology issued in 1993. Carr's intervention seems to fly in the face of Australia's long-standing policy of not commenting on Japanese domestic politics. Actions like this, together with the Australian government's legal challenge to Japanese whaling in the southern oceans currently before the International Court of Justice in the Hague,

---

[21] Ibid., xii.

[22] 'Japan, Australia Agree to Boost Security Cooperation with U.S.', *The Japan Times*, 14 January 2013, at www.japantimes.co.jp/text/nn20130114a5.html.

appear on the surface to pose a major threat to the Australia–Japan relationship. On the other hand, perhaps the relationship documented so meticulously by Neville Meaney has become close enough that it can admit frank discussions between friends. There is a common expression in Japanese, *kenka o suru hodo naka ga ii*: 'they are so close they can argue'. Only time will tell if this holds true.

3

Pondering Australia's World: Neville Meaney on the Role of Culture, Ideology and Geopolitics in American and Australian Foreign Policy History

Matthew Jordan

Neville Meaney pioneered the teaching and study of both Australian and American foreign relations history in Australia and established himself as one of the country's leaders in the field. In 1956, after completing undergraduate studies at the University of Adelaide, Meaney was awarded a scholarship to undertake graduate work at Duke University in North Carolina. He was the first Australian historian to be awarded an American PhD, in 1959. His doctoral dissertation examined US attitudes to the British Empire after the First World War and the effect of these views on America's decision not to join the League of Nations.[1]

In taking this focus, Meaney combined the two main interests that would dominate his teaching and research over his long and distinguished career; namely, the history of US foreign relations, and the external relations of Australia and the countries of the British Empire and Commonwealth. This chapter will look closely at this record, and especially Meaney's large and remarkably unified corpus of published material, providing an introduction to the main aspects of his thinking and the scope and originality of his contribution to the discipline in Australia. It shows that Meaney, in emphasising the role not merely of domestic politics, strategic considerations and diplomacy but also of culture and ideology in shaping the American and Australian experiences in the world, has done much to overcome what he himself referred to as the enduring perception of foreign policy history as 'a poor relation to the more flourishing areas of social and political history'. His work has reinforced the critical importance of understanding the behaviour of nations and national leaders at a time when 'international politics remains as anarchic, violent and unpredictable as at any time in the modern era'.[2]

The American National Myth and US Relations with the World

In 1963, after a short stint at the University of New South Wales, Meaney was appointed to the University of Sydney's history department to teach US history, a novel field at that time in a curriculum that was heavily focused on European and especially British imperial history.[3] As Meaney himself later commented, 'For Sydney, as for British universities

---

[1] Neville Meaney, 'The American Attitude Towards the British Empire from 1919 to 1922: A Study in the Diplomatic Relations of the English-Speaking Nations', PhD thesis, Duke University, 1959.

[2] See Meaney, 'Preface', in *Australia and the World: A Documentary History from the 1870s to the 1970s*, ed. Meaney (Melbourne: Longman Cheshire, 1985), vii–viii.

[3] See Roslyn Pesman Cooper, 'The Years of Plenty: The Department in the 1950s and 1960s',

generally, America did not exist as a historical subject after the War of Independence and the colonies' separation from the British Empire.' What US history was taught was picked up by lecturers with little expertise in the area and the teaching reflected this: 'It was said for example that "Arkansas" was commonly pronounced "Ar-kansass" in lectures.'[4] Following his appointment, Meaney sought to overcome this deficiency by developing and teaching not only a general course on the history of the United States but also specialist courses such as 'American Political and Social Thought' and, later, 'Themes in American Civilisation'. Drawing on the areas of interest that had provided the focus for his PhD, Meaney from 1964 also began teaching a course on British–US relations from 1760 to 1900.[5] By the late 1960s, this had developed into the first dedicated history course on US foreign relations taught in an Australian university—'The American Foreign Policy Tradition', which became 'America and the World' in the 1980s.[6]

During his time in the United States, Meaney had been fascinated with the intensity of American nationalism, a phenomenon that seemed totally foreign to the laconic, self-consciously unemotional attitude of his fellow Australians towards the idea of nationhood. Unlike Americans, including scholars and intellectuals, who, as creatures of their culture, uncritically accepted the self-justifying myths of American nationalism, Meaney concluded that US 'exceptionalism', like all nationalisms, was historically contingent and artificial. For him, this provided the key to understanding American perceptions of itself and the US approach to the world. Beginning in 1979, he offered a fourth-year honours course on 'The Making of the American National Myth', which focused on 'the origins and nature of American nationalism' and how it 'responded to changing social structures, political experience, economic expectations, continental opportunities and foreign relations and the values which these changes engendered'.[7] In seeking to understand the role of nationalism in shaping the US approach to the world, this course was the first of its kind offered in an Australian university.

The same preoccupation with the broader cultural and ideological context in which US foreign policy was formulated and implemented has informed Meaney's research and publications in the field. Taking these ideas as his starting point, Meaney in the bicentenary year of the American Revolution examined this key event with the objective of shedding light on the nature, source and accuracy of the American projection of its place and role in world affairs. For all Americans—including its historians, who Meaney showed were representative of views held in the general community—the Revolution was the cornerstone of a superior international morality, an 'exceptional' approach to foreign affairs defined not by the power politics of the Old World but by a redemptive mission to spread the 'American' principles of liberty, freedom and democracy to the wider world:

---

in *History at Sydney, 1891–1991: Centenary Reflections*, eds Barbara Caine, et al. (University of Sydney: Department of History, 1992), 55–58, 61–62; and W. F. Connell, et al., *Australia's First: A History of the University of Sydney*, vol. 2, *1940–1990* (Sydney: University of Sydney in Association with Hale and Iremonger, 1995), 160, 163.

[4] See Meaney, 'American History', in *History at Sydney*, eds Caine, et al., 178–79.

[5] University of Sydney, *Faculty of Arts Handbook, 1964* (hereafter *Arts Handbook*), 88–90.

[6] See *Arts Handbook, 1971*, 122; *Arts Handbook, 1983*, 263; and *Arts Handbook, 1989*, 186.

[7] *Arts Handbook, 1979*, 254.

> America was 'the land of the free' ... [American] mythmakers maintained that in the American Revolution the Founding Fathers had successfully defended the liberty of the New World against the despotism of the Old and that they had laid down the blueprint for moral and material progress which was to be a guide to America's providential future and an inspiration for people everywhere.[8]

Meaney showed, however, that the events of 1776 had not always been viewed this way, and certainly not by the main protagonists of the Revolution. Indeed, the colonists did not actively seek independence; they were imbued with a deep affection for the Crown, constitution and culture of the British nation. At the same time, they had developed a strong sense of political community which recognised that the American colonies possessed distinct interests from Britain and would not agree to any proposal in which those interests were subordinated to the whims and prejudices of an imperial parliament.[9]

It was only when the British sought to exert closer control over colonial affairs that the Americans, reluctantly, sought separation. And even then, there was no spontaneous outpouring of patriotic support for the cause of liberty and freedom. George Washington, the commander-in-chief of the Continental Army, constantly complained of the American people's lack of interest in the war; sectional groups formed alliances with the enemy not because they were Loyalists but because they wanted the British to secure their land titles; and in order to win French support the Americans guaranteed all French possessions in the country, thus committing themselves to a permanent 'entangling alliance' with the kind of Old World regime from which they claimed to be distancing themselves.[10] The American Revolution, though marking the birth of the nation in 'a practical political sense', as Meaney concluded, was not 'regarded seriously by the Revolutionaries as an epoch-making ideological and moral event which would transform their lives and the life of the world'. The nation that emerged from the Revolution 'was not held together by a concept of mission'.[11]

For Meaney, the American sense of a redemptive mission only emerged in the 1820s and 1830s, when American society began to experience enormous changes in its composition, nature and economic conditions—a phenomenon that was reflected most dramatically in the whirlwind expansion westwards during the first half of the nineteenth century. Like other nations undergoing these modernising processes, the US responded by cultivating a national myth which, in accordance with the artificial and historically contingent nature of all nationalisms, grew out of its local experiences and circumstances and which was therefore peculiar to itself. While this was common to the phenomenon elsewhere, the US experience of nationalism was indeed exceptional in one important respect. Unlike classical European nationalisms, which dealt with the trauma of modernisation by taking emotional comfort in the idea of themselves as peoples of common descent or race speaking a distinct language and sharing primeval customs and cultures, America, by its very definition as a New World society which had self-consciously disclaimed its ancestral roots in Europe, could not fall

---

[8] Meaney, 'Introduction: The American Revolution in Search of a Future', in *Studies on the American Revolution*, ed. Meaney (South Melbourne: Macmillan Company of Australia, 1976), 32.

[9] Ibid., 20–23.

[10] Ibid., 25–27.

[11] Ibid., 31.

back on a ready-made national myth. Under these circumstances, the American myth-makers looked to the only source of legitimacy available—the Revolution—and from it cultivated a sense of themselves as the avatars of liberty with a heavenly mandate to spread the 'universal' principles of democracy and freedom to the world. Thus:

> The Declaration of Independence, rescued from obscurity, became, along with the Constitution, holy writ; the Founding Fathers, the legendary guardians of the ark of the covenant; and the struggle against the British became the starting point of a new era in the history of human liberty.[12]

According to this formulation, which defined American nationalism not in cultural or (more commonly) racial terms but in civic egalitarian terms, American values were universal values. In this sense, as Meaney put it, 'America has been imagined not culturally but ideologically, not exclusively but inclusively—or better still in an exclusively inclusive way'.[13]

This myth, though present from the 1820s in the work of myth-makers like George Bancroft, remained on the fringes as the nation focused its energies on expanding and developing its ever-growing territory, rebuilding after the trauma of the Civil War and maintaining its hegemony in the Western Hemisphere against the intrusion of the wicked Old World nations. At the end of the nineteenth century, as the US grew in power and self-confidence, it came to fully embrace this image of itself as the saviour of mankind. The Monroe Doctrine, originally conceived, applied and justified in fundamentally pragmatic terms, was increasingly given a moral character which reflected the American sense of worldwide mission. During the Venezuelan Crisis of 1895, Secretary of State Richard Olney claimed not only that the US as the pre-eminent power in the Western Hemisphere had a right to intervene in the dispute but also that its involvement was morally justified because American democracy was 'for the healing of all nations' and the US therefore had 'a vital interest in the cause of self-government'.[14] There was still a latent hostility to Europe and the power politics it was thought to embody, so the US remained aloof from the Old World, continuing to 'spread' its ideals to neighbouring Latin American countries—even when these countries were reluctant recipients. During the late nineteenth and early twentieth centuries, the US government intervened in the region frequently and aggressively, claiming that the US was acting out of a desire to help these countries by making them more like America:

> This amplification and idealisation of the Monroe Doctrine conflated the well-being of the United States' neighbours with their subordination to its national ego and glorification of its national honour.[15]

President Woodrow Wilson more than any other previous American leader was the most articulate and persistent advocate of this 'moral nationalism', and the role of Wilson in

---

[12] Ibid., 7.

[13] Meaney, 'American Nationalism, the Monroe Doctrine and Woodrow Wilson's New World Order', in *Relacoes Internacionais Dos Paises Americanos: Vertentes da Historia*, eds Amado Luiz Cervo and Wolfgang Dopcke (Brazil: University of Brasilia, 1994), 231–32.

[14] Cited in ibid., 234.

[15] Ibid., 235.

shaping and applying the myth both regionally and internationally has featured prominently in Meaney's writings on American foreign policy. Like previous US presidents, Wilson, in making this myth the first principle of American foreign policy, initially focused his energies on Latin America. Indeed, he intervened in the affairs of neighbouring countries more than any other president, attempting unsuccessfully to impose US attitudes and political norms on Mexico between 1913–17 while simultaneously attaining a large degree of hegemony over countries such as Cuba, Panama, Haiti, the Dominican Republic and Nicaragua—all the time claiming to be acting as 'the nearest friend' of these countries. Meaney, in contrast to other scholars who have either taken this language at face value or dismissed it as subterfuge, argued that for Wilson there was no contradiction in such a position, since America would be acting out of the purest motives and indeed was only imparting 'universal' principles which these countries would choose of their own volition if free to do so: 'American intervention and influence was merely the benevolence of a near neighbour, a good neighbour—but self-evidently a neighbour who knew what was best for the neighbourhood.'[16] When, therefore, Wilson found himself in a position to influence the peace negotiations following the First World War, he brought these simplistic presumptions of 'egoistic altruism and unilateral universalism' with him. In accordance with the national myth, Wilson now clothed his original motives for entering the war—'the honour and self-respect of the nation'—in the language of a redemptive mission to 'make the world safe for democracy'. The war thus became a moral crusade 'to vindicate the principles of peace and justice' and 'to fight for the things we have always carried nearest our hearts—for democracy, … for the rights and liberties of small nations', for the very 'principles that gave her [America] birth'.[17]

However, as the Americans discovered in Latin America in the late nineteenth century—and as they would discover after both world wars in the twentieth century—the international community was unmoved by the claims American nationalism made for itself. Following the First World War, Wilson pushed hard for a League of Nations which, by redefining the Monroe Doctrine as a world doctrine, would guarantee peace through collective security and allow America to 'redeem the world by giving it liberty and justice'. In thus making these 'American' values the source of global renovation, Wilson, in the spirit of 'egoistic altruism and unilateral universalism', gave a privileged place to the role of the US in leading and directing the activities of the League. As in Latin America, Wilson seemed to assume that the international community, far from resenting the arrogance and presumptuousness of the American national myth, would both welcome the US as the 'predestined mediators of mankind' and swallow American intentions and objectives at face value. They would, in effect, accept an American League on American terms. When, however, Europe rejected American leadership, there was a huge backlash in the United States—not because those at home disapproved of Wilson's vision of America's redemptive

---

[16] Ibid., 237–38.

[17] Cited in ibid., 239. For more on Wilson's self-interested motives, and his seamless convergence of these interests with the national myth, see Meaney, 'Woodrow Wilson as Machiavelli's "*Prince of Peace*": A New Point of Departure of the Study of Wilson's Foreign Policy', in *Australian and New Zealand American Studies Association: First Biennial Conference Proceedings*, ed. Norman Harper (Melbourne: ANZASA, 1964).

mission, but on the contrary, because the myth was so ensconced in the fabric of national life that Europe's failure to automatically accept America's image of itself convinced many US political leaders that the Old World remained unregenerate and unworthy of American beneficence. As a result, the US Senate rejected the League of Nations—an organisation of America's own making—and withdrew into isolation for the next two decades.[18]

Likewise, following the Second World War and America's emergence as the dominant military and economic superpower, US leaders, answering the call of destiny, resurrected Wilson's plans and played a central role in creating the United Nations. With the 'promised land' in sight, however, the US was confronted with a new adversary in the Soviet Union, which not only challenged American prescriptions for the post-war world but also offered a rival myth of universal redemption in the form of communism. True to past form, the US was highly indignant at the claims of this 'false prophet' and, emboldened by the flow of history which seemed to confirm American promise and expectations, became evermore assured of its own myth. If the US redemptive mission was foreordained, as the myth claimed, then the Soviet Union must be an imposter, and it was in these essentially Manichean terms of good and evil, freedom and oppression, democracy and totalitarianism that American leaders in the two decades after the Second World War understood and formulated US foreign policy. In doing so, they created the very conditions which would contribute to the myth's undoing. As Meaney saw it, because the American national myth 'is about the future not the past, because it is a universal redemptive ideology to be achieved through history', it can be 'tested against history and is therefore at the mercy of history'. In contrast to its charmed existence in the first half of the twentieth century—the 'first great American Century'—history was not especially kind to the US during the 1960s and 1970s. Despite the prescribed triumph of America in this Cold War morality play, Meaney observed:

> the outcome was not what the myth had led Americans to expect. After two decades of containment and confrontation the Communist powers had not crumbled. Despite herculean efforts on behalf of freedom the United States was defeated by Communist guerrillas in Vietnam. The United Nations, America's mythic structure for collective security in the new dispensation, turned against its maker. The accompanying economic reverses [that began in the 1980s] might then be seen as the material confirmation to the loss of the mandate of heaven.[19]

By the time the US did 'win' the Cold War, the damage was already done. The national myth, following the experience of nationalism in other Western countries, was unravelling under the weight of new historical circumstances. Indeed, at the very moment that this great triumph occurred, the US was in the throes of collective hand-wringing over its future as the world's number-one nation. The extent of this cultural crisis was reflected in the national debate that followed the publication in 1987 of Paul Kennedy's *Rise and Fall*

---

[18] Meaney, 'Woodrow Wilson's New World Order', 242–43.

[19] Meaney, 'American Decline and American Nationalism', *Australian Journal of International Affairs* (hereafter *AJIA*), 45 (1), 1991, 94–95. See also Meaney, 'Introduction', 5–6. For the role of the myth in shaping the American decision to become embroiled in the Vietnam War, see Meaney, 'From the Pentagon Papers: Reflections on the Making of America's Vietnam Policy', *Australian Outlook*, 26 (2), 1972, 163–92.

of Great Powers, which, as well containing a magisterial survey of 500 years of Western history, seemed to take considerable pleasure in reminding Americans that they were not 'exceptional' and were, in fact, destined to experience the same decline as all other great powers. Kennedy's claim that the American economy was unable to cope with the demands of its global responsibilities—a phenomenon he called 'imperial overstretch'—and must therefore accept its new role as an equal among many powers was met with overwhelming hostility from Americans. Their objections centred largely on the belief that the US possessed a 'self-renewing genius' which guaranteed continued American dominance in the world. For Meaney, however, both sides of the debate missed the larger, more important point about what happened to a national mythology when it lost its virtue. Like so much of his writing, Meaney's focus was the dominant role played by culture and ideology in shaping people's attitudes and their responses to the world. In the debate over decline, Kennedy as a European disciple of balance-of-power politics was overly focused on the material substructure of international relations and too dismissive of ideological factors, while his American critics, 'being creatures of their culture', found it hard to understand the problem let alone contemplate the possibility of American decline.[20]

In this sense, Meaney felt that that it was mythological—not imperial—overstretch that posed the greatest impediment to the evolution of a foreign policy worthy of the United States. Writing shortly before the American-led invasion of Iraq in 2003, of which he was deeply critical because it represented the latest example of the national myth's tendency to understand international relations as a Manichean battle between the forces of good and evil—this time an 'axis of evil' led by Iraq—Meaney argued that this simplistic view of the world had produced the totally indefensible doctrine of pre-emption, which not only 'defied Western tradition' but also threatened to produce 'international anarchy':

> The comic strip *Superman*, an American creation, is not a proper model for international behaviour. The US, if it is to act with an intelligent moral sensibility, has to learn to live with the tensions of a world shaped by historical contingency.[21]

While conceding that this myth of US exceptionalism remained strong with the American people and its leaders, Meaney, pointing to then-Senator Barack Obama's criticism of the imminent invasion of Iraq in 2003 as a 'dumb war' because it was premised on these comic-book assumptions, argued that some US leaders were capable of transcending the myth. That Obama went on to become president despite expressing views that defied the White House, his own Democratic Party leadership and an overwhelming majority of the American people convinced Meaney that under the right leaders the US could abandon the simplicities of this redemptive mission and 'when we look back to Abraham Lincoln we can say, yes, these miracles do happen'.[22]

---

[20] Meaney, 'American Decline', 90–91, 94.

[21] Meaney, 'War Aims Clouded by Aggressive Intent', *Australian*, 20 January 2003.

[22] Meaney, 'The "Imperial Presidency" and American Foreign Policy', Paper to the Australian Institute of International Affairs, Sydney, 9 October 2012, available at www.youtube.com/watch?v=oW9LDBlv8iE.

Matthew Jordan

Australia and the World

While much of Meaney's teaching and research was, in his early years at the University of Sydney, devoted to the history of US international relations, he had maintained a keen and continuous interest in his home country and especially in the attitudes and ideas which shaped its approach to the world. In the late 1960s, he began teaching an honours course on the subject which in the 1980s was repackaged as 'Australia and the World'. Like its American counterpart, it was the first course dedicated to covering the whole history of Australia's foreign relations to be offered in an Australian university. In it students were encouraged to understand the broader cultural and ideological context in which Australian attitudes and policies to the world were conceived and put in place. As the *Faculty of Arts Handbook* put it, the course promoted:

> A study of the forces shaping Australia's role in the world, including geo-politics, cultural identity, racism and domestic divisions. The emergence of a distinctive foreign policy tradition out of the tensions created for a European society in an Asian-Pacific environment.[23]

These 'tensions' and the corresponding emergence of 'a distinctive foreign policy tradition' became one of the central elements of Meaney's understanding of Australia's role in the world.

At the same time, Meaney's insights on nationalism and its influence on US attitudes to international affairs played a pivotal role in shaping his views on the Australian experience. Influenced especially by American historian David Potter, who had drawn a distinction between cultural and political consciousness in the American Civil War, Meaney observed similar elements at work in Australian nationalism.[24] Unlike the European style of nationalism, which invariably combined the practical need for territorial and political integrity with the emotional need for a distinctive cultural myth, Australian behaviour was marked by a strong attachment to its British cultural inheritance—as opposed to a self-sufficient and uniquely Australian cultural identity—which was nevertheless balanced by an even more powerful sense of Australia's distinctive security interests in the Pacific region. This competition between sentiment and self-interest had created confusion among historians, who, enamoured of the romanticism and traditional dominance of cultural nationalism, had either bemoaned the professed non-existence of an independent Australian foreign and defence policy or made ludicrously inflated claims for the existence of a distinctly Australian national character.[25] Much of Meaney's published record has been directed at overcoming these ahistorical views and providing a more nuanced understanding

---

[23] *Arts Handbook, 1983*, 269.

[24] See David Potter, 'The Historians' Use of Nationalism and Vice Versa', *American Historical Review*, LXVII (4), 1962, 924–50. For the influence of his American experiences in shaping his attitudes to the Australian situation, see Meaney, 'American History', in *History at Sydney*, eds Caine et al., 181.

[25] For an early exposition of this argument, see Meaney, '"A Proposition of the Highest International Importance": Alfred Deakin's Pacific Agreement Proposal and its Significance for Australia–Imperial Relations', *Journal of Commonwealth Political Studies*, 5 (3), 1967, 200–01, 208.

of the nature of Australian identity and its influence on the Commonwealth's approach to the world.

'The Riddle of Australian Nationalism': Sentiment and Self-Interest in the Formation of Australian National Identity

In 1969, in a groundbreaking essay which presented some of his earliest thoughts on the nature of the Australian foreign policy tradition, Meaney criticised those policymakers and expert commentators who, following Britain's withdrawal east of Suez, foreshadowed a 'new era' when Australia could no longer automatically assume 'the protection of Great Britain' and would need to abandon its historical tendency to associate itself with 'the national attitudes, animosities and allies of Britain'. Far from agreeing with this 'myth', Meaney wrote that 'the most cursory examination of past Australian attitudes to defence and foreign policy ... quickly reveal the inadequacy of this picture'. Indeed:

> successive Australian governments have held a distinctive view of Australia's position in the world—a Pacific centred world—which has differed markedly from, and even conflicted with, that of the British government. From the entry of contending European powers into the South Pacific at the end of the nineteenth century to the present time, Australian defence and foreign policy has been dominated by one idea—the search for security in the Pacific.[26]

Taking this 'search for security in the Pacific' as the sub-title of his major history of the development and formulation of Australia's foreign and defence policies in the first decade of the twentieth century, Meaney insisted that there was 'little to be said' for the 'superficial judgment' that Australia was merely an appendage of Great Britain, willing and indeed happy to leave relations with the rest of the world to the 'mother country'.[27]

Contrary to this perception, Australia, deeply disturbed by the intrusion of European imperial powers in the Pacific from the 1870s, had developed distinctive strategies and policies to meet this perceived threat. Against the wishes of the British government, Queensland in 1883 had unilaterally taken possession of the eastern half of New Guinea on behalf of the British Empire, and when Whitehall annulled this action there was widespread resentment in the Australian colonies and renewed calls for a British 'Monroe Doctrine' in the Pacific. During the 1880s and 1890s, the colonists continued to demand that the British take possession of the remaining unclaimed Pacific territories; they established a Federal Council of Australasia which would be authorised to act with respect to 'the relations of Australasia with the islands of the Pacific'; and for the first time they took steps to build up their defence capability, which included the creation of a small permanent corps in each of the colonies, fortifying land and harbour defences and financing an auxiliary naval squadron.[28] Australia's acute sense of its own interests in the Pacific produced a strong push for federation in these years and, conversely, a persistent refusal to accept the idea

---

[26] Meaney, 'Australia's Foreign Policy: History and Myth', *Australian Outlook*, 23 (2), 1969, 173.

[27] Meaney, *A History of Australian Defence and Foreign Policy, 1901–23*, vol. 1, *The Search for Security in the Pacific, 1901–14* (Sydney: Sydney University Press, 1976), ix–x, 1–3.

[28] Ibid., 8–12, 15–30. See also Meaney, 'History and Myth', 174–81.

of an imperial union or federation. This reluctance, according to Meaney, stemmed from 'an Australian perception of a conflict of interest, of an instinctive Australian sense that the colonies' economic, political and strategic interests were so different from those of the Mother Country that [imperial] union was impossible'.[29]

The failure of historians to recognise this 'plain evidence of a nation-state'—leading to either uncritical acceptance of the 'folk tradition' of Australian subservience or in 'slavish imitation of European and American national religions and rites' efforts to fill the perceived void with local equivalents—was, as Meaney contended, due to their fixation on the cultural dimension of nationalism. But this was reinforced by the sheer intensity of the Australian attachment to its British cultural and—as it was increasingly understood—racial inheritance; what Meaney has variously called 'British race patriotism', 'Anglo-Saxon race patriotism', or more simply, 'Britishness'.[30] The roots of this intense identity, which found its most fervent expression in the Sudan (1885) and Boer Wars (1899–1902), were to be discerned in the emergence in the late nineteenth century of new ideas about nation and identity. The rapid modernisation of the colonies from the 1870s was a profoundly traumatic experience, prompting Australians, like other Western peoples caught in this social maelstrom, to seek psychological security in a more intense, exclusive sense of community. The strategic urgency of protecting Britain's Australian colonies from the intrusions of the European imperial powers at this time was one symptom of this development; but an even more striking manifestation of these new ideas of social belonging was the fervour with which Australians embraced an idea of themselves as members of an organic global community of British peoples, bound inexorably together by the 'red line of kinship', as New South Wales premier, Henry Parkes, put it. It was a process, in Meaney's view, 'which equated nation with race, thus defining each people by fusing the cultural with the biological'.[31]

This intense racial identity was further exaggerated by Australia's proximity to what were frequently referred to as the 'teeming hordes' of Asia and the 'awakening' at this time of regional nations—especially China and Japan—which were regarded as a direct threat to the 'British type' of the Australian population.[32] Possessed of this racially exclusive

---

[29] Meaney, *Search for Security*, 6, 30–38.

[30] See ibid., vii–viii, 3–7. These ideas have been thoroughly explored in Meaney, 'Britishness and Australian Identity: The Problem of Nationalism in Australian History and Historiography', *Australian Historical Studies*, 32 (116), 2001, 76–90; Meaney, 'Britishness and Australia: Some Reflections', *Journal of Imperial and Commonwealth History*, 31 (2), 2003, 121–35; and Meaney, '"In History's Page": Identity and Myth', in *Australia's Empire*, eds Deryck M. Schreuder and Stuart Ward (Oxford: Oxford University Press, 2008), 363–87. Australia's British identity pervades all aspects of Meaney's landmark documentary history *Australia and the World*, as well as his general survey of the subject, 'Australia and the World', in *Under New Heavens: Cultural Transmission and the Making of Australia*, ed. Meaney (Port Melbourne: Heinemann, 1989), 379–450.

[31] See Meaney, 'In History's Page', 367–70 and Meaney, 'Australia and the World', 393–97.

[32] For the centrality of White Australia to Meaney's work, see Meaney, 'Australia and the World', 399–403; Meaney, 'The End of "White Australia" and Australia's Changing Perceptions of Asia, 1945–1990', *AJIA*, 49 (2), 1995, 171–90; Meaney, '"The Yellow Peril", Invasion Scare Novels and Australian Political Culture', in *The 1890s: Australian Literature and Literary Culture*, ed. Ken Stewart (St Lucia: University of Queensland Press, 1996), 228–63.

view of society, the Australian colonies during the 1880s moved to close the doors first against the Chinese and later against all non-European, though more specifically Asian, peoples. Unlike earlier scholars, who tended to interpret this episode as the inevitable consummation of restrictive laws first introduced in the 1850s, Meaney, noting the limited nature of this earlier legislation and the colonies' subsequent decision to rescind it, argued that the late nineteenth century transition to complete exclusion was a product of the same ideas about race and national identity that had prompted Australians to so fervently embrace the religion of Britishness. Convinced that race and blood were all, they not only endeavoured to cultivate Australia as a cradle of British civilisation but also resolved to keep out peoples who were, by virtue of their race, permanently 'alien' and therefore incapable of assimilating or becoming useful members of the community. The White Australia policy, as this national orthodoxy became commonly and appropriately known, was entrenched in the Commonwealth's first major piece of legislation. It was, as Meaney argued, 'a foundation policy of the Federal union, a fundamental principle of national life'.[33]

Understanding the dynamic between these competing claims on Australian identity—the cultural nationalism of British race patriotism and the political nationalism of strategic self-interest—was the key to understanding what Meaney referred to as 'the riddle of Australian nationalism'. While Australia's affection for Britain and emotional dependence on the British cultural tradition helped shape its passionate support for the empire at times of international crisis—especially during the First and Second World Wars—its peculiar geographical anxieties and perspectives, its fear of being exposed in the Pacific in the event of a European war preoccupying the United Kingdom, prompted the first federal leaders to develop a distinctive world view which by force of expediency produced defence policies as sophisticated as anything the British government devised in response to the so-called 'German menace' in the first decade of the twentieth century. From 'uncertain beginnings' in the immediate post-federation years, Commonwealth leaders came to view the emergence of Japan as the premier military power in the Pacific with great trepidation. Following Japan's humiliation of Russia in the Russo-Japanese War of 1905—the first time that a European country had been defeated by an Asian power—Australia, 'in spite of herself', as Prime Minister Alfred Deakin put it in 1910, set aside its imperial hopes and aspirations and in the years leading up to the First World War accepted the realities of divergent security interests between Australia and Britain and developed the substance of a foreign and defence policy in which its own needs were paramount.[34]

Imperial Sentiment, the Japanese Threat and the First World War

In the first of his two major histories of Australian foreign and defence policymaking in the early decades of the twentieth century, Meaney, in accordance with his views about political and cultural nationalism, argued that Australia's approach to the world during the early years of the new Commonwealth was heavily conditioned by its status as a

---

[33] Meaney, 'End of "White Australia"', 174. For the policy's application to Japan in particular, see Meaney, 'The Problem of Nationalism and Race: Australia and Japan in World War I and World War II', *Journal of the Oriental Society of Australia*, 42 (2010), 1–30.

[34] See generally Meaney, *Search for Security*, preface, chs 3–5.

constitutionally dependent part of the British Empire. In this context, Australian leaders were 'exceptionally deferential' to the British authorities and for the most part accepted the British government's 'exclusive right to treat with foreign countries and to act for the empire in matters of high policy'. Lacking the 'forms and frills' of a fully developed foreign policy and 'direct contact with the extra-imperial world', Australia's view of international relations was unusually brusque, dismissive of 'the niceties of diplomatic relations' and characterised by 'a stark realism and egocentricity' which was narrowly self-interested and often expressed in the crude language of racial intolerance. And yet, moved by the military rise of the Japanese in the Pacific, they worked hard within this framework to influence British policy and thereby bring the whole weight of the empire's power and prestige to bear on Pacific problems. When this failed, successive Australian governments formulated diplomatic initiatives and defence programs aimed at safeguarding the nation's security. Because of Australia's cultural attachment to Britain and its expectation that the interests of the two countries should coincide not only culturally but also strategically Australian policy during these years was necessarily pursued in 'an indirect, almost clandestine, manner', but it nevertheless bore the substantive signs of a foreign policy. More than that:

> in the carrying out of the first function of a nation's external policy, namely, the safeguarding of its citizens and territory, the Australian achievement will stand comparison with many other countries which had all the advantages of a full and independent international status.[35]

As evidence of this claim, Meaney pointed out how Deakin, just two weeks after Japan's crushing blow on the Russian navy at the Battle of Tsushima, spoke openly of the threat to Australia from Japan—a nation, Deakin said, invoking what was rapidly becoming a dominant theme in Australian foreign and defence policy thinking, which was, 'so to speak, next door, while the Mother Country is many streets away'. With these concerns in mind, Deakin called not only for the fortification of Australian defences but also, and more importantly, for the creation of an Australian navy and the introduction of a compulsory military training scheme.[36] On becoming prime minister in 1905, therefore, he pushed hard but mostly unsuccessfully for British recognition of these claims. Still a good imperialist, he used the Colonial Conference of 1907 to promote a new theory of empire not defined by the old British race patriot dream of imperial federation but by the idea of an empire of equal parts in which the rights of the self-governing colonies would be protected and duly taken into account. In proposing this idea, Deakin hoped to create a more cooperative empire which would give the self-governing colonies a greater share in the making of imperial policy, including defence arrangements for the Pacific dominions.[37] When these efforts at an imperial solution were met with indifference from the British authorities, Deakin, spurred on by parliament, the press and public opinion, set about devising a defence program which would be conceived and implemented independently of Britain. In December 1907, he presented parliament with a comprehensive plan for strengthening every aspect of the Commonwealth's land and sea defences, including the purchase of a

---

[35] Ibid., viii–ix, 11–14.
[36] Ibid., 121–22, 129.
[37] Ibid., 141–42, 147–49.

local flotilla for coastal and harbour defence, which would be built, manned and exclusively controlled by Australia despite opposition from the British admiralty. He also committed the Commonwealth government to a system of universal military training for young men which would produce a national guard of 200 000 men in eight years and ultimately an army of as many as 800 000 men.[38] At the same time, Deakin sought to cultivate a 'special relationship' with 'our kinsmen' from the United States and, defying accepted protocol, personally invited the American Great White Fleet—which was then touring the world—to visit Australia.[39]

The overwhelming success of the visit and the spontaneous outpouring of public enthusiasm was, for Meaney, a telling symbol of the intense strategic and racial fears held by the Australian community in response to the growing military might of Japan in the Pacific and the prospect that the very existence of white Australia might be at risk if the situation in Europe continued to deteriorate. The visit had been understood by Australians not merely as a show of Anglo-Saxon strength—and a veiled warning to Japan as the most potent symbol of the so-called Yellow Peril—but also as a way of shaming Britain into taking a greater interest in the Pacific region, a strategy which seemed to pay off when the British government at the Imperial Defence Conference of 1909 surprised Australia by offering to create an Imperial Pacific Fleet which would be large enough to take care of coastal and trade defence in the region.[40] The Australian government, for its part, received the offer with alacrity, only demanding that the proposed navy not come under imperial control in peace or war without the explicit consent of the Commonwealth authorities. The new Labor administration of Andrew Fisher went so far as to reject the British government's offer of a £250 000 annual subsidy to assist with the fleet's upkeep, thereby securing what cabinet referred to as 'complete local control' over the Pacific unit. Fisher, like Deakin, also promoted the idea of an 'English-speaking alliance', which would include the US, a proposal that found no favour with either Britain or isolationist America.[41]

The British government's later decision to renege on the 1909 agreement following the outbreak of a new arms race in Europe produced considerable anxiety and recrimination in Australia. By 1913, it was 'but a scrap of paper', as Meaney put it, and Anglo-Australian relations were more severely strained than at any time since federation. When, in early 1914, First Lord of the Admiralty Winston Churchill not only publicly challenged Australia's strategic concerns in the Pacific but also called upon the dominions to return to a policy of contributions—a suggestion which would presumably involve Australia surrendering the 'superfluous' navy it had developed at considerable expense to itself under the 1909 arrangement—Australian leaders were livid. They refused to accept this assessment and publicly challenged Churchill's claim that the Anglo–Japanese alliance provided a sufficient guarantor for Australian security.[42] So convincing and uncompromising were

---

[38] Ibid., 153–54.

[39] Ibid., 163–67.

[40] Ibid., 182–83.

[41] Ibid., 201–02, 211–12.

[42] Ibid., 242–44, 249–51.

their arguments that the Colonial Office refused to be associated with Churchill's weak and blustering efforts to dismiss Australian complaints—the first lord was in the process of succumbing to the Colonial Office's demands that 'the Admty [sic] … climb down from a wholly indefensible position' and 'do something to mollify the wrath of Australia' when war erupted in Europe and, as Meaney noted, 'Australia's defence efforts were turned towards rallying support for the Mother Country'.[43] In the interim, however, Australian foreign and defence policymaking had consistently demonstrated that:

> Australian statesmen were not by any means innocents abroad, colonial 'Dads and Daves', forced into a strange and alien world of power politics. Australians, by the time of World War I, had their own sophisticated perspective on international diplomacy and had been through a baptism of fire in an effort to reorder imperial diplomacy and internal defence to serve the national interests … One did not need a foreign office to unveil the self-evident. Japan in Asia, like Germany in Europe, was indisputably the 'coming power', searching for its place in the sun … [Australians] were compelled to fall back finally on what they could do for themselves in order to augment national security.[44]

The outbreak of the First World War, as Meaney recently argued in the second volume of his foreign and defence policy history titled *Australia and World Crisis*, produced a spontaneous outpouring of British race patriotism. Possessed of a Britishness which was, because of Australia's 'structureless democracy' and 'geopolitical isolation', more intense than that evinced by the people of the British Isles, Australians—in marked contrast to their British brethren—were virtually unanimous in their support for the mother country's entry into the war. The response of Australia's four major political leaders—Liberal prime minister Joseph Cook and his attorney-general William Irvine along with their Labor shadows Andrew Fisher and William Morris Hughes—was identical in its emotional simplicity. 'All our resources', the prime minister declared, 'are in the Empire and for the Empire, and for the preservation and security of the Empire'. Not to be outdone in these expressions of loyalty, Fisher the following night promised to stand by Britain 'to help and defend her to our last man and last shilling'.[45] Even the Australian Irish Catholic community fell in behind the mother country. John Gavan Duffy, the son of a Young Ireland nationalist and long-time supporter of Home Rule, called on the Irish community to:

> forget old injustices and stand shoulder to shoulder, knee to knee, to fight the battle of the Empire … an Empire whose flag flew all over the world, from east to west, the greatest empire the world had ever seen.[46]

At the same time, however, there were strong practical reasons for supporting Britain in the war. Recognising that Australia had been created under the protective cover of Pax Britannica, its leaders understood that the country's survival was inextricably bound up with the fortunes of Britain and the Empire. As Meaney explained, should Great Britain be

---

[43] Ibid., 256–57.

[44] Ibid., 259–261.

[45] Meaney, *A History of Australian Defence and Foreign Policy, 1901–23*, vol. 2, *Australia and World Crisis, 1914–23* (Sydney: Sydney University Press, 2007), xi, 6–10.

[46] Cited in ibid., 23.

defeated in the European war, 'Germany—and Japan also, if it switched sides—would be able to impose whatever peace they chose on Australia, including a commanding influence over policy and even possibly cessions of territory'.[47]

Fisher, who was elected prime minister shortly after the outbreak of war, agreed that Australia's interests were best served by promoting a rapid British victory but he was equally concerned about Australia's isolation in the Pacific. Following his 'last man and last shilling' statement, he almost immediately began to backpedal. Having fought for recognition of Australia's strategic concerns against British indifference in the years leading up to the war, he remained concerned about overcommitting the nation to the European theatre given its own geopolitical vulnerability. Within days of his pledge to give everything to Britain's cause, he claimed that Australia's priority was 'to first provide for our own defence and if there was anything to spare offer it as a tribute to the Mother Country'.[48] As prime minister, he remained committed to the social reform platform on which the Labor Party had been elected to office and he was therefore cautious about further recruitment and was absolutely opposed to compulsory overseas service. This approach was reinforced by the potential threat from Japan, which was in turn intensified by the latter's occupation and thinly veiled objective of taking permanent ownership of the German Pacific territories north of the equator in late 1914.[49] Despite Australia's best efforts, the Japanese assumed control of the islands, prompting Fisher to privately assess that the country was facing a crisis which had 'no parallel in our history'. He worked assiduously though unsuccessfully for an imperial conference 'for Defence and for Pacific Administration as well as Imperial Policy'. In January 1915, he visited New Zealand to promote the idea of a Pacific fleet and when this initiative also failed he called on the British to demand limitations on Japan's post-war tenure over the north Pacific islands. This too proved a fruitless avenue, and indeed by the middle of 1915 an emboldened Japan was exerting further pressure on Australia to adhere to the Anglo-Japanese Commercial Treaty—all of which convinced Australian leaders that Japan had every intention of exploiting its dominant position in the Pacific and Britain's preoccupation in Europe as a means of exacting concessions from them.[50] During this the first critical year of the war, according to Meaney, Australian defence and foreign policy was thus 'pulled in two different directions':

> On the one hand Australians for strategic and sentimental reasons identified with Britain in its struggle against Germany. They appreciated that at a global level Australia's survival was linked to a British victory in Europe and so continued to send reinforcements for the A[ustralian] I[mperial] F[orces]. On the other, however, they saw that Japan's rise to power in the Pacific posed a dangerous problem for Australia's immediate security, a problem for which Britain had little sympathy, and this caused them to look to their own defences hopefully supported and sustained by the cooperation of the other Pacific Dominions.[51]

---

[47] Ibid., xi–xii.

[48] Cited in ibid., 11–14.

[49] Ibid., 33–43, 66–69, 71–76.

[50] Ibid., 78–84, 89–90.

[51] Ibid., 109–10.

This balancing act became increasingly difficult for 'a sensitive and thoughtful leader like Fisher' to sustain, especially as it became clear that the war was not going to be easily won. In October 1915, as calls for the introduction of conscription for overseas military service increased, he resigned to take up the post of high commissioner in London.[52] Hughes, who took over from Fisher, had no such internal doubts when it came to prosecuting the war. A 'gnome-like figure with a potoroo head perched on a wizened frame', in Meaney's description, Hughes had the appearance of someone who might 'spring at any enemy who should dare to cross his path or thwart his will'. In marked contrast to Fisher, Hughes was 'stridently imperious' in his belief that the war was a clash between contending races for supremacy. This racial view of international relations was held in some form by most Australian leaders at the time, but in Hughes it took an especially virulent form, prompting him to introduce a raft of laws that discriminated against naturalised German-Australians and even Australian-born citizens of German extraction. After all, Hughes reasoned, giving expression to his belief that racial biology made the person:

> If I were in Germany for 100 years … I should still be British or Australian, and I would not think it wrong to do what I could for Great Britain or Australia. I put a German in Australia on exactly the same footing. His sympathy is for Germany in this struggle … Naturalisation is nothing but a form if the substance does not accompany it—that is, if there is no change in the heart and mind.[53]

These uncompromising views were even more pronounced in the 'Win-the-War' strategy which Hughes adopted as prime minister. Because nothing less than the survival of the British race was at stake, there could be no half-measures. Unlike Fisher, who hesitated to commit the nation to total war because of regional anxieties and his hopes for social reform, Hughes offered a simple solution to the problem: all aspects of national life must be subordinated to achieving a comprehensive victory for the British Empire. By adopting this approach, Hughes hoped to restore the British Empire to its former glory and thereby provide for Australia's future security in the Pacific.[54]

No sooner was he prime minister than Hughes announced the government's support for a new recruiting target of 50 000 men over and above the accepted level of 9500 monthly reinforcements and authorised the Parliamentary War Committee to approach all eligible men and ask them to complete a card indicating their intentions regarding enlistment—a move that many members of the labour movement saw as 'veiled conscription'.[55] The labour constituency which Hughes ostensibly represented became increasingly critical of his draconian recruiting tactics, a challenge to which Hughes in his usual fashion responded by denouncing all doubters as 'men [who] know no nationality, no religion or principle'.[56] This

---

[52] See ibid. For Fisher's record as high commissioner, see Meaney, 'The First High Commissioners: George Reid and Andrew Fisher', in *The High Commissioners: Australia's Representatives in the United Kingdom, 1910–2010*, eds Carl Bridge, Frank Bongiorno and David Lee (Canberra: DFAT, 2010), esp. 45–50.

[53] See Meaney, *Australia and World Crisis*, 18–20, 35–36, 115–16.

[54] Ibid., 116, 135–36.

[55] Ibid., 119–21.

[56] Cited in ibid., 123. See generally chs 5–6.

served to alienate rather than galvanise the labour movement, and by the time of the first conscription referendum in October 1916 Hughes had almost single-handedly divided the country down the middle. Both sides, in making their respective cases, shared a common obsession with Japan and its intentions in the Pacific. Hughes, though circumspect in his public pronouncements, in a closed session of parliament urged conscription so that Britain could win the war quickly and in so doing ward off

> the dangers to which Australia was exposed by her close proximity to the hordes of the coloured races, with particular reference to Japan, who although our Ally in the World War, might at some future time be our enemy.

J. H. Catts, a Labor parliamentarian who was both director for recruiting in New South Wales and a member of the federal Parliamentary War Committee, argued the opposite case on the grounds that Australia's geopolitical circumstances—and he openly identified the threat from Japan—required the retention of 'the manhood of Australia … for home defence'. Reiterating the prime minister's key line, he warned that '[t]here have been instances in previous wars where allies fighting together one day have fallen out among themselves on the cessation of hostilities'.[57]

When the referendum for conscription was narrowly defeated, Hughes and his mostly 'establishment' supporters were greatly shocked. While the reasons for this failure were many and complex—and Meaney has shown that the majority of 'no' votes came from traditionally conservative electorates fearful of the economic consequences of conscription, not to mention AIF soldiers in the trenches on the Western front, three-quarters of whom voted against conscription[58]—Hughes was swift to lay the blame on the labour and Irish Catholic sections of society. For Meaney, Hughes, in his denunciations following the vote, further intensified 'the bitterness and rancour generated in the campaign', and through his actions 'caused recruiting, the war and the Empire to become symbols of domestic division and strife'. More than that:

> it was Hughes's decision to push willy-nilly for conscription and to steamroll all opposition which led, through a spiral of provocations, to the breaking of the bonds of mutual trust. His action … hardened hearts and steeled resolve and his authoritarian and vindictive referendum campaign intensified these feelings … Hughes and the conscriptionists … put half the nation outside the pale, vilifying those who would not surrender to the necessities of war and Empire as disloyalists or fellow-travellers with the disloyal.[59]

While largely responsible for this general sickness in the body politic, Hughes maintained the rage. He continually attacked 'shirkers', Australians of German extraction, 'wobblies', prominent (if deliberately provocative) Irish Catholics such as Archbishop Daniel Mannix and anti-conscription labour leaders such as Queensland premier T. J. Ryan; he introduced further draconian laws targeting those sections of society he held responsible for the outcome of the referendum; and far from taking any lessons from the defeat of the conscription referendum and altogether ignoring the large numbers of American troops

---

[57] Both cited in ibid., 160–61, 172–80.
[58] Ibid., 180–82, 195.
[59] Ibid., 181, 190–91.

joining the European war by this time, he called for a second conscription vote in November 1917.[60] Again, the 'yes' campaign failed—this time by a larger margin—and recrimination quickly followed with yet another round of official persecution and censorship of the anti-consriptionist lobby. Only with the war's end, in November 1918, did the whole issue of conscription become moot.[61]

While war-weary European leaders and their American counterpart, Woodrow Wilson, committed themselves to a liberal peace based on national self-determination and the formation of an international organisation that would prevent the possibility of such a destructive event ever occurring again, Hughes refused to fall into line with these post-war plans. He instead called for a peace of 'annexation and indemnity', which would strip Germany of its wealth, overseas territories and capacity to wage war and thereby ensure the survival and indeed pre-eminence of the British race and empire. To this end, he was scathing in his criticism of Wilson's Fourteen Points, which provided the blueprint for the post-war settlement. Indeed, Hughes had by this time so alienated these world leaders that British prime minister Lloyd George deliberately excluded him from the War Cabinet's discussions which essentially accepted the Fourteen Points as the basis for peace talks. Furious that the British government had refused to honour its promises and consult the dominions on the peace terms, Hughes expressed his anger so publicly and so aggressively that the Australian cabinet itself urged him to refrain from 'hanging British family linen on the line for the information and amusement of other nations, including enemies'.[62] Thus chastened, Hughes toned down his assault on the 'British family' but leading up to and during the Versailles peace conference in early 1919 he clashed frequently with Wilson over the status of Germany's Pacific territories—north and south[63]—refused to accommodate a moderate Japanese proposal to include a racial equality clause in the covenant of the new League of Nations[64] and promoted completely unrealistic reparations objectives which were doomed to fail.[65] While Hughes was pleased with his efforts in vetoing the Japanese racial equality clause, the failure to crush Germany convinced him that the Treaty of Versailles was '*not* a good peace for Aus: nor indeed for Britain'.[66]

Hughes' unhappiness stemmed not merely from his desire to inflict a 'vindictive' peace on the enemy, in Meaney's assessment, but also 'to punish and crush the German nation which he saw as an enduring threat to the supremacy of the British Empire'. All that Australia had fought for—the restoration of the British Empire to a pre-eminent position in the world, which would in turn accommodate Australia's perennial 'search for security in the Pacific'—had come to nought. This was why, as Meaney also noted, Hughes was equally contemptuous of the US—'she who did not come into the war to make anything but made

---

[60] Ibid., 196–200, 204–11, 219–22, 225–30.

[61] Ibid., 223–24.

[62] Cited in ibid., 297–98.

[63] Ibid., 317–26, 347–58.

[64] Ibid., 366–72, 376–79.

[65] Ibid., 388–90, 393–95.

[66] Cited in ibid., 397 (original emphasis).

thousands of millions from it', as Hughes complained, thus emerging from the conflict as a potential rival to Pax Britannica.[67] Because the fundamental issue of Australian regional security thus remained unresolved—and indeed for many Australian policymakers the country's position was even more precarious because of the great losses suffered during the war—there was a continuation of what Meaney referred to as the 'cold war' against Japan in the Pacific. While Hughes was still in Paris, acting prime minister William Watt, at the behest of his director of intelligence, E. L. Piesse, set up a Pacific branch in the Prime Minister's Department which was to study the affairs of the countries of the Far East and the Pacific and advise the government accordingly. Piesse, who became its first director, remained concerned about Japanese intentions in the Pacific and, amongst other things, recommended a significant watering down of the White Australia policy to meet Japanese sensitivities. He was rebuffed by Hughes because such views, to use Meaney's phrasing, 'offended his biological determinism'.[68] Only when the major powers met in Washington in 1923 and agreed to set limits on their respective navies did Australia take a more relaxed attitude to Japanese intentions in the Pacific.[69]

'Yellow Peril' to 'Red Peril': Japan, the Second World War and the Coming of the Cold War to Asia

The Washington Conference and its entrenchment of the territorial status quo in the Pacific allowed Australian leaders to breathe easy throughout the 1920s. For the first time since the Russo-Japanese War of 1905 the Australian people were confident, as Piesse put it, that Japan had 'no aggressive intentions towards us', and indeed that the decisions taken at the Washington Conference 'might well justify us in abandoning much of our preparation for defence'.[70] With Australia's traditional geopolitical fears somewhat calmed, Australians, far from re-evaluating the British race patriotism that had led to their involvement in the First World War, became even more comfortable with this identity. They took great pride in the role they played fighting for the British cause in the war, which had provided a focus for national feelings, and emerged from the conflict not chastened from the huge loss of life and national treasure but convinced that Australia provided the political, economic and material conditions for a regeneration of the British race. Meaney, citing a speech written by Australia's official historian of the war, C. E. W. Bean, has argued that this egalitarian race vision was the essential motivating factor for Australia's enthusiastic participation in the war:

> It was Bean's view that the Australian soldier 'knew only one social horizon, that of race', by which he meant the white British race. Bean believed that it was for this the AIF had fought and that in the process they had proved themselves to be better Britons than the British of the Mother Country.

---

[67] Cited in ibid.

[68] Ibid., 413–14, 418. See also Meaney, *Fears and Phobias: E. L. Piesse and the Problem of Japan, 1909–1939* (Canberra: National Library of Australia, 1996).

[69] Meaney, *Australia and World Crisis*, 492ff.

[70] Cited in Meaney, *Fears and Phobias*, 34.

Because the war had validated this British racial identity, Anzac Day, commemorating the 'blooding' of the Australian troops and nation, 'became a national holiday, or, perhaps more aptly, a holy day, dedicated to the memory of the fallen'.[71]

The peace of the 1920s did not last. When, in the 1930s, Nazi Germany rose to challenge the power of Britain and more ominously, Japan embarked on an imperial course in North-East Asia, Australia's historical fear that a European war would leave it exposed to its putative enemy in the Pacific caused great consternation. Because of the favourable conditions of the 1920s, Australia had taken full advantage of this rare convergence of its cultural and political interests by promoting ever closer economic and social ties with the 'mother country'—embodied in Prime Minister S. M. Bruce's slogan 'Men, Money and Markets'— as well as military enmeshment, symbolised most reassuringly for Australia by Britain's construction of a purpose-built naval base at Singapore. Now, as before the First World War, Australia was again forced to turn its attention to its own region, and with this end in mind its leaders began appeasing the Japanese, first by attempting to encourage British and US recognition of Japanese claims in Manchuria, then by seeking a non-aggression pact between the US, Japan and other Pacific powers. In both respects, Australia's efforts went unrewarded.[72]

E. L. Piesse, who had earlier called for a reassessment of the White Australia policy to meet Japanese objections and in so doing lost Hughes' confidence, weighed into the debate on Japan and Australian security during the 1930s. By now a freelance writer, he was deeply disturbed by developments in Japan and absolutely convinced of the danger to Australia. Against the general complacency of Australian leaders, Piesse in 1935 self-published a long tract which criticised the 'Singapore solution' and, using language reminiscent of that employed by Deakin before the First World War, called upon Australian leaders to plan:

> in the expectation, not that the British Navy will be available after local means of defence have served us for a few months, but that we shall have to rely solely and finally on our own resources and preparations.[73]

While this strategic analysis was slow to gain acceptance in Australian official circles, by the late 1930s the government recognised the impending danger. In April 1939, R. G. Menzies, among the most ardent of Australia's British race patriots, in his first act as prime minister announced that Australia would establish direct diplomatic relations with the three major Pacific powers: the US, Japan and China. In taking this 'painful' step, as Meaney put it, which 'went against his deepest instincts', Menzies implicitly accepted the limitations of British power. 'What Great Britain calls the Far East', he said, 'is to us the Near North'. He still saw Australia as 'an integral part of the British Empire', but even as he reassured himself in this way he accepted that Australia as a principal must act for itself given that 'the primary risk in the Pacific is borne by New Zealand and ourselves'.[74]

---

[71] Meaney, *Towards a New Vision: Australia and Japan Across Time* (Sydney: University of New South Wales Press, 2007), 31–32. See also Meaney, 'Australia and the World', 410–11.

[72] Meaney, 'Australia and the World', 416–17.

[73] Meaney, *Fears and Phobias*, 40–42. For Piesse's earlier critique of 'White Australia', see generally ch. 2.

[74] Cited in Meaney, 'Australia and the World', 417.

When war came to the Pacific following Japan's attack on Pearl Harbor in December 1941, Prime Minister John Curtin famously declared that in these dire circumstances Australia looked to the United States for help 'free of any pangs as to our traditional links or kinship with the United Kingdom'. He refused to countenance any policy which treated the Pacific as a subordinate segment of the general conflict and promised that under his government 'Australia shall not go'.[75] Curtin's comment, or more specifically its tone, has been interpreted by many historians as a turning point in Australian attitudes to the world; the moment at which Australia abandoned its historical dependency on Great Britain and assumed a less subservient and more independent role for itself in international relations. For Meaney, however, Curtin's comment, far from expressing particularly novel sentiments, was entirely consistent with an established foreign policy tradition, articulated by leaders such as Deakin, Fisher, Hughes and most recently Menzies, who recognised Australia's strategic vulnerability and acted accordingly. Like all these leaders, Curtin was a committed British race patriot whose view of Australia's place in the world accorded with the same ideas of an organic community of British peoples connected by the ties of blood and race. Until the Japanese attack on Pearl Harbor, Curtin too had understood Australia's war effort not independently but as 'an integral part of the British Commonwealth of Nations'. As the war was coming to an end, moreover, Curtin, in accordance with his conviction that Australia was a British outpost in the Pacific, gave life to the long-held aspiration of a workable imperial union by calling for the creation of 'some imperial authority' which would allow the British Commonwealth to have, 'if not an executive body, at least a standing consultative body' to formulate British global policy.[76] For Meaney, this was hardly evidence for a paradigmatic shift to the US—indeed Australia found the American embrace 'suffocating' and in 1944 promulgated the ANZAC Agreement which in response to US incursions into Australia's 'sphere of influence' called for a 'hands-off' policy in the Pacific. Despite Curtin's opportunistic statement in 1941, his defence policies and those of his post-war successor Ben Chifley:

> looked towards working more closely than ever with Britain. The egregious failure of the Singapore base had not prompted any reassessment of assumptions. Australia's defence was linked to British Commonwealth global and regional strategy. In the case of [a potential] war with the Soviet Union Australia was considering proposals to send troops and aircraft to join Commonwealth forces in the Middle East and in the case of regional troubles it planned to join with Britain and New Zealand in a common effort in South-East Asia.[77]

Curtin, Chifley and the post-war minister for external affairs, H. V. Evatt, all of whom are often celebrated by 'radical nationalist' historians for 'standing up' to the British authorities in defence of Australia, had what Meaney has called 'feet of British clay'.[78]

While committed to this historical vision of a global British community, Australia, as always, remained concerned about its geopolitical vulnerability in the Pacific. Following

---

[75] Cited in ibid., 418–19.
[76] Cited in ibid., 418, 420.
[77] Ibid., 422.
[78] Meaney, 'Britishness and Australian Identity', 80.

the war, therefore, Chifley and Evatt in particular worked hard to ensure that Japan could never be a military threat to Australia again. Like Hughes, who was largely moved by the same fear and the same sense that Australia's great-power allies were totally indifferent to Australian anxieties, the post-war Australian government was deeply incensed by the British (and American) decision to act unilaterally for the Pacific during the Second World War. The solution for Evatt, according to Meaney, was not to 'reject the special ties to Britain and the Commonwealth', but, like Australian policymakers before him, 'to fashion them anew to ensure that consultation was effective and that Australia should assume the leading role for the Commonwealth in the Pacific'.[79] Accordingly, at every stage of the Japanese peace settlement, Australia insisted on its role as a 'party principal', successfully securing British approval to command the Commonwealth forces in Japan and to represent the Commonwealth on the Allied Council in Tokyo.[80] Even as Australia won this practical recognition for its claim to represent the Commonwealth in the Pacific, there was the unhappy realisation that in Britain's weakened post-war state this amounted to very little without US backing. To Evatt's chagrin, the Americans even more than the British refused to consult Australia over matters affecting its vital interests, most notably the peace settlement with Japan. When the US, in response to rising tensions between itself and Russia, began promoting a 'soft' peace which it was hoped would restore Japan's industrial capacity, encourage its alignment with the Western camp and thereby make Japan a bulwark against communist expansion, Evatt publicly questioned the wisdom of this strategy. He warned that rebuilding Japan for one purpose might be used for another: 'it might ultimately be used according to the wishes of the Japanese leaders and turned in the direction of the South Pacific to the detriment of this country'. It would be 'an evil day for Australia', he added, 'if Japan is given capacity to rearm'.[81]

For Meaney, this was the old dilemma in a new guise; namely, that Australia's Pacific concerns were being ignored by its great-power allies because in devising a 'soft' peace for Japan to accommodate the emerging Cold War they were once again pursuing a 'Europe first' policy. When, therefore, Britain approached the Australian government in January 1948 seeking its cooperation in the formation of a 'Western Union' to combat Soviet expansion, Australia alone among the dominions expressed strong disapproval for the scheme. In taking this stance, it was deeply critical of the great powers and their failure to prevent this latest international crisis. Far from accepting that this approach represented a major shift to a liberal internationalist foreign policy, Meaney argued that it was just another symptom of the problem that had wracked Australia's relations with its great-power allies since the late nineteenth century. That is, Evatt, through Chifley, used the British request to vent his spleen about the continuing neglect of Australian concerns in the Pacific.[82]

---

[79] Meaney, *Primary Risks and Primary Responsibilities in the Pacific: The Problem of Japan and the Changing Role of Australia in the British Commonwealth, 1945–1952* (London: Suntory Centre, LSE, 2000), 5.

[80] Ibid., 10–11, 15–18. See also Meaney, *Towards a New Vision*, 160–68.

[81] Cited in Meaney, *Primary Risks and Primary Responsibilities*, 53. See generally 37, 47–49,

[82] Meaney, 'Australia, the Great Powers and the Coming of the Cold War', *Australian Journal of Politics & History*, 38 (3), 1992, 318–20. See also ibid., 51–52; and Meaney, 'Dr H. V. Evatt and the

Indeed, having castigated the Americans (and implicitly the British) for pursuing policies of expediency and for bypassing United Nations 'principles of justice', Chifley made it clear that his primary concern was the Pacific and the possibility that the Cold War would again leave Australia isolated and exposed. Australia's interests 'were very much bound up in the Pacific area', he said, and 'in the event of European conflict, our whole manpower might well have to be directed to the protection of our interests in this area'.[83]

For all the latent hostility to the United States, Evatt and Chifley were not, as the Americans mistakenly understood them, 'fellow travellers' who sympathised with the Soviet Union. Meaney has demonstrated conclusively that Evatt worked frantically during the second half of the 1940s to secure Australia against Japan by persuading the Americans to agree to a Pacific pact, first by openly pleading with the US for such a scheme, and when this failed, by offering US access to Australian bases in exchange for a defence agreement, which was also unsuccessful.[84] The same objective was pursued with equal vigour by Evatt's successor, Percy Spender, who became minister for external affairs in the coalition government of R. G. Menzies. So similar were the objectives and styles of the two men that the British secretary of state for Commonwealth affairs, Patrick Gordon Walker, after meeting Spender, commented: 'Scratch a Spender and you'll find an Evatt'.[85] And Spender had success where Evatt had persistently failed; in 1951, Australia, New Zealand and the US signed the ANZUS Treaty, the mutual defence pact Australia had been seeking since the beginning of the twentieth century. However, as Meaney noted,

> the Menzies Coalition Government had obtained what Chifley and Evatt had long sought not because they were superior diplomats but because the Americans after the outbreak of the Korean War [in 1950] had embraced a policy of worldwide containment of Communism through the creation of alliances along the East Asian archipelagos from Japan in the north to Australia and New Zealand in the south.[86]

Reassessment and Reorientation

ANZUS, while in many ways the culmination of hopes that had been held by Australian policymakers for half a century, was a significant departure in Australian foreign policy. Following on from Evatt's recognition in the 1940s that British power was on the wane and that Australian security was therefore dependent on a strong American presence in the Pacific, Spender had blatantly pursued his aims with little regard for British objections. 'Australia was a principal power in the [Pacific] area', he had complained to the Americans, using the same phrasing as Menzies and Evatt before him, 'but the United Kingdom was

---

United Nations: The Problem of Collective Security and Liberal Internationalism', in *Australia and the United Nations*, eds James Cotton and David Lee (Sydney: Longueville, 2012), 34–65.

[83] Cited in Meaney, 'Australia, the Great Powers and the Coming of the Cold War', 326.

[84] Ibid., 325.

[85] Cited in Meaney, 'Look Back in Fear: Percy Spender, the Japanese Peace Treaty and the ANZUS Pact', *Japan Forum*, 15 (3), 2003, 402.

[86] Meaney, *Primary Risks and Primary Responsibilities*, 75. See also ibid., 404, 408–9.

not'.[87] Importantly, when the treaty was signed, it did not include Britain; indeed, it was the first political treaty into which Australia had entered without British participation.[88] At the same time, however, the ANZUS Treaty did not alter the continuing importance that Australia attached to its strategic relationship with Great Britain; nor did it signify a serious diminution of the emotional intimacy Australians felt for the mother country. Menzies, perhaps more so than any other leader since Parkes, was a staunch British race patriot and in this regard he worked hard to maintain the ties between the two countries. He readily agreed to assist Britain with its efforts to develop a nuclear weapons capability, allowing it to test nuclear devices at Emu Field and Maralinga in South Australia and in the Monte Bello islands off the Western Australian coast. In 1955, he sent an infantry battalion and three squadrons to Malaya to assist British forces in suppressing a communist-led insurgency; the following year he gave uncritical support to Britain's heavy-handed tactics during the Suez Crisis, a decision which alienated Australia from the US as well as its Asian neighbours.[89] In taking all these decisions, Menzies still believed that Australia and Britain 'must at all times nourish our ancient structural unity which remains the best thing in the free world'.[90] To demonstrate that these sentiments were broadly shared by the Australian community, Meaney pointed to the visit of Queen Elizabeth II in 1954. The first time that a reigning monarch had visited Australia, it evoked:

> the greatest outpouring of British race sentiment in Australian history … The imperial drones swarmed reverentially around their Queen. It was a civil religious occasion which eclipsed Anzac Day in its pageantry and popularity. It was reported that the crowd of a million people who turned out in Sydney to greet the Monarch was 'almost hysterical in its excitement' and that 'some scattered rose petals along the path of the Royal Car' … The Queen [according to the *Sydney Morning Herald*] symbolised 'the supreme achievement of the British race'.[91]

By the early 1960s, however, Australia's British race dream had started to unravel. This process was assisted by the declining potency of nationalism itself, which had been severely discredited by the experience of two world wars and the emergence of independent African and Asian nations that were highly critical of Western race nationalism. Australians, like other Western peoples exposed to modernisation in the late nineteenth century, became more inured to the permanence of change. Moreover, the emotional need for a strident and exclusive sense of community became less pressing—a development that found its fullest expression in the gradual liberalisation and abandonment of the White Australia policy during the 1950s and 1960s.[92] Reinforcing this decline in the ideological appeal of British race patriotism was the sundering of Australia's formal ties with Britain as the waning power of the United Kingdom forced Australia to seek new markets and strategic relationships elsewhere. Trade with Japan had boomed following the signing of

---

[87] Cited in Meaney, 'Look Back in Fear', 405–07.
[88] Meaney, 'Australia and the World', 427.
[89] Ibid., 428–30.
[90] Cited in ibid.
[91] Ibid., 425.
[92] Meaney, 'In History's Page', 383.

a commercial treaty between the two countries in 1957, and by the end of the next decade Japan had overtaken Britain as Australia's largest and most important export market.[93] The logic of ANZUS was also played out during the 1960s as the United States quickly eclipsed Britain as its pre-eminent strategic partner. In these years, Australia, in much the same way that it had permitted the British to conduct nuclear tests on Australian soil, allowed the US to erect bases on its territory. In 1965, Australia, in contrast to Britain, committed troops to America's war in Vietnam. The extent of the Anglo-Australian rupture was symbolised most powerfully in Britain's successful application to join the European Economic Community, thus turning its back on 'Greater Britain'. Though Australians were at first disconsolate with this turn of events, complaining that the British had abandoned them, the finality of these new circumstances, as Meaney put it, forced them 'to recognise at last that the Empire wore no clothes'.[94]

While Australians could take some comfort in the continuing presence of the United States in the region during the 1960s and, even after US president Richard Nixon's promulgation of the Guam Doctrine, in the more benign geopolitical circumstances of the 1970s and 1980s it was much more difficult for them to fill the emotional void left by the collapse of British race patriotism. There was, as Donald Horne put it in the late 1960s, 'a commendable emptiness in Australians about their place in the world, the need for a new rhetoric, a new approach, as if Australia were beginning again'.[95] This search for a new approach, a new identity to replace Australia's defunct myth of Britishness, has taken several forms. Meaney himself identified at least three types of responses to this crisis of identity. The first, which he recently referred to as 'Anglo-conservative nostalgic', had sought to reinvigorate and therefore privilege the Anzac myth—that is, the myth most commonly associated with Australia's British race patriot past. In the post-British multicultural era, as Meaney observed, such a myth could not serve a viable purpose: 'There is a need to link the British past to Australia's present but it seems anachronistic to do it through that element of the past which is so closely related to exclusive ideas of ethnic unity and British race loyalty'.[96] A more common response to the dilemma was what Meaney called 'radical nationalism'. This school, far from making its peace with Australia's British past, denied that Britishness was the dominant cultural myth in Australia and instead claimed that subterranean nationalist stirrings—'latent from the time of the arrival of the first European settlers'—were 'thwarted' by 'British manipulations' and 'cultural hegemonic practices' which 'frustrated again and again the achievement of the national destiny'. Apart from the conspicuous lack of evidence for this perspective, the main weakness of this thinking was that it uncritically accepted, as Meaney argued, 'nationalism's own teleological view

---

[93] See Meaney, *Towards a New Vision*, 172–87. See also Meaney, 'Australia and Japan: The Historical Perspective', in Meaney, Sol Encel and Trevor Matthews, *The Japanese Connection: A Survey of Australian Leaders' Attitudes Towards Japan and the Australia–Japan Relationship* (Melbourne: Longman Cheshire, 1988), 20–22.

[94] Meaney, 'Australia and the World', 431–33.

[95] Cited in Meaney, 'In History's Page', 383–84.

[96] See Meaney, 'Gallipoli Versus Kokoda: Did Australians Fight Other People's Wars?', *Sydney Papers Online*, 2–3, available at www.thesydneyinstitute.com.au/speaker/neville-meaney/.

of history, namely that all history is a struggle by "peoples" towards achieving self-realisation'—a view which most scholars are agreed has lost both its moral virtue and intellectual moorings in the post-nationalist world.[97]

A third strand of thinking, eschewing the presumption of these first two schools that in seeking a unifying social idea Australia must subscribe to a nationalist myth—whether British or distinctly Australian—turned its back altogether on nationalism and emphasised Australia's redefinition of itself as a multicultural society. In doing so, however, those who promoted this alternative vision overlooked the fundamental ambiguity of multiculturalism; namely, the inherent tension between what Prime Minister Malcolm Fraser referred to simultaneously as the goal of 'a cohesive, united, multicultural nation'—which seemed to assume the equality of all cultures and the privileging of none—and those 'aspects of life in Australia that, irrespective of our ethnic backgrounds, we treasure and want to preserve'— which seemed to imply the continuing dominance of British cultural, political and legal traditions in Australia.[98] In ignoring this dilemma, Meaney recently argued,

> it is as though the culture makers and perhaps even the public at large have been fearful that if any attempt should be made to look for a unifying social idea the only answer would be some form of nationalism with all its potential for reviving the evils that multiculturalism has endeavoured to eradicate.

As a first step, in Meaney's opinion, Australia must come to terms with its British past, not for the purposes of either celebrating or whitewashing it, but to re-examine the British inheritance 'free of the emotional trammels of the past' and in doing so perhaps discover 'a more certain way of legitimizing the values and institutions which in practice hold the commonwealth together'.[99]

For Meaney, this concept of the Commonwealth—even more so than the much-touted idea of a republic—provides the greatest promise as a legitimising myth in post-nationalist Australia. It has special meaning for Australia not only because of the importance that the architects of federation attached to the term with its 'host of allusions and connotations about liberty and community' but also because it reflects the political community of Australianness as opposed to the cultural community of Britishness:

> Commonwealth is the symbol of Australian nationhood. Since the nation was formed around political community rather than cultural identity it lacks the exclusiveness and intolerance of [British race] nationalism. It is able to embrace the shared and affective experience of the community without stifling or suppressing the diversity of cultural traditions.[100]

Commonwealth in the most fundamental sense, therefore, is capable of linking the past to the present but at the same time accommodating the cultural pluralism of modern Australia. By embodying the central principle that has defined Australian nationhood since

---

[97] Meaney, 'Britishness and Australian Identity', 76–79.

[98] See Meaney, 'End of "White Australia"', 185–87.

[99] Meaney, 'In History's Page', 386–88.

[100] See esp. Meaney, 'The Commonwealth and the Republic: An Historical Perspective', *Papers on Parliament No. 27: Reinventing Political Institutions*, ed. Kathleen Dermody (Canberra: Department of the Senate, 1996), 22ff.

federation—the pursuit of the 'common weal'—it provides a firm basis for unifying the diverse elements of the Australian community as it continues to change.

The Essays

The essays that comprise this festschrift are replete with the themes and intellectual preoccupations that have dominated Neville Meaney's work over many years. The all-important, but often neglected, role of ideas in shaping peoples' views of themselves, and the influence of these ideas on their understanding of and engagement with the world, figures prominently.

The essays have been organised into sections according to distinct, though interconnected, themes. Following the historiographical focus of the first section and its appraisal of Meaney's role in the formation and advancement of foreign relations history in Australia, the second section covers the centrality of race and racial imaginings in shaping Australia's white British identity in the late nineteenth century and the resilience of these ideas even after the emergence in the mid-twentieth century of Asian nations that were highly sensitive to racial discrimination. Matthew Jordan looks at the Chinese immigration crisis of 1888 and shows how this seminal event focussed the colonial mind on the idea of race as the defining principle of the settler society and led directly to the adoption of the White Australia policy in 1901. Eric Meadows, by looking at Asian criticism of the policy following the Second World War demonstrates how Australia refused to modify the policy even when the changes proposed were largely cosmetic and might have created more amicable relations between Australia and India.

The third section examines what Meaney has referred to as the 'riddle' of Australian nationalism; that is, the inherent tension between its cultural identification with a global British community and determination to protect its peculiar geopolitical interests in the Asia-Pacific region. By examining three significant Australian public and intellectual figures—the first chief of Australia's military forces, General E. T. H. Hutton; one of the most important architects of the Commonwealth and perhaps its most eminent public servant, Robert Randolph Garran; and A. C. V. Melbourne, a leading public intellectual in the 1920s and 1930s—Richard Lehane, Colin Milner and James Cotton explore how Australians sought to reconcile these competing claims and find that, invariably, the community of interest trumped the community of culture.

The fourth section focuses on the idea of British race patriotism, not exclusively in the Australian context, but as a worldwide phenomenon. Ross McKibbin, in comparing the economic and social circumstances of Britain and Australia in the first quarter of the twentieth century, argues that although both societies shared a sense of belonging to a worldwide community of British peoples their separate experiences produced interesting differences. Stuart Ward, on the other hand, by tracing out the central role that Britain's withdrawal from empire played in bringing Australia as well as Canada and New Zealand to free themselves from this British race vision, shows that there was a remarkable similarity in the separate responses of these British settler-colonial societies. All three countries, independently of each other, sought to fill the void left by the collapse of Britishness by embracing a 'new nationalism' which, while having often embarrassing consequences, reinforced how fundamental British race patriotism had been to defining these societies and how profound their post-imperial disorientation was.

The fifth section looks at the development and nature of Australia's alliance relationship with the United States since the signing of the ANZUS Treaty in 1951 and the way that relationship has been understood and interpreted in the last fifty years. James Curran, by recreating the Australian response to the visit of US president Lyndon Baines Johnson in 1966, the first visit to Australia of a serving American head of state, questions the common belief that it represented a significant shift in US–Australia relations and explains the undeniable 'optics' of the visit in the context not of a 'turn' to America but of traditional Australian geopolitical anxieties. David McLean, in a forensic reading of the recent literature on Australia's decision to follow the US into Iraq in 2003, convincingly argues that the persistence of Cold War myths about the nature of the alliance—what he calls the triumph of 'mismemory' over history—not only influenced Prime Minister John Howard's unquestioning support of the US in Iraq but also made it easier for him to accommodate his strong cultural bias for the US.

The sixth section examines another major theme of Meaney's work, namely, the role of nationalism in shaping American self-perceptions and the application of these myths to US foreign policy since the early twentieth century. David Rowlands, taking on a major concern of Meaney's research in the American field, explores the origins of President Woodrow Wilson's adoption of the American national myth and shows that his conversion to the idea of an American redemptive mission came so late in life as to make the myth's own claims for itself as 'self-evident' and 'universal' highly questionable. Likewise, Michael Thompson, in looking at Reinhold Niebuhr's critique of nationalism and especially American nationalism from the 1920s to the 1950s, takes on a figure whose philosophical response to this distinctly modern phenomenon exerted an important influence over Meaney's own thinking on the subject. In this way, Thompson shows how Niebuhr and the various theological schools with which he was associated viewed American nationalism as artificial and historically contingent several decades before its decline made such a reappraisal conceivable for most of the country's political leaders and culture-makers. Tom Switzer, focusing on the period when this decline began, examines how future US president Richard Nixon, in questioning one of the shibboleths of the American national myth—the US rejection of the People's Republic of China—came to abandon the myth of US exceptionalism and accept its limitations in a multipolar world.

Each of these essays, though dealing with complex ideas and the way in which those ideas have shaped people's attitudes and actions, has been written on the simple premise that the study of the past can bring insight and understanding to the present human condition. This fundamental principle goes to the heart of Meaney's approach to the discipline of history, both as a teacher and a scholar, and it provided the justification for his decision in 1985 to publish the first documentary history covering the whole sweep of Australia's engagement with the world of nations—to which he gave the appropriate title *Australia and the World*.[101] In an introduction with the equally apt title 'The Meaning of the Past',

---

[101] See Meaney, *Australia and the World*, vii. Meaney is set to publish an updated, two-volume version of the documentary history in 2013.

Meaney lamented 'the poverty of politics, not least of foreign policy', which suffered from a tendency to understand events in the context not only of the foreshortened past but also of the 'uncritical mythology by which events are understood and made sensible for decision'. While history with its focus on change and human contingency could never produce laws of a scientific character and would always be a focus of passion and argument, it could provide a sound basis for understanding the broad patterns of human behaviour:

> All that the historian can hope to achieve by bringing the past to life, by probing the causes of events and by looking at the alternatives out of which the present has emerged, is to mediate the passion, clarify the argument and enlighten the judgement.[102]

This book, as well as formally acknowledging Neville Meaney's enormous contribution to the discipline, is a modest attempt to elaborate on the themes that have dominated his work and in so doing mediate the passion, clarify the argument and enlighten the judgement.

---

[102] Meaney, 'Introduction: The Meaning of the Past', in ibid., 1–2.

II

Race, Nationalism and White Australia

4

The Chinese Immigration Crisis of 1888 and the Coming of White Australia

Matthew Jordan

On 16 May 1888, New South Wales premier, Sir Henry Parkes, rushed emergency legislation through the colony's Legislative Assembly that provided for the virtual exclusion of Chinese migrants. This followed a fortnight of mass demonstrations in the city in response to the arrival of several ships carrying illegal Chinese passengers. The highpoint of this agitation occurred on 3 May, when a meeting organised by the colony's anti-Chinese league attracted a crowd of over 5000 people who gathered at Sydney Town Hall and were then led by the city's mayor to Parliament House. There the mob demanded an audience with Parkes, who refused, and attempts were made to rush the Legislative Assembly before the premier agreed to receive a deputation the following morning.[1]

After chiding its leaders for encouraging such an unruly rabble, Parkes nevertheless assured them that he was 'entirely with them in the matter', and indeed, that he 'had been at all times'.[2] For this reason, he told them, the government had decided not to allow any Chinese to land in Australia except for those possessing bona fide naturalisation papers. This 'precipitate action', as Parkes called it, foreshadowed the introduction of the Influx of Chinese Restriction Bill from which, he said, 'we do not mean to turn back'. Not even the imperial government would be allowed to sway the colonists from their course, which, as Parkes explained it, 'is to terminate the landing of Chinese on these shores forever, except under the restrictions imposed by the bill, which will amount, and which are intended to amount, to practical prohibition'.[3]

Unlike earlier restrictions in New South Wales in the 1860s and early 1880s, which were invariably a response to the number of Chinese entering the colony and therefore mainly aimed at circumscribing their admission, the laws introduced in 1888 had the specific objective of keeping the Chinese out altogether. Equally novel was the consensus of opinion in New South Wales over the decision to introduce further restrictions. In the 1860s legislators had adopted restrictive measures only reluctantly, and when these discriminatory laws had served their purpose and the number of Chinese in the colony declined somewhat, they had been quick to repeal them. In 1888, by contrast, Parkes' proposals represented not a retreat from but a hardening of the restrictive laws that had been reintroduced at the beginning of the decade.[4] While Parkes was widely criticised in the

---

[1] *Sydney Morning Herald* (hereafter *SMH*), 4 May 1888.

[2] Cited in ibid., 5 May 1888.

[3] *New South Wales Parliamentary Debates* (hereafter *NSWPD*), Legislative Assembly (hereafter LA), XXXII (16 May 1888), 4787.

[4] The experience was similar in the other major colonies from the 1850s to the 1880s. See Matthew Jordan, 'Rewriting Australia's Racist Past: How Historians (Mis)Interpret the White Australia

colony during May and June 1888 for a litany of sins—despotism, disloyalty to the Crown and especially disregard for the law—there was wholesale agreement on the principle of near-complete exclusion, and more than that, strong pressure to introduce completely prohibitive laws in New South Wales. And this aspiration was not confined to the premier colony. Events there prompted the other colonies to convene an Intercolonial Conference in June 1888 with the specific purpose of devising uniform laws that would advance the common objective of prohibiting Chinese migrants from coming to the whole continent once and for all.

Historians who have attempted to understand these events agree almost unanimously that the Chinese immigration crisis of 1888 was a crucial turning point in colonial attitudes to race. The only significant exception is Keith Windschuttle, who claims that the colonists were mainly concerned with 'the number of Chinese entering the Australian colonies and the high proportion of them who were illegal immigrants'.[5] At the most basic level this interpretation fails to acknowledge that overall numbers of Chinese were by this time declining in the colonies; that the existing laws were sufficient for the purposes of controlling Chinese immigration levels; and that, in contrast to earlier anti-Chinese measures, when Chinese numbers declined even further in the following decade there was no corresponding urge to rescind the laws of 1888.

If scholars basically agree that the events of 1888 were a pivotal moment in Australian race relations, they differ over the motives of the colonists in introducing these near-prohibitive laws. Historian Andrew Markus has emphasised the role of the burgeoning labour and trade union movements, and more especially their fear of Chinese economic competition, to account for the 'sense of panic' that gripped New South Wales and the other colonies in 1888.[6] A recent variation of this view has been advanced by Jeremy Martens, who claims that 'massive popular protests' and 'extra-parliamentary populism' provide the key to understanding the events of May and June 1888.[7] But neither Markus nor Martens demonstrate the economic sources of this 'panic' and 'populism', nor do they explain why those who supported the new restrictions—and this included people who had no real sympathy for the labour movement—wanted to exclude all Chinese, not merely those from the labouring classes.[8]

Policy', *History Compass*, 3 (1), 2005, 8–11.

[5] Keith Windschuttle, *The White Australia Policy* (Sydney: Macleay Press, 2005), 90–101.

[6] See generally Andrew Markus, *Fear and Hatred: Purifying Australia and California, 1850–1901* (Sydney: Hale and Iremonger, 1979), 140, 155.

[7] Jeremy Martens, '"Disturbing and Most Poisonous Agitations": Henry Parkes, Populism and the Usurpation of Law in New South Wales, 1888', in *Orb and Sceptre: Studies on British Imperialism and its Legacies, In Honour of Norman Etherington*, ed. Peter Limb (Clayton, Vic.: Monash University ePress, 2008).

[8] Phil Griffiths, recognising that this argument virtually exonerates the 'ruling class' of any culpability in the creation of anti-Chinese legislation in the late nineteenth century, has recently argued that the more important consideration for the colonists—at least in terms of Queensland's Chinese Immigrants Regulation Act 1877—was strategic: 'Fear of Chinese numbers was overwhelming amongst ruling class legislators'. But Griffiths goes further, tracing this motive through to the Commonwealth's creation of White Australia in 1901. In so doing, he fails to

Charles Price has instead suggested that at the most primal level—'the dark realm of basic social motives and group psychology'—the events of 1888 stemmed from a strong cultural aversion to the Chinese: 'that deep fear of the strange and different' and 'that intolerance of anyone or anything that does not seem to be completely "with it".'[9] Like the economic argument, however, this view ignores the fact that the new restrictions were prohibitive in character and as such targeted even the most 'cultured' and 'adaptable' Chinese, including those who were naturalised British subjects from Crown colonies.

Because of the obvious shortcomings of these interpretations, the most common explanation for the events of 1888 is that the colonists were primarily driven by considerations of race. In taking this position, most historians argue that the source of this thinking was new ideas about racial hierarchy and the alleged inferiority of non-European races. These ideas, according to Graeme Davidson, were reinforced by 'neo-Darwinian ideas of racial competition', which, he claims, were widely shared by politicians and colonial leaders of an intellectual bent, including Alfred Deakin and C. H. Pearson, both of whom purportedly 'accepted the idea of a hierarchy of the races without question'.[10] And yet, few scholars make any genuine effort to explain the source and nature of these notions—and indeed, terms such as 'social Darwinism' are often used in a throwaway manner as though their meaning and prevalence are self-evident. But an examination of the 1888 debates suggests that ideas associated with racial hierarchy—let alone a systematic philosophy of racial superiority—were not central to colonial attitudes towards Chinese immigration, and indeed, that such ideas were expressed by a minority of legislators who were just as likely to be repudiated for advancing them.

At the same time, it is clear that in devising the legislative framework for Australia's 'great white walls' the colonists were almost exclusively motivated by racial considerations. Myra Willard, the first historian to write a comprehensive history of the White Australia policy, in 1923, while accepting and indeed endorsing its main racial orthodoxies, denied

---

acknowledge the real differences between 1877 and 1888—specifically, the fact that Queensland in the former period experienced a true Chinese influx, whereas the move to exclude Chinese in 1888 and all 'coloured' people in the 1890s occurred at times when non-European numbers were declining or negligible and that any such fears could have been addressed with restrictive as opposed to prohibitive legislation. Griffiths, 'The Strategic Fears of the Ruling Class: The Construction of Queensland's Chinese Immigrants Regulation Act of 1877', *Australian Journal of Politics and History*, 68 (1), 2012, 16–18.

[9] C. A. Price, *The Great White Walls Are Built: Restrictive Immigration to North America and Australasia, 1836–1888* (Canberra: ANU Press, 1974), 254, 260–61, 269–70.

[10] Graeme Davison, 'Unemployment, Race and Public Opinion: Reflections on the Asian Immigration Controversy of 1888', in *Surrender Australia? Essays in the Study and Uses of History: Geoffrey Blainey and Asian Immigration*, eds Andrew Markus and M. C. Ricklefs (Sydney: Allen and Unwin, 1985), 101–11. For the same general argument, see also A. T. Yarwood and M. J. Knowling, *Race Relations in Australia: A History* (Sydney: Methuen, 1982), 185–88; Raymond Evans, 'Keeping Australia Clean White', in *A Most Valuable Acquisition: A People's History of Australia Since 1788*, eds Verity Burgmann and Jenny Lee (Ringwood, Vic.: Penguin Books, 1988), 177, 181; Andrew Markus, *Australian Race Relations 1788–1993* (Sydney: Allen and Unwin, 1994), 76, 111; James Jupp, *From White Australia to Woomera: The Story of Australian Immigration* (Melbourne: Cambridge University Press, 2002), 7.

that in adopting the policy the colonists were 'actuated by any idea of the inferiority of the mentality or physique of the excluded peoples'. Nevertheless, she praised the wisdom of the founders in creating and cultivating a White Australia: 'They knew'—not believed, but knew—'that racial unity … was essential for national unity, for true national life', and in taking this course they were cognisant of 'the well-marked social and political evil inevitably connected with the co-existence of distinct races in one country'.[11] As a creature of her culture, Willard may have been fundamentally wrong about the supposedly fixed barriers to non-European absorption, but the mentality was an essentially accurate reflection of the racial ideas which had moved Australians to end Chinese immigration in 1888.

The nature and source of these ideas—of the mentality underlying the creation of White Australia—is the concern of this chapter. The events of May and June 1888 provide a useful window, not only in terms of demonstrating the colonial consensus on the need to exclude Chinese migrants altogether but also in terms of shedding light on the essential attitudes shaping colonial thinking on the question of Chinese immigration. In doing so, this chapter contends that the colonists, both in New South Wales and in Australia generally, were driven primarily by new ideas of identity, nation and race which dictated that Chinese migrants were biologically and eternally separate from British-Australians and as such incapable of adapting to the culture of the host community. While not necessarily based on notions of racial superiority, this conflation of culture and colour prompted the colonists to resolve against any further encroachment by these potential Chinese 'hordes', a decision that would be extended to all 'coloured' people in the 1890s and lead to the formal adoption of the White Australia policy as the foundation principle of the federal Commonwealth in 1901.

Conflict in Consensus: The Scene in New South Wales

Following the arrival on 28 April of the steamship *Afghan*, which was reported to have fifty-three illegal Chinese passengers on board, Parkes, as promised, ordered that no Chinese be allowed to land. All ships carrying Chinese passengers, including the recently arrived *Tsinan*, *Guthrie* and *Menmuir*, were ordered into quarantine and placed under police guard while the relevant authorities scrutinised their naturalisation papers. While those Chinese holding bona fide naturalisation certificates would be entitled to land pending validation of their papers, all others, as the *Sydney Morning Herald* told its readers approvingly, would be 'turned back'; even those Chinese willing to pay the poll tax—a £10 entry fee that had been levied exclusively against Chinese migrants since the early 1880s—as well as those holding exemption certificates issued by the colonial authorities would be returned to China.[12]

Because this action was illegal under the *Influx of Chinese Restriction Act 1881*—a law which Parkes himself had been responsible for introducing—the premier on 15 May 1888 called for a suspension of the standing orders so he could introduce 'legislation of a drastic character' that would not only indemnify the government but also establish the future legislative framework for the 'practical prohibition' of the Chinese. Accordingly, the Influx

---

[11] Myra Willard, *History of the White Australia Policy to 1920*, 2nd edn (Melbourne: Melbourne University Press, 1974 [1923]), 190, 192.

[12] *SMH*, 8 May 1888.

of Chinese Restriction Bill proposed a reduction in the number of Chinese who could come to the colony from one for every one hundred tonnes of a ship's weight to one for every 300 tonnes. The poll tax for Chinese, which had been set at £10 since 1881, was to be increased to £100. Under the terms of the draft legislation, the Chinese would henceforth be excluded from all mining pursuits in the colony. They would also be confined to specified parts of New South Wales and, even more importantly, prohibited from being naturalised 'on any ground whatever'.[13]

While Parkes was met by a barrage of criticism in parliament, those who attacked him did so not because they objected to the substance of the legislation but because they regarded his actions as rash, unlawful or unnecessarily cruel. The leader of the opposition, George Dibbs, attacked Parkes for pushing through legislation 'pell-mell with all its blemishes and imperfections' and without 'giving the measure calm consideration and dealing with it from a judicial point of view'. In doing so, Parkes had trampled upon the law of the land. Indeed, the government, according to Dibbs, had:

> broken the law, and the Premier has told us tonight that he will snap his fingers at the technical law, that he will ignore the power of the empire, that he will refuse the right of these poor unfortunate Chinamen who went away on the good faith of the colony that they would be allowed to return to their wives and families who are in the colony now whilst their bread-winners are imprisoned, not by the law, but by order of the imperial dictator of New South Wales—Sir Henry Parkes.

At the same time Dibbs, far from championing the cause of the Chinese in the colony, assured the House that this was 'no party question': 'It is a grave national question. Hon[ourable] Members on this side of the House are decided in their views upon it; we all go for the exclusion of the Chinese.' Indeed, he criticised the proposed legislation because it 'does not go far enough'. If the colony was to be preserved for the 'pure Anglo-Saxon type', he said, employing a favourite phrase of the premier's, 'we do not want the Chinese here at all'. With that in mind, Dibbs called upon the government to 'eradicate every vestige of the evil' by adopting legislation 'so drastic in its character that it would prevent any future influx of Chinese to these shores'. More than that, he said, 'let us pass a stronger law. Let us pass a law of exclusion if necessary'.[14]

A number of opposition politicians actually broke ranks and claimed that under the circumstances the government's unlawful actions were warranted. James Fletcher, convinced that the matter was urgent 'and should be dealt with without a moment's delay', felt that the executive was justified in 'using every means in their power to prevent the evil which has occurred in other parts of the world from occurring here'; Parkes therefore had his 'hearty support in making the bill … the law of the land'. Fletcher's only objection to the proposed legislation was that it 'does not absolutely prohibit the landing of Chinamen in the colony'.[15] Ninian Melville was deeply apologetic to his colleagues for supporting the government, but for him the issue transcended party politics:

---

[13] *NSWPD*, LA, XXXII (15 May 1888), 4696–97, 4833–35.

[14] Ibid., 4793–800. Similar sentiments were expressed by Dibbs' political allies, including Thomas Slattery, John McElhone and Thomas O'Mara. See ibid., 4807–08, 4812–13, 4814–15 (respectively).

[15] Ibid., 4801–02.

> I cannot afford, even for party purposes, even though it might lead to a division of friendship—I cannot afford to think of all these things when the interests of my native land are at stake, when the people of this country are asking for protection against a race who are a curse to every land they enter.

Far from taking issue with Parkes on constitutional grounds, Melville congratulated him for taking 'a determined stand' and felt that

> even if the Government had strained the law to such an extent as to justify their removal from office it would be the patriotic duty of any statesman opposed to them to condone their action in view of the public interest.

Like others, he only regretted that the legislation was not more severe but was confident that it would 'lay the foundation for total prohibition before many years'.[16]

When the bill went into committee, the level of consensus over the general principle of Chinese restriction was even more pronounced. Dibbs remained committed to complete exclusion and introduced an amendment to that effect, which garnered support from 'prohibitionists' on all sides of parliament. The government, believing that absolute legislation of this kind would fail to receive the royal assent, accused the opposition of using the crisis for political advantage. Parkes too favoured the total exclusion of the Chinese but legislation to that effect would be 'stupid, impracticable and resultless':

> Does any member of the Committee suppose that if the Government had thought that a bill to entirely exclude Chinese form the colony would receive the royal assent they would not have brought in such a bill? … We have gone as near to exclusion as it is possible for any set of men to go.[17]

This difference of opinion, as Dibbs himself admitted, centred around the proposed method for excluding the Chinese, not the principle itself, on which, he said, there was 'a consensus of opinion'.[18]

Not surprisingly, therefore, when the bickering over method and legal propriety petered out, the committee adopted a number of amendments that actually made the proposed legislation more stringent. This included increasing the entry restriction to 300 tonnes—Parkes had been content to leave it at one hundred tonnes—and imposing a £20 fine for non-resident Chinese who traded or travelled in 'any place or part of the colony' without the express written authority of the colonial secretary.[19] Parkes, who saw the bill through a twenty-seven hour sitting of the Legislative Assembly, later claimed that on the general question of further restricting Chinese immigrants 'the feeling of the House was so strongly with me that no division was called for'.[20]

While Parkes could claim a moral victory in seeing the Influx of Chinese Restriction Bill through the Legislative Assembly in a single night, he was less successful in convincing opinion outside the chamber that the government was justified in overriding the law. The

---

[16] Ibid., 4802–05.

[17] Ibid., 4822–24.

[18] Ibid., 4825.

[19] Ibid., 4834–35.

[20] Henry Parkes, *Fifty Years in the Making of Australian History*, vol. II (London: Longman's, Green and Co., 1892), 209–10.

mainstream press, led by the *Sydney Morning Herald*, became ever more critical of the government for its constitutional transgressions. As early as 4 May, when the government's intentions were still not entirely known, the *Herald* struck a cautious note by warning against any flouting of the existing law:

> The Act as it stands sanctions the introduction of Chinese under certain conditions, and until it is repealed it must be respected. Of course if Chinese appear at our doors with sham naturalisation papers, we are warranted in turning them away; but those who comply with the law are entitled to admission. The Government … must keep in view its obligations to the law.[21]

But, like those who criticised the premier's unlawful actions in the Legislative Assembly, the *Herald* almost invariably qualified this criticism with expressions of strong support for the principle of further restricting Chinese immigration. When, on 15 May, Parkes introduced his draft bill to the Legislative Assembly, the *Herald* took this line. The government's behaviour, according to the newspaper, while 'rash or ill-judged' from a constitutional point of view, was nevertheless correct: 'In proposing to introduce legislation to still further restrict the admission of Chinese the Government pursues a course to which no exception can be taken … [Here] the Government is on firm ground'.[22]

The New South Wales Supreme Court meanwhile decreed that Parkes had acted illegally in detaining the passengers of the *Afghan*. It thus ordered the release of all Chinese in possession of bona fide naturalisation and exemption certificates, a decision that was eventually extended to those passengers willing and eligible to pay the poll tax under the existing law.[23] While Parkes spent the next two weeks attempting to frustrate the court's orders, he soon discovered that the Legislative Council was equally disapproving of the government's precipitate action and refused to be stampeded into adopting rash legislation.[24] And yet, in the Council as in the Assembly, there was no disagreement on the fundamental need for harsher anti-Chinese laws. Richard Bowker claimed that there was 'no-one in this House and country who has a greater horror of the Chinese coming here than I have', while Dick O'Connor was 'strongly of the opinion that some urgent and drastic legislation of the character proposed in the bill is absolutely necessary'.[25] Moreover, when debating whether the bill should be read for a second time on 30 and 31 May, not a single member of the Council spoke against the general principle of further restriction.[26]

When the bill went into committee a week later, although the Legislative Council baulked over the question of discriminating against Chinese already residing in the colony, it was again unanimous on this fundamental point. The three most vocal opponents of the government's draft provisions, Andrew Garran, William Bede Dalley and William

---

[21] *SMH*, 4 May 1888.

[22] Ibid., 16 May 1888.

[23] See ibid., 18, 21, 29 and 30 May 1888.

[24] See, for instance, comments by Andrew Garran, Dick O'Connor and John Macintosh in *NSWPD*, Legislative Council (hereafter LC), XXXIII (17 May 1888), 4855–57, 4861, 4864 (respectively).

[25] See ibid., 4860 (O'Connor) and 4863 (Bowker).

[26] See ibid. (30–31 May 1888), 5018ff.

Manning, claimed to be 'entirely in favour of a large restriction, and a close regulation of this immigration' (Manning). Garran frankly admitted that 'he did not want to see these Chinaman back. He had rather that they stopped at home'. Dalley asked that the government 'make the measure as stringent for the exclusion of Chinese as it could possibly be'. There was therefore no desire to 'in any way weaken or emasculate the bill', as Garran put it, or to 'diminish the severity of the measure'.[27] But they and many other Council members agreed that the main purpose of the bill could be accomplished without indulging in 'wretched, contemptible, petty' legislation which deprived resident and (in certain instances) naturalised Chinese of the right to leave the colony and return at their own convenience, or to live, travel and work where they pleased. This inclination to discriminate against residents of the colony—even if they were, as Garran put it, 'despised Chinamen'—was 'a monstrous thing' (Henry Dangar), 'an act of injustice' (John Macintosh) and 'not at all necessary for the purposes we had in view' (Manning).[28]

In accordance with these sentiments, the Council removed a number of the bill's most objectionable features. Clauses restricting Chinese to 'defined areas' of New South Wales, making their 'unauthorised' movement between the colonies a criminal offence and subjecting them to discriminatory license fees were expunged.[29] But beyond these perceived obligations to resident Chinese the Council approved completely of the bill. It expressed no qualms over the government's stated intention of issuing no more exemption certificates. Likewise, while unwilling to sanction retrospective action against Chinese already residing in the colony, the Council readily approved of a clause prohibiting new arrivals from engaging 'in the work of any gold, silver, or other mine, or in any mining pursuit whatever'.[30] Significantly, the Council retained the clause prohibiting any further naturalisation of Chinese. While some members, including Garran, Macintosh and Manning, questioned the necessity of such a provision, mainly because 'the cases were likely to be exceedingly few' (Manning) under the new restrictions, they nevertheless voted in favour of an amendment which endorsed this discriminatory practice.[31] Those Council members who opposed it—the bill still passed eighteen to eight—did so not because they disagreed with the principle but because they wished to go further still and divest naturalised Chinese who temporarily left the colony of their status as British subjects. As the government's representative in the Legislative Council, Julian Salomons, put it, 'the policy of the Government of the country is not to allow [naturalised] Chinese to come back if they go away. We do not compel them to go; but if they do go, the policy of the country is to allow them to become residents of some other country'.[32]

This near-universal consensus in the colony's legislative and constitutional organs on the need for further restrictive legislation was even more pronounced in the community

---

[27] See ibid. (6 June 1888), 5249 (Manning), 5260 (Dalley), 5242, 5340 (Garran).

[28] See ibid., 5265 (Manning), 5268 (Dangar), 5270 (Macintosh). The reference to 'wretched, contemptible, petty' laws was John Hay's (5267).

[29] See Price, *Great White Walls*, 195–96.

[30] *NSWPD*, LC, XXXIII (7 June 1888), 5346.

[31] Ibid. (6 June 1888), 5265.

[32] Ibid., 5267.

at large. During the course of the crisis, a series of anti-Chinese rallies and meetings were held across New South Wales which, while more orderly than earlier demonstrations, were highly critical of the Supreme Court and Legislative Council for focusing on the legality and propriety of the government's methods instead of taking equally decisive action to end Chinese immigration. Meetings at Newtown, Paddington, Newcastle and Tumut all expressed unwavering approval for the premier's actions. Led by ministers of parliament, mayors, aldermen and unionists, these rallies, as well as frequently condemning the Supreme Court, invariably passed resolutions to the effect that 'the Legislative Council will deserve the thanks of New South Wales by passing into law the Chinese Restriction Bill, as it left the Legislative Assembly'.[33]

Not one to miss a political opportunity, Parkes himself, at a meeting at Centennial Hall ostensibly convened to discuss the 'political situation' in the colony, but focusing primarily on 'the Chinese question', said that in his opinion 'a great error had been committed by the high legal tribunal of this country'. To rapturous cheers and applause, Parkes promised that the government 'would not turn back (hear, hear)' and, indeed, that he would 'push on [with] this measure until it became law, and until a Chinaman's tail would be seen in our streets no longer (laughter)'.[34] The climax of this anti-Chinese activity was a procession on 4 June along George Street in Sydney, which was reportedly attended by as many as 50 000 people—or one in seven of the city's population. There the gathering called upon Parkes to 'lead the people in driving the Chinamen from these shores in spite of the Supreme Court and its orders'.[35]

The Principle of Chinese Exclusion Goes National: The Intercolonial Conference

While the relevant colonial authorities—including Parkes—were unwilling to accommodate such extreme demands, there was in New South Wales a near consensus on the principle of virtually prohibiting Chinese migrants. And this clearly extended to the other colonies, all of which had keenly observed the events in New South Wales and likewise accepted that the virtual prohibition of Chinese immigration was essential. They, like the premier colony, had been unsure of the best way forward and initially felt that the Chinese should be excluded by way of a formal treaty along the lines of one recently negotiated between China and the United States.[36] But with the crisis in New South Wales bringing the issue to a head, they now looked to introduce nationwide legislation. Several days before Parkes rushed his emergency legislation through the Legislative Assembly, the premier of South Australia, Thomas Playford, perhaps sensing that his New South Wales counterpart was predisposed to drastic action, wrote Parkes and the other colonial leaders suggesting an Intercolonial Conference to discuss the so-called 'Chinese difficulty'. Playford felt that

---

[33] See *SMH* for reports of anti-Chinese meetings at Marrickville (10 May 1888), Bulli (22 May 1888), Paddington, Newtown and the Queen's Statue (23 May 1888).

[34] Cited in ibid., 26 May 1888.

[35] Ibid., 4 June 1888.

[36] See Willard, *History of White Australia*, 77–80.

'unity of action amongst all the Colonies of Australasia is most likely to satisfactorily effect our common purpose of restricting Chinese immigration'.[37]

After several weeks of negotiating a date and venue for the proposed conference, senior representatives of each of the self-governing colonies gathered in Sydney on 12–14 June 1888. Following the election of Parkes as conference president, Playford introduced a series of resolutions which, amongst other things, accepted that 'the further restriction of Chinese immigration is essential to the welfare of the people of Australasia' and stipulated that any uniform legislation should 'apply to all Chinese', including those in Crown colonies such as Hong Kong and the Straits Settlements (part of present-day Malaysia and Singapore). To achieve these objectives, the conference initially anticipated a mix of diplomatic action by the imperial government—especially in the form of a treaty with China—and uniform Australian legislation including a poll tax of £30 and the limitation of one Chinese to every 200 tonnes of a ship's weight.[38] Far from adopting a less extreme view than their colleagues in New South Wales, the conference delegates regarded this latter provision as not sufficiently prohibitive, and on an amendment proposed by Victorian premier Duncan Gillies, they resolved to limit the number of Chinese which any vessel could bring to any Australian port to one for every 500 tonnes of a ship's weight. This provision being so comprehensive, the colonial leaders, in deference to the mother country's desire to avoid offending Chinese sensitivities, agreed to waive the poll tax altogether. At the same time, they felt that this nationwide legislation made the urgency of a diplomatic solution less pressing. A committee, consisting of Alfred Deakin (Victoria), James Murtagh Macrossan (Queensland) and Charles Cameron Kingston (South Australia), was therefore appointed to draft a bill which, it was anticipated, would form the basis of future uniform legislation.[39]

The decision to waive the poll tax was as much as the colonists were prepared to concede. They refused to budge on the increased tonnage restriction, which, like the poll tax, discriminated against Chinese but no other immigrants. A suggestion by the British colonial secretary, Lord Knutsford, that the most effective means of overcoming Chinese objections was to introduce measures that discriminated equally against all foreign labourers—thereby meeting working-class objections to Chinese immigration but removing the offence caused by a policy of virtual Chinese exclusion—met 'great disfavour' with the conference delegates, according to the *Sydney Morning Herald*, and 'could not be acceded to'.[40] When Lord Knutsford pointed to the potential commercial benefits to the colonies of maintaining friendly relations with China, Parkes, in his capacity as conference president, cited import and export figures to demonstrate that China 'offers no present outlet of importance for Australasian trade'. At the same time, the delegates called on Britain to 'induce the Governments of the Crown Colonies of Hongkong, Straits Settlements and Labuan to at once prohibit the emigration [to Australia] of all Chinese',

---

[37] See Thomas Playford to Parkes, 9 May 1888, in NSW, *Votes and Proceedings of the Legislative Assembly during the Session 1887–8, with the Various Documents Connected Therewith* (hereafter *Votes*), vol.II (Sydney: Government Printer, 1888).

[38] Parkes, 'Minutes of Proceedings of Conference on Chinese Question', 12 June 1888, in ibid.

[39] Parkes, 'Minutes of Proceedings', 13 June 1888, in ibid.

[40] *SMH*, 15 June 1888.

including naturalised British subjects. In conveying this resolution, Parkes simply noted that 'the Chinese who may claim to be considered British subjects in those Colonies are very numerous'.[41]

Given this broad consensus, the colonies not surprisingly moved quickly to adopt a policy of near-complete exclusion. New South Wales persisted with its own Chinese exclusion bill, which, after incorporating the Legislative Council's various amendments, became law in July 1888. Accordingly, while the euphemistically titled *Chinese Restriction and Regulation Act* expunged most of the internal discriminatory measures originally proposed in the draft bill, it retained the spirit of virtual prohibition by endorsing the entry restriction of one Chinese to every 300 tonnes of a ship's weight and increasing the poll tax to £100. Adopting the strident tone of the original bill, it decreed that 'after the passing of this Act no certificate of naturalisation shall be issued to any Chinese on any ground whatever', and, effectively ending the system of exemption certificates, it further stipulated that 'all Chinese leaving the Colony except those who have been naturalised therein shall on returning be subject to all the provisions of this Act'.[42]

Due to the niceties of diplomatic relations, Chinese government officials were exempted from the provisions of the act. All others were to be excluded, and the miniscule number henceforth admitted under the new law would be denied the opportunity of becoming full members of the community in the way that more racially acceptable groups were. Those who were to be excluded included not merely non-British Chinese from the mainland, or Chinese labourers who might pose a threat to the living standards of the colony's working classes, but 'any person of Chinese race', as the act put it.[43]

The other major colonies followed with legislation based heavily on the measures agreed to at the Intercolonial Conference. In Victoria, Gillies accordingly introduced a 500-tonne entry restriction. As in New South Wales, the Victorian Legislative Council was sensitive to the rights of resident Chinese in the colony, and shaped the new laws accordingly, but Gillies successfully defeated all attempts to make special exemption for wives and children and for returning Chinese residents. Queensland also passed legislation closely modelled on the intercolonial draft. So severe were some of its additional provisions, however, such as the imprisonment of the master of a vessel even accidentally infringing the law, that the new law only received the royal assent in 1890, after Queensland agreed to modify some of its more strident penalties. South Australia, despite remonstrations from colonists who believed that Chinese labour was essential to developing the tropical areas of the Northern Territory, likewise adopted the main characteristics of the draft bill. While the colonial secretary of Western Australia, Malcolm Fraser, returned home from the conference saying that all the agitation in the eastern colonies was 'somewhat premature', in 1889 he too passed a law of prohibition. Only Tasmania, which remained largely untouched by Chinese immigration, refused to adopt further restrictions along the lines agreed to at the Intercolonial Conference. There the existing £10 poll tax and one hundred tonne entry restriction remained in place.[44]

---

[41] Parkes to Lord Knutsford, n.d. [c. 14 June 1888], in NSW, *Votes*, vol. II.

[42] *Chinese Restriction and Regulation Act 1888*.

[43] Ibid.

[44] Price, *Great White Walls*, 190–95.

Matthew Jordan

The Reasons Offered for Chinese Exclusion: What Do They Say About Colonial Motives?

The push for wholesale Chinese exclusion, which was embraced by all the self-governing colonies except Tasmania, meant that by the early 1890s there was a virtually uniform barrier against any further Chinese immigration to Australia. Why was this so? What convinced the colonists at this time that the Chinese were so objectionable as a race that they should be absolutely excluded from Australia? With these questions in mind, it might be instructive to explore the reasons actually offered by public figures, particularly in New South Wales but also at the Intercolonial Conference, to justify their positions and to test these claims against the available evidence.

At first glance, the contention that the colonists were concerned about a Chinese influx seems partly convincing. Edward O'Sullivan, referring to the colony's determined efforts forty years earlier to exclude convict ships 'freighted with men of our own race', accordingly reasoned: 'If it was justifiable to send back these people because they were objectionable … how much more justifiable is it now, when we find our very civilisation menaced by the extraordinary influx of Chinese?'[45] But talk of a Chinese influx, of an actual surge in the number of Chinese arrivals, was greatly exaggerated. Certainly, large numbers of Chinese were arriving in the Northern Territory from the mid-1880s—a rare occasion when the use of the word 'influx' was probably justified—but the issue hardly touched New South Wales. At the same time, the numbers entering the colony remained small and indeed, New South Wales had experienced an overall decline in the Chinese proportion of its population. As Price has shown, while there was a slight surge of Chinese migrants to the colony in the mid- to late 1880s, the strength of the Chinese population in New South Wales dropped from 1.4 per cent in 1881 to 1.2 per cent in 1891.[46] At a time, therefore, when the visibility of the Chinese community in New South Wales was at best static if not actually receding it is difficult to believe that the colonists, in adopting prohibitive laws, were driven mainly by concerns over a perceived Chinese influx. Many of the colony's policymakers recognised this vital point. As Dalley observed:

> Now, with so small a proportion of Chinese immigrants, and with their proportion to the whole population so slightly altered from what it was more than six years ago notwithstanding our proximity to China, what could be said in favour of the urgency of dealing with the whole Chinese question under the apprehension of the country being instantly overrun and overwhelmed by them?[47]

---

[45] *NSWPD*, LA, XXXII (16 May 1888), 4764. Similar references to preventing the 'further influx' of Chinese were made by W. J. Allen (4775), John Hurley (4876), William Wall (4777) and Thomas O'Mara (4815).

[46] The trend was similar elsewhere in Australia. In Queensland, the Chinese proportion of the population dropped from 9.3 per cent in the 1870s to 2.5 per cent in 1888; in Victoria from 2.4 per cent to less than one per cent over the same period; in Western Australia it was steady at about two per cent; and in Tasmania and South Australia the Chinese population was virtually unnoticeable. In the last of these colonies, which had a population of only 300 or 400 Chinese, the anti-Chinese movement was as vocal as those in New South Wales and Victoria. See Price, *Great White Walls*, 235, 238.

[47] *NSWPD*, LC, XXXIII (30 May 1888), 5021.

If the 'Chinese influx' thesis comprehensively fails to account for this shift in colonial attitudes, does the evidence instead suggest that the decision to exclude Chinese migrants was taken on the basis of economic considerations? This fear of Chinese competition and the threat the Chinese posed to the colony's working classes was even more pronounced in the parliamentary debates than talk of a surge in numbers of Chinese immigrants. Melville claimed to object not to the Chinese as a people but more specifically to the types of Chinese who were coming to the colony. Thus he claimed to oppose the arrival of Chinese 'not because of their immorality' but because 'they are neither more nor less than ... slaves in the hands of certain capitalists'.[48] Likewise, Parkes, while careful to point to 'the great though homely virtues' of the Chinese, nevertheless felt that it was precisely because of these qualities that they posed a threat to the colony's working classes:

> Can it be surprising to any of us that the mothers of those [working] families ... look with something like aversion—with even stronger antipathy—towards the Chinaman, who is a direct competitor with her husband—the father of her children—and with the future of her household? Is it to be wondered that the mother ... should ... cultivate a feeling of hostility to the persons who come in direct competition with the bread-winners of her household for the daily food of the family?[49]

This view, interestingly, was even more marked in the Legislative Council. Many members claimed to support the principle of exclusion because, as Bowker put it, assuming the same racial positivism as Parkes, if the Chinese were allowed to 'come in numbers here, owing to their good qualities—to their being too good, and not too bad—our working men would have no chance with them, owing to their industry, frugality and other good qualities'.[50]

However, the economic objection to Chinese immigration, though pronounced, cannot by itself explain the wholesale shift to a policy of absolute exclusion at this time. As Price has argued, there were many politicians and social commentators who claimed no affinity for working-class aspirations or objectives but who nevertheless were equally strident in their calls for further Chinese restriction. More importantly, the threat from Chinese competition, like the actual numbers arriving in the colony, was grossly exaggerated. The level of actual competition from Chinese residents was very slight. Apart from playing a relatively minor role in certain specific industries—especially furniture making and shop keeping—most Chinese were merchants trading directly with China or employed in establishments catering almost exclusively to the Chinese themselves. Many others were employed in market gardening, railroad building, domestic services and similar industries in which Europeans showed little if any interest.[51] And again, the more percipient contemporary observers recognised this vital fact. Garran, who cited economic reasons to

---

[48] Ibid., LA, XXXII (16 May 1888), 4805.

[49] Ibid., XXXI (16 May 1888), 4783–84.

[50] Ibid., LC, XXXIII (17 May 1888), 4863. For other examples of this view in the Legislative Council, see comments by Manning, Edmund Barton, John Davies, Alfred Stephens and John Lucas, in ibid. (30–31 May 1888), 5032, 5103, 5108, 5112–13 and 5123 (respectively).

[51] See esp. Price, *Great White Walls*, 227–30; and Davison, 'Unemployment, Race and Public Opinion', 105–07.

justify the further exclusion of Chinese, nevertheless felt that this argument 'has perhaps been overstated', and contrariwise, that:

> the utility of the Chinese to the working-classes has perhaps been underestimated. For all the trades have not suffered; quite the contrary, the Chinese have touched only a few. The working-classes, as consumers, are the persons who receive the greatest benefit from the cheapness of Chinese labour. They may be cut out as producers, certain individuals may suffer; but, taken as a whole, they owe their cheap furniture and their cheap vegetables to the Chinese.[52]

Most tellingly, the legislation subsequently introduced in New South Wales and the other colonies targeted not merely Chinese from the labouring classes, but all Chinese regardless of economic background. This principle had been firmly established at the Intercolonial Conference, which had rejected all efforts by the British government to have the new restrictions applied equally to all foreign labourers and thereby avoid any stigma of racial discrimination.

For similar kinds of reasons, the cultural argument fails to provide a sufficiently plausible explanation for the unanimous decision to introduce a policy of complete prohibition. Certainly, some policymakers phrased their objection in cultural terms, accusing the Chinese of making little or no effort to become good colonists. Taking up this theme in the Legislative Council, John Macintosh claimed that he would:

> almost go to the length of prohibiting Chinese from coming into the country, because I do not think they are a desirable kind of immigrant. I do not think we ought to allow them to come here to disturb our social relations. They do not come as colonists … The Chinese have not altered in any respect since they came amongst us. They are just the same now as they were twenty years ago.[53]

But this complaint ignored the presence of Chinese in the colony who were thoroughly assimilated. Some parliamentarians recognised this problem, explicitly citing the example of the wealthy Sydney merchant, Quong Tart, a close friend of Parkes' and the living antithesis of everything the premier claimed for the Chinese as a race—proudly British, highly respected and indeed admired by the mainstream community, and according to another close political acquaintance, George Reid, 'the only man living who has got the true original Gaelic accent'.[54] And yet, those who cited the example of these assimilated Chinese did so not to demonstrate how the Chinese, with encouragement and the passage of time, might become assimilated and valued members of society, but rather to emphasise what rare exceptions they were. Salomons, who conceded the existence of 'what I may call Quong Tarts among the Chinese of the colony', insisted that 'we cannot legislate in the light of exceptional circumstances'.[55]

---

[52] *NSWPD*, LC, XXXIII (30 May 1888), 5026.

[53] Ibid. (31 May 1888), 5116–17.

[54] Cited in Robert Travers, *Australian Mandarin: The Life and Times of Quong* Tart (Kenthurst, NSW: Kangaroo Press, 1981), 182.

[55] *NSWPD*, LC, XXXIII (30 May 1888), 5016. Consistent with one of the key objectives of the intercolonial conference, which had called upon the mother country to exclude Chinese who were naturalised British subjects, cultured and productive colonists such as Quong Tart were, under the

The Chinese Immigration Crisis of 1888

What clearly offended Salomons and his fellow colonists was the race itself. Does this mean that they were mainly driven by a coherent doctrine of racial superiority? While attitudes of this nature have received considerable attention in the literature on the subject, language associated with Chinese racial inferiority, not to mention the more contested concept of social Darwinism,[56] was conspicuous by its almost complete absence during the crisis in New South Wales. It is true that certain colonists were wont to speak of the Chinese as 'wretched, miserable, dirty devils' (John Want), an 'alien and inferior race' (Edmund Barton) whose 'habits and morals are exceedingly bad' and who were responsible for the introduction of 'loathsome diseases' (John Davies).[57] Perhaps the closest anyone came to articulating an ideology of racial hierarchy was Salomons. When introducing the Influx of Chinese Restriction Bill to the Legislative Council on 30 May, he spoke in terms that clearly relegated the Chinese race to a lower form of humanity. While conceding that the Chinese were 'a thrifty, quiet and industrious people', Salomons nevertheless felt that they belonged to 'a civilisation which tends downwards rather than upwards'. Their habits and customs were disagreeable, and when they came into contact with Europeans they infected them with 'habits of life, views of duty, and impressions alien to the proper standard of morality'—like 'a drop of deadly poison in a large goblet of pure water'. They came from 'a lower civilisation', and as if to emphasise the permanence of this situation, Salomons claimed that in every respect the Chinese were in 'as unfortunate a position as people … who are born paralysed, with hereditary diseases, or who are maimed'.[58]

But this view that the Chinese were biologically inferior to Europeans—in a manner that was as unavoidable as a congenital disease—was one to which few decisionmakers in New South Wales openly resorted. On the contrary, Salomons, after expressing these sentiments, was met by a barrage of criticism from his colleagues who rejected the unflattering racial qualities attributed to the Chinese. Dalley mocked those who accused the Chinese of immorality, 'loathsome vices' and 'every species of odious and abominable offence', and pointed to their tolerance, industry and 'extreme inoffensiveness of demeanour'.[59] Garran likewise talked up the many good qualities of the race and deplored

> those vituperative orators whose vulgarity, whose cruelty, whose vindictiveness, and whose hypocritical accusations are a disgrace to themselves and their country, and reveal to us how thin often is the veneer of civilisation that overlies the subjacent barbarism, and how much of the wild beast still lingers in the man.[60]

---

new laws in New South Wales, as unwelcome as all other Chinese.

[56] For an excellent critique of the use, abuse and general misunderstanding of the term 'social Darwinism', see Mark Francis, 'Social Darwinism and the Construction of Institutionalised Racism in Australia', *Journal of Australian Studies*, 20 (50–51), 1996, 90–105.

[57] See *NSWPD*, LA, XXXII (16 May 1888) and LC, XXXIII (31 May 1888), 4765 (Want), 5103 (Barton), 5108, 5111 (Davies).

[58] Ibid., LC, XXXIII (30 May 1888), 5013–15. The only other legislators who referred to Chinese 'inferiority'—although even here this seemed to refer to the social position of the Chinese and not any biological inferiority—were Parkes (4781) and the cosmopolitans Garran (5031) and Alfred Stephens (5113–14).

[59] Ibid., 5022–23.

[60] Ibid., 5031.

Some went further still, not only accusing these detractors of the very barbarism for which they denounced the Chinese, but also demonstrating that the same vices and habits of life that supposedly made the Chinese such a despicable race were equally prevalent in European communities. William Manning pointed to the dens of London, 'where he would see several families living in one room', and wondered what a representative of China might make of such conditions. Indeed:

> would he be justified on his return to his own country in reporting that the English lived in dens and amidst all kinds of abominations? ... Let us not, therefore, base our objections to the Chinese on the ground of their inferior civilisation, or if we do consider ourselves a people of superior civilisation, let us show it by nobility of conduct towards those whom we consider our inferiors.[61]

As Manning's comment suggested, a number of colonial legislators were unconvinced by accusations of Chinese inferiority, and even when they entertained notions of racial hierarchy this was done grudgingly, and then only to dismiss such ideas as a primary motivating factor.

'No Chinaman is One of Us, and He Never Can Be': The Source and Nature of Australian Race Thinking

None of these interpretations are therefore capable of serving as a self-contained explanation for the decision of the colonists at this time to introduce legislation that provided for the wholesale exclusion of Chinese migrants. Some colonists certainly regarded the Chinese as a threat to their living standards while others saw them as a people that refused to assimilate and were therefore culturally objectionable, but in both cases the existing restrictions were more than sufficient for weeding out these undesirables and allowing more cultured and economically acceptable Chinese to continue migrating to the colonies without resorting to a policy of total prohibition. Likewise, the numbers arriving in the colonies, with the single exception of the Northern Territory, were so insignificant that the adoption of wholesale restrictions was simply unwarranted.

The invocation of these economic, cultural and numerical objections even when the evidence to support them was so sparse suggests that there was something more fundamental, even visceral, about colonial objections to the Chinese; that indeed, their primary complaint against the Chinese was simply that they were Chinese. This is not to suggest that the colonists were moved by an all-embracing or even tangible doctrine of racial superiority. Some colonists—perhaps even a majority of colonists—regarded the Chinese as an inferior race. A cursory glance at populist newspapers such as the *Bulletin* and the Brisbane *Worker* demonstrates that certain sections of society—especially those that felt most threatened by Chinese immigration—were given to crude racial slogans and notions of Chinese inferiority when expressing their objections.[62] But those responsible

---

[61] Ibid., 5032–33.

[62] See, for instance, Markus, *Fear and Hatred*, 200–05. See also Neville Meaney, '"The Yellow Peril", Invasion Scare Novels and Australian Political Culture', in *The 1890s: Australian Literature and Literary Culture*, ed. Ken Stewart (St Lucia: University of Queensland Press, 1996).

for introducing the prohibitive laws of 1888 rarely drew on this kind of language—indeed, just as many flatly eschewed it. This would suggest that such ideas were not sufficiently prominent to provide a coverall explanation for the colonial consensus on Chinese exclusion.

And yet, the racial aversion to the Chinese was undeniable. Time and again, those who called for complete exclusion spoke as if the Chinese were not merely unwilling but actually incapable of partaking in the political, economic and cultural life of the community by virtue of their race. John Macintosh, who had been careful to phrase his objection to the Chinese in cultural terms, could not overcome what was basically a racial conception of the problem. 'No Chinaman is one of us', he said emphatically at one point, 'and he never can be'.[63] William Manning, who had taken great umbrage at the suggestion that the Chinese were racially inferior to Europeans, nevertheless argued that 'we all know from experience … the antagonism that exists between the races'. For him, 'you cannot get races that are totally different from each other to amalgamate', and with this in mind, Manning felt that it was 'well … for those in power to take care that the two races are not brought into antagonism more than can be helped'.[64] Garran too focused on the racial aspect of the question, acknowledging the labour movement's concerns but then claiming that this was only one aspect of a much broader problem:

> Apart altogether from the wage argument, there is another which will weigh with persons who, like myself, think that up to the present time the working men of this colony have been more frightened than hurt by Chinese labour—namely, the social argument, that is the inexpediency of having any large pariah class in the community—a class that never can, and never will, amalgamate with the rest of the community.

In Australia, where they were 'beginning a new country in a new way', it was undesirable to have 'a large number of persons who cannot, or should not, be allowed to exercise the suffrage; who are, in fact, a sort of slave class'. The United States had squandered the opportunity for a truly homogeneous society and was 'now suffering from the difficulties of having 7 000 000 negroes, nominally citizens, and yet socially outcasts' in the body politic.[65]

These comments revealed a great deal about the colonial aversion to Chinese immigration. Like Macintosh, Manning and almost every other legislator, Garran was convinced that Chinese dissimilarity—which he understood in specifically racial terms—made the Chinese undesirable migrants and a danger to the peace and prosperity of New South Wales. This racially determinist view of society was at the core of colonial attitudes to Chinese immigration in the late 1880s. But where did these ideas come from? A possible answer is to be found in the great changes that occurred throughout colonial society in the 1870s and 1880s. Like other Western industrial societies, Australia at this time experienced a period of rapid modernisation which produced an increasingly skilled, literate and mobile population. In the process, the certainty and security of the village community, of the cycle of the seasons and established social orders gave way to a highly

---

[63] *NSWPD*, LC, XXXIII (31 May 1888), 5116.

[64] Ibid. (30 May 1888), 5032.

[65] Ibid., 5030.

industrialised, capitalist and urban society.⁶⁶ The psychological trauma and disorientation created by this process produced an intense need for a new identity, one that would help the colonists understand these disturbing social changes and restore the sense of purpose and belonging that had been lost with the onset of modernisation. The ideology of nationalism, which took hold in nearly all developed Western or Western-derivative societies around this time, seemed to fill the void. For societies deeply traumatised by these changes, the seemingly natural and spontaneous emergence of nationalist sentiment, which borrowed extensively from the past to give meaning to the present and promise to the future, offered great emotional comfort to communities that yearned for unity and purpose under these difficult new circumstances. Reflecting this urge and the homogenising tendencies inherent in modernisation, nationalism in Australia—which assumed the form of British race patriotism—embraced the familiar and spurned the foreign; it promoted the emergence of a community of identical individuals and sought to expunge all alien elements from the body politic.⁶⁷

In a society that required sameness and homogeneity, both for practical and psychological purposes, race became a convenient, if crude, benchmark. While not necessarily based on notions of hierarchy, and indeed quite capable of assimilating an egalitarian race view of humanity that emphasised the positive attributes of different races, this racial view of society nevertheless presumed the existence of fundamental dissimilarities between Chinese and British Australians. According to this thinking, no amount of exposure to British customs and laws, political institutions and economic practices could alter the inherent inability of the Chinese to amalgamate, let alone contribute to colonial society. Indeed, under these circumstances it was immaterial whether the colonists regarded the Chinese as inferior, or as economic competitors, or as a people who did not 'mix'. Nor did it matter that they were entering the colonies in relatively small numbers and that the ratio of Chinese to British Australians was actually declining by this time. These objections were merely symptomatic of a much broader set of ideas which stipulated that a person's race dictated their culture and their capacity to contribute to the political, social and economic life of Australia. Indeed, because this absolute belief in racial dissimilarity informed all aspects of colonial thinking on the subject, those who called for Chinese exclusion often cited one or more of these reasons simultaneously. Parkes was one of many legislators who

---

⁶⁶ For the most succinct and compelling introduction to this process and its ideological consequences for modern societies, see Ernest Gellner's classic study of *Nations and Nationalism* (New York: Cornell University Press, 1983), chs 2–3. See also Benedict Anderson, *Imagined Communities: Reflections on the Origins and Spread of Nationalism* (London: Verso, 1991 [1983]), esp. 37ff; Hans Kohn, *The Idea of Nationalism: A Study of its Origins and Background* (New Brunswick: Transaction Publishers, 2005 [1944]), 10–13.

⁶⁷ See Jordan, 'Rewriting Australia's Racist Past', 19–25; Neville Meaney, 'The End of "White Australia" and Australia's Changing Perceptions of Asia, 1945–1990', *Australian Journal of International Affairs*, 49 (2), 1995, 171–75; and Neville Meaney, 'Britishness and Australian Identity: The Problem of Nationalism in Australian History and Historiography', *Australian Historical Studies*, 32 (116), 2001, 76–90. For the most lucid contemporary account of these developments and their effect on the identity of the Australian colonies, see Charles Henry Pearson, *National Life and Character: A Forecast* (London: Macmillan, 1893), 15–18, 84–85, 180–90.

could talk interchangeably of protecting the working classes from Chinese competition, preserving 'the type of the British nation' in New South Wales, saving the colony from 'a plague', 'a pestilence' or 'a famine', and excluding 'any element that of necessity must be of an inferior nature or character'.[68]

But at the core of all these arguments was a racial conception of society which sprang from the intense psychological need of the colonists to create a homogenous and essentially monochrome nation. When, in March 1888, the British government had sought clarification from the colonies on the nature and extent of their anti-Chinese laws, Parkes, in citing all the usual arguments, nevertheless focused on two fundamental but interrelated principles: the supposedly inherent and immutable differences between the two races, which made peaceful coexistence impossible, and the geopolitical necessity of preventing China's multitudes from descending upon the colonies in such numbers that Australia's British character and inheritance would be overturned.

> (1) The Australian ports are within easy sail of the ports of China … (3) The working classes of the British people in all the affinities of race are directly opposed to their Chinese competitors. (4) There can be no sympathy, and in the future it is to be apprehended that there will be no peace between the two races. (5) The enormous number of the Chinese population intensifies every consideration of this class of immigration in comparison with the emigration of any other nation. (6) The most prevailing determination in all the Australian communities is to preserve the British type in the population. (7) There can be no interchange of ideas of religion or citizenship, nor can there be intermarriage or social communion between the British and the Chinese.[69]

Parkes later made the same key points, only more forcefully, at the Intercolonial Conference, urging the British government to support the colonists in

> their endeavour to prevent their country from being overrun by an alien race who are incapable of assimilation in the body politic, strangers to our civilisation, out of sympathy with our aspirations, and unfitted for our free institutions, to which their presence in any large number would be a source of constant danger.[70]

While the actual numbers of Chinese entering New South Wales (and Australia) during the 1880s was relatively insignificant, the spectre of these unassimilable 'hordes' descending upon the country and entrenching their racially acquired cultural traits and standards of living filled the colonists with such dread that they resolved to exclude the Chinese as completely as possible and thereby prevent any chance of a fifth column ever threatening the racial homogeneity of the emerging nation. This sense of an impending 'invasion by numbers' was expressed dramatically in the New South Wales debates. Bowker warned that 'the Chinese were like a reservoir of water hanging over the country; and it was only necessary to turn on a tap to overwhelm us'.[71] Invoking a similar analogy, Manning regarded them as 'a heavy cloud … which might eventually … let down rain enough to

---

[68] *NSWPD*, LA, XXXI (16 May 1888), 4782.
[69] Parkes to Lord Knutsford, 31 March 1888, in NSW, *Votes*, vol.II.
[70] Parkes to Lord Knutsford, n.d. [c. 14 June 1888], in ibid.
[71] *NSWPD*, LC, XXXIII (17 May 1888), 4863.

flood the country'.⁷² Thomas Walker, speaking in the Legislative Assembly, warned not of an invasion by force, which he conceded 'we can sometimes foresee and provide against', but of 'an insidious invasion'. Like 'the creeping into wood of white ants', this form of encroachment was not seen immediately; rather '[i]t goes on silently, until it works its way into the whole fabric of society; and before we realise what is going on, we find that our birth right is stolen from us'.⁷³

These fears were as manifestly unrealistic as talk of Australia's economic, cultural and moral norms being overturned unless the colonies adopted a policy of wholesale exclusion. But Australia's proximity to Asia and the growing expectation that China would emerge as a regional power further intensified the already strident sense of collectivism in the colonies and their determination to keep Australia white and preferably British. Not surprisingly, the same racially determinist motives were conspicuous in the justifications offered by senior legislators in the other colonies. Gillies, responding to the same inquiry from the British government to which Parkes had already replied, claimed that Victoria's discriminatory legislation against Chinese was due to 'the totally different character of Chinese immigration from all other immigration'. While 'members of the European family of nations joining our community become amalgamated with the general population', he said, echoing Parkes' sentiments, 'the Chinese stand out in marked contrast'. They did not bring their women or children, had no intention of settling and always occupied an 'isolated position' in the community:

> Nor is it the mere fact of this isolation, but the impossibility of it being otherwise. The Chinese, from all points of view, are so entirely dissimilar as to render a blending of the peoples out of the question. They are not only of an alien race, but they remain aliens. Thus, we have not a colonisation in any true sense of the word, but practically a sort of peaceful invasion of our land by Chinese.

In the infancy of the emerging nation, he concluded, 'the question of race is of paramount importance' and the issue was whether the British government would agree to 'admit hordes of the Mongolian race' or reserve it 'for those peoples—our own, or kindred to our own—that have led the van of the world's civilisation'.⁷⁴

Similar sentiments were expressed in March 1888 by Queensland premier Sir Samuel Walker Griffith, who likewise explained the problem to the British in specifically racial terms. Thus, after referring to the threat posed by Chinese competition, he claimed that 'the main, and in the opinion of the Government, the insuperable objection to allowing the immigration of Chinese is the fact that they cannot be admitted to an equal share in the political and social institutions of the colony'. This was not because they were inferior. On the contrary, Chinese civilisation was 'of a complicated and in many respects marvellous character'. But, he added, it was 'essentially different' from European civilisation. For him, race and culture were entwined, and because of the permanence of this situation, 'the

---

[72] Ibid. (30 May 1888), 5035.

[73] Ibid. LA (17 May 1888), 4880–81.

[74] Duncan Gillies to Lord Loch, 11 April 1888, in House of Commons (Great Britain), *Correspondence Relating to Chinese Immigration into the Australasian Colonies* (hereafter *Correspondence Relating to Chinese Immigration*) (London: Stationery Office, 1888).

presence in considerable numbers of an alien race occupying an inferior position could not fail before long to bring about very serious troubles, and', he added, reiterating the common fear that this must lead inevitably to the kind of peaceful invasion referred to by Gillies, 'would probably necessitate a radical change in our political institutions, and entirely alter the future history and development of Australia'.[75] Playford, when later justifying his calls at the Intercolonial Conference for the exclusion of all Chinese regardless of whether they were naturalised British subjects, did so in unmistakably racial terms. As he told the South Australian Legislative Assembly in July 1888:

> the objection is to the race (hear, hear). A Chinaman was not the less a Chinaman because he was born under the British flag in Hongkong or Singapore (hear, hear). If we allowed British-born Chinese to come in we should be flooded by immigrants holding some kind of nationalisation papers (hear, hear).

According to Playford, at the Intercolonial Conference Parkes had baulked at this provision but was swayed by Gillies, who reminded the New South Wales premier that 'he [Sir Henry] had all along objected to the Chinese, not because of their vices, but because they were different to us, and would not assimilate with our people so as to form a homogeneous whole by-and-bye; in fact he had objected to Chinamen on the score of race'.[76]

Even Tasmania, which like Western Australia was somewhat out of accord with all the other colonies on the issue of Chinese immigration, seemed to understand the problem in these racial terms. Premier Philip Oakley Fysh, who had attended the Intercolonial Conference and, in typical liberal humanitarian style, was deeply uncomfortable with the notion that the Chinese were intrinsically poor colonists, had admitted to Parkes several months earlier that the Australian aversion to Chinese immigration was probably unavoidable: 'However selfish it may be to cry "Our country for our own people", the cry is in accordance with the instincts of nations, and indeed is in accord with the sacred instincts of the family when "kith and kin" are sheltered to the exclusion of strangers'.[77] When, moreover, he had received the British request for information on the nature of Tasmania's discriminatory laws, Fysh had replied by enclosing 'an exhaustive memorandum' by his attorney-general, Andrew Inglis Clark, which, he said at the time, embodied his own views on the question of Chinese immigration.[78] Clark's screed contained the same ideas about race that characterised the thinking of other prominent colonial leaders. Accordingly, he felt that Tasmania should support the other colonies in their efforts to further restrict Chinese immigration because, 'although the influx to Tasmania has not been so great as to create a similar local necessity for … more stringent measures', the continued admission of Chinese would produce 'a combined political and industrial division of society upon the basis of a racial distinction'.[79]

---

[75] S. W. Griffith to Sir Anthony Musgrave, 24 March 1888, in ibid.

[76] *Debates in the House of Legislature … of South Australia*, Legislative Assembly, 3rd Session, 3 July 1888, 202.

[77] P. O. Fysh to Parkes, 25 November 1887, in NSW, *Votes*, vol.II.

[78] Fysh to Sir Robert Hamilton, 1 May 1888, in House of Commons, *Correspondence Relating to Chinese Immigration*.

[79] Andrew Inglis Clark to Fysh, 24 April 1888, in ibid.

To Clark's mind, because the Chinese were racially distinct from British Australians, they would either occupy an inferior political and social position—and for him, societies so divided, like the United States he otherwise deeply admired, 'produce particular vices in exaggerated proportions, and are doomed to certain deterioration'—or they would continue to come in numbers, and if they should

> at any time become as numerous … in any colony as the residents of European origin, the result would be … an attempt on the part of the Chinese to establish separate institutions of a character that would trench on the supremacy of the present legislative and administrative authorities.

Further expounding on this fundamentally racial view of humanity and society, Clark added:

> Both the virtues and the vices of the Chinese are bred in them by a civilisation stretching back, in an unparalleled fixedness of character and detail, to an age more remote than any to which the beginnings of any European nation can be traced, and the experience of both America and Australasia proves that no length of residence amidst a population of European descent will cause the Chinese immigrants who remain unnaturalised to change the mode of life or relinquish the practices that they bring with them from their native country.

Having seemingly suggested that this was a cultural problem—that is, that Chinese separateness might be remedied by naturalising them—Clark almost immediately back-pedalled, saying that granting them political equality 'suggests a result equally menacing to the permanence and the civilisation and structure of the society now existing in these colonies', and this, he concluded, encapsulating the fundamentally racial view of society which had moved the colonists to prohibit Chinese immigration altogether, was because

> the indurated and renitent character of the habits and conceptions of the Chinese immigrants make their amalgamation with populations of European origin, so as to become constituent portions of a homogenal community retaining the European type of civilisation, an impossibility.[80]

Conclusion

The Chinese immigration crisis of 1888 was a crucial event in the development and consolidation of Australian attitudes to race. In New South Wales, where the crisis was initially and most dramatically played out, the arrival of relatively small numbers of Chinese occasioned widespread anti-Chinese demonstrations and unilateral action by the government to legislate for their virtual exclusion. While Parkes was lambasted for flouting the law and pandering to mob rule, there was universal support for the principle of prohibition. Those who approved of the premier's motives, if not his methods, offered a variety of reasons—and these often simultaneously—for their support. Some colonists undoubtedly wanted the Chinese excluded because they regarded them as racially inferior; still others had convinced themselves that the Chinese were coming in such numbers that the 'influx' must be stopped or Australia would be inundated; and others identified

---

[80] Ibid.

the Chinese as an economic or cultural threat to the colonies. But at the core of these specific objections was the overarching conviction that the Chinese were incapable of assimilation by virtue of their race. In this context the economic, cultural, invasion and racial hierarchy arguments were merely by-products of a much broader belief that because of the biologically acquired traits of the Chinese—their 'indurated and renitent' habits and 'unparalleled fixedness of character', as Clark put it—their absorption into Australia's British society would not just be difficult but 'an impossibility'. This fixed view of humanity, which was made more intense by the peculiar geopolitical anxieties of the colonists, convinced them that allowing Chinese to migrate in even small numbers would result inevitably in inundation and the economic, cultural, and perhaps even the moral degradation of white Australians.

This racially determinist view of society became entrenched in the Australian mindset in the late 1880s as the colonists responded to the homogenising tendencies of modernisation by seeking to create an essentially monochrome nation while at the same time expunging all 'coloured' elements. In this sense, the events of May and June 1888 were not directly responsible for the adoption of racially exclusive laws but served as a catalyst for decisive action. At the same time, Parkes' action prompted the other colonies to convene an Intercolonial Conference, which used the occasion of the crisis to draft measures that were in some ways more prohibitive than those adopted in New South Wales and which sought to establish once and for all the statutory wall behind which a racially British nation could be cultivated. This blood-based sense of community—'the crimson thread of kinship', as Parkes put it—could be strengthened by promoting the immigration of the colonists' 'kith and kin' from Britain and even small numbers of racially acceptable groups from Europe, but it also required the complete exclusion of the unassimilable 'hordes' of Asia. Because of the fundamentally racial nature of this thinking, the extension of these absolute laws to other 'coloured' people was only a matter of time and from the 1890s there was an inexorable move to exclude all non-Europeans from Australia.[81] When, in 1896, the colonies resolved to adopt this course 'without delay', the *Sydney Morning Herald*, invoking the very language used by the colonial legislators to justify the complete exclusion of Chinese in 1888, claimed that this was not:

> a mere matter of sentiment or racial prejudice, but the grave question of whether we shall preserve our existence as an Anglo-Saxon people, and prevent the Australian continent from being swarmed over by races that do not assimilate, but might in their multitudes sweep away the institution we are building for ourselves and our children.[82]

Following the adoption of this racial view of society as the founding principle of the Commonwealth in 1901, Deakin, emphasising the nation's geopolitical anxieties and determination to maintain its 'racial exclusiveness', told a British readership that Australians 'with little more than nominal occupation of half the continent is so stubbornly British in sentiment that it proposes to tolerate nothing within its dominion that is not British in

---

[81] See A. T. Yarwood, *Asian Migration to Australia: The Background to Exclusion, 1896–1923* (Melbourne: Melbourne University Press, 1964), 7–9, 11.

[82] *SMH*, 20 February 1896. See also Jordan, 'Rewriting Australia's Racist Past', 25.

character and constitution or capable of becoming Anglicised without delay'. He admitted that 'a less attractive aspect' of this thinking was 'the fear exhibited of confessedly inferior stocks'—a sentiment with which he himself clearly sympathised to some extent—'and the affront afforded to the abler peoples and higher classes of Asiatic origin'. But these concerns were merely peripheral according to Deakin, who seemed to imply that even if Australians generally regarded non-Europeans as inferior this was not their primary objection to 'coloured' immigration. The 'solid argument' for the Commonwealth's adoption of a White Australia, he instead claimed, was 'the unsuitability of mixed races for constitutional government'. This belief in the dominance and permanence of racial difference was the fundamental motive animating the founders and their single-minded commitment to a nation of white, preferably British migrants. 'For all outside that charmed circle', Deakin said, encapsulating Australia's approach to immigration for the next seventy years, 'the policy is that of the closed door'.[83]

---

[83] See Alfred Deakin, *Federated Australia: Selections from Letters to the Morning Post, 1900–1910*, ed. J. A. LaNauze (Melbourne: Melbourne University Press, 1968), 80–81.

5

'He No Doubt Felt Insulted': The White Australia Policy and Australia's Relations with India, 1944–1964

Eric Meadows

The Australia–India relationship in the post-war period, and indeed until quite recently, has often been characterised as one in which bouts of enthusiasm are followed by periods of neglect; a stop/start relationship, as it were. Meg Gurry has argued that there were structural reasons for this: a solid relationship between two countries required a multi-strand context to develop a depth that was lacking in the past.[1] The relationship was one of 'missed opportunities, mutual incomprehension, and benign neglect'.[2] Gurry also recognised the importance of the lack of personal rapport between Indian prime minister Jawaharlal Nehru and his Australian counterpart, R. G. Menzies, at a time when leaders put much stress on the personal factor in successful foreign relationships.[3] Nehru thought Menzies did not belong in the twentieth century, regarded his speeches with 'wry amusement' and considered him a fit subject for a Victorian museum.[4] Although Gurry felt that the lacklustre relationship was Australia's fault, Australia was low on India's list of priorities. In Nihal Kuruppu's view, Australian views on India were dominated by out-of-date British attitudes.[5] Andrea Benvenuti firmly put the blame for the benign neglect on the different views of the Asian Cold War which both countries held. Australia saw in the Cold War a potential threat to Australian security and was committed to a 'realist' policy firmly anchored in creating alliances with great powers with the capacity for global reach. India, in contrast, was opposed to any military alliances and steered a resolutely independent path between the Cold War opponents.[6]

Australia worked hard to put depth into the political relationship, for instance, suggesting exchanges on strategic matters and proposing official talks between the

---

[1] Meg Gurry, *India: Australia's Neglected Neighbour? 1947–1996* (Griffith University: Centre for the Study of Australia–Asia Relations, 1996).

[2] Gurry, 'Neither Threat Nor Promise: An Australian View of Australian–Indian Relations Since 1947', *South Asia*, XIII (1), 1990, 85–101.

[3] Gurry, 'Leadership and Bilateral Relations: Menzies and Nehru, Australia and India, 1949–1964', *Pacific Affairs*, 65 (4), 1992–93, 510–26

[4] Cited in Chris Waters, 'Diplomacy in Easy Chairs: Casey, Pearson, and Australian–Canadian Relations, 1951–7', in *Parties Long Estranged: Canada and Australia in the Twentieth Century*, eds Margaret MacMillan and Francine McKenzie (Vancouver: University of British Colombia Press, 2003), 220.

[5] Nihal Henry Kuruppu, *Non-Alignment and Peace Versus Military Alignment and War* (New Delhi: Academic Foundation, 2004).

[6] Andrea Benvenuti, 'Difficult Partners: Indo-Australian Relations at the Height of the Cold War, 1949–1964', *Australian Journal of Politics and History* (hereafter *AJPH*), 57 (1), 2011, 53–67.

two external affairs ministries. For a time it was also active in seeking solutions to the Kashmir dispute. Moreover, it posted its best and most senior diplomats to New Delhi. New Delhi responded, with very few exceptions, by posting lacklustre heads of mission. Nothing seemed to spark a deeper connection: the relationship was always full of potential but enthusiasm wasted away. The principal structural and political link between the two countries remained mutual membership of the Commonwealth. Beyond this, mutual interests hardly existed. Trade, normally a key determinant of bilateral strength, was not a major factor.[7] Defence links did not spark until after India's 1962 war with China, and then only briefly. There was a strong connection to Australian aid via the Colombo Plan but India seemed largely indifferent to Australia's small but effective aid program.

An under-examined factor in the historiography of the bilateral relationship is the impact of the White Australia policy throughout this period. Given that its relationship with Australia was not significant for India, it is probable that the policy did not affect the minimal ties that existed. But it was certainly an impediment to a better relationship and, in the eyes of the Indian press, the policy called into question Australia's good faith in its protestations of friendship with India. It was also an irritant in the relationship, felt keenly by Australia's high commissioners and reported at length by them, as well as by India's high commissioners in Canberra. Independence had established India as a sovereign country in the international system. White Australia seemed to imply that Indians were not equal and this offended elite opinion in India, even though it was claimed that the policy was not intended to insult overseas opinion but rather to protect an isolated, homogenous British society from external threat.

Neville Meaney has written about how the federation's ideal of a White Australia was replaced in the 1970s by a multicultural society which facilitated a positive relationship with Asia.[8] All governments in Australia until that time were committed to the preservation of a homogenous, white British society, one which continued the inheritance from Britain of a stable political culture. Asia was the Other, a threat to the British community created so far away from its cultural roots. Until the departure of the British from east of Suez and the United States from Vietnam in the late 1960s and early 1970s, Australia saw no need to reassess these basic assumptions or to come to terms with the nations closest to it.

Some tentative first steps along these lines, in the form of a measure of Asian immigration, were being urged on the Australian government by its diplomats in India from the 1940s onwards, aware as they were of the shifts in influence and power taking place in Asia. That they had little influence says volumes about the impact of Australia's diplomats on key policy issues. What changes there were came from the quiet work of immigration officials.[9] The most important exception to this generalisation is the crucial work of Sir Peter Heydon who had been high commissioner to India before becoming secretary of the Department

---

[7] Kuruppu, *Non-Alignment and Peace*, 18.

[8] Neville Meaney, 'The End of "White Australia" and Australia's Changing Perceptions of Asia, 1945–1990', *Australian Journal of International Affairs* (hereafter *AJIA*), 49 (2), 1995, 171–89.

[9] See Matthew Jordan, 'The Reappraisal of the White Australia Policy Against the Background of a Changing Asia, 1945–67', *AJPH*, 52 (2), 2006, 224–43.

of Immigration in 1961.[10] The specific issue of White Australia, despite public statements to the contrary, was also of considerable interest to the Indian government from the start of its diplomatic representation in Canberra in 1944.

The 1940s

In 1944, Australia was the first country with which India established a full diplomatic relationship. All the old dominions had been asked to do this by the then British secretary of state for India and Burma, Leo Amery, as part of India's transition to independence, but Australia was the first to do so. The instructions to the first Indian high commissioner to Australia were anodyne and generalised. Significantly, the one area of policy instruction concerned Australia's immigration policy where Sir Raghunath Paranjpye, the first high commissioner, was instructed to 'educate the mind of the Australian public so that it would be reconciled in due course to the idea of admitting Indians as immigrants on an equal footing with other members of the British Commonwealth'. He was instructed to avoid public recrimination or criticism. It was expected that the number of Indians in Australia would increase after the war and Paranjpye was to stand ready to help where he saw fit.[11]

Dr N. B. Khare, who was responsible for Commonwealth relations in the government of India and to whom Paranjpye therefore reported, amplified the instructions in his early letters to the Indian mission in Canberra. Paranjpye was to convince Australians that India did not want mass Indian migration to Australia, but rather a token quota such as the United States was likely to grant. The point of this was to remove the racial stigma against Indians. Khare noted, however, that this was not an urgent problem and that any change in Australia would only come from better understanding between the two countries.[12]

Paranjpye was to report on race issues more than any other. White Australia was often raised with him and he reported on calls within Australia from religious leaders, intellectuals and journalists for it to be modified. At first, his inclination was to agree with Australia's line that the White Australia policy was not based on racial prejudice but on the wish for a homogenous society, without pockets of 'coolie labour'; one in which all workers were paid fairly.[13] Khare disputed this, but Paranjpye insisted that in Australia, unlike Britain, there was little evidence of racial prejudice.[14] Nonetheless, fairly soon into his posting Paranjpye began to doubt that social homogeneity was the only reason for the policy. In June 1945, for instance, he asked New Delhi to send only the top Indian scientists to Australia on tours in order to remove the misconceptions about the capabilities of Indians in Australia:

---

[10] See Sean Brawley, 'The Department of Immigration and Abolition of the "White Australia" Policy Reflected Through the Private Diaries of Sir Peter Heydon', *AJPH*, 41 (3), 1995, 420–34.

[11] Letter, R. N. Banerjee to Sir Olaf Caroe, 'Instructions to the High Commissioner for India in Australia', 1 November 1944, National Archives of India (NAI): File 682(35)-FE/44.

[12] Letter, R. P. Paranjpye to N. B. Khare, 2 March 1945, Nehru Memorial Museum and Library (NMML): Papers of R. P. Paranjpye (hereafter Paranjpye Papers), List No.5.

[13] Letter, Paranjpye to Khare, 11 January 1945, NMML: Paranjpye Papers.

[14] Letter, Paranjpye to Khare, 2 March 1945, NMML: Paranjpye Papers.

> Although it is officially stated that white Australia is based on purely economic considerations there is certainly an undercurrent of feeling among Australians that Indians are in some way inferior to the white population of the country.[15]

The Indian government's Standing Committee on Commonwealth Relations asked Paranjpye in 1947 to survey the extent to which Indians in Australia were discriminated against.[16] His report noted that at the urging of the government of India in the 1920s, legal discrimination which had existed in some of the Australian states had been removed. Some 2000 people of Indian origin lived in Australia and temporary entry for students and merchants, among others, was permitted; migration entry restrictions, of course, remained. After independence a file was opened by the Indian Ministry of External Affairs to collect material on the White Australia policy. As the official who started it noted, 'Sometime or other this question is bound to assume greater importance for us'.[17] The file was to contain reports on the ever-increasing calls from many sections of Australian society for modifications to be made to the policy.

In his extensive tours of the country Paranjpye made a point of meeting Indians who had settled in Australia. They were, he noted, mostly 'humble people' who did not associate with India. Many were born in Australia and reported no experience of racial prejudice. In Townsville Paranjpye reported that the Indians lived 'very shabbily' compared to Australians even though they had money. Because of this situation, Paranjpye added, 'the prejudice of Australians to any further influx of Indians appears not unreasonable'.[18] In a speech to Wollongong Rotary he noted that Indians permanently settled in Australia 'suffered practically no difficulties compared with those in South Africa'. Nonetheless, there was an implicit slight in the term 'White Australia' because it debarred any Indian, regardless of his or her social status, from settling in Australia. The introduction of a quota of one hundred Indian migrants by the United States had greatly increased that country's standing in India. Paranjpye's speech hardly raised any eyebrows in contrast to what was to happen when one of his successors, General H. M. Cariappa, made similar points in public speeches in the 1950s, by which time the issue of migration policy had become much more politically contentious within Australia.[19]

In his last report to New Delhi before his departure Paranjpye summed up his attitude to Australia: 'The people are generally friendly and hospitable though their white Australia policy is almost a fetish with all sections of the people'.[20] His adult daughter's memoirs of their time in Australia, written soon after their return to India, contained a chapter on 'White Australia'.[21] Here she described the policy as one born out of a real fear that the country would be swamped by 'the teeming millions of Asia'. There may not have been much colour prejudice in Australia but the loud cries of support for this unfortunately

---

[15] Letter, Paranjpye to New Delhi, 14 June 1945, NAI: File 532-EPI/46.
[16] 'Disabilities of Indians in Australia', NAI: D-4382-IANZ/50.
[17] Ministry of External Affairs (India), 'White Australia Policy', NAI: File 208(2) IANZ 1948.
[18] Letter, Paranjpye to Jawaharlal Nehru, 30 October 1947, NMML: Paranjpye Papers.
[19] Cited in *Daily Telegraph*, 17 July 1946.
[20] Letter, Paranjpye to New Delhi, 10 November 1947, NMML: Paranjpye Papers.
[21] Shakuntala Paranjpye, *Three Years in Australia* (Poona: self-published, 1951).

named policy, from all sides of politics, offended Asia and would isolate Australia from the Asia-Pacific region. The policy, intentionally or not, was a slur on Asia and offended its amour-propre: 'People are prone to be offensive when terrified of extinction. Besides Australia is an adolescent country and adolescence is seldom considerate.'[22]

In contrast to this relatively uncritical, even bemused assessment, press coverage in India of the policy was consistently critical. The English-language press reflected elite opinion, and was the voice of those who traditionally ran India's major institutions. Various journals ran a consciously provocateur role, a kind of chorus off stage to say the things it thought the main actors would not or could not say. Some senior correspondents were close to government officials and were perhaps used by them to float a line with which the government did not wish to be associated. But, above all, the press commentary on Australian migration policy reflected the day-to-day comments with which Australian officials in India had to deal in their social interactions with members of the Indian elite.

In a series of articles in 1946 titled 'Australia Our Neighbour', the Cawnpore *Telegraph*, for instance, noted that for trade to flourish Australia would need to treat India as an equal and repudiate the White Australia policy, under which Indian merchants were only permitted entry into Australia under annual 'certificates of exemption'.[23] Citing Sydney's *Daily Telegraph*, the *Hindustan Times*, a newspaper closely aligned with the Indian National Congress and the independence movement, warned that countries could not expect their neighbours to defend them in wartime if they had not been treated as friends and equals in peace time.[24] Another series of articles in April and May 1947, in the *The Statesman*, a newspaper which spoke for elite interests in Calcutta, called for an end to the policy in order to bring in more people to populate the north of Australia before it was inevitably invaded from Asia.

In a well-argued and moderately toned despatch in 1946, the Australian high commissioner, Sir Iven Mackay, recommended the introduction of a quota for Indian migrants. This was to become a regular feature of the reporting from New Delhi. Australia's policy was based on racial as well as economic and social grounds, he noted; there was no other way to explain why Australia would refuse to take such a small number of Westernised Indian professionals, which would greatly assist its economic expansion. Some thirty Indians entered for temporary residence each year under the current regulations. These, Mackay reasoned, were necessarily merchants or students. Adding twenty professional migrants would remove the resentment felt by educated Indians about the policy of complete exclusion from migration. He noted the goodwill felt towards the United States because of the introduction of an annual quota of a hundred Indian migrants. Australia's stocks stood high in India apart from the White Australia policy. Mackay's main argument was, however, that this act of goodwill would be in Australia's strategic self-interest given the likely importance of independent India and that it would make no appreciable difference to the social make-up of Australia.[25]

---

[22] Ibid., 123.

[23] *Telegraph*, 12 November 1946.

[24] Summarised in cablegram, New Delhi to Canberra, 7 April 1947, National Archives of Australia (NAA): A1066, 645/1/1.

[25] Dispatch 52/46, Iven Mackay to H. V. Evatt, 22 December 1946, in *Documents on Australian*

The Department of External Affairs (DEA) summarised the despatch and sent it to Sir Tasman Heyes, secretary of the Department of Immigration, in March 1948. This was by no means an endorsement of a quota system by the DEA. Its secretary, John Burton, distanced himself from Mackay's arguments, noting that they were personal views and did not represent the considered assessment of the DEA.[26] Not surprisingly, therefore, Mackay's proposals made little impact on Immigration officials. In his position as post-war immigration minister, Arthur Calwell had promised that there would be no 'watering down' of White Australia and he accordingly administered the *Immigration Restriction Act 1901* with an apparent disregard for the impact of his decisions on Asian opinion. If proof were needed that the White Australia policy was based on racial and not economic grounds, in January 1949 Heyes told Burton that Calwell had decided to refuse entry to 'persons not of pure European descent'.[27] Burton protested, knowing the kind of criticism this explicitly racial ruling would provoke in Asia were it to become known, but to no effect.

Mackay's despatch had an eye to the then-forthcoming Asian Relations Conference at which Australia was to be represented. This conference in March 1947 brought together leaders of independence movements in Asia to discuss issues of common interest. The primary concern for Australia at the conference was that its immigration policy would be attacked. R. N. Banerjee, secretary of the Indian Commonwealth Relations Office, told one of the Australian official observers at the conference that while India desired Australia's friendship, 'an adjustment of our [Australia's] migration policy would be requested at a later stage'.[28] Official secretary to the Australian High Commission in New Deli, Colin Moodie, who reported on the success of the conference, highlighted the divisions within Asia over migration and the internal discrimination which existed in many Asian countries. These provided a means for Australia to avoid challenge over its immigration policy. And yet, Moodie added:

> While principles on which Australian migration policy is based must remain, it may be possible to make our rules somewhat more flexible and less apparently exclusionist. Certain cultured and deserving types of Asiatics who do not fit into present categories might usefully be admitted and in such cases, the necessity for renewing their permits annually might be waived.[29]

The Asian Relations Conference was a success in creating a commitment to a common cause in a newly post-colonial Asia. A second pan-Asian conference, this time on the question of Indonesia's independence was called in January 1949 at which Australia was again represented and influential. A serious misunderstanding between India and Australia

---

Foreign Policy (hereafter *DAFP*), vol. X, *July–December 1946*, eds W. J. Hudson and Wendy Way (Canberra: Australian Government Publishing Service, 1993), 534.

[26] Letter, J. W. Burton to T. H. E. Heyes, 1 March 1948, in *DAFP*, vol. XIV, *1948–49*, ed. Pamela Andre (Canberra: DFAT, 1998), 315. The text refers to the despatch but dates it a year later, in 1947.

[27] Heyes to Burton, 20 January 1949, in ibid., 322.

[28] Supplementary report by Gerald Packer, 24 April 1947, NAA: A1068, M47/9/6/15 part 2.

[29] Colin Moodie, report on Asian Relations Conference, 11 April 1947, in *DAFP*, vol. XII, *1947*, eds W. J. Hudson and Wendy Way (Canberra: Australian Government Publishing Service, 1995), 802.

over immigration matters occurred shortly after it. Nehru, by now Indian prime minister, gave an interview to Australian Associated Press in which he was reported to have said that Australia's immigration policy was legitimate if based on maintaining its standard of living and 'not on a racial plane'. He noted that 'no discrimination should, however, be exercised within Australia … against the rights and privileges of Asians living there'.[30] The interview was given at a time of considerable controversy in Australia over the attempts by the Commonwealth government to deport Annie O'Keefe.[31] The Australian minister for external affairs, H. V. Evatt, answering a question in the House of Representatives, claimed that Nehru's comments showed he supported Australia's immigration policy.[32] This provoked Nehru into making a statement in the Indian parliament on 23 February 1949:

> It is not quite clear what Dr Evatt meant by the report attributed to him. Presumably this is based on some newspaper report which appeared in Australia. In the record of an interview with an Australian newspaper correspondent some time ago I stated that I could understand an emigration [sic] policy based on economic considerations with a view to maintaining certain standards and ways of living but that I thought a racial policy was wrong and to be deprecated. We inquired into this matter and found that Dr Evatt told our representative that he regretted he had not been quite understood.[33]

The English-language Indian press had a field day over the perceived incongruity of Australia being present and active in the New Delhi conference on Indonesia's freedom while at the same time announcing it would deport an Indonesian woman married to a white Australian and her children. The Ambala *Tribune* felt that the O'Keefe case was an 'index to the injustice and selfishness of high government policy' while the *Bombay Chronicle* thought Evatt, by his outrageous statement that Nehru supported White Australia, would fritter away the popularity he had gained for Australia through his support of freedom for an Asian country.[34]

Calwell's speech to the Australian Natives Association on 21 February 1949, in which he stated that there would 'be no quota system for the admission of Asiatics, no appeasement …which imperils the hard won living standards which we inherited', provoked a sharp rebuke from the *Bombay Chronicle*. In a single speech, it argued, Calwell 'has very nearly destroyed all prospects of Asia and Australia maintaining friendly relations'. 'Living standards', it argued, was code for racial superiority in white skin and coloured skin was inferior no matter who its owner might be: an uncouth white criminal was clearly superior

---

[30] Cited in *SMH*, 24 January 1949.

[31] Mrs Annie Jacob and her husband and children were wartime refugees from the Dutch East Indies. After the death of her husband Mrs O'Keefe married an Australian citizen, Jack O'Keefe. Despite the marriage the Department of Immigration moved to deport the O'Keefe family along with about 600 other wartime refugees. The family fought this in the High Court and was allowed to stay. The case provoked strong criticism of Calwell for administering Australia's immigration policy too inflexibly.

[32] *Commonwealth Parliamentary Debates*, House of Representatives, vol. 201, 9 February 1949, 55.

[33] Cited in *The Statesman*, 24 February 1949.

[34] 'White Australia Policy', *Tribune*, 3 February 1949; 'Australian Perversion', *Bombay Chronicle*, 11 February 1949.

to the best person from Asia.[35] This was not a view endorsed by the government of India, which, as we have seen, had a more nuanced view of Australia's motives, but the stridency of the commentary reflected the offence felt by many English-language speakers. Were they not the equal of the white citizens of the Commonwealth?

Most of the Indian press focused on the apparent contradiction between Australia's desire for a larger population to advance its development, and its racially exclusive policy. How was it possible for such an under-populated continent to justify holding the land with so few people when Asia had so little land and such pressing needs? This was the kind of complaint which supporters of the policy in Australia also made: no matter how many Asians Australia accepted, it would make no difference to Asia's population problem and only create for itself the possibility of racial disharmony or of racial ghettos.

The Indian high commissioner, Colonel Daya Singh Bedi, reported all the twists and turns of Calwell's administration of the policy and the disaster that was the Australian government's goodwill mission to South-East Asia in 1948 led by W. Macmahon Ball.[36] Much of Bedi's reporting consisted of accounts of appeals by various Australian lobby groups or newspaper clippings calling for a quota or, alternatively, arguing that a quota would lead inevitably to the racial tragedies plaguing the United States and South Africa. The high commissioner noted that a minimum quota in proportion to Australia's population 'would be infinitesimal' and would be worth considering by Australia if it removed the complaint of discrimination.[37] The high commissioner's political report for September 1949 noted that in private Evatt was 'bitterly critical' of Calwell's attitude and thought the issue of wartime refugees ought to be handled more diplomatically but that Australian prime minister Ben Chifley supported the hardline approach.[38] A month later, he noted that although there was a lot of criticism of Calwell's methods, no one seemed able to suggest an alternative approach.[39]

Following the Australian general election of December 1949, which brought Menzies into power as the head of a Liberal-Country Party coalition government, Bedi, after a conversation with the new prime minister, reported to New Delhi that the result of the election indicated significant shifts within Australia. Labor's policy had been to improve the living standards of the workers—restricting immigration was a part of this policy—and by so doing satisfy the trades unions. Yet Labor had lost the election.[40] Bedi continued that there was a mood of insecurity in the country: Calwell's policy was widely seen to have 'alienated the goodwill and inspired the enmity of all Asian people' and hence the electorate wanted a government with a complete reliance on the defence shield of the United Kingdom and the United States. At the same time, Bedi reported, the new minister for immigration,

---

[35] *Bombay Chronicle*, 25 March 1949.

[36] Rather than build goodwill, the mission was the occasion for trenchant criticism of Australia's immigration policy. See Chris Waters, 'The MacMahon Ball Mission to East Asia 1948', *AJPH*, 40 (3), 1994, 351–63.

[37] D. S. Bedi, 'Publicity Report', February 1948, NAI.

[38] Letter, Bedi to Subimal Dutt, 15 September 1949, NAI: File 208 (2).

[39] Letter, Bedi to Dutt, 17 October 1949, NAI: File 208 (2).

[40] Letter, Bedi to Dutt, 23 December 1949, NAI: File 105/IANZ/50, 1949.

Harold Holt, had promised that the coalition government would take a more humane and considerate attitude towards Asians in Australia, a commitment which was manifested almost immediately in its decision to reverse Calwell's deportation proceedings against Annie O'Keefe and the other wartime refugees. To what extent 'they will allow Asians to settle in this country', he added presciently, 'remains to be seen but general feeling is against Asiatic immigration'.[41]

For its part the Australian High Commission in New Delhi kept up its line that a token quota of Indian immigration would do much to improve the relationship. The reporting from post was sharp and to the point. In 1949 a despatch reported that the foreign secretary, Sir Girija Bajpai, had told the High Commission that the Indian government did have an official position regarding the White Australia policy but preferred not to share it with journalists. The despatch emphasised the feeling with which Bajpai spoke about Australia's immigration policy and added that the conversation demonstrated the resentment felt by even well-disposed Indians towards Australia. Given sufficient provocation, the Indian government might be 'tempted to ventilate its objections rather more forcefully'.[42] A quota would remove the basis of those objections.

Within the DEA, there was an acute awareness of the difficulties that the policy caused to the relationship between Australia and India. Colin Moodie, who returned from his posting in Delhi in 1948, wrote a minute which captured much of the department's thinking about India and Pakistan in the period immediately after Partition and was to prove substantially correct for years to come: avoid acting as a mediator between the two countries as this would 'probably antagonise one side or the other'; and in determining the line to follow, 'the fundamental principle should be to cultivate Pakistan rather than India if we must make a choice'. Turning to immigration, Moodie was clear. To secure the goodwill of both countries the White Australia policy must be modified: 'All other gestures would be futile without this.' He felt that the term 'White Australia' should not be used in any official pronouncements, an objective which the Department of Immigration had been attempting to enforce with mixed success for some time. Finally, he repeated his appeal that the application of the policy be more elastic with the introduction of a quota system.[43]

The 1950s

The Australian High Commission line was restated forcibly by Francis Stuart who had been posted in Singapore at the time of the Macmahon Ball fiasco.[44] He was sent to New Delhi to replace Moodie in early 1950 and lost no time in urging a quota which, he reported, was also the view at senior levels in the Indian Ministry of External Affairs. The 'racial bias

---

[41] Letter, Bedi to Y. D. Gundevia, 31 December 1949, NAI: File DO No. E (3) 5HC. For the coalition government's more liberal administration, see Jordan, 'Reappraisal of "White Australia"', 231–32.

[42] Despatch 21/49, New Delhi to Canberra, 19 May 1949, NAA: A1838, 169/10/1 part 1.

[43] Minute, 11 February 1948, NAA: A1838, 169/10/1 part 1.

[44] See his wry account of the Macmahon Ball mission in *Towards Coming of Age: A Foreign Service Odyssey* (Griffith University: Centre for the Study of Australia–Asia Relations, 1989), 147–48.

of Australia's immigration policy is a stronger antagonistic force to Australia's neighbours than the economic and technical development of Australia is an attractive one', he warned, and would prevent Australia from gaining the goodwill of Asia.[45] For most of the external affairs officers who advocated it, a quota did not imply a wholesale abandonment of the need for an immigration policy which had as its first premise the need for social harmony and therefore the capacity for migrants to assimilate into the prevailing culture. A quota would have dealt with the issue of immigration from India, at least in the medium term, and perhaps have influenced Indian opinion makers, without in any way retreating from the fundamental principles of the policy.[46]

While Australian officials argued in vain for a token quota to end the charge of racial discrimination, Canada, with Nehru's urging, introduced one.[47] Canada quickly grasped that if a new, multiracial Commonwealth was to have any meaning, it should be open to citizens of newly independent Commonwealth countries. Its active role in the United Nations gave an additional reason to avoid any suggestion that its population was selected on racial grounds.[48] Indeed Canada was a leader in the creation of the new Commonwealth; in 1949 it had advocated the formula of recognising the King as the symbol of the free association of the Commonwealth's independent member nations and head of the Commonwealth thus allowing India to remain a member. This formula avoided a two-tiered membership, where the old white dominions would constitute an inner club leaving the newly decolonised nations in an outer grouping. In January 1951, Canada signed an agreement with India for a quota of 150 Indian migrants each year which for the first few years was not filled, a total of only 327 arriving by 1955. The work load for the Canadian High Commission in New Delhi was considerable but the goodwill Canada gained in India more than made up for this. A review in 1955 showed that of those who had arrived a high percentage had British or American engineering qualifications.[49] By 1957 the quota was increased to 300 and in February 1962 Canada introduced a new immigration policy which allowed applicants equal opportunity regardless of race thus dispensing with the need for quotas.[50]

---

[45] Despatch 47, New Delhi to Canberra, 28 August 1950, NAA: A1838, 169/10/1 part 1.

[46] See Gurry and Gwenda Tavan, ' "Too Soft and Long-Haired"? The Department of External Affairs and the White Australia Policy, 1946–1966', *AJIA*, 58 (1), 2004, 131.

[47] It is instructive to ask why India and Canada had such a good relationship in this period, a question Australian minister for external affairs R. G. Casey asked Canadian prime minister Lester Pearson in their exchange of letters so well described by Chris Waters. See generally Waters, 'Diplomacy in Easy Chairs'. Benvenuti has noted that Canada could afford to have a warm and constructive relationship with India given that it was far from Asia and less nervous than Australia about possible communist expansion and was a member of NATO. Pearson acknowledged this but his firm commitment to a multi-racial Commonwealth and anti-imperialism led him to positions more in sympathy with India's. Moreover, Canada had technical exports, which India needed, in particular, nuclear reactors. See Benvenuti, 'Difficult Partners', 66.

[48] See Brawley, *The White Peril. Foreign Relations and Asian Immigration to Australasia and North America 1919–1978* (Sydney: University of New South Wales Press, 1995), 262–63.

[49] Memorandum from Canadian Department of Citizenship and Immigration, 27 May 1955, NAA: A1838, 581/1 part 4.

[50] Memorandum 437/64, Ottawa to Canberra, 30 April 1964, NAA: A1838, 229/10/1/6 part 1.

Holt's more flexible administration of the Australian policy had initially made a favourable impression on the Indian press, but this soon dissipated. By June 1951 an editorial in the *Hindustan Times* captured the mood of the press well:

> the people of India wish that Australia had taken a more progressive line in regard to her immigration laws. They hope, however, that Australia will consider itself more an Asian nation than an outpost of the West. We say this because the Menzies regime has revealed tendencies in the latter direction.[51]

The Indian high commissioner reported the emphasis in the early 1950s on preserving a 'British way of life' or a 'white democracy' in the push for greater migration. He noted that a shortage of manpower was the greatest hindrance to development in Australia and that all new immigrants seemed to need was a superficial knowledge of English, an 'easily assimilable way of life and an anti-communist outlook'. Given this focus, the high commissioner felt that it should be relatively straightforward for the Australian government to accept carefully selected, 'readily assimilable' Asian migrants along the lines of a quota already adopted in Canada and the United States. In fact, the high commissioner noted, this was the private view of Holt, but it was not politically possible according to him: the Labor opposition would claim that since Asians multiplied quickly, they would inevitably dominate the European component of the population in years to come. Australia above all wanted to avoid the social problems of South Africa, according to the minister.[52] The high commissioner might have commented on how convenient it was for Holt to duck the issue of a quota by blaming the opposition. Holt's commitment to a 'British way of life' meant, at least in part, a commitment to a racially homogenous society which would avoid the social tensions so obvious in other white settler countries. In this he was no different from his colleagues in cabinet and senior members of the public service in Canberra.

The problems created by Australia's restrictive immigration policy would be a constant theme of Walter Crocker's two tenures as Australian high commissioner to India (1952–55, 1958–62). His postgraduate study at Stanford had been in demography and he was interested in the impact of race on foreign relations in particular. His inaugural lecture at the Australian National University on this subject was subsequently published.[53] In his first despatch from India on the topic he argued that if Australia were to understand India it had to accept that communism did not touch the deeper feelings of Indians whereas colonialism and racial issues did. Racial discrimination was a preoccupation and led sometimes to unbalanced views, for example on colonial matters or on Nehru's ambivalence towards Indo-China or Korea. Australia's immigration policy was always in the background of exchanges with Indian officials. The attitude to Canada was friendlier because of that country's introduction of a quota for Indian immigration, a face-saving gesture which removed the total bar against Indians. Racial questions had the potential to blur traditional

---

[51] *Hindustan Times*, 16 June 1951.

[52] Indian High Commission, Canberra, 'Annual Political Report for 1951', NAI: 3 (31) – R&I/52.

[53] W. R. Crocker, *The Racial Factor in International Relations* (Canberra: Australian National University, 1956). The Australian Natives Association complained to Casey that this lecture was an attack on the White Australia policy. See letter, ANA to Casey, 25 June 1956, NAA: A1838, 581/1 part 4.

loyalties to the Commonwealth and thus make the Soviet Union a more attractive partner to India.[54] He put the issue succinctly in a subsequent despatch: 'no policy dealing with India which does not give a prior place to this pre-occupation [with racial issues] can be soundly based'. Geography could not be denied and the goodwill of Asia must be a 'cardinal item' in Australia's foreign relations; the current immigration policy was the chief obstacle to this goodwill.[55] In his farewell despatches at the end of his first posting, Crocker noted that Australia was beginning to count for little more in Nehru's mind 'than the country with a disapproved immigration policy'.[56] Issues of race to do with Australia always made the headlines, whereas similar issues involving Canada would be in small print in an obscure part of the newspaper. Few Indians would deny the reasonableness of Australia controlling immigration but 'the implication of inferiority due to skin colour and the total exclusion of non-whites' rankled with politically-minded Indians.[57]

It clearly rankled General Cariappa, who took up his post as Indian high commissioner to Australia in 1953.[58] Both external affairs departments, in Canberra and New Delhi, were contemptuous of his abilities and his personal vanities; his reporting was regarded as superficial and he was clearly out of his depth. His first intervention into what was seen as Australia's domestic affairs occurred in Darwin shortly after his arrival when he called for Indian ex-servicemen to migrate to the north of the continent to assist in its development; this was a sensible way of dealing with Australia's labour shortage.

This was treated in both Canberra and New Delhi as naïve rather than malicious. In a subsequent conversation with officials in Canberra, however, it became clear that issues of race were uppermost in his mind. As he saw it, the White Australia policy encouraged communism in Asia and it was incredible to him that Italians, former enemies, could migrate, while Indians, allies and a fellow member of the Commonwealth, could not.[59] In a conversation with with External Affairs Minister R. G. Casey, Cariappa made it clear that he was calling for a token quota which would help ex-servicemen. Casey explained that the policy was expressly designed to prevent the emergence of minorities which would not assimilate. Australia, he added, was anxious to prevent 'the sort of situation which had arisen with regard to Indians in South Africa'.[60] There is no evidence that Cariappa challenged Casey to explain how a small quota of Indian professionals would lead to a situation akin to South Africa.

But it was Cariappa's statement in Brisbane in June 1954 that caused the most controversy. Here he openly criticised the policy, again called for a quota and, reminiscent

---

[54] Despatch, Crocker to Canberra, 'Indian Feelings on Race Relations', 26 October 1952, NAA: A462, 618/2/6.

[55] Despatch 1, Crocker to Casey, 5 January 1954, NAA: A4231, 1954/New Delhi.

[56] Despatch 18, Crocker to Canberra, 6 December 1954, NAA: A5954, 2271/3.

[57] Despatch 23, Crocker to Canberra, 6 December 1954, NAA: A5954, 2271/3.

[58] See David Walker, 'General Cariappa Encounters "White Australia": Australia, India and the Commonwealth in the 1950s', *Journal of Imperial and Commonwealth History*, 34 (3), 2006, 389–406.

[59] Note by Francis Stuart, 8 November 1953, NAA: A1838, 169/10/7 part 1.

[60] Record of conversation, General Cariappa and Casey, 31 March 1954, NAA: A1838, 169/10/7 part 1.

of his remarks in Darwin, questioned the reasons behind the current migrant intake. The Australian press took up the speech and Calwell issued a statement attacking the high commissioner's comments. Here, as in some of the departmental commentary on the speech,[61] Calwell assumed that Cariappa was promoting the idea of mass migration, which he was not. Even on the question of a limited quota, Calwell reasoned that it was:

> more insulting to Asian feeling than our present system, quite apart from the dangers that lie hidden in it. The quota system has been advocated by some eminent people but for the most part its advocates are appeasers, escapists, sentimentalists, and those who cannot or will not think of the disasters to which their policy inevitably will lead.[62]

No 'disaster' had occurred in Canada from the introduction of a quota, which Calwell in his emotional outburst seemed to forget. Even a hundred or so Indian professionals would threaten the British race make-up of Australia by this reasoning, because once Indian opinion was appeased in this, there would be a flood of demand for a larger quota which an appeasing government would have no principled basis to refuse. Calwell was fond of using the term 'appeasers' or 'appeasement' in comments about any retreat from the policy, an indication of the depth of political emotion with which he approached it.

The acting minister for external affairs, Sir Phillip McBride, called in Cariappa and a report of this conversation was sent to Crocker in New Delhi which included this commentary:

> We appreciate that Cariappa and possibly the Indian Government would like to see some modification of our policy. If they do Cariappa is going about it in the worst possible way from his own point of view. Cariappa seemed more concerned about the risk of his government criticising him for a reported reference by him to the dangers of India going communist.[63]

Cariappa's official secretary, Perelal Ratnam, who was disliked in Canberra for being a 'thruster type',[64] called on Stuart and proceeded to undermine his high commissioner by dissociating himself from the speech. In addition he claimed that the White Australia policy had 'at no time' been given undue prominence in the High Commission's reporting and that the ministry in Delhi had not raised the matter. Nonetheless the policy was an impediment to good relations with Asia and 'it was the hope of the Ministry that at some time the Australian Government would be able to introduce a token quota system'.[65]

The storm over this continued for some months and reached new heights when it was reported that Cariappa had told a journalist on a non-attributable basis that the Indian government would soon ask for a quota system. Cariappa seemed to be making it up as

---

[61] See, for instance, note, Patrick Shaw to secretary, 23 June 1954, in which the assumption is made that Asian immigration would be proposed to help 'Asia's population problem'. NAA: A1838, 169/10/7 part 1.

[62] Statement by Calwell, 25 June 1954, in NAA: A1838, 169/10/7 part 1.

[63] Cablegram 125, Canberra to New Delhi, 25 June 1954, NAA: A1838, 169/10/7 part 1.

[64] This was the opinion of the DEA's advisor on Commonwealth relations, J. E. Oldham. See note, Oldham to acting minister, 23 June 1954, NAA: A1838, 169/10/7 part 1.

[65] Record of conversation, Perelal Ratnam and Stuart, 24 June 1954, NAA: A1838, 169/10/7 part 1.

he went along and the Indian ministry in talks with Crocker distanced itself from him. Nehru was annoyed and Cariappa was sent a sharp reprimand, which stated that the Indian government had no official interest in, or complaint, against the Australian immigration policy.[66] Cariappa wrote home wishing to be relieved of his post,[67] which was refused. Undaunted, he approached the ABC to speak on the matter but Casey intervened to have this stopped. To the annoyance of the ministry, Cariappa made a further speech in Adelaide on 26 August 1954, but by now everyone was weary of the matter. Both external affairs ministries were playing it down. The Indian press for its part was mildly critical of Cariappa, making the point that there was a matter of diplomatic propriety involved. In January of the following year he was told that the Ministry did not wish him

> to make any approach, however informal, to the Australian authorities regarding immigration into Australia. If there is to be any change in Australian immigration policy, that is a matter entirely for their decision and initiative.[68]

South Africa and Australia

Throughout this period Australia, for the most part, escaped Indian criticism because South Africa's apartheid policy was the primary concern of official and press commentary. The Indian government was explicitly in opposition to apartheid whereas White Australia had not attracted its public criticism. Since Paranjpye's time the Indian government had understood that within Australia there were no major official disabilities for non-Europeans, no matter what might have happened to particular individuals. This was reaffirmed in 1955 in the Indian parliament when the parliamentary secretary to the minister for external affairs responded to a question by saying that he was unaware of any discrimination against the 2000 Indians living in Australia. Nehru, answering a further question, noted that the Indian government did not know if there had been any particular change in the White Australia policy and added that it was 'not particularly interested in this matter either.'[69]

Nonetheless, there were occasional comparisons between apartheid and White Australia. In 1949 the Australian High Commission reported that the Indian press was increasingly linking Australia and South Africa. During debates in the Constituent Assembly on the London Declaration, in which India affirmed its acceptance of the monarch as head of the Commonwealth of Nations, members opposed to India joining the Commonwealth argued that India should only ratify it if the Commonwealth prevented discrimination in South Africa and Australia.[70] In the late 1950s and early 1960s, there was, again, a tendency to link the two countries, as pressure on South Africa mounted and as Australia's policy, at least in regard to creating any kind of program of Indian migration, remained static.[71]

---

[66] Record of conversation, Dutt and Crocker, 2 September 1954, NAA: A1838, 169/10/7 part 2.

[67] Cariappa to N. R. Pillai, 7 July 1954, NAI: Cariappa Papers, Part II, Group IX.

[68] Dutt to Cariappa, 27 January 1955, NAI: Cariappa Papers.

[69] Memorandum 1659, 13 December 1955, NAA: A1838, 169/10/1 part 3.

[70] Despatch 21/49, 19 May 1949, NAA: A1838, 169/10/1 part 1.

[71] Considerable softening of the regulations embodied in White Australia occurred quietly throughout the 1950s and 1960s. See, in particular, Gwenda Tavan, *The Long Slow Death of White*

'He No Doubt Felt Insulted': The White Australia Policy

The generally calm way India responded to comments by the South African prime minister, Dr D. F. Malan, linking Australia's immigration policy with South Africa's, showed that Indian opinion could make a distinction between the two countries. Malan at a lunch for Menzies in Capetown in July 1953, had spoken of the common danger of India to both Australia and South Africa and that Australia with its White Australia policy had built a 'wall of colour' similar to South Africa's. In his reply Menzies had avoided the issue. Indian press commentary was strongly critical of Malan and sympathetic to what it assumed was Menzies' embarrassment when listening to Malan's comments, although as the high commissioner pointed out, 'Australian immigration policy remains unaccepted and suspect'.[72] There was some feeling in official government circles that Malan's 'hallucinations' might have caused embarrassment to Australia, and a recognition that the two policies were quite different. The kerfuffle was smoothed somewhat by a statement from the now-retired Paranjpye that there was hardly any racial discrimination in Australia and that India had never claimed that countries should allow free entry and had, moreover, accepted that every country could determine the character of its own population.[73]

Unfortunately, the positive effect of these comments was largely lost some weeks later following an ABC broadcast reporting on Menzies' trip overseas for the coronation of the Queen and visit to South Africa. He pointed out that for the sake of Commonwealth unity, one country should not sit in judgement on another country's problems. He wondered if Australia's circumstances had been similar to South Africa's whether it would have devised better answers to the problems. Crocker reported that the broadcast was interpreted by the Indian press as a commentary on Nehru's speeches on racial issues in South Africa and a retreat from the studied silence with which Menzies had greeted Malan's recent lunch address. The effect of the broadcast 'was unlucky as regards its effects in Asia'.[74] He urged, however, that the negative reaction be ignored as it would blow over.[75]

White Australia was even less of an issue as the decade wore on and South Africa's policies became more extreme. The Indian press, however, never let go of it entirely. The press remained completely independent but officials, who often floated their own concerns and not those of the government, regularly briefed its correspondents. Because of this, some members of the press urged on occasion for a quota to be introduced, even though the government had never said so officially and when pushed, was not especially concerned. Nonetheless, the press recognised that the political climate in Australia was not favourable to such a revolutionary step. By 1961 when the crisis over South Africa's remaining in the Commonwealth was reaching its inevitable conclusion, the Indian press had begun to

---

Australia (Carlton North: Scribe, 2005).

[72] Cablegram 140, New Delhi to Canberra, 13 July 1953, NAA: A1838, 169/10/1 part 2.
[73] Despatch 18, New Delhi to Canberra, 14 July 1953, NAA: A1838, 169/10/1 part 2.
[74] Despatch 21, New Delhi to Canberra, 9 August 1953, NAA: A1838, 169/10/1 part 2.
[75] The Indian high commissioner called on Menzies to seek clarification. Menzies was 'very distressed' at the misunderstanding caused by the misquotation of his comments. Situation report from Australia 8/53, NAI: File No.9-R&I/53.

mention Australia's policy in the same breath as apartheid.[76] But this did not last long. Once South Africa had left the Commonwealth and the membership criterion of racial equality had been established, Indian press commentary on Australia's policy seemed to revert to a periodic airing of grievances.

The South African crisis at the Commonwealth Prime Ministers Conference in March 1961 exposed Australia's vulnerabilities. The Afro-Asian prime ministers urged the conference to adopt a statement disapproving of apartheid. Macmillan's near final draft stated that apartheid was inconsistent with the ideals on which the unity and influence of the Commonwealth rested. Menzies thought this was tantamount to giving South Africa notice to quit the Commonwealth and 'in view of our plainly discriminatory immigration policy we have a good chance of being next in line'.[77] As the conference wore on Menzies became increasingly disenchanted with Macmillan's partiality towards India: 'I sometimes doubt whether the Government of the United Kingdom appreciates the fact that old friends are best and some of the new boys are in the Commonwealth for what they can get out of it'.[78] By the end of the conference Menzies was clearly yesterday's man, unable to respond to change and increasingly isolated.

Indian press commentary on Australia's role at the conference was predictable. The *Bombay Free Press Journal* noted on 17 March that 'Dr Verwoerd's sole supporter at the London Conference was, significantly enough, Prime Minister Menzies of Australia, the Dominion's White Australia policy being only one rung separated from apartheid'. The *Times of India* on 20 March noted that if Australia's 'racialist immigration policies' were raised by Asian and African members of the Commonwealth with the same determination as they had shown on apartheid, then the Commonwealth might disintegrate.[79]

The 1960s

As the 1950s wore on Australian policy papers on the bilateral relationship increasingly assumed that the immigration policy did not have an impact on wider objectives. After all, the few public comments on it by Nehru seemed to suggest this. Australian officials in New Delhi, however, had to live with press and public criticism of the policy. Heydon noted that after almost every speech he made in New Delhi, the first question would always be on Australia's immigration policy.[80] Crocker reported the same in 1961, that the criticism of the policy by the press would always be sharp.[81] From his travels in India, Casey was aware that there was a good deal of emotion around the policy among elite opinion, but was unwilling to raise the matter in any forceful way in cabinet. Menzies had made his

---

[76] Cablegram 154, New Delhi to Canberra, 21 March 1961, NAA: A1838, 169/10/1 part 5.

[77] Menzies to John McEwen, 14 March 1960, cited in A. W. Martin, *Robert Menzies: A Life*, vol. 2, *1944–1978* (Melbourne: Melbourne University Press, 1999), 426.

[78] Ibid., 428

[79] Both newspapers in cablegram 167, New Delhi to Canberra, 26 March 1961, NAA: A1838, 169/10/1 part 5.

[80] Cited in Brawley, 'The Department of Immigration', 422.

[81] Memorandum 248, New Delhi to Canberra, 1 March 1961, NAA: A1838, 169/10/1 part 5.

position clear. In 1955, prior to the Bandung meeting,[82] Casey tried to have provisions in both federal and state legislation which 'could offend Asian susceptibilities', removed. Menzies opposed this on the grounds that to do so would only provoke debate and, in any case, 'Asians' had not complained.[83]

Heydon's role in the reappraisal and eventual liberalisation of the White Australia policy was influential. Having been high commissioner to India he had a firsthand understanding of how the policy was regarded in Asia. As secretary of the Department of Immigration, from 1961, he was in a key position. In 1962 he sent a senior official to India to tidy up immigration procedures and make them more palatable to Indian opinion.[84] There were by now some fourteen categories of exemption from the absolute bar which allowed 'distinguished' and 'highly-qualified' Asians to settle in Australia under 'certificates of exemption' from the blanket ban on migration. Accordingly, officers overseas could not assert that Asians were permitted to migrate as such. Heydon, along with Tange and other senior officials, remained opposed to a quota. The matter was too delicate from the point of view of domestic politics for any minister to introduce. Officials urged the introduction of a greater range of exemptions, which would mean much the same thing, but successive ministers remained opposed. The prime minister was also opposed and so too was Casey.[85] Casey thought, moreover, that the issue had not been seriously considered which seems to suggest he had not absorbed the constant despatches on the matter from New Delhi. He even wondered if a quota would in fact be offensive to Asians because other migrant groups would not be subject to one.[86] The comparison with Canadian practice was often raised by Indians. In 1962, for instance, an Indian parliamentary delegation used the Canadian example to challenge Australian policy while in Canberra. Internally, departmental officials dismissed the Canadian example as irrelevant, apparently because Canada had a cold climate whereas Australia with its hotter climate would soon be unable to manage a quota were it introduced.[87] It seems that perhaps officials in Canberra still believed the old racialist line so influential in Deakin's time that Asians were more suited to living in hot climates and were only waiting to swamp Australia.[88] Crocker, home on briefing in 1963, told a departmental meeting that the White Australia policy was 'resented by all Asians, especially Indians'. Although he admitted it was not possible to point to it having had direct policy consequences, it nevertheless underlay the relationship.[89]

---

[82] The meeting of African and Asian 'non-aligned' countries held in Indonesia in April 1955.

[83] Casey to Menzies, 5 April 1955; and W. K. Brown (Department of Immigration) to Casey, 21 September 1955, NAA: A1209, 1957/5056.

[84] Note, A. S. Landale (DEA) to Arthur Tange, 9 February 1962, NAA: A1838, 169/10/1 part 6.

[85] Minute, Casey to Tange, 23 May 1958, NAA: A1838, 581/1 part 4.

[86] Letter, Casey to P. R. Heydon, 27 May 1958, NAA: A1838, 581/1 Part 4.

[87] Note, Tange to J. C. G. Kevin, 15 September 1958, NAA: A1838, 581/1 part 5.

[88] Alfred Deakin, as prime minister of Australia had introduced the *Immigration Restriction Act* of 1901. Deakin had read Charles Pearson's highly influential *National Life and Character: A Forecast* (London: Macmillan, 1893), which advocated such views.

[89] DEA, 'Policy Intelligence Bulletin', undated (c. 1963), NAA: A1838, 169/10/1 part 6.

Eric Meadows

Conclusion

If the White Australia policy underlay the relationship, influencing Indian attitudes to Australia, it cannot be said to have affected it in any significant way. The policy remained in force throughout the period Nehru was in office (1947–64) and beyond, although with greater flexibility in its administration. To Indian officials it represented an Australia mentally trapped by outdated imperial thinking and misunderstanding of the depth of Indian feeling about racial exclusion. Introducing a quota for Indian migration might have created a better climate for the bilateral relationship to develop; it certainly did for Canada.[90] But it is doubtful if even then the relationship would have had much substance: unlike Canada, Australia did not have nuclear technology to sell to India and its government was not sympathetic to many of the international issues which involved India. Furthermore, Australia was aligned with the West in the Cold War and, for the most part, took a publicly uncritical line of the policy of the United States. India saw itself as not aligned to either side but was often sharply critical of Western policy. This fundamental difference inevitably led to disagreements on a wide range of post-war security issues. Australia might have wanted a better relationship with more substance, noting India's obvious importance and influence in Asia, but India remained indifferent to Australia; at many times it did not seem to matter to India's security or trade or development and it seemed not to have its own voice on strategic matters.

There was no official Indian commentary on White Australia or any active campaign against it as there was with South Africa's racial policies. Nonetheless, it remained an irritant to opinion makers. The Indian press from time to time reflected this irritation. The high commissioners found the policy uncomfortable to defend and would have preferred a modification of it to allow for some Indian migration. As Heydon said in an interview in 1970, Nehru 'would not admit to being insulted [by the policy], though he no doubt felt insulted, but it was always in the background'.[91]

---

[90] See M.S. Rajan, 'The Indo-Canadian Entente', *International Journal*, 17 (4), 1962, 358–84.

[91] Mel Pratt, interview with Sir Peter Heydon, 2 December 1970, NLA: Oral History Program.

III

Sentiment and Self-Interest in Australian Public and Intellectual Life

6

A Military Mission for Greater Britain: Edward Hutton's 'A Co-operative System for Defence of the Empire'

Richard Lehane

On Primrose Day, April 1898, Colonel E. T. H. Hutton addressed an assembly of the Royal Colonial Institute on the subject of the military defence of the British Empire. He used the occasion to outline a scheme he had developed to enable Great Britain to share this burden with its self-governing colonies. Hutton's scheme, entitled 'A Co-operative System for Defence of the Empire', called for each member to divide its troops between garrison and field forces. The garrison forces would ensure local defence while the field forces would be ready in wartime to combine to form a federal militia of six army corps available for the general defence of the empire. Hutton described his proposal as an 'offensive–defensive system'.[1] With this cooperative system, Hutton sought to give a practical form to Colonial Secretary Joseph Chamberlain's statement earlier that year that 'the sons of Britain throughout the world shall stand shoulder to shoulder to defend our mutual interests and our common rights'.[2] That goal, to focus British sentiment towards a practical end, makes Hutton's scheme a useful vehicle for understanding the nature and dynamics of the relationship between Great Britain and its self-governing colonies in the late nineteenth century.

This chapter explores the origins of Hutton's cooperative system, examining in particular his exposure to the ideas of imperial apostles John Seeley and Garnet Wolseley and his experience of commanding the New South Wales militia in the period leading up to Australian federation. Hutton claimed to have introduced his scheme in both Canada and Australia. This chapter concludes by exploring both attempts and the colonial responses.

The Origins and Nature of 'Greater Britain'

The last quarter of the nineteenth century was, as Neville Meaney puts it, the 'classical era of British race patriotism'.[3] During those years a wave of British nationalism swept through Great Britain and her self-governing colonies, binding them together with a vision of an empire united as one. This was reflected in the creation of new institutions, especially the Royal Colonial Institute (founded in 1868) and the Imperial Federation League (1884), and in the writings of scholars such as John Seeley, Sir Charles Dilke and James Froude. It

---

[1] E. T. H. Hutton, 'A Co-operative System for Defence of the Empire', April 1898, reproduced in Royal Canadian Military Institute, *Selected Papers*, No. 1/05 (Toronto: RCMI, 2005), 5.
[2] Joseph Chamberlain, speech in Liverpool, 18 January 1898, cited in ibid., 6.
[3] Neville Meaney, 'Britishness and Australia: Some Reflections', *Journal of Imperial and Commonwealth History*, 31 (2), 2003, 123.

was given early official voice by British prime minister Benjamin Disraeli in his June 1872 Crystal Palace speech. Chamberlain, colonial secretary from 1895 to 1902, made the most concerted effort to apply it in government policy. Queen Victoria was embraced as the movement's figurehead and General Charles Gordon, killed at Khartoum in 1885, became its martyr. *Britannia* premiered in English musical halls in the wake of Gordon's death and reassured its audiences with the refrain:

> There's little fear for England
>
> With brave Colonial sons
>
> Ready at the hour of need
>
> With money, men and guns.[4]

In seeming response, the Colonial Defence Committee began coordinating defence policies around the empire in the same year. Two years later, during the 1887 Jubilee, representatives from the self-governing colonies gathered for the first colonial conference ever held. This seemingly organic coalescence of the British diaspora moved Seeley to announce the birth of 'a new state, English in race and character', comprising the United Kingdom, Canada, parts of South Africa and the Australasian colonies. He named that new state 'Greater Britain'.[5]

Late Victorian imperialism can be understood as a form of nationalism, or to borrow Alfred Cobban's colourful description, '[a] kind of bastard imperialism which is merely nationalism writ large',[6] and it can be placed within the broad context of the flowering of Western nationalism in the period 1880 to 1914.[7] In both Great Britain, where imperial disciples such as Seeley, Dilke and Chamberlain pressed for an empire bound together by the ties of culture and politics, and the self-governing colonies, which responded to the trauma of modernisation by embracing even more fervently than the mother country the idea of an organic community of worldwide British peoples, the idea of Greater Britain took hold of the collective imagination. This characterisation of Greater Britain as a nationalism is legitimate. Hans Kohn, one of the earliest scholars to identify nationalism as a historically contingent phenomenon, argued that it was 'first and foremost a state of mind, an act of consciousness' and 'not a natural phenomenon, not a product of "eternal" or "natural" laws'. As an 'idea' or 'artificial product of historical and intellectual development', nationalism produced a curious condition in modern societies, defining 'our identification with the life and aspirations of uncounted millions whom we shall never know, [and] with a territory

---

[4] Penny Summerfield, 'Patriotism and Empire: Music-Hall Entertainment 1870–1914', in *Imperialism and Popular Culture*, ed. John M. Mackenzie (Manchester: Manchester University Press, 1986), 28.

[5] John Seeley, *The Expansion of England*, ed. John Gross (Chicago: University of Chicago Press, 1971 [1883]), 14, 17. Seeley borrowed 'Greater Britain' from the title of Sir Charles Dilke's 1868 travelogue *Greater Britain: A Record of Ttravel in English-Speaking Countries During 1866 and 1867*, 2 vols (London: Macmillan, 1868).

[6] Alfred Cobban, 'The Idea of Empire', in *Ideas and Beliefs of the Victorians: An Historic Revaluation of the Victorian Age*, eds Noel Annan et al. (London: Sylvan Press, 1949), 329.

[7] E. J. Hobsbawm, *The Age of Empire: 1875–1914* (London: Weidenfeld and Nicolson, 1987), 142.

which we shall never visit in its entirety'.[8] This fundamental characteristic of nationalism was no less true for the members of Greater Britain—on both sides—who 'imagined' themselves (to paraphrase Benedict Anderson's well-worn phrase) bound together by a common British folk-myth.[9] And there was much talk of knitting those bonds more tightly. In a speech in London a year before Hutton's address, Wilfred Laurier, the Canadian prime minister, exclaimed: 'As thoughts of separation disappear, thoughts of union, of a closer union, take their place. To-day the sentiment exists in Canada in favour of a closer union with the motherland.'[10]

As a nationalist phenomenon, however, Greater Britain posed the special problem that competing with these sentimental considerations was self-interest; the fact that both Britain and the self-governing colonies, being separated by a vast geographical divide, still remained conscious of their local autonomy and jealous of their local interests. If, as Ernest Gellner contends, nationalism is the modern impulse to align national (community of culture) and political (community of interest) units—the same impulse that was at the heart of the idea of Greater Britain—then this task was made that much more difficult by the demands of local interests and geopolitical circumstances.[11] For Britain and the self-governing colonies, these two communities would sometimes align but they would more often than not shear apart. In the same speech in which Laurier had talked up 'a closer union with the motherland', the Canadian prime minister, wary of sacrificing any Canadian autonomy, went on to sound a warning note, discouraging attempts at formalising the connection in an imperial federation:

> It is not in the genius of English history to write Constitutions and to devise theories, but it is in the genius of English history, and it is in the genius of the British race to proceed slowly ... to proceed only so far as may be necessary to meet existing exigencies.[12]

This noncommittal attitude to imperial federation was even more pronounced in Australia, where the intense sense of strategic vulnerability made the colonies implacably opposed to any suggestion of surrendering their autonomy—and least of all control over their local defence forces—to the mother country. As New South Wales premier, George Reid, put it in 1897:

> The great test of our relations, I submit, will be the next war in which England is engaged ... Our money would come; our men would come ... that feeling of patriotism, we may call it—would flame out just as practically in the Colonies, in

---

[8] Hans Kohn, *The Idea of Nationalism: A Study in Its Origins and Background* (New York: The Macmillan Company, 1958 [1944]), 6, 8–9, 10–11.

[9] See generally Benedict Anderson, *Imagined Communities: Reflections on the Origins and Spread of Nationalism* (London: Verso, 1991 [1983]). See also Meaney, 'Britishness and Australian Identity: The Problem of Nationalism in Australian History and Historiography', *Australian Historical Studies*, 32 (116), 2001, 76–90.

[10] Cited in *Times*, 14 June 1897.

[11] See Ernest Gellner, *Nations and Nationalism* (Ithaca: Cornell University Press, 1983), esp. chs 1, 5.

[12] Cited in *Times*, 14 June 1897.

the hour of danger, as in England; but it is only in those moments that you can make the people one in the sense of sacrifice.[13]

How is this wariness of a formal commitment to be balanced against the growing enthusiasm for the cultural connection? Is a concern to protect local interests evidence of a competing local identity? In the age of nationalism, what proved the more important impulse in determining identity for the members of Greater Britain? Hutton's cooperative defence system provides a useful window for understanding this problem. In his Primrose Day speech he explicitly identified and attempted to reconcile the competing claims of culture and interest:

> It will be readily conceded by all observers of recent events in our history that a mutual, though unwritten, understanding exists between all portions of the Queen's dominions. The ties of sentiment and self-interest alike render the maintenance of the Empire necessary for the commercial and political development of each and all.[14]

Hutton's understanding of the importance of those twin forces of sentiment and self-interest can be traced to his colonial commands.

The Influences on Hutton: Seeley and Wolseley

Among British army officers of his day, Hutton was one of the most experienced in commanding colonial forces. At the time of his Primrose Day speech he had already served as general officer commanding in New South Wales and he was soon to take command of the Canadian militia. He would later lead a combined colonial mounted force on campaign in the Boer War and he served as post-federation Australia's first (and only) general officer commanding. In these positions Hutton conceived of himself as being much more than a mere commander:

> Humble individual though I was, some inner voice seemed to force me into undertaking the mission of showing that *military service is the main factor for training democratic communities in their primary duties of citizenship*. It was a new role for a soldier to undertake.[15]

Hutton's cooperative system had its genesis in his first colonial command, in New South Wales (1893–96). It was here that he was first confronted with the realities of colonial politics and colonial opinion, of imperial sentiment and colonial self-interest. By the time of that appointment, Hutton had come under the influence of two key figures: Sir John Seeley and Garnet Wolseley.

Sir John Seeley was one of the leading late Victorian theorists of empire. His history, *The Expansion of England*, when published in 1883, was a blockbuster, selling 80 000 copies in its first two years in print. Hutton admired it as an 'epoch-making book' which he claimed

---

[13] Cited in Meaney, *A History of Australian Defence and Foreign Policy, 1901–23*, vol. 1, *The Search for Security in the Pacific, 1901–14* (Sydney: Sydney University Press, 1976), 36.

[14] Hutton, 'A Co-operative System', 2.

[15] Hutton, unpublished memoirs, first typed draft, British Library (BL): Hutton Papers, ADD 50113, 16. Original emphasis.

to have 'carefully studied'.[16] Although Seeley spent most of the work dwelling on British problems in India and America, it was the self-governing colonies that he viewed as being vital to the empire's future. According to John Clive, these colonies were in fact his essential theme.[17] Seeley asserted an essential unity between Britain, Canada, New Zealand and the Australian and southern African colonies. He introduced the notion of Greater Britain and suggested that the British should stop thinking of the empire as an assortment of colonies but rather as 'a new state, English in race and character'.[18] Seeley suggested that bonds of 'nationality, language and religion' constituted 'natural ties which unite Englishmen'.[19] Seeley's position was non-prescriptive. Although he was a member of the Imperial Federation League and looked to the eventual embodiment of Greater Britain in a political federation, he believed that the work of the League itself should be primarily educational. He never promoted a particular scheme for imperial unification, believing that closer ties would naturally evolve from the basic, cultural connection.[20] Even though this process could not be structured, it could be encouraged, and Seeley believed that civic education was vital. He argued that only a broad education compassing moral as well as intellectual cultivation could enable Greater Britain to achieve its 'potential as a world power'.[21]

Hutton accepted Seeley's views entirely. When serving at Aldershot in the late 1880s he invited Seeley to present a lecture to the military society, an occasion he remembered reverently. 'I was an enthusiastic disciple', he wrote in his unpublished memoirs, 'and even now recall with a glow the peroration of his address'.[22] Hutton not only embraced Seeley's vision of a more tightly knit empire but also adopted his proposed means—education—to assist with the process of natural evolution. Hutton was encouraged by the role Seeley allowed for soldiers in this process. Seeley overturned the traditional idea that the army must be neutral and encouraged the assembled officers to consider themselves not just specialists, but also 'citizens and patriots'.[23] He attacked the notion that the army was a burden on the economy, asserting that it was essential to the expansion of trade, and he challenged colonial reluctance to assist in imperial defence:

> You may tell English trade that you have been from the outset its instrument, that you sprang into existence along with the trading policy of England, and grew with its growth. You may tell the Colonies that it has been your great work from the outset either to found or to protect them, that England has not engaged in

---

[16] Hutton, unpublished memoirs, second draft, BL: Hutton Papers, ADD 50113, 296.

[17] John Clive, 'Introduction', in Seeley, *The Expansion of England*, xiv.

[18] Ibid., 17.

[19] Ibid., 234.

[20] Peter Burroughs, 'John Robert Seeley and British Imperial History', *Journal of Imperial and Commonwealth History*, 1 (2), 1973, 202; Deborah Wormell, *Sir John Seeley and the Uses of History* (Cambridge: Cambridge University Press, 1980), 96, 167.

[21] Deborah Wormell, 'John Robert Seeley (1834–95): Educational Reformer, Historian and Political Scientist', PhD thesis, University College London, 1977, 99–101.

[22] Hutton, unpublished memoirs, second draft, 296.

[23] Seeley, 'Lecture 17: The Empire', *Military Lectures*, Aldershot Military Society, 24 April 1889, 14.

> European wars against their interest, but that the wars of England have been from first to last undertaken in the cause of the Empire, so that it would be far truer to say that the Colonies have dragged England, than that England has dragged the Colonies, into war.[24]

Hutton was deeply affected by this. He quoted extensively from the passage in his memoir.[25] At the conclusion of Seeley's address he was the first (besides the chair) to respond. Claiming to speak for the 'rising generation,' he assured Seeley that British officers felt keenly their role 'with reference to the Empire here and throughout the world':

> I can only assure Professor Seeley that we feel our responsibility deeply, very deeply, and in the discharge of our duties as officers towards those superior to ourselves and towards those whom we command we have the maintenance and welfare of the Empire profoundly at heart, and that we are in the best sense of the term both patriots and citizens.[26]

If Seeley moved Hutton's sentimental side, then it was Garnet Wolseley who influenced Hutton as a practical soldier. Driving this was fear of an impending great European war. This was widespread in Britain from the mid-1870s and it was particularly common among members of the British army.[27] It was based on a belief that the European balance of power could not be maintained given the rapid expansion of the continental armies (conscript forces had been introduced throughout Europe after the dramatic French defeat in the Franco-Prussian War). According to M. D. Welsh, the late Victorian idea of inexorable progress led many to fear that unrestrained and rapid advances in military science and technology must inevitably produce a war of catastrophic proportions.[28] Hutton belonged to this group. 'The enormous and increasing armaments of the European Powers', he cautioned, 'cannot much longer exist and statesmen solemnly acknowledge that a great crisis is at hand.'[29] He warned that 'a war if it does come will require all the military resources that we possess', echoing Colmar von der Goltz's theory of total war (published only a few years earlier), which prophesied that '[t]he day of cabinet wars is over. It is no longer the weakness of a single man, at the head of affairs, or of a dominant party, that is decisive, but only the exhaustion of the belligerent nations.'[30] In November 1897, Hutton gave a lecture to the Aldershot Military Society based on his recent inspection of the German and French military manoeuvres.[31] That experience, he declared, had shown him that, in their current

---

[24] Ibid., 12.

[25] Hutton, unpublished memoirs, second draft, 296.

[26] Seeley, 'The Empire', 12.

[27] M. D. Welsh, *Science in a Pickelhaube: British Miltiary Lesson Learning at the RUSI (1870–1900)* (Whitehall: Royal United Services Institute for Defence Studies, 1999), 8.

[28] Ibid., 39.

[29] Hutton, 'Modern Warfare', lecture delivered to the Inns of Court Volunteers, 16 December 1886, BL: Hutton Papers, ADD 50111, 179.

[30] Ibid. See also C. Von Der Goltz, *The Nation in Arms: A Treatise on Modern Military Systems and the Conduct of War*, trans. P. Ashworth, 5th edn (London: Hugh Rees, 1906 [1883]), 9

[31] Hutton, 'The German and French Military Manoeuvres: Some Retrospective Deductions', lecture to Aldershot Military Society, November 1897, reproduced in Hutton, *The Defence and*

state, the empire's auxiliary forces, on which would rest the bulk of its defence, were not capable of an adequate resistance and that, as a result, 'the existing condition of the military defence of the United Kingdom and the Empire is nothing less than perilous'.[32]

Wolseley, the Victorian army's chief reformer, was responsible for preparing the British army to face the growing threat posed by the new national armies on the continent. In the 1880s, when adjutant general, he considered this dilemma facing Britain's small, professional army and responded by campaigning for the establishment of a field army, comprising two army corps and one cavalry division.[33] Edward Stanhope, the secretary of state for war, affirmed that aim in his famous 1888 memorandum. This was Wolseley's signal achievement: to form from the British army a corps ready for mobilisation for service at home or abroad. Hutton's cooperative system essentially attempted to apply the same model to the militias of the self-governing colonies.

Hutton in New South Wales, 1893–96

In his New South Wales command it was Seeley's influence that helped Hutton engage with colonial British race patriotism: Seeley minimised questions of interest and emphasised instead the fostering of imperial sentiment. Wolseley, however, had taught Hutton expediency and had impressed on him the desperate need to bolster the British army against a coming war on the continent.

Hutton's main initiative, in his New South Wales command, was the development of a scheme for Australian federal defence. He originally drafted this at Premier George Dibbs' request and first publicly aired it in a speech in January 1894 at Bathurst where he claimed that, while 'committees, speeches, and reports [had] availed little' in advancing imperial union, federation for defence 'was distinctly within practical politics'.[34] The scheme was most fully expressed in Hutton's draft Australian Federal Defence Agreement of 1896.[35] Containing the clear influence of Wolseley, this involved each colony dividing their units into two separate forces: a garrison-type local defence force and a mobile field army capable of joint action anywhere in Australia (and potentially abroad, as Hutton's critics suspected). A federal defence council would administer these combined field forces and appoint a federal general commanding to lead them. Hutton promoted his federal defence scheme at two separate commandants' conferences (October 1894 and January 1896), the second to which he presented his draft 'Federal Agreement', and the whole matter was considered by the Australian colonial premiers in 1896. However the scheme was never adopted; the premiers at that time decided that a solution to the problem of federal defence must await full political federation. Its only concrete achievement was to encourage South Australia to

---

Defensive Power of Australia (Melbourne: Angus and Robertson, 1902), 44.

[32] Ibid., 80.

[33] Stephen Badsey, 'Fire and Sword: The British Army and the *Arme Blanche* Controversy c. 1871–1921', DPhil thesis, University of Cambridge, 1981, 95.

[34] 'Major-General Hutton at Bathurst', unidentified newspaper extract, 25 January 1894, NLA: MS 1215, Hutton Letters and Press Cuttings, vol. 6, 110.

[35] Hutton, *Australian Federal Defence Agreement, Schedule C to Report and Schedules of the Intercolonial Military Committee* (Sydney: Government Printer, 1896).

pass an act allowing its troops to serve throughout Australia.[36] It was, however, a milestone in Hutton's own thinking on imperial defence cooperation.

In its underlying concept, Hutton's federal defence scheme was not at all new. In large part it was based on the report of Sir Bevan Edwards, a British general who had examined the state of Australian defences in 1889. Edwards stressed the importance of a federal approach to defence and mooted the possibility of an Australian mobile force, about 30 000 strong, being available for imperial service.[37] A meeting of Australian commandants echoed these recommendations in 1890. In 1892 the British commandant in Victoria, Major-General Alexander Tulloch, led the Royal Commission into the State of the Defence Forces of New South Wales and again recommended a federal defence policy.[38] Federal defence was a sensible solution to the problem of continental defence. Separate defence acts, equipment, uniforms, and training meant that, were the colonies ever required to cooperate against an aggressor, legal and military impediments would intervene. For example, in December 1892, shortly before Hutton arrived, when the Echuca Company of the Victorian Rangers was invited to visit the town of Moama, across the Murray in New South Wales, it required the assent of both colonial parliaments and both commandants.[39] Bringing the colonial armies together under the control of a central council would strengthen Australian continental security.

It also promised to be an advantage in an imperial context, and this was where Hutton sought to bring his concept of an offensive–defensive system into play. Due to British naval supremacy, Hutton argued, following the logic of Bevan Edwards' view, it seemed unlikely at that time that Australia would ever face an invading force. The mobile force that Hutton proposed for the protection of Australia against possible foreign incursion would therefore have little chance of actually being deployed for this purpose. It was, however, potentially very useful as a ready-made Australian expeditionary force that might, in the case of Britain being at war with a European power, attack foreign assets in the region, especially the European Pacific colonies. At the second commandants' conference, the definition of 'Australia and Tasmania' was enlarged to include a large segment of the Pacific with this very end in mind.[40] Furthermore, this force—provided members would volunteer for such service—could, if necessary, support British forces anywhere in the world. Captain Matthew Nathan, the secretary of the Colonial Defence Committee, wrote that since there was no likely Australian defensive need for a mobile force, the expeditionary function of such an army was 'the chief raison d'être of the whole scheme'. The military defensive justification

---

[36] L. D. Atkinson, 'Australian Defence Policy: A Study of Empire and Nation (1897–1910)', PhD thesis, Australian National University, 1964, 38.

[37] Bevan Edwards, 'Proposed Organization of the Military Forces of the Australasian Colonies', The National Archives (TNA): CAB 9/1/40.

[38] Major-General Alexander Tulloch, 'Report of the Military Service Enquiry Commission', attached with despatch, Earl of Jersey to Colonial Office, No 936, received 18 January 1893, TNA: CO 201/613.

[39] Bob Nicholls, *The Colonial Volunteers: The Defence Forces of the Australian Colonies* (Sydney: Allen and Unwin, 1988), 151.

[40] Hutton, *Australian Federal Defence Agreement*, 9.

for it, he added, 'is far less obvious, the conference having accepted the principle "that the most probable form of attack on the Australian littoral would be by means of raids of an enemy's cruisers".'[41] Hutton, aware that Australians would resist a scheme designed to support imperial interests at the expense of Australia's local defence, was more circumspect than either Edwards or Nathan and said nothing publicly about this ultimate objective. Nevertheless, when replying confidentially to Nathan, he claimed to be in full agreement:

> I have kept this object steadily in view throughout all the Schemes, both for N. S. Wales, and for Australia, which I have drawn up, but I have never dared to hint publicly at the possible necessity of moving Australian Troops out of Australian Waters, until the 31st ultimo, when at a Banquet I indicated the principle as applied to England. This has not been adversely criticized, and I propose to go a step further upon the next occasion that offers![42]

Hutton's scheme ultimately failed, with the colonial premiers opting for full federation instead. It was the issue of who would control the new force that disrupted Hutton's plans. The main flaw in Hutton's Australian Defence Scheme was his proposed Federal Council. It was ill-defined. He suggested that two members be appointed by New South Wales and Victoria and one from each of the other colonies, but never elucidated the manner, tenure, or timing of the appointments, and proposed that these members be assisted by three ex-officio members, the federal general commanding and the chief of the military staff (both to be appointed by the council itself) and a naval officer to represent the admiral on the Australian station.[43] The federal general commanding would enjoy the sort of powers Hutton fancied for himself as general officer commanding: the entire responsibility for 'discipline, organisation, minor allotment, and the distribution of troops, apart from the policy of Australian defence.'[44] It was a poor substitute for an elected parliament, as the *Sydney Morning Herald* had editorialised when Hutton first mooted the scheme in 1894: 'To call into existence an army subject to the orders of no responsible Government would be opposed to the traditions and principles of Englishmen.' The same editorial damned Hutton's system as one step away from federation, an attempt 'to pluck the fruit of federation before we have planted the tree.'[45] This resistance to Hutton's scheme for Australian federal defence should not be read as colonial nationalism beating back unwelcome British imperialist advances. Rather, it represented a colonial determination to preserve control over the military forces for which they were paying: local control, as opposed to imperial, and parliamentary control, as opposed to military.

Despite this failure, Hutton was not wholly disheartened and this was because, with Seeley, he had come to value sentiment as much as schemes. National education was as worthwhile as any definite agreement. Following Seeley, Hutton believed in the development, in the nurturing, of the British nations comprising Greater Britain, through education and through the cultivation of civic values. 'We are', he had suggested to the British army's commander-in-chief, the Duke of Cambridge, in 1894,

---

[41] Letter, Matthew Nathan to Hutton, 27 November 1895, BL: Hutton Papers, ADD 50087, 150.

[42] Letter, Hutton to Nathan, 5 January 1896, BL: Hutton Papers, ADD 50087, 158.

[43] Hutton, *Australian Federal Defence Agreement*, 42.

[44] Ibid.

[45] *Sydney Morning Herald*, 25 October 1894.

> I venture to think most likely to reach our ideal of military perfection by a system of evolution, and by educating public opinion to our ultimate requirements rather than by expecting a species of cataclysm to attain our ends which only an acute war crisis would give us.[46]

Thus he was eager to engage with the sentimental side of colonial identity. In public speeches Hutton appealed to race, to common kinship, to religion, to what Seeley believed were the 'natural ties which unite Englishmen [and which will] resume their influence as soon as the counteracting pressure is removed.'[47] The fact that Hutton regarded the cultivation of this sentiment as an evolutionary process with great long-term potential is evident in the care he took not to risk that sentiment in his attempts at implementing federal defence. Bevan Edwards had promised a troop of 30 000; Hutton, on the other hand, was far more circumspect.[48] In the minutes of the Federal Defence Conference of 1894, Hutton was revealed as the most conservative of all the colonial commandants in his objectives. It was he, for instance, who amended Clause 11 of the report to ensure that the colonies would control their forces at all times apart from 'national emergency'.[49] Hutton demonstrated this sense of caution in a letter to Cambridge written after the conference: 'we have endeavoured in our Report to … propose just so much as the existing condition of public opinion is likely to concede to us.'[50] In his time in New South Wales, Hutton had come to appreciate the depth of sentimental attachment to Greater Britain but he also realised that Australians had a keen sense of their own geopolitical interests and would not sacrifice their local defence to imperial schemes.

Hutton's proposal for a 'Co-operative System of Defence'

Hutton took these lessons home with him. On his return from New South Wales in 1896, Hutton in a lecture at Aldershot warned his fellow imperialists in England that:

> A certain influential body of those who are pressing Imperial Federation seek to bind all portions of the empire hand and foot to one given policy both of defence and of finance. Attractive as this may seem, a sojourn in our Colonies, even of short duration, will soon demonstrate the impossibility of such a system being accepted by the majority of our fellow subjects of Greater Britain.[51]

Hutton's 'sojourn' in New South Wales had taught him the true value of Seeley's emphasis on the sentimental bonds of empire. He did attempt to translate colonial loyalty into practical military assistance but, in the absence of such a commitment, he was willing to accept that in a moment of crisis the essential ties of empire would impel the colonies to Britain's aid.

---

[46] Letter, Hutton to Duke of Cambridge, 5 November 1894, BL: Hutton Papers, ADD 50078.

[47] Seeley, *The Expansion of England*, 234.

[48] Atkinson, 'Australian Defence Policy', 33.

[49] Federal Defence Committee, Minutes and Summary of Proceedings of Conference, 1894, TNA: CAB 11/23.

[50] Letter, Hutton to Duke of Cambridge, 5 November 1894, BL: Hutton Papers, ADD 50078.

[51] Hutton, 'Our Comrades of Greater Britain', lecture to Aldershot Military Society, 24 November 1896, reproduced in Hutton, *The Defence and Defensive Power of Australia*, 14.

Accordingly, Hutton set about applying his New South Wales experiences to the problems of imperial defence. He presented a lecture entitled, 'Our Comrades of Greater Britain', to his own old comrades at the Aldershot Military Society in November 1896. The lecture ranged over the entire self-governing empire, arguing for the essential unity of soldiers from Britain, Canada, Australia and Africa, and it discussed practical problems such as the extent of political influence in the colonies, the importance of forming complete field armies from their existing forces, and the necessity of popularising these armies.[52] Hutton impressed upon his audience the grave danger of impending war and of the importance of imperialist sentiment in meeting that threat: 'This is not the spirit of bluster or pride which has been deservedly stigmatised as "Jingoism"; it is a national purpose, it is a national and indeed a natural instinct of self-preservation!'[53] The military could contribute to the education of Greater Britain by teaching 'those manly qualities which are vital to the well-being of any great people', qualities which had established, and protected, 'our freedom and free institutions'.[54] Hutton suggested that the imperial sentiment of the colonies might be harnessed, but he warned of the dangers of attempting to impose any single, fixed military or financial policy on the empire.[55] The solution, he believed, must be flexible and he concluded that his own cooperative system best harnessed the type of nationalist sentiment that he had witnessed in New South Wales, a combination of imperial loyalty and an awareness of local interests:

> Those who, like myself, have had peculiar facilities for knowing the real feeling existing in our Australian Colonies can alone realize the depth of loyalty and generous affection for, and pride in, the old country. England, throughout Australia, is always known and spoken of as 'Home', and with that word are embraced all that makes a 'Home' dear to the distant members of a family. Entwined, however, with this deeply rooted loyalty for and love to the old country, is that truly British love of liberty and that freeborn and independent spirit which resents an injury and brooks no interference—a spirit which is and has been for the last three hundred years the heritage of our race. Overlying all lies that very human failing of self-interest. Having realized the important influences of loyalty, sentiment, and self-interest which exist, we shall find it is wisest in the best interests of the Empire to base our schemes upon these and upon the force of public opinion, which has nowhere in the world so quick and intelligent exponents as in the Australian press.
>
> A co-operative system of defence it is which seems best adapted to fulfil our objects, such, for instance, as that which I have sketched as proposed for the five Australian Colonies and Tasmania. A co-operation based on loyalty to Her Majesty the Queen and to our common country, upon the sentiment of race and of common birth, and upon self-interest.[56]

---

[52] Ibid., 25, 28, 34–35.

[53] Ibid., 37.

[54] Ibid., 38.

[55] Ibid., 44.

[56] Ibid.

In this lecture, Hutton harmonised the ideas of both Seeley and Wolseley, and created from that potent mix his 'Co-operative System for the Defence of the Empire'.

Hutton's formal enunciation of a cooperative system for the defence of the empire followed soon after. In its substance, the scheme was very similar to the scheme for Australian federal defence: calling for each member to divide its troops between garrison and field forces, the combined imperial field forces forming a federal militia of six army corps available for mobilisation in wartime to serve wherever the empire was threatened. In framing this scheme he was, however, faced with the same problem that had confronted his scheme for Australian federal defence: who would control his proposed force? Parliamentary democracy, he admitted, prevented 'the establishment of an ideal system' and ways must be adapted to means.[57] Hutton advocated proceeding as cautiously as possible and making little change to existing military structures, instead relying on existing militia acts to provide the necessary manpower. He also realised that the self-governing colonies would require a say in the disposition of their forces: 'It may be taken for granted that the only plan of co-operative defence which would be acceptable to Great Britain and to her Colonies would be one based upon a representative system.'[58] In his final answer, however, the creation of a 'central controlling council', Hutton gave no detail, and simply hoped that the bonds of sentiment would find a way:

> Surely in the case where the sentiment of race, of religion, of language, of political inclinations are common to all, it should not be difficult to so plan a central controlling authority which would make possible a system of cooperative defence, such as that framed in the Australian Federal Defence Scheme.[59]

The intractability of this problem had hamstrung his plans for Australian federal defence. The dilemma of how to reconcile loyalties of sentiment and self-interest would haunt Hutton in his successive attempts at introducing the scheme in Canada and Australia.

Hutton's Canadian Command, 1898–1900

When Hutton was appointed as general officer commanding the militia of Canada in 1898, he took up his post with the firm objective of implementing his cooperative system of defence. Indeed, he would boast a few years later that in this this quest he had been largely successful in the two key self-governing colonies: 'The idea … of a Co-operative System of Military Defence', he wrote the permanent under-secretary for the colonies, Sir Montagu Ommanney, in 1902, 'has been officially presented to both the Canadian and Australian Governments!'[60] In the case of Canada, Hutton's claim seemed to rest on the publication of his 1899 annual report to the Canadian parliament. Hutton always held that the great value of this report lay not in the specific reforms outlined but in the general statement of principles governing Canadian defence. This statement, closely following the tenets of his cooperative system, described two principles on which any organisation of Canadian

---

[57] Hutton, 'A Co-operative System for Defence of the Empire', 3.
[58] Ibid., 4.
[59] Ibid.
[60] Letter, Hutton to Sir Montagu Ommanney, 8 April 1902, BL: Hutton Papers, ADD 50078.

defence must be based: firstly, the defence of Canadian soil and, secondly, the ability to participate in a general defence of the British Empire.

> It is justly claimed for Canada that she is now a nation. In establishing this claim it must equally be accepted that with her birth as a nation are indisputably born the responsibilities of self-defence … Canada is, moreover, a part of that larger empire which has given her birth, and it is the pride of Canada that in the past, whenever British or Imperial interests have been threatened, she has been the first to offer her assistance. If public opinion has been rightly judged there is, at the present time, a universally held determination to uphold at all costs the integrity of the empire, and at all hazards to maintain its interests against hostile aggression or foreign interference.[61]

As commandant in New South Wales Hutton had certainly envisaged colonial military assistance to the empire but he had never been so bold as to state this aim in his official reports nor claim it as the basis of a new defence arrangement. He had always been mindful of local sensibilities and had justified his reforms solely on the basis of local needs.

Hutton's annual report was submitted to the Canadian government, received his minister's signature, and his estimates were passed by parliament with hardly even a debate. Hutton was fairly astonished, believing he owed his success to the pressure of public opinion upon a reluctant cabinet.[62] He wrote proudly to Chamberlain in July 1899 suggesting that the calm reception of the report gave 'good ground for the hope that Canada purposes to take a foremost part in solving the question of a Co-operative System of Defence for the Empire'.[63]

Why was the Canadian government so accommodating? First, contrary to Hutton's claims, the Canadian parliamentarians, in allowing him to express these views, did not necessarily assent to them. Not even Dr Frederick Borden, one of the more imperial-minded members of the Canadian cabinet and Hutton's minister, actually agreed with Hutton, but he was quite willing to let him talk:

> His report is *his own*. This has always been the rule with regard to the Report of the General Officers Commanding, who are Imperial Officers. I saw his Report before it was published and pointed out the respects in which I thought it impossible to have his suggestions adopted, but gave him permission to have the whole published, as he prepared it. I thought it only just to him to do this.[64]

Despite his boasts to Chamberlain, Hutton was no doubt himself aware at the time of the limits of parliamentary approval. In fact, he seems to have been slightly upset that his report was received so quietly, hoping to have created more of a splash. He sent a proof copy to Dr George Parkin, a principal figure in the Canadian imperial federation movement,

---

[61] Department of Militia and Defence for the Dominion of Canada, 'Report for the Year Ended December 1898', TNA: CAB 18/4.

[62] Letter, Hutton to Garnet Wolseley, 31 December 1899, BL: Hutton Papers, ADD 50085, 146.

[63] Letter, Hutton to Chamberlain, 28 July 1899, Birmingham University Library (BUL): Joseph Chamberlain Collection, JC 29/2/2/156.

[64] Letter, Frederick Borden to Lt-Col Leverett de Veber Chipman, 10 April 1899, Public Archives of Nova Scotia: Borden Collection, Borden Letter Book 9, MG 2 90, 456. Original emphasis.

claiming that although he had the 'good will' of cabinet he would need 'Public Opinion' on side to have any real effect and asking Parkin to lend the report his 'powerful support' in the public arena.[65] He wrote in a similar fashion to Bevan Edwards and to Sydenham Clarke.[66] Clearly, if Hutton was convinced that he needed public sympathy to push his reforms, he was hardly confident of government support.

Nevertheless it is still significant that the Canadian government allowed Hutton to publicise the case for imperial cooperation. They seemed to have fewer of the Australian fears of becoming embroiled and entangled in imperial commitments against their will, or losing control over their defence forces. In March 1899, for example, discussing British contingency planning for a possible war with France, Canadian prime minister Wilfred Laurier surprised the governor-general, Lord Minto, by assuring him that in his opinion the British government was entitled to mobilise the Canadian militia for service overseas.[67] Hutton's public conflation of Canadian and imperial defence did not challenge Canada's sense of cultural identity—indeed, it was entirely consistent with it—nor, more importantly, did it challenge its sense of its own local interests.

There are two reasons why Canada was willing to permit their commandant to express such views. Firstly, it made strategic and economic sense for the Canadian government to accommodate the British as far as possible. The 1895–96 Venezuelan war scare had awakened the Canadian people to the possibility of war with the United States, and the only realistic defence Canada had was the British navy. The Canadians also relied on British power to press their claims in boundary disputes with America over Alaska. Some members of cabinet, particularly Borden and Richard Cartwright, felt that Canada should reciprocate and participate in some form in the defence of the empire.[68] Britain had also become vital to Canadian trade, especially since the introduction of the McKinley tariff in the United States in 1890, and this had sparked Laurier's interest in imperial preferential tariffs.[69] Secondly, the Canadian government was happy to play along because in peacetime the militia was of only limited importance. As Peter Durrans points out, the militia was simply not a priority for Laurier and his government (before the Boer War), whose efforts

---

[65] Letter, Hutton to George Parkin, 13 March 1899, National Archives of Canada: Parkin Fonds, 3839.

[66] Letter, Hutton to Bevan Edwards, 12 February 1899, BL: Hutton Papers, ADD 50096, 38; letter, Hutton to Sydenham Clarke, 1 March 1899, BL: Hutton Papers, ADD 50108, 257.

[67] Letter, Lord William Seymour to Under Secretary of State for War, 14 December 1898, TNA: WO 32/6367, Despatch C 112; memorandum of conversation, Lord Minto and Wilfred Laurier, 27 March 1899, in *Lord Minto's Canadian Papers: A Selection of The Public and Private Papers of the Fourth Earl of Minto*, vol. 1, *1898–1904*, eds John Saywell and Paul Stevens (Toronto: The Champlain Society, 1981), 44.

[68] Letter, Hutton to Chamberlain, 20 February 1899, BL: Hutton Papers, ADD 50078, 174: 'The Minister of Defence (Doctor Borden), Sir Richard Cartwright, and several other members of the Cabinet have, in conversation, repeatedly said that the Reforms made should be such as would not only guarantee the security of Canadian soil, but would enable Canada to participate in the defence of the Empire.'

[69] Guy Maclean, 'The Imperial Federation Movement in Canada, 1884–1902', PhD thesis, Duke University, 1958, 87.

were bent almost wholly towards economic growth.[70] In 1898 Canada spent less per capita on its defence than any other country in the world.[71] Laurier could therefore assure the British of their right to call out his militia in the secure knowledge that in its current underfunded and ill-trained state the Canadian militia was hardly likely to do anyone any good.

The Canadian response to Hutton's attempt to introduce the central principles of his cooperative system in that country is interesting because it occurred at a time when Canada's geopolitical interests were temporarily aligned with Britain's: when the communities of culture and interest were in relative harmony. Even so, there was never a question of Canada subjecting control of its military to the empire nor even of the Canadian government fully endorsing Hutton's proposals (as Borden made clear). Yet Hutton was permitted to officially and publically make the case for imperial defence cooperation, something that he was never able to do in Australia.

The Australian Command, 1902–04

Hutton arrived in Melbourne on 29 January 1902 and for the first few months of his final colonial command he enjoyed remarkably clear sailing. A fortnight before his arrival, Chamberlain had requested additional Australian contingents for the ongoing war in South Africa and the government of Edmund Barton had responded with two Commonwealth contingents, and was shortly to announce a third. Imperial sentiment was high and Hutton enjoyed a warm reception from the public, the troops and his government.[72]

Hutton was fortunate to have as his minister one of the staunchest imperialists in the government. In 1902 John Forrest was busy developing his 'Minute on Naval Defence'. This was an important document that led to the restructuring of Australia's naval agreement with Britain. Forrest approached Hutton for assistance in drafting the minute. Impressed, Hutton likened its contents to his own views on defence: '[it] is based upon a System of Co-operation'.[73] Forrest's naval minute was imperially-focused and in its sentiments it nicely matched the military changes Hutton hoped to make:

> In regard to Defence we must altogether get rid of the idea that we have different interests to those of the rest of the Empire, and we must look at the matter from a broad common standpoint. If the British nation is at war, so are we; if it gains victories or suffers disasters, so do we, and therefore it is of the same vital interest to us as to the rest of the Empire that our supremacy on the ocean shall be maintained … That this is the sentiment deep-rooted in the hearts of the Australian people, has, I am proud to say, been shown during the South African war, which we have made our own, proving unmistakably to the world that our

---

[70] Peter Durrans, 'Imperial Defence: The Canadian Response during Joseph Chamberlain's Tenure of Office as Colonial Secretary 1895–1903', MA thesis, Carleton University, 1964, 121.

[71] Norman Penlington, 'General Hutton and the Problem of Military Imperialism in Canada, 1898–1900', *Canadian Historical Review*, 24 (2), 1943, 156–71.

[72] Letter, Hutton to Ommanney, 3 February 1902, BL: Hutton Papers, ADD 50078, 259.

[73] Letter, Hutton to Ommanney, 8 April 1902, BL: Hutton Papers, ADD 50078.

interests in war as well as in peace, are indissolubly bound up with the Country from which our fathers came, and to which we are all proud to belong.[74]

On 7 April 1902 Hutton delivered his own statement of policy to the government, his 'Minute upon the Defence of Australia'. As in Canada, Hutton explored the potential for Australian forces to share in the general defence of the empire, but he was much more circumspect, phrasing the notion in the language of local interests. He warned that defence could only ever be assured by a capacity to take the offence and argued that:

> The defence of Australia cannot, moreover, be considered apart from the defence of Australian interests. Australia depends for its commercial success and its future development firstly upon its seaborne trade; and secondly upon the existence, maintenance, and extension of fixed and certain markets for its produce outside Australian waters. It is hardly consistent with the present development of Australia as a young and vigorous nation to neglect her responsibility for defence outside Australian waters, and in the robust period of her youth thus to rely upon the strong arm of the Mother Country. It may be assumed, therefore, that Australia will determine not only to defend her own soil, but to take steps also to defend those vast interests beyond her shores upon maintenance of which her present existence and her future prosperity must so largely depend.[75]

Hutton recommended dividing the Australian military into garrison and field forces and proposed that a large portion of the field force be mounted. He suggested that this accorded with the natural aptitudes of Australians and, moreover, it

> provides exactly that description of fighting man which has proved so valuable in South Africa, and which, without doubt, would constitute a most powerful, if not controlling, factor in any campaign in which Australian troops might be engaged.[76]

Hutton did not baldly state that the field force would be available for imperial service but the subtext of his minute was clear. He explained the line he was trying to follow to the British secretary of state for war, William St John Brodrick:

> I have been careful to avoid any direct reference to assistance to the Empire in time of war except inferentially. There is a certain section in Australia who are little Englanders & who would restrict the use of Australian troops to Australian soil. My minute was written to prove the utter fallacy of such principles but I have preferred to allow this inference to be drawn rather than to actually state it.[77]

Hutton's April minute received a positive response from his government and Barton and Forrest both congratulated him on it.[78] Barton and Forrest were at that time preparing to leave for the June 1902 Colonial Conference and Hutton believed that with the two minutes on naval and military defence they were well equipped to discuss imperial cooperation.[79]

---

[74] Letter, John Forrest to Hutton, 10 April 1902, BL: Hutton Papers, ADD 50084.

[75] Hutton, 'Minute upon the Defence of Australia', 7 April 1902, TNA: CAB 11/24 1902–13.

[76] Ibid.

[77] Letter, Hutton to William St John Brodrick, 7 April 1902, BL: Hutton Papers, ADD 50085.

[78] Letter, Edmund Barton to Hutton, 6 April 1902, BL: Hutton Papers, ADD 50084; letter, Forrest to Hutton, 10 April 1902, BL: Hutton Papers, ADD 50084.

[79] Letter, Hutton to Ommanney, 8 April 1902, BL: Hutton Papers, ADD 50078.

Unfortunately for Hutton, events in London would threaten these early hopes. On the basis of the Boer War, St John Brodrick had decided that arrangements for colonial military assistance ought to be formalised. For the last few years he had been considering the problems of imperial defence and had actually approached Hutton in early 1901 for advice on the question.[80] Hutton had suggested the calling of a colonial conference to discuss a general scheme for the defence of the empire.[81] Brodrick evidently decided that the June 1902 Colonial Conference, held in conjunction with the Royal coronation, would be a suitable forum. At that conference, he asked the assembled leaders of the colonies for a formal contribution to imperial defence. Brodrick based his proposal on a paper by Lieutenant-Colonel Altham, a British intelligence officer, which put the case for definite colonial peacetime military commitments. Altham had discovered in Hutton's proposed Australian field force the ideal unit for such a purpose and had suggested renaming it the 'Imperial Australian Force' and making it available for defensive or offensive operations in any part of the world.[82] Brodrick approached Barton and Forrest and in putting this idea to them formally requested the creation of an 'Imperial Australian Force' consisting of 9000 men ready to be handed over to war office control in emergency.[83]

Barton was embarrassed by this direct request. He wrote privately and apologetically to Chamberlain requesting a private conversation before the conference to explain 'the reasons why we hold certain views', and, he continued: 'We should all understand the limitations which may at the present moment hold back the completion of some things we all want to see achieved.'[84] Believing that he could never get the Australian parliament to acquiesce to the cession, during peacetime, of control over forces for which it was paying, Barton ultimately rejected Brodrick's proposal. Brodrick was bitterly disappointed and complained to Chamberlain that 'from a military point of view it is the wreckage of the scheme which would have saved us heavy expenditure'.[85]

Hutton was also disappointed by the conference but for different reasons. He was angry that Brodrick pushed for a guarantee of Australian defence assistance. As he confided to fellow general Sir Thomas Kelly-Kenny: 'I fondly hoped that I had persuaded Mr Brodrick of the absurd supposition that our Colonies would accept any definite military contribution to the Military strength of the Empire without due representation.'[86] He realised from long experience that Australian public opinion would never stomach such a scheme and that there were constitutional issues at stake: 'The cost of the system which I propose to create would naturally fall on the Commonwealth government, and it would equally rest with that Government to employ their troops how or where they might decide.' This was why Hutton insisted that, although he was preparing colonial troops for imperial service, the eventual

---

[80] Letter, Hutton to Lord Minto, 27 March 1901, BL: Hutton Papers, ADD 50081.

[81] Letter, Hutton to Brodrick, 30 January 1901, BL: Hutton Papers, ADD 50085.

[82] Lt-Col Edward Altham, 'The Organization of Colonial Troops for Imperial Service', appendix to Memorandum No 293M, 13 June 1902, TNA: CAB 8/3.

[83] Meaney, *Search for Security*, 62.

[84] Letter, Barton to Chamberlain, 9 June 1902, BUL: Chamberlain Collection, JC 17/2/4.

[85] Letter, Brodrick to Chamberlain, 11 August 1902, BUL: Chamberlain Collection, JC 17/1/9.

[86] Letter, Hutton to Sir Thomas Kelly-Kenny, 4 August 1902, BL: Hutton Papers, ADD 50097, 163.

offer of such service must be voluntary. Hutton was fairly certain that, without a prior formal commitment, Australian support could still be relied upon in emergency:

> Co-operation in the Defence of the Empire under the circumstances that exist would be solely a matter of sentiment, and in the present condition of public feeling it would be unwise to press anything more. The strongest possible feeling of sympathy with, and determination to be considered a part of the Empire exists in every part of Australia. This feeling has been intensified a hundred fold by the recent Campaign and nothing has struck me so much since my return to Australia as the extraordinary development of public feeling in this respect.[87]

Barton mirrored Hutton's position when rejecting Brodrick's proposal at the conference: 'Our people are like their countrymen here, they will do much in time of warlike emergency which in time of peace they would decline to bind themselves beforehand to accomplish.'[88]

Hutton had come to believe, unlike many in the British administration, that a formal assurance of Australian assistance was not necessary. He had faced this problem in New South Wales and in Canada and he realised that such a cession of control ran against the constitutional grain:

> I am absolutely convinced that given a National Emergency involving a menace to the unity and solidarity of the Empire that Australia would be found determined at all hazards to take a foremost part, and that any Government which advocated any other policy would not last a week ... It is however idle to imagine that any self-governing Colonies whether it be Canada or whether it be Australia will for a moment admit the *right* of the Imperial Government to bind them to defined military assistance without representation in the Imperial Councils which may make such assistance necessary. In other words the Military assistance to be rendered in time of National Emergency by either Canada or Australia must be purely one of sentiment and self-interest so long as the existing condition of non-representation continues.[89]

Conclusion

The cooperative system was therefore Hutton's attempt at marshalling colonial and British sentiment for the purpose of formalising the bonds of Greater Britain. In his scheme he attempted to fuse the ideas of Seeley with the methods of Wolseley and at one stage, he actually signalled his willingness to pursue his plans for cooperative defence alone, if need be, evoking his two mentors as justification:

> No statesman under either Liberal or Conservative administrations had up to that date [1898] enunciated a military defence policy or laid down the requirements for the military defence of the Empire. It was left, therefore, to the members of the Wolseley school of military experts to frame such a policy for themselves and to act thereon ... The disciples of the great Seeley, no less than the followers of

---

[87] Letter, Hutton to William Nicholson, 23 July 1902, BL: Hutton Papers, ADD 50086.

[88] Barton, speech to Colonial Conference, 30 June 1902, BUL: Chamberlain Papers, JC 17/1/1.

[89] Letter, Hutton to Sir Frederick Matthew Darley, 20 January 1903, BL: Hutton Papers, ADD 50082. Original emphasis.

the Wolseley school of military thought, were thoroughly in accord with these primary principles of defence.[90]

In New South Wales, Hutton had witnessed first hand the extent of that colony's allegiance to the idea of Greater Britain, balanced against its unwillingness to cede control over its own forces or sacrifice its local interests. His cooperative system highlights his understanding of that central problem of Greater Britain. In his attempts to implement the scheme in Canada and Australia, he demonstrated a nuanced understanding of the separate loyalties of sentiment and self-interest, making the case for imperial cooperation only so far as local interests would permit. Ultimately, however, despite his attempts to overcome these local interests with small steps and with appeals to sentiment, the inherent and perhaps insurmountable problems of applying the aspirations of Greater Britain to imperial defence policy prevented Hutton's cooperative system from ever coming to fruition.

---

[90] Hutton, 'John Gilbert, 4th Earl of Minto. Governor General of Canada, 1898–1904. A Narrative', BL: Hutton Papers, ADD 50081, 237–38.

7

Robert Randolph Garran and the Creation of the Australian Commonwealth

Colin Milner[1]

One of the most important things learnt by students in Neville Meaney's honours seminar on the history of Australian defence and foreign policy, at the University of Sydney in the late 1970s, was that the Australian (formerly Commonwealth) public service could provide not only an opportunity to pursue an honourable profession but, more broadly, an arena where youthful aspirations to good citizenship might be usefully directed and, hopefully, realised. Given the seminar's subject matter, those areas of the public service which were closely involved in Australia's engagement with the world were a particular focus of attention.

Meaney had an evident respect for E. L. Piesse, the insightful foreign policy analyst who had served as director of the Pacific branch created in the Prime Minister's Department during the aftermath of the First World War.[2] This was later confirmed by his entry on Piesse in the *Australian Dictionary of Biography* and a subsequent monograph devoted to Piesse's work on Australian policy towards Japan.[3] Meaney saw Piesse as 'a practical scholar, a man of independent mind who believed that public policy must be based on knowledge and understanding'.[4] It was essentially this ideal of the frank and fearless public servant which had been encouraged in his seminar.

These lessons were reinforced for the author a couple of years later when, working as a part-time research assistant for Meaney while studying at law school, he again had the opportunity to attend the honours seminar when it was addressed by the late Alan Renouf. With a long and distinguished diplomatic career behind him, Renouf retired after serving as Australia's ambassador in Washington during the late 1970s. He was then researching the foreign policy of H. V. Evatt, the Australian minister for external affairs, with whom he had worked during the 1940s.[5] A career combining scholarly interests, a

---

[1] The author is employed as an official in the Australian Department of Foreign Affairs and Trade. He serves in a private capacity as a member of the Steering Committee for Historians of Australia's Foreign Relations. The views expressed in this chapter are his own.

[2] Neville Meaney, *A History of Australian Defence and Foreign Policy, 1901–23*, vol. 1, *The Search for Security in the Pacific, 1901–14* (Sydney: Sydney University Press, 1976), 12, 14.

[3] Meaney, 'Edmund Leolin Piesse (1880–1947)', in *Australian Dictionary of Biography* (hereafter *ADB*), vol. 11, ed. Geoffrey Serle (Melbourne: Melbourne University Press, 1988), 227–29; Meaney, *Fears & Phobias: E.L. Piesse and the Problem of Japan, 1901–1939* (Canberra: National Library of Australia [NLA], 1996).

[4] Meaney, 'Edmund Leolin Piesse', 227.

[5] See Alan Renouf, *Let Justice Be Done: The Foreign Policy of Dr H. V. Evatt* (St Lucia, Qld: University of Queensland Press, 1983).

legal qualification (which, as it happened, Piesse and Renouf both possessed) and practical public service employment (with the possibility of international experience) clearly had much to recommend it.

Robert Randolph Garran was another distinguished Australian who embodied this combination of qualities in pursuing ideals of public service and good citizenship. Garran had a strong interest in both the advancement of scholarship—he was one of the founders of the Australian National University in Canberra—and Australia's engagement with the wider world. In particular, he recognised the value of historical perspective informing judgement, not only in meeting the challenges of Australia's international relations, but also for understanding the nation's fundamental law (of which he was an acknowledged authority).

The preface to *The Annotated Constitution of the Australian Commonwealth* (or 'Quick and Garran', as it is commonly known) suggested the strong feeling that he and co-author John Quick had for history and its practical applications. As they put it:

> Our chief aim has been a practical one. Clear as is the language of the Constitution, it cannot be fully understood without the study of a large correlated literature … It has been built on traditional foundations. Its roots penetrate deep into the past. It embodies the best achievements of political progress, and realizes the latest attainable ideals of liberty … Such an instrument of government must needs be rich in historical associations … There is hardly a phrase in it without a history.[6]

Such insights added weight to a student's choice of history as a subject. Along with Piesse and Renouf—and others, like Frederic Eggleston, also encountered in the Meaney seminar—Garran's example could have an inspiring effect on a callow undergraduate uncertain of which career path to follow.

Garran was undoubtedly a substantial figure in Australian history, even if the extent of his contribution still has to be fully assessed. His contemporaries knew his quality. Kenneth Bailey, one of his successors as secretary of the Attorney-General's Department and solicitor-general, wrote shortly after Garran's death that he was 'revered in his lifetime as one … of the Fathers of Federation'.[7] Eggleston, who had worked with Garran at the Paris Peace Conference in 1919, regarded him as 'the greatest of all the Commonwealth Public Servants'.[8] The writer and pioneering critic of Australian literature, Tom Inglis Moore, who knew him in Canberra during his later years, admired Garran for his common sense and liberal tolerance.[9]

One of the best summations of Garran's life and work is found in R. S. Parker's elegantly written entry in the *Australian Dictionary of Biography*.[10] It is noteworthy that the Prime

---

[6] John Quick and Robert Randolph Garran, *The Annotated Constitution of the Australian Commonwealth* (Sydney: Legal Books, 1976 [1901]), vii–viii.

[7] K. H. Bailey, 'Sir Robert Garran', *Australian Quarterly,* 29 (1), 1957, 11.

[8] Cited in R. S. Parker, 'Robert Randolph Garran (1867–1957)', in *ADB*, vol. 8, eds Bede Nairn and Geoffrey Serle (Melbourne: Melbourne University Press, 1981), 623.

[9] Pacita Alexander and Elizabeth Perkins, *A Love Affair with Australian Literature: The Story of Tom Inglis Moore* (Charnwood, ACT: Ginninderra Press, 2004), 224.

[10] Parker, 'Robert Randolph Garran', 622–25.

Minister of Australia, Julia Gillard, in her Robert Garran Oration delivered in Hobart on 26 August 2011, directly quoted the following words from Parker's entry on Garran:

> His personality, like his prose, was devoid of pedantry and pomposity and, though dignified, was laced with a quizzical turn of humour. He was capable of strong and decisive administrative action when required; what people of all kinds most remembered were charity, modesty, courtesy and charm.

And the prime minister added:

> It is hard to imagine a more perfect description of public sector leadership as we wish it always to be.[11]

In light of these judgments, the aims for this chapter are firstly, to highlight Garran's substance as an historic figure; secondly, to contend that, as a result, a more comprehensive account of Garran's life and work than has yet been published is justified; and, thirdly, to suggest some ideas which might be usefully developed in a detailed biographical effort in the future.

A Man of Many Careers

A brief outline of Garran's career—or, rather, careers—should be sufficient to highlight his substance as an historic figure. This has been well done elsewhere on more than one occasion, so the point hardly needs restating, except as an appropriate prelude to pursuing the second and third aims of this chapter.

One of Australia's native sons, born in the British colony of New South Wales in 1867, Garran was a young Sydney barrister who became involved in what he called the 'popular movement' for Australian federation from the early 1890s.[12] He established himself as an expert on the text that was developing into the constitution of the 'Coming Commonwealth', as he titled the handbook he wrote for federalists, and served as secretary to the drafting committee of the 1897–98 Constitutional Convention.[13] Having proved his mettle as one of the team of young men assisting the leader of the popular federal movement, Edmund Barton—who was to become Australia's first prime minister in 1901—Garran, at the request of Barton's deputy, Alfred Deakin, was appointed the inaugural secretary of the Commonwealth Attorney-General's Department.[14] He was only thirty-three years old.

Assuming this position on 1 January 1901, the day the Commonwealth was proclaimed, Garran served as secretary until his retirement from the public service in 1932. He also served concurrently as the first Commonwealth solicitor-general from 1916. In these roles, Garran became the expert legal adviser on the constitution to a succession of Commonwealth

---

[11] Julia Gillard, Robert Garran Memorial Oration, 26 August 2011, available at www.pm.gov.au/press-office/robert-garran-memorial-oration-institute-public-administration-australian-national-conf.

[12] Garran, *Prosper the Commonwealth* (Sydney: Angus and Robertson, 1958), 101–09.

[13] Garran, *The Coming Commonwealth: An Australian Handbook of Federal Government* (Sydney: Angus and Robertson, 1897).

[14] Parker, 'Robert Randolph Garran', 622.

governments of all persuasions. As such, he achieved a degree of bipartisan acceptance and influence that was evidently denied his colleague Atlee Hunt. Another of Barton's young men, Hunt had been appointed secretary of the first Department of External Affairs in 1901, only to come under the suspicion of Labor Party leaders for his 'conspicuous political associations', especially after the advent of the first Labor majority government led by Andrew Fisher in 1910.[15] Garran, whose own political associations were similar to Hunt's, may have been more circumspect in this regard but he also may have been more indispensable to Labor governments because of his great expertise on the constitution.

In addition, Garran served as the parliamentary draftsman (the equivalent position is now the statutory office of first parliamentary counsel) throughout his thirty-one years in the public service. In this role, he was also able to exercise that significant if subtle influence on policy outcomes which emanates from the way Commonwealth legislation is drafted or, in the words of Justice Mary Finn, 'the real power in our legal and political system' that comes from 'the truth … that in the end legislative ideas will only work according to how they are in fact expressed in the statute book.'[16] Overall, Garran was well placed to influence the shape and substance of Australia's federal institutions over the first three decades of their history.

During the First World War, Garran developed a close working relationship with W. M. Hughes, Fisher's attorney-general and, from October 1915, prime minister of Australia. When first observed, theirs seems a curious relationship, given stark differences of background and personality. But the famous statement attributed to Hughes that 'the best way to govern Australia was to have Sir Robert Garran at his elbow, with a fountain pen and a blank sheet of paper, and the *War Precautions Act*' draws attention to their partnership.[17] The severity of that wartime legislation and also, more generally, the serious rifts engendered and exposed in Australian society by the conscription crisis over which Hughes presided provide a highly charged historical context for analysing that partnership.

A study of Garran during this period promises an insight into how one influential Australian, a British Empire loyalist who loved German lyric poetry and song, dealt with the tensions created within Australia and, more particularly, the Commonwealth government, by the terrible and costly conflict with Germany and its allies.[18] An early indication of Garran's wartime perspective is found in a lecture he delivered in Melbourne during 1915:

> We can never forget—we need not wish to forget—the great services that the Germany of past generations has rendered to civilization, in literature, in science, in philosophy, and in music. But the Germany of Goethe, and Heine, and Hegel, and Beethoven is not the Germany of to-day—the Germany of Nietzsche, and

---

[15] See Helen M. Davies, 'Atlee Arthur Hunt (1864–1935)', in *ADB*, vol. 9, eds Bede Nairn and Geoffrey Serle (Melbourne: Melbourne University Press, 1983), 404.

[16] Cited in Carmel Meiklejohn, *Fitting the Bill: A History of Commonwealth Parliamentary Drafting* (Kingston, ACT: Office of Parliamentary Counsel, 2012), 260.

[17] Cited in Parker, 'Robert Randolph Garran', 623. Garran had been knighted in 1917.

[18] See Heinrich Heine, *The Book of Songs*, trans. Garran (Melbourne: Edward A. Vidler, 1924); and Garran, *Schubert and Schumann: Songs and Translations* (Melbourne: Melbourne University Press, 1946).

Bernhardi, and Von Goltz. The madness which has overcome the nation has placed her, for the time being, outside the pale.[19]

It was in this wartime context that Garran developed an important international dimension to his professional life. At the outset, Garran and his department were confronted by unfamiliar international legal problems generated by the outbreak of the First World War. Ever the practical scholar, Garran turned to the writings of Australian-born and Oxford-educated Pitt Cobbett, foundation professor of law at the University of Sydney from 1890 and a pioneer in the study and teaching of international law in Australia. To Garran, Cobbett was a 'practical and useful' source of guidance in these matters, while all the other textbooks 'seemed in comparison to be the armchair speculations of academic lawyers.'[20]

International engagement could only increase for the new nation in the circumstances of war and its aftermath. Indeed, the end of the war drew Australia into active multilateral engagement beyond the strict bounds of the British Empire. In 1919 Garran played a key diplomatic role as official adviser to Hughes at the Paris Peace Conference where Australia gained recognition, along with the other self-governing dominions of the empire, in its own right—not only as a founding member of the League of Nations, but also for rather less admirable reasons as a prominent opponent of the Japanese proposal for inclusion of a racial equality clause in the league's covenant.[21] Among the other overseas gatherings that Garran attended as an Australian official were the Imperial Conferences of 1923 and 1930.[22]

After retiring from the public service in 1932, Garran continued a life of active community service for another twenty-five years. The foundation professor of law at the Australian National University's Research School of Social Sciences, Geoffrey Sawer, who knew Garran well in his later years, captured a key focus of that contribution by naming him in an obituary as 'the Father of Canberra, nurturer of its educational, religious and cultural life, and advocate for its political rights'.[23] This is a theme well worth exploring, especially as the centenary of the proclamation of Canberra as the nation's federal capital falls in 2013.

Garran was a 'Father of Federation' who actually lived in the fledgling national capital during its formative early stages of development after the seat of government was transferred there from Melbourne in 1927. He was committed to Canberra as the 'political Capital and a symbol of Australian unity'.[24] This surely had much to do with Garran's devotion to the Commonwealth of Australia he had helped to create—from conception, gestation and birth through long decades of growth to maturity as an independent nation.

That devotion was the leitmotiv of Garran's life. It was reflected in the repeated use of the word 'Commonwealth' in the titles of three major publications by Garran—*The*

---

[19] Garran, 'Trade and the War', *University of Melbourne War Lectures* (Melbourne: George Robertson, 1915), 87–88.

[20] Garran, *Prosper the Commonwealth*, 221. See also F. C. Hutley, 'William Pitt Cobbett (1853-1919)', in *ADB*, vol. 8, 40–41.

[21] Garran, *Prosper the Commonwealth*, 257–81.

[22] Parker, 'Robert Randolph Garran', 624.

[23] Geoffrey Sawer, 'Sir Robert Garran', *Australian National University News*, 31, March 1957, 1.

[24] Garran, *Prosper the Commonwealth*, 292.

Coming Commonwealth, *The Annotated Constitution of the Australian Commonwealth* and his substantial memoir, *Prosper the Commonwealth*, which was published posthumously in 1958. Garran's emphasis on the term 'Commonwealth' in describing the Australian nation-state reflected what historians James Curran and Stuart Ward have called 'a sense of national idealism and the idea of a free community dedicated to the advancement of the common good'. This has a renewed resonance for contemporary Australians given, as Curran and Ward have stated, that term's capacity to 'transcend the vast changes that Australia has undergone in the past several decades and … potential to connect the nation's past to its present and future'.[25]

As his son Andrew related in a prefatory note, the title of Garran's memoir was chosen after his death from the last line of the 'Federation Hymn' which he had written at the time the Commonwealth of Australia was established. The final lines are reproduced below:

> Thou who, in peace and war-time,
>
> Hast, with ungrudging hand,
>
> Prospered our sires aforetime,
>
> Prospered our Motherland,
>
> Guard Thou the daughter nation
>
> From danger, strife and stealth;
>
> Through trial, drouth, temptation,
>
> Prosper the Commonwealth![26]

For those close to Garran, that last line must have summed up his life and legacy like none other.

The Historiographical Problem

Garran was, therefore, a major figure in the creation of the Australian Commonwealth in the most complete sense. As historian Jeff Brownrigg has observed, 'Garran not only helped to construct the engine, he also laid important sections of the tracks along which the newly built Commonwealth would travel'.[27] Such a pioneer deserves more scholarly attention than Garran has received. Unlike quite a few 'Fathers of Federation' and one or two 'Mothers', Garran has never been the subject of a comprehensive biography.[28]

Garran tended to be modest about his own contribution and significance, so establishing the extent of his influence is a real challenge for the historian. But the problem affecting the historiography on Garran goes beyond that. Brownrigg has set it out in straightforward terms:

---

[25] James Curran and Stuart Ward, *The Unknown Nation: Australia After Empire* (Melbourne: Melbourne University Press, 2010), 265–66.

[26] Garran, *Prosper the Commonwealth*, v.

[27] Jeff Brownrigg, 'Federation's Prodigy: The Private Life of Robert Randolph Garran', in *Makers of Miracles: The Cast of the Federation Story*, eds David Headon and John Williams (Melbourne: Melbourne University Press, 2000), 97.

[28] Ibid., 96.

Others have received less attention than they deserve, even after having written memoirs that present a view from within the federal movement. Robert Randolph Garran is perhaps the best example of this group, having suffered for being a bureaucrat and a closet academic rather than a regular politician. This fact has tended to steer attention away from the central role he played.[29]

In particular, it seems that, from 1901 until 1932, Garran was always the loyal public servant, attuned to the requirements of the elected government of the day and imbued with a commanding sense of propriety in whatever he said or wrote. Indeed, the constitutional lawyer (and past occupant of the Robert Garran Chair at the law school of the Australian National University) Leslie Zines has concluded that because he was a public servant, 'there is no way one can accurately determine what contribution Garran made to the formulation of government policy'—thus framing a formidable challenge for any budding biographer.[30] In doing his job properly, Garran obscured his overall importance.

Brownrigg points out too that Garran has not always been well served by those who have written about him. A prime example is Alfred Deakin's single reference to Garran in *The Federal Story* depicting him as a 'counsellor upon legal and constitutional matters' advising an apparently weak George Reid—the New South Wales premier who was lampooned in the press as 'Yes–No' Reid for his indecision on the federal cause.[31] This image of Garran dutifully serving the political players, including even a federation doubter, does him an injustice even if the damage is only collateral in nature.[32] Once again, Brownrigg is insightful:

> The image of Garran as the compliant drafter of pointed and elegant English, attending on the lions of Federation, somehow off to one side of the main game is unsatisfactory, too simplistic, too easy … Garran the gifted polymath … deserves to occupy a loftier place than he does at present in the Federation pantheon.[33]

The image of Garran created by Deakin in the federation historiography, of a figure lurking in the shadows rather than firmly planted centre stage, tends to be reinforced in the absence of a comprehensive biography.

Most of the more specific historical writing on Garran consists either of general and necessarily brief accounts of his life and work, such as Helen Irving's perceptive biographical entry in *The Oxford Companion to the High Court of Australia*,[34] or chapters in books with a larger or different focus, such as the official centenary history of the Attorney-General's

---

[29] Ibid.

[30] Leslie Zines, 'Sir Robert Garran', in *Papers on Parliament No. 44: Democratic Experiments*, ed. Kay Walsh (Canberra: Department of the Senate, 2006), 127.

[31] Alfred Deakin, *The Federal Story: The Inner History of the Federal Cause 1880–1900* (Melbourne: Melbourne University Press, 1963 [1944]), 101.

[32] There is not much doubt, as Brownrigg notes, that Deakin's real target was Reid. See J. A. La Nauze, 'Introduction', in ibid., vi.

[33] Brownrigg, 'Federation's Prodigy', 97.

[34] Helen Irving, 'Robert Randolph Garran', in *The Oxford Companion to the High Court of Australia*, eds Tony Blackshield, Michael Coper and George Williams (South Melbourne: Oxford University Press, 2001), 292–93.

Department (in which Garran figures prominently).³⁵ However, Noel Francis generously self-published a book on Garran entitled *The Gifted Knight* in 1983. This included a biographical introduction and usefully brought together a collection of Garran's writing, particularly his verse.³⁶

Brownrigg's chapter on Garran in the collection of federation essays entitled *Makers of Miracles* gives a sense of the richness and creativity of Garran's private life and the connection between his diversity of interests and the achievements of his public life. One of the valuable insights gained from an analysis of Garran's wider interests is that the creative artist was a crucial aspect of Garran's being.

The greatest work on which Garran was engaged as a creative artist was the Commonwealth of Australia. A process of creation can be cumulative and this accords with the reality that Garran's entire adult life was engaged creatively with the Commonwealth. Pre-eminently, this was the ongoing process, over several decades, of implementing and interpreting the Commonwealth constitution and developing the institutions that were set up under it. Indeed, examining this as Garran's main calling in life would establish a context for better appreciating all of his many other activities and interests and achieving a suitably coherent assessment of the man. A larger study with a more holistic approach might well reveal Garran as an admirable figure around whom a story stretching over several dramatic decades of Australia's political, intellectual and cultural history could be constructed.

This is a big claim to make on behalf of a public servant (as civil servants are commonly known in Australia). In his biography of the long-serving secretary of the Department of Defence, Frederick Shedden, historian David Horner observed that 'civil servants are assumed to be nameless, boring and pedestrian'.³⁷ Horner also noted that Shedden 'in the traditions of the civil service … eschewed publicity and concentrated on his departmental work to the exclusion of wider interests'. In contrast, Garran had the talents, the temperament, and somehow found the time to be a polymath, which certainly helps to make him even more interesting as a potential biographical subject. In short, Garran was no ordinary public servant—'not just any old departmental head or just any old constitutional lawyer', to quote Zines.³⁸

All this writing on Garran is well done, but the overall treatment of him is, inevitably, incomplete. Ironically, the most complete work on this modest man so far produced is Garran's own memoir, *Prosper the Commonwealth*. What is needed, in the author's view, is a study that grapples comprehensively with Garran's central contribution to the creation of the Australian Commonwealth. A study that deals with his roles as constitutional expert, legal adviser, parliamentary draftsman and pioneering diplomat in the Commonwealth

---

[35] Meiklejohn, ed., *100 Years: Achieving A Just and Secure Society, Attorney-General's Department, 1901–2001* (Canberra: Attorney-General's Department, 2001).

[36] Noel Francis, *The Gifted Knight: Sir Robert Randolph Garran, GCMG, QC* (Canberra: N. Francis, 1983).

[37] In making this point, Horner also noted Garran's long and outstanding service and his varied activities. See David Horner, *Defence Supremo: Sir Frederick Shedden and the Making of Australian Defence Policy* (St Leonards, NSW: Allen & Unwin, 2000), 3–4, 354.

[38] Zines, 'Sir Robert Garran', 121–22.

government, sets these into the broader context of Garran's other activities and interests, and gives some coherence of analysis to the whole, would be ideal. A good biography of Garran would be a welcome addition to Australian historiography.

A Father of Federation

Such a biography would need to examine Garran's role in the federation movement as a key issue. It is worth exploring a little here Brownrigg's contention that Garran deserves a loftier place in the federation pantheon.

As the story goes, the movement for the federation of the Australian colonies began in earnest in 1889 with the famous Tenterfield Address of Henry Parkes, premier of New South Wales and the 'grand old man' of Australian politics, on the occasion of the receipt of the report by Major-General J. Bevan Edwards on colonial defence. Edwards, who had been chosen by the United Kingdom government to inspect the armed forces of the Australian colonies and advise on their organisation following a recommendation by the 1887 Colonial Conference, had emphasised that they 'should at once be placed on a proper footing' which was 'quite impossible without a federation of the forces of the different colonies'.[39]

Parkes' motivations in making the speech at Tenterfield and its real significance have, of course, been the subject of discussion by historians.[40] Clearly, the terms of the Edwards report enabled Parkes to insist on the necessity of political federation of the Australian colonies to ensure that any federal army would be responsible to a federal government. Otherwise, the colonial governments would be at the mercy of the United Kingdom government on issues of command and control of such an army, leading to outcomes which might not accord with Australia's distinctive interests.

Garran's considered assessment was that Parkes was a 'man of imaginative vision' who 'dreamed great dreams, and the greatest of them was his dream of a united Australia'.[41] Certainly, the movement initially gained some momentum under Parkes' leadership. The National Australasian Convention—at which Garran was a keenly interested spectator—was held in Sydney in 1891 and a constitutional text for an Australian federation was drafted.[42]

It is well known that the federal movement stalled in the years immediately afterwards. Parkes had attempted to achieve federation from the top down, with the colonial political leaders setting the pace and himself being in charge of proceedings. In fact, practical day-to-day politics got in the way of making further progress and the rather elitist approach that Parkes had adopted could not overcome the resistance. Garran would later acknowledge

---

[39] Cited in A. J. Hill, 'James Bevan Edwards (1834–1922)', in *ADB*, vol. 4, ed. Douglas Pike (Melbourne: Melbourne University Press, 1972), 130.

[40] See, for example, A. W. Martin, *Henry Parkes: A Biography* (Melbourne: Melbourne University Press, 1980), 383–85. This was also the subject of the author's honours thesis under Meaney's supervision. See Colin Milner, 'Sir Henry Parkes: Defence and Federation', BA honours thesis, University of Sydney, 1978.

[41] Garran, *Prosper the Commonwealth*, 92.

[42] Ibid.

that Parkes himself ultimately recognised the need for a stronger popular base to the movement.⁴³

Garran became an important figure in the popular movement that took up the federal cause, helping to keep the ideal alive until an official convention process became politically feasible again. He was one of the first members of the Australian (later the Australasian) Federation League, serving as a councillor from 1893 until 1900. During this time, he attended the important federation conference at Corowa, which was organised under the league's auspices in 1893, as well as the People's Federal Convention held at Bathurst in 1896.⁴⁴

The Corowa Conference was a crucial event for Garran, who attended as a Sydney delegate for the league. Working with John Quick from Victoria—and one can see here the beginnings of their close working relationship—Garran evidently assumed an important role, both publicly and behind the scenes. For example, Garran moved the first resolution on the 'early union of Australian colonies' and made an eloquent speech in its support. The record states that Garran said:

> We had nothing whatever to wait for. Federation became a practical matter when taken in hand by practical men, as had been done in the Convention which drafted the Commonwealth Bill. Federation had now taken a definite form and shape … No doubt there were difficulties in the way, but they were not insuperable. The longer the question was delayed the greater would the difficulties become … The great aim was to advance not on provincial but on national lines.⁴⁵

The main conference outcome was a resolution, proposed by Quick and adopted unanimously, setting out a plan for an elected convention process to consider and adopt a federal constitutional text which would then be submitted for popular approval by referendum in each of the colonies. In the words of 'Quick and Garran', this 'marked a new epoch and initiated a new mode of dealing with the question'—one that would eventually lead to success.⁴⁶

Significantly, Barton was not at Corowa and Deakin arrived late. In *The Federal Story*, Deakin mentions the Corowa Conference only briefly, ignores Garran altogether and lauds the role played by Quick.⁴⁷ For his part, Parkes turned up in Corowa at the very end to make a speech. In a comment written on his personal copy of the record of the Corowa meeting (now held by the National Library of Australia), Garran expressed his view about Parkes' appearance in what were, for him, fairly blunt terms:

> Parkes made no reference to the plan—& does not seem to recognise that the power has passed from his hands. If he did, he certainly did not come to Corowa to give his blessing to a new movement under other leadership. He was now a frustrated old man, out of office—& never to return. He died within three years.⁴⁸

---

43 Ibid., 101. See also Quick and Garran, *Annotated Constitution*, 148–49.

44 Garran, *Prosper the Commonwealth*, 102–05, 108–09.

45 *Official Report of the Federation Conference held in the Court-House, Corowa on Monday 31st July, and Tuesday, 1st August, 1893* (Corowa: James C. Leslie, 1893), 19.

46 Quick and Garran, *Annotated Constitution*, 153.

47 Deakin, *The Federal Story*, 57–58.

48 Annotation initialled 'RRG' on copy of 'Sir Henry Parkes at Corowa', Appendix A of the *Official*

This is a good example of how Garran allowed his feelings to show, the kind of personal revelation which helps to inject flesh and blood into the biographical study of the man.

Garran took pride in the popular basis of the Commonwealth and its constitution.[49] He had faith in responsible government under a system of parliamentary democracy. This was a feature of the 'utilitarian consensus' which has been characterised by political scientist Hugh Collins as the 'dominant ideology' of Australian politics.[50] Pride and confidence in Australia's democratic institutions and in the protections afforded by its legal system derived from English common law combined with the practical approach of its people towards resolving problems, were central to Australian political culture from the late nineteenth century onwards. Garran was naturally sympathetic to these elements of what would prove to be a resilient political tradition. And, in particular, the Corowa Conference of 1893, in which Garran was closely engaged, was crucial in ensuring that federation could be celebrated as a great democratic political achievement of the Australian people.

A Randolph Cousin

Garran could draw inspiration from his family background for his life's work. In *Prosper the Commonwealth*, Garran briefly noted his claim to descend from the Plantagenet dynasty of England.[51] The connection was evidently quite meaningful to Garran, whose serious verse included a series on people and events from the Plantagenet era of English history, written for a pageant performed at the University of Sydney in June 1939.[52]

That descent was claimed on Garran's maternal side, through the famous Randolph family of colonial Virginia.[53] He elaborated further on this more recent connection in his memoir. One of Garran's great-grandmothers was a Randolph by birth and her husband—Garran's great-grandfather—was surnamed Eppes, another prominent family name in the history of Virginia.[54] Few Australians could match Garran's direct family links with the

---

Report of the Federation Conference Held in the Court-House, Corowa.

[49] Some compromise changes to the text of the constitution were required by the United Kingdom government prior to its enactment by the parliament at Westminster. See Quick and Garran, *Annotated Constitution*, 228–49.

[50] Hugh Collins, 'Political Ideas and Practices', in *Under New Heavens: Cultural Transmission and the Making of Australia*, ed. Meaney (Port Melbourne: Heinemann Educational Australia, 1989), 102.

[51] Garran, *Prosper the Commonwealth*, 13–14.

[52] Francis, *The Gifted Knight*, 136–42

[53] A descent of Thomas Jefferson from King Edward III of England and his Queen, Philippa of Hainault, through William Randolph of Virginia by his wife Mary Isham, is set out in *Ancestors of American Presidents*, compiled by Gary Boyd Roberts (Santa Clarita, California: Carl Boyer, 3rd, in association with the New England Historic Genealogical Society, 1989), 140, 273–74. Garran claimed to share in this descent.

[54] Garran, *Prosper the Commonwealth*, 13. Jefferson's mother-in-law and one of his sons-in-law were from the Eppes family. See Annette Gordon-Reed, *The Hemingses of Monticello: An American Family* (New York: W. W. Norton & Company, 2008), 52–57, 416–17, 670–71; and Jonathan Daniels, *The Randolphs of Virginia* (Garden City, New York: Doubleday & Company, 1972), xiv.

history of the United States, at a time when American influence on the nation was growing. His ancestral pride had perhaps helped to stimulate the statement in 'Quick and Garran' that

> Virginia may be regarded as the type and model of modern colonies, in which representative and responsible government is the prevailing system, with a Governor appointed by the Crown as the agent of the sovereign to watch imperial interests.[55]

Here were hints of what might have sparked the youthful Garran's interest in what would become his life's work. 'Quick and Garran' demonstrated his fascination with the British and American (and also Canadian) antecedents of the mixed federal and parliamentary form that the Commonwealth of Australia took. Garran was genuinely interested in the development of a constitutional monarchy in England and later in the United Kingdom, of colonial self-government in the North American colonies, of federalism in the United States and of dominion status in Canada. In a sense, Garran's family tree connected him with many of these developments.

Before venturing any further down this track, the sage warning of Robert Skidelsky, a biographer of Garran's contemporary John Maynard Keynes, should be heeded:

> Family trees are apt to be tedious except to members of the family and genealogists. Nor are they always illuminating from a biographical point of view, since the laws of heredity are so little understood.

Thus fortified, Skidelsky goes on to make a point about the significance of young Keynes having delved into his own ancestry, stating that 'the subject of this biography discovered his Keynes family past at an impressionable age, was fascinated by it, and thought he had a name to live up to.'[56]

Similarly, the interest that Garran took in his family tree possibly helped to direct his attention towards the great constitutional achievements of the English-speaking world, such as the Magna Carta or the drafting and interpretation of the United States constitution, in which his ancestors and relatives had been engaged and to which Australia's own federal constitution would be added in his lifetime. Near the end of his life, Garran advocated the unity of the English-speaking peoples in terms similar to the contemporaneous writings of Winston Churchill:

> Amid all tensions and conflicts of the world today, I believe that one of our greatest assets is the fundamental oneness of the British and American peoples … We all know this in our hearts, and we know that it is a first duty of Britons and Americans to deepen their mutual understanding and goodwill and to learn to see our differences in their proper perspective.[57]

Garran's Randolph descent connected him with many important figures in the history of colonial Virginia and the formative period of the United States. These included Edmund

---

[55] Quick and Garran, *Annotated Constitution*, 15–16.

[56] Robert Skidelsky, *John Maynard Keynes*, vol. 1, *Hopes Betrayed 1883–1920* (New York: Penguin Books, 1983), 3.

[57] Garran, *Prosper the Commonwealth*, 363. See also Winston S. Churchill, *A History of the English-Speaking Peoples*, 4 vols (London: Cassell, 1956–58).

Randolph, the first attorney-general of the United States and later secretary of state in President George Washington's administration, and the politician and diplomat John Randolph of Roanoke. The wider Randolph family included even more eminent folk, such as President Thomas Jefferson (whose mother was a Randolph) and Chief Justice John Marshall.

These are the four historic figures mentioned by Garran as distant Randolph relatives in his memoir but he could have included more.[58] From his own time, for example, Garran could have cited Francis Biddle, solicitor-general and then attorney-general in President Franklin Roosevelt's administration, and chief American judge at the post-war Nuremberg war crimes trials, as a distant cousin.[59] The elder of Biddle's sons was named after his direct ancestor, Edmund Randolph.[60] As Garran noted in his memoir, when he visited the United States on a goodwill lecture tour in 1940–41, he made a point of contacting and visiting some of his Randolph relatives. Maybe, too, he took time to reflect on the Jefferson Memorial then being built on the shore of the tidal basin in Washington, although it was the already completed monument to Civil War president Abraham Lincoln which particularly caught his attention.[61]

Law and diplomacy as vocations, scholarship, literature and music as avocations, and the pursuit of ideals of public service and good citizenship, were recurring traits in the Randolph family and ones which would have attracted Garran towards emphasising his kinship with them. An American historian later referred to the Randolph family's 'manic-depressives, schizoids, perverts, sadists, idiots and geniuses' but Garran, who may not have been fully aware of these other family traits, would only allow that John Randolph of Roanoke was 'picturesque'.[62]

All this contrasted strongly with Jefferson's self-consciously egalitarian comment in the opening pages of his autobiography that the Randolph family 'trace their pedigree far back in England and Scotland, to which let every one ascribe the faith and merit he chooses'.[63] Garran, growing up over a century later in the more open and democratic colony of New South Wales, had nothing of what Jefferson had derisively referred to as the 'patrician order'—of privileged families (including the Randolphs) which had ruled colonial Virginia—to rail against. Indeed, it could be argued that, in his own time and place, Garran plausibly filled the role of a Jeffersonian natural aristocrat; that is, one of the 'aristocracy of virtue and talent' best fitted, in Jefferson's view, to lead and govern a society.[64]

---

[58] Garran, *Prosper the Commonwealth*, 14.

[59] Daniel, *The Randolphs of Virginia*, xviii.

[60] Francis Biddle, *A Casual Past* (Garden City, New York: Doubleday & Company, 1961), 279.

[61] Garran referred incorrectly to 'Lincoln's Tomb' in his memoir when he clearly meant the Lincoln Memorial in Washington. See Garran, *Prosper the Commonwealth*, 368.

[62] Forrest McDonald, 'John Randolph (1773–1833)', in *Encyclopedia of American Biography*, 2nd edn, eds John A. Garraty and Jerome L. Sternstein (New York: Harper Collins, 1996), 915; ibid., 14.

[63] Cited in Gordon S. Wood, 'The Trials and Tribulations of Thomas Jefferson', in *Jeffersonian Legacies*, ed. Peter S. Onuf (Charlottesville: University Press of Virginia, 1993), 402.

[64] Letter, Thomas Jefferson to John Adams, 28 October 1813, cited in ibid., 403.

Perhaps for these reasons, Garran could more readily acknowledge and be inspired by his Randolph family connections. He evidently knew about them from his youth; as a lad, he was presumably curious about the origin of his middle name. In due course, Garran's eldest son Richard would also be given 'Randolph' as his middle name.[65]

In a playful letter written in 1901 to his soon-to-be wife Hilda Robson, Garran toyed with the possibility that his branch of the Randolphs might give him a descent from the famous Native American 'Princess' Pocahontas.[66] Garran's friend, Dr Llewelyn Bevan, had evidently suggested this possibility to Hilda and Garran wrote to her in reply:

> So which of us does he think are like Red Indians? Mother says that her Mother was supposed to have the Red Indian ear—without any curl—over on the top rim. But in spite of that, I am afraid there is a weak spot in the genealogy. Some of the Randolphs did marry descendants of Pocahontas, & there are representatives of that branch still living; but I can't make out that Pocahontas is in *our* direct ancestral line.[67]

Garran's letter reads curiously, to say the least, when set against his responsibilities that same year in the drafting of the *Immigration Restriction Act 1901*, the new nation's first major piece of legislation which embedded the White Australia policy as a foundational principle of the Commonwealth. As Myra Willard, an early historian of the subject, wrote, using language current among white Australians at the time, '[t]he desire to guard themselves effectively against the dangers of Asiatic immigration was one of the most powerful influences which drew the Colonies together'.[68] But, though it was also typical of its era in the forms of expression used, there is little sense of 'danger' apparent in Garran's response to the thought that he might have had a strain of Native American blood flowing in his veins.

This raises the broader question of Garran's own actions and views on racial matters. Race is a major theme in the study of Australian history. Racial discrimination remained a feature of the nation's immigration policy throughout Garran's lifetime (finally being fully dispatched in the early 1970s) and British race patriotism prevailed as a unifying sentiment until it unravelled in the years after his death in 1957.[69] It was a decade afterwards, in 1967, before a successful referendum amended the Commonwealth constitution to remove discriminatory provisions affecting Aboriginal and Torres Strait Islander Australians and allow the Commonwealth government to assume a special responsibility in Indigenous affairs.

The distinguished Indigenous Australian leader, Lowitja (Lois) O'Donoghue, expressed the significance of this question, in compelling terms that demand attention, in her Robert Garran Oration, delivered in 1991:

---

[65] Parker, 'Robert Randolph Garran', 625.

[66] John Randolph of Roanoke was, for example, a descendant of Pocahontas. See William Cabell Bruce, *John Randolph of Roanoke*, vol. 1, *1773–1833* (New York: G. P. Putnam's Sons, 1922), 16.

[67] Letter, Garran to Hilda Robson, 9 October 1901, NLA: MS 2001/3/6. Original emphasis.

[68] Myra Willard, *History of the White Australia Policy to 1920* (Melbourne: Melbourne University Press, 1967 [1923]), 119.

[69] See generally Curran and Ward, *The Unknown Nation*.

> It has been traditional to begin this speech by making some mention of the contribution made by Sir Robert Garran. For me, however, this is a little more difficult.
>
> In matters concerning Australia's [I]ndigenous people, Sir Robert was very much a man of his time. He was one of the drafters of the Australian Constitution, which mentioned Aboriginal people only twice and then only to exclude them from being counted in the population, and from the power of the commonwealth. For the policy-makers of 1901 Aboriginal people were irrelevant.

Moving on to examine developments in Aboriginal and Torres Strait Islander affairs since the 1967 referendum, O'Donoghue observed:

> Accompanying these developments has been a thoroughgoing reappraisal by white Australians of the Aboriginal contribution to this nation. We have rolled back the 'great Australian silence' which is how anthropologist W. E. H. Stanner … in his 1968 Boyer Lectures, described the almost total exclusion of the Aboriginal point of view from accounts of national history and culture—the silence that reigned in Sir Robert Garran's time.[70]

The question of Garran's actions and views regarding the 'great Australian silence' and on other racial matters cannot be examined in detail here but its pertinence—to understanding him in the context of his times and properly appreciating him in terms of our own—must be acknowledged. For all his playfulness with his sweetheart—and future mother of his four sons—in contemplating the possibility of claiming descent from a heroine of history and romance, Garran's letter about Pocahontas also suggests that he may have been a bit more relaxed about the reality of racial mixing and intermarriage in colonial societies than was common in a time and place (such as Australia in 1901) where notions of racial 'purity' held sway.[71] This line of thinking should perhaps not be taken very far, however. Despite any nuances which might be uncovered about him, Garran's overall attachment to British race patriotism—'the idea that all British peoples, despite their particular regional problems and perspectives, ultimately comprised a single indissoluble community through the ties of blood, language, history and culture', as Stuart Ward has defined it—remained strong.[72]

Garran's direct Randolph ancestors were evidently Loyalists during and after the American Revolution.[73] The Loyalist creed was one of sacrifice for the imperial cause, a lost cause as far as the first British Empire in America was concerned but one which could still be pursued in the growing expanses of the second British Empire.[74] Some of Garran's

---

[70] Lois O'Donoghue, 'Ending the Despair', Sir Robert Garran Oration, reproduced in *Australian Journal of Public Administration*, 51 (2), 1992, 214–15.

[71] The 'mixed-blood descendants' of Pocahontas and her colonist husband, John Rolfe, have been estimated to number around three million. See Paula Gunn Allen, *Pocahontas: Medicine Woman, Spy, Entrepreneur, Diplomat* (New York: Harper Collins, 2003), 305.

[72] Stuart Ward, *Australia and the British Embrace: The Demise of the Imperial Ideal* (Melbourne: Melbourne University Press, 2001), 2.

[73] Garran, *Prosper the Commonwealth*, 13–14.

[74] See Maya Jasanoff, *Liberty's Exiles: The Loss of America and the Remaking of the British Empire* (London: Harper Press, 2011).

Loyalist ancestors had done this for a time in India, before a later generation moved to Australia where, as Meaney has shown, being loyal Britons was not spurned but, in the late nineteenth century, became the defining characteristic of Australian identity and community.[75]

Those who suffer defeat can exert a powerful influence on the imagination of their descendants. As the architectural historian, Marc Girouard, writing of the poet and novelist Walter Scott, observed:

> Families which are distantly allied to the great, or conscious of landed property which should, but for mischance or misfortune, have been theirs, or who live in the city but have roots in the country, tend to be especially romantic about their ancestry and connections.[76]

Girouard noted that all of the above conditions applied to Scott. Much the same might be said of Garran, although he did not seek to recreate any lost, landed estate on the scale that Scott, with the ardour of an early Romantic enthusiast, attempted at Abbotsford in Scotland. Instead, Garran and his wife simply adopted a place name associated with the Randolph family in Virginia—'Roanoke'—for their handsome suburban home on Mugga Way in Canberra.[77] But just as Garran's own most direct Randolph ancestors remained Loyalists in the American Revolution, so too did Garran, like nearly all Australians of his time, remain loyal to Australia's British connection throughout his life. Yet, Garran always remained grounded in the land of his birth. His entire formal education was received in his native land and, although he spent significant periods of time working overseas, Garran's later life was also firmly Australia-based.

Garran's immediate family background was quite different from the world lived in by his Anglican landowner ancestors in colonial Virginia. Garran's father, Andrew, was a journalist who became editor of the *Sydney Morning Herald* newspaper and his mother, Mary Isham (née Sabine), pursued interests such as the welfare of orphaned and neglected children. Both parents attended the Pitt Street Congregational (now Uniting) Church, along with the Fairfax, Jones and Foss families and other leading members of Sydney's commercial and professional classes in the mid-nineteenth century.[78] Historian Alan Atkinson has described this group as 'members of a small communion endowed with clean hands, pure hearts, growing wealth and a wish to do good'. Atkinson noted that '[u]nlike other Sydney empire builders, such as Tooths, their dominion was one of soul and intellect as well as commerce; power was extended by conscientious work on boards and committees, and at editorial desks'.[79]

---

[75] Meaney, 'Britishness and Australian Identity: The Problem of Nationalism in Australian History and Historiography', *Australian Historical Studies*, 32 (116), 2001, 76–90.

[76] Marc Girouard, *The Return to Camelot: Chivalry and the English Gentleman* (New Haven: Yale University Press, 1981), 31.

[77] Garran, *Prosper the Commonwealth*, 368.

[78] Susan Emilsen, et al., *Pride of Place: A History of the Pitt Street Congregational Church* (Beaconsfield, Vic.: Melbourne Publishing Group, 2008).

[79] Alan Atkinson, *Camden: Farm and Village Life in Early New South Wales* (Melbourne: Oxford University Press, 1988), 51.

This was the world into which Garran was born and in which he grew up. The men in such families considered themselves to be gentlemen, in the expanding Victorian sense of the term, but they were part of the new urban liberal elite. This group was distinct from the conservative colonial landed gentry who, under the leadership of James Macarthur and others, had failed by the 1850s to establish a 'family compact' in the colony of New South Wales, like those which had ruled colonial Virginia and, during the early nineteenth century, Loyalist-dominated British colonies such as Upper Canada (now Ontario) and Nova Scotia.[80] Notably, for a time, the Pitt Street congregation appears to have included an ambitious Henry Parkes, his wife Clarinda and their family, aspirants for recruitment to this new breed.[81]

Garran's father, like Parkes, had experienced Birmingham Congregationalism during his formative years and would be politically associated with him in years to come, being nominated by Parkes in 1887 to be a member of the Legislative Council in the New South Wales parliament.[82] In 1889, the elder Garran presided jointly with Parkes over two lectures on federation given by James Jefferis, the minister at the Pitt Street Congregational Church.[83] For all his royal Plantagenet and conservative Loyalist ancestry, there can be little doubt that Robert Randolph Garran grew up in an environment congenial to liberal democracy and to giving thoughtful and progressive consideration to political issues affecting the relationship of the Australian colonies with the British Empire as a whole.

An Australian Nationalist and a British Imperialist

By focussing on Garran's work in the creation of the Commonwealth, we can perhaps discern an answer to what Meaney has described as the 'riddle of Australian nationalism'.[84] The issue is essentially to understand how people of Garran's time and place reconciled their British cultural nationalism with their Australian political nationalism. Garran was enamoured of the British imperial ideal, even though he did not in fact visit the United Kingdom until he was a mature adult—in 1907, when he was forty. The British race patriotism of the time helped to inspire the verse which Garran wrote to celebrate the coming of the Commonwealth in 1901, along with a spiritual dimension grounded in his Christian faith and late Romantic appreciation of the distinctive Australian landscape. Here is an extract from Garran's poem 'One People, One Destiny'—its title derived from the toast to which Parkes had famously spoken at the banquet marking the opening of the 1891 convention in Sydney—which owed something to all three sources of inspiration:

---

[80] For colonial Virginia, see David Hackett Fischer, *Albion's Seed: Four British Folkways in America* (New York: Oxford University Press, 1989), 212–25. For the other colonies, see John Manning Ward, *James Macarthur, Colonial Conservative, 1798–1867* (Sydney: Sydney University Press, 1981).

[81] See Peter Cochrane, *Colonial Ambition: Foundations of Australian Democracy* (Melbourne: Melbourne University Press, 2006), 272–73, 296–97. Cochrane described Parkes as 'the epitome of colonial ambition'.

[82] E. K. Bramsted, 'Andrew Garran (Gamman) (1825–1901)', in *ADB*, vol. 4, 233–34.

[83] Susan Emilsen, et al., *Pride of Place*, 103–04.

[84] Meaney, *Search for Security*, viii–ix. See also Meaney, 'Britishness and Australian Identity', 78–79.

> Then forth from the isles of the freemen,
>
> Questing for worlds unknown,
>
> England sent England's seamen,
>
> Who found it, and knew it their own,
>
> And the solitudes sang of endeavour,
>
> And the cities arose by the sea;
>
> God spake: 'One destiny ever,
>
> One people that is to be!'[85]

To use historian Keith Hancock's famous phrase, Garran was typical of the 'independent Australian Briton'. Defining himself culturally as a Briton, he, like nearly all his fellow Australians, nevertheless had an instinctive sense of Australia's separate national interests, especially in the Pacific region.[86] For virtually his entire career as a Commonwealth public servant, it appears that Garran acted according to that instinct, with a keen sense of the practical reality of Australian autonomy, but he did so firmly within the imperial framework. A key theme for any comprehensive study of Garran will be to examine his contribution to the development of the relationship of the new Commonwealth of Australia with the broader British Empire. Exploring Garran's role in shaping Australia's views at the various imperial conferences which took place during his working years in the public service should provide good guidance on that contribution.

Generally, the Australian approach at imperial conferences during this period emphasised the preservation of imperial unity. A case in point was the debate about the dominions entering treaties with foreign powers. The view expressed in 'Quick and Garran' in 1901 was that 'the Commonwealth, being a dependent part of the Empire, has no power to make treaties except so far as such power may be expressly delegated to it by the Imperial Government'.[87] There had been a specific reference to treaties under the external affairs power in a draft text of the Commonwealth constitution but this had been deleted subsequently, prior to its enactment.[88] The issue of treaty-making by the dominions was raised prior to the 1923 Imperial Conference where it became a major topic of discussion, but Australia remained more focused on gaining a voice in the formation of 'a true Empire foreign policy acceptable to all the Dominions'; that is, on finding the necessary machinery for consolidating the sentimental bonds of empire. Before leaving to attend the conference in London, the new Australian prime minister, S. M. Bruce, suggested that laying down a basis for such a policy might mean that 'the claim of certain Dominions to make their own treaty arrangements will disappear'.[89] It was a forlorn hope as, in the event, others pressed

---

[85] This 1901 poem was republished in a special edition of the *Canberra Times* on 1 January 1951.

[86] W. K. Hancock, *Australia* (London: Ernest Benn Limited, 1930), ch. 3.

[87] Quick and Garran, *Annotated Constitution*, 768.

[88] J. A. La Nauze, *The Making of the Australian Constitution* (Melbourne: Melbourne University Press, 1972), 184–85.

[89] See *Commonwealth Parliamentary Debates* (hereafter *CPD*), House of Representatives (hereafter

the issue and the 1923 conference accepted that the dominions, including Australia, could conclude treaties in their own right.[90]

Garran was himself involved in pursuing Australia's foreign policy interests on the margins of the 1923 conference. He engaged in discussions with the Foreign Office regarding methods for improving communication between the United Kingdom and dominion governments on foreign policy subjects when imperial conferences were not sitting.[91] These and other discussions led to the appointment in 1924 of R. G. Casey, a future minister for external affairs and governor-general of Australia, as the first Australian liaison officer attached to the cabinet secretariat in London. In this capacity, Casey was charged with being a direct channel of communication between the two governments on external affairs matters that affected Australian interests.[92]

Garran did not attend the 1926 Imperial Conference at which the important Balfour Declaration was issued. This settled the main characteristics of the dominions: equality of status, autonomy in internal and external affairs, common allegiance to the Crown and free association in the British Commonwealth of Nations.[93] But Garran chaired the drafting committee for the 1930 conference, at which it was agreed that the legislative supremacy of the United Kingdom parliament over the dominions should be abolished.[94] A recommendation was made that this step should be formalised in what was to become the Statute of Westminster enacted by the United Kingdom parliament the following year. Once again, Australia was reluctant, yet the statute may be seen as the foundation of Australia's independence as a nation-state.[95]

On many of these issues, Garran's views appear to have been conservative, stressing the importance of imperial unity. But he tended to take a pragmatic view of the implications of the Balfour Declaration and the evolution of dominion status overall. During the 1930s, Garran adjusted well to the increasingly separate diplomacy of the dominions, as he demonstrated in his views on Australia's diplomatic activity in the Pacific. He approved of the visit by the then attorney-general and minister for external affairs, J. G. Latham, to the Far East in 1934, which Garran observed was 'the first mission of a diplomatic character that Australia has sent to foreign countries', reflecting 'the fact that friendly relations with the East are of great importance to Australia'. He also appeared to foreshadow the likelihood that Australia would follow some of the other dominions in making its own 'ambassadorial appointments' to overseas capitals, as indeed happened.[96] Garran pursued his interest in

---

HR), vol. 104, 24 July 1923, 1483–84.

[90] W. J. Hudson and M. P. Sharp, *Australian Independence: Colony to Reluctant Kingdom* (Melbourne: Melbourne University Press, 1988), 72–76.

[91] *CPD*, HR, vol. 106, 27 March 1924, 42–43.

[92] Hudson and Jane North, 'Introduction', in *My Dear P.M.: R. G. Casey's Letters to S. M. Bruce, 1924–1929*, eds Hudson and North (Canberra: Australian Government Publishing Service, 1980), vii–xxii.

[93] W. D. McIntyre, *Colonies into Commonwealth* (London: Blandford Press, 1966), 141.

[94] Parker, 'Robert Randolph Garran', 623.

[95] Hudson and Sharp, *Australian Independence*, 138.

[96] Garran, 'Diplomatic Relations in the Pacific', held by the NLA.

such developments further during this period as a founder of the Australian Institute of International Affairs, a parallel organisation to the Royal Institute of International Affairs at Chatham House in London and the Council on Foreign Relations in the United States.[97]

Looking back from the perspective of writing his memoir, Garran identified the existence of two possibilities for resolving the issue of the relations of nation and empire which had so exercised him and his contemporaries. The first had been 'some form of imperial federation'.[98] Garran had met the ardent imperial federationist, Lionel Curtis, on his visit to Australia in 1910 and duly became a foundation member of the Melbourne group of the organisation Curtis was promoting to further the cause, namely the Round Table. Yet Garran's own views, along with those of quite a few of the Australian Round Table members, were evidently more equivocal, certainly as events developed over time. Historian Leonie Foster, in her book on the Australian Round Table, relates how Garran, along with Eggleston, chastised the United Kingdom government at a Round Table moot in England in late 1918 for not consulting with the dominions on the terms of the armistice with Germany.[99] For these Australians, the Round Table was more a forum for informed debate and discussion about questions of imperial relations, broadly defined. Garran noted in his memoir that imperial federation 'had considerable support in England, but very little in Australia, where the emphasis was on autonomy without the complications of any implied legal obligations'.[100]

The second possibility identified by Garran was 'a looser form of union advocated by Richard Jebb in a book entitled *Studies in Colonial Nationalism*' whereby the 'Dominions should retain the status of a group of autonomous nations loosely linked by a common allegiance to the Crown.'[101] Notably, Meaney later assessed that Jebb's book provided 'by far and away the most percipient introduction to the subject' of '[t]he development of an instinctive sense of common interest by the Australian colonies'—as well as the other self-governing colonies of the empire. In Meaney's words, Jebb 'concluded that in its relation with the mother country neither subordination nor constitutional integration were viable alternatives for the future' and the 'only feasible and proper relation was, in his view, that of alliance'.[102]

The answer to this conundrum was found within that second possibility, in the British Commonwealth of Nations, as established by the Balfour Declaration of 1926 and the Statute of Westminster of 1931. Thus was created an alliance of self-governing dominions united with the mother country and each other only by a common allegiance to the Crown. Garran himself was content with this resolution of the issue:

---

[97] J. D. Legge, *Australian Outlook: A History of the Australian Institute of International Affairs* (Sydney: Allen & Unwin with AIIA and ANU Department of International Relations, 1999), 31–37.

[98] Garran, *Prosper the Commonwealth*, 298.

[99] Leonie Foster, *High Hopes: The Men and Motives of the Australian Round Table* (Melbourne: Melbourne University Press in association with the Australian Institute of International Affairs, 1986), 84.

[100] Garran, *Prosper the Commonwealth*, 298.

[101] Ibid., 298–99. See also Richard Jebb, *Studies in Colonial Nationalism* (London: Edward Arnold, 1905).

[102] Meaney, *Search for Security*, 7.

> It was the looser form of association that the course of history ultimately followed, acting upon the sound principle that the larger the area the looser should be the union.[103]

Garran's distant Randolph cousin, Thomas Jefferson, has been credited with perhaps the earliest expression of a vision of the British Empire so transformed, in his pamphlet *The Summary View of the Rights of British America*, published in 1774.[104] This pamphlet cleverly applied the Whig idea of the social contract, entered into by the people in a state of nature as the basis for their government, to the British colonists in America. Jefferson's vision, of course, could not be fulfilled at that time, partly because King George III refused to cooperate and continued to support his parliament in its quarrel with the American colonies. There were no royal visits to America in the eighteenth century to kindle an ongoing sense of loyalty to the Crown, strengthen the sentimental bonds of kinship linking Britons across the seas and help calm the tempests arising in the imperial relationship. As one of King George's descendants has stated:

> George III's cardinal error was that he 'failed' in history—he failed to retain the American colonies, and in the search to find a scapegoat for this national disaster the King became the obvious target … The tragedy is that the American colonies never received a visit from him—if a royal tour had been a conceivable undertaking in the eighteenth century the leaders of the colonies might have understood him better.[105]

Instead, a new political opportunity ripe for exploitation opened up, which Thomas Paine skilfully used in his famous pamphlet *Common Sense*, and as a result, 'broke down the British-Americans' cultural constraints and, metaphorically speaking, killed King George III', as Meaney has written.[106]

Jefferson himself soon adopted the alternative republican vision advanced by Paine. He gave practical expression to it as the principal drafter of the United States Declaration of Independence of 1776, which listed the colonial grievances against King George III and announced the dissolution of the political ties that had bound the Americans with the British people.[107] But, long after 1776, developments in the second British Empire—which had taken lessons of its own out of the American Revolution—saw Australia and the other dominions attain their independence but remain allied (for the most part, although Ireland's neutrality during the Second World War would be an exception) with each other and the United Kingdom in a personal union through the Crown. In other words, Jefferson's vision

---

[103] Garran, *Prosper the Commonwealth*, 299.

[104] David Starkey, *Crown and Country: A History of England through the Monarchy* (London: Harper Press, 2006), 436–37. See also the reprint of Thomas Jefferson, *A Summary View of the Rights of British America* (Brooklyn: Historical Printing Club, 1892).

[105] H. R. H. The Prince of Wales, 'Foreword' to John Brooke, *King George III* (London: Constable, 1972) vii, ix.

[106] Meaney, 'Introduction: The American Revolution in Search of a Future', in *Studies on the American Revolution*, ed. Meaney (South Melbourne: Macmillan Company of Australia, 1976), 22.

[107] See *The Declaration of Independence as Written by Thomas Jefferson and Changed by the Congress Before its Unanimous Adoption on July the Fourth, 1776* (Newark, Delaware: Curtis Paper Company, 1955).

outlined in the *Summary View* found space and support to be transformed into reality in the Australian context.

This fulfilment of the earlier, albeit less sentimentally expressed, Jeffersonian vision was, ultimately, entirely acceptable to Garran. He celebrated it with great warmth in a radio broadcast on 21 February 1954, on the occasion of the first visit by Queen Elizabeth II to Australia. In Garran's view, this visit was '[a] spectacular climax to the development of Dominion status'.[108] Specifically, he saw a connection between 'the enthusiasm and affection shown' to 'the Queen and her gallant husband' and the development of the status of the dominions through the Balfour Report (which had led to the endorsement of the Balfour Declaration at the 1926 Imperial Conference) and the Statute of Westminster to the point where '[o]ur Queen comes to us … as our own Queen of Australia, who reigns here, not in accord with her own despotic will, but by and with the advice of her Australian Ministers'.[109]

It is perhaps difficult now for many Australians—and others—to comprehend fully the deep emotions that were stirred in people like Garran by this first visit to their native soil by the reigning monarch. This was, and remains, in fact, 'the most popular public event in the history of the nation', as Meaney has acknowledged.[110] There is a sense in which Gough Whitlam, as Australian prime minister in 1972–75, carried Garran's mature views forward to a logical conclusion by seeking 'to impart a distinctively Australian character to the monarchy', through initiatives such as the local *Royal Style and Titles Act 1973* which gave added emphasis to Queen Elizabeth's title as Queen of Australia.[111]

A strong public contrast with Garran's style and perspective on the subject of royal visits to Australia was evident, however, only a decade later. Perhaps aiming to be an antipodean Thomas Paine, the journalist Donald Horne argued a case for a republic in his book *The Lucky Country*. Highlighting a 'drop in interest' for the Queen's second visit to Australia in 1963, Horne commented that: 'Australia is no longer short of visiting "celebrities". Even Liz Taylor has been to Australia.'[112] This was a portent of a new way of thinking, speaking and writing about the British connection in Australia—particularly, in its initial stages, among intellectuals. Yet the words of Garran's 1954 broadcast convey a sense of 'the Crown and the People', a favoured concept at the time, which many of his fellow Australians would have felt instinctively was valid for them.[113]

Garran and his contemporaries had been nurtured on the cultural and political self-confidence of the worldwide British raj during the high imperialism of the late Victorian and Edwardian periods. At the end of the historical introduction in 'Quick and Garran', the

---

[108] Garran, *Prosper the Commonwealth*, 333.

[109] Ibid., 334–36.

[110] Meaney, *Search for Security*, vii.

[111] Gough Whitlam, *The Whitlam Government: 1972–1975* (Ringwood, Vic.: Viking, 1985), 130–32, 147.

[112] Donald Horne, *The Lucky Country: Australia in the Sixties* (Ringwood, Vic.: Penguin Books, 1964), 110.

[113] For example, see H. R. H. The Duke of Windsor, *The Crown and the People 1902–1953* (London: Cassell, 1953).

hope had been expressed that the destiny of the Australian people would 'always be linked with that of the mighty Empire of which they form a part'.[114] By 1954, Quick was long dead, the empire was in retreat, India had become a republic within the renamed Commonwealth of Nations and Garran's vision had moved on to encompass an independent Australian sovereignty vested in the Queen of Australia and her Australian parliament, but still maintaining a residual yet, for him, meaningful British connection through the person of the monarch. In other words, he had accepted the divisibility of the old imperial Crown and the existence of a separate Australian Crown. This resolution of historical forces which had played out during the course of their lifetimes is how Garran and many other Australians ultimately reconciled their continuing British sentiment with their consciousness of Australia's separate national interests in the first half of the twentieth century.

Conclusion

When the distinguished Jefferson scholar from the United States, Annette Gordon-Reed, delivered the 2011 Allan Martin Lecture at the Australian National University, she asked at the end, 'is there anybody who resembles Jefferson in your national history?'[115] One answer to that question, despite the obvious difference in their respective levels of fame and fortune, could be Robert Randolph Garran. The two distant cousins even resembled each other physically, especially in height, build and profile. Overall, a number of interesting points of comparison—and contrast—can be drawn between the two men.

But one important resemblance between Garran and Jefferson stands out. Although he was a man with an education, tastes and achievements which might seem to set him apart from most Australians during his lifetime, rather as Jefferson might seem in the context of his own time and place, Garran had a profound Jeffersonian faith in the Australian people. The success of the popular movement in creating the Commonwealth of Australia had taught him that.

Paradoxically, Garran—a man who, like Edmund Barton, had received the education of a gentleman, first at Sydney Grammar School and then in reading classics at the University of Sydney—was quick to see the need for a popular federal movement and worked hard with Barton and others to develop one. In contrast, the self-taught, self-made and self-regarding Henry Parkes—in his origins, more the common man than either Barton or Garran—had been determined to dominate the federal cause himself and ended up losing his way, sadly overcome by old age, ill health and political defeat.[116]

In *Prosper the Commonwealth,* which he completed shortly before his death in 1957, Garran stressed that this was not 'a text-book on constitutional law'. Instead, he stated the following conviction:

> The parts of this book that deal with constitutional law are meant for the general reader as well as the lawyer. Accordingly, they have been written in language as little technical as possible … after all, the law claims to be, and is, the sublimation

---

[114] Quick and Garran, *Annotated Constitution*, 252.
[115] Annette Gordon-Reed, 'Slavery at Thomas Jefferson's Monticello', Allan Martin Lecture, 10 May 2011, School of History, Research School of Social Sciences, Australian National University, 24.
[116] Martin, *Parkes*, 394–424.

> of common sense, and it is an article of faith with me that there is nothing in the Constitution or in its history that is incapable of comprehension by an attentive mind really interested in public affairs.[117]

Garran committed his life to the service of the Australian people in seeking to create strong Commonwealth government institutions which might serve them well, and be well understood by them, as citizens in a liberal democracy. He believed fervently in the capacity of his fellow Australians to deal intelligently with the issues which faced them as a civil and political community. Garran's article of faith in the people, which seems to be calling on later generations to follow him in pursuing ideals of public service and good citizenship, is a decisive reason why the contribution of this gifted and generous man should be more thoroughly understood and appreciated.

---

[117] Garran, *Prosper the Commonwealth*, vii–ix.

8

A. C. V. Melbourne in Australian International Thought: Nationalism and Appeasement Between the World Wars

James Cotton

In December 1938 Associate Professor A. C. V. Melbourne was in a state of agitation. On foreign policy, he had become something of an influence upon Prime Minister Joseph Lyons. Earlier in the year he had written to Lyons to express his views on the decision, mistaken in his view, to ban the export of iron ore from Yampi Sound to Japan. Having excluded Japan from Australian markets during the trade diversion episode in 1936, on which issue Melbourne had tirelessly sought to encourage a compromise, now Australia was obstructing the supply of resources, putting further pressure on Japan.

Australia–Japan relations were thus in disarray. And a new and disturbing context was evident in the form of the 'new order' doctrine articulated by Japan in November which prefigured domination of the whole Asian continent. On 21 December Melbourne sent Lyons a summary of his bleak views of Australia's predicament. His main concern was to impress upon the prime minister the necessity for genuine Commonwealth solidarity on policy towards China, given reports that Britain was contemplating offering financial support to the Nationalist government which would be regarded by Japan as a hostile act. Japan was 'strongly anti-British' and 'quite determined to take the fullest possible profit from her military success' in Asia; if this step provoked war, Australia would bear the brunt. Australia's role should match this risk. Thus, the exigencies of regionalism required that 'Australia should exercise an exceptional influence in the determination of British Commonwealth policy in eastern Asia', and in seeking to exert that influence the greatest priority should be placed on encouraging 'the conclusion of a reasonable agreement between the United Kingdom and Japan'.[1] Melbourne favoured appeasement in the Far East.

In the literature on Australian international thought, Melbourne is credited with eloquent and persistent advocacy of Australia's particular interests in the Asia-Pacific. These interests were not, he argued, sufficiently recognised nor protected by the prevailing imperial machinery, and consequently a new approach was required, the first step being to provide for separate Australian representation in the capitals and trading centres of Asia. In the accepted historical account, Melbourne is given an honourable mention in the process leading to the legislation of 1933 which provided for the appointment of trade commissioners, and in the later decision by the Lyons cabinet that Australia should

---

[1] Letter, A. C. V. Melbourne to Joseph Lyons, 21 December 1938, National Library of Australia (NLA): Melbourne Papers.

dispatch full diplomatic ministers to the United States, Japan, and (later) China.[2] While the motivation for this advocacy is generally ascribed to Melbourne's nationalism, its deeper springs in his intellectual outlook remain obscure. In particular, the radical transformation in Melbourne's career, from constitutional historian to student of and traveller in Asia, at a time when the latter activities were decidedly more demanding and dangerous than for later generations, has not received extended analysis. This chapter seeks to situate Melbourne's more familiar views in the wider context of his work. In particular, Melbourne's acceptance of policies of appeasement and his apparently close relationship with Japanese interests are related to his unabashed nationalism. In turn, these ideas are linked to his more general notions about national identity and the international system. Finally, Melbourne's advocacy of a prudent appeasement of Japanese interests is situated in relation to the imperial management of the British position in the Far East.

Nationalism

Geoffrey Bolton detects in Melbourne's writing 'hints of a robust Australian nationalism ready at all times to question the wisdom of British policies'.[3] David Bird, while similarly recognising that nationalistic strain, suggests that there was some inconsistency in his conduct: 'his connections with the Japanese government were deeper than publicly revealed in the Thirties and of a questionable nature for one who so vocally espoused Australian nationalism'.[4] 'Nationalism' was a word Melbourne frequently employed, but given the many ambiguities of the term his specific usage requires further analysis of his published and unpublished work.

Melbourne was by training a constitutional and political historian. After teaching at Queensland University and being assisted by the award of a Rockefeller Fellowship—his field of study is recorded as 'political science' in his Rockefeller file[5]—Melbourne travelled to London to undertake doctoral study with A. P. Newton at King's College. Newton was Rhodes Professor of Imperial History, with a particular interest in the Atlantic and the West Indies. Under Newton's supervision, Melbourne studied early Australian constitutional development, and chapters on the subject of responsible government appeared in *The Cambridge History of the British Empire* of which Newton was one of the editors.[6]

---

[2] Shannon Smith, 'Towards Diplomatic Representation', in *Facing North: A Century of Australian Engagement with Asia*, vol.1, *1901 to the 1970s*, ed. David Goldsworthy (Melbourne: Melbourne University Press with DFAT, 2001), 61–96.

[3] Geoffrey Bolton, 'A. C. V. Melbourne: Prophet without Honour', in *The Discovery of Australian History 1890–1939*, eds Stuart Macintyre and Julian Thomas (Melbourne: Melbourne University Press, 1995), 113.

[4] David Bird, *J. A. Lyons, the 'Tame Tasmanian': Appeasement and Rearmament in Australia 1932–39* (North Melbourne: Australian Scholarly Publishing, 2008), 41.

[5] Card Index, 'Australia Fellowships Social Sciences', Rockefeller Foundation Archives, Tarrytown, NY: RG310.

[6] These were 'New South Wales and its Daughter Colonies' and 'The Establishment of Responsible

Prior to his sojourn in London, however, Melbourne devoted sustained attention to Australia's relations with New Guinea.[7] In these studies, Melbourne depicted the British government as having limited interest in issues that had excited some public concern in Australia, with the result that known strategic disadvantages had been incurred by the Australian colonies. Into this early writing can be read a sensitivity towards the particular interests of the Australian colonies and also a judgement that the British authorities, even when cognisant of those interests, were quite prepared to set them aside for reasons derived from Britain's more immediate concerns. This early work, then, betrays a nationalist spirit if that is understood to elevate to pre-eminence a perception of Australian national interest.

Having by that time become associate professor of history at Queensland, Melbourne came to prominence beyond academia as a result of the study he wrote for the university following a tour of China and Japan from December 1931 to April 1932 in search of markets for Australian produce, the traditional outlets for which had been seriously diminished by the global depression.[8] In the narrative of Australia's 'engagement' with Asia, Melbourne occupies an honourable position. The conditions of the time had prompted others to pursue thinking along the same lines. Melbourne's extensive report, published in 1932, covered some of the same ground as that of Sir Herbert Gepp.[9] As David Walker observes, in the contributions of Melbourne and Gepp can be discerned 'a new thoroughness in the examination of Asia's trade potential together with a new determination to create those structures needed to place trade with Asia on a secure footing'.[10] Melbourne's efforts in particular were extremely systematic, and his work was sufficiently recognised to gain him an appointment to the Queensland Advisory Committee on Eastern Trade, as well as to the Federal Advisory Committee on Eastern Trade. He served as chair of both committees from 1933 to 1935. Having originally sought data and introductions from the Japanese Consulate in Sydney for his field expedition, he began a correspondence with these Japanese officials that became an important source of information for both parties until 1940.

In every department, Melbourne trenchantly argued, the infrastructure to support and promote Australia's trade with Asia was lacking. It was beyond the existing competence of Australian banks to deal directly in Asian currencies, freight rates were exorbitant, tariffs were obstructive, the administration of immigration regulations was unhelpful, the absence of bilateral commercial treaties favoured competitors, and many exporters did not attend to the essentials of presentation and quality control. The most important of his recommendations related to the necessity to appoint Commonwealth trade officials in

---

Government', in *The Cambridge History of the British Empire*, vol. VII, pt 1, *Australia*, eds J. Holland Rose et al. (Cambridge: Cambridge University Press, 1933), 147–84 and 273–329 (respectively).

[7] 'The Relations between Australia and New Guinea, up to the Establishment of British Rule in 1888: Part 1', *Royal Australian Historical Society Journal and Proceedings*, 12 (5), 1926, 288–314; 'The Relations between Australia and New Guinea, up to the Establishment of British Rule in 1888: Part 2', *Royal Australian Historical Society Journal and Proceedings*, 13 (3), 1927, 145–72.

[8] Bolton, 'A. C. V. Melbourne', 114.

[9] H. W. Gepp, *Report on Trade between Australia and the Far East* (Canberra: Parliament of the Commonwealth of Australia, 1932).

[10] David Walker, *Anxious Nation: Australia and the Rise of Asia 1850–1939* (St Lucia: University of Queensland Press, 1999), 204.

Tokyo and Shanghai. With a fraction of the market stake, Canada had already seen fit to do so (in addition to stationing a minister in Tokyo). Altogether, Melbourne's report is an impressive piece of work which compares well with the study produced more than half a century later by Ross Garnaut pointing to the need for many of the same measures.[11]

Moreover Melbourne's efforts had an impact on national policy. In 1933 the Commonwealth government, on the advice of Melbourne's Advisory Committee on Eastern Trade, passed legislation for the appointment of trade commissioners, and for a time it appeared that Melbourne himself would receive the post in Japan which was eventually filled by Longfield Lloyd in 1935. His recommendation that Australia dispatch an 'economic mission' to China and Japan may be seen as the original impulse for the quasi-diplomatic Eastern Mission undertaken by Sir John Latham to South-East Asia, China and Japan in 1934. After a lengthy correspondence, Latham, while not unreceptive to Melbourne's ideas, would neither include him in the delegation, nor would he follow Melbourne's advice and take business or commercial figures with him on the mission. While a useful diplomatic initiative, the mission was a lost economic opportunity.

For the purposes of this essay, the most noteworthy aspects of Melbourne's report are those concerned with the disconnect between the political and economic manifestations of what Melbourne referred to as 'Australian nationalism'. For him, Australian political nationalism, which was clearly discernible, was a consequence of the Great War and subsequently led to Australia becoming a 'virtually independent' member of a Commonwealth that had meanwhile been transformed into a 'voluntary association'. In the economic sphere, however, Australian trade was 'still essentially a trade with the United Kingdom'. Australian policy makers had pursued evident national objectives through their use of the tariff, but 'a false interpretation of the protective theory' had led to the establishment in Australia of 'many manufacturing industries for which there is not the slightest economic justification'. As a result, consumers were forced to purchase many goods in the marketplace at prices far in excess of comparable goods that could be imported from abroad. In short, 'the Australian tariff law has been used deliberately to depress the import trade'.[12]

Melbourne clearly favoured tariff reform. Under current arrangements, he opined, there was 'no satisfactory method of insisting on either economy or efficiency in the management of ... [the local] monopolies' that were the creatures of the prevailing regime.[13] However, in the era that was very shortly to produce the Ottawa Agreement, he was undoubtedly aware that reform was a forlorn hope. Nevertheless the objective conditions of the international market had to be acknowledged. Almost all of Australian exports were primary commodities, and while he regarded the fostering of intra-imperial trade as 'eminently wise', the imperial market for these items was limited. Additional markets needed to be found. Trade data indicated that there was a large and growing market in Asia,

---

[11] See Ross Garnaut, *Australia and the Northeast Asia Ascendancy* (Canberra: Australian Government Publishing Service, 1989), esp. Introduction.

[12] Melbourne, *Report on Australian Intercourse with Japan and China* (Brisbane: Government Printer, 1932), 32, 37.

[13] Ibid., 57.

especially in Japan, but neither government nor business showed much inclination to look beyond traditional commercial relations.

According to Melbourne, international trade depended upon reciprocity, but imports from those countries that constituted growing markets faced formidable barriers. The prevailing import tariff regime provided for a triple scale of duties, granting most advantageous rates to imperial producers, then intermediate rates to goods from countries with which Australia had negotiated favoured nation status, and above these a general rate for all other imports. So far, there had been no attempt to negotiate commercial agreements with Asian countries which would permit them to land their imports under the intermediate rate. For a scholarship boy and the son of a union official it was evident that state action was required to foster trade linkages with Asia, principally through the appointment of resident trade officials. Their task would be to provide Australian exporters with the necessary information and introductions to enter the local market while acting as agents of the Commonwealth in negotiation with the national government. Regarding the qualifications and duties of these officials Melbourne offered some sagacious and highly practical suggestions, in particular that their business should be 'principally [that] of establishing good relations with people of Japanese and Chinese race rather than with the foreign residents'.[14] Although there had been a series of ad hoc appointments of trade representatives prior to the 1933 federal legislation, its enactment may be considered one of the foundation stones of Australian international diplomacy.[15]

In his 1932 report Melbourne was careful to affirm the value of the imperial relationship, a value that was reaffirmed in some later writings. It was an aspect of his nationalist thinking, however, to regard that relationship as by no means assured of permanence. In framing policy, Australia should 'look centuries ahead' to the possibility that unique national challenges might be faced alone.[16]

To this point, it would appear that Melbourne can confidently be placed in the narrative of developing Australian awareness of Asia. Indeed, contemporary resonances can be detected in his argument that resources should be expended to provide scholarships for the study of Asia and also in the fact that he was personally responsible, assisted by Peter Russo,[17] for arranging for the appointment of Seita Ryonosuke as the first lecturer in Japanese at the University of Queensland in 1938. Melbourne believed that the administration of the White Australia policy could be more sensibly managed to facilitate visits by merchants, students and tourists from Asia. As he remarked: 'If Australia is to obtain and keep a footing in the East, some indication must be shown of a willingness to meet the peoples of the East on equal terms.'[18] Nevertheless, his suggestion that northern Australia could be developed by contract Chinese labour while preserving the White Australia policy is a

---

[14] Ibid., 44.

[15] Boris Schedvin, *Emissaries of Trade. A History of the Australian Trade Commissioner Service* (Canberra: Austrade and DFAT, 2008).

[16] Melbourne, *Report on Australian Intercourse*, 60.

[17] Prue Torney-Parlicki, *Behind the News. A Biography of Peter Russo* (Crawley: University of Western Australia Press, 2005), 74, 103.

[18] Melbourne, *Report on Australian Intercourse*, 79.

reminder that though holding an internationalist outlook, Melbourne was still bound by specific preoccupations with race.

Melbourne took every opportunity to expound the ideas essential to his 1932 work, even writing a letter to Prime Minister Lyons summarising his views.[19] He was an assiduous contributor on these themes in the Queensland press.[20] And he was not afraid to draw the conclusion from his developing acquaintance with Asia that 'it is highly probable that Australia's future will be determined by … relations with Japan'. Given that 'the government's most important obligation' was to frame a foreign policy, he therefore concluded that those relations should be cultivated through, in the first instance, a commercial treaty with that country.[21]

Through his work on the state and federal advisory committees, and also his prominence at academic venues, Melbourne's ideas entered the policy arena. The Queensland branch of the newly formed Australian Institute of International Affairs (AIIA), under the energetic leadership of T. P. Fry, organised in October 1934 a roundtable on Australian foreign policy at Southport, the proceedings of which were published under AIIA auspices. Significantly this was the first book to appear with the phrase 'Australian Foreign Policy' in its title.[22] Melbourne's conference presentation, entitled 'A Foreign Policy for Australia', was its centrepiece. It is both a digest and an extension of his 1932 report, and in the months preceding the conference he had distributed a cyclostyled version to a number of his correspondents, including to Prime Minister Lyons.

In it he argued that the Ottawa Agreement, designed to boost intra-imperial trade was as much as could be expected from the empire. The gains thus obtained would not be permanent, and as Britain in the future was likely to take fewer Australian goods there would be a growing need for Australia to find additional markets. Australian foreign policy should therefore be oriented 'towards maintaining and developing the association with existing markets, while seeking to gain a footing in others where Australian goods are not yet sold'.[23] In this effort Australia's geographical position was something of a handicap, giving rise to a sense of 'exclusiveness' and also to an 'unjustifiable feeling of superiority'. Significantly, Melbourne recommended objectives beyond the commercial in China, suggesting the provision of technical advice since 'Australia may someday need China's help'.[24] In pursuing these objectives, Melbourne felt that it was vital to recognise the role of culture and to avoid any 'colour sense' in dealings with the Chinese.

As for Japan, Melbourne took the view that the current extent of Australia's relations with that country was almost exclusively commercial. He therefore urged a more concerted effort

---

[19] Melbourne to Lyons, 18 July 1932, NLA: Melbourne Papers.

[20] See, for instance, *Brisbane Daily Mail*, 14–19 August 1933, NLA: Melbourne Papers.

[21] 'The Obligations of Australian Nationalism', *Brisbane Daily Mail*, 19 August 1933, NLA: Melbourne Papers.

[22] Hector Dinning and J. G. Holmes, eds, *Australian Foreign Policy 1934* (Melbourne: Melbourne University Press with Oxford University Press, 1935).

[23] Melbourne, 'A Foreign Policy for Australia', in ibid., 25, 28.

[24] Ibid., 31–32.

to improve the existing pattern of 'ill-balanced trade'. At the same time, he acknowledged 'latent possibilities of trouble' in the political and diplomatic spheres. The Manchukuo venture was still an experiment; any failure in Japan's continental policy would 'lead her to attempt the formation of a maritime Empire', which could in turn prompt an attempt to occupy 'the northern portion of Australia'.[25] To deal with such long-term contingencies, Melbourne recommended developing relations with China and the other regional powers, including the United States. Altogether, this program represented 'the basis of a systematic, consistent, and non-aggressive foreign policy for Australia'. Diplomatic representation should be extended to the major capitals in Asia and elsewhere. A program should be developed for the preparation of a cadre of future diplomats as well as to improve the standard of public debate. In addition, so as to provide for training in the necessary foreign languages and in knowledge of the international sphere, a school of international studies should be established in Canberra.[26] Melbourne also believed that a number of federal departments had overlapping responsibilities for external matters and some administrative reform was needed in order to coordinate their activities.

Minister for Commerce Frederick Stewart also participated in the Southport meeting. In February 1933, he had convened in Sydney the Conference on Eastern Trade which had heard Melbourne elaborate his views and which had endorsed the appointment of trade representatives in Asia. Stewart's remarks were devoted to explaining the advantages of such representatives, in phrases so close to those of Melbourne that it would appear that this successful and somewhat iconoclastic business figure had fallen under the academic's spell.

Melbourne's next venture was a tour of universities in China and Japan, again with the support of the University of Queensland and with the assistance of the consular staff representing China and Japan in Australia. While international academic tourism is now commonplace, it should be recalled that Melbourne travelled to these destinations at a time when few of his countrymen took the trouble to make such visits. (There were some exceptions, including when Institute of Pacific Relations meetings were held in these countries, or when individuals such as Ian Clunies Ross made contact with their Asian counterparts.) Lawlessness and disease were widespread in China, but Melbourne was undeterred and travelled to Canton (Guangzhou), Shanghai, Nanjing and Wuhan, though an apparently serious bout of illness (his health never seemed to have been robust as a result of wounds sustained at Gallipoli) prevented a planned expedition to Beijing. Upon arrival in Japan, Melbourne found himself in receipt of unusual hospitality. Ahead of the visits to Japanese cities he was taken on a tour of Manchukuo, visiting, by way of Dairen, the major cities of Mukden (Shenyang) and Hsinking (Changchun) and returning by way of Seoul. He also discussed sheep rearing and wool production at an agricultural research station at Kungchuling (Gongzhuling). The South Manchuria Railway Company provided transportation for this leg of his trip; until the outbreak of the Sino–Japanese War in the following year it was the principal agent of Japanese imperialism in the Northeast and its

---

[25] Ibid., 32, 35–36.

[26] Ibid., 37–38.

representatives were astute promoters of the notion of the mission of Japanese capital as the only hope for the development of the region.[27] In Japan he lectured to classes and met academics and administrators in universities in Tokyo, Sendai, Sapporo, Kyoto and Kobe.

This study tour was evidently an important experience for Melbourne. He came back convinced that there was great scope for the exchange of university staff with institutions in China and Japan, and that the improved mutual understanding that would result would be further facilitated by the funding of scholarships for students and the provision of Asian language instruction in Australia. In particular, he proposed that the University of Queensland initiate such contacts by the appointment of a teacher of Japanese. His observations on conditions in both countries reveal a keen intelligence at work. In China the scholar was 'revered', and students generally were strongly patriotic and 'hostile to Japan'. Writing before the Xian incident of 12 December 1936, when former Manchurian warlord Zhang Xueliang kidnapped Chiang Kai-shek as a strategy to convince his nominal superior to enter a united front with the Communist Party forces in order to resist Japan, Melbourne was convinced that if the central government did not oppose Japanese encroachments many students would follow the communists.[28]

As a result of the disarray in the national administration, he encountered limited interest amongst Chinese government officials in possible cooperation with their Australian counterparts. In many respects, Japan was a contrast. Government control was pervasive, scholars played little part in public life, and there was a good deal of censorship which obstructed manifestations of the interest many students held for liberal and progressive ideas. Discussing the case of Minobe Tatsukichi, professor of law at the University of Tokyo, who was humiliated because his interpretation of the constitution implied that the emperor's powers were limited (albeit obscurely), Melbourne observed that 'the university professor who deals with controversial subjects must exercise the greatest care'.[29] He even noted the case of a student from Manchukuo he encountered whose preference was to study in China but who feared that following such a course would have led to the persecution of his family.

It may be surmised that the contrast he observed between what he was shown in Manchukuo and what he saw of China reinforced the argument advanced by Japanese spokesmen, and noted by Melbourne in his subsequent writings, that Japan was fulfilling a developing and 'civilising' role in China. In a paper he wrote in 1938 on the Sino–Japanese question, that is, after the outbreak of the Japanese war with China, Melbourne suggested that Japan had assumed the role of 'leadership' in China, and that the Manchurian venture was the consequence of Japan's industrialisation and its quest for materials and markets. He did add that the army's expansion into north China was not popular with the people, and he also made an attempt to explain the perspective of the Nanjing government. At any rate, Australia should not be seen to be 'taking sides' in this conflict.[30]

---

[27] R. H. Myers, 'Japanese Imperialism in Manchuria: The South Manchuria Railway Company, 1906–1933', in *The Japanese Informal Empire in China, 1895–1937*, eds Peter Duus, R. H. Myers and M. R. Peattie (Princeton: Princeton University Press, 1989), 101–32.

[28] Melbourne, *Report on a Visit to the Universities of China and Japan* (Brisbane: University of Queensland, 1936), 19–20.

[29] Ibid., 39.

[30] Melbourne, 'The Sino-Japanese Question', NLA: Melbourne Papers.

Melbourne and the Trade Dispute with Japan

Melbourne was in Japan in 1936 when Australia introduced a recalculation of import duties (a measure which was followed by a licensing scheme) which had the effect of obstructing imports of textiles from Japan that had been progressively displacing those traditionally supplied from Britain. After Sir Henry Gullett (responsible for trade treaties) and Prime Minister Lyons made plain that these measures were specifically directed at particular imports from Japan, Tokyo responded with countermeasures that were introduced just as Melbourne arrived back on his return voyage.[31] The timing of this dispute was doubly disadvantageous for Melbourne. While he was in Japan the Australian government had requested, without success, that Japan voluntarily limit exports of certain textile items. In Tokyo, Melbourne had argued that Japan's interests would not be affected by import quotas and that Japan must recognise that preference for British goods was a fundamental feature of Australia's trading system. In an account of a meeting with Baron Sakatani (former finance minister and mayor of Tokyo, then president of the Japan–Australia Society) and senior business figures, he recorded: 'I told them frankly that, in my opinion, Japan alone was to blame for the distrust which had developed in Australia.'[32] Melbourne then referred to the popular books of Ishimaru[33] and Ishiharo and other writings, all of which implied that Japan had designs upon Australia. His words seem to have had some effect, though only temporarily, with Sakatani subsequently disavowing any Japanese designs on Australia in remarks in the House of Peers.[34]

The literature on the trade dispute suggests that, at the very least, Gullett acted without sufficient consultation or thought for the full consequences of his decision, especially the alienation of Japanese sentiment, given that Latham's mission had led to the initiation of lengthy negotiations for a bilateral commercial treaty.[35] This opinion has been generally supported by subsequent work on the bureaucratic and political background to the dispute.[36]

Melbourne felt compelled, upon his return to Australia, to make serious efforts to reconcile the contrasting Japanese and Australian government views. These efforts took two forms. In correspondence he exchanged with Gullet and then with Lyons, he endeavoured to familiarise them with the fundamentals of Japanese sentiment, while making contact

---

[31] Yamakawa Tadao, 'The Yosemite Conference and Japan', *Pacific Affairs*, 9 (4), 1936, 515–523.

[32] Letter, Melbourne to Henry Gullett, September 1936, NLA: Melbourne Papers.

[33] Ishimaru Tōta, *Japan Must Fight Britain,* trans. G. V. Rayment (London: Hurst and Blackett, 1936).

[34] Letter, Melbourne to Gullett, September 1936, NLA: Melbourne Papers.

[35] D. B. Copland and C. V. Janes, *Australian Trade Policy: A Book of Documents 1932-1937* (Sydney: Angus & Robertson, 1937), 259–323; F. C. Benham, 'Japan or Manchester', in *Some Australian Take Stock,* ed. J. C. G. Kevin (London: Longmans, 1939).

[36] Herbert Burton, 'The "Trade Diversion" Episode of the 'thirties', *Australian Outlook*, 22 (1), 1968, 7–14; D. C. S. Sissons, 'Manchester v. Japan: The Imperial Background of the Australian Trade Diversion Dispute with Japan, 1936', *Australian Outlook*, 30 (3), 1978, 480–502. See also A. T. Ross, 'Australian Overseas Trade and National Development Policy 1932-1939: A Story of Colonial Larrikins or Australian statesmen?', *Australian Journal of Politics and History* 36 (2), 1990, 184–204.

with Murai Kuramatsu, consul-general for Japan in Sydney, to explore possible grounds for a settlement. Later in the dispute he also publicised his own somewhat critical views.

On 25 June Lyons had delivered a radio broadcast, *The Truth About the Japanese Trade Position*, in which he claimed that the dispute arose because of Japan's pursuit of a monopoly of sections of the Australian textile market, and that by engaging in a trade boycott until that market was opened, Japan was seeking to infringe on Australia's sovereign authority to set its own tariffs for its own reasons.[37] He also adverted to the need to retain entry to the British market in order to dispose of excess agricultural produce. Lyons' own intervention, especially in a manner calculated to appeal to nationalist sentiments, was unhelpful for the prospects of a settlement. From the first, Melbourne had suspected the machinations of British business, and in his first letter to Consul-General Murai, having stated that he believed the policy was a 'mistake', sought information that would strengthen his critique: 'anything showing that the government's policy is due to the influence of British interests would be particularly useful'.[38]

It was not Melbourne's intention, however, to embarrass the government, but rather to find some means of resolution. Melbourne had first corresponded with Lyons in 1932, and was not slow to offer his views in this instance. They exchanged letters on the trade issue in early July, and two weeks later Melbourne travelled to Canberra where he met Gullett, R. G. Casey, and several other officials. On the way he had stopped in Sydney and met Consul-General Murai and Japanese business figures. Thus briefed, he wrote a long letter to Lyons which ranged well beyond the trade dispute to the broad picture of trends in and forces behind Japanese policy.[39] He claimed to have no quarrel with the British orientation of Australian policy but 'this British aspect of Australian policy may be overemphasised. It may be given effect without offending Japanese opinion'. There was no doubt that the Japanese had been offended, he warned, as much by the tariff and licensing measures as by the way they had been introduced. The idea of 'expansion' was predominant in Japan, and currently there were three schools of advocacy: those who looked north and west, a view associated with the army; those who looked south, which was the position of the navy; and those—mostly civilians—who supported a simultaneous movement. The idea of southern expansion which would entail a collision with a number of major powers was held by many to be suicidal. Melbourne, recounting his experiences with Baron Sakatani, argued that the failure to conclude a commercial treaty was a lost opportunity, and that the current dispute had strengthened the hand of the southern party. This raised the issue of Australian defence. Although a Japanese attack on Australia was considered to be unlikely for a long time, should it eventuate, even in the form of raids upon coastal cities, it followed from the improbability of any assistance from Britain that Australia would be thrown on its own resources. Melbourne considered that it would be 'unprofitable to sacrifice Australia to British interest' and that 'it is very advisable to maintain friendship with Japan'.[40] He then offered some practical advice on the trade in various commodities, given that it was

---

[37] Copland and Janes, *Australian Trade Policy*, 269–72.
[38] Letter, Melbourne to Murai Kuramatsu, 2 July [1936], NAA: C443 J45.
[39] Letter, Melbourne to Lyons, 22 July 1936, NLA: Melbourne Papers.
[40] Letter, Melbourne to Lyons, 22 July 1936, NLA: Melbourne Papers.

necessary for Australia to respond to the threatening Japanese decision not only to buy less Australian wool but also to find substitutes. In the future, Japan would buy a reduced quantity of other commodities, such as wheat. This deterioration of trading relations could only be arrested through a compromise, and Melbourne provided actual figures for quotas of imports in cotton and rayon cloth which he believed Tokyo might accept. He put these and other suggestions to Lyons in person when the prime minister was in Brisbane on 5 August 1936.

On 13 August Melbourne was able to inform Murai, in a letter marked 'personal and confidential', that the prime minister was 'prepared to go a long way towards the conditions I had suggested as a basis of settlement'.[41] Bird's view, that his connections with the Japanese were 'of a questionable nature' for an avowed nationalist, should now be recalled. The files of the Japanese Consulate show that various sums of money were expended on hospitality for visitors; Melbourne's name is listed three times, but for the most modest sums (£1.3.0 in 1936, 2/6 and 1/4 in 1937; in 1937, by contrast, Peter Russo and party were entertained to the tune of £7.2.0).[42] In light of the fact that, of his discussions with the prime minister, he wrote to Murai that 'I thought it wiser not to ask him for details', Melbourne cannot be characterised as acting as an interested party. The following passage, which Melbourne himself quoted to other correspondents in order to demonstrate his own position, illustrates his personal view:

> I gathered that the government has been disturbed by what it regards as a Japanese attempt to restrict its right to give preference to the products of other British countries. I am certain that the government will persist with its determination to maintain this right … Unless Japan is willing to accept the principle of imperial preference it will be impossible to obtain a settlement. I feel also that the government will insist on establishing quotas in cotton and rayon goods. I know that Japan objects, in principle, to the idea of a quota … I cannot see that there is anything derogatory to Japan in the quota principle, especially if it is associated with a provision which will give Japan an added share in expanding trade … I feel … that the government will insist on establishing quotas, and if your Foreign Office refuses to negotiate on this basis, the present unfortunate trouble will continue.[43]

Despite Melbourne's efforts, Lyons delivered a second broadcast on 17 August, the hectoring tone and poor logic of which did little to improve the atmosphere. He therefore turned his attention to Sir Henry Gullett, repeating some of his earlier proposals, and reproducing the above comments to Murai. He then adverted to what he considered to be one of the obstacles facing Australia: 'what is needed, particularly now, is the presence of someone at Tokyo who will be able to put the arguments directly to representatives of the Japanese government'.[44] Unfortunately, Trade Commissioner Longfield Lloyd had been forced to labour under the disadvantage of not functioning as Australia's voice in Tokyo,

---

[41] Letter, Melbourne to Murai, 13 August 1936, NLA: Melbourne Papers.
[42] Japanese Consulate, NAA: C443 J45.
[43] Letter, Melbourne to Murai, 13 August 1936, NLA: Melbourne Papers.
[44] Letter, Melbourne to Gullett, 22 September 1936, NLA: Melbourne Papers.

since the government 'continues to communicate with the government of Japan through the British Embassy in Tokyo', a position that Melbourne regretted as reflective of 'an ultra-British attitude and a tendency to place British before Australian interests'. In a subsequent letter to Murai, Melbourne referred to his efforts to educate Gullett. He also speculated on the current position of the cabinet:

> Probably the government, being encouraged by the maintenance of wool prices, will hold out longer, expecting that Japanese buyers will be forced to weaken their position by coming into the market at some of the early sales. If they do this, it will strengthen the hand of the Australian government and make it still more difficult to arrive at a compromise.

Here Melbourne was advising against a quick return to the wool market, otherwise the dispute would be prolonged.[45]

In publicising his views, Melbourne held his fire (and was thanked on 14 September by Gullett for doing so) until efforts to heal the breach appeared fruitless. He did, however, work on a series of three articles under the title 'Australia and Japan', which were in draft by early September, reviewing in great detail the background to the trade dispute and its implications for bilateral relations. At one stage Melbourne had plans to turn these materials into a book, but he never did.

These articles exhibit a very thorough knowledge of Australia–Japan trade and of the positions of both governments.[46] In them, Melbourne entered a plea for 'the preservation of Australian national interests' in a situation where, in essence, 'Australian interests are being sacrificed to sentiment', that is, to the imperial relationship.[47] Unfortunately this sentiment was not reciprocated by Great Britain which preferred to purchase supplies of meat and butter from Argentina and Denmark rather than from Australia. As British critics pointed out, its overall effect on Australia's trade restrictions policy was to reduce international trade and provide another source of grievance for the dissatisfied powers. If British imports were falling it had to be acknowledged that British cotton manufacturing was a sunset industry increasingly uneconomic for an advanced industrial country; remarkably, Australia had actually been importing a relatively constant proportion of declining exports.[48] Damage to Australian exports of wheat and beef could be expected, and the impact upon the wool industry would be grave. Perhaps the greatest error had been not to assess properly Japan as a trading partner.[49]

Bird suggests that this material was considered by Murai as helpful to Japan's case,[50] and indeed the consul-general did offer several comments on the draft to correct some of the data.[51] However Melbourne's text was nothing more than an accurate summary of the

---

[45] Letter, Melbourne to Murai, 23 Oct 1936, NAA: C443 J45.
[46] Melbourne, 'Australia and Japan', NLA: Melbourne Papers.
[47] Ibid., paper 1, NLA: Melbourne Papers.
[48] Ibid., paper 2, NLA: Melbourne Papers.
[49] Ibid., papers 3, 6, NLA: Melbourne Papers.
[50] Bird, *Lyons*, 163.
[51] Letter, Murai to Melbourne, 10 September 1936, NAA: C443 J45.

existing situation, the inconsistencies in the Australian government's position being plain to many contemporary observers. His own contribution to the arrangements that resolved the textile issue—which required Japan to accept some quotas—is difficult to estimate given that many interests, not least some members of the wool growing fraternity, urged the government to compromise. As Sissons has shown, Murai was also in contact with other figures sympathetic to Japan, notably Ian Clunies Ross and Charles Hawker, who played a role in bridging the gap between the positions of the two governments.[52] However, as Melbourne observed in a letter to Murai on the dispute, 'as far as I can see it was settled almost on the terms I suggested some months ago'.[53] If Melbourne and his fellows, with their close knowledge of the Japanese industries involved, had not promoted this compromise, it is doubtful whether Gullett and Lyons would have had the wit to stumble upon its like.

In a frank communication with Longfield Lloyd in Tokyo, Melbourne clearly attributed this sorry episode to the absence of a thorough-going nationalist perspective on the part of Australian politicians. He complained that the government's ministers 'cannot free themselves from the dictation of British politicians'; both the 'jingoistic' Hughes and the 'dogmatic unimaginative' Gullett were 'essentially anti-Australian' in being unable to realise that Australia has interests 'apart from the interest of the United Kingdom'.[54] It should not be concluded, however, that Melbourne's was an entirely lone voice. Clunies Ross was similarly a consistent advocate of paying much more serious attention to Japan,[55] and had made his own attempt, seeking funds from the Carnegie Corporation, to introduce the teaching of Japanese at the University of Sydney.[56] Charles Hawker, formerly minister of commerce, was another like-minded figure with whom, indeed, Melbourne had conducted a sympathetic correspondence.[57]

Even with the fading of the trade diversion controversy, Australia–Japan relations remained fragile. Further difficulties were encountered when, on 17 March 1938, cabinet decided to prohibit, after a three month grace period, the further export of Australian iron ore, ostensibly on the grounds that this resource was needed for local industry. As the government was well aware, this decision particularly affected exports from Yampi Sound, ore extraction at that site being developed through the investment of considerable sums of capital from Japan. The British had counselled caution lest offence be caused to the Japanese; the Department of External Affairs, though taking the view that this investment

---

[52] D. C. S. Sissons, 'Private Diplomacy in the 1936 Trade Dispute with Japan', *Australian Journal of Politics and History*, 27 (2), 1981, 143–59.

[53] Letter, Melbourne to Murai, 25 December [1936], NAA: C443 J45.

[54] Letter, Melbourne to Longfield Lloyd, 11 January 1937, NLA: Melbourne Papers.

[55] Ian Clunies Ross, 'Australia's Trade and Diplomatic Relations with Japan', *Australian Quarterly*, 5 (17), 1933, 79–92; 'Australian Representation in Japan' *Australian Quarterly*, 6 (22), 1934, 61–68; 'Factors Influencing the Development of Australia's Trade with Japan', in *Australia and the Far East: Diplomatic and Trade Relations*, ed. Clunies Ross (Sydney: Angus & Robertson/AIIA, 1937), 153–202.

[56] Letter, Clunies Ross to Frederick P. Keppel, 21 March 1935, Butler Library Columbia University: Series 3A, Box 52, Folder 5.

[57] Geoffrey Hawker, 'The Japan–Australia Trade Dispute', *Austral-Asiatic Bulletin* 1 (1), 1937, 4–6.

was a further instance of Japan's meddlesome 'Southward advance' strategy, had offered similar advice.[58] As has been noted, once again Melbourne took the initiative, writing to seek to influence the prime minister directly. Japan 'must import raw materials and she must export manufactured goods', he explained, identifying the crux of Tokyo's dilemma. '[I]f other countries refuse to sell the raw materials, of which possibly they have a surplus, or refuse to buy the manufactured goods, Japan will be forced to choose between fighting for markets and allowing her industries to perish.'[59]

It is against the frustration of Melbourne's hopes for improved bilateral relations that aspects of his close relationship with Japanese consular officials are to be understood. In a letter to the Japanese consul-general, Torao Wakamatsu, marked 'confidential', Melbourne observed that while he knew that it was 'possible to make out a good case for Japan',[60] Tokyo's propaganda was unconvincing. He even offered to 'draft the skeleton of a book suggesting titles for chapters and sections with proposed contents for each' so that this case could be made more effectively. Yet in addressing a Japanese audience, Melbourne was not afraid to state that from his viewpoint, which was based upon 'the requirements of Australian security', Australian fears of Japan were not without foundation. In a letter to the business group the Association of Far Eastern Affairs in Sydney, Melbourne argued that, despite his many personal efforts to improve relations, it was not in Australia's interests for Japan to control China 'as a military dependency'.[61] If Japan was successful in subduing China, this outcome would be likely to stimulate yet further expansionism. As he observed, 'triumphant militarism does not recognise any limitations'. By this time Japanese armies were advancing into southern China and some commentators were even predicting the complete collapse of the national government.

If the Australia–Japan relationship was to be rescued from further deterioration and the threat of conflict, what steps could Australia take? In the remaining period before the outbreak of the Pacific War, Melbourne sought to promote three major changes. First, Australia must adopt a new approach to its place in the Commonwealth, speaking with an independent voice in the region and shaping Commonwealth policy to match Australia's exposure to the risks generated by such a policy. Second, Australia should contribute to the opening of markets that would mitigate Japan's sense of grievance. Third, Australian diplomacy must be devoted to associating other powers, notably the United States, with a new modus vivendi with Japan, Melbourne suggesting that the government should make renewed efforts to conclude a Pacific pact. Reliance upon Britain was not a prudent policy, since 'as Rome was forced to withdraw her legions from outlying provinces, the United Kingdom might be forced to recall her ships and planes from eastern areas to meet a crisis nearer home'.[62]

---

[58] Memorandum, W. R. Hodgson to R. G. Casey, 13 December 1937, in *Documents on Australian Foreign Policy* (hereafter *DAFP*), vol. I, *1937–38*, ed. R. G. Neale (Canberra: Australian Government Publishing Service, 1975), 240–2.

[59] Letter, Melbourne to Lyons, 14 July 1938, NLA: Melbourne Papers.

[60] Letter, Melbourne to Torao Wakamatsu, 26 April 1938, NAA: C443 J45.

[61] Letter, Melbourne to Association of Far Eastern Affairs, 18 October 1938, NAA: A1608 B41/1/6.

[62] Melbourne, 'Australia's Relations to other Pacific Countries', Australian Supplementary Papers

Australian Initiatives on Appeasement

Following the intervention considered at the beginning of this chapter, Melbourne pursued further the possibility of an Australian initiative in the Far East. Writing to Lyons again he offered the view that the evidence now showed that the 'Japanese expansionists' were committed to the goal of regional domination. In pursuit of this goal they regarded the reaction of the other powers as hypocritical:

> The Japanese can not understand why, in giving expression to the policy of 'appeasement', the United Kingdom has condoned Italian aggression in Africa and German aggression in Europe, while it refuses to recognise the Empire of Manchoukuo.[63]

Japanese opinion had reached the point where collusion between the United Kingdom and the United States in assisting China was suspected at every turn. At the same time, Japan was frustrated by the fact that the UK could 'exert pressure on Japan in China without subjecting the vital interest of the United Kingdom to undue risk.' Sooner or later Britain and Japan would come to blows, and the ensuing conflict would unavoidably and necessarily embroil Australia. The only expedient that would delay this conflict would be a Japan–UK agreement. Here Melbourne suggested that this proposal 'reduces, to a practical form, the ideal which inspired you to suggest the conclusion of a general "Pacific Pact"'. The idea of a regional pact to replace the failed Washington Treaties was advanced by Lyons at the 1937 Imperial Conference, only then to lose plausibility with the outbreak of the Sino-Japanese War. In retrospect, it was probably as well for Australia's international reputation that the distance between Devonport and Tokyo is somewhat greater than that between London and Munich. With Melbourne having suggested to Lyons that an Australian plenipotentiary might be sent to Japan as an emissary, it is not beyond the bounds of possibility—given Lyons' apparent faith in the potential for personal diplomacy—that the prime minister might not himself have considered assuming this role. As Bird characterises this episode, 'the consensus builder was asked himself to intervene in the Anglo-Japanese dispute as a go-between'.[64] Lyons did not, however, have long to live, and his successor, R. G. Menzies, was as yet a tyro in foreign affairs. Melbourne wrote to other contacts in the government, putting the same case that as the costs of a conflict between Japan and Britain would be borne principally by Australia, they should take the initiative to divert the forces of destruction while there was still a chance of so doing.[65]

Such was the impact of Melbourne's ideas on Prime Minister Lyons that he arranged a meeting for Melbourne with Stanley Melbourne Bruce, the Australian high commissioner in London who had returned to Australia for consultations (given Lyons' increasingly poor health, his visit also involved political manoeuvres). Melbourne, disappointed that Bruce had evidently not read any of his communications with the prime minister, reported to

---

Series E, No 2, Prepared for the British Commonwealth Relations Conference, Lapstone NSW (AIIA, 1938), 15.

[63] Letter, Melbourne to Lyons, 24 January 1939, NLA: Melbourne Papers.

[64] Bird, *Lyons,* 281.

[65] Letter, Melbourne to Archie Cameron and Arthur Fadden, 11 February 1939, NLA: Melbourne Papers.

Lyons that it was Bruce's view that the time for any intermediary role for Australia had passed.[66] However, Melbourne felt that Bruce did not know about the current state of Japanese opinion; the high commissioner was an undoubted expert on European affairs, 'but Australia is a Pacific country' and for full intra-Commonwealth consultation to be effective Australia needed the best information. If Bruce himself did not want to travel to Tokyo, perhaps Casey should be sent.

Although Melbourne wrote to Menzies to congratulate him upon his decision to send ministers to Washington and Tokyo, the new prime minister did not share his predecessor's interest in Melbourne's views. Nevertheless, Melbourne felt that he had been vindicated by events and especially by the establishment of a diplomatic post in Tokyo. As he wrote to Wakamatsu:

> The opposition to the idea has been very strong. It came from people who would not agree that Australia has special interests in the Pacific and eastern Asia. I feel that, with this decision, we will make a great step forward and that the relations between Japan and Australia will be put on a much better basis.[67]

Melbourne's chief activities were thereafter directed to writing and broadcasting, and in 1940 he produced a series of texts on the basis of Japan's foreign policy. In the broadcast 'The Population Problem of Japan', Melbourne considered the contradictory nature of Japanese imperialism, an imperialism at once 'ambitious and aggressive' but also 'fearful'.[68] Of the two impulses, fear was the most significant, in particular the fear of questions springing from the prospect of the government being unable to feed the burgeoning population. Japan had copied other countries in its economic and industrial strategy but had been denied the fruits expected from that strategy. The choice for Japan's policy makers was now stark: 'if the markets of the world are closed to Japanese goods, and if Japan fails to get sufficient relief from Manchoukuo, war seems inevitable'.[69] Melbourne's advocacy of economic concessions to Japan may be understood as a consequence of these views.

Appeasement and Australia Before the Pacific War

In the 1930s there was a considerable current of opinion in Australia supporting policies of accommodation with Japan.[70] Latham, for whom the 'vigorous efficiency' of Japan was in marked contrast to the 'pitiably poor' condition of China, had reported confidentially to Lyons on his discussions with Foreign Minister Kōki Hirota conducted during the 1934 Eastern Mission. He was clearly in favour of conciliating Japan. As there was not 'the slightest probability that Manchukuo will cease to exist', and as this issue would prevent any prospect of Japan returning to the League of Nations, he recommended that some means had to be found to recognise what had become the reality in Asia:

---

[66] Letter, Melbourne to Lyons, 7 March 1939, NAA: A1608 B41/1/6.
[67] Letter, Melbourne to Wakamatsu, 28 April 1939, NAA: C443 J45.
[68] 'The Population Problem of Japan', NLA: Melbourne Papers.
[69] Ibid.
[70] Robert Murray, 'Munich Revisited', *Quadrant,* 42 (6), 1998, 46–52.

> Accordingly it appears to me that consideration should be given to the possibility of discovering some formula which would enable both Japan and the League to 'save face' and get rid of what threatens to be a permanent source of poison in the relations between Japan and other countries.

That the 'factions' in China—Latham did not dignify them with the name of the national government—would be prepared to accept such a formula he regarded as 'improbable', but that situation he evidently felt did not stand in the way of such international acceptance of Japan's control of Manchuria.[71]

Regarding the more general question of appeasement, as Eric Andrews argues, the position of informed opinion even after the Abyssinia debacle was generally sympathetic to the dictatorships: 'there was a fairly general support for the policy of appeasement, especially economic appeasement, among certain intellectuals'.[72] As Paul Twomey's careful survey shows, among officials and political leaders only William Morris Hughes stood against the proposition that forms of conciliation could be successfully negotiated with Germany. At various times Casey, Bruce, Lyons and senior external affairs officials Keith Officer and W. R. Hodgson all demonstrated sympathy for treaty revision and for corresponding economic measures, that is, 'the intellectual pattern for the later policy of appeasement'.[73] Ritchie Ovendale notes that, at the Imperial Conference of 1937, Casey had expressed the view that as Britain would not be likely to defend Czechoslovakia, this position should be explained in eastern Europe.[74] Even in early 1939, Menzies and Casey were in favour of concessions over Danzig and the Polish corridor. The highly detailed study of Christopher Waters elaborates this story further.[75] If Melbourne's position can be assimilated to the idea of appeasement, he was in a numerous and influential company.

How did these Australian views appear in the wider imperial context? In the account by William Roger Louis of the British management of imperial decline in Asia, even after the articulation of the 'new order' doctrine, Foreign Office officials remained focused on devising terms that would both strengthen China's position and conciliate Japan. In January 1938, for example, Sir John Brenan proposed a settlement of hostilities that would see a Japanese withdrawal beyond the Great Wall, China's recognition of Manchukuo,

---

[71] 'Australian Eastern Mission, Confidential Report on Trade between Australia and Japan', 3 July 1934, NAA: A981, Far 5 part 17.

[72] E. M. Andrews, *Isolationism & Appeasement in Australia: Reactions to the European Crises, 1935-1939* (Canberra: Australian National University Press, 1970); Andrews, *The Writing on the Wall: The British Commonwealth and Aggression in the East, 1931-1935* (Sydney: Allen & Unwin, 1987).

[73] Paul Twomey, 'Munich', in *Munich to Vietnam. Australia's Relations with Britain and the United States since the 1930s*, ed. Carl Bridge (Melbourne: Melbourne University Press, 1991), 15.

[74] Ritchie Ovendale, 'Appeasement', in *Between Empire and Nation: Australia's External Relations From Federation to the Second World War*, eds Carl Bridge and Bernard Attard (Melbourne: Australian Scholarly Publishing, 2000), 185–204; see also Garry Woodard, 'The Diplomacy of Appeasement', *Quadrant*, 43 (1/2), 1999, 48–53.

[75] Christopher Waters, *Australia and Appeasement. Imperial Foreign Policy and the Origins of World War II* (London: I. B. Tauris, 2012).

retention of the current customs administration, and the internationalising of Shanghai.[76] The problems entailed in any course of action were complex:

> The Foreign Office agonized as acutely over the issue of assisting China as that of appeasing Japan. Each argument in favour of stiffening Chinese resistance could be refuted by one demonstrating the adverse impact on Anglo–Japanese relations.[77]

Japan's espousal of the 'new order' stimulated generalised alarm on the future of imperial interests in the Far East. The clear implication of this doctrine was the supersession of the 1922 Nine-Power Treaty order, guaranteeing China's political integrity. The affirming of this integrity, aiming at finding some resolution of the Sino–Japanese War, was the purpose of a conference of the relevant powers (Japan declining to attend) convened, partly at the instigation of Bruce who was in attendance in Brussels, on 3 November 1938.[78] Prime Minister Fumimaro Konoe's initial announcement of Japan's alternative doctrine was delivered the same day.[79] Japanese forces had occupied Canton the previous month. However, the Japanese military had just suffered a serious reversal at the hands of the Soviet Union at Changgufeng (Zhanggufeng) on the Manchurian border with Russia.

The documents on the preparations for the conference throw light upon the interesting relative roles of Melbourne and of the British secretary of state for dominion affairs, Malcolm MacDonald. In October 1937, MacDonald dispatched to Lyons an assessment of the British government's view of the possibilities to be entertained at Brussels for the achievement of a peaceful settlement.[80] Three options were suggested: taking no action, expressing moral condemnation of Japan without taking any other steps, and providing assistance to China and/or exerting economic pressure on Japan. Quite apart from the practical difficulties in the way of the final option, and the need for coordinated action by all parties not least the United States, economic sanctions could well have elicited 'violent action' from Japan.[81] Given the prominence of Lyons in the crafting of the response to Hitler's designs on the Sudetenland, MacDonald and his colleagues must have been aware that any message that sanctions might occasion war would have been most unwelcome. Such was the case, with the Commonwealth responding to MacDonald that the last option was neither warranted by the Nine-Power Treaty, nor likely to be of practical effect, even if all parties (including, by implication, the United States) were in agreement. Even 'moral censure' was undesirable, as it would 'probably antagonise and harden feeling in Japan to

---

[76] Wm. Roger Louis, *British Strategy in the Far East 1919-1939* (Oxford: The Clarendon Press, 1971), 248–50; see also Peter Lowe, *Great Britain and the Origins of the Pacific War. A Study in British Policy in East Asia 1937–1941* (Oxford: The Clarendon Press, 1977).

[77] Louis, *British Strategy,* 260.

[78] Alfred Stirling, *Lord Bruce: The London Years* (Melbourne: Hawthorn Press, 1974), 48–55.

[79] Yagami, Kazuo, *Konoe Fumimaro and the Failure of Peace in Japan, 1937–1941* (Jefferson NC: McFarland, 2006), 68.

[80] Letter, Malcolm Macdonald to Commonwealth government, 19 October 1937, in *DAFP*, vol. I, 210–12.

[81] Ibid., 211.

such an extent as to preclude any possibility of a settlement'.[82] Thus the Commonwealth favoured nothing beyond the conference identifying a mediator. Even before the Brussels meeting, Eden had said in the Commons on 31 October that the object of the conference was 'appeasement'.[83]

In 1934 MacDonald, then parliamentary under-secretary in the Dominions Office, visited Australia. He was also present at the Southport conference of the AIIA, and had offered some rather conventional remarks as well as responding to a series of questions regarding British policy on certain international matters (including India, Ireland and disarmament) and also on the domestic program of the post-1931 National government in Britain. As has been noted, Melbourne had argued vigorously at the same meeting for a distinctive Australian policy towards Asia. He also suggested a future strategy for the 'potential danger' posed to Australia if Japan failed to achieve her ambitions on the mainland of Asia and was forced, as an alternative, towards the South Pacific.[84] In this eventuality, good relations with all the powers of the region, and especially the United States, would be vital, and a prominent Australian diplomacy would be the necessary vehicle. MacDonald was called upon to offer some discussant's comments. Of Melbourne he observed: 'he ... underestimates the willingness of Great Britain to help Australia—if she may have the honour and privilege of doing so'. The conference record indicated 'laughter' at this point.[85] MacDonald subsequently wrote to Chatham House with some impressions of his visit. In a later letter dated 1 February 1935 he stated: 'Generally, with the exception of the Queensland Branch of the Australian Institute of International Affairs, I thought that the personnels [sic] of the Branches are of a high quality'.[86] Three years later, MacDonald, knowing full well that Britain could spare no forces with which to defend its Far Eastern interests, played his part in a government which would take no decisive steps to defend Britain's Far Eastern position. When the Foreign Office attempted to organise, in concert with the United States and Soviet Russia, a common embargo on trade with Japan, Macdonald claimed that 'the situation in Europe was too critical to justify our taking any risks in the Far East'.[87] But neither, it seems, could the British government countenance a comprehensive rapprochement with Japan. As Antony Best notes, after the Nazi–Soviet Pact, there were strong arguments in London for 'limited appeasement' in the Far East.[88]

---

[82] Letter, Commonwealth government to Macdonald 28 October 1937, in ibid., 217.

[83] Ovendale, 'Appeasement', 80.

[84] Melbourne, 'A Foreign Policy for Australia', 36.

[85] MacDonald's remark cited in ibid., 46.

[86] Royal Institute of International Affairs (RIIA), 'Imperial Committee Agenda and Minutes, 8th Meeting', 22 May 1935, RIIA, London.

[87] Cabinet meeting, 13 October 1937, cited in Bradford A. Lee, *Britain and the Sino-Japanese War, 1937–1939* (Stanford: Stanford University Press, 1973), 67; see also B. J. C. McKercher, 'National Security and Imperial Defence: British Grand Strategy and Appeasement 1930–1939', *Diplomacy and Statecraft*, 19 (3), 2008, 391–442.

[88] Antony Best, *Britain, Japan and Pearl Harbor: Avoiding War in East Asia, 1936–41* (London: Routledge/LSE, 1995), 87.

At the time, then, Melbourne was evidently not alone in believing that the best strategic interests of the empire would be served by an accommodation with Japan, though he was especially clear-sighted in recognising that such a step would be at the expense of China.

As Japan continued to test British resolve in China, Bruce in London counselled conciliation. Discussing further provocations in Tientsin and the deteriorating situation in the Far East, he recommended to the prime minister in June 1939 that 'every possibility of resolving the trouble ought to be explored—short of accepting intolerable humiliation'.[89] By this time Bruce had formed the view that the dispatch of any sizeable British fleet to Singapore was a remote possibility, yet British policy makers had not thought through the consequences. Accordingly, he wrote to Menzies shortly after the European war began:

> As to Japan—I have had a growing feeling for some time that though the Far East is a major problem to us, it is a relatively minor one to Whitehall, and that the British Government is more engaged in hanging on in China, hoping for something to turn up, than in any clear process of thinking about the future.[90]

The suggested measures Bruce offered to his British interlocutors included extensive concessions, a joint program with the United States offering capital to assist the funding of development in China which would generate markets for Japanese produce, the abandonment of extra-territorial rights, and the recognition of the status quo in Manchukuo. Such measures would recognise the 'special problems' of Japan, namely, population pressure, lack of raw materials and restrictions on international markets.[91] Clearly Bruce had come around to Melbourne's view. But despite, in this instance, conveying his opinions to the noted appeaser R. A. Butler, his opinions on this question counted for little in Whitehall.

In characterising the British reaction to Japanese encroachments in Asia, Aron Shai discerns 'a gradual process of erosion' rather than any grand gesture comparable with the Munich Agreement, though he notes the humiliation involved in the acceptance of Japanese demands over the Tientsin foreign concession and the temporary closure of the Burma Road in 1940.[92] Despite sympathy for Japan on the part of British figures, Chamberlain not least, Whitehall was very reluctant to abandon the privileges of the established order in China. It is the view of Louis that both economic interests and prestige were at stake:

> the Japanese noted that the British seemed to be more enthusiastic about making trade concessions to the Germans or Italians than to them … In short, political appeasement sounded appealing in principle, especially because it seemed like a reasonable price to pay for strategic security; but it became more and more elusive when examined in the light of concrete steps to achieve it. The British did not yield easily when the issues boiled down to specific economic concessions.

---

[89] Record of meeting held in U.K. Prime Minister's Room at House of Commons, 28 June 1939, in *DAFP*, vol. II, *1939*, ed. R. G. Neale (Canberra: Australian Government Publishing Service,1976), 142.

[90] Letter, Bruce to Menzies, 11 September 1939, in ibid., 257.

[91] Letter, Bruce to R. A. Butler, Enclosure, 21 September 1939, in ibid., 279–81.

[92] Aron Shai, 'Was There a Far Eastern Munich?', *Journal of Contemporary History*, 9 (3), 1974, 163.

The great act of appeasement did not occur in the Far East, but eventually in Central Europe, where the British Empire had no direct involvement.[93]

The inference may be drawn that the safety of the Pacific dominions would never be secured at the price of conceding to Japan uncontested hegemony in China. Melbourne's hope, then, for a new Anglo-Japanese accord was bound to be frustrated even though imperial policymakers were aware of their woeful lack of leverage in the Far East.

Conclusion

The trajectory of Melbourne's career provides ample evidence that he came to regard the better understanding of the Asian region—and especially of Japan—as a national necessity, and the widest propagation of the knowledge he obtained as a personal vocation. Though he suffered many reverses his energies were undiminished. At a time of some personal despondency he remarked that were he to be unable to make a further contribution his plan would then be to return to his constitutional writings, the research for which he had already completed. But he remained engaged on the question of the better management of relations with Asia which he saw as the most important requirement for the protection of the Australian national interest. In particular, Melbourne's assessment of the trade diversion policies of Lyons and Gullett found them not only to have been clearly contrary to the demands of Australian nationalism but also to have set a course entailing subsequent further damage to bilateral relations.

It has been shown that as late as 1940, Melbourne continued to believe that conciliation, or appeasement, of Japan was both possible and desirable. Despite his expressed understanding of the mainsprings of Japan's militarism, he did not hold that further aggressive expansion on Japan's part was necessitated and unavoidable. However, any possible role for Australia in influencing the strategic decisions of Japan's leaders was constrained by the predominance of imperial assumptions as well as by the lack of appropriate diplomatic machinery. Australia's leaders were never prepared to offer a policy of thoroughgoing appeasement of Japan without such being part of a strategy conceived in London, and the British government was never willing to adopt such a policy. The fact of this inability vindicated Melbourne's contention that, in the absence of a thoroughgoing integration of the empire, Australia's national interests in the Far East were bound to be sharply distinct from those of Britain.

---

[93] Wm. Roger Louis, 'The Road to Singapore: British Imperialism in the Far East, 1932–42', in *The Fascist Challenge and the Policy of Appeasement*, eds Wolfgang J. Mommsen and L. Kettenacker (London & Boston: George Allen and Unwin, 1983), 368.

IV

The British World Compared

9

The Political Cultures of Australia and Britain: How Alike Were They?[1]

Ross McKibbin

A major theme in Neville Meaney's work has been the Britishness of Australia: throughout much of its history it is Britishness, British race patriotism and imperial loyalties that have trumped so much else in Australian life, even the predominant types of Australian nationalism. In Meaney's work Australians often appear as disappointed suitors, people with a clearer idea of what it is to be British than the British, constantly depressed by the failure of the British to behave towards Australia as Australians believed they should.[2] That Australians for so long should have thought of themselves as fundamentally British was not unreasonable. As societies they were (and still are) very alike, and Australia was unquestionably an offshoot of Great Britain—even if originally a product of the leavings of British society. Until the 1950s they were demographically also remarkably alike. Both were overwhelmingly Anglo-Celtic: about ninety-five per cent of both populations were of British or Irish origin. Australia is more Irish—from both north and south—than Britain itself, though that difference was significantly diminished by the huge migration of southern Irish to Britain in the 1950s, when Ireland's net population increase was simply decanted to mainland Britain. Both are now multiethnic in a way unimaginable in 1950—Australia even more than Britain[3]—and although their respective ethnicity has different biases, their experience of multiethnicity is broadly similar. Population movement continues to nourish ties. Until recently the British were the largest single national grouping migrating to Australia (those of Chinese and Indian origin now are) and, apart from those claiming Australian ancestry, more Australians are of British origin than any other nationality. At the same time, by far the biggest of Australia's expatriate communities is in Britain, particularly London, and always has been—though that might well change as UK immigration rules become increasingly stringent.[4]

---

[1] This is an enlarged version of an essay that originally appeared in *History Australia*, which was based upon a lecture given at the conference of the Australian Historical Association in Perth in 2009. See Ross McKibbin, 'Britain and Australia: Historical Contrasts and Comparisons', *History Australia*, 7 (3), 2010.

[2] See particularly Neville Meaney, 'Britishness and Australian Identity: The Problem of Nationalism in Australian History and Historiography', *Australian Historical Studies*, 32 (116), 2001, 76–90.

[3] About one quarter of Australia's working population was born outside Australia, probably the highest in the developed world. In Britain that is true only of London where indeed the figure might well be higher.

[4] It is worth noting that the present (2013) Australian Prime Minister Julia Gillard and Leader of the Opposition Tony Abbott are British born.

For much of their history most Australians, certainly at the level of public rhetoric, thought of themselves as fundamentally British, and the rhetoric of Britishness was acceptable both to the Australian right and left, even if that involved different conceptions of Britishness. 'We are an integral, proud and British community, and to preserve those attributes must practice a community of sacrifice', Prime Minister R. G. Menzies told the Australian people after the fall of France in 1940.[5] This was not an untypical comment. The language of the right was suffused with the vocabulary of Anglo-imperial institutions and values, and that remained so at least until the 1960s.[6] When Labor prime minister Ben Chifley told the British that Australia, New Zealand and Britain itself alone 'fully represent the British tradition' he was identifying Britishness with social democracy, a definition which therefore excluded South Africa and Canada and virtually all other members of the Commonwealth,[7] but one which clearly aligned Australianness with Britishness, and even subordinated it to Britishness. Australian civilisation was thus, in Prime Minister John Curtin's formulation, 'British-speaking'.[8] Furthermore, Britishness survived the Second World War and Australia's apparent continuing dependence on the United States for its security (at least as Australians conceived their security). Arguably Australian Britishness reached its peak in 1954 with the Queen's first visit, a visit that to those who participated in it was almost a transcendent experience. Indeed, dealings with real Americans during the war actually reinforced Britishness, as it did for Curtin, the man who had first openly announced such dependence.[9] This sense of umbilical Britishness was demonstrated at the outbreak of the First and Second World Wars—from Labor prime minister Andrew Fisher's 'last man and last shilling' commitment in 1914 to Menzies' simple assumption in 1939 that because Britain was at war so was Australia. This was even though, as Meaney has argued, Australia in peacetime was very reluctant to enter imperial arrangements that did not recognise the primacy to Australia of Australia's defence interests.[10]

Similarly, for much of their joint history, Australia and Britain were culturally alike for the obvious reason that Australian culture was, for the most part, British culture, and even 'Australian' culture was often a variant of the British original.[11] For those raised as late as the 1940s and 1950s, when American influence via film and popular music was becoming ever stronger (in both countries), *William*, *Biggles* and Enid Blyton were as important to

---

[5] Cited in Paul Hasluck, *The Government and the People, 1939–1941* (Canberra: Australian War Memorial, 1952), 216.

[6] See Menzies' radio broadcast from Cairo on his way to Britain in 1941, in ibid., 314.

[7] Cited in Meaney, 'Britishness and Australian Identity', 81.

[8] Hasluck, *Government and the People*, 558.

[9] For Curtin's position, see David Day, *John Curtin: A Life* (Sydney: HarperCollins, 1999), 518–60. Chifley likewise commented in 1946: 'We have great respect for our American friends, but we simply say: "We are part of the British Empire and we are prepared to help the United Kingdom".' Cited in L. F. Crisp, *Ben Chifley: A Biography* (London: Longmans, 1960), 282.

[10] See Meaney, *A History of Australian Defence and Foreign Policy, 1901–23*, vol. 1, *The Search for Security in the Pacific, 1901–14* (Sydney: Sydney University Press, 1976), esp. 3–14.

[11] Andrew Milner, 'On the Beach: Apocalyptic Hedonism and the Origins of Post Modernism', in *Australian Popular Culture*, ed. I. Craven (Melbourne: Cambridge University Press, 1994), 200.

Australian youth, certainly middle-class youth, as any Australian or American literature.[12] In any case, American influences could be contained within Britishness: though the films were usually American (and after 1956 most of the TV programs) the most popular radio programs, other than Australian, were British. As a measure of this popularity, the British programs were broadcast at night, whereas the American ones were broadcast in the morning—that is, in school hours and thus when they were unavailable to schoolchildren. In the 1940s and 1950s the most popular Second World War books tended to be British—*The Cruel Sea*, *HMS Ulysses*, *The Dam Busters*, *Reach for the Sky*—and that too reinforced Britishness.[13] Such books were rarely about the American experience of the Second World War and even less the Australian.

Even though the United States is now almost certainly the most powerful external cultural influence on both Britain and Australia—though more on Australia than Britain—and even though we must presume that cultural relationships between Britain and Australia will continue to weaken, both are still surprisingly strong influences on each other. British usage and idioms, for example, enter Australian speech quickly, and Australia must surely be the last country in the world where bed linen is still called 'manchester'. Thus Australians are 'gobsmacked' if things go 'pear-shaped'. Those they dislike are 'wankers' or 'pratts'. Embarrassing events are 'naff'. Australians are now 'gifted' something. Their university-aged children have a 'gap year'. 'At the end of the day' there might be a 'window of opportunity'. Sportsmen's wives are 'WAGs'. Australia's political leaders want a 'level playing field' to ensure the success of 'privatisation'. These are all British coinages which have rapidly entered Australian speech. The reverse is also true. Anyone who teaches in Britain is aware of the Australianisation of British English, both its vocabulary and pronunciation, probably via the Australian TV soaps watched by generations of British teenagers—one reason why British students now go to 'uni'. While today most successful Australian film actors drift to Hollywood if they can, most successful popular musicians still go to Britain, or at least London, to make or confirm a reputation. For Kylie Minogue, pop music queen and London resident, it was easier than most since she was already very well-known to the millions of British who watched *Neighbours*.[14]

But there is Australianness as well as Britishness. Both Britain and Australia had (and have) well-developed notions of each other which they probably do not have of any other country. Hugh Dalton, the first chancellor of the exchequer in Clement Attlee's post-war Labour government, wrote in his memoirs that 'those people in the South Pacific, most of them our kinsmen, are closer to us, except in physical distance, than any other people in the world. Very literally they are our own people.'[15] These notions might be irrational, skewed or

---

[12] That was true also of what we might call hobby literature. At my school aircraft recognition was immensely popular, and the most influential literature was almost all British—esp. *Flight*, *Aeroplane* and the *Observer's Book of Aircraft*.

[13] When I was at school Douglas Bader, the subject of *Reach for the Sky*, visited our town. Schoolchildren lined the main street while he drove in an open-top car to greet them.

[14] The same is true of her sister, Dannii, who made her name in Britain via *Home and Away*.

[15] Hugh Neale Dalton, *The Fateful Years: Memoirs 1931–1945* (London: Frederick Muller, 1957),

stereotypical but they undoubtedly existed. Just as for many Australians in the nineteenth and earlier twentieth centuries Britain was 'home'. British conservative politician Henry Channon, who escorted Menzies and his party to Britain in 1941, noted that 'the excitement of Menzies' Australian entourage was touching to see as they approached England for the first time'.[16] For many British, Australia was for a long time—and probably still is—their idea of paradise, a view held not just by the ordinary man. Dalton also wrote in his diary after a visit to Australia and New Zealand in 1938: 'How much more worth defending are these sunny, healthy British Democracies in the South Pacific than the Counting Houses of the City of London, or the Snob Home Counties, or the slums of Glasgow!'[17]

The British, in fact, had and have a fairly clear idea of Australia. Australian visitors to Britain complain of the extent to which Australian affairs are unreported in the press.[18] But they usually look in the wrong part of the press. There is little paucity of reporting in the sports pages (or indeed in the financial). In the story of Anglo-Australian relations sport plays an important part. The Ashes and its immediate predecessors are the oldest international sporting competitions in the world.[19] And because Australia has so many football codes cricket has traditionally been the only national sport. Equally, though football (soccer to Australians) is unquestionably Britain's national sport, because of British football's long self-imposed isolation from the rest of the world,[20] Anglo-Australian cricket was what most British historically considered 'international' sport. Australia, not Germany or France or the United States, became the 'old enemy'. One curious feature of the modern Olympics is the extent to which the Australian and British sporting establishments regard Anglo-Australian rivalry as the centre of the games. Britain compares itself not, say, to Germany, which would be a better comparator, but to Australia. The Australians compare themselves not, say, to Canada, but to Britain. The two countries' sports ministers had a bet on the outcome of the 2012 Olympics. It is unlikely that ministers of any other two countries have a similar bet. It was 'nice to beat the old enemy on their home ground', one man said of England's victory in the Rugby World Cup in Sydney in 2003.[21] But 'old enemy'

153.

[16] Henry Channon, *Chips: The Diaries of Sir Henry Channon*, ed. R. Rhodes James (London, Weidenfeld and Nicolson, 1967), 293. The 'entourage' consisted of Sir Frederick Shedden, the secretary of the cabinet, N.C. Tritton, Samuel Landau and John Storey, men who were not easily excited. It was not, of course, Menzies' first visit. Nor was he an uncritical admirer of Britishness in wartime. See generally David Day, *Menzies and Churchill at War* (Oxford: Oxford University Press, 1993).

[17] Dalton, *Fateful Years*, 160.

[18] Kevin Foster, 'National Fictions and the Spycatcher Trial', in *Australian Popular Culture*, ed. Craven, 127. Foster notes the absence of political reporting but (in my view) underrates the significance of sporting relationships.

[19] The first Anglo-Australian cricket test match was in 1877. The Queen was present at the centenary test in 1977. Australia won by forty-five runs on both occasions.

[20] McKibbin, *Classes and Cultures: England 1918–1951* (Oxford: Oxford University Press, 1998), 378.

[21] To the author of this essay. See also Richard Hinds' comment on those Australians who went to

The Political Cultures of Australia and Britain

is (at least) a semi-affectionate description and implies shared experiences and a shared history.

Similarities

It must be admitted immediately that the social contexts in which the Australian and British political systems developed were significantly different. Australia did not have an aristocracy or a gentry with acknowledged political rights—though in some parts of rural Australia the squatters claimed such rights and were sometimes given them.[22] The monarchy as the bearer of a historically-sanctioned hierarchy pressed more lightly on Australia than it did on Britain. Social relationships were less formal and the language of politics more democratic, as was for much of the time the franchise. To that degree Neville Kirk reasonably argues that the overall 'politico-economic structures and experiences of Australia and Britain were very different'.[23] Yet it is easy to exaggerate these differences. The Australian and British socio-political systems clearly belong to the same family—something Australians acknowledge when they speak of the 'Westminster System': a phrase used more sparingly in Britain itself. They all (with the exception of Queensland, which abolished its upper house) are based upon bicameral legislatures and all adopted many of the assumptions of British anti-democratic thought. Indeed, the upper houses in the Australian colonial and later state parliaments, especially those elected on very restrictive franchises, were remarkably successful in defending the status quo, and especially successful in defending electoral boundaries heavily biased in favour of rural districts. In some states, like South Australia, such boundaries were scandalous, and in the case of South Australia these were not nineteenth century hangovers but products of the 1930s. The upper houses which defended such systems were not reformed until the last quarter of the twentieth century when, as blemishes on democracy, they were eventually, but reluctantly, recognised as indefensible. The House of Lords, of course, was (and is) equally a blemish but the Parliament Act 1911 was a mechanism by which the obstruction of an unrepresentative upper house could be overcome.[24] That was much more difficult in the Australian colonies/states system. And since the federal Australian Constitution can only be changed by referenda with strict requirements and since federal legislation is subject to review by an often conservative judiciary[25] it can be argued that for much of their joint

---

Ascot to support the Australian sprinter Black Caviar. 'To those loyalists, Black Caviar is a dinkum sheila set to land a telling blow against the Pom in this summer's eagerly (or depending on your Oi Oi Oi levels, nauseously) anticipated smackdown of the Old Enemy'. *Sydney Morning Herald*, 23–24 June 2012.

[22] There is a very good discussion of Australia's class and social system in the late nineteenth century in Beverley Kingston, *The Oxford History of Australia*, vol. 3, *Glad, Confident Morning, 1860–1900* (Melbourne: Oxford University Press, 1988), 237–90.

[23] Neville Kirk, *Labour and the Politics of Empire: Britain and Australia 1900 to the Present* (Manchester: Manchester University Press, 2011), 72.

[24] The House of Lords also lost its right to reject a money bill; a right most Australian upper houses (including the federal Senate) possessed, and in the case of the Senate still possesses, and a right sometimes used destructively.

[25] Not only must a majority of the electors vote for change so must a majority of the states,

history British bicameralism has actually been more responsive politically to social change than Australian bicameralism. A result of this is that Labour governments in Britain have faced many fewer institutional and judicial obstacles to their legislation than Australian Labor governments: one reason why the welfare legislation of the Attlee government was more extensive and complete than that of the Curtin and Chifley governments. The greater willingness of the Australians to experiment with voting procedures than the British and the undoubted fact that Australian systems of voting are more representative than the British has been only a partial counter to this.[26]

Furthermore, Australia is a monarchy and until the 1970s few Australians wished it otherwise. The monarch's representatives in Australia, the governors-general of the Commonwealth and the state governors, often members of the British elite until the mid-twentieth century, presided over little courts which were very important elements in Australian social and political life. The vice-regal pages of the *Sydney Morning Herald* or the *Age* in Melbourne were modelled on the court page of the London *Times* and there were many who read them. An inappropriate choice of viceroy excited much hostility. When William McKell, the Labor premier of New South Wales was made governor-general in 1947, Menzies described the appointment as 'shocking and humiliating'[27] and there was a whole anecdotage testifying to McKell's social unfitness for the job. (Something of the same occurred in Britain when Labour figures first became mayors and lord mayors.) The function of the viceroys was not merely ceremonial. They could (though rarely did) intervene in politics, either publicly or privately, and act in a manner which hardly any British monarch would or could have done at the same time.[28] The whole quasi-monarchic structure was, as in Britain, underpinned by the imperial honours system. As in Britain they were given in profusion, and, as in Britain, they were frequently given for political services rendered. And, yet again as in Britain, they were widely sought by a society as status-conscious as most. Even in the Labor Party, which was officially opposed to imperial honours, a number of its members were tempted and accepted them (including McKell).[29]

---

requirements almost impossible to achieve.

[26] Though not, of course, the voting procedures for the Scottish, Welsh and Northern Irish legislatures.

[27] Cited in Crisp, *Chifley*, 279.

[28] The dismissal of the Lang government in New South Wales in 1932 was probably the most defensible of these interventions since it is hard to see how the crisis which Lang's policies had created could otherwise have been resolved. Bede Nairn, *The 'Big Fella': Jack Lang and the Australian Labor Party, 1891–1949* (Melbourne: Melbourne University Press, 1986), 254–62. The dismissal of the Whitlam government by the governor-general in 1975 was, of course, immensely controversial. Arguably King George V crossed a boundary when he persuaded Ramsay MacDonald to form a 'National' government in Britain in 1931. But MacDonald needed little persuading and the Labour government had already resigned. Nonetheless, the overwhelming victory of the National government in 1931 owes something to the King. For the best single account of the 1931 crisis, see Andrew Thorpe, *The British General Election of 1931* (Oxford: Oxford University Press, 1990). For George V's role, see Kenneth Rose, *King George V* (London: Weidenfeld and Nicolson, 1983), 371–79.

[29] He was knighted when his term as governor-general was completed. Being made a privy

The 'Australianisation' of honours was not achieved until the early 1970s by the Whitlam government, a reform then partly undone by its successor.

In any case, as historian Beverley Kingston has pointed out, Australia for much of its history had a concealed and absentee ruling class as much as a quasi-monarchic one: 'investors, land and company owners, Colonial Office bureaucrats, those members of the British Establishment who made decisions or approved decisions made in Australia'.[30] Furthermore, the vacuum created by the absence of elites with inherited prestige was filled in Australia by others who claimed it and to whose standing people would defer. The social and political status of doctors in Australia, for example (a status now somewhat reduced) greatly exceeded that of doctors in Britain except for the very grandest, and that status allowed them to obstruct any reforms which they thought might undermine their standing or their incomes, as the Chifley government found after the Second World War.[31] Australia was also good at mimicking those British institutions which propped up a privileged social hierarchy. It created, for example, a system of independent schools modelled more or less on the British public schools; a system now further entrenched by lavish state funding, something inconceivable in Britain itself.

Differences

All this is to suggest that Britain and Australia have an intimate, if edgy, relationship even though Britishness matters much more in Australia than does Australianness in Britain: we can imagine Britain without Australia but not Australia without Britain. Nonetheless, it is possible to ask genuine counterfactual questions on the basis of Anglo-Australian comparisons which are real and not simply fanciful—which is what Andrew Scott and Neville Kirk have attempted in their comparative studies of the British and Australian labour parties.[32] Because of their likenesses the differences are interesting and sometimes puzzling. Why Britain is not more like Australia, and the other way round, are questions worth asking.

Many such questions doubtless could be asked, but I would like to concentrate on three themes: Britain's continued adherence to free trade when Australia adopted protection, and

---

councillor, however, was usually acceptable—at least until Whitlam refused the honour. Arthur Calwell, Whitlam's predecessor, the last Labor politician to be made privy councillor, was happy to accept one although he was not in office when he received it. (He also accepted a papal honour.) The British labour movement, despite initial hostility, especially to the peerage, eventually made its peace with the honours system in a way the Australian Labor Party never did. See McKibbin, *The Ideologies of Class* (Oxford: Oxford University Press, 1990), 19–20. See also Nicholas Owen, 'MacDonald's Parties: The Labour Party and the "Aristocratic Embrace", 1922–1931', *Twentieth Century British History*, 18 (1), 2007, 1–53.

[30] Kingston, *Glad, Confident Morning*, 278.

[31] Crisp, *Chifley*, 316–18. Something attested to in the social pages of the Australian press by the habit, for instance, of referring to 'Dr Jack and Mary Bloggs' rather than 'Jack and Mary Bloggs', as the other stars of society were. See McKibbin, 'Politics and the Medical Hero: A. J. Cronin's *The Citadel*', *English Historical Review*, CXXIII (502), 2008, 651–78.

[32] Andrew Scott, *Running on Empty: 'Modernising' the British and Australian Labour Parties* (Sydney: Pluto Press, 2000); Kirk, *Labour and the Politics of Empire*.

the consequences of such adherence; the comparative absence of sectarianism and anti-communism in Britain as compared to Australia; and the significance of the First World War in the shaping of British and Australian political culture.

Protection Versus Free Trade

Before the First World War Australia could claim to be a model democracy—even if as a model it was flawed—and that is something most Australians believed. It had most of the political institutions of a model democracy, including universal suffrage, that is men and women, but Australia, like New Zealand, also had a markedly 'social' element which was largely absent in that other model, the United States. Australia's social legislation, together with its industrial arbitration system and its large number of state-owned enterprises— 'socialism without doctrine', as Albert Métin called it[33]—was widely known in Britain and admired by many. One of the most striking features of the model was its relationship to and reliance on tariffs. The victory of protection over free trade, which meant the victory of protectionist Victoria over predominantly free-trade New South Wales, implied not just the imposition of tariffs but the development of a political and legal form of wage determination which was part of the bargain between labour and capital: protected markets meant protected wages. But it was also a statement about the kind of society most Australians wanted. We should remember that Mr Justice Henry Bournes Higgins' famous judgement in the Harvester case, designed to allow ordinary Australians 'frugal comfort', as Higgins put it, was given under customs and excise legislation, not under the arbitration acts. As John Howe has argued, 'to all intents and purposes the tariff legislation was labour law'.[34] Protection was a result of many things, but it was especially a characteristic response by a society with a small market whose costs of production were uncompetitive and where the state had, therefore, a role as 'developer' and borrower, a role it did not have in Britain. Thus one of the characteristics of Australia's doctrine-less socialism was, as we have seen, the large number of state-owned and managed enterprises. Protection was also a response to pressures from a comparatively small industrial working class which was, however, also comparatively highly unionised. It was in addition a response by a commodity-rich society which could, in a sense, afford the high production costs that protection brought with it. The extent to which protection and wage rates were intimately tied was demonstrated in the 1980s when a government determined to open the economy by reducing tariffs felt obliged to drastically reform the traditional nature of Australian wage negotiation.

In Britain, however, the same debate at the same time ended in the victory of free trade. This victory was not inevitable, even if it seemed to some that it was. Why might the same debate have gone the other way? In the first place, the Harvester judgement was

---

[33] Albert Métin, *Socialism without Doctrine*, trans. Russel Ward (Chippendale, NSW: Alternative Publishing Co-operative Ltd, 1977).

[34] John Howe, 'The Broad Idea of Labour Law: Industrial Policy, Labour Market Legislation and Decent Work', draft paper prepared for 'The Idea of Labour Law' workshop, Cambridge University, 7–8 April 2010, 2.

well-known in Britain and Higgins was a widely-admired lawyer.[35] Secondly, aspects of the Australian system, including compulsory arbitration and conciliation, always had supporters within the British labour movement. Many Fabians (including Sidney and Beatrice Webb), for example, and a number of trade union leaders like Ben Tillett and Arthur Henderson looked to the Australian system—Henderson even tried unsuccessfully to persuade the Trade Unions Congress to accept compulsory arbitration.[36] In the third place, there were close relations between Australian and British unions and in several cases, like the Engineers, the Australian unions were simply affiliates of their British founders. Some of the legislation supported by British unions, like that on the sweated trades, was based on Australian examples.[37]

Most importantly, however, the triumph of the Australian system in Britain was a real possibility because Joseph Chamberlain led an attack on free trade which converted the Conservative Party to protection in some form.[38] Even after the mid-Victorian triumph of free trade and the Peelite-Gladstonian system based upon it, protection never entirely went away. It lurked in agricultural pressure groups particularly, often in the guise of 'fair trade' and began to make headway in those parts of British industry feeling the bitter wind of German and American competition. It was Chamberlain's decision to campaign for imperial preference and a measure of industrial protection in 1903 which brought these movements together. Many of those, like E. E. Williams, author of the famous quasi-protectionist manual, *Made in Germany* (1896), became unqualified protectionists, which most always had been (even if only privately). Chamberlain's motives were mixed. He was worried that the Conservative Party was losing its working-class support (as it was);[39] he was sensitive to those parts of British industry, like chemicals, electrics and fine steel, which were wilting before German competition; he argued that industry was being neglected in the interests of finance and the City of London; and he became convinced that Britain's status as a great power could be preserved only by mobilising the empire—not through sentiment alone but via the distribution of economic privileges—as a British zollverein (a word he himself used). Although he devised what he thought was a policy attractive to as many people as possible, his appeal to the unions was in fact quasi-socialist. Why should

---

[35] B. S. Rowntree has a quotation from Higgins as epigraph to both editions of his *Human Needs of Labour* (London: Thomas Nelson and Sons, 1918 and 1937), which argued for a 'living wage' and was a departure from the subsistence wage Rowntree had used as a benchmark in *Poverty: A Study of Town Life* (London: Macmillan and Co., 1901).

[36] McKibbin, *Parties and People: England 1914–1951* (Oxford: Oxford University Press, 2010), 19.

[37] Kirk, *Labour and the Politics of Empire*, 19–23.

[38] For the fiscal debate in Britain see Alan Sykes, *Tariff Reform in British Politics, 1903–1913* (Oxford: Oxford University Press, 1979); E. H. H. Green, *The Crisis of Conservatism: The Politics, Economics and Ideology of the British Conservative Party, 1880–1914* (London and New York: Routledge, 1995); F. Trentmann, *Free Trade Nation* (Oxford: Oxford University Press, 2008); Anthony Howe, *Free Trade and Liberal England, 1846–1946* (Oxford: Clarendon Press, 1997).

[39] Chamberlain's campaign began when it became obvious from by-elections that the post-Boer War Conservative Party was in a bad way. It is important to note that its electoral decline predated that campaign. See A. K. Russell, *Liberal Landslide: The General Election of 1906* (London: David & Charles, 1973), 26–9.

bodies whose function within Britain was to obstruct the workings of the free market not wish to obstruct the workings of the international free market? Protection was simply their usual policy in a different sphere. Tariffs guaranteed jobs for all and higher wages for many. Free trade, he argued, was therefore incompatible with the society the unions sought to create.[40]

There was thus a strong intellectual and economic case for protection. Yet, as we know, Chamberlain's campaign failed. Part of the problem was that Chamberlain tried to do either too much or too little. By attempting to combine imperial preference—a system whereby the primary products of the white settler colonies would gain preferential access to the British market in return for their giving British manufacturers preferential access to their markets—with proposals to guarantee the British working man full employment, to rescue both the empire and the British economy, he ensured that both would fail. And it was unlikely that he himself could have lived with a wage structure which, however protected the market, significantly raised the labour costs of employers. Furthermore, much of his potential support turned out to be only potential. Although Chamberlain promised that raw materials, like American cotton, would not be subject to duty,[41] virtually the whole of the Lancashire cotton textile industry was against the proposals, and there was surprisingly little comfort to be had from those industries most harmed by German and American competition, or, less surprisingly perhaps, from of the City of London, or from the trade unions. Indeed, there was apparently little working-class support.

Even allowing for the muddled nature of Chamberlain's proposals this absence needs explaining. Some of it was a result of simple economic self-interest. There were too many people who were convinced that free trade served them better than protection, that individual trade treaties between Britain and other countries resolved the problem of protection, even if the evidence for this was becoming increasingly doubtful, and that keeping food prices low (the 'cheap loaf' as against the 'dear loaf') was both politically and economically necessary in a country seventy-five per cent of whose population belonged to the manual working class and who could not, unlike those in Australia, possibly feed themselves. Above all, free trade lay at the heart of a pluralist system of government and an ideological consensus which hardened into a religion: something, like all religions, it became dangerous to question. Free trade not only apparently favoured the textile magnates[42] and the City of London, it was very favourable both to working-class politics and to legally unconstrained union activity, and with that the unfettered free collective

---

[40] See Chamberlain's speech at Liverpool, October 1903, in *Mr Chamberlain's Speeches*, vol. 2, ed. C. W. Boyd (London: Constable and Co., 1914), 199–218.

[41] A promise which drew from H. H. Asquith the almost unanswerable question: since the bulk of Britain's imports from a country like the United States (whose tariffs had done real damage to British manufactures) were raw materials what, then, was Britain going to retaliate upon? See 'Mr. Asquith's Speech at Cinderford', in H. H. Asquith, *Trade and the Empire: Mr Chamberlain's Proposals Examined in Four Speeches and a Prefatory Note* (London: Methuen and Co., 1903). The policy of retaliation was A. J. Balfour's attempt to devise a compromise on protectionism.

[42] Though it is arguable that the Indian market, rigged in favour of British cotton exports such that India became in effect a protected British market, was just as significant.

bargaining which was to remain the basis of Britain's industrial relations until the 1980s.[43]

The British determination to preserve free trade, however, had one important further consequence. The attraction of Australian protectionism was that it suggested to many British that tariffs alone allowed an advanced social policy. But Britain's Edwardian Liberal governments, precisely to preserve the hegemony of free trade, undertook an ambitious social welfare policy which suggested that free trade could do the same. That, and constitutional legislation which much weakened the House of Lords, made the Australian model less attractive or important.

One complicated variable in all this is race. It could be argued that a necessary condition for Australia's comparatively high-wage protected economy was racial exclusion. W. K. Hancock, for instance, argued in 1930 that the White Australia policy 'was the indispensable condition of every other Australian policy'.[44] Marilyn Lake and Henry Reynolds have suggested that it 'was the White Australia Policy that distinguished Australia from Britain in 1901 and underpinned assertions of sovereignty; it was the White Australia Policy, as Alfred Deakin had proclaimed, that "was the founding creed of our nationality"'.[45]

Just how necessary White Australia actually was to the system of wage determination and fiscal policy that emerged in Australia before and after the First World War must, however, be doubtful. It might have required regulated immigration but certainly did not depend on a colour bar as such. It is more likely that it was driven by racial ideologies mixed up with a secondary belief that an Asian workforce would be a cheap workforce and thus opposed to the economic interests of Anglo-Celtic Australia.

Racism was less obviously central to Britain. Though certainly not absent its origins were probably more conventionally economic and political. Before 1905 there were no formal bars on entry to Britain by anyone, though the Home Office had the power to exclude those thought undesirable—a power rarely used. The first formal restriction was the Aliens Act 1905 which attempted to exclude Russian Jewish paupers and followed a political agitation in East London against 'cheap' and 'unfair' Jewish labour. But the 1905 Act was not, in fact, very strict, and came when Jewish migration had started to decline anyway. There was similar anti-alien legislation at the beginning of and immediately after the First World War (the Aliens Registration Act 1914, Aliens Restriction (Amendment) Act 1919 and the Aliens Order 1920). The victims on this occasion were either Germans thought to be bent on Britain's ruin or Russians thought to harbour bolshevism, but they technically brought all foreign citizens within the 1905 legislation. It was this legislation that made it difficult for German and Austrian Jewish refugees to gain entry into Britain in the 1930s—though in

---

[43] I think the legal significance of free trade for British unions is rather underplayed by Keith Ewing in his otherwise excellent comparison of the evolution of British and Australian labour law. See Keith Ewing, 'Australian and British Labour Law: Differences of Form or Substance?', *Australian Journal of Labour Law*, 11 (1), 1998, 11–32.

[44] W. K. Hancock, *Australia* (London: Ernest Benn Limited, 1930), 77–81. Hancock's treatment of the White Australia policy was largely sympathetic.

[45] Marilyn Lake and Henry Reynolds (with Mark McKenna and Joy Damousi), *What's Wrong With Anzac?* (Sydney: University of New South Wales Press, 2010), 20. For a more general discussion, see Marilyn Lake and Henry Reynolds, *Drawing the Global Colour Line: White Men's Countries and the Question of Racial Equality* (Melbourne: Melbourne University Press, 2008).

the end about 60 000 were admitted.[46] This was in some senses racist legislation. However, neither this nor the labour movement's hostility to the use of Chinese labour in South Africa was of the White Australia kind. The objection here was not to the Chinese *qua* Chinese but as indentured cheap labour introduced by the mining companies which would apparently deprive the white man of the best jobs in South African mining. While there was always controversy in the British port towns about foreign merchant seaman—some of whom were British subjects—there were few formal restrictions on right of entry for citizens of the empire, while the 1948 British nationality legislation specifically gave full right of entry to all citizens of the Commonwealth regardless of colour. Such automatic right was not abolished until 1961 when Britain was experiencing for the first time large scale non-white immigration—legislation which in the long term proved relatively ineffective.[47]

What most distinguished Britain from Australia, however, was that much the largest source of 'foreign' labour to Britain was Ireland; labour that could not be excluded even after the creation of the Irish Free State in 1922 or the proclamation of the Irish Republic in 1948. The Irish always had (and still have) uninhibited right of entry to Great Britain despite their religion (Catholic) and nationality (disloyal). To this degree it was not possible for Britain to have a 'White Britain' policy regardless of how many British wished to exclude the 'black' Irish.[48]

Yet even if we conclude that White Australia was not a necessary condition for protection and the judicially-established basic wage, many Australians thought it was. Was there a similar relationship between Britain's immigration policies and free trade and free collective bargaining? Some have argued that the relative openness of Britain before 1914 was a function of free trade: as a factor of production free movement of labour was as much a part of free trade as freedom of capital.[49] To the extent that free trade was an intellectually coherent system this should have been true. Furthermore, we might argue that the British were themselves an emigrant and mobile nation. Except for comparatively brief periods (the 1930s, the later 1990s and early 2000s) many more have left Britain than have arrived. But Britain was not all that open—we might say it was more porous than open—and the history of British immigration policy, particularly when 'colour' was the issue, suggests that whenever openness came under pressure it buckled. Given these considerations it would not, therefore, have required much for Britain to have adopted protection. The balance, though it usually favoured free trade until the early 1930s, was always fine. Australia was the

---

[46] Louise London, *Whitehall and the Jews, 1933–1948: British Immigration Policy, Jewish Refugees and the Holocaust* (Cambridge: Cambridge University Press 2000).

[47] It had some part in the exclusion of West Indian migrants, but just as significant were changes in American and Canadian legislation which made it easier for West Indians to migrate to North America. As a means of excluding or even seriously regulating the inflow of non-white migrants over the next forty years it largely failed—primarily because for much of the time the asylum laws were liberally interpreted and the legislation itself was weakly enforced.

[48] Since 2008 there has been another big Irish migration to Britain. In 1912 there were 360 000 Irish nationals in Britain; a number exceeded only by the Poles whose numbers are somewhere between 500 000 and 700 000.

[49] See, for example, John Garrard, *The English and Immigration, 1880–1910* (London and New York: Oxford University Press, 1971).

alternative; never adopted but always in view. The consequences, however, of not adopting it became all too clear after the First World War. Free trade was preserved in circumstances which were highly unfavourable to Britain, as John Maynard Keynes eventually came to admit.[50] It precluded until the 1930s one of the few strategies then available to British governments to deal with high unemployment. The problem of unemployment was deemed secondary to the demands of the London money market and the city's institutions, and it kept in place, at the insistence of the unions, a form of free collective bargaining which did little to maintain employment or raise real wages; or if did raise them it was at the expense of the unemployed. But what the Australian example in the early 1930s could suggest, and not only to conservatives, was the dangers rather than the advantages of protection. In 1931 Winston Churchill, still a free trader, told Harold Nicolson that the policy of Oswald Mosley's New Party (which favoured protection and with which Nicolson was associated) that was 'based upon High Tariffs plus the conciliation of the Trades Unions would lead England to a crisis of bankruptcy equalled only by that which Australia has obtained'.[51]

What would a visitor to Britain and Australia at the end of the First World War have observed? He would see in Australia a state, either on its own or through the judicial system, much more active in economic development—and borrowing much more than it should have done to promote it—and much more active in the determination of wages and conditions. As Keith Hancock said of Australia in the 1920s: 'Australian democracy has come to look upon the State as a vast public utility, whose duty it is to provide the greatest happiness for the greatest number'.[52] The observer would not have seen the same in Britain. On the contrary, he would have seen a state determined to restore the pre-war financial and fiscal system and ready to deflate its economy heavily in order to do so. But he would have seen a state capable of providing a kind of wage through unemployment benefit that kept large numbers of people alive and not starving almost indefinitely—a perverse but nonetheless almost unique form of social generosity. He would also have noted that as a social laboratory Australia was, rightly or wrongly, no longer a model to the rest of the world. Although the arbitration system was largely put in place after the First World War, particularly the federal system, it was something with which people were already familiar. Australia continued to develop structures which, as C. Hartley Grattan pointed out, were largely Edwardian.[53] As a dynamic system the Australian model was almost played out, as the abandonment of the Lyons government's national insurance legislation seemed to show. Australia, however, was always only a model to the British left, never to the British right. Thus in the interwar years, insofar as the British left looked abroad for models after 1935, it was to Sweden or New Zealand[54] since Australia only offered a pattern of industrial

---

[50] Though Keynes tended to favour tariffs when he concluded no one would devalue the pound. When the pound was devalued by about one third in 1931 he thought tariffs were less necessary.

[51] Harold Nicolson Diary, 8 June, 1931, MS Nicolson, Balliol College Archives, Oxford. Nicolson became an MP in 1935.

[52] Hancock, *Australia*, 72.

[53] C. Hartley Grattan, 'The Future in Australia', *Australian Quarterly*, 10 (4), 1938, 7–29.

[54] See McKibbin, *Parties and People*, 157; and Peter Baldwin, *The Politics of Social Solidarity: Class Bases of the European Welfare State* (Cambridge: Cambridge University Press, 1990).

relations which was for historic reasons, as I have suggested, unacceptable to most of the British labour movement, but apparently offered little else.[55]

Sectarianism and Anti-communism

The observer, especially if he were long-lived, would further have noted the degree of religious sectarianism in Australia as compared to Britain. Sectarianism was not, of course, unknown in Britain. That would scarcely have been possible in a country with such a large Irish population. In areas of Irish settlement, such as Merseyside, Clydeside and parts of London, sectarianism drove politics.[56] Yet it never had the corrosiveness of Australian sectarianism. No-one growing up in Australia, before the 1960s at least, particularly in relatively small communities like country towns, could be unaware of how fundamental the Protestant–Catholic divide was and how carefully nurtured were these resentments and hostilities. Nor could anyone be unaware of the extent to which conservative politics was suffused with anti-Catholicism, either directly, or indirectly via its associated temperance or anti-betting societies or Orange lodges. In Britain such distinctions were never so fundamental. Why? Part of the answer lies in the different character of the Catholic Church in Britain. Its episcopacy was less Irish, drawn from a wider social background, and more conscious of the Established Church and its standing.[57]

The episcopacy was also more cautious. There were no hell-raisers like the Australian Archbishop Daniel Mannix. However, it also seemed to be more divided. Thus in 1926 Cardinal Francis Bourne, the Archbishop of Westminster, who presided over a diverse and socially ambitious flock, was bitterly opposed to the general strike, while the Archbishop of Liverpool, whose constituency was overwhelmingly Irish and working class, was sympathetic. It was therefore difficult to promote an agreed 'Catholic' position on anything much, except perhaps on issues like the Spanish Civil War or ethical issues such as birth control—and even on birth control Catholic practice clearly differed from Catholic teaching. In Britain the desire for acceptance was more open than in Australia, where it was more concealed, if just as strong.[58] Britain's Irish community was probably less cohesive and more mobile than Australia's. It tended to drift back and forth between Britain and Ireland and the drama of Ireland's history was more likely to take place in Ireland itself rather than in Britain.[59] In fact, the kind of politics with which Australians became familiar was exported from Britain to Northern Ireland. With the creation of the Irish Free State in 1922 the 'problem' of Ireland lost its force in Britain while the bulk of Britain's Irish found their political home in the Labour Party and in its (mostly) secular politics.[60]

---

[55] Though Keynes believed that the Premiers' Plan did offer a model other similarly stressed economies could adopt.

[56] For an indispensable study of this, see P. J. Waller, *Democracy and Sectarianism: A Political and Social History of Liverpool, 1868–1939* (Liverpool: Liverpool University Press, 1981).

[57] See McKibbin, *Classes and Cultures*, 285–88.

[58] The late Tony Cahill, who knew Australian Catholicism as well as anybody, said of Cardinal Gilroy's knighthood that 'it is what they always wanted'. Private communication to the author.

[59] J. A. Jackson, *The Irish in Britain* (London: Routledge and Kegan Paul, 1963).

[60] Illustrated in December 1929 when the seat of Liverpool Scotland, the only constituency in

Finally, the question of state aid to Catholic education, which was to become such a divisive issue in Australia, was avoided in Britain because state aid was never abandoned, as it had been in Australia in the late nineteenth century. The determination of the Conservative Party to protect the Anglican elementary schools—which in 1900 educated more than half of Britain's children—by granting them state assistance meant that on grounds of fairness the Roman Catholic schools also had to be supported. This was 'Rome on the rates'—the funding of Catholic as well as Anglican schools by the state—so disliked by many nonconformists. The Education Act 1902, which introduced such state support, had two consequences.[61] First, it kept the Catholic schools within the state system. The British Catholic schools thus never nourished that sense of alienation and exclusion which characterised the Australian Catholic school system for much of the twentieth century. If the Catholics in Britain had a grievance it was over the amount of state payment; the principle was not at issue. Second, it was more difficult in Britain, precisely because of nonconformist hostility to the Established Church and its pretensions—especially educational—to create that anti-Catholic 'Protestant' front so easily mobilised in Australia. In Britain, there has always been doubt both within and without the Church of England how 'Protestant' it actually was, other than for the purposes of the royal succession. In Australia there was little doubt for most of its adherents that Anglicanism was Protestant. Indeed, the archdiocese of Sydney became notorious for a low-church Anglicanism indistinguishable from evangelical Protestantism.

The observer would also have noted the strength of anti-socialism and, often the same thing, of anti-communism in Australia as compared to Britain. Writing of the interwar years, Kirk has suggested that 'the tarring of labour was more evident and sustained in Australia than in Britain'.[62] Partly because that has become a historical commonplace it is easy, in fact, to exaggerate the comparative absence of tarring in Britain. Our observer would, for example, have seen the relentless tarring that kept Ramsay MacDonald out of parliament in 1921, in a campaign that did not differ much from the campaign that denied Hugh Mahon a return to the federal Australian parliament at almost the same time.[63] If he observed the anti-bolshevism of the 1924 elections, or the conservative press before and after the 1926 general strike, or during the 1931 election campaign, he might further

---

Britain to be held by an Irish Nationalist, T. P. O'Connor, passed on his death into the hands of the Labour Party.

[61] For a good general discussion of the Education Act 1902, see S. J. Curtis, *History of Education in Great Britain* (London: University Tutorial Press, 1968), 310–21.

[62] Kirk, *Labour and the Politics of Empire*, 126.

[63] In January 1921 the Labour Party decided to return MacDonald (who had been defeated in the 1918 election) to parliament via a by-election in the safe Labour seat of East Woolwich. After a vicious 'patriotic' campaign MacDonald was defeated by Capt. Gee, a non-political soldier who had won the Victoria Cross at Cambrai. The seat returned to Labour at the 1922 election. For this episode, see David Marquand, *Ramsay MacDonald* (London: Jonathan Cape Ltd, 1977), 272–75. Hugh Mahon, a minister in the Watson, Fisher and Hughes governments, was expelled from the House of Representatives at Hughes' instigation in 1919—for making an 'unpatriotic' speech—and lost his seat of Kalgoorlie at the subsequent by-election in 1920. He is the only member to have been expelled from the federal parliament. The speech, almost inevitably, was about Ireland.

wonder how emollient and open British society really was. Equally, it is questionable how electorally successful such strategies were in Australia, at least in isolation. Rather they were one part of conservative rhetoric and not necessarily the most important. Nonetheless, its promoters thought it effective and it indirectly led to the split in the Australian Labor Party (ALP) in 1954–55, a boon to the conservative forces which had worked so hard to achieve it. The historian, like anyone who lived through the period, is immediately struck by how much more central anti-communism was to the political culture of Australia than it was in Britain. Britain did not try to ban the Communist Party after the Second World War; the British Labour Party was not seriously divided about the issue of communism; the British unions, except in the case of the Electricians' Union, were not riven by it. Where the unions did have a partly communist leadership (as the miners did), that leadership tended to behave as unionists rather than communists.[64] How do we explain these differences? Why did communism seem to be so much more of an issue in Australia than in Britain?

One explanation must lie in the different character of the countries' labour movements. For much of this period, until the end of the Second World War, the ALP was much stronger than the British Labour Party. Even during its worst days in the 1920s and 1930s the ALP mobilised much more of the electorate than did its British equivalent, and it continued to match the popularity of the conservative parties in the states. In Australia, therefore, the anti-labour forces had more to worry about. The one moment in Britain when it appeared that the Labour Party's growth might be unstoppable—the early 1920s—was the moment when the rhetoric of anti-socialism and anti-bolshevism was most vigorous. As it became clear that the old party system was more deeply rooted than in Australia, the rhetoric flagged. Within the two labour movements the position of the trade unions in Australia was always more alarming to their opponents than in Britain. The history of the British Labour Party cannot, of course, be written without the unions, but their attachment to the party was less fundamental than in Australia. No British union, for example, had a relationship to politics like that of the Australian Workers' Union. And because, for reasons we shall see, the Australian unions were more radical and less parliamentary that relationship was destabilising. The history of the New South Wales Labor Party in the 1920s or 1930s, for example, a story of conservatism, socialism, communism, trade unionism, tammany, Sinn Fein, general corruption and colossal personal egoism—all summed up in Premier J. T. Lang's second government—could not be replicated in Britain.[65] The fact that in office many of these ALP governments were anything but radical did not necessarily change the way outsiders saw them.

The differing fiscal systems were important. Protection and compulsory arbitration in Australia to some extent shielded the unions. It gave them a freedom of manoeuvre that free trade, whatever its other advantages, denied the British unions. Free trade implied market discipline: it made production costs more central to debate in Britain than in Australia, where the workforce could hide beneath tariffs. Free trade also brought with it

---

[64] For a good example of this, see Nina Fishman, *Arthur Horner: A Political Biography*, vol. 2, *1944–1968* (London: Lawrence and Wishart, 2010), 774–801, 955–72. The British Communist Party was, of course, never monolithic.

[65] Nairn, *The 'Big Fella'*, 183–261.

free collective bargaining, which was intended to be essentially non-political. Rather than being dependent on law it depended on the absence of law. It therefore made the British unions very ambivalent about political action and their relationship to the Labour Party. On the whole, they wanted to keep politics and the law out of it; whereas politics and the law were central to the Australian system. The general strike in 1926, for example, was conducted with virtually no regard to the British Labour Party, for which the Labour Party rather than the unions actually paid the penalty.[66]

The increasing salience of anti-communism in Australia was partly due to the degree to which the Catholic Church there had become politicised. As I have suggested, Britain had no equivalent to Archbishop Mannix and the Catholic Church in Victoria. The British church was more like the Catholic Church in New South Wales under Cardinal Gilroy—cautious and reluctant to become too involved.[67] But the church in Victoria under Mannix had become used to ideological politics, to taking public positions. As a defence of Ireland and its independence became more or less redundant after 1922 the threat of communism became Mannix's idée fixe and that of those around him, like B. A. Santamaria.[68] Thus the corporatist teaching of the Catholic Rural Movement had a place in Catholic thought in Australia which similar ideas, like those of G. K. Chesterton and Hilaire Belloc, never had in Britain. Equally, the church in Australia became involved in the anti-communist politics of the trade unions, through the industrial groups, in a way that had no equal in Britain. Even if we argue that the split in the Australian Labor Party in the 1950s was avoidable it is undeniable that Catholic activity of this sort was deeply disruptive, and that there was no similar disruption in Britain.

The depth of this dispute in Australia probably reflects a comparatively weak sense of national identity and less agreement on fundamental social values. In Britain, that sense was wider and stronger. Britain's dominant social and political values, those represented by the Conservative Party, tended to be the values shared by all, or nearly all. One measure of this is the fact that in Britain in both world wars it was possible to form all-party governments whereas in Australia it was not. And even before such governments were formed the parties agreed on a wartime electoral 'truce'—an agreement not to oppose each other in by-elections. This also was not possible in Australia. Outsiders visiting Australia in the Second

---

[66] I have discussed this elsewhere. See McKibbin, *Parties and People*, 55–57, 74–77. For the relationship between the Labour Party and the unions in the interwar years, see generally H. A. Clegg, *A History of the British Trade Unions since 1889*, vol. 2, *1911–1933* (Oxford: Clarendon, 1985); David Howell, *MacDonald's Party: Labour Identities and Crisis, 1922–1931* (Oxford: Oxford University Press, 2002), esp. Part II. The best account of the general strike is still G. A. Phillips, *The General Strike: The Politics of Industrial Conflict* (London: Weidenfeld and Nicolson, 1976).

[67] Mannix was never made a cardinal and his politics was probably the reason. It is also worth noting that Australia has had six prime ministers of Irish origin, all Labor or ex-Labor, and all Catholic. Britain in the modern era has had only one, James Callaghan, and he was not raised a Catholic.

[68] For a good sense of these politics, see B. A. Santamaria, *Daniel Mannix: The Quality of Leadership* (Melbourne: Melbourne University Press, 1984). See also B. A. Santamaria, *Santamaria: A Memoir* (Melbourne: Oxford University Press, 1997).

World War were sometimes struck by this comparative lack of social cohesion.[69] A second measure is that the Labour Party's conception of the state was fundamentally a Tory one, which is why it has found large-scale reform of the state—even of the electoral system— so difficult.[70] That is perhaps one reason why Australian trade unions were much more reluctant to detach themselves from the communists than were the British, more reluctant to abandon unity tickets, since the dominant values, though very like the British, were less widely or more weakly held. One consequence, as we have seen, was that in Britain the Catholic Church, though equally anti-communist, felt little need to intervene in politics as actively as parts of the Australian church did. The other was that many Australians believed that the British Labour Party was overconcerned with respectability. In April 1940, for example, Chifley wrote to his future ministerial colleague, Arthur Drakeford, that he hoped the Australian Labour Party

> is not trying to grow too respectable. The Labour Party in England has been making itself very patriotic and the only result is that nobody takes any notice of Attlee—unless it is to quote his utterances as regards the Reds.[71]

Kirk has suggested that geographical contiguity, Australia's closeness to Asia, was one reason why political anti-communism was stronger in Australia than in Britain. By 1948, he argues, the British no longer feared the advance of communism and were, in any case, about to be protected by the atom bomb.[72] In Asia, on the contrary, communism continued to advance. There is doubtless some basis for Australia's fear of communism. Even so, Canberra was much more distant from communism than London and we still must ask how rational the Australian fear really was. That the 'threat' was Asian is probably more important than that it was communist. It fits all too well with historic Australian racial fears of being overwhelmed from the north—something which almost certainly still drives the Australian obsession with boat people and 'illegal' asylum seekers. Furthermore, although many people on the Australian right appear to have thought a third world war imminent in the early 1950s, the politics of anti-communism was so polluted by domestic electoral considerations as to make one suspicious of 'rational' arguments.

The Impact of the First World War

If we agree, as I think we should, that for much of the twentieth century, for all their likenesses, Australia was a less cohesive society than Britain, arguably the most important single reason for this was their different experience of the First World War. It was for every participant, with the possible exception of the United States, probably a disaster. It certainly was for Australia. Quite apart from the huge human and physical losses for which the war was responsible, it profoundly embittered political life, aggravated sectarianism, destroyed the hegemony of the Labor Party and with it of Australian radicalism, enthroned

---

[69] For examples, see Max Hastings, *Nemesis: The Battle for Japan, 1944–45* (London: Harper Perennial, 2008), 363–72.

[70] See McKibbin, *Parties and People*, 199–201.

[71] Cited in Crisp, *Chifley*, 125–26.

[72] Kirk, *Labour and the Politics of Empire*, 197–98.

a narrow and semi-authoritarian conservatism and entrenched an imperial-minded British race patriotism which the British themselves did not necessarily share. It directly and indirectly shattered personal lives in ways no amount of Anzac rhetoric could conceal.[73] It significantly strengthened the conservative–nationalist forces, already strong, in Australian life. Australia ended the war a more conservative and arguably less democratic society than it was when it began.

The British experience was different. The human and physical losses were, of course, also huge and in 1918 Britain was a diminished power. Yet in many respects it ended the war a less conservative and more democratic society. Even during the war itself the Defence of the Realm Act 1914 (UK) was never used as ferociously as the Australian *War Precautions Act 1914*, nor did Liberal wartime prime ministers Henry Herbert Asquith or Lloyd George behave as Hughes did and was allowed to do. The war also had different consequences to party structures. In Australia the war did immense damage to the Labor Party. In Britain the war gave the British Labour Party its opportunities, and though its record in the interwar years was disappointing, its mere existence acted as a brake on more ambitious plans for a conservative political and economic reconstruction. Thus, despite the predictions of Keynes and others, the general strike was not followed by an attack on real wage levels since that was now thought too risky. Nor did the program of the National government in 1931 have the remorselessness of the Premiers' Plan. By the late 1930s that government had even become cautiously interventionist and there was a steady, if haphazard, expansion of a proto-welfare state. Furthermore, the definition of the good life had broadened in Britain after the war even if what actually followed was less broad.[74] At the non-state level, the level of voluntarism and quasi-politics, it can certainly be argued that Britain was significantly more democratic and participatory than it had been, and it did not require state compulsion[75] to achieve this.[76]

The principal reason for such differences lies in distinct forms of post-war political reconstruction. In Australia electoral mobilisation during and after the war was conservative–nationalist. It was upon this that post-war Australian politics rested. In Britain, reconstruction, though it could have taken the Australian form (and almost did), was dependent upon a different form of mobilisation. The determination of the Conservative Party to assimilate the Liberal Party and liberalism significantly modified its traditional attitudes. One of the main functions of Baldwinite conservatism was to make itself acceptable to former Liberals. Thus, for instance, liberal internationalism and liberal imperialism replaced more traditional and aggressive conservative policies. A comparison between the Australian Returned Services League (RSL) and its British equivalent, the British Legion, is instructive. Both came to be the accepted voice of ex-soldiers, even though most

---

[73] A theme well captured in Roger McDonald's novel *1915* (1979) and in the ABC television series based upon it.

[74] McKibbin, *Parties and People*, 196.

[75] As in the introduction of compulsory voting in Australia.

[76] Although I would not go as far as she does, this case has been strongly made by Helen McCarthy, 'Whose Democracy? Histories of British Political Culture Between the Wars', *Historical Journal*, 55 (1), 2012, 221–38.

ex-soldiers did not belong to them, and both eliminated left-wing alternatives. Both were part of conservative political associationalism. But there the comparison stops. The British Legion was politically cautious, reluctant to alienate the Labour Party and always eschewed conservative–nationalist rhetoric. Its politics were Baldwinite rather than diehard. It never sought the political prominence that the RSL in Australia sought and obtained. Nor did it express the same views as loudly and publicly.[77]

Conclusion

For all the continuing connections, by the 1960s the distances between Australia and Britain were becoming apparent and the distances will almost inevitably grow wider. For the generation of Australians for whom the cultural and political links with Britain were central to their lives this could cause much sorrow and cultural disorientation.[78] Increasing ignorance has played its part. The British have never known much about the details of Australian political structures, but the Australians, through an anglicised educational system, knew a great deal about Britain's. That is no longer true, and it is sometimes the most educated who know the least.[79] Several of the issues that seemed most fundamental to both countries, the sectarian divide (especially in Australia) for example, have for now lost much of their significance, as has the old class system which underpinned the politics of both societies, to be replaced by others, race and immigration for example.

Paradoxically, however, though the cultural differences between the two have widened, the political and economic differences have narrowed. Much of the neoliberal program and its vocabulary (not least, as we have noted, the word 'privatisation'), dominant in the last thirty years, was borrowed by Australia from Britain as well as America, just as what we might call neoliberal policies to the universities were originally borrowed by Britain from Australia. Indeed, it is now arguable, with the great days of Australian protectionism gone, along with the world of the C Series Index and the metal trades award, that the political economies of Britain and Australia are now more alike than they have been since the late nineteenth century. Furthermore, Australia has once again become a possible model. Although I have argued that for much of their history Britain's was the more cohesive society, it is now significantly less cohesive than it was. Apart from social strains now common to all European states, the main reason for this has been the slow disintegration of the

---

[77] For the British Legion, see G. Wootton, *The Official History of the British Legion* (London: Macdonald and Evans, 1956); A. P. Latcham, 'Journey's End: Ex-servicemen and the State During and After the Great War', DPhil, Oxford University, 1997; McKibbin, *Classes and Cultures*, 96.

[78] For two very good examples of this (Keith Hancock and Owen Dixon), see Jim Davidson, *A Three-Cornered Life: The Historian W. K. Hancock* (Sydney: University of New South Wales Press, 2010); and Philip Ayres, *Owen Dixon* (Melbourne: Miegunyah Press, 2003).

[79] I heard an instance of this in Australia in 1998. On the day of the 1998 election I was talking to a woman serving on the Liberal how-to-vote table and a man on the One Nation table. The Liberal wanted to know how the British elected their senate and was told rather sharply by the One Nation man that Britain had a House of Lords, which was not elected. (He also lamented the likely disappearance, as it then appeared, of the pound sterling.) It is scarcely conceivable that a politically active Australian conservative of an earlier generation would not have known about the House of Lords.

historic United Kingdom. Britain has become, both formally and informally, increasingly federalised and Britons thus look to federal states, Australia, Canada, Germany (but rarely the United States) as models, even if they do so without any clear idea of what a federal Britain might look like and how it might be achieved.

What the future historian of Anglo-Australian neoliberalism or British federalism will make of them we cannot know. But historical comparisons, where they are legitimate, can be telling and oblige us to see individual histories in different ways. For the historian of Britain's political culture, in particular, there are two such 'lessons'. The first is that Britain could have been a very different and perhaps more egalitarian society had it abandoned free trade at the moment Australia did. The second is that the First World War had important but different consequences in Australia and Britain. Before the war, Australia was by most criteria a more democratic and possibly more cohesive society than Britain. After 1918 that was less true. The political and religious divisions which marked Australian life during and after the First World War, though not absent, were significantly weaker in Britain, while anti-democratic influences in Australia became probably more powerful than in Britain. Popular conceptions of Australia as democratic and open and Britain as closed and hidebound, while not without truth, thus become more fragile under close examination—especially when we remember the long-term consequences in Britain of the social and constitutional policies of Edwardian Liberal governments which significantly diminished the difference between Australia and Britain as democratic societies.

10

The 'New Nationalism' in Australia, Canada and New Zealand: Civic Culture in the Wake of the British World

Stuart Ward

Writing in August 1964, the editor of the Montreal newspaper *Le Monde*, Claude Ryan, offered a penetrating commentary on the contemporary plight of 'les Canadiens anglais':

> *La project Pearson est une reaction contre ce vieux nationalisme. Il exprime, gauchement peut-etre, un nouveau nationalisme qui se voudrait plus completement canadien.*

> [The Pearson project is a reaction against the old nationalism. It expresses, perhaps awkwardly, a new nationalism that seeks to be more completely Canadian.]

Ryan was writing in the context of the bitter flag debate that had assumed centre stage in the spring and summer of that year. The Pearson government's determination to invest the *nouveau nationalisme* with new civic emblems and ideals was an exercise fraught with political pitfalls. As Ryan argued, it ran the risk of aggravating the existing divisions between French and English Canadians by prising open latent divisions within English Canada itself—namely between Pearson's converts to the Maple Leaf, and the conservative adherents to the Union Jack and the ideal of an imperial Canada.[1]

Four years later in Australia, Donald Horne (writing in *The Bulletin* and completely independently of Ryan) coined precisely the same phrase, 'the New Nationalism', to describe the political and rhetorical style of Australian prime minister John Gorton. Like Pearson in Canada, Gorton seemed to represent the dawning of a new era in Australian politics, heralding 'the beginnings of what is likely to be the most coherent and determined attempt of an Australian Prime Minister to identify himself with a nationalist spirit'. While recognising that the new nationalism would arouse distrust among 'certain kinds of Australians', Horne nonetheless hoped that Gorton might take a leaf (excuse the pun) out of Canada's book by pressing for a new flag and anthem in order 'to provide something of our own'.[2]

Within three months, the first New Zealand-born governor-general, Sir Arthur Porritt, was proudly proclaiming that 'the events of the last year or two have given New Zealand a new sense of national entity'.[3] Porritt offered little in the way of explanation or example, but he was clearly indulging in the same tentative probing for new objects of civic identification that had characterised recent politics in Canada and Australia. Within three years, New Zealanders, too, would have a political leader capable of exploiting the language and rhetoric of new nationalism, in Labour's Norman Kirk.

---

[1] 'Le Dilemme du Drapeau', *Le Devoir*, 15 August 1964.
[2] Donald Horne, 'The New Nationalism?', *Bulletin*, 5 October 1968.
[3] *Evening Post* (Wellington), 2 January 1969.

When political observers spoke about 'new nationalism', they were referring to a process of redefining settler-colonial communities for a post-imperial era. It was a nationalism stripped of its British underpinnings—a self-conscious striving for a more self-sufficient, self-sustaining idea of the people, in place of the 'old' nationalism with its entanglements in wider networks of British belonging. The new nationalism referred primarily to the realm of civic culture—the formal trappings of nationhood as manifested in official rites and rituals, public holidays, flags, anthems and so on. But it also referred to a new self-sufficiency in governance in areas such as citizenship, foreign policy, and the role of the state in the promotion of 'national' culture.

The new nationalism in its many manifestations provides a useful window, not only into the comparative settler-colonial experience of the demise of the British world, but also into the meaning and significance of Britishness in settler-colonial conceptions of nationalism. By examining how Canadians, New Zealanders and Australians sought to adapt their national symbols to a post-imperial (and post-British) world, we might gauge the function and significance of Britishness in determining the outlines and contours of settler-colonial identities over the preceding generations.

The Problem of 'Colonial Nationalism'

Indeed, one of the unresolved issues in 'British world' scholarship remains precisely the extent to which colonial nationalism in the nineteenth and twentieth centuries should be understood as nationalist discourse at all. The debate has multiple origins and contexts, but a useful starting point is a series of articles published in the early 1970s by the Canadian historian Douglas Cole. At a time when historians were uncovering the historical roots of settler-colonial identities, Cole offered the provocative view that what had been unearthed was not 'nationalism' in the true sense of the term.[4] He drew a distinction between nationalism on the one hand—embodying an ethnic, linguistic and cultural community—and a more localised patriotism on the other, which expressed affection for a homeland and its inhabitants, but which stopped short of an exclusive, self-sufficient folk myth. He argued that Canadians and Australians (and by extension New Zealanders) had traditionally located their ethno-national selves in the worldwide community of the British race—or 'Britannic nationalism' as he termed it. It was the British world that possessed all of 'the most potent elements for nationhood—language, origin, cultural heritage, common loyalty, the inspiration of past achievement, a foreign menace', and so on.[5] What had often been mistaken for colonial nationalism, he insisted, was really an expression of pride of place and community of interest. Or, as he put it in the case of English Canadians, 'there is a recognition of a distinction of interest between the Canadian state and the United Kingdom, and a feeling that colonial status is humiliating, but not a feeling that Canadians constitute

---

[4] Douglas Cole, 'The Problem of "Nationalism" and "Imperialism" in British Settlement Colonies', *Journal of British Studies*, 10 (2), 1971. Cole was specifically taking issue with Carl Berger's *The Sense of Power* (Toronto, 1970), which, he claimed, had made 'the strongest case for a Canadian nationalistic consciousness' (171).

[5] Ibid., 178.

a new group'.[6] He found support for this view in a wide variety of sources, not least in W. K. Hancock's maxim: 'among the Australians pride of race counted for more than love of country'.[7] This was not to dismiss patriotism as an important reference point for settler-colonial identity formation, but merely to stress how the more narrow 'patriotisms' of the British world remained 'vitally dependent on Anglo-Saxonism and Caucasian racialism'. As such, they lacked the capacity to evolve into 'full-blown' nationalism, monolithic in their exclusive loyalties to a settler-colonial nation-state.[8]

Cole's ideas failed to make an impression on his fellow Canadian historians, who were more inclined to follow Carl Berger's designation of Canadian imperialism as 'one variety of Canadian nationalism'.[9] But there have been traces of Cole's basic model (if not his nomenclature) in Australian and New Zealand studies of the problem. Neville Meaney's long-established claim that 'in the nationalist era Britishness was the dominant cultural myth in Australia, the dominant social idea giving meaning to "the people"' is a case in point.[10] Meaney's central purpose has been to lay to rest the 'thwarted nationalism' paradigm, which has assumed the existence of deep-rooted national sensibilities in Australia that were consistently frustrated by the malign influence of British or 'imperial' delusions. Similarly in New Zealand, there are shades of Cole in James Belich's two-volume history, particularly in his interpretative challenge to the nationalist generation of historians led by Keith Sinclair. Again, the terminology differs, but Belich's concept of recolonisation is almost exactly coterminous with Meaney's 'nationalist era', and echoes Cole in claiming that during this period 'collective [New Zealand] identity was intense, but not nationalist'.[11]

This view is not without its critics, however. Neville Meaney has been taken to task by John Rickard and others for his assertion that 'nationalism is a jealous God', that the 'Australian puzzle cannot be resolved by a glib assertion that Australians shared two equal

---

[6] Ibid., 166.

[7] W. K. Hancock, *Australia* (London: Ernest Benn Limited, 1930).

[8] Cole, '"The Crimson Thread of Kinship": Ethnic Idea in Australia, 1870–1914', *Historical Studies*, 14 (56), 1971, 523.

[9] See Phillip Buckner, 'The Long Goodbye: English Canadians and the British World', in *Rediscovering the British World*, eds Buckner and R. Douglas Francis (Alberta, Canada: University of Calgary Press, 2005), 182.

[10] Neville Meaney, 'Britishness and Australian Identity: The Problem of Nationalism in Australian History and Historiography', *Australian Historical Studies*, 32 (116), 2001, 79. Meaney's view can be traced to his 1976 monograph, *A History of Australian Defence and Foreign Policy, 1901–23*, vol. 1, *The Search for Security in the Pacific, 1901–14* (Sydney: Sydney University Press, 1976), through his edited collection *Under New Heavens: Cultural Transmission and the Making of Australia*, ed. Meaney (Port Melbourne: Heinemann, 1989) to, most recently, his essay 'Britishness and Australia: Some Reflections', in *The British World: Diaspora, Culture and Identity*, eds Carl Bridge and Kent Fedorowich (London: Frank Cass Publishers, 2003), 121–35.

[11] James Belich, *Paradise Reforged: A History of the New Zealanders from the 1880s to the Year 2000* (Honolulu: University of Hawaii Press, 2001), 30. Belich's argument was in many respects an answer to Keith Sinclair's *A Destiny Apart: New Zealand's Search for Identity* (North Sydney: Allen & Unwin in association with Port Nicholson Press, 1986), which was an attempt to locate the origins of New Zealand nationalism in the late nineteenth century.

and complementary myths'.[12] According to Rickard this 'curious passage' in Meaney's work overlooks the way in which 'Australian mythology both competed with and depended on the mythology of Britishness', and fails to grasp the complex processes whereby the two loyalties could be reconciled.[13] John Hirst implicitly endorses this approach, in his detailed documentation of a latent, late-nineteenth century Australian nationalism that became manifest in the drive towards federation, but which remained inherently conservative, coexisting happily with British and imperial sentiment.[14] Phillip Buckner, too, has taken on what he terms the 'nationalism is a jealous mistress' school (with Douglas Cole chiefly in mind). He regards the attempt to distinguish between nationalism and patriotism as misguided, overlooking the fundamental vagueness of nationalism as a historical concept which makes it near impossible to sustain such a distinction. 'Today', he argues,

> we accept as normal that immigrants to Canada and their descendants can easily negotiate between the identity of their home country and of their adopted country. Why then should it be so difficult to accept that most British immigrants and their descendants were able to hold on to more than one national identity?[15]

Buckner is right to point to the problem of drawing rigid distinctions between concepts which were used imprecisely—even indiscriminately—by the peoples who invented and made use of them. But there are arguably good grounds for regarding settler-colonial nationalism as more complex and ambiguous than a 'dual identity'. What Cole, Meaney and Belich share is not a belief that Canadian, Australian and New Zealand identities could not be reconciled with a wider British nationalism, but simply that they lacked the means to exert an exclusive, or 'monolithic' claim over the allegiance and loyalties of their adherents (and to that extent, fell short of the requirements of 'nationalism'). Or put simply, so long as they relied on Britishness for their ethnic categories of inclusion and exclusion, settler-colonial identities provided no basis for the development of a self-sufficient national myth. Indeed, Cole emphasises that this is precisely the reason why Australian and Canadian identities 'blurred and blended' so easily with Britishness: because they were essentially alternative expressions of a common ethnic consciousness.[16] It is this dependence on an ethnic Britishness that placed settler-colonial 'nationalisms' on a less sure footing than other more conventional nineteenth-century national ideologies. They cannot be regarded as analogous to the phenomenon of dual nationalities today, which depend on the arbitrary personal histories of the individuals who can claim them.[17] It is for this reason that the 'two hats' model of settler-colonial dual nationalism is misleading, and why the very concept of

---

[12] Meaney, 'Britishness and Australian Identity', 78.

[13] John Rickard, 'Response: Imagining the Unimaginable?', *Australian Historical Studies*, 32 (116), 2001, 128–31.

[14] John Hirst, *The Sentimental Nation: The Making of the Australian Commonwealth* (South Melbourne: Oxford University Press, 2000).

[15] Buckner, 'The Long Goodbye', 185.

[16] Cole, '"The Crimson Thread of Kinship"', 522.

[17] My own children, for example, are both Australian and Danish nationals, but this is solely by virtue of the accident of their parentage. It is not because the one category is determined by the other.

nationalism is problematic when applied to the outlook, sentiments and self-interest that Canadians, Australians and New Zealanders undoubtedly shared with their own, more limited communities.

The experience of new nationalism in the 1960s and early 1970s is particularly instructive here, because it underlines the necessary adjustments that had to be made when Britishness could no longer serve as a key determinant of belonging to the settler-colonial state. As Britishness was slowly consumed by the receding wake of empire, it was widely assumed that Canada, Australia and New Zealand were somehow incomplete as national entities, that they were in urgent need of a national cultural makeover. Each case necessarily differed according to varying contextual factors, but the underlying language and assumptions of new nationalism were strikingly similar. In particular, three broad areas of common experience can be identified.

First, as the appeal of Britishness dwindled, a palpable sense of something lacking in Australian, Canadian and New Zealand civic culture emerged. The diminishing certainties of empire seem to have prompted reflection about the flimsiness of post-imperial nationhood. Second, this growing awareness of the nation's shortcomings led to government intervention at various levels to place the formal trappings of nationhood on a new, post-imperial footing. Examples of this abound, from the appointment of national citizens as governor-general;[18] the fate of Empire Day and the corresponding revival, renaming, or reinvention of Canada Day, Australia Day and New Zealand Day respectively; the establishment of the Canada Council (1957), the Australia Council (1967) and the QEII Council for the Arts (New Zealand, 1963) for the purpose of promoting a more 'truly' national culture; and the renovation of national symbols, best illustrated by the adoption of the Canadian flag in 1965 (yet to be mirrored in Australia and New Zealand) and the process of selecting new, home-grown national anthems in the 1960s and 1970s. These issues arose at different times and according to divergent political contexts, but in each instance there is a subtext of obsolescent Britishness.

Third, and most significantly, these processes of civic cultural renovation were typified neither by a robust sense of liberation from the stultifying imposition of Britishness, nor by an unproblematic switching of hats to a ready-made local nationalism that had long coexisted alongside British sentiment. The whole point of the 'new' nationalism was that it raised unprecedented questions about the cultural and ideological roots of the settler-colonial nation. Finding answers to these questions was anything but self-explanatory, nor were the 'national' alternatives to Britishness in any way self-evident. While few raised any objection to the principle of new nationalism, there was very little consensus as to what it might entail. Rather, there prevailed an ambivalent blend of hesitation, indecision and discord, as advocates of national renewal sought to translate their cause into new emblems that might strike a chord in the community. It is this post-imperial civic void that underlines the vital function that Britishness had traditionally performed in framing a sense of the people in the several communities of the British world, and which allows us

---

[18] 1952, 1965 and 1967 in Canada, Australia and New Zealand respectively. Although the appointment of Richard Casey to the post in 1965 was not the very first Australian vice-regal appointment, it was regarded as significant in signalling the last of the British-born governors-general.

to view the demise of Britishness in Canada, Australia, and New Zealand within the same interpretive frame.

Something's Missing ...

Recent research has emphasised the durability of Britishness in the settler-colonial world, well into the post-Second World War era. The language, sentiments and civic culture of the British world were extremely resilient in the face of unprecedented strains on the material and cultural ties of the empire and Commonwealth. Jose Igartua, for example, has shown how the Suez Crisis was not the watershed in Canada's British sensibilities that it is often thought to be, while Phillip Buckner makes a persuasive case for the ongoing appeal of Britishness among English Canadians into the 1960s. In Australia, recent works by James Curran, David Goldsworthy, myself and others have attempted to demonstrate the recurrent recourse to British rhetoric in post-war Australian political culture, while in New Zealand it is widely accepted that both official and popular awareness of the redundancy of Britishness was particularly belated.[19]

Into the 1960s, however, as it became abundantly clear that neither empire nor Britishness could provide credible myths of identity and belonging, attention turned towards the shortcomings in the trappings of settler-colonial nationhood. This climate of national self-examination emerged initially in Canada, where the simultaneous rumblings of Quebec separatism gave the issue added urgency. Typical was the annual navel-gazing of newspaper editorials on the occasion of the 1 July holiday (known variously at the time as 'Dominion Day' and 'Canada Day'). As the *Globe* and *Mail* editorialised on 1 July 1961:

> Three basic tasks face Canada in the years ahead. First, to recover a sense of national identity and purpose, to be less imitative of other countries, to set our own standards—in short to be a real nation.[20]

And again there years later:

> Ninety-seven years ago some frock-coated gentlemen created a political entity called Canada. But it was not then and it is not now a nation, and what has begun to trouble a lot of Canadians is the thought that it may never become a nation. Yet it is in this thought, perhaps, that our greatest hope of eventual nationhood lies.[21]

The tension between a sense of the past and the future was indicative of the problem. Were Canadians to strive to 'recover a sense of identity and purpose' that they had somehow discarded, or were they to look ahead to a species of nationhood that had hitherto eluded them? Resolving this dilemma generated volumes of expert commentary, but few coherent answers. Mathew Seddon observed wryly in the *Calgary Herald*:

---

[19] James Curran, *The Power of Speech: Australian Prime Ministers Defining the National Image* (Melbourne: Melbourne University Press, 2004); David Goldsworthy, *Losing the Blanket: Australia and the End of Britain's Empire* (Melbourne: Melbourne University Press, 2002); Stuart Ward, *Australia and the British Embrace: The Demise of the Imperial Ideal* (Melbourne: Melbourne University Press, 2001).

[20] *Globe and Mail*, 1 July 1961.

[21] Ibid.

> Some day in the future an historian studying the Canadian people will surely assume that they were a melancholy lot. He will if he uses for the basis of his report any of the remarks made by those Canadians who, in 1961, are torturing their souls and tearing their hearts out in agonized self-examination of Canadians. More particularly they say they are trying to decide 'what is a Canadian' ... What a wailing, miserable, tear-soaked, self-pitying, moaning, timid bunch they were, the historian will conclude.[22]

In Montreal that same year, the *Gazette* was more sanguine about the significance of Canada's national shortcomings:

> Dominion day celebrates not the formation of a 'Nation' but the effective participation of the Canadian peoples in a common state, irrespective of their national backgrounds. This is a momentous achievement of which Canadians have every reason to be proud ... there is no reason why they should be regarded as some great source of weakness.[23]

Thus, while agreeing wholeheartedly that Canada was not a nation, the *Gazette* saw no cause for collective hand-wringing. On the contrary, it was the very absence of a home-grown nationalist tradition that was Canada's finest 'national' achievement. But not everyone could reconcile the dilemma in this way, and the rhetorical search for a new nationalism proceeded apace throughout the decade. In the mid-1960s, Charles Hanly pronounced (pre-empting Douglas Cole by nearly a decade) that 'In a psychological sense there is no Canadian nation as there is an American or French nation ... there is a legal and geographical entity, but the nation does not exist'.[24] It was presumably within this prevailing climate of self-doubt that the organising committee for the Canadian pavilion at the 1967 World Expo in Montreal opted for the theme 'knowing ourselves'.

In Australia, too, these years saw the beginnings of a broad debate about the quality of Australian nationhood. On 15 July 1964, Rupert Murdoch's *The Australian* arrived on the scene, proudly trumpeting its status as 'Australia's first truly national newspaper'. But in the inaugural editorial, readers were frankly informed that something was amiss in the national consciousness:

> We Australian have always been proud—and perhaps a little self-conscious too—about describing our country as a 'young country' ... Yet something we all know in our hearts when we are very young is that sooner or later we will be grown up ... We have fought successfully against British control of our political affairs. We have made a lot of money, speaking of us collectively. But have we really grown up? It seems we have not ... We are growing up. But we have manifestly not yet achieved maturity.[25]

Again, 'real' nationhood was something discussed in the future tense. Robin Boyd in his 1967 Boyer Lectures looked forward to

---

[22] Seddon, 'Oh Canada', *Calgary Herald*, 2 March 1961.

[23] *Gazette*, 1 July 1961.

[24] Charles Hanley, 'A Psychoanalysis of National Sentiment', in *Nationalism in Canada*, ed. Peter Russell (New York & Toronto: McGraw-Hill, 1966), 312.

[25] *Australian*, 15 July 1964.

> the real stuff of creative progression which will give us eventually a real Australian civilization—instead of a second-hand British, or a second-hand American, or second-hand, second-rate, second-best anything else.[26]

But achieving this goal could not be taken for granted. He reflected ruefully on the fact that 'many Australians who appear to be thoroughly good men … excellent Aussie men … are unmoved by the prospect that Australia may never have a culture of its own'.[27] Donald Horne, by contrast, saw potential in this situation, commenting in January 1968 that 'there is a commendable emptiness in Australians about their place in the world, the need for a new rhetoric, a new approach, as if Australia were beginning all over again'.[28] This 'emptiness' implicitly referred to the historic baggage of British race patriotism that had seemingly evaporated with the departure of Sir Robert Menzies from the prime ministership in 1966. Menzies' successors took up Horne's call for a 'new rhetoric', particularly John Gorton, who was at pains to distance himself from the taint of Menzies' 'British bootheels'. But like Robin Boyd, Gorton felt bound to use the future tense:

> For a long time we stood not really as a nation in our own right, but as the nation the people of whom spoke of 'home' and meant another nation, meant Great Britain … it is essential that we should develop a feeling of nationhood … I hope you will all help me in the years ahead to foster this feeling of real nationalism.[29]

It is unclear how enthusiastically Australians responded to Gorton's call for a 'real' nationalism. This is partly because Gorton was at a loss to develop the concept in any meaningful way. The underlying difficulty, as law professor Geoffrey Sawer noted at the time, was a fundamental 'lack of any strongly indigenous Australian national symbols and feelings' that might have provided Gorton with a genuine purchase on the theme. Although most Australians seemed prepared to dispense with Menzies' worship of the Queen, there had been no 'immediate development of an indigenous focus of loyalty' to supplant the monarchy.[30] Thus, five years later, Governor-General Paul Hasluck could be heard on television exhorting his fellow Australians: 'Our patriotism has to be patriotism for the Australia of today—the Australia that exists—not to an Australia of a different kind that no longer exists … patriotism and loyalty are our own thing'.[31] It is hard to imagine a French or American head of state making the same kind of utterance. But in a settler-colonial context in the early 1970s, Hasluck's message required no elaboration.

In New Zealand too, the 1960s brought increasingly vocal demands for an overhaul of the nation's key symbols and traditions. Keith Sinclair confessed in a 1963 lecture that 'for us to want to be British is a poor objective, like wanting to be an understudy or a

---

[26] Robin Boyd, *Artificial Australia: The Boyer Lectures* (Sydney: Australian Broadcasting Commission, 1968), 9.

[27] Ibid., 44.

[28] Cited in Curran, *Power of Speech*, 47.

[29] *Bulletin*, 5 October 1968.

[30] See Jeppe Kristensen, '"In Essence still a British Country": Britain's Withdrawal from East of Suez', *Australian Journal of Politics and History*, 51 (1), 2005.

[31] Paul Hasluck, 'Patriotism and Loyalty', governor-general's televised Australia Day address, 26 January 1973, Hasluck Papers, National Library of Australia: MS 5274, Box 38.

caretaker—or an undertaker'. He spoke of the 'very many changes in New Zealand, of a kind which make me believe that a New Zealand civilization is not impossible'.[32] That same year, the journalist Len Fanning launched a campaign for 'a national song worthy of New Zealand'. Both the national anthem, *God Save the Queen*, and the unofficial 'national hymn', *God Defend New Zealand*, had their roots in an outmoded conception of nationalism that failed to address contemporary New Zealand attitudes. 'Not one line', Fanning complained, 'indicates what New Zealanders have done, or what they could or should do'. But as in Australia, the problem lay in devising adequate alternatives. The poet Alistair Campbell frankly conceded: 'What the alternatives are to the sentiments expressed in our national song I just don't know'. He thought that a nationwide competition might help, but that he himself would be unable to summon up a sufficiently 'rousing and widely acceptable' entry. His compatriot, Denis Glover, was more scornful: 'All this nationalism seems to be childish and a great, great laugh.'[33]

Again, the call for new national symbols was predicated on the assumption that New Zealand was not truly a nation. W. B. Sutch constantly reiterated this theme throughout the 1960s, in lectures, essays and publications such as *Colony or Nation?* (1965) and *Take Over New Zealand* (1972). Sutch's main grievance was the colonial dependency of the New Zealand economy, but the basic elements of his theme were easily transposed into cultural policy. Taking his cue from Sutch, the chairman of the New Zealand Arts Council, Bill Sheat, warned in 1972 that 'the problem of a small country such as ours retaining its identity or even of developing any identity, is just as great as that of Canada [situated] immediately alongside the United States.'[34] But the good news, as his colleague Mike Nicolaidi frequently pointed out, was that 'the visual arts of this country have come of age—and that the country itself is coming of age … recognising its past, its traditions and, I believe, its uniqueness and individuality which may yet make it a nation in the true sense of the word'.[35] As in Canada and Australia, real or true nationhood remained the ultimate long-term goal. It received prime ministerial endorsement in Norman Kirk's address on the inaugural New Zealand Day in February 1974:

> For 134 years we have been making a nation and we are perhaps to ask ourselves: 'are we yet a completed nation? Have we yet achieved a true New Zealand civilization?' Not yet … Now as a nation we are independent and on our own. As Britain joins her destiny with Europe's, we must draw more upon the spiritual and cultural strength of the people who make our nation.[36]

Like Gorton a few years earlier, Kirk pointed to the direct causal relationship between the fraying ties of Britain, and the urgency of putting the national house in order. It was the

---

[32] Keith Sinclair, 'The Historian as Prophet: Equality, Inequality and Civilization', in *The Future of New Zealand*, ed. M. F. Lloyd Prichard (Christchurch, NZ: Whitcombe & Tombs for the University of Auckland, 1964).

[33] *New Zealand Herald*, 27 July 1968.

[34] W. N. Sheat, 'The Silent Takeover', address to the Auckland Society of Arts, 8 May 1972, Archives of New Zealand (ANZ): AANV 972/66d 8/21/1.

[35] Mike Nicolaidi, speech at opening of exhibition 'New Zealand Painting, 1900–1920', Nelson, 22 July 1972, ANZ: AANV972/66d 8/21/1.

[36] Norman Kirk, New Zealand Day address, 6 February 1974.

unavoidable fact that New Zealanders could no longer ground their ethnic selves within an imagined community of British peoples that brought the fundamental flimsiness of their nationhood sharply into focus.

A Spur to Legislative Action

There was more to the new nationalism than rhetorical flourishes and editorial self-examination. As the calls for national renewal grew more insistent, the new nationalism became a legitimate rationale for legislative action. In all three countries, governments took steps towards renovating the key symbols of nationhood—flags, anthems, royal styles and titles, national holidays, cultural policies and royal honours were all suddenly up for grabs. This process did not unfold in an orderly or uniform manner; some symbols seemed ripe for change in, say, Canada, but less so in other settings. Nor was the timing of these changes predictable or indeed logical. To some extent a change in one country clearly sparked a debate in the other two, while in other instances they were allowed to pass virtually unnoticed.

It is impossible here to consider in detail the haphazard (and in many ways incomplete) inner workings of the new nationalism in all three countries during this critical phase of redundant Britishness. Instead, I wish to look at one key symbol of change (or change of symbol) in each of the countries concerned, in order to convey a sense of the range of items under discussion, and the variety of contexts within which the discussion took place. I therefore turn now to examine briefly the flag debate in Canada, the national anthem competition in Australia, and the short-lived invention of 'New Zealand Day'. My emphasis is not so much on the detailed narrative of events which have been recounted elsewhere, but on the fundamental dilemmas inherent in constructing new national emblems out of the remnants of the imperial past. Each case study involved an event or symbol that pointed to the obsolescence of Britishness. Yet each of them had to be forced through parliament by left-leaning governments in the face of opposition from conservative parties, and widespread dissent, disenchantment or indifference within the community. At the very moment when colonial 'nationalism' had an opportunity to rely on its own devices, the depth and emotive power of a residual Britishness loomed larger than ever. But more significant than the lingering appeal of Britishness was the difficulty of devising stand-alone, self-sufficient national ornaments that might speak meaningfully to 'the people'.

The Maple Leaf

The story of Canada's maple leaf flag is now a familiar one. Prime Minister Pearson's initiative emerged at a time of growing concern about the unity of the French and English peoples of Canada. Pearson's chief advisor on the flag issue, John Matheson, recalls that the whole issue emerged against the background of Pearson's 'one paramount and desperate objective, the saving of the confederation'.[37] But it was also consistent with Pearson's long-held convictions and experience as external affairs minister in the 1950s that Canada needed to become more visible as a sovereign entity in world affairs. The debate came

---

[37] Ross Matheson, *Canada's Flag: A Search for a Country* (Boston: G. K. Hall, 1980), xiii.

The 'New Nationalism' in Australia, Canada and New Zealand

on the heels of a series of debates in the 1940s and 1950s that had unfolded along similar lines. An earlier flag debate in 1945, followed by disputes over the question of Canadian citizenship in 1946, the appointment of a Canadian as governor-general in 1952, the naming of the 1 July holiday, and Canada's opposition to British actions at Suez in 1956, had drawn the battle lines that would determine the course of the flag debate in 1964. On the one hand was the predominantly liberal view that Canadian sovereignty and self-respect was compromised by symbols that implied an ongoing colonial relationship with Britain. On the other was the passionately held conservative view that to tamper with those symbols was to deny Canadians the only 'distinctive' identity they had at their disposal. Ironically, both sides of the debate had one eye firmly on the threat of cultural extinction on the doorstep of the American monolith. For liberals, it was a question of cementing Canada's status and identity on the North American continent. For conservatives, it was precisely the British connection that provided the necessary bulwark against US domination. As Harold Innis urged in 1952:

> We are indeed fighting for our lives ... the jackals of communications systems are constantly on the alert to destroy every vestige of sentiment toward Great Britain, holding it of no advantage if it threatens the omnipotence of American commercialism. This is to strike at the heart of cultural life in Canada.[38]

Thus, Pearson anticipated a hostile reaction from certain quarters, and indeed he deliberately sought out hostile territory to launch his flag initiative—namely an address to the Royal Canadian Legion in Winnipeg in May 1964. In setting out his aims, he drew on language and imagery that was vintage new nationalism:

> I believe most sincerely that it is time now for Canadians to unfurl a flag that is truly distinctive and truly national in character; as Canadian as the maple leaf which should be its dominant design; a flag easily identifiable as Canada's; a flag which cannot be mistaken for the emblem of any other country; a flag of the future which also honours the past; Canada's own and only Canada's.[39]

Pearson's design of choice was three red maple leaves on a single stem on a white background, flanked by two blue bars representing a 'sea to sea' motif. Dubbed the 'Pearson pennant' by opposition leader John Diefenbaker, it became the object of one of the most bitter public wrangles in Canadian history. From the outset, there were profound reservations about the possible impact of a flag debate on the increasingly sensitive problem of Quebec separatism. *The Globe and Mail* expressed concern that the prime minister had

> chosen to press the divisive issue of a national flag at a time when emotions are already deeply stirred by the question of national unity—or rather, by the lack of unity ... He should now understand the danger of the course he has taken.[40]

Letters to the editor frequently objected to the idea of 'bowing to pressure from Quebec', and appealed to the spirit of the pioneers of 1783. As one anonymous letter-writer proclaimed:

> These proud people we call United Empire Loyalists [and] their descendants are scattered throughout Canada and are not going to take kindly to any removal

---

[38] Harold Innis, *The Strategy of Culture* (Toronto: University of Toronto Press, 1952), 19.
[39] *Ottawa Journal*, 19 May 1964.
[40] *Globe and Mail*, 19 May 1964.

of the Union jack from Canada's flag as a result of anti-British agitation from Quebec. Can Canadians today not take a lesson from these brave Loyalists and object to this tinkering with our background?[41]

The Progressive Conservative opposition had no quarrel with the basic proposition that Canada needed a flag of its own, but their preferred choice was the 'Red Ensign' which had served as an unofficial Canadian flag for several generations. They insisted that any design for a Canadian flag should feature the Union Jack in some way (alongside the fleur-de-lis if necessary). The use of the maple leaf was regarded as entirely inappropriate for a national flag—not because it was not a recognisable Canadian symbol, but because it lacked the dignity, decorum and gravitas required of a flag emblem. As conservative MP Michael Starr from Ontario protested: 'stickers are being made, baloney, beer and all the other products are being sold under this insignia. This is what we are being asked to adopt as a flag'. His senior colleague, Gordon Churchill, was equally appalled, describing Pearson's flag as 'this frightful atrocity which the Prime Minister is trying the ram down our throats'.[42]

John Diefenbaker's opposition to the maple leaf was trenchant and unrelenting. As early as 1926 on the campaign trail in Saskatchewan, he had made his position clear: 'I want to make Canada all Canadian and all British. The men who wish to change our flag should be denounced by every good Canadian'.[43] At that time he was probably referring to the Union Jack as 'our flag'. Forty years later he was equally ready to jump to the defence of the red ensign. His objection was two-fold. First, he found Pearson's methods repugnant, particularly his refusal to put the flag issue to a popular vote. He railed in parliament in June 1964:

> You cannot force a flag on the people of Canada and secure from them that mystic something which some ridicule as nationalism … A flag design is not a trick by which one group imposes upon others some evidence of a Canadianism that all will not accept.[44]

Second, he felt that the maple leaf, while a perfectly adequate symbol of Canada as a distinctive place, was completely inadequate as the embodiment of Canadians as a distinctive people. He harped on this theme at length throughout 1964:

> In what way does the design now proposed embody our history? It denies Cardinal Newman's saying that all greatness rests upon the shoulders of past generations. In what way does it represent the sacrifices, the experiences, the achievements of the past? … Edmund Burke said all human society was a partnership between the living and the dead. This design denies that partnership. There is nothing in this design for memorial, sorrow or old renown. There is nothing for those who with sword and crucifix went into the wilderness where they left their names and often their bones as sacred heritage for us all … Are we as Canadians to have a flag

---

[41] *Ottawa Journal*, 20 May 1964.

[42] *Globe and Mail*, 15 December 1964.

[43] Alistair B. Fraser, 'A Canadian Flag for Canada', *Journal of Canadian Studies*, 25 (4), 1990–91, 66.

[44] Cited in Gregory A. Johnson, 'The Last Gasp of Empire: The 1964 Flag Debate Revisited', in *Canada and the End of Empire*, ed. Buckner (Vancouver: University of British Columbia Press, 2005).

which treats our memories, our past sacrifices, all the milestones of greatness as irrelevancies? … Is it beyond the realm of possibility that, should this new design become our flag in a few months hence, Canadians as a whole will feel their past has been forgotten?[45]

For Diefenbaker, Canada's British and imperial past were inseparable from the idea of 'the people' that English Canadians had long cherished. If national symbols were the embodiment of a people's struggle for self-realisation, then Canadians had been more than adequately served by the symbols and sentiments associated with forging a new British frontier out of the wreckage of the American Revolution. To attack these symbols was, as Harold Innis had argued twelve years earlier, to 'strike at the heart' of Canadian culture and ultimately to erase it entirely.

In his memoir of the flag debate, John Matheson painstakingly reconstructs how the flag evolved in strict adherence to the rules of heraldry and the traditional symbolism of Canada. The red and white colours that were eventually chosen had been Canada's official colours since the 1920s, while the maple leaf had long-established heraldic connotations reaching well back into the nineteenth century. Yet opponents continued to see in the flag an abandonment of tradition—the very antithesis of the feeling of deep-rootedness that is fundamental both to the stability and plausibility of national myths. Thus the dilemma of post-imperial nationhood was not the absence of imagery that conveyed a sense of place. Rather, it was a question of how to package these materials as credible conveyors of a sense of the people, in place of the traditional British markers of ethnic distinction.

The flag debate was ultimately resolved by the enforcement of closure in the House of Commons—the first time in living memory that a debate had been summarily shut down in the Canadian parliament. This was widely regarded as an unfortunate and unedifying means of bringing a new national flag into being. Pearson appealed, in his closing parliamentary speech, for united support for the new flag, 'but in the tumult caused by the members of both sides of the House he could barely be heard'.[46] The *Globe and Mail* deeply regretted that 'a great national occasion was marked to the end in political squalor', and pondered whether Canada had ever possessed any genuinely national traditions. The very nature of its adoption had undoubtedly inscribed the flag with an unmistakable symbolism. But it was 'a symbolism that looked to the future while carrying with it the only true Canadian tradition that has ever existed—that of our historic purpose in the creation of a unique national framework for the fulfilment of two cultural destinies'.[47]

Advance Australia Fair

Australia's national anthem debate emerged in a less fraught and emotional setting, and without the threat of national fragmentation. But some of the general features of the Canadian flag dilemma were played out in Australia in the first year of the Whitlam Labor government in 1973. Gough Whitlam had been elected in December 1972 on a broad

---

[45] Cited in Matheson, *Canada's Flag*, 159–60.
[46] *Ottawa Journal*, 15 December 1964.
[47] *Globe and Mail*, 16 December 1964.

platform of national and social renewal, and had made effective political use of Australia's perceived national shortcomings. His electoral promise to introduce a new national anthem to replace *God Save the Queen* was part of a series of measures designed to disentangle Australia's political, constitutional and sentimental symbolism from its outmoded British moorings. Thus, he pressed for the abolition of knighthoods and other imperial honours (replacing them with an Australian honours system), sought to bring an end to Privy Council appeals (unsuccessfully), and placed the Queen's Royal Style and Title on a more national footing (replacing her former cumbersome litany of crowns with the more straightforward: 'Queen of Australia'). The national anthem was the initiative that caught the greatest amount of public attention, and, perhaps for that very reason, became the one that would cause the Labor government the greatest degree of political embarrassment.

Whitlam's case for a new anthem was couched in the now-familiar rhetoric of the new nationalism. While campaigning in rural New South Wales in November 1972 he announced:

> In the great issues facing us it's time for a national approach. It's time we had our own symbols of our nationhood. It's time ... that we had our own national anthem ... The choice of the Australian people, not the musical tastes of George II, should determine Australia's national anthem.[48]

James Curran has described Whitlam as the 'second coming' of new nationalism in Australia, following John Gorton's faltering attempt to breathe life into the concept in the late 1960s. While Whitlam could not claim authorship of the phrase, he was 'happy to adopt and affirm' it as prime minister.[49] There is evidence that public opinion had warmed to the logic of new nationalism within a surprisingly rapid timeframe. In 1965, for example, Gallup polls showed only thirty-eight per cent of Australians in favour of a distinctively Australian anthem. By 1967 this had increased to 44.1 per cent, 51.4 per cent in 1969, and 72.3 per cent on the eve of Labor's victory in 1972.[50] Whitlam therefore wasted little time in launching the national anthem quest, announcing a nationwide competition on Australia Day 1973 for the composition of new music and lyrics. The idea was to select the best of these entries and place them alongside 'several popular songs' with a 'long and colourful history' that might conceivably lay claim to the affections of the people. This selection of old and new compositions would then be put to 'the people' to select the most popular tune—a process of democratisation of the new national symbolism which seemed a far cry from Lester Pearson's exercise in national cultural engineering.[51]

But almost from the very beginning this auspicious plan started to unravel. The Australia Council appointed a panel of judges, consisting of prominent Australian artists and intellectuals such as the historian Manning Clark, playwright David Williamson and

---

[48] Cited in Curran, *The Power of Speech*, 79.

[49] Ibid., 78.

[50] These figures were tabled in parliament by the minister for immigration, Al Grassby. *Commonwealth Parliamentary Debates* (hereafter *CPD*), House of Representatives (hereafter HR), vol. 80, 6 December 1973, 4382.

[51] Gough Whitlam, 'National Anthem', Australia Day broadcast, 26 January 1973, National Archives of Australia: A3211, 1973/128 Part 1.

Aboriginal poet Kath Walker, whose task it was to select a short list of twelve that would go into the final competition. But even before the three-month deadline for entries had closed, a note of scepticism had crept into proceedings. In April, a group of Australia's leading composers voiced their doubts that anything worthwhile could come out of the competition. Peter Sculthorpe revealed to the *Melbourne Age* that he personally had no intention of entering the fray. 'I suspect they want a national anthem that's stirring and heroic—and I don't think things are like that anymore. The thought of that kind of anthem being written now is laughable—society's changed too much'. Adelaide composer Richard Meale concurred, surmising that 'it's something we should have done years earlier—it's as though we have missed the boat for a national anthem'. This was backed up by the *Age* music critic, Felix Werder, who predicted that 'With a competition, you'll just get hundreds of synthetic 19th-century pastiches.'[52]

And this is precisely what occurred. Despite some 2500 entries for lyrics, and a further 1500 entries for the music, it soon became apparent that there was no credible anthem to be found amid the reams of earnest, chest-thumping doggerel that descended on the judging panel. The judges were at a loss to find a dozen worthy finalists, and were duly given permission to reduce the shortlist from twelve to six. Yet even these, upon release to the press in July, were bitterly savaged by the critics. Australia's leading poets queued up to announce the winning verses as 'comic stuff' (A. D. Hope), 'hopelessly bad' (James McAuley) and 'posing an impossible task' (Judith Wright). One of the judges, David Williamson, agreed wholeheartedly with this assessment, and confessed publicly: 'if you think these are bad, you should have seen the rest of the 2500 or so we rejected'.[53] The *Australian* was particularly unforgiving in its assessment, declaring that the public was now faced with the 'unbearable' and the 'unforgiveable'. Not a single one of the six finalists, the editorial jeered,

> could be sung in public without a deep sense of embarrassment. They carry a 19th-century air of wide-eyed zeal and mawkish sentimentality which is certainly not appropriate today, and might well have embarrassed all but anthem composers in the last century.

If this were the best Australia had to offer, 'we may as well go back to *God Save the Queen*'.[54]

That nothing of any merit emerged from 4000 entries clearly suggests that it was the process itself that was flawed. The very idea of devising newfangled national symbols was a contradiction in terms, given the function of national symbols in providing a tangible connection between a people and their past. Composers were faced with only two options—something couched in nineteenth-century heroic mode that might stimulate some ancient collective lineage, or a more contemporary verse that might improve with age. Most of the short-listed entries fell into the former category—only Bob Ellis seems to have attempted the latter, and even his composition read more like a plea for new nationalism than its lyrical realisation:

---

[52] *Age* (Melbourne), 14 April 1973.

[53] *Sydney Morning Herald* (hereafter *SMH*), 4 July 1973. A selective rummage through the five boxes of entries that remain in the possession of the National Archives of Australia fully bears out Williamson's assessment.

[54] *Australian*, 4 July 1973.

> Lift your head Australia
>
> The hour to stand alone
>
> Without the proud regalia
>
> Of Kingdoms not our own
>
> Approaches every minute
>
> And bids us speak the right;
>
> Oh, come let us begin it
>
> Before the fall of night.

Ellis, like so many of his contemporaries, projected nationalism as a future potential rather than an established fact of Australian life. Indeed, he confessed to the *Sydney Morning Herald* that he had experienced great difficulty saying anything meaningful about Australian nationhood in the present tense:

> You've got to leave out all the gum trees and wallabies, and you can't talk about defending the country from the yellow hordes, so there's not much to talk about except an independent stance and pride in ourselves. Anything else would embarrass the audience.[55]

This merely underlines the conceptual void at the heart of the new nationalist project. Australians had lost their connection to the symbols and sensibilities of 'being British', and in so doing had forfeited the traditional conceptual apparatus for understanding themselves as Australians.

From this point onwards the Whitlam government's approach to the anthem was essentially one of damage control. The six finalists were quietly forgotten, and in December it was announced that an indicative plebiscite of 60 000 voters would be conducted to select an anthem from three more familiar alternatives: *Waltzing Matilda*, *Advance Australia Fair*, and *Song of Australia*. But even this strategy brought cries of consternation from the opposition parties. Their grievance was twofold—first, that the method chosen for ascertaining the 'choice of the people' was woefully unrepresentative; and more critically, the voters polled would not be given the choice of retaining *God Save the Queen*. Thus, the government was taking for granted the central issue at stake—whether Australians really desired or needed an anthem of their own. Liberal MP Michael MacKellar introduced a motion in parliament within days of the government's announcement which barely concealed his scepticism about the new nationalistic assumptions behind the entire project. Those assumptions, he said, could 'be tested only by a full vote of the Australian people, with the opportunity of expressing an opinion on the present anthem being given to them'. MacKellar was at pains to avoid any 'expression of opinion as to what should or should not be the anthem', leaving this for the decision of the Australian people. But it is clear from the contribution of his conservative colleagues to the debate that what was really at stake was the fate of *God Save the Queen*. Conservative backbencher N. M. Cooke, for example,

---

[55] *SMH*, 4 July 1973.

intimated that a switch to a new national anthem inevitably carried republican overtones, which he personally did not welcome. Liberal MP Harry Turner concluded the debate in terms reminiscent of Diefenbaker's conservatives in the Canadian flag debate nine years earlier:

> 'God Save the Queen' may indeed have been the choice of George II. If that is so, he chose a pretty good tune, anyway, and I would not substitute that choice with the Prime Minister's choice, nor do I think that half the Australian people would substitute that choice.

Although the opposition produced evidence that public sentiment was flowing back to *God Save the Queen* in the aftermath of the anthem competition debacle, the government dismissed their intervention as 'merely another device to deny Australia a badge of independence'.[56] The indicative plebiscite went ahead as planned in April 1974, and *Advance Australia Fair* proved to be the first choice of the voters, despite the fact that it was far less widely known than *Waltzing Matilda*. This was most likely because its brassy, Victorian cadence and earnest, upright lyrics, complied with the majority of voters' sense of what a national anthem should sound like. The result provided the government with the means to lay to rest the endless speculation and argument of the previous twelve months. Yet even this solution raised further problems relating to the song's origins as a late-nineteenth century hymn to imperial Australia. Of the five stanzas in Peter Dodd McCormick's 1878 original, only two were really appropriate as a national anthem in 1970s Australia. The other three were peppered with heartfelt declarations of Australia's devotion to empire and Britishness. The second stanza, for example, referred to 'Albion', 'British courage', 'old England's flag', and 'Britannia rules the waves', before mentioning 'Australia' in the last line almost by way of afterthought. And the final stanza was virtually unprintable in the prevailing new nationalist climate of the 1970s:

> Britannia then shall surely know,
>
> Beyond wide ocean's roll,
>
> Her sons in fair Australia's land
>
> Still keep a British soul.

In other words, the people had voted for a song that was steeped in precisely the sentiments that having an 'anthem of our own' was designed to bury. The government responded to this dilemma in two steps. Whitlam initially declared, upon announcing the winner of the poll, that the result related only to the music of *Advance Australia Fair*. Although 'words for the tune existed', they would not be regarded as part of the official anthem. Whitlam claimed, somewhat disingenuously, that he 'had always taken the view that it was the music that mattered'. This untenable position was subsequently modified by some judicious editing of the text, which resulted in *Advance Australia Fair* being reduced from five stanzas to two. Both of the remaining verses were primarily concerned with Australia's material and natural bounty, and had little to say about the spiritual, cultural or

---

[56] See speeches by Michael MacKellar, Al Grassby, N. M. Cooke, Robert King and Henry Turner in *CPD*, HR, vol. 80, 6 December 1973, 4380–90.

New Zealand Day

If the maple leaf flag and *Advance Australia Fair* ran into difficulties due to the residual claims of Britishness on popular sensibilities, this was hardly the case with the public row over New Zealand Day. Here, the issue was not so much the substitution of a British tradition for a national one, but rather the invention of a new national occasion entirely from scratch. While it may be argued that New Zealand Day was somehow an alternative to Empire Day (which had fizzled out in the late 1950s), there was no sense that it presented a moment where New Zealanders were compelled to choose between the old and the new. As such, there were no entrenched interests or 'loyal' lobby groups who might have been expected to oppose the initiative. And yet, New Zealand Day became caught up in a widespread controversy over the date, name and the commemorative practices designed to mark the occasion.

February 6 had been marked each year as 'Waitangi Day' since the early 1930s, but it had never acquired the status of a national holiday. The anniversary of the signing of the Treaty of Waitangi in the Bay of Islands had become a prominent event on the Northland regional calendar, but it had never really caught on in other parts of the country where its relevance seemed less immediate. This was borne out by attempts in the early 1960s to enhance the status of Waitangi Day by making it a national holiday. The Waitangi Day Act 1960, one of the last initiatives of Walter Nash's Labour government, sought to substitute a single national holiday on 6 February for the various provincial anniversary holidays. But in order not to offend provincial sensibilities (or add an additional day off to the working calendar), Nash left it to each province to decide whether to make the switch or not. In the event, only Northland opted to replace Auckland Anniversary Day with Waitangi Day, while the rest of the country continued to honour the provincial holidays. As the Christchurch *Press* commented, the idea of 'upsetting local arrangements' to mark the Treaty of Waitangi was 'greeted with a national yawn'.[58]

It might be assumed that the upgrading of Waitangi Day to the New Zealand Day national holiday in 1974 reflected a greater public awareness of issues relating to indigenous rights, and the need to address the legacies of colonisation. And there can be no doubt that the 1960s and 1970s witnessed far greater attention to Maori grievances, heavily influenced by the civil rights movement in the United States and Australia, and the rapid processes of

---

[57] Even this was not the end of the debate. The change of government in 1975 resulted in a partial reinstatement of *God Save the Queen*, a further plebiscite in 1977 (which also favoured *Advance Australia Fair*), but no final resolution to the problem. It was not until the Hawke Labor government came to power in 1983 that *Advance Australia Fair* (expurgated version, with some further alterations to the text) was permanently installed as Australia's national anthem. Unsurprisingly, the question continues to arise each year on Australia Day as a kind of ritual pondering of whether there isn't a more suitable alternative. See for example Mark O'Connor, 'Search for an Australian Anthem', *Australian*, 26 January 2005.

[58] *Press*, 2 January 1973.

decolonisation in Africa. But a closer examination of the priorities and motives of the Kirk Labour government that came to office in November 1972 indicates that a focus on Maori issues was by no means the decisive factor in the establishment of New Zealand Day. On the contrary, New Zealand Day was originally conceived as an event that might distract attention from internal distinctions and divisions by emphasising national unity.

While it is true that Kirk's minister for Maori affairs, Matiu Rata, played a leading hand in placing the New Zealand Day proposal on the Labour Party's 1972 election manifesto, his aims to promote better race relations were quickly superseded by the new nationalist enthusiasms of the prime minister and the minister for internal affairs, Henry May. In introducing the New Zealand Day Bill to parliament in August 1973, May devoted almost the entirety of his speech to the idea that 'all nations feel a need to express their independence and nationhood, and the event which Waitangi Day commemorates is clearly connected with New Zealand's first step towards nationhood'. The bill, he declared, reflected 'the growing awareness among New Zealanders of the need to have a national day that we can observe in an appropriate manner'. He underlined that in changing the name from 'Waitangi Day', the government was seeking to ensure that the message of maturity, independence and national unity was not lost in the detail of the Treaty of Waitangi. He freely conceded the government's concerns that 'keeping the name Waitangi Day could have led to the day being associated much more with one particular event'.[59] Opposition spokesman and former internal affairs minister, Allan Highet, was in full agreement.

> I prefer to call our national day New Zealand Day because, unfortunately, Waitangi Day has over recent years become an occasion for airing Maori discontents, and therefore I think … it is far better we should call it New Zealand Day and try to come together and live as one people.[60]

Similar arguments arose in the deliberations of the organising committee for the inaugural New Zealand Day celebrations. The prime minister had given verbal instructions that 'the celebrations should desirably differ from those marking Waitangi Day'. The emphasis should instead be placed on 'New Zealand as one country of many people', drawing in the wider participation of the many nationalities which made up contemporary New Zealand. The committee discussed the various ways in which this could be achieved—recruiting the many nationalities represented in Auckland to participate in a New Zealand Day pageant, featuring the varieties of national dress and national flags. The committee chairman, A. J. Faulkner, fully supported Kirk's 'multi-cultural' theme, and emphasised that New Zealand Day 'was really the total concept, not just Maori and British Pakeha'.[61] Playing down the imperial dimensions of New Zealand's past, therefore, necessarily meant a watering down of the Maori dimensions of Waitangi.

---

[59] *New Zealand Parliamentary Debates*, HR, vol. 185, 1 August 1973, 2886–87. As a concession to Rata, who clearly preferred retention of the original name, the full text of the Treaty of Waitangi was included as a schedule to the bill.

[60] Ibid., 2898.

[61] New Zealand Day Celebrations Steering Committee, notes of discussion, 2 October 1973, ANZ: AAAC/7536, W5084 Box 231 CON/9/3/14.

But this left the government with several problems that were typical of the post-imperial dilemmas faced by Canada and Australia. First, imperial memories of the meaning of Waitangi could not be erased overnight. Organisations like the Maori Women's Welfare League lobbied continuously for the retention of the original label, protesting that

> for over one hundred years it has been known as 'Waitangi Day' and to give a Pakeha name at this stage, to a day which is for both Maori and Pakeha, causes concern to the minority group who needs to identify themselves to this particular day.[62]

And it was not only Maori who felt that something had gone missing in the name change. The Auckland Historical Society lobbied the minister for a reversion to the original, arguing that 'the former name has some significance and interest, referring to the picturesque occasion of the signing of the Treaty by which New Zealand became British'.[63] Even Norman Kirk, when pressed on the subject, conceded that 'in my heart I will probably still call it Waitangi Day'.[64] The Wellington branch of the New Zealand Labour Party offered a solution to the naming problem in February 1974 which merely underlined the intractability of the dilemma: it suggested that the relevant legislation should be amended to include the words: 'the 6th day of February each year shall continue to be known as Waitangi Day and shall henceforth be known as New Zealand Day'. The formulation was deliberately vague and inconclusive. As the branch secretary, David Walker, explained to the minister for Maori affairs: 'Those who wanted to refer to the day as Waitangi Day would not be officially wrong, while those who followed the more general usage of New Zealand Day would also be officially correct'.[65] Needless to say, this proposal hardly served to clarify matters and was politely ignored.

Others felt that the problem was not so much the use of the name 'New Zealand Day', as the date which had been chosen to celebrate it. Newspaper editorial opinion on this point reveals a stark regional divide, with Northland endorsing the choice of 6 February to the hilt, and enthusiasm waning steadily southwards. South Island newspapers seemed particularly puzzled by the 'nationalisation' of Waitangi Day. In Christchurch, the *Press* argued that at least two other dates had claims as valid—Anzac Day on 25 April and Dominion Day on 26 September. While the former was already a holiday, the latter seemed to hold out real potential.

> If a new national holiday—a 'New Zealand Day'—must be found, the occasion in 1907 when New Zealand received the title of "Dominion" might have the best claim of all. By this time New Zealand was a country with a rugged sense of individuality, well aware of its separateness from Britain.[66]

---

[62] Submission by Maori Women's Welfare League to the Maori Affairs Committee, undated [1973], ANZ: AAAC/7536, W5084 Box 231 CON/9/1/5.

[63] Letter, Margaret R. McCormick, honorary secretary of the Auckland Historical Society, to Henry May, 21 March 1975, ANZ: AAAC/7536, W5084 Box 227 CON/9/2/3.

[64] *Dominion Post*, 7 February 1974.

[65] Letter, David Walker to Matiu Rata, 6 February 1974, ANZ: AAAC/7536, W5084 Box 227 CON/9/2/3.

[66] *Press*, 2 January 1973. Two years later the *Christchurch Star* described the occasion as an 'ill-

This was closely related to a more fundamental problem faced by Labour in breathing life into the occasion—finding a coherent set of meanings for a 'new' New Zealand nationalism around which the annual festivities might be constructed. The inaugural New Zealand Day pageant, performed in the presence of Her Majesty the Queen at Waitangi in February 1974, featured a heady mixture of song, ceremony, cabaret, sketch comedy, Maori ritual and multi-cultural spectacle. The pagent received a mixed reaction from a record television viewing audience, with the *New Zealand Herald* summing up the diversity of opinion in a single headline: 'Imaginative Pageantry or Tasteless Vulgarity?'[67] Either way, it was clear that nobody had the stomach to see the performance repeated annually. Henceforth the government made it clear that it would not take the lead in staging the event, and that it would rely on community leaders to come up with appropriate forms of commemorative practice. As Henry May put it in a press release:

> Each town in New Zealand has its own history and its own present day composition which makes it unique. This diversity forms a colourful patchwork of both the Nation's history and of its present identity. It is appropriate that these particular features of any area be commemorated.[68]

This was an extraordinary admission of creative and imaginative bankruptcy. By devolving responsibility for commemorative innovation to the 'colourful patchwork' of regional diversity, the government undermined one of its key arguments in creating New Zealand Day—the need for a single occasion that would emphasise the burgeoning spirit of New Zealanders as one people. New Zealanders had long enjoyed a holiday for each region—what purpose then would be served by a single national holiday with a regional emphasis?

Not surprisingly, the regions failed to respond to May's challenge, and New Zealand Day 1975 proved to be a phenomenal fizzer. Editorials around the country—with the exception of Northland—proclaimed the day a singular non-event, with headlines such as 'Do-it-yourself New Zealand Day', 'Just Another Day', 'Another Holiday' and 'Just Another Day Off'.[69] The *Nelson Evening Mail* asked 'Are These Wasted Days?', and pointed the finger squarely at Wellington:

> The point surely is that if the Government considered, as it must have done when it enacted the necessary legislation with so much patriotic trumpeting, that a special New Zealand Day should be inaugurated, it might well also have given a lead on how it suggested such an occasion might be appropriately marked, except by the luxury of not having to set the alarm clock on the night of February 5.[70]

---

timed holiday', and asked 'how many spared a thought today for the reason for the holiday—the signing of the Treaty of Waitangi 135 years ago? How many of those who did cared?', 6 February 1975.

[67] *New Zealand Herald*, 7 February 1974.

[68] Henry May, 'Future Observance of New Zealand Day', press statement, 25 September 1974, ANZ: AAAC/7536 W5084, Box 227 CON/9/2/3

[69] See, respectively, *Te Awamutu Courier*, 30 January 1975; *Greymouth Evening Star*, 1 March 1975; *Marlborough Express*, 5 February 1975; and *Evening Post*, 6 February 1975.

[70] *Nelson Evening Mail*, 31 January 1975. The *Greymouth Evening Star* (1 March 1975) and Wellington *Evening Post* (6 February 1975) made almost exactly the same point.

The non-spectacle of New Zealand Day 1975, where literally *nothing* happened outside of the Bay of Islands (not even in the capital) was indicative of the skin-deep penetration of New Zealand's brand of new nationalism. Indeed, it spoke volumes for New Zealand's 'incomplete nationhood' in a way that the perceived lack of such an occasion could never have done. Like Gough Whitlam in Australia, Kirk had promoted the cause of New Zealand Day to help fill the post-imperial void. But in the final analysis he merely succeeded in accentuating it.

And like Whitlam's national anthem, Kirk's New Zealand Day was partially revoked by the conservatives when they were returned to power in 1975. The precise reasons for this remain obscure, but on New Zealand Day 1976 Prime Minister Robert Muldoon announced that henceforth the occasion would be referred to by its original name, Waitangi Day. He stopped short, however, of revoking the nationwide holiday. Apart from some muffled cries of complaint in the *New Zealand Herald* ('Is this nationhood?' pondered the editorial[71]) there were few who identified any great national setback in these measures. On the whole there seemed to be general agreement with the verdict of the *Oamaru Mail* that 'efforts to make it a day of national significance and a rallying point for nationhood appear to have failed'.[72] And Maori community leaders were invariably gratified that the real significance of the occasion would no longer be airbrushed for the sake of some nebulous national spirit.

'Shorn of Empires'

On the eve of Canada's centennial in June 1967, the *Ottawa Journal* surveyed the Canadian propensity for selling themselves short as a nation. 'We as Canadians', it was argued, 'have become too impressed with our misgivings'. Politicians, the press and the general public had become so consumed with their national shortcomings that they failed to see the real value of being Canadian. The *Journal* suggested that Canada fared far better than most comparable nations, and asked readers to consider: 'Would we prefer to be as Britons, French, Italians—shorn of world empires and having to adjust to lesser ways?'

Yet, as I have tried to establish here, Canadians, Australians and New Zealanders too, had been 'shorn of empires' in a very real sense. And this inevitably entailed profound adjustments, not so much to 'lesser ways' as to their lesser selves, in place of the former reliance on 'Greater Britain' as the primary category of ethnic and cultural distinction. In the realm of civic culture, the formal definition and outward representation of the nation became subject to an ambivalent process of downsizing—of finding a language and imagery that would convey a more limited sense of the people. It was one thing to proclaim an abiding pride of place—an enduring affection for the settler-colonial homeland and its physical and material bounty. But it was quite another to articulate a coherent, self-sufficient folk myth, embodying a deep-rooted sense of an exclusive national community. As the *Globe and Mail* framed the problem in July 1964: 'Can the tenants live up to the real estate?'[73]

---

[71] *New Zealand Herald*, 9 February 1976.
[72] *Oamaru Mail*, 16 February 1976.
[73] *Globe and Mail*, 1 July 1964.

The three case studies examined here represent only a small facet of a far wider problem that resonated throughout the British world from the 1950s to the 1970s and beyond. They indicate that the switch from an imperial or 'dominion' civic culture to something more 'truly' national was neither straightforward nor consensual. It was not simply that a strong residue of British sentiment militated against the expression of a more exclusively defined national idea. Far more onerous was the problem of devising alternatives to Britishness as credible objects of civic identification—of filling the conceptual void left by the receding wake of the British world. Examined in this light, the upending of empire appears not so much as a process of national self-realisation as a species of post-imperial disorientation.

Moreover, the very dilemmas raised by the unravelling of Britishness suggest that there remains much to be said for the 'nationalism is a jealous God' school of British world historiography. Without buying in to Douglas Cole's overly rigid categories, it is possible to share his scepticism about treating Canadian, Australian and New Zealand identities as variants of nationalism, on a par with other nineteenth-century national ideologies including Britishness itself. The fact that these countries were so widely considered, in the very moment of their emancipation from Britishness, to be fundamentally lacking the stuff of 'real' nationhood, is surely indicative that they were qualitatively different. The solution lies not in the suggestion that these countries somehow missed out on the intellectual and cultural forces of nineteenth-century nationalism, but rather—following Cole, Meaney and others—that their experience of these forces was predominantly British and imperial. It was a Britishness for the most part home grown, tailored to the outlook, aspirations and anxieties of a settler-colonial population, but it was also crucially an expansive concept that was believed to be shared equally by fellow Britons around the globe. It was only when this concept became unimaginable with the collapse of the imperial infrastructure that the articulation of a more circumscribed national consciousness could be understood as a search for 'real' or 'true' nationhood.

Even today, annual national holidays in Canada, Australia and New Zealand are punctuated by an almost ritualised probing into the depth (or lack thereof) of the national soul. And there are signs that Britain itself is finally catching up in this regard. Just as dominion identities in the past had relied heavily on Britishness for national self-definition, so too the several nationalities of the British Isles had become harnessed to the common imperial project of being British. Recent moves to bring civic cultural practices into line with the developed version of the United Kingdom have therefore raised similar problems about the philosophical roots of Scottish, Welsh and now English nationalism. One key difference is that all three can point to pre-imperial ethnic categories that provide a ready-made treasure trove of symbols, rituals and commemorative occasions, but in many respects these are merely modern fabrications of a half-remembered past. Jeremy Paxman's popular history of Englishness describes a people 'simultaneously rediscovering the past that was buried when "Britain" was created, and inventing a new future'. And in a significant turn of phrase, he refers to this ambiguous process as England's own 'new nationalism'.[74] Yet Paxman, like virtually all recent authorities on Englishness, Britishness and so on, is entirely oblivious of his settler-colonial predecessors. A 'greater British' perspective has much to recommend itself in laying bare the disoriented identities of the post-imperial world.

---

[74] Jeremy Paxman, *The English: A Portrait of a People* (London: Penguin, 2007), 265.

V

Dependent Ally?
Australian–American Relations

11

Cold War 'Love Feast': The First US Presidential Visit to Australia, October 1966

James Curran

In October 1966, the United States ambassador in Canberra, Ed Clark, reported directly to the White House that 'the air in Australia is still charged' following Lyndon Johnson's visit to the country earlier in the month. It was the first time that a serving American president had set foot in the country, and Clark was convinced that the visit would 'have a tremendous lasting effect on Australia's thinking, on its economy, the policy in terms of Asia and elsewhere, and of course in US–Australian relations'.[1] Johnson spent nearly four days in Australia on his way to the Manila Security Conference, greeting mostly rapturous crowds and grateful officials in Sydney, Melbourne, Canberra and Townsville. At the time, the visit symbolised for many on both sides of the Pacific not only the high point of the relationship, but the dawn of a new era in American–Australian cooperation in the Asia-Pacific region. According to the Melbourne *Age*, the president's ability to tap such 'a fantastically rich vein of affection in the Australian people' meant that 'the warmth of this tribute so far overstepped the bounds of formal politeness that it also became a mass approval of his policies'. On the morning of Johnson's arrival in Australia, the *Sydney Morning Herald* discerned the 'first faint outline of a "special relationship" between Australia and the United States in the Pacific which may come to parallel the former special relationship between the United States and Britain in Europe'.[2] The Australian federal election was held the month following the president's tour, a poll which essentially became a referendum on Australian involvement in the Vietnam War. The governing Liberal–Country Party coalition—in power since 1949—won its biggest victory on record. Little wonder that early the following year the US Embassy in Canberra viewed Australia's rock-solid support for its government's policy in the region as evidence of 'what almost amounts to a bi-national US–Australian foreign policy in Asia' and a 'reaffirmed and nearly total commitment to the alliance'.[3]

Such confidence and euphoria was not altogether misplaced. Johnson's visit came at a time when Australian popular support for the war was peaking. Polling taken in August 1966 showed that sixty-four per cent of the electorate strongly approved of Prime Minister Harold Holt's support for American policy in Vietnam, while an even larger majority backed the call-up for military training of nineteen-year-olds. The commitment of 8000

---

[1] Telegram 2287, Ed Clark to Lyndon Baines Johnson (hereafter LBJ), 25 October 1966, Papers of Lyndon Baines Johnson (hereafter Johnson Papers), Lyndon Baines Johnson Library (LBJL), Austin, Texas: Confidential File, Box 95 (2 of 2).

[2] *Age* (Melbourne), 24 October 1966; *Sydney Morning Herald* (hereafter *SMH*), 22 October 1966.

[3] US Embassy, 'United States Annual Policy Assessment', 20 January 1967; US Embassy, 'Australia: Annual US Policy Assessment', 19 January 1968, National Archives and Records Administration (NARA), Washington DC: RG 59, Subject Numeric Files, Box 1863.

Australian troops at the height of the conflict had given the Australia, New Zealand, and United States (ANZUS) security alliance—signed in 1951—a new meaning.[4] On his first visit to Washington as prime minister in June 1966 Holt had famously adapted the Democratic Party's election campaign slogan, declaring that Australia was 'all the way with LBJ'—this at a time when the administration was attracting widespread condemnation for its bombings of the major population centres in North Vietnam. Such unqualified support from a close ally provided much succour to a White House keen to avoid the appearance of international isolation. Indeed when Walt Rostow, special assistant to the president, suggested a visit to Australia around the time of the Manila Conference, he pointed out to Johnson that there were 'no difficult issues outstanding in our relations with Australia' and was confident that 'the whole atmosphere of the visit will be excellent'.[5] Even before his departure from Washington, there can be little doubt that the Australian leg of the tour was seen in Washington as a much needed tonic for an increasingly beleaguered president and nervous officials concerned with the lack of progress on the ground in Vietnam. And, as Mitchell Lerner has shown, Johnson's vice-presidential travels had already displayed a considerable talent for using these types of trips as 'remarkably successful exercises in cultural diplomacy'.[6] Johnson lived and breathed for this type of election campaign-style communion with the public.

Given the significance of this presidential visit and its implications for the alliance at the height of the Cold War, it is intriguing that the archival record has remained relatively untouched. Moreover, the historiography on the events of October 1966 is miniscule. The major works on Australia's participation in Vietnam have touched only briefly on the visit and its ramifications. Where the Johnson visit has featured in studies of American–Australian relations, it has inevitably formed part of a wider backdrop—not only to Australia's contribution to the Vietnam War and the debate over the electoral boost the visit gave to the Liberal Party on the eve of the November 1966 election, but also to the question of the growing Americanisation of Australian political and popular culture.[7] Peter Edwards argues, for example, that the euphoria of the visit turned Harold Holt's 'All the way' gaffe into a 'political asset', while Glen Barclay suggests that the whole experience was 'reminiscent of the chairman of the board checking up on his branch managers'.[8] In other studies, the

---

[4] Neville Meaney, 'Australia and the World', in *Under New Heavens: Cultural Transmission and the Making of Australia*, ed. Meaney (Port Melbourne: Heinemann, 1985), 432–33.

[5] Memorandum, Walt Rostow to LBJ, 3 October 1966, Johnson Papers, LBJL: National Security Files, Manila Conference.

[6] Mitchell Lerner, ' "A Big Tree of Peace and Justice": The Vice Presidential Travels of Lyndon Johnson', *Diplomatic History*, 34 (2), 2010, 359–60.

[7] Paul Williams is an exception, though his article is expressly concerned with disproving the oft-made assumption that Johnson's visit resulted in an electoral boost for the Australian government on the eve of the 1966 election. See Paul Williams, 'Holt, Johnson and the 1966 Federal Election: A Question of Causality', *Australian Journal of Politics and History* (hereafter *AJPH*), 47 (3), 2001, 366–383.

[8] Peter Edwards, *A Nation at War: Australian Politics, Society and Diplomacy during the Vietnam War, 1965–1975* (Sydney: Allen & Unwin, 1997), 114–15; Glen St J. Barclay, *Friends in High Places: Australian–American Diplomatic Relations since 1945* (Melbourne: Oxford University Press, 1985),

dominant interpretation offered is that Johnson was rewarding Australia for its loyalty and obedience at a time when criticism of the president both in Washington and abroad was making his task of selling the war all the more problematic. Australian public enthusiasm for the visit is therefore usually depicted as a symptom of American cultural dominance and a fawning, obsequious government in Canberra unable to prosecute an independent Australian foreign policy. Thus historians Robin Gerster and Jan Bassett have described the visit as the 'apotheosis of Australia's love-affair with America'. For them, American cultural imperialism had 'so conquered Australia by the mid-1960s that a visiting President was virtually a de facto leader'.[9] Public intellectual Donald Horne saw the visit as a presidential payback for services rendered, with all the pomp and ceremony of a visiting monarch:

> here was the faithful ally being rewarded by an imperial visit, offering the spectacles of the triumphal motorcade, the imperial limousine, the imperial lectern, the imperial secret service guard, the impromptu stops, the hand shakings.[10]

More recently Stuart Macintyre, employing a familiar theme of Australian radical nationalism—the idea that an innate, self-sufficient vision of national 'independence' has been thwarted by the nefarious activities of London or Washington—claimed that Johnson's presence only confirmed a simple switch in Australian loyalties, as the country's political elite shifted their allegiance from one great power to another: 'As before with Britain, so now with the United States—obeisance to a powerful protector was payment in kind for defence on the cheap.'[11] Such interpretations, as David McLean demonstrates, allow little for the peculiar cultural and historical forces shaping the world view of Australian political leaders in the Cold War and, moreover, the particular anxieties that fuelled the concerns of the Australian public during this period. Furthermore it assumes all too easily that Australia adhered uncritically to the demands of Washington and was unable to express its own national interests.[12] As an isolated European outpost on the edge of an alien Asia, Australia had long sought the protection of a great power; during the Cold War Australia had sought to use the alliance to further Australia's interests in the region to its north. The visit of President Johnson in 1966—at the very peak of Australian–American cooperation in the containment of Asian communism—offers a powerful means of understanding alliance dynamics and their implications for Australia's cultural identity and strategic stance during this period.

Two key themes are discussed here as a means of revising the interpretative framework within which scholars of Australian foreign relations have assessed the significance of the visit. Firstly, although the rhetorical and symbolic optics of the visit should not be lightly dismissed, it needs to be asked what, precisely, both countries gained from the visit. Although Australia's continued support for American objectives in Vietnam was greatly

---

157.

[9] Robin Gerster and Jan Bassett, *Seizures of Youth: The Sixties and Australia* (Melbourne: Hyland House, 1991), 33–34.

[10] Donald Horne, *Time of Hope, Australia 1966–72* (Sydney: Angus & Robertson, 1980), 53.

[11] Stuart Macintyre, *A Concise History of Australia* (Cambridge: Cambridge University Press, 2009), 215.

[12] David McLean, 'Australia in the Cold War: A Historiographical Review', *International History Review*, XXIII (2), 2001, 320.

appreciated in Washington, there were some signs of US frustration with the relatively low number of troops contributed from its antipodean ally. Indeed, against the dominant view in Australian history writing that Australia went 'all the way with LBJ', it is too often forgotten how few concessions Australia had to make in order to maintain the American presence in South-East Asia—a key pillar of its Cold War policy. On this point it is instructive to note the Australian prime minister's confidence in May 1966 regarding the situation in Vietnam. Speaking to senior cabinet colleague Peter Howson about the benefits his government would reap from minimal military commitment, Holt surmised: 'The USA are [sic.] there to stay … We will win there and get protection in the South Pacific for a very small insurance premium'.[13] The widening gulf between ongoing Australian enthusiasm for the conflict as opposed to growing American doubts about the progress of the war around this time provides a further example of Australian alliance management—a style which would ultimately prove to have significant limits once the US began to scale down the war.

Secondly, this chapter will consider what the visit symbolised about shifting Australian loyalties and priorities. The assumption here is that the period of the visit and the 1966 election marked not only Australia's transformation from 'British sycophant' to 'American lickspittle'—as historian Humphrey McQueen so colourfully put it—but also, in the words of Greg Pemberton, the beginning of a 'new era in Australian political culture'.[14] Against the background of British military withdrawal from South-East Asia and attempts by the British government to join the European Economic Community, the tendency has been to assume that Johnson's tour put the final ceremonial gloss on Australia's exit from the bonds of the British Empire and heralded its entry into an American orbit. Unquestionably, Johnson's visit brought to the fore the growing American influence on Australia—strategic, cultural, political and economic—but it also pointed to a lingering suspicion of Americans as somewhat 'foreign', echoes of which had been heard at other key moments of American–Australian cultural interaction, namely the visit of President Theodore Roosevelt's Great White Fleet in 1908 and during the Second World War, when over a million American servicemen—including a young Lyndon Johnson—spent recreational leave in Australia.

'Friend, Saviour and Big Brother'

At the outset it is instructive to note briefly the closeness of the American–Australian alliance during the Cold War. By the end of the 1950s Australia had a sense that in the future they could not expect effective help from Britain in the case of a major threat to their territory. Everything would depend on the United States, and to this end the Australians reorganised their military structures and armaments to fit those of the US armed forces. Furthermore they saw the need to integrate America's defence needs with Australia so that American authorities would come to see the defence of Australia as being assimilated to the defence of America. The construction of US intelligence bases at Northwest Cape,

---

[13] Peter Howson, *The Howson Diaries: The Life of Politics*, ed. Don Aitkin (Ringwood, Melbourne: The Viking Press, 1984), 219, 223.

[14] Gregory Pemberton, *All the Way: Australia's Road to Vietnam* (Sydney: Allen & Unwin, 1987), 324.

Woomera and Pine Gap in the 1960s and the commitment of troops to Vietnam in 1965—the first time Australia had fought a war in which Britain was not involved—meant that the revolution in Australia's strategic orientation was complete. Indeed Australia and New Zealand were the only powers who contributed freely to the American cause in Vietnam. The United States' European partners in the South-East Asia Treaty Organisation (SEATO) stayed on the sidelines.[15]

Nevertheless despite the intimacy of the alliance and its foundation in shared values, Australians had found that their priorities and interests in the region collided with those of Washington as much as they coincided. In the early 1960s the two countries disagreed over Indonesian claims to the Dutch-held territory of West New Guinea[16] and Jakarta's policy of Confrontation towards the new Malaysian Federation.[17] These episodes, and Washington's reluctance to promise military assistance in the event of Australia becoming involved in armed conflict with Indonesian forces, raised doubts about the meaning of the ANZUS alliance, and about Australia's ability to rely on America for support or even consultation about issues which touched its vital interests in the region. Following this pattern of divergence, it is perhaps unsurprising that the Australian government viewed the presence of Johnson in their country as the most tangible proof of American strategic reassurance.

At the time, Johnson's seventeen-day trip abroad was the longest ever taken by an American president, and certainly the longest since John F. Kennedy's assassination in November 1963. His swing through Asia and the Pacific also included stops in Hawaii, New Zealand, Thailand, Malaysia and South Korea. According to Joseph A. Califano, one of Johnson's senior domestic aides, the president was 'enthusiastically received everywhere, and came away convinced that Asia was the future'.[18] Even in New Zealand, previously feared by some American officials as the 'worse launching pad' imaginable—a 'bucolic WASP utopia that does not specialize in enthusiasm'—the crowds came out. According

---

[15] For a general overview of US–Australian relations in the Cold War see T. R. Reese, *Australia, New Zealand and the United States: A Survey of International Relations, 1941–68* (London: Oxford University Press, 1969); Glen St J. Barclay, *Friends in High Places*; Coral Bell, *Dependent Ally: A Study in Australian Foreign Policy* (Melbourne: Oxford University Press, 1988).

[16] On US policy more broadly on this issue, see David Webster, 'Regimes in Motion: The Kennedy Administration and Indonesia's New Frontier, 1960–1962', *Diplomatic History*, 33 (1), 2009, 95–112. For an Australian perspective see Pemberton, *All the Way*, 101; and Richard Chauvel, '"Up the Creek without a Paddle": Australia, New Guinea and the "Great and Powerful Friends"', in *Menzies in War and Peace*, ed. Frank Cain (Sydney: Allen & Unwin, 1997), 55–71.

[17] On negotiations over the scope of ANZUS during Confrontation, see esp. John Subritzky, *Confronting Sukarno: British, American, Australian and New Zealand Diplomacy in the Malaysian-Indonesian Confrontation, 1961–5* (New York: St. Martin's Press, 1999), ch. 4. See also memorandum of conversation, McGeorge Bundy, Sir Howard Beale, and Michael V. Forrestal, 'ANZUS Treaty and Malaysia', Washington, 16 October 1963; and memorandum of conversation, President Kennedy and Sir Garfield Barwick, 17 October 1963, both in *Foreign Relations of the United States, 1961–63*, vol. XXXIII, *Southeast Asia*, ed. Edward C. Keefer (Washington: US Department of State, 1994), 747–50, 750–53 (respectively).

[18] Joseph A. Califano Jr, *The Triumph and Tragedy of Lyndon Johnson: The White House Years* (New York: Simon & Schuster, 1991), 150.

to British diplomats in Wellington, the 'New Zealanders, normally undemonstrative, surprised themselves by the enthusiasm with which they reacted to the President'.[19]

The Australian leg of the tour was not altogether a new experience for the Democratic president. As a young naval lieutenant in the Second World War, Johnson had spent some time in the country as part of his war service in the Pacific theatre, a service which he increasingly drew on as his political career took shape in the aftermath of the conflict. As Robert A. Caro has shown, Johnson was prone to exaggerating the extent and the effect of his time in uniform, a charade he was still performing with journalists at the White House the week before he left for his Asian tour in October 1966. Caro's description of Johnson's time in Australia provides a short but revealing portrait of an emerging political style. On a flight from Darwin to Melbourne, his company's plane was forced to land in desert country due to a navigational failure. Once landed, the lieutenant commander, according to a firsthand account given to Caro, got 'busy' meeting the local Australian farmers. Johnson was 'shaking hands all round', telling his comrades that 'these are real folks—the best damn folks in the world except maybe the folks in … Texas'. And as one of Johnson's travelling companions noted: 'Pretty soon he knows their first names … and there's no question he swung that county for Johnson before we left. He was in his element'.[20]

It is hardly surprising then that once he arrived in Australia as president twenty-four years later, Johnson was eager to reminisce about his previous visit, and his speeches were peppered with vignettes of his wartime experience: it had been a 'mission of war' whereas he was now on a 'mission of hope'; he could 'feel … as I did in 1942, the confidence that comes from the steadfast support of a united people in Australia'; he was in the country, he said on another occasion, to 'retrace some of the tracks that I made a quarter of a century ago'. Leaving Australia from Townsville in Northern Queensland, he confessed it had been a 'sentimental journey'.[21] Tempting though it might be to dismiss this kind of rhetoric, it nevertheless gave Johnson an immediate emotional connection to the Australian collective memory of the Pacific War—a time when in the face of the Japanese southward advance and the inability of Britain's Royal Navy to provide for Australia's defence, the nation's prime minister had made a dramatic appeal to America for military assistance.[22] The rhetorical bridge between the 'struggle for freedom' in the Second World War and the struggle against communism in the post-war period was never a difficult one for Johnson to construct.

---

[19] Telegram, Bill Moyers to William Bundy, 9 October 1966, LBJL; Telegram 537, British High Commission, Wellington, to Foreign and Commonwealth Office, 26 October 1966, TNA: FCO 49/78. Only in Malaysia was the response to the president characterised as 'limp', since according to the British high commissioner there, the Malaysians were 'not normally demonstrative'. See despatch, British High Commission, Malaysia, to Herbert Bowden, 'Malaysia: Visit of President Johnson', 1 December 1966, TNA: DO 169/471.

[20] Robert A. Caro, *Means of Ascent: The Years of Lyndon Johnson* (New York: Alfred A. Knopf, 1990), 44.

[21] See, for example, LBJ, 'Remarks Upon Arrival at the RAAF Fairbairn Airport', Canberra, Australia, 20 October 1966; LBJ, 'Remarks at Townsville Upon Departing from Australia', 23 October 1966, both in *Public Papers of the Presidents, Lyndon Baines Johnson: Containing the Public Messages, Speeches and Statements of the President* (hereafter *PPP: LBJ*), vol. 3, bk 2, *1 July–31 December 1966* (Washington: US Government Printing Office, 1967), 1238–56.

[22] See generally James Curran, *Curtin's Empire* (Melbourne: Cambridge University Press, 2011).

In Australia the fervour of the welcome for the president seemingly knew no bounds. 'For 65 hours', journalist Alan Ramsey observed, Johnson 'hypnotized Australia with his magnetic personality and wide smile, his Texan drawl and folksy rhetoric'.[23] The *Age* hailed it as 'the most spectacular reception ever given by Australia to one man'.[24] The *Canberra Times*' description of the president's reception in Sydney gave something of the flavour, noting a little sarcastically:

> Rising like the ocean waves were joyous shouts of 'All the way with LBJ' … while in their hearts the surging masses felt love for their great leaders and derision for the cardboard dragon of Chinese imperialism. Through the night loyal printers had laboured to produce 'one million hoorays' printed on strips of coloured paper eight inches long, 100,000 lapel badges and 1,000 cardboard banners 15 inches by 20 inches, all carrying portraits of President Lyndon—friend, saviour, big brother and father of friendship between the American and Australian peoples'.

As if this was not sufficiently effusive, 'some loyal cadres', as the *Canberra Times* described sections of the crowd, 'had even produced posters proclaiming "the 51st State welcomes LBJ"'.[25]

Certainly, there were protests, but they were not allowed to impinge on Australia's moment in the international sun. Anti-war demonstrators were warned by a nervous press and officialdom not to stain the national reputation and sully Australia's image in the eyes of the world. In Brisbane, the *Courier Mail* branded the visit as a 'test of good manners' even suggesting that the local police allow a demonstration by an anti-war group 'before the presidential arrival' which 'should satisfy both the demonstrators, who will get the protests off their chests, and the waiting crowd, who will have the opportunity of watching a preliminary to the big event'. Putting aside the bizarre reduction of the visit to the rules and regulations of a major sporting event, the plaintive tone of such reporting showed that nothing less than the 'national prestige' was at stake.[26] In general, the press tended to portray the protests as aberrant, isolated incidents, or, in the words of one report, 'unrepresentative of Australian feeling'.[27] Others stressed that now was simply not the time to pick a fight with the US commander-in-chief—political discord could wait for the November election. 'As the guest of Australia, the president will not be able to argue with minority groups', the Melbourne *Age* observed. 'We can do that between ourselves before the year is out'.[28] Although one incident—where paint bags were thrown at the presidential limousine in Melbourne—captured international headlines, more attention was given to the agreement of the paint bombers to pay compensation to the injured and their readiness

---

[23] *Australian*, 24 October 1966.

[24] *Age* (Melbourne), 24 October 1966.

[25] *Canberra Times*, 19 October 1966.

[26] *Courier Mail*, 15 October 1966. See also an editorial in the wake of the visit in the *Sydney Morning Herald* which cautioned that 'the technique of protest requires a discipline and responsibility which some of our demonstrators have not learnt … demonstrators should stick to the ground rules laid down for non-violence in India by Gandhi'. *SMH*, 29 October 1966.

[27] *Courier Mail*, 22 October 1966.

[28] *Age* (Melbourne), 20 October 1966.

to accept psychiatric testing. Indeed, in a subsequent letter to the president, the Australian lawyer acting on behalf of the paint bombers stressed that their actions were not 'inspired by any malevolent feeling towards you or the great Nation you represent', but 'rather ... the effervescence of youthful gaiety and jocularity excited to fever pitch by your presence and the consequent air of exaltation and triumph'.[29]

For the British high commissioner in Canberra, Charles Johnston, it was the very novelty of the whole experience for Australians, as much as the lure of the limelight of international opinion, that captured the essence of Johnson's effect on the country: 'The President's double function as Head of State and of Government, and the consequent mixture of majesty and campaigning folksiness, was something quite new to Australians and had an overwhelming impact'. In the main, he told the secretary of state for Commonwealth affairs, Herbert Bowden, 'they were flattered that so much attention should be paid to them by the most powerful man in the world'. The post-Dallas security procedures and overall sense of grandeur were particularly novel features for Australian crowds:

> the security arrangements were a prominent part of the proceedings. They were carried out with a certain ruthless 'colonialism' which characterised the whole visit. With a good deal of courtesy the Americans made it absolutely clear who was the boss. When their security people arrived in advance at a place which the President was going to visit, they practically took it over, and everyone from the State governor down had to keep out of the way, and no questions asked. Perhaps the most extraordinary impression was created by the bubble-top car. When the President stopped it and emerged from it to talk to people on the route, he resembled a diver coming up for air. Below him, inside the bowl of thick plate glass, the portly form of Ambassador Ed Clark could be faintly discerned like a monster of the deep. At other times, when the car was moving, the President's voice coming out of it over the bull horn produced a sort of science fiction effect—like a Dalek.

The whole episode, Johnston observed with obvious relish, 'was new and exciting and slightly macabre'.[30]

American Doubt, Australian Conviction

No matter how spontaneous the welcome from the Australian public was or how much effort the White House and secret service put into stage-managing the visit, there were points of contention. Certainly, private discussions between the president and Australian politicians, as historian Peter Edwards has noted, constituted a 'blunt reiteration of the public rhetoric'.[31] Nevertheless, evidence of underlying American frustration at the numbers of Australian and other allied troops committed and significant divergences between respective understandings of the situation on the ground in Vietnam point to ongoing tensions in the alliance dynamic at this time.

---

[29] Correspondence, Frank Galbally to LBJ, 24 October 1966, Johnson Papers, LBJL: TR100.

[30] Despatch, Charles Johnston to Bowden, 'Australia: Visit of President Johnson', 24 November 1966, TNA: DO 193/80.

[31] Edwards, *A Nation at War*, 116.

As American doubts about the progress of the war increased throughout 1966—with a growing number of senior American officials, including Assistant Secretary of State for East Asian and Pacific Affairs William Bundy and Secretary of Defense Robert McNamara, almost at the point of despair—Australian leaders only seemed to gain in confidence. That confidence derived less from the situation on the ground in the war but rather from an assessment of how the alliance could best serve Australian national interests in the wake of the British decision to start withdrawing militarily from east of Suez. In March 1966, cabinet had decided that Australia's primary consideration in being in Vietnam was the 'continued commitment of the United States to the defence of South East Asia'.[32] Accordingly Australian statements and policies at this time all pushed in that direction. In late June 1966 Secretary of State Dean Rusk found Holt 'one thousand per cent in support of what we are trying to achieve in South East Asia'. Taking the matter further Holt had explained that

> the general feeling in Australia is that Australia is more directly threatened by the situation in Vietnam than is the US, and that there is a widespread feeling the US is fighting Australia's battle there, rather than the other way around.[33]

It was an accurate summation of the Australian attitude.

Although Holt's visit to Washington in July 1966 is remembered primarily for first using the 'all the way with LBJ' slogan, perhaps all the more remarkable was Holt's response to an American journalist following his speech at the National Press Club during the same visit. The Australian prime minister was told that 'we are not used to having our policies so enthusiastically supported', and when asked, 'Isn't there anything wrong with American foreign policy?', Holt's response was revealing: 'Well, frankly, not in our eyes'.[34] As Glen Barclay has argued, Holt, 'temperamentally the Australian politician most sympathetic to American concerns, did not seem to recognise as serious circumstances that were rendering the Americans desperate'.[35] From December 1965 until the end of 1966 American forces increased from 184 000 to 385 000.[36] Australian leaders, however, were always wary of being trapped in a cycle of automatic commitment, where Canberra would be expected to systematically match US troop increases.[37] Indeed in a speech upon his return from Washington, Holt extolled Australia's worth to the United States as a 'country of influence' in the Asia-Pacific area, but was sure to add in the next breath that 'there is no escalation … in contemplation' in relation to Australia's Vietnam military contribution.[38]

On 21 October, when Johnson addressed the Australian cabinet in Canberra, he made a point of again expressing his disappointment with Britain and Washington's SEATO

---

[32] Cited in ibid., 102.

[33] Cablegram, Dean Rusk to LBJ, 27 June 1966; memorandum of conversation, Rusk and Holt, 28 June 1966, both in LBJL: National Security Files—Country Files, Box 233.

[34] Cited in Glen St J. Barclay, *A Very Small Insurance Policy: The Politics of Australian Involvement in Vietnam, 1954–1967* (St Lucia, Qld: University of Queensland Press, 1988), 138.

[35] Ibid.

[36] Edwards, *A Nation At War*, 100.

[37] Pemberton, *All the Way*, 304.

[38] Holt, speech to National Press Club, Canberra, 18 July 66, in *Current Notes on International Affairs,* 37 (7), 1966, 451–61.

partners for staying out of the conflict. Although he stressed that he 'had not come to Australia to ask for a man or a dollar', his listeners around the cabinet table would not have missed his subsequent statement that 'if the United States were to pull out of Vietnam tomorrow, other countries of South East Asia would quickly fall. And the aggressor would get to Australia long before he got to San Francisco'.[39] It was a line he repeated in his public speeches during the visit. 'It is time', he told one audience, 'for you to stop, look, and listen, and decide how much your liberty and your freedom mean to you and what you are willing to pay for it'.[40] There is evidence to support the suggestion that Johnson and his advisers were growing increasingly frustrated with the unwillingness of Australia and New Zealand to contribute more troops to the war effort. Privately, the Americans were putting a great deal of pressure on Prime Minister Holt to add a third battalion to the two that were already in Vietnam, though Holt maintained that the policy would remain the same until 'the people have had a chance to vote on it'.[41] At the official reception for the president in Melbourne, the governor of Victoria was shocked to hear Johnson 'declaiming violently against New Zealand for the smallness of its contribution in Vietnam', reportedly telling guests: 'Here are 100 American boys being killed every week … and yet New Zealand only sends 200 odd men there. Such a country does not deserve to be free'.[42] The unnerving thought for Australian politicians and officials was whether or not Johnson had unloaded in a similar vein on the level of their military commitment.

Australia, it would seem, did not entirely escape a certain measure of American frustration. A staunch opponent of the war in Washington, Democrat senator J. William Fulbright, already had Australia's troop numbers in his sights and sought to maximise Canberra's embarrassment on this point, with his remarks earlier in the year that

> they believe that the United States will carry the whole load, and that our men will do the dying and that we will pay the bill. Otherwise, I am unable to understand why they do not send more than a token force.[43]

Harry Macpherson, a Democratic party aide from Texas accompanying the president, noted the gulf between Australian rhetorical support—along with other US allies in Asia—and actual troop commitments:

> The Australians and New Zealanders, the Filipinos, the Thais, the Malaysians and Koreans, the Japanese and Indonesians all are glad to have a counterweight to China in the region. All say, publicly and privately, that resistance to the communists in Vietnam is terribly important to them. Then why has none of them, except for the Koreans, sent substantial numbers of troops there? Because we have. If the strongest, richest country in the world proclaims that stopping

---

[39] Cabinet decision 670, 'Meeting with President Johnson', 21 October 1966, NAA: A5839, 670.

[40] LBJ, 'Remarks at a Reception at Government House', Melbourne, 21 October 1966, reported in correspondence, Johnston to Sir Neil Pritchard, 8 November 1966, TNA: DO 169/471.

[41] Holt cited in despatch, Johnston to Bowden, 'Australia: Visit of President Johnson', 24 November 1966, TNA: DO 193/80.

[42] Correspondence, Johnston to Pritchard, 8 November 1966, TNA: DO 169/471.

[43] Fulbright cited in *Report on the US Senate Hearings: The Truth about Vietnam*, eds Frank M. Robinson and Earl Kemp (San Diego: Greenleaf, 1966), 63, 383–4.

> North Vietnam is critical to its own security, surely that makes it unnecessary for lesser countries to contribute much to that fight? Prime Minister Holt … could not survive the deficits and long casualty lists that would follow a deeper commitment.[44]

And as Johnson prepared to depart from Townsville, Macpherson's incredulity only seemed to have intensified:

> Together we … shall what? Fight Asia's wars … What are white men doing out here on this stalagmite of a continent, praying the ancient English prayers and talking about a war between brown men four thousand miles away? Presumably making sure that the North Vietnamese or Chinese troops do not someday camp in the New Guinea mountains across the Coral Sea. At the moment, as we stand on the baked, barren ground at Townsville, that seems far-fetched.[45]

Such questions cut through the rhetorical gloss of the visit, but these differences were not given public expression, and for Australian leaders there can be no doubt that Johnson's tour carried enormous symbolic appeal. As Howson noted in his diary after listening to Johnson's speech in Canberra, the president's words had 'cemented the US–Australian alliance and confirmed a common policy in South East Asia. There can now be no doubt that Australia has an umbrella or shield' in the region. 'Three years ago', he added, 'this was not really a certainty'.[46] Australian ministers publicly acknowledged that the US relationship was at the core of their Vietnam involvement, and the presence of Johnson provided the heavyweight personal assurance that successive leaders struggled to find in the language of the ANZUS Treaty itself—a moment, at least, where the legacy of difference and disagreement with Washington over West New Guinea and Confrontation could be easily forgotten, momentarily carried away, as it were, on a sea of sentimental affection for the visiting president. With British moves to withdraw from the region, and ongoing Australian doubts about the longevity of an American regional presence, Johnson's four days provided that reassurance and a public relations coup for the government. And in the wake of Holt's commanding win at the polls in November, the Americans had their answer on an extra military commitment, with the announcement of a force increase for Vietnam, bringing the total number of Australian troops at that time to 6300.

'No Need for Us to Despair': Johnson and the Fate of Australian National Loyalties

The presidential visit also came at a time of growing American appreciation for a more nationalistic Australia. Although this new nationalism came to be more fully identified with the outlook of the subsequent Whitlam Labor government from 1972–75, it had its first stirrings during the predecessor administrations of Holt and John Gorton. Holt was the first Australian leader to use the term 'Australian identity', while Gorton regularly

---

[44] Harry Macpherson, *A Political Education* (Boston: Little, Brown and Co, 1972), 313–14.
[45] Ibid., 306–07.
[46] Howson, *Howson Diaries*, 244–45.

appealed to the population to help him 'foster a real sense of nationalism'.[47] Both prime ministers recognised the need to bolster the flimsy foundations of Australian nationhood once the defining idea of national life—the idea of being British—collapsed under the weight of changing circumstances in the 1960s. US assessments of Australia's new spirit of national purpose typically focussed on the redundancy of Australia's imperial outlook in defence and economic terms, highlighted the need for America to consult more widely and intimately with political leaders in Canberra and assumed, in the words of one Central Intelligence Agency (CIA) report, that the US now provided Australia's 'shield' in South-East Asia.[48] But American support for a more independently minded Australia was highly qualified—independence was to be welcomed in so far as it entailed a nation willing not only to fall into line with American objectives in Vietnam, but also to assume a greater responsibility for the defence of South-East Asia in the wake of British announcements of their intention to withdraw from the region; an expectation that would assume concrete form with the promulgation of the Guam, or Nixon, Doctrine several years later.[49]

In the meantime, American officials might have been forgiven for thinking that Australians were drifting inexorably out of the British imperial embrace. A Gallup poll in May 1965 found that 'Australians are slightly more likely to name the US as the "best friend" of their country than they are to choose the British motherland' (forty-three per cent to thirty-nine per cent).[50] In his memoirs Johnson himself drew attention to the turbulence in Australian strategic thinking around this time, underlining that 'New Zealand and Australia were reappraising their roles in the world community' and that 'a profound, and doubtless painful, readjustment was under way'.[51] That Johnson's arrival in Canberra coincided with the announcement by British defence minister Dennis Healey of the departure of the first 10 000 British troops from Borneo was not missed by the Australian press. As the *Sydney Morning Herald* editorialised: 'The tide of history is washing Britain slowly out of South East Asia … And now we only hear "its melancholy, long withdrawing roar".'[52] Or as the *Bulletin* observed: 'Britain? That is a memory, it seems, a phase Australia has passed through on its way to American inter-dependence, even if in this inter-dependence we are the junior partners'.[53] A harsher verdict on that transformation was handed down by historian Geoffrey Serle the following year. 'We have been making the transition from a British colony to an American province', he wrote, 'with only a fleeting

---

[47] Curran and Stuart Ward, *The Unknown Nation: Australia after Empire* (Melbourne: Melbourne University Press, 2010), 5–7.

[48] CIA Intelligence Report, 'Australia Today', 11 October 1966, Johnson Papers, LBJL: National Security Files—International Meetings and Travel Files, Box 10.

[49] Jeffrey Kimball, 'The Nixon Doctrine: A Saga of Misunderstanding', *Presidential Studies Quarterly*, 36 (1), 2006, 59–74.

[50] Gallup poll, 'Australian Public Slightly More Likely to see US than Britain as "Best Friend" Country', 19 May 1965, Johnson Papers, LBJL: National Security Files—Country Files, Box 232.

[51] Lyndon Baines Johnson, *The Vantage Point: Perspectives of the Presidency, 1963–69* (New York: Holt, Rinehart and Winston, 1971), 361.

[52] *SMH*, 22 October 1966.

[53] *Bulletin*, 20 October 1966.

glimpse of independence on the way'. For Serle, the Australian political elite had 'such an inbuilt sense of dependence, is so little conscious of what sense of Australian nationality there is … that it can be expected to defer and stand aside'. Australians were destined to 'become just slightly different sorts of Americans'. The more Australians pronounced their independence, he added, the 'more and more Americanised and dependent' they would become, eventually becoming a hybrid nation, 'Austerica'.[54]

Yet despite the signs of Britain's imminent withdrawal from the region, along with Holt and Johnson's barely concealed criticism of Harold Wilson's reluctance to commit British forces to Vietnam, there is every reason to resist the lure of Geoffrey Serle's 'logic of satellitism'—the belief that amidst the hysteria of Johnson's visit Australians were duly sucked into the American vortex and there located an alternative pole of cultural attraction to Britishness. And not least because Australian leaders always tried to use the alliance to serve their own ends. Serle himself suspected that the 'British tradition may have more lasting appeal than appears at the moment'. It is telling, for instance, that the reception accorded Johnson could only have one point of comparative reference: British royal tours. Thus while the president's visit became the occasion for much discussion about presidential style, the superiority of his speechmaking and American political glitz and glamour, it was equally a moment when many were forced to reflect on the style of the monarchy, its continuing hold on the Australian imagination, the current state of the British connection and therefore the fate of Australian loyalties in a post-imperial era.

As argued above, the very spectacle of Johnson's presence had a beguiling effect on Australian crowds. Though such an impression was easy to dismiss as one of 'slightly bogus folksiness, of homely country manners served up as it were in cellophane for the consumption of big city voters', the civic and ceremonial space of Australian culture up to that time had been mostly reserved and restrained: even the splendour of royal tours, it seems, were no competition for the Johnson effect. According to Charles Johnston, what seems to have attracted the Australian eye the most was the 'happy hand-shaking manner' of the president. Here was a head of state that was tangible and seemingly genuinely pleased to be among the people. Johnson's 'apparent lack of respect for timing and protocol (and his consequent readiness to keep dignitaries waiting in order that he could chat with ordinary men and women in the crowd) were contrasted with the formality and rigid timing of some Royal Tours'.[55] Or, as a Queensland newspaper editor put it more directly, Johnson's visit was 'as different from the royal tour type of visit as a choirboy's bunfight is from afternoon tea with the bishop'.[56] Other tests were more superficial and amounted to little more than counting the number of miniature US flags being frantically waved by feverish onlookers. Journalist Alan Ramsey opined: 'Never has a head of state received such prime ministerial attention. Not even royalty, not even the Queen was treated like this. And never before have

---

[54] Geoffrey Serle, 'Austerica Unlimited', *Meanjin*, September 1967.

[55] Letter, Johnston to Sir Saville Garner, 'Austalian Attitudes towards the Monarchy', 26 January 1967, in *Documents on Australian Foreign Policy: Australia and the United Kingdom, 1960–1975*, eds S. R. Ashton, Carl Bridge and Stuart Ward (Canberra: DFAT, 2010), 919.

[56] *Courier Mail*, 15 October 1966.

the stars and stripes so overwhelmingly outnumbered the Union Jacks'.⁵⁷ Thus by the time the president reached Townsville—the last stop on his Australian visit—British observers discerned a ray of hope for the future of the Anglo-Australian relationship, but only in purely heraldic terms: 'in the absence of mass-produced American flags, a large number of Union Jacks [were] being waved in the streets'. ⁵⁸

The comparison with Australians' reactions to royal tours also provoked a certain defensiveness on the part of British officials. The enthusiastic reception of Johnson was not confined to Australia—Johnson had received a rapturous welcome in New Zealand, with protesters even dropping their placards to shake the presidential hand.⁵⁹ Ironically, in the wake of Johnson's departure from the country British officials lamented:

> One of the more regrettable notes struck by the press, especially in the big circulation papers, has been the repetition of the comment that in warmth, size and enthusiasm the reception accorded the President and his lady by the populace of Wellington has far exceeded that of Royal visits.⁶⁰

In Canberra similar comparisons were being made, though with different conclusions. Almost with relief the British high commissioner noted that 'Press coverage, though prodigious, was actually no greater that that given to the first days of Her Majesty's latest visit'.⁶¹ With no hint of irony, the media arrangements in general were judged to be similar for those put in place for Churchill's funeral. Lord Carrington, leader of the opposition in the House of Lords and a future defence secretary, flatly rejected any talk of Anglo-American rivalry in securing Australia's loyalty as an ally. Carrington dismissed the cry that the presidential visit, and Australia's reaction to it, meant that 'Australia is going American … The fact that Australia and America have strong ties is quite irrelevant to British relationships with Australia'.⁶² Others divined a more earthy form of solace in the Australian countryside. The 'typical Australians' were sticking with Liz, not Lyndon. The British Foreign Office was subsequently reassured that 'one hears stories of shearers and other people in the country area who said things like "if it was the Queen I would go in to see her, but B[ugger] Johnson" '.⁶³ It followed from this anecdote that if the rugged Australian outdoor frontiersman was remaining faithful to the Queen, Australia's essential Britishness was very much in safekeeping.

On other frontiers however, the reaction was less encouraging. At times, Johnson appeared to some observers as nothing less than the irreverent American cowboy crudely

---

⁵⁷ *Australian*, 24 October 1966.

⁵⁸ Despatch, Johnston to Bowden, 'Australia: Visit of President Johnson', 24 November 1966, TNA: DO 193/80.

⁵⁹ Telegram, Moyers to William Bundy, 9 October 1966, Johnson Papers, LBJL: National Security Council Histories, Box 45.

⁶⁰ Telegram 533, British High Commission, Wellington, to Foreign and Commonwealth Office, 'United States President's Visit: Press Roundup', 21 October 1966, TNA: FCO 49/78.

⁶¹ Telegram 1485, Johnston to Bowden, 'Publicity Coverage of Johnson's Visit', 24 October 1966, TNA: DO 193/80.

⁶² *SMH*, 25 October 1966.

⁶³ Correspondence, Johnston to Pritchard, 8 November 1966, TNA: DO 193/80.

indifferent to formal diplomatic protocol. The British high commissioner saw in the visit an 'interesting clash between the dignified procedures traditional in Australia and the hustling, electioneering methods of the Presidential Court in America today', a confrontation 'curiously symbolised when the President tried to *howdy* four Vietnam veterans of the Australian army whom he found standing on guard at the Canberra War Memorial with heads bowed and arms reversed'. And nowhere was this tension more apparent than at a barbecue held for Johnson by the US ambassador at a property in Tharwa, just outside Canberra. Despite an invitation requesting the wearing of lounge suits, Johnson apparently 'appeared in full Texan kit complete with everything except a six-shooter'. With a security helicopter backfiring overhead, and guests enjoying pink ice creams shaped in the form of kangaroos, the British high commissioner could barely conceal both his displeasure and discomfort when 'the President, who was chewing a mouthful of steak at the time, greeted us courteously but without obvious enthusiasm'. In the middle of this 'Vietnam oriented Australian–American love-feast', he wailed, 'the representative of the British Government was decidedly the skeleton at the barbecue'.[64]

Wailing or not, the reception accorded President Johnson was of such magnitude that it prompted a number of considered British assessments concerning Anglo–Australian relations, Australian attitudes to the monarchy and the future of Australian republicanism. The conclusions were mixed. First and foremost, according to Johnston, 'the visit should certainly not be interpreted as an explosion of pro-Republican feeling'. The lack of republicanism on any of the party platforms, the difficulty for Australians in accepting a local politician as a president and the lack of an aristocracy from which to draw an appropriate candidate for such a role all provided a measure of reassurance for the high commissioner that the 'Monarchy as an element of dignity, stability and continuity would be hard to replace'.[65] The state of Australian relations with Britain was far more problematic, officials conceding that the ledger was very much stacked against Whitehall: no British involvement in Vietnam; uncertainty arising from plans for military withdrawal from the region; various economic difficulties, particularly doubts on the long-term future of the British sterling; and 'the failure of combined resistance to Indonesia to move the public imagination in the same way as Vietnam'. Nevertheless, there was:

> no need for us to despair. The links which bind Australia and Britain are still strong. Australians are above all an independent-minded people. They have no wish to pass from British into American tutelage. They have no wish to follow in Canada's footsteps. The British connection so far has been a family affair, taken for granted and regarded as something solid if slightly boring. Now the Australians have a conscious motive for needing Britain to help hold the balance. We shall however have to work harder than ever to prove to the Australians that we are still around.[66]

---

[64] Despatch, Johnston to Bowden, 'Australia: Visit of President Johnson', 24 November 1966, TNA: DO 193/80.

[65] Letter, Johnston to Garner, 26 January 1967, in *Australia and the United Kingdom*, eds Ashton, Bridge and Ward, 917.

[66] Telegram 1483, Johnston to Bowden, 24 October 1966, TNA: DO 193/80.

The solution to working harder was to encourage not only a British prime ministerial visit, but more importantly, the introduction of a more informal type of royal tour. The Foreign and Commonwealth Offices wanted a piece of the presidential magic. Thus in March 1967 Charles Johnston could happily report a successful 'experiment': the first visit by members of the royal family, Princess Alexandra and her partner Angus Ogilvy 'with the object of private business plus fun and relaxation'. Against the background of Johnson's visit, he confessed that the High Commission had 'felt the need for a new and more informal type of visit to Australia by members of our own Royal family'. In short, Johnston added, 'the more we can show the Australians that members of the Royal Family enjoy coming here without fuss or formality, the better pleased the Australians will be'.[67]

It is tempting to consider that the real legacy of Johnson's visit was a spate of royal tours that were designed to bring the Queen closer to her people. By any measure, the strategy worked. Despite a period in which the nation's constitutional bonds with Britain were progressively loosened—be it in the form of dropping the words 'British subject' from Australian passports, or in Whitlam's attempts to end Privy Council appeals, inaugurate a new national anthem to replace *God Save the Queen* and institute a new Australian honours system—the country continued to welcome royal visits. Indeed the Queen visited Australia twice during the period of supposedly the most nationalist government of the post-war era—the Whitlam Labor government. And while those visits lacked the fervour of the 1954 royal visit, they nevertheless lent a certain credence to Geoffrey Dutton's view that such occasions acted as a kind of symbolic and rhetorical syrup that 'oozed over any cracks' in the Australia–Britain relationship.[68] By contrast, Presidents Nixon, Jimmy Carter and Ronald Reagan did not visit Australia during their terms in office. Just over a quarter of a century would elapse before the next serving US president, George H. W. Bush, landed in Australia in late December 1991.

Conclusion

In his analysis of the American–Australian alliance in the Cold War, David McLean makes the important point that

> the impulse behind Johnson's welcome in 1966 was similar to that underlying the reception of President Roosevelt's Great White Fleet in 1908. In both cases the fervour of the response expressed goodwill and gratitude towards a culturally related great power to which Australians looked for protection against a threatening region, in particular against what were feared to be the expansionist ambitions of Japan in one case, China in the other.[69]

The presidential visit of 1966 was by no means the first time that Australians wildly embraced the phenomenon of the visiting American. But just as in 1908, and again following the so-called 'friendly invasion' of nearly a million American servicemen in the Second World War, real gains—in terms of greater Australian influence or access to the centre of US

---

[67] Correspondence, Johnston to Garner, 9 March 1967, TNA: FO49/78.
[68] Geoffrey Dutton, 'British Subject', *Nation*, 6 April 1963.
[69] David McLean, 'From British Colony to American Satellite? Australia and the USA during the Cold War', *AJPH*, 52 (1), 2006, 74.

policymaking—were thin on the ground. In 1908, Roosevelt was uninterested in Prime Minister Alfred Deakin's proposal for the extension of the American Monroe Doctrine to the South Pacific. And during the Second World War, the Australian reception of American troops did not result in Australia gaining more access to the innermost allied councils of the war, or to a more sympathetic American ear to repeated Australian proposals for a defence pact or security arrangement with Washington in the immediate post-war years. Indeed on both occasions, the hysteria that greeted the visitor was followed by a measure of ambivalence, if not downright disappointment in subsequent years.[70]

In the case of 1966, the euphoria was perhaps even more short-lived. Holt himself confided to a senior British diplomat in the immediate wake of the visit that while he 'admired President Johnson very much', he 'found it difficult to get on the same wavelength with him', not only during the president's Australian visit but also at the subsequent Manila Conference. According to the British diplomat, Holt claimed a greater personal affinity for Harold Wilson, even if 'Johnson probably means more to me and my country'.[71] It was a revealing comment: Holt appeared to be telling his British friends precisely what they wanted to hear—that whilst American power could not be lightly dismissed, the personal chemistry between prime minister and president simply did not match the equivalent relationship that an Australian leader enjoyed with his British counterpart. In truth, British officials had probably worried a little too much about the fate of Australian loyalties in the wake of the Johnson visit. Certainly Holt, as Jeppe Kristensen has shown, was 'in no way inclined to dance on the grave of British Australia'. During a visit to Britain in September 1967, Holt conceded that America was going to loom larger on the Australian horizon, but this was not to imply that the last rites were to be delivered to the British connection. The prime minister told an audience in London that Australia was 'in essence still a British country … The Australian situation geographically, politically and in terms of trade, draws us into the Pacific Ocean of affairs … But this is not to kiss goodbye to Britain'.[72] Holt's language may have lacked the conviction and certainty of old, but it nevertheless showed that amidst a time of turbulence and change in the Australian outlook, the gravitational pull of the American superpower had by no means entirely extracted the political elite from the comfort of their familiar British orbit.

The White House was particularly sensitive to the perception that the relationship with Australia was sustained by little else than pleasantries and platitudes: in preparation for Holt's visit to Washington in June the following year US secretary of state for East Asia and the Pacific, William Bundy pointed to the 'danger that this visit, particularly with its formalities, will be construed in some quarters as overdoing it from a personal standpoint'.

---

[70] See esp. Meaney, *A History of Australian Defence and Foreign Policy, 1901–23*, vol. 1, *The Search for Security in the Pacific, 1901–14* (Sydney: Sydney University Press, 1976), 163ff; Meaney, *Primary Risks and Primary Responsibilities in the Pacific: The Problem of Japan and the Changing Role of Australia in the British Commonwealth, 1945–1952* (London: Suntory Centre, LSE, 2000); and more generally, John Hammond Moore, *Over-Sexed, Over-Paid and Over Here: Americans in Australia, 1941–1945* (St Lucia, Qld: University of Queensland Press, 1981).

[71] Correspondence, Johnston to Pritchard, 8 November 1966, TNA: DO 169/471.

[72] Cited in Jeppe Kristensen, '"In Essence still a British Country": Britain's Withdrawal from East of Suez', *AJPH*, 51 (1), 2005, 48.

Bundy recommended that the president prioritise the discussion of 'major serious Asian topics' rather than the 'personal cordialities', including the need for public presidential statements to put 'Vietnam in the context of an Asia that may be turning the corner'.[73] Even the Americans, then, were conceding that the alliance required an injection of substance over show.

On that score, the Australians were aware before Johnson's arrival that the general line in his speeches would be 'essentially a projection' of his White Sulphur Springs speech of 12 July 1966 which White House advisers were portraying more and more as a turning point in Johnson's approach to Asia.[74] In those remarks Johnson had attempted to set out the administration's regional view—the foundation for peace in Asia. For the president the 'untold story of 1966' was 'the story of what free Asians have done for the themselves, and with the help of others, while South Vietnam and her allies have been busy holding aggression at bay'.[75] It shows that amidst the discussions over the future of the war, Johnson was giving tentative shape to his grand design for Asia: containing communist China, to be sure, but also looking towards the creation of a zone of independent neutral states in South-East Asia, including eventually Vietnam; an understanding with the Soviet Union on spheres of influence; and even an attempt at reconciliation with Peking. This was interpreted as a signal that Johnson understood that in the long run Asia had to be left to the Asians while America remained discreetly in the background. The 'New Asia' was in essence a self-reliant Asia—in which most emphasis was placed on the role of the most economically developed and politically stable nations, such as Japan and Korea in the north and Australia and New Zealand in the south. Australian newspapers generally welcomed Johnson's regional emphasis, and his positioning of Australia at the crossroads between East and West:

> We are not British, and we are not American, but we are Australian and, as the Canadians know better than we, there are problems in living in the shadow of a giant. But if there are problems, and the maintenance of our identity and policies are only two of them, there are enormous compensations too … To nobody is America's commitment to Asia more important than it is to Australians. We have a broad continuity of interests in this region, in holding the line against Communism as it once had to be held in Europe, and in bringing China into a sane relationship with the rest of the world as soon as may be.[76]

For all the talk of a 'New Asia' on the American side, however, Australians were still very much conceiving of the region through the prism of a reassuring American presence. And there were limits to the aiding and abetting of this American strategy. Such enthusiasm stood in the way of a more independently minded Australian assessment of developments in Asia—a blind spot that made the task of engaging with the region in the following decades just that much more complicated.

---

[73] Memorandum, William Bundy to Rostow, 24 May 1967, LBJL.

[74] Cablegram 4207, Washington to Canberra, 15 October 1966, NAA: A1838, 250/9/9/13.

[75] LBJ, 'Remarks to the American Alumni Council: United States Asian Policy', 12 July 1966, in *PPP: LBJ*, vol. 3, bk 2, 718ff.

[76] *Canberra Times*, 21 October 1966.

More significantly, however, the 1966 visit did not result in closer consultation and coordination of policy in Vietnam. Though Holt gained great domestic political kudos from Johnson's visit to Australia in October 1966 it did not translate into a greater level of access to the US policymaking process. Indeed all the major American decisions relating to the withdrawal of troops from Vietnam and its efforts to reach terms with the enemy were carried out without any prior discussions with the Australians. It provoked yet again another round of introspection in Canberra as to the meaning of the alliance. When in April 1968 President Johnson decided to scale down the war in Vietnam, the Australian minister for the air, Peter Howson, confided in his diary: 'To my mind it's the first step of the Americans moving out of South East Asia and … within a few years, there'll be no white faces on the Asian mainland … [F]rom now on, and to a much greater extent, we shall be isolated and on our own'.[77] An American research report into Australia's reaction to the Guam Doctrine in 1969 concluded that Australian behaviour in international policy was characterised by 'much incoherence and drift', while the *Economist*, noting that 'the desire of most Australians to keep America actively involved in Asia is strong', nonetheless asked pointedly: 'But … who stays in the posse when the marshal decides to get out of town?'[78] This latter development, as Stuart Ward has argued, constitutes the clearest indication of the 'transience of the special attention showered on Australia by the United States during the Johnson-Holt era'.[79] By 1971 the administration in Washington was breaking the ice with China, a metamorphosis in American policy that caught the Australian government hopelessly flatfooted.[80] And so the 'special relationship' welcomed by the Australian press one morning in October 1966 had become very much strained and stressed, ushering in an unprecedented period of doubt, discord and disagreement in the history of the Australian–American alliance.

---

[77] Howson, *Howson Diaries*, 415.

[78] Bernard K. Gordon, *The Guam Doctrine: Elements of Implementation*, Study III, *The Strategy Gap in Asia: Japan and Australia*, October 1970, Research Analysis Corporation, US Embassy Canberra, Classified Central Subject Files, NARA: RG 84, Box 54; 'The Qualms Hit Australia', *Economist*, 1 November 1969.

[79] Kimball, 'The Nixon Doctrine', 60; Stuart Ward, 'Security', in *Australia's Empire* (Oxford History of the British Empire Companion Series), eds Deryck M. Schreuder and Ward (Oxford: Oxford University Press, 2008), 252.

[80] Roderic Pitty, 'Way Behind in Following the USA over China: The Lack of any Liberal Tradition in Australian Foreign Policy, 1970–72', *AJPH*, 51 (3), 2005, 440–50.

12

Too Much Memory: Writing the History of Australian–American Relations During the Howard Years

David McLean

In the history of Australian–American relations since 1945, two periods have been marked by conspicuous and unquestioning Australian support for the United States. One period was dominated by the Asian Cold War. In 1965 when Australia became the only Western country to send forces in support of American military intervention in Vietnam (apart from a tiny New Zealand contingent), it confirmed US senator William Knowland's judgment of a decade earlier that Australia, with Turkey, South Korea and Taiwan, was one of America's most dependable friends.[1] During the second period, that of Prime Minister John Howard's government, Australia was one of the most enthusiastic and uncritical supporters of the US invasion of Iraq and one of few countries to send forces to both the Afghanistan and Iraq wars.

This essay examines the works of those scholars, journalists and former diplomats who have written about this more recent period. This body of writing on a short but significant episode in the history of Australia's relations with the United States highlights some widely held Australian beliefs about the relationship and its past. In particular, it reveals the persistence of interpretive assumptions and explanatory patterns that have their origins in the Cold War years; therefore the essay also examines connections between the literature on the Howard period and the historiography of Australian–American relations during the Cold War. The continuing influence of older interpretive frameworks cannot be accounted for by their intrinsic persuasiveness. They reflect the political divisions of the time—the domestic Cold War in one case, the Howard years in the other. The earliest works on Australian–American relations in the 1950s and 1960s were written by participants in the foreign policy debates of that period, culminating in the debate over Australia's involvement in the Vietnam War. Interpretive approaches established in that context had an irresistible appeal to a later generation of writers who took sides in political controversy arising from the Howard government's decisions to associate Australia closely with the United States in its 'war on terror' and invasions of Afghanistan and Iraq.

A number of authors are influenced also by nationalist assumptions. These assumptions are most clearly evident in a Whig interpretation of Australian history which maintains that a struggle for national independence has been central to the country's history, that this nationalist impulse was expressed from time to time in acts of assertiveness towards Britain, but that until recently it was thwarted by resistance from the colonial power and its local supporters, who for their own self-interested reasons worked to obstruct the realisation of

---

[1] Cited in Trevor R. Reese, *Australia, New Zealand and the United States: A Survey of International Relations, 1941–1968* (London: Oxford University Press, 1969), 148.

an Australian national identity.[2] Though the most prominent strand in this interpretation views the labour movement and Labor Party as forming the vanguard of nationalist forces, its influence is not limited to the left wing of Australian political life. Even the journalist Paul Kelly, who defends the Howard government's foreign policy, offers a curious variation on the radical nationalist theme that Australians have always 'fought other peoples' wars' in his claim that there is a 'proud and honorable' tradition, 'extending from World War I to Iraq', of Australia 'fighting in all of America's big wars'.[3] Indeed, Howard's own nationalism drew on the radical nationalist idea that egalitarianism and mateship are central to the Australian ethos, though for him the roots of mateship and Australia's national identity lay not in the experience of workers and trade unions but in the Anzac legend: in his view national independence arose not from the rejection of Australia's British past but from Australians' participation, as Britons, at Gallipoli, and the preservation of the British heritage, though stripped of British class consciousness, remained crucial to national cohesion.[4]

Political divisions and the influence of nationalism help to explain a third characteristic of these works: many of them are limited by the triumph of memory—'a poor guide to the past', as Tony Judt reminds us[5]—over history, that is, the systematic, disciplined and professional study of the past. Those authors who have tried to understand the development of Australian–American relations in the Howard years have often done so by drawing on distorted versions of the past, and their works have suffered as a result.

The Historiography of Australian–American Relations During the Cold War in Asia

The first interpretations of Australian–American relations during the Cold War reflect the myths which arose from the political arguments of the period.[6] Some of the first scholarly works on the subject echoed the common view that whereas under Labor Party governments in the 1940s Australia followed an independent foreign policy, under the coalition government of Robert Menzies from 1949 Australia became an American satellite. Writing in the late 1970s, Joseph Camilleri and L. G. Churchward argued that the US alliance had trapped Australia in a relationship of unquestioning compliance which

---

[2] See Neville Meaney, 'Britishness and Australian Identity: The Problem of Nationalism in Australian History and Historiography', *Australian Historical Studies*, 32 (116), 2001, 76–78.

[3] Paul Kelly, 'The Australian–American Alliance: Towards a Revitalization', in *The Other Special Relationship: The United States and Australia at the Start of the 21st Century*, eds Jeffrey D. McCausland, Douglas T. Stuart, William T. Tow, and Michael Wesley (Carlisle, Pa.: Strategic Studies Institute, US Army War College, 2007), 57, available at www.strategicstudiesinstitute.army.mil/pdffiles/pub760.pdf.

[4] See James Curran, *The Power of Speech: Australian Prime Ministers Defining the National Image* (Melbourne: Melbourne University Press, 2004), 241–65; and Judith Brett, *Australian Liberals and the Moral Middle Class* (Cambridge: Cambridge University Press, 2003), 202–06.

[5] Tony Judt, *Postwar: A History of Europe Since 1945* (New York: Penguin, 2005), 829.

[6] The argument summarised in this and the following paragraph is developed in David McLean, 'Australia in the Cold War: A Historiographical Review', *The International History Review*, XXIII (2), June 2001, 299–321.

deprived it of its autonomy and benefited only the United States.[7] The main challenge to these interpretations came from scholars who took a sympathetic view of the Menzies government's policies. The starting point for writers such as T. B. Millar and Norman Harper was the judgment that Australia depended for security and survival on the goodwill of its great-power friends, that as a small power Australia could not afford to overplay its hand in relations with the United States and Britain, and that Australia's subservience to America amounted to the payment of 'insurance premiums'. As an explanation for Australia's willingness to send forces to Korea in 1950, to follow the US lead on non-recognition of the People's Republic of China, to allow American defence and intelligence installations to be built on Australian soil, and to send forces to Vietnam, they cited Australia's need to prove its loyalty as a means of strengthening the US commitment to protect Australia. They were in no doubt that Australia had little choice but to act as it did: to fail to participate in the US military intervention in Vietnam would have jeopardised the American alliance and would therefore have put Australia's security at risk.[8] These opposing views thus occupied some common ground: both sides to the debate maintained that the Australia, New Zealand, and United States (ANZUS) security alliance left Australia little choice but to send its forces to Vietnam and to support the United States there as on other issues.

These interpretations, formed before the release of the official documents in the 1980s and reflecting the political conflicts of the Cold War era, proved remarkably resilient. Though later works based on archival research added greatly to the store of knowledge on Australian policymaking, only in a few cases did they attempt to revise interpretive frameworks derived from the earlier period. A curious disjunction therefore emerged. The specific research results of the best archival studies showed that during the 1950s and 1960s Australian leaders, far from acting in uncritical subservience to the United States, made their own assessments of Australia's interests and tried to exploit the US alliance for Australian purposes; that Australian policies and perceptions differed from those of the US government, on some questions—notably Indonesia—markedly; that even Australia's military commitment to Vietnam arose not from servility towards Washington, not from a belief that the ANZUS alliance required Australian involvement, and not from a general hope of winning American goodwill, but from the Australian government's attempt to persuade the United States to commit itself to the defence of South-East Asia and Australia—and at the lowest possible cost to Australia; and that the Vietnam conflict presented Australia with real choices, one of which was to decide against military intervention. Yet despite these findings, the interpretations that prevailed in most of these later studies were derived from the pre-archival works and, in turn, from the political conflicts of the Menzies years. These studies presented, on the one hand, the view that Australia between 1949 and the end of the 1960s rejected the independent course charted by the Labor governments of the 1940s and

---

[7] J. A. Camilleri, *Australian–American Relations: The Web of Dependence* (Melbourne: Macmillan, 1980), esp. 15–18; L. G. Churchward, *Australia and America, 1788–1972: An Alternative History* (Sydney: Alternative Publishing, 1979), 165–95.

[8] T. B. Millar, *Australia in Peace and War: External Relations, 1788–1977* (Canberra: Australian National University Press, 1978), 153, 177, 199–201, 216, 221–22, 410; Norman Harper, *A Great and Powerful Friend: A Study of Australian American Relations between 1900 and 1975* (St Lucia: University of Queensland Press, 1987), 116, 153, 191–92, 247, 318, 329, 334, 342–5, 349, 352–53.

acted as a mere client, colony or satellite within an American empire; on the other, the view that Australian policymakers, constrained by the country's circumstances and its alliance with the United States, had little choice but to act as they did.

The Howard Years and the Rebirth of a 'Special Relationship'

The enduring influence of these two interpretive approaches is evident in what amounts to the first draft of the history of Australian–American relations during the Howard years—a body of work written mainly not by historians but by international relations and strategic studies specialists as well as by scholars from other academic fields, journalists, and former diplomats, and often written for polemical rather than scholarly or even journalistic purposes.

In the period between the end of the Asian Cold War and the election of the Howard government, the level of Australian dependence on the United States that marked Australia's involvement in the Vietnam War gave way to the development of a relationship in which Australia's role was more like that of a 'normal' American ally, one in which Australian governments aimed to maximise Australia's independence within the alliance. Yet in 1999 Howard seemed to embrace a journalist's description of Australia's role in Asia as that of 'deputy sheriff' to the United States (thenceforth known as the Howard Doctrine), a position which he repudiated only in response to widespread criticism from both within Australia and the wider region. In the years that followed the terrorist attacks of 11 September 2001 (9/11), Australia was again one of a very small number of American allies that proved willing to give unhesitating support, even committing military forces to a US military intervention which, in the eyes of many, was politically and morally indefensible. Australian leaders echoed US justifications for the invasion of Iraq and criticisms of the United Nations and uncritically supported US positions on security issues generally. Howard publicly endorsed President George W. Bush's pre-emptive strike doctrine, even to the point of declaring that Australia itself would be prepared to launch a first strike against a neighbouring country in order to prevent a terrorist attack on Australia.

The central question presented by the Howard period is why the 'normal' relationship of the quarter-century after 1969 was replaced by one which, at least at first glance, resembled closely the relationship as it stood in the 1960s. Most of the writers who have written on the subject do not acknowledge the problem, let alone give it the systematic attention it warrants. Nonetheless, these works do contain material that is relevant to answering this question, and most of them offer some answers, at least implicitly. They reflect three main perspectives.

The First Perspective: Australia as a US satellite

The first perspective seeks to understand Howard's policies in the context of what is claimed to be an Australian tradition of colonial servility towards great-power allies. For these writers Howard, in his uncritical support for the policies of the Bush administration, acted as previous Australian prime ministers had done. These writers regard it as axiomatic that the ANZUS alliance, seen as the product of a colonial relationship with the United States, led inevitably to Australian involvement in the wars in Afghanistan and Iraq.

This view is central to Alison Broinowski's two books on the subject.[9] Until the Second World War, Broinowski explains, 'Australia accepted its foreign and defence policies direct from London; and, after that, from Washington.' In the second half of the twentieth century, she claims, 'the aspects of Australia's foreign and defence policies that were not cut and pasted from those of the United States became fewer and fewer', to the point where Australian leaders could 'hardly wait to send troops to most of the United States' wars, asking for no guarantee of American defence in return'. For Broinowski, Howard's actions confirmed the trend and turned Australia into 'a hand-in-glove puppet' of America, so that Australia's own interests, especially in Asia, were inevitably damaged.[10] These views are supported by Erik Paul, who describes Australia's support for American military intervention in Afghanistan and Iraq in 2001–03 as the inevitable result of Australia's 'colonial modality',[11] and by Anthony Burke, for whom Australia's behaviour over 200 years has been that of 'an anxious and threatened outpost of Europe'. Hamstrung by a colonial mentality, Burke suggests, 'we'—Australians—have been unable to 'think for ourselves.'[12] Though Labor governments sometimes attempted to carve out an independent foreign policy, their efforts failed, and Australia came to be tied 'more closely to the strategic imperatives and outlook of the United States.'[13]

These interpretations fall down in a number of respects. First, the image of Australia as an American puppet, eager to do as it was told by Washington and to send troops to American wars without asking anything in return, is not consistent with the nature of Australian military contributions to the wars in Afghanistan and Iraq, where small contingents were deployed in such a way as to minimise Australian casualties and the costs of involvement while maximising the (supposed) political benefits.[14] Second, the argument

---

[9] Alison Broinowski, *Howard's War* (Melbourne: Scribe, 2003); Broinowski, *Allied and Addicted* (Melbourne: Scribe, 2007).

[10] See Broinowski, *Howard's War*, 13–14, 16.

[11] Erik Paul, *Little America: Australia, the 51st State* (London: Pluto, 2006), 48.

[12] Anthony Burke, *Fear of Security: Australia's Invasion Anxiety* (Melbourne: Cambridge University Press, 2008), 234–35. The use of the pronoun 'we' and the adjective 'our' to refer to Australians of earlier generations (typically in a sentence like 'We had no foreign policy of our own before 1942') is a strikingly common feature of the works reviewed in this chapter. It suggests, firstly, either parochialism (the author wants his or her work to be read only by Australians) or pessimism (the author expects that only Australians will be interested); or perhaps both. It also betrays the influence of nationalism's teleological view of history. Australians are viewed as a people, the essence of which has remained unchanged since the beginning of the nation. Though the practice of referring to Australians as 'we' need not in itself prevent intellectual detachment, it does nonetheless suggest that the author concerned may not be conscious of the distinction between writing as a scholar or journalist and writing as an Australian; and not conscious of the risk of superimposing on the past the values and beliefs of the present. On the problem of the teleology of nationalism and its use in writing on Australian history, see Meaney, 'Britishness and Australian Identity', 76–90.

[13] Burke, *Fear of Security*, 99.

[14] By February 2012 a total of thirty-four members of the Australian Defence Force had been killed in the conflicts in Iraq and Afghanistan (two in Iraq, thirty-two in Afghanistan). By comparison, Canada, which did not participate in the Iraq War, had suffered 158 deaths in

that Howard's support for the United States damaged Australian interests in Asia is not persuasive. Michael Wesley and other scholars have shown that on the whole, despite some errors of judgment, Howard managed Australia's regional interests successfully, and that Australia's position in Asia was not harmed by its alliance with the United States or by its participation in the war on terror.[15]

Above all, these attempts to explain the Howard foreign policy as the continuation of an Australian foreign policy tradition of colonial dependence on great-power protectors fly in the face of the best historical scholarship of the last four decades, which shows that from 1901 Australian leaders made policy according to their own assessments of Australia's interests; that dependence on Britain and America was chosen independently, not as a matter of unthinking subservience; that Australian governments attempted to exploit relations with 'great and powerful friends' to serve Australian purposes; that on many issues Australia was at odds with Britain and the United States; and that these generalisations apply to the Menzies years as well as to periods of Labor government.[16] Indeed, the evidence of independent Australian policymaking is so overwhelming that Broinowski and Paul cannot adhere consistently to their claims that Australia behaved as a mere colony or satellite. Both authors, albeit inadvertently, point to cases in Australian history where foreign policy was formed on the basis of policymakers' perceptions of Australian interests, and to cases in which Australia acted independently of—and found itself in conflict with—the United States.[17]

Broinowski, Paul, and Burke have difficulty in identifying the sources of what they allege to be a history of Australian obsequiousness towards the United States. Broinowski and especially Paul have much to say about American cultural influence in Australia, and we might infer that they believe this influence has helped shape Australian foreign policy.

Afghanistan. Denmark, a country with a population around a quarter the size of Australia's, had forty-two servicemen killed in Afghanistan and seven in Iraq. See AP News Research Center Web Services, Iraq War Casualties Database, at nrcdata.ap.org/casualties/data_summary.aspx; and Congressional Research Service, Afghanistan Casualties: Military Forces and Civilians, February 29 2012, at www.fas.org/sgp/crs/natsec/R41084.pdf.

[15] Michael Wesley, *The Howard Paradox: Australian Diplomacy in Asia 1996–2006* (Sydney: Australian Broadcasting Corporation, 2007). See also David Martin Jones and Andrea Benvenuti, 'Tradition, Myth and the Dilemma of Australian Foreign Policy', *Australian Journal of International Affairs* (hereafter *AJIA*), 60 (1), 2006, 114–16; and Roger Bell, 'Extreme Allies: Australia and the USA', in *Trading on Alliance Security: Australia in World Affairs 2001–2005*, eds James Cotton and John Ravenhill (South Melbourne: Oxford University Press, 2007), 47–51.

[16] The outstanding examples of this body of scholarship are Meaney, *A History of Australian Defence and Foreign Policy, 1901–23*, vol. 1, *The Search for Security in the Pacific, 1901–14* (Sydney: Sydney University Press, 1976); and Meaney, *A History of Australian Defence and Foreign Policy, 1901–23*, vol. 2, *Australia and World Crisis, 1914–23* (Sydney: Sydney University Press, 2009). On the historiography of the immediate post-World War II decades, see McLean, 'Australia in the Cold War'; and McLean, 'From British Colony to American Satellite? Australia and the USA during the Cold War', *Australian Journal of Politics and History* (hereafter *AJPH*), 52 (1), 2006, 64–79.

[17] See Broinowski, *Howard's War*, 13, 18, 36; Broinowski, *Allied and Addicted*, 7, 26, 74, 86, 96–97, 104, 106; Paul, *Little America*, 6, 15, 18, 46, 99–102, 111–12, 115–43, 149, 156–57, 161, 165, 193–94.

But neither author tries to demonstrate that this is the case. Ultimately all three authors seem to think that they have found the answer in the problematic notion of manipulation by powerful elites, along with the related idea that threats—whether terrorism from 2001 or communism in the 1950s and 1960s—were invented.[18] But they fail to show who these elites were, or how they benefited from subordinating Australian interests to those of the United States or by warning of threats which they knew to be illusory, or why the attitudes and beliefs of the Australian public should be dismissed as the products of manipulation. None of these authors attempt to suggest that there were not good reasons for Australians in the 1950s and 1960s to be concerned about communist-led insurgencies in South-East Asia and the prospect of Chinese and communist influence in Indonesia, or for Australians in the first decade of the twenty-first century to be concerned about terrorist activities in the same region.

The Second Perspective: A Tradition of Pragmatism

A second group of writers also seek to understand the Howard government's policies as the continuation of an Australian foreign policy tradition or 'strategic culture'. Most of these writers, too, are highly critical of these policies, either on the realist ground that Australia damaged its interests through uncritical support for the United States or on the liberal ground that Howard's actions undermined the international and regional regimes, centred around the United Nations, international organisations and other forms of cooperation between states, on which all countries depend for their security and prosperity. This interpretive approach, however, does not claim that Australia behaved as a US colony or satellite. Instead, the works of Owen Harries, Bruce Grant, Dennis Altman, and Robert Garran, as well as a number of academic studies, suggest that Australian leaders, at least since the Second World War, have acted according to hard-headed—albeit flawed—assessments of Australian interests and that Howard continued this tradition.[19] Altman writes that both in Vietnam in the1960s and in Iraq in 2003,

> conservative governments assumed that Australia's security depended more upon a close alliance with the United States than it did upon the specific issues of the wars, and, close as the two countries may have appeared, our government

---

[18] See Broinowski, *Allied and Addicted*, esp. 13, 22, 106, 110; Paul, *Little America*, 2, 4, 26–27, 71, 162, 181–82, 190, 224; and Burke, *Fear of Security*, esp. 96–99, 103, 115, 209, 236.

[19] Owen Harries, *Benign or Imperial? Reflections on American Hegemony* (Sydney: Australian Broadcasting Corporation, 2004); Bruce Grant, *Fatal Attraction: Reflections on the Alliance with the United States* (Melbourne: Black Inc., 2004); Dennis Altman, *51st State?* (Melbourne: Scribe, 2006); Robert Garran, *True Believer: John Howard, George Bush and the American Alliance* (Crows Nest: Allen and Unwin, 2004). See also Bell, 'Extreme Allies', 37, 40, 42–43; Gary Smith and David Lowe, 'Howard, Downer and the Liberals' Realist Tradition', *AJPH*, 51 (3), 2005, 468–69; Mark Beeson, 'With Friends Like These: Reassessing the Australia–US Relationship', in *Bush and Asia: America's Evolving Relations with East Asia*, ed. Mark Beeson (London: Routledge, 2006), 216; Alan Doig, James P. Pfiffner, Mark Phythian and Rodney Tiffen, 'Marching in Time: Alliance Politics, Synchrony and the Case for War in Iraq, 2002–2003', *AJIA*, 61 (1), 2007, 25–26; and Brendon O'Connor and Srdjan Vucetic, 'Another Mars–Venus Divide? Why Australia Said "Yes" and Canada Said "Non" to Involvement in the 2003 Iraq War', *AJIA*, 64 (5), 2010, 529, 539–42.

was more influenced by old-fashioned calculations of Realpolitik than was the United States.

He regards Australia's role in Iraq as

> a calculation of self-interest by a conservative government following a century-old practice of Australian governments, which is to engage in foreign wars alongside its more powerful allies as a guarantee of support in a world perceived as potentially hostile.[20]

For Grant, too, Howard's 'particular interest' in Iraq 'would have been, *as always*, in bringing Australia into as close a relationship as possible with the Americans to ensure future benefits from the alliance'.[21] Harries views this policy as an example of a 'Menzies tradition' in the history of Australian foreign policy. He suggests that Howard's policy 'can be and has been defended … on Menziean grounds—that is, protecting one's own security and paying one's insurance premium to a great and powerful friend'.[22] Though Garran claims that Howard was 'a true believer in Bush's radical story about America's imperial role', and that he was personally committed to the Bush mission to impose democratic change on the Middle East, he too in the final analysis contends that Howard in 2003, like Menzies in 1965, adopted 'a hard-headed power politics approach to international affairs' and acted above all from the conviction that Australian security interests demanded strong support for the American alliance.[23]

These authors therefore have in common the view that a pragmatic (if misguided) concern for the health of Australia's alliance with the United States provides the key to understanding the Howard government's policies. Yet the fact that most US allies declined to commit military forces to the invasion of Iraq should invite scepticism; and indeed these writers do not demonstrate that the alliance in itself accounts for those policies. The view that Australian policy primarily represented the payment of insurance premiums—a view that is explicit in the works of most of these authors and implicit in Garran's, and one that was hinted at in Howard's various public assertions about his motives in 2001–03—needs scrutiny.

First, the history of Australian foreign policy suggests that the idea of insurance premiums as a motive should be treated with caution. As Grant concedes, Australia's involvement in Vietnam was not a matter of updating insurance but an attempt to persuade and encourage the United States to commit military forces to the defence of Australia's region.[24] Moreover, though it is true that Australian leaders in the 1960s sometimes justified involvement in Vietnam as a means of earning American goodwill, these claims were made in a particular regional context—one in which policymakers believed that Australia was threatened by two regional powers (China and Indonesia) and that American protection was essential.

---

[20] Altman, *51st State?*, 6, 31.
[21] Grant, *Fatal Attraction*, 83. My emphasis.
[22] Harries, *Benign or Imperial?*, 84.
[23] Garran, *True Believer*, 194, 207; see also 1–3, 11, 21, 101, 200.
[24] Grant, *Fatal Attraction*, 145.

No such context lent plausibility to the insurance premium argument in 2001–03. As Robert Manne has written:

> At the time of the onset of the War on Terror, Australia faced no conventional military threats of any kind in the short- or middle-term for which we needed American protection. The only real security threat we faced—from an Islamist terrorist group—was obviously increased rather than diminished by our participation in the invasions of Afghanistan and Iraq.[25]

In attempting to apply the logic of insurance through ANZUS, Howard and Foreign Minister Alexander Downer alluded publicly to the prospect of a North Korean attack on Australia as a justification for Australia's participation in the invasion of Iraq.[26] In this case such logic involved the assumptions not only that North Korea possessed, or might one day possess, the missile capacity to attack Australia and that it would want to do so, but the assumption that such an attack might occur outside the context of a war involving South Korea and Japan and, therefore, the United States, for only then would it be necessary for Australia to take out insurance to secure US military action against North Korea. The improbability of this contingency highlights the difficulty that policymakers encountered in trying to fit the insurance rationale to Australia's circumstances in 2003. Even if the records of Australian policy deliberations, once released, reveal that insurance premium arguments were paramount, the question will remain as to why Howard and his cabinet were persuaded by such considerations.

The Third Perspective: Realism and Values

A third group of writers, among whom Michael Wesley, Paul Kelly, and Greg Sheridan are pre-eminent, offer a defence as well as an explanation.[27] They argue not only that Howard made his own assessments of Australian interests but that his foreign policy was characterised by a sophisticated realism. For these writers there was a clear and tough-minded logic to Howard's approach to relations with the United States. America enjoyed overwhelming international pre-eminence, and Howard believed in the permanence of US primacy. Moreover, Wesley states:

---

[25] Robert Manne, 'Little America: How John Howard has Changed Australia', *The Monthly* (March 2006), 24.

[26] John Howard, 'Address to the Nation on Committing Australian Forces to War in Iraq', 20 March 2003, at usrsaustralia.state.gov/us-oz/2003/03/20/pm1.html; Garran, *True Believer*, 161.

[27] See Wesley, *The Howard Paradox*; Wesley, 'Panel III Chairman's Introduction', in *The Other Special Relationship*, eds McCausland et al., 135–43; Paul Kelly, *The March of Patriots: The Struggle for Modern Australia* (Melbourne: Melbourne University Press, 2009); Kelly, 'Australian–American Alliance', 39–62; Greg Sheridan, *The Partnership: The Inside Story of the US–Australian Alliance Under Bush and Howard* (Sydney: University of New South Wales Press, 2006). See also, as examples of the third perspective, Jones and Benvenuti, 'Tradition, Myth', 103–24; David Martin Jones, 'Australia, China and the Region', in *Australian Foreign Policy in the Age of Terror*, ed. Carl Ungerer (Sydney: University of New South Wales Press, 2008), 182–99; Rod Lyon, 'Australia–US Relations: The Future of the ANZUS Alliance', in *Australian Foreign Policy*, ed. Ungerer, 52–73; Michael Evans, 'Security and Defense Aspects of the Special Relationship: An Australian Perspective', in *The Other Special Relationship*, eds McCausland et al., 279–309.

the tie with the United States was one of the few of Australia's external relationships that yielded tangible benefits: military equipment and technology; access to a global intelligence gathering network; and shelter under the American nuclear umbrella. These appealed intuitively to John Howard's preference for tangible returns and practical benefits.[28]

These considerations, it is suggested, helped shape Howard's reaction to 9/11. 'Howard's strategic view of the US alliance', Kelly writes, 'was that Australia's national interest dictated unity with America—this was not the time to hedge bets or wait until more was known'.[29] For Kelly, Howard's 'alliance thinking would have been familiar to Billy Hughes and Menzies who knew Australian statecraft was about extracting the best deal from the "great and powerful friends"'.[30] Howard's version of this approach, he suggests, was 'full-scale rhetorical support for the United States but niche military commitments of limited duration and a quick withdrawal', a strategy 'designed to maximize Australia's political leverage with the Americans and minimize military casualties'.[31] For Sheridan, too, the Howard government's response to 9/11 demonstrated its strategic sophistication. Howard and Downer, unlike 'most of the community of strategic analysts and commentators in Australia', understood that 9/11 had produced a fundamentally new strategic environment.[32] They recognised that 'Australia's interests are global', that defending them would require participation in 'coalition operations' beyond Australia's region, and that 'Coalition operations primarily mean US-led coalitions'. Unlike their critics, Sheridan claims, they understood Australia's 'strategic culture', for 'Australia had always deployed the army overseas in coalition operations.'[33]

Yet Sheridan does not rest his case for the merits of the alliance and of Howard's policies— or his explanation for those policies—entirely on these realist grounds. The alliance, he asserts, also has a 'moral worth', derived from the fact that the United States 'proceeds from the same core values as Australia does and it has the same core objectives'.[34] Sheridan is in no doubt that America commands a position of international moral leadership. Australian policymakers, therefore, are able to 'take advantage of the access and opportunity which the US system offers to advance Australia's national interests and also our values, and by so doing to advance the cause of mankind'.[35] Though Wesley and Kelly are less inclined to adopt the role of advocate for ANZUS, they also emphasise the importance of values to Howard. Howard, they suggest, identified strongly with 'Western values'; in particular, he referred repeatedly to Australia's links with the 'Anglo-Saxon' countries.[36] His response to the war on terror, Kelly observes, reflected his 'outlook as a cultural traditionalist dedicated

---

[28] Wesley, *The Howard Paradox*, 110. See also Kelly, *March of Patriots*, 439, 477, 571; and Sheridan, *Partnership*, 202, 266.

[29] Kelly, *March of Patriots*, 586.

[30] Ibid., 440.

[31] Ibid., 591; Kelly, 'Australian–American Alliance', 48.

[32] Sheridan, *Partnership*, 38.

[33] Ibid., 131–34.

[34] Ibid., 14, 322.

[35] Ibid., 171; see also 15, 84.

[36] Wesley, *The Howard Paradox*, 39–40, 47–52; Kelly, *March of Patriots*, 439, 585–86.

to Western civilisation … His belief that the US alliance was about values was ignited'. His reaction to 9/11 was an emotional one: 'For Howard, a true friend of America must take an unequivocal stand at this point. It was time to "stand shoulder-to-shoulder with the Americans".'[37]

Kelly, Wesley, and Sheridan judge this amalgam of realism and culture to have been highly successful. For Wesley, the fact that 'Howard was feted by Bush after the war', and Bush's insistence that negotiations for a free trade agreement with Australia be given priority, are evidence that Australia's strong support on the Iraq issue 'resonated strongly in Washington' and earned Howard 'substantial political capital' in the United States.[38] Kelly, too, suggests that there is 'a near-consensus on Howard's personal response to the [9/11] crisis—that it was effective, controlled and instinctual. Its impact on the Americans he saw was enduring.'[39] Sheridan writes that Howard succeeded in his determination 'to intensify the Australian–US relationship across the board', established the alliance on a more intimate footing, and took advantage of opportunities to transform ANZUS 'from a predominantly regional affair to a truly global partnership' and 'as close a security alliance as there can be'.[40] These authors agree that Howard's approach yielded clear benefits for Australia at little cost: they included gains in 'access and goodwill', visa free entry for Australians to the United States, a free trade agreement, increased access to US intelligence, closer defence cooperation, and, in Sheridan's view, Australian influence on Washington decision making as well as increased US involvement in the Asia-Pacific region and 'the greater prestige in Asia that comes from being close to and able to influence Washington'.[41]

Like the first and second perspectives, this interpretive approach fails to provide a convincing explanation for the Howard government's decisions to 'intensify' Australia's relations with the United States. First, the relationship between values and realism is not established. Wesley, having suggested that values were important to Howard, fails to make clear how they contributed to his foreign policy; his explanation for Howard's uncritical support for the Bush administration points rather to the importance of realism and says nothing about values.[42] In Kelly's case it is difficult to reconcile the two views that emerge from his account. On the one hand, there is the Howard who identified so strongly with America that he regarded 9/11 as an attack on Australia's 'way of life' and who ignored Lord Palmerston's fundamental principle of realism, that states have no permanent friends or allies, only permanent interests.[43] On the other hand, there is the practitioner of Realpolitik who shrewdly exploited the opportunities to advance Australian interests provided by the war on terror, cultivating political ties with the United States while committing only niche military forces to Afghanistan and Iraq and thus carefully minimising the costs to

---

[37] Kelly, *March of Patriots*, 585–86.

[38] Wesley, *The Howard Paradox*, 114–15; Wesley, 'Chairman's Introduction', 137.

[39] Kelly, *March of Patriots*, 582.

[40] Sheridan, *Partnership*, 13–14, 39.

[41] Ibid., 13; Wesley, *The Howard Paradox*, 114–15; Wesley, 'Chairman's Introduction', 137–38; Kelly, *March of Patriots*, 592.

[42] Wesley, *The Howard Paradox*, 110–17.

[43] Kelly, *March of Patriots*, 585–86.

Australia of its special relationship with Washington. Moreover, Kelly does not show how a commitment to 'Western civilisation' and 'Western values' (presumably liberal democratic values)—a commitment shared by critics of the Bush administration's policies in both America and Australia and by those liberal democratic governments that opposed the US invasion of Iraq—helps to explain Howard's unquestioning support for the United States.

Similarly Sheridan, having claimed that the United States and Australia are influenced by the same core values, does not show what these values are—except to point out that America, Australia and Britain are all liberal democracies—or how they caused the United States, with its British and Australian allies, to embark on a pre-emptive strike on Iraq or generally to frame their response to the problem of Islamic terrorism as a 'war'. Consistent with his claims that idealism underlies the alliance and that 'naturally Australia would not commit to a bad cause because of alliance solidarity', Sheridan accepts at face value Bush's and Howard's claims that the invasion of Iraq was morally justified.[44] It is true, he argues, that no 'weapons of mass destruction' (WMDs) were found in Iraq, but Bush, British prime minister Tony Blair, and Howard had all believed that under Saddam Hussein's regime Iraq had WMDs, and they had 'acted in good faith'. The decision to invade 'would not have been taken if the governments had known the truth of Saddam's WMD capacity'. As for the other American justification for the invasion, Saddam's alleged connection with Islamic terrorists, Sheridan sees no reason to question the Bush administration's sincerity: he has it on the authority of Deputy Secretary of State Richard Armitage that this was ' "at the top" of American concerns'. Nor does he question Howard's assertion after the event that 'removing Saddam was moral justification enough'.[45] Sheridan ignores the weight of evidence and argument that points strongly to other conclusions: that Iraq's WMDs and alleged terrorist links were mere pretexts for invasion; that Bush and his cabinet (and therefore Blair and Howard) did not know the truth of Iraq's WMD capacity precisely because they went out of their way not to know, and used their intelligence agencies cynically to this end; that even if Saddam Hussein's regime had been shown to possess WMDs, the case for invasion, as opposed to managing the problem by deterrence, would have remained weak; and that the humanitarian benefit of removing Saddam's regime was greatly undermined by the human suffering that resulted from the invasion and its aftermath.

As in its handling of the role of values, so too on the question of Howard's realism the third perspective is flawed. This case, unlike that of such writers as Harries, Grant, Altman, and Garran, is based not only on the fact that Howard largely justified his policies in these terms, and not only on the assumption that this is the way that Australian governments normally conduct defence and foreign policy, but on the authors' judgment that the Howard approach was, after all, successful. Yet none of these authors demonstrate that those 'tangible benefits' which Wesley suggests that Australia gained from the alliance would have been lost if Australia had limited its support for the United States to that of a normal ally. As for the additional benefits which, according to Wesley, Kelly, and Sheridan, Australia gained as a result of Howard's unquestioning support for Bush, there is, firstly, no evidence that Howard's policies were carefully calculated with these in mind; and secondly,

---

[44] Sheridan, *Partnership*, 17, 321.

[45] Ibid., 62–63, 73.

the supposed gains range from the minor (such as visa-free entry to the United States) to the questionable. These writers make no attempt to show that the alleged benefits—increased access and goodwill in Washington, greater access to US intelligence, increased defence cooperation, a free trade agreement—advanced Australia's interests (as opposed to the interests of particular individuals, groups and organisations).[46] Sheridan's larger claims are harder to sustain. No evidence is offered in support of the assertion that Australia has influenced the nature of US involvement in Asia and the Pacific. On the claim that Australia's prestige and influence in Asia were enhanced by its close ties with Washington, Wesley, who has looked closely at the evidence, concludes that there is 'little evidence that Australia's access in Washington increases its diplomatic stocks in Asian capitals', and that 'the impact of the American alliance on Australia's relations with Asian states is not positive or negative, but neutral'.[47]

Nor is it clear that the relatively minor Australian gains suggested by Wesley, Kelly, and Sheridan outweighed the costs: the loss of Australian lives, the economic costs, increased exposure to terrorist threat, loss of international reputation, and not least the undermining of what James L. Richardson calls 'Australia's larger interest in international order and security'.[48] Costs are not considered by these authors, but they need to be if the case for Howard as a hard-headed custodian of Australian interests—as the heir to the legacy of Hughes and Menzies (or, as Sheridan would have it, Percy Spender)—is to be supported.[49]

Common to these accounts is an unwillingness to examine the assumptions underlying the Howard foreign policy. As Kelly observes, Australia under Howard drew closer to the United States at a time when many other countries kept their distance.[50] As Sheridan points out, in these years the alliance moved from a regional to a global footing. These developments

---

[46] The most authoritative studies of the Australia–US Free Trade Agreement suggest that though it is too early to be certain of long-term costs and benefits, in negotiating the agreement Australia made significant concessions to the US and gained little, while the US gave up little. See esp. Ann Capling, *All the Way with the USA: Australia, the US and Free Trade* (Sydney: University of New South Wales Press, 2005); Linda Weiss, Elizabeth Thurbon, and John Mathews, *How to Kill a Country: Australia's Devastating Trade Deal with the United States* (Crows Nest: Allen and Unwin, 2004); Maryanne Kelton, *'More than an Ally'? Contemporary Australia–US Relations* (Aldershot: Ashgate, 2008), 161–79; and Don Russell, 'Economic and Business Aspects: An Australian Perspective', in *The Other Special Relationship*, eds McCausland et al., 223–28.

[47] Wesley, *The Howard Paradox*, 135–36.

[48] James L. Richardson, 'Comment on Special Issue (July 2002) Australian Foreign Policy: New Challenges and Changing Practices', *AJIA*, 57 (1), 2003, 36.

[49] For Sheridan on Spender, see *Partnership*, 306–11. For sensible comments on the costs of Howard's approach to relations with the US, of Australia's alliance with the US, and of the broader Australian–American relationship, see esp. Mark Beeson, 'Australia's Relationship with the United States: The Case for Greater Independence', *Australian Journal of Political Science*, 38 (3), 2003, 387–405; Beeson, 'With Friends Like These', 213–27; Linda Weiss, Elizabeth Thurbon, and John Mathews, *National Insecurity: The Howard Government's Betrayal of Australia* (Crows Nest: Allen and Unwin, 2007); Harries, *Benign or Imperial?*, 83–92; Grant, *Fatal Attraction*, 5–7, 110–11, 163–71, 125–33; Jim George, 'Will the Chickenhawks Come Home to Roost? Iraq, US Preponderance and its Implications for Australia', *AJIA*, 57 (2), 2003, 235–42.

[50] Kelly, 'Australian–American Alliance', 39.

in the Australian–American relationship are treated as self-evident achievements rather than as the basis of a historical problem, namely, how these developments can be accounted for. That Australian interests are global is in itself an unexceptionable position: all countries have global interests in that all can be affected by global developments. But to go beyond that simple observation and assert that Australian interests required participation in US military operations in Iraq and Afghanistan, to assume that Australia's interests were not damaged by these actions, and to assert moreover that this participation represented the continuation of the Australian tradition in defence and foreign policy, is to make much larger claims which demand close scrutiny.

Old and New Directions

Even when allowances are made for difficulties inherent in writing the history of very recent events, the failure of so many authors to deal convincingly with the central historical problem posed by the Howard government's handling of relations with the United States is striking. The influence of nationalist assumptions and the dominant role of Australia's political divisions largely explain this failure. Their role is most clearly apparent in the first and third perspectives. The first perspective adopts without qualification the Camilleri and Churchward interpretation of the Menzies foreign policy and applies it to Howard's attitudes and policies towards the United States. It reflects directly the influence of the radical nationalist narrative of thwarted Australian nationalism. The third perspective views Howard's approach through a very similar lens to that employed by Millar and Harper in their understanding of Australia's commitment in Vietnam: as pragmatic, reasonable, and, from the point of view of preserving the American alliance and protecting Australian interests, even a necessary response to the circumstances of the day. In contrast to the radical nationalist assumptions of the first group, the readiness of those who write from the third perspective to accept at face value the Howard government's own justification for its policies suggests an emotional commitment to a version of Australian national identity which regards it as axiomatic that Australia should act in unison with America and Britain.

Though the second perspective may appear to be free of the grip of older explanatory patterns, here too the history is sometimes confused, and the conclusions are closer to those of the other two perspectives than may at first be evident. Grant's analysis of a foreign policy based on the calculation of Australian interests sits alongside a radical nationalist version of Australian history in which the pragmatism which he regards as central to Howard's uncritical support for the United States is interpreted as evidence that Australia's quest for national maturity had, yet again, been thwarted.[51] This, then, would appear to be a form of 'pragmatism' that is not far removed from the colonial mentality that Broinowski, Paul and Burke object to. Similarly, Altman's analysis, though appearing to place hard-headed considerations of Australian interest at the centre of the country's foreign policy tradition, is not consistent. Having suggested that Australia's role in Iraq was the continuation of 'a century-old practice' of Australian governments trying to use great-power alliances for purposes of Australian security, he also asserts that Australia had no foreign policy before the 1940s. His claim that the Howard government showed an 'enthusiasm for

---

[51] See Grant, *Fatal Attraction*, 84–91.

satrapy status … an enthusiasm which has at times resembled a schoolboy crush rather than a carefully thought-through foreign policy', is hard to reconcile with his emphasis elsewhere on Howard's pragmatic support for the American alliance.[52] For his part Garran appears to suggest that Howard's alleged belief in the Bush mission for the Middle East was not independently arrived at but rather the result of uncritical acceptance of American perceptions—and here his interpretation is indistinguishable from that of Broinowski, Paul and Burke.[53] Moreover, in their readiness to accept pragmatism or realism as an explanation for Howard's policies, these authors, like those associated with the third perspective, again reveal the enduring influence of one of the interpretive frameworks derived from the Cold War period.

In addition to the influence of nationalism and Cold War interpretive approaches, the misuse of history marks this body of writing. Most of the authors under review, in attempting to understand the origins of the Howard foreign policy, have relied on flawed interpretations of Australian foreign policy history: that Australia had no foreign policy of its own until very recently; that Australia, either under Australian governments in general or non-Labor governments in particular, acted as a mere colony or satellite first of Britain, then America; that Australian governments' approach to relations with great-power friends has usually been one of keeping insurance premiums up to date; that Howard acted in Iraq as Menzies did in Vietnam. These claims are in most cases based on simple assertion and are advanced with such certainty, such indifference to other possibilities, including those suggested by the best scholarship in the field, that it is difficult to avoid the suspicion that they reflect aspects of collective memory which have enduring appeal because they serve political, ideological or emotional needs.

Some writers, however, have taken other approaches. One is Maryanne Kelton, whose *'More than an Ally'? Contemporary Australia–US Relations* is the most detailed study of the Howard foreign policy to date. Kelton does not adopt fully any of the three main perspectives, though she shares some common ground with both the second and third. Similar to the second perspective, she is in some respects critical of Howard's attempts to transform Australia's relationship with the United States. The criticisms are cautious, however: Kelton rests her case on a charge of possible miscalculation, believes that the success of Howard's strategy 'remained questionable',[54] and stops short of claiming that Howard's policies were morally wrong or strategically dangerous. Moreover, she does not believe that Howard belonged to an Australian foreign policy tradition. On the contrary, she cites Chris Reus-Smit in support of the suggestion that Howard's approach 'represents a unique posture amongst Australian governments', and comments that though 'in the past former governments have supported the US alliance, most have done so cognisant of the need for either a balance of power and/or the necessity of institutional constraint'— something which she apparently does not believe was true of the Howard government.[55]

---

[52] Altman, *51st State?*, 26–27, 31, 125.

[53] See Garran, *True Believer*, 206.

[54] Kelton, *'More than an Ally'?*, 1. See also 2, 36–37, 42–43, 54, 57, 102, 140–43, 170–73, 176–79, 186.

[55] Ibid., 188.

In trying to explain why Howard followed this course, Kelton, like Wesley, Kelly, and Sheridan, emphasises the interaction of realism and values, though she gives more weight to the former. The Howard government, she argues, was motivated primarily by 'material perceptions of threat'—especially perceived threats arising from the rise of China and terrorism—though cultural and ideological connections with the United States and domestic political considerations also played a part.[56] Kelton's book contains a wealth of information and valuable insights into various aspects of Australian–American relations in the Howard years, but her analysis mistakes context for cause. Since these perceived threats, along with culture and domestic politics, could just as plausibly account for policy choices very different from those adopted—including decisions to avoid involvement in American wars in Afghanistan and Iraq and to concentrate Australia's attention and resources on its region—their explanatory value is limited.

A different explanation is given by Linda Weiss, Elizabeth Thurbon and John Mathews, who argue that Howard's 'hyper-American stance' was 'driven by an intensely personal quest for recognition and standing, and an intensely political calculation that one's "enemies" at home can be silenced in the alliance's name'. Though they suggest Howard's pursuit of a close relationship with the Bush administration and the United States was 'necessarily constructed in the official terms of alliance building', they contend that it was 'powerfully driven by a status-deficit, a quest for the recognition sorely missing in Howard's 25-year climb up the political ladder.' Howard, they argue, 'framed his political choices … in such a way that his standing and prestige would be enhanced.' For by 'edging closer to the US President, and delivering favours to the United States, and being rewarded with recognition abroad, he found that his prestige at home grew as well'.[57]

That opportunities for personal and political aggrandisement through a close relationship with the Bush administration and America influenced Howard is suggested by the fact that, as Weiss, Thurbon and Mathews point out, other, commonly accepted explanations for his behaviour that emphasise alliance building are so unconvincing.[58] That it is only a partial explanation, however, is underscored by the counterfactual exercise of asking whether Howard would have acted in the same way if the hyperpower in question had been not the United States but, say, China, or Japan, or Germany. The scenario is implausible: neither Australian political culture nor Howard's own political outlook would have encouraged a similar cultivation of intimate ties. For cultural reasons, as Weiss, Thurbon and Mathews themselves suggest, the United States 'has long been the Prime Minister's preferred other.'[59]

Identifying the values and beliefs that underlie Howard's attraction to America is central to understanding his foreign policy. Though a number of the authors discussed above, especially those writing from the third perspective, recognise that there was a cultural dimension to Howard's policies, their attempts to understand it are, as we have seen, not convincing. More persuasive are the insights of Manne and Joseph Camilleri. Camilleri, declining to take the Howard government's claims to pragmatism at face value, argues

---

[56] Ibid., 3–10, 17–38, 126, 140, 181–82, 188, 190.
[57] Weiss et al., *National Insecurity*, 228, 234–35, 245.
[58] Ibid., 7–8.
[59] Ibid., 238.

that for all the government's rhetorical emphasis on 'the national interest', all the evidence suggests that 'in defining its response to international terrorism Australia's policymaking process had not sought to engage in an interest-based calculus of costs and benefits'. Rather, he suggests, policy was driven 'largely by domestic political considerations on the one hand … and by a preconceived determination to align Australia firmly with US priorities and strategies', and that 'what mattered most was the political and emotional pull of the US alliance'.[60] It was for these reasons, Camilleri suggests, that Howard embraced the US alliance 'with a consistency and enthusiasm unmatched by any other ally of the United States, the United Kingdom included, and, the historical record might in due course show, by any previous Australian government, the Menzies and Holt governments included'.[61] Camilleri does not elaborate on the role of 'domestic political considerations', but his insight into the 'emotional pull' of the US alliance is valuable. He maintains that 'central to the direction of Australia's external relations under Howard has been a certain conception of the world, as much psychological as intellectual, in which the West generally and the United States in particular loom large.'[62] Camilleri sees Howard's world view as mirroring his image of Australia:

> When he speaks of Australia's 'national character', of its 'distinct and enduring values', and of 'an Australian way', he is using code language to refer to key aspects of the white Anglo-Australian heritage. Placed in this context, the 'national interest' becomes another linguistic device which conveys the same culturally and ideologically charged view of the world and of Australia's place in it. The United States assumes a pervasive presence in the Howard mind-set precisely because it finds in it much needed psychological comfort and sustenance.[63]

Manne similarly rejects the facile comparison between Howard's policies and Australian involvement in the Vietnam War and the 'common suggestion' that 'Australia has supported the War on Terror as a kind of down payment on its insurance policy with the US'. He argues that the explanation for Howard's decisions to send Australian forces to Afghanistan and Iraq lay 'far less in rational calculation and far more in sentimental dreaming than he or his supporters either understand or would be willing to admit'. On the basis of an analysis of Howard's speeches on the American alliance, Manne points to a 'romantic attachment to American civilisation and a vision of Australia's future as ally of the great American Empire'. Howard, he claims, though often misunderstood as an Anglophile, is instead an Americanophile who 'feels attached to the contemporary US in the way his great hero, Sir Robert Menzies, once felt attached to the British Empire'. He concludes that America represents for Howard 'a shiningly positive country. Integration with it is his vision of our future. It was for these reasons, rather than as a matter of cool calculation … that his government sent Australian troops into Afghanistan and Iraq'.[64]

---

[60] Joseph A. Camilleri, 'A Leap into the Past—In the Name of the "National Interest"', *AJIA*, 57 (3), 2003, 439, 444.

[61] Ibid., 435.

[62] Ibid., 448.

[63] Ibid., 449.

[64] Manne, 'Little America', 23–24.

Both Manne and Camilleri, then, argue persuasively that rational calculations of 'the national interest' cannot account for the Howard government's enthusiastic support for the American war on terror and that Howard's sense of cultural and ideological affinity with the United States provides a more convincing explanation for those policies. Despite, however, Manne's insistence that Howard was no Anglophile, he is also struck by his cultivation of the Anzac myth—a myth which arose from the story of 'British' Australians' participation at Gallipoli.[65] In Howard's case there appears to have been a connection between sentimental attachment to America and reluctance to let go of Australia's British past. For Howard, as Camilleri's insight cited above suggests, close association with the United States in the war on terror arose naturally from Australia's origins as a British community and its 'organic' ties with the English-speaking powers.[66] This view is supported by James Curran, who in his study of Howard's nationalism comments that 'Australia's bilateral relationships with the English-speaking powers make him much more comfortable about his and Australia's place in the world', and that for Howard 'the United States and the United Kingdom constitute the world community'.[67] These studies constitute the first step towards understanding the cultural underpinning of Howard's attitudes and policies towards the United States.

Cultural values and beliefs and, as a secondary motive, Howard's quest for personal and political recognition and standing through close association with America, help to account for his government's unquestioning support for the Bush administration's policies, but the record of Australian policy towards the United States in these years suggests that something else also played a part. It concerns the role of memory in the government's decision making. Policymakers are inevitably influenced by their understanding of the past; moreover, the history of international relations suggests that policymakers normally use history badly.[68] The most prominent case of a distorted view of the past helping to shape flawed policies is the attempt by Western, especially American, leaders during the Cold War to apply the 'lessons' of the 1930s. And, indeed, between 2001 and 2004 Howard, like Bush, repeatedly drew on the 'Munich analogy' to warn of the perils of 'appeasing' dictators such as Saddam Hussein.[69] Yet for Howard, unlike Australian and American leaders of the 1950s and 1960s, the impression made by the 1930s was not deeply personal. His own political outlook was formed instead during the era of the Cold War; it is likely that his thinking on foreign policy owed most to his experience of that period, and that the 1930s analogy was employed mainly for purposes of advocacy or as a way of rationalising policies arrived at for other reasons.

---

[65] See Meaney, 'Gallipoli Versus Kokoda: Did Australians Fight Other People's Wars?', Address at The Sydney Institute, 11 May 2010, Sydney Papers Online, at www.thesydneyinstitute.com.au/issue-number/sydney-papers-online-issue-7/.

[66] On Howard and the Anzac myth, see Manne, 'Little America', 26–27; Curran, *The Power of Speech*, 241–52; and Mark McKenna, 'Howard's Warriors', in *Why the War Was Wrong*, ed. Raimond Gaita (Melbourne: Text, 2003), 167–200.

[67] Curran, *The Power of Speech*, 262.

[68] The seminal work on the subject is Ernest R. May, *'Lessons' of the Past: The Use and Misuse of History in American Foreign Policy* (New York: Oxford University Press, 1973).

[69] Curran, *The Power of Speech*, 261–62; McKenna, 'Howard's Warriors', 192; Garran, *True Believer*, 137, 139.

Especially compelling for Howard was a set of beliefs, the origins of which lay in the Cold War years, about Australia's alliance with the United States and the history of this alliance. These beliefs can be inferred from some of his statements (and are shared with some of the authors discussed above). Howard believed that Australia had always been loyal to the United States—presumably because of its willingness to participate in American wars—and that as long as Australia kept American goodwill in this way, the United States could be relied on to come to Australia's assistance when required. On the other hand, he believed that if Australian governments failed to meet their alliance responsibilities, Australian security would be endangered.

The influence of these beliefs was evident in 1999, when Howard felt betrayed by the US refusal to send ground forces to support the Australian-led military intervention in East Timor. It was, he thought, 'a poor repayment of past loyalties and support'.[70] From 2001 his public comments justifying the unconditional promise of Australian military support for America and the deployment of Australian forces in support of the 2003 invasion of Iraq suggest that he saw these contributions as an essential price to pay for maintaining the American alliance. 'The Americans have helped us in the past', he told the Australian public, 'and the United States is very important to Australia's long-term security'. Australians would 'never forget the vital assistance we received from the United States during World War II'. Clearly, Howard suggested, Australia needed to pull its weight in support of the alliance, to the satisfaction of the Bush administration, in order to ensure that this 'vital assistance' would be available in future. To fail to participate in the Iraq invasion would have amounted to leaving it to the United States 'to do all the heavy lifting', and would have undermined 'one of the most important relationships we have'. It was 'critical' for Australia to 'maintain the involvement of the United States in our region where at present there are real concerns about the dangerous behaviour of North Korea'.[71] Foreign Minister Downer shared this view of Australia's strategic predicament, declaring that

> It wasn't a time in our history to have a great and historic breach with the United States. If we were to walk away from the American alliance it would leave us as a country very vulnerable and very open, particularly given the environment we have with terrorism in South-East Asia, the North Korean issue.[72]

There is, therefore, merit in the view of those writers who suggest that the motives behind the Howard government's policies towards the United States were largely or primarily pragmatic. Howard and Downer appear to have hoped that Australia would derive practical benefits from its loyal support for Bush's America. The most fundamental of these practical considerations was the belief, emphasised by authors who write from the

---

[70] John Howard interview with Paul Kelly, US Studies Centre, 'Reflections on the Australia–United States Alliance', 15 February 2011, at ussc.edu.au/events/past/Reflections-on-the-Australia-United-States-Alliance.

[71] John Howard, 'Address to the Nation on Committing Australian Forces to War in Iraq', 20 March 2003, at usrsaustralia.state.gov/us-oz/2003/03/20/pm1.html; John Howard, speeches to Parliament, *Commonwealth Parliamentary Debates*, House of Representatives, vol. 219, 4 February and 18 March 2003, 10648, 12508 (respectively).

[72] Cited in Garran, *True Believer*, 161.

second perspective, that sending military forces to American wars in Iraq and Afghanistan constituted a form of insurance premium on Australia's security. But this was a confused pragmatism which cannot be taken at face value. It exaggerated the external threats facing Australia, the rewards that Australia stood to gain from military involvement in Afghanistan and Iraq, and the likely costs of declining to participate in these wars. It can be understood as the product of a misreading of history. Howard's expectations of what the alliance might deliver for Australia, of what Australia might gain by offering uncritical support for an American war when other American allies declined to do so, and of what Australia might lose if it failed to offer such support, ignored the inescapable lessons of the history of ANZUS: that as the US refusal to support Australia on the issues of West New Guinea and Confrontation in the 1950s and early 1960s showed, the United States did not regard itself as committed by the alliance to send forces to support Australia when US interests were not at stake; that the penalties suffered by US allies that failed to respond to American preferences were usually minor, and that American allies which did not send troops to help fight American wars—such as Canada and Britain in the Vietnam War—did not suffer as a result; that when the Menzies government sent military forces to Korea in 1950 and Vietnam in 1965 it did so for specific purposes arising from its view of Australian regional interests, not for the general purpose of demonstrating loyalty and storing up credit with Washington.[73]

Conclusion

The first body of writing on Australian–American relations during the Howard years reflects a broad—and persistent—misunderstanding of the history of Australia's relationship with the United States. The first step towards answering the central question for historians of the Howard years is to reject those myths, arising largely from political conflict and nationalist assumptions (though the myths do appear to have a life of their own), which have led to the triumph of memory—or mismemory—over history. They include the belief that Australia always fights other peoples' wars (for better or worse, depending on one's point of view); that the history of Australian defence and foreign policy has been one of colonial dependency, first on Britain, then America; that the history of Australia's relations with the United States has centred on the pragmatic payment of insurance premiums in order to guarantee American protection as well as other perceived benefits of the alliance; and that because of Australia's British heritage it should support the foreign policy of the United States as the leading 'Anglo' power.

Some of these myths influenced the Howard government's policymaking. They helped shape Howard's understanding of ANZUS and of Australia's place in the world, and in this way they form part of an explanation for Australia's uncritical, conspicuous support for the policies of the Bush administration. Howard's sense of cultural attachment to the United States was also important: it provided an emotional impetus for the government's actions, and it partly explains why he was attracted to a distorted version of the history of the Australian–American relationship. Finally, the opportunity for Howard to increase his

---

[73] See McLean, 'Australia in the Cold War', 307–14; and McLean, 'British Colony to American Satellite?', 76–79.

personal and political standing through close association with the US president created an additional motive for unquestioning support of American policy. Exploring these three influences and the relationship between them is the main challenge for historians of this period of Australia's relations with the United States.

VI

The Making and Unmaking of American Nationalism

13

Becoming Wilsonian: Woodrow Wilson's Conversion to the American National Myth

David T. Rowlands

In order to illuminate the relationship between the myths of American nationalism and the Wilsonian vision of America's role in the world, it is helpful to examine the process by which Woodrow Wilson himself became—intellectually—an American nationalist. By adopting what may be termed a 'post-nationalist' approach, this reading of Wilson's intellectual development offers an alternative interpretation of the important subject of the origins of Wilsonianism, treating it not as a natural or inevitable phenomenon but as the outcome of Wilson's calculated appropriation of the American national myth. After reviewing the evidence, I conclude that it was only in 1910, at the beginning of his political career, that Wilson became a convert to the world view that equated—and continues to equate—the universal projection of US power with a selfless, messianic mission to the world.

If excessive military spending coupled with a bent for so-called idealistic or humanitarian intervention in strategically important regions might be described as a present-day US pathology, the roots of this 'illness' go back to Woodrow Wilson's day. As president of the United States from 1913 to 1921, Wilson made considerable use of national myths in the formulation of foreign policy settings. During the nineteenth century the United States' expansion had taken place across the North American continent, but by the time Wilson took office the process had acquired hemispheric and even global dimensions. It was an 'imperial moment' and the beginning of a new era of US dominance of the international system. Wilson was not the first to refer to America's 'mission', but in response to the demands of the times he made it the centrepiece of his official rhetoric with a coherence surpassing that of any predecessor. In so doing, Wilson established a principle which continues to define the 'parameters [of] the policy debate', according to one highly regarded authority on the subject of American imperialism. This principle, 'so authoritative as to be virtually immune to challenge', is the 'Wilsonian tradition … to which all recent occupants of the Oval Office … have adhered'. Wilsonianism proclaims 'the imperative of America's mission as the vanguard of history, transforming the global order [by] perpetuating its own dominance [and projecting its] military supremacy'.[1]

As a result of Wilson's pivotal role in the First World War and the Paris Peace Conference, Wilsonian idealism came to be regarded by many US scholars as equivalent with a pure and benevolent liberal internationalism.[2] Others, such as Wilson's chief biographer Arthur S.

---

[1] Andrew Bacevich, *American Empire: The Realties and Consequences of US Diplomacy* (Cambridge: Harvard University Press, 2002), 215.

[2] The tendency to straightforwardly equate Wilsonianism with liberal internationalism is a feature

Link, viewed his liberal internationalism as flawed in its execution, but still praised Wilson for the substance of his ideals.[3] Although this view still enjoys widespread currency, it is based on a fundamental misunderstanding. While it is true that Wilsonianism drew on elements of the liberal internationalist vision of universal peace and democracy, it did so in order to nationalistically assert America's moral, material and strategic pre-eminence. Although it is standard to refer to Wilson as a liberal internationalist, he was in fact an ultranationalist, as Neville Meaney has pointed out, seeking to recast the world in the image of the US. Meaney is one of the few scholars to place Wilsonianism in the broader context of the American national myth.[4]

The American National Myth

Nations, as has been rightly suggested by a series of scholarly commentators, are social and historical constructs, or 'imagined communities'.[5] Nationalism came into being with the onset of the modern age and its ensuing identity crisis. Traditional European societies beset by technological, economic and political change found in the myth of the nation state a new idea of community. Individuals and class groupings within such societies acquired a sense of solidarity through a new nationalistic sense of common historical, ethnic, linguistic and/or religious identity that was unique, supposedly, to the nation in question.

American national ideology, as with other varieties of nationalism, developed in the disruptive context of modernity and widespread social change. Originally, the American Republic established in the 1780s had been based on notions of classical republicanism that bore very little relation to the democratic evangelical nationalism that came later. The

---

of the following well-known works: Mark T. Gilderhus, *Pan-American Visions: Woodrow Wilson in the Western Hemisphere, 1913–1921* (Tucson: University of Arizona Press, 1986); Kendrick A. Clements, *Woodrow Wilson: World Statesman* (Boston: Twayne Publishers, 1987); Clements, *The Presidency of Woodrow Wilson* (Lawrence: University Press of Kansas, 1992); Akira Iriye, 'The Globalizing of America 1913–1945', in *The Cambridge History of American Foreign Relations*, vol. 3, ed. Warren Cohen (Cambridge: Cambridge University Press, 1993); Tony Smith, *America's Mission: The United States and the Worldwide Struggle for Democracy in the Twentieth Century* (Princeton: Princeton University Press, 1994); and Thomas J. Knock, *To End All Wars: Woodrow Wilson and the Quest for a New World Order* (Princeton: Princeton University Press, 1995).

[3] See esp. Arthur S. Link, *Wilson: The Struggle for Neutrality* (Princeton: Princeton University Press, 1960).

[4] See, for example, Neville Meaney, 'American Nationalism, the Monroe Doctrine and Woodrow Wilson's New World Order', unpublished conference paper, 1994. See also N. Gordon Levin, Jr., *Woodrow Wilson and World Politics: America's Response to War and Revolution* (New York: Oxford University Press, 1968); Ernest Lee Tuveson, *Redeemer Nation: The Idea of America's Millennial Role* (Chicago: University of Chicago Press, 1968); Michael H. Hunt, *Ideology and US Foreign Policy* (New Haven: Yale University Press, 1987); and Walter A. McDougall, *Promised Land, Crusader State: The American Encounter with the World since 1776* (Boston: Houghton Mifflin, 1997).

[5] Texts that deal with this subject include such classic works as Ernest Gellner, *Nations and Nationalism* (Ithaca: Cornell University Press, 1983); Benedict Anderson, *Imagined Communities: Reflections on the Origin and Spread of Nationalism* (London: Verso, 1983); and E. J. Hobsbawm, *Nations and Nationalism since 1780: Programme, Myth, Reality* (Cambridge: Cambridge University Press, 1990); and Elie Kedourie, *Nationalism* (Oxford: Blackwell Publishers, 1993).

writings and speeches of founding fathers such as George Washington, John Adams, James Madison and Alexander Hamilton were as one in their suspicion of the demos and fear of popular government. 'Had every Athenian citizen been a Socrates', according to Madison, 'every Athenian assembly would still have been a mob.'[6] Adams claimed to be 'fully sensible of the real misery, as well as the dangerous tendency, both of democratical licentiousness and monarchical tyranny', preferring a 'well-tempered aristocracy to all other governments … Orders of men, watching and balancing each other, are the only security; power must be opposed to power, and interest to interest'.[7] Philosophically, as these remarks show, they were conservatives, not liberals. Here, among the ruling elite at least, was a sceptical view of human nature, a cyclical understanding of history and an unequivocal rejection of popular sovereignty.[8]

During the first half of the nineteenth century, as new socio-economic conditions arose in the westwardly expanding republic, a democratic political culture of sorts supplanted the republicanism of the revolutionary generation. With democracy came a new definition of the nation and the seeds of a nationalism grounded on America's supposedly exalted place in the vanguard of human progress. Whereas the rebels of 1776 had in many cases seen themselves as the defenders of traditional English liberties, the new generation of Americans saw their country as an experiment in freedom ordained by Providence and unrelated to anything that had gone before.

In 1826, on the fiftieth anniversary of the Declaration of Independence, this new vision was spectacularly proclaimed in an oration by George Bancroft, an up-and-coming historian whose ideas about America embodied the intellectual trends of this period. Having studied in one of the great German universities, the University of Göttingen (a not uncommon sojourn among early nineteenth-century Bostonians), Bancroft had been directly influenced by the Hegelian concept of nation-states as progressive agents in human affairs. Conditioned also by liberal Protestantism and its optimistic faith in the possibility of collective temporal redemption,[9] Bancroft was led to equate America with democracy, and democracy with universal progress:

---

[6] Cited in Robert D. Kaplan, 'Was Democracy Just a Moment?', *The Atlantic Monthly*, 280 (6), December 1997, 56.

[7] Cited in Paul A. Rahe, *Republics: Ancient and Modern,* vol. 3 (Chapel Hill: University of North Carolina Press, 1994), prologue.

[8] The philosophical orientation of the founding of political economy is a subject likely to be contested for some time to come. For the purposes of this chapter, I have drawn on the republican interpretation exemplified in works such as G. A. Pocock, 'Between Gog and Magog: The Republican Thesis and the *Ideologia Americana*', *Journal of the History of Ideas*, 48 (2), 1987, 325–46; Rahe, *Republics: Ancient and Modern*; and M. N. S. Sellers, *American Republicanism: Roman Ideology in the United States Constitution* (New York: New York University Press, 1994).

[9] For a general study of the wider context of developments in nineteenth-century liberal Protestant theology, see Karl Barth, *Protestant Thought: From Rousseau to Ritschl* (New York: Harper & Brothers, 1959). See also Bernard M. G. Reardon, *Liberal Protestantism* (Stanford: Stanford University Press, 1968); Claude Welch, *Protestant Thought in the Nineteenth Century* (New Haven: Yale University Press, 1985); and Gary J. Dorrien, *The Making of American Liberal Theology: Imagining Progressive Religion 1805–1900* (Louisville: Westminster John Knox Press, 2001).

> When the names of our venerated Fathers were affixed to the instrument which declared our Independence, an impulse and confidence were imparted to all efforts at improvement throughout the world. The festival which we keep is the festival of freedom itself; all the nations of the earth have an interest in it, and humanity proclaims it sacred.[10]

Here was something altogether new and startling in the American imagination, foretelling a sense of national mission linked inextricably with assertions of predestined moral supremacy:

> The events of the last fifty years lead us to hope, that liberty, so long militant, is at length triumphant. From our own revolution the period derives its character. As on the morning of the nativity the astonished wizards hastened with sweet odors on the Eastern road, our government had hardly come into being and the star of liberty shed over us its benignant light, before the nations began to follow its guidance and do homage to its beauty.[11]

America, Bancroft concluded, was the prime mover of world history and had come into being as a veritable Christ of nations entrusted with the 'dearest interests of mankind'. The universal establishment of democratic liberty (a principle supposedly embodied in the institutions of the United States) was held up as the altruistic goal of America's mission, and the nation's history was presented exclusively in such a light:

> Our moral condition is, then, indeed superior to that of the old world in the present, or in any former age. We have institutions more free, more just, and more beneficent, than have ever before been established … The dearest interests of mankind were entrusted to our country … the nations of the earth turned towards her as to their last hope. And the country has not deceived them.[12]

Bancroft had formulated an American nationalist typology which vastly exceeded the claims of earlier generations. Here, in the image of the 'nations of the earth' turning to democratic America 'as to their last hope' was what the United States, according to Bancroft, had always represented.

Woodrow Wilson's presidential public addresses were absolutely consistent in their application of this Bancroftian typology. The following extract from one of Wilson's impassioned speeches during the 1919 Western Speaking Tour captures Wilson's American nationalism at its rhetorical peak. Characteristically, he urged a Nevada audience to:

> look at [the League of Nations] as a fulfilment of the destiny of the United States, for it is nothing less. At last after this long century and more of blood and terror, the world has come to the vision that the body of 3,000,000 people, strung along the Atlantic coast of this continent had in that far year 1776.[13]

---

[10] George Bancroft, *Oration, delivered on the Fourth of July, 1826 at Northampton, Massachusetts* (Northampton: T. Watson Shepard, 1826).

[11] Ibid.

[12] Ibid.

[13] Wilson, 'An Address in Reno', 22 September 1919, in *The Papers of Woodrow Wilson* (hereafter *PWW*), ed. Arthur S. Link (Princeton: Princeton University Press, 1994), 63: 441.

Like Bancroft before him, Wilson understood the American nation not as a transitional phase in history, but as the ultimate meaning of history itself, the inevitable outcome of fixed eternal laws. Hence, it was prescribed a priori that the world must identify with the universal establishment of an American-style democracy. It was a vision that drew on the liberal internationalist ideal, moulding it to equate the triumph of that ideal with the establishment of American power on the world stage:

> Men in Europe laughed at them, at this little handful of dreamers, this little body of men who talked dogmatically about liberty, and since then that fire which they started ... has consumed every autocratic government in the world.[14]

During his years in public office, Wilson was careful to convey the impression that his commitment to these ideas was as ancient as it was absolute. 'A true American conceives America in the atmosphere and the whole setting of ... her destiny', he remarked on 12 September 1919, adding: 'I have taken pains since I was a boy so to saturate myself in the traditions of America that I generally feel a good deal of confidence that the impulses which I find in myself are American impulses.'[15] Yet, in reality, Wilson's relationship with what he called 'American impulses' was far less straightforward. In fact, as we shall now examine, he was a late and unlikely convert to nationalism.

Wilson's Political and Theological Point of Origin

The historical school most responsible for cultivating and perpetuating the American national myth may be termed the national liberal school, which has captured the mainstream of American historical writing by narrating the story of US history as a predestined and inevitable progress toward the triumph of American 'democracy' on the domestic and global stage. Liberal nationalist historiography has tended to see in Wilson an exemplary case of straightforward identification with American ideals, which are considered equivalent with liberal internationalist values. For liberal nationalist historians convinced of the self-evident nature of 'American principles', the nature of Wilson's world view presents no conceptual problem and so its ultimate provenance requires no explanation outside nationalist terms. It has been stated or implied many times that Wilson's democratic world view (pure in its selfless American idealism) was a constant factor throughout his life. Having been raised in a Presbyterian manse, his commitment to the national mission was lent a peculiarly dutiful intensity. According to Link, for example,

> Wilson's thoughts about international relations grew out of his attempt to define the role of the United States in world affairs within the context of American democratic traditions and his own ... religious faith ... America's mission in the world was not to attain wealth and power, but to serve mankind through leadership in moral purposes and in advancing peace and world unity.[16]

---

[14] Ibid.

[15] Wilson, 'An Address in Coeur d'Alene', 12 September 1919, *PWW*, 63: 212–13.

[16] Arthur S. Link, *Woodrow Wilson: Revolution, War and Peace* (Arlington Heights, IL: Harlan Davidson, 1979), 6.

This has been the dominant interpretation of the origins of Wilsonianism, and it can only be described as a literally nationalist interpretation. There have been numerous well-researched studies dealing with the evolution of Wilson's thinking during his formative years. Many of them contain important insights, but they miss the all-important questions of when, how and why Wilson became an American nationalist.[17]

Of course, it is only when one becomes conscious about the ideological character of American nationalism that one can begin to ask such questions—and the fact is that most American historians, having been conditioned to a greater or lesser extent by the myths of American nationalism, simply do not see the problem.[18] While there exists an excellent body of literature on Wilson and Wilsonianism, the point that has been consistently missed by the Wilson historiography is that from the period of his southern childhood until the end of his tenure as Princeton's reforming leader, the future president had never once given expression to ideas that were in any sense Wilsonian; that is, that the United States alone of all nations had a pre-ordained mission to democratise the world. In fact, his entire outlook on politics, America and international affairs, although subject to change and development over time, was consistently unrelated to the nationalist tone of his presidential foreign policy vision.

Thomas Woodrow Wilson was born in Staunton, Virginia on 28 December 1856 to the Reverend Doctor Joseph Ruggles Wilson, a high-ranking minister in the southern Presbyterian Church. Joseph Wilson had played an important role in the founding of this breakaway movement.[19] The antebellum separation of southern Presbyterians from their northern brethren was provoked by the upsurge of liberal theology then deeply affecting American Protestantism.[20] Joseph Wilson's southern church was vehemently opposed to liberal theological developments. They were diehard conservatives, determined to cling to the pre-modern Calvinism in whose defence the ancestral Scottish Covenanters had

---

[17] See, for example, John Milton Cooper, Jr., *The Warrior and the Priest: Woodrow Wilson and Theodore Roosevelt* (Cambridge: Harvard University Press, 1983); and Cooper, *Woodrow Wilson* (New York: Alfred A. Knopf, 2009). See also Henry W. Bragdon, *Woodrow Wilson: The Academic Years* (Cambridge: Harvard University Press, 1967); Arthur Walworth, *Woodrow Wilson* (Boston: Houghton Mifflin, 1965); John M. Mulder, *Woodrow Wilson: The Years of Preparation* (Princeton: Princeton University Press, 1978); and August Heckscher, *Woodrow Wilson* (New York: Collier Books, 1991). Niels A. Thorsen's *The Political Thought of Woodrow Wilson 1875–1910* (Princeton: Princeton University Press, 1988), while in some respects a thorough work, ignores the issue of Wilson's changing regard for democracy and American nationalism.

[18] Meaney is to be credited with opening my eyes to that issue, just as he has opened the eyes of many who have written about the problem of Australian nationalism. As numerous ex-students will agree, to be taught by Meaney is to experience a paradigm shift in one's perception of history.

[19] For a comprehensive overview of southern Presbyterian religious culture, see Ernest Trice Thompson, *Presbyterians in the South* (Richmond: John Knox Press, 1973).

[20] See George Marsden, 'Kingdom and Nation: New School Presbyterian Millennialism in the Civil War Era', *Journal of Presbyterian History*, 46 (2), 1968, 254–73. More generally, see Lloyd L. Averill, *American Theology in the Liberal Tradition* (Philadelphia: The Westminster Press, 1961); Kenneth Cauthen, *The Impact of American Religious Liberalism* (New York: Harper and Row, 1962) and Daniel Day Williams, *The Andover Liberals: A Study in American Theology* (New York: Octagon Books, 1970).

mounted their seventeenth-century dissent. The theology of Joseph Wilson was centred on the problem of individual salvation and was firmly convinced that human trial and torment was a permanent condition for imperfect humanity.

Dr Wilson's surviving sermon notes embody this pre-modern brand of theology. He would speak of unredeemed human nature as 'a running sore of corruption that everywhere spreads infection: and which no surgery can cure except the divine surgery that shall take the man all apart'.[21] Congregations were urged to 'face the fact that there are individuals—not a few—who are by-and-by to be set aside as of no account in this universe: each one a nuisance and an obstruction of the world's chaff ... to be taken ... along with much of the same sort, only to be burned!'[22] The liberal vision of unfolding perfection, with its promise of upward moral progress, had little appeal to the conservative Dr Wilson. 'Human nature', he argued, 'is all the while repeating itself. Change of persons, change of times, change of countries, produce no radical change.' In this cyclical view of history, there was a 'uniformity which thus characterizes those leading principles of conduct ... you may expect the men of this day to do what, under similar circumstances, men have always done.'[23]

Nineteenth-century liberal theology, by contrast, had progressed so far as to virtually dispense with the literalism that typified earlier Christian thought. Christ was not primarily regarded as a supernatural redeemer of individual souls, but as an historical figure whose ethical example had set a noble standard for personal emulation. In northern centres of advanced learning such as Massachusetts, the milieu of an increasingly influential Bancroft had embraced this teaching and saw in their rising democratic America the nation-state avatar of humanity's temporal redemption. In the South, however, these ideas were roundly condemned. Joseph Wilson's pulpit, like those of his fellow Confederate preachers, became a point of prolonged Calvinist resistance to the modern industrial age and its religious ethos.[24] Wilson's intellectual point of origin was, in fact, utterly divorced from the liberal theology and politics out of which American nationalism had emerged.

His father's conservative Calvinism rejected the progressive and generally benevolent view of human nature upon which this new democracy was grounded. Committed to preserving an old theocratic status quo in the rigid class and racial hierarchy of southern civilisation, southern Presbyterians tended to mistrust schemes of radical social innovation in the form of a 'democratic' political economy. Their preferred model of Commonwealth was not democracy, but the measured balance of eternally competing interests supposedly enshrined in the British constitution. Traditional British rights and liberties, the outcome of an organic process of historical development (as Burke argued), were to be defended at all costs against the encroachments of monarchs or masses alike.

---

[21] J. R. Wilson, sermon on Matthew 3:12, Wilson Papers, Library of Congress.

[22] Ibid.

[23] Ibid.

[24] See Thompson, *Presbyterians in the South*; James Oscar Farmer, Jr., *The Metaphysical Conspiracy: James Henley Thornwell and the Synthesis of Southern Values* (Macon: Mercer University Press, 1986); and, more generally, William Warren Sweet, *Religion in the Development of American Culture, 1765–1840* (New York: Charles Scribner's Sons, 1952).

The Civil War served to polarise and solidify the divergent strands of American Protestantism. Always strongest in the archaic reaches of the South, the old Calvinism made its stronghold there while the modernising North was given over to liberal theology, democracy and its attendant nationalism. During the closing years of the war with their darkening outlook for the southern cause, Joseph Wilson's parish church in Georgia was made available as a hospital for the Confederate's wounded. The kirk grounds were made to serve as a holding yard for Union prisoners, and the pulpit, of course, as an ongoing platform for southern propaganda. Many a 'flail of rebuke' did Dr Wilson threaten to swing over the heads of meddling northern abolitionists who sought to destroy a system of slavery that apparently fed the 'mutual good will of white and black'.[25] Joseph Wilson's belief system survived the fall of the South and its re-absorption by the United States. The years of Reconstruction were a time of deep disillusionment and growing bitterness, but the Reverend Doctor remained a staunch Confederate Anglophile and an unyielding theological conservative.

Dr Wilson defiantly undertook to cast his son's developing mind in the same theological and political mould. 'The true principle unquestionably is', he advised in a letter to Woodrow, 'the owners of a country ought to be its rulers. That is, let there be property qualification—and all the more, because, ordinarily, property and intelligence go together'. Either 'a limitation of suffrage or anarchy in twenty-five years or sooner', he warned. 'I do not refer', Dr Wilson stipulated, 'to the Negroes any more than to the ignorant Northern voters.'[26] This teaching had a noticeable impact on the young Woodrow's emerging political views. At the age of nineteen he would venture that, 'universal suffrage is at the foundation of every evil in this country'.[27]

He elaborated on this theme on 4 July 1876 in response to the centenary of the Declaration of Independence. Across the nation, this was a day of officially sanctioned patriotic celebration and speech-making. In Massachusetts, for example, Charles Francis Adams, an eminent lawyer, politician (and the grandson of President John Adams), delivered an address that was typical of many. Over the past century, he argued,

> Devotion to the principle of liberty [has been] the pillar of fire illuminating the whole of our later path as an independent people … steadily directing us toward the attainment of new and great results, beneficial … to ourselves [and] to the progress of the other nations of the world.[28]

Wilson's response differed very sharply from the Bancroftian sentiment flowing so freely up north:

> The one hundredth anniversary of American independence. One hundred years ago America conquered England in an unequal struggle and this year she

---

[25] Cited in John M. Mulder, 'Joseph Ruggles Wilson: Southern Presbyterian Patriarch', *Journal of Presbyterian History*, 52 (3), 1974, 249.

[26] 'Two Letters from Joseph Ruggles Wilson', *PWW*, 1: 477.

[27] Wilson, diary entry, 19 June 1876, *PWW*, 1: 143

[28] Charles Francis Adams, *The Progress of Liberty in a Hundred Years, An Oration Delivered Before the Citizens of Taunton, 4th July 1876* (Taunton, MA: C. A. Hack & Son, 1876), 8, 9–10.

> glories over it. How much happier she would be now if she had England's form of government instead of the miserable delusion of a republic.²⁹

Still very much the young, embittered southerner, Wilson was here completely dismissive of the nationalist ideas that would later form the foundation of the Wilsonian vision. As a consequence of the intensive conditioning he had received from his father, Wilson offered an uncompromising rejection of the world view associated with the claims of American nationalism. Remarkably, he not only scoffed at the idea of democracy but predicted the imminent demise of the US political system:

> A republic too founded upon the notion of abstract liberty! I venture to say that this country will never celebrate another centennial as a republic. The English form of government is the only true one.³⁰

Today such thoughts would surely be labelled 'anti-American' and they unmistakeably testify to Wilson's profound feelings of alienation from the nation he would later lead.

In the months and years to come, there were further remarks in this Anglophile, anti-Yankee, anti-democratic vein. On reading a then well-known work of English history, for example, Wilson was moved to comment: 'It is a grateful thought that this History of the English people is a history of the American people as well; it is a high and solemn thought we [are] a lusty branch of a noble race.'³¹ This prompted him to question the validity of the 'democracy' that sought to set America on a path divergent from that of the broader sweep of British political history. 'Is the principle of universal suffrage', he asked,

> consistent with those principles of government which bear the sanction of the wisest Englishmen of eight centuries and which have secured personal freedom and political liberty to a great nation for more than eight hundred years[?] Is it necessary or even compatible with the healthy operation of a free government?³²

Referring to the British inheritance of a balanced constitution, Wilson warned:

> With what diligence should we guard so precious a legacy of privileges! How careful should we be in this experiment of ours, in which sacred principles are stretched to the utmost, the place of the Goddess of Liberty be not usurped by the Harlot.³³

In 1879, Wilson argued more explicitly that the 'democratic idea [was] the cant of our times'.³⁴ In an essay from the same period concerning the desirability of British-style cabinet government in the United States, he continued in the same vein: 'It is indisputably true that universal suffrage is a constant element of weakness, and exposes us to many dangers which we might otherwise escape.'³⁵

---

[29] Wilson, diary entry, 4 July 1876, *PWW*, 1: 148–49.
[30] Ibid., 149.
[31] Wilson, 'Review of Green's *A History of the English People*', *PWW*, 1: 375.
[32] Wilson, marginal notes, *PWW*, 1: 388.
[33] Wilson, 'Review of Green'.
[34] Wilson, 'Self-government in France', 4 September 1879, *PWW*, 1: 515.
[35] Wilson, 'Cabinet Government in the United States', August 1879, *PWW*, 1: 494.

David T. Rowlands

Wilson's Discovery of Liberal Protestantism and Democracy

In 1883, Wilson embarked on graduate study in historical and political science at the new and forward-looking Johns Hopkins University. There, under the dynamic tutelage of the prominent 'ethical-historical' economist and Social Gospel theologian, Richard T. Ely, Wilson discovered the heady doctrines of evangelical progressivism. 'The most modern movement in economics', claimed Ely, may 'be regarded as in part a return to the teaching of Christ … The doctrine of brotherhood is a powerful economic factor. Let us bear one another's burdens.'[36] Ely's national influence was at that time very great; it has been said that there 'was probably no other man of the period who had as much influence on the economic thinking of parsons and the general religious community'.[37] His general position was that the management of the nation-state must reflect Christian ethics and improving social principles, not the selfishness of laissez-faire and the invisible hand. Ely dismissed the doctrines of classical economics that reduced society to a perpetual competition between materialistic individuals. Prominently allied with the burgeoning labour movement of the era, he, like other leading economic thinkers such as John Bates Clark, called for a new economics dedicated to the equitable redistribution of America's industrial wealth. Underlying Ely's economic program was the liberal Protestant vision of social redemption, a Kingdom of God on earth.

Wilson's engagement with Ely's milieu at Johns Hopkins led him to view democracy in a more positive, accepting light. Social Christianity—and all it implied from the perspective of political economy—had come to command his attention. On reading the influential *Philosophy of Wealth* by John Bates Clark, Wilson felt drawn to its democratic social philosophy. In a personal letter to Clark regarding the book, Wilson wrote: 'I feel under special obligations to its author. I feel that it has fertilized my own thought not only in the field of economics but also in the field of practical politics in which my special studies lie.' In language that would have shocked his father, he declared that a 'sane, well-balanced sympathizer with organized labor is very dear to my esteem'.[38]

During the mid-1880s, Wilson produced a number of works that owed at least a slight debt to the liberal Protestant, democratic world view he had encountered at Johns Hopkins. These revealed the extent to which the progressive climate of that institution had produced a change in Wilson's outlook. His little-known treatise on the modern democratic state was, as Wilson put it later, 'a task, not of origination, but of interpretation. Interpret the age: i.e. interpret myself. Account for the creed I hold in politics.'[39] It was a turning point in Wilson's intellectual development, revealing that while this former implacable opponent of universal suffrage still viewed democracy with some reservation, he had at least come to regard it in

---

[36] Richard T. Ely, *Outlines of Economics* (New York: Macmillan, 1893), 383.

[37] See John R. Everett, *Religion in Economics: A Study of John Bates Clark, Richard T. Ely, Simon N. Patten* (New York: King's Crown Press, 1946), 75. Later, Wilson would write Ely: "I shall take the more heart in what I have to do because men like yourself are so generous in believing in me'. See *PWW*, 12: 434.

[38] Wilson to John Bates Clark, 26 August 1887, *PWW*, 5: 565.

[39] Wilson, confidential journal, 28 December 1889, *PWW*, 6: 463.

a more sympathetic light. Like many liberals of the era, Wilson saw in democracy a way to ameliorate the worst tendencies of industrial proletarian radicalism:

> It is, indeed, more than ever a matter of deep moment to the world whether the Democratic State proves a success or failure. If not the capstone, it must in any case be the foundation of the future structure of politics. Men cannot turn back to the systems which they have rejected; advance or catastrophe is their alternative: and if a democratic polity based on individual initiative prove a failure, they will, apparently, be tempted to grope on, in the doubtful light of Socialism, towards a democratic polity based on communal initiative. Democratic in any case the future system must be.[40]

Here it can be seen that although Wilson had clearly liberated his thinking from the strictures of Calvinist conservatism, he had not cast off the teachings of his father in their entirety. The charismatic progressive movement at Johns Hopkins had helped turn Wilson into a liberal Protestant democrat, albeit one who still bore the influence of the conservative intellectual tradition in which he had been raised. Wilson's best-known work of the 1880s, *Congressional Government,* still reads very much like an Anglophile critique of rampant American democracy. In the United States, warned Wilson, the directly elected representatives of the people had been allowed to monopolise the legislative process. It was high time to reform this corrupt popular supremacy and return to an effective system of checks and balances such as had preserved the republican health of the polity in the early days of self-administration. 'Only the Senate', he noted with some relief, 'saves us often from the headlong popular tyranny'. The country 'may be said to be a limited democracy because of the Senate. This has proved the chief value of that upper chamber … It is valuable in our democracy in proportion as it is undemocratic'.[41]

During the 1890s and beyond, Wilson tended to view American democracy as a political-cultural expression of British ethnicity. Whereas Bancroft had insisted that the principle of democratic governance was capable of instantaneous and universal extension, Wilson considered it suitable only for Anglo-Saxon or Teutonic peoples whose stable character had equipped them for the responsible enjoyment of liberty. He considered 'the democracy of other peoples which is bred by discontent and founded upon revolution' as fundamentally different to 'the democracy, or rather the popular government, of the English race, which is bred by slow circumstance and founded upon habit'.[42] While conceding at times that there might exist 'certain influences astir in this century which make for democracy the world over', he insisted that 'it was not such forces that made us democratic, nor are we responsible for them'.[43] By 'we' he meant the United States, and here was an unequivocal rejection of the idea that the country had been founded with a special role to play in the advancement of humanity. Those 'who planned our constitution were aware that they were not inventing a new kind of rule'.[44] The first American government 'founded one hundred years ago, was

---

[40] Wilson, 'The Modern Democratic State', *PWW*, 5: 62.

[41] Wilson, 'Congressional Government', *PWW*, 4: 127.

[42] Ibid.

[43] Wilson, 'Nature of Democracy in the United States', 10 May 1889, PWW, 6: 224.

[44] Wilson, 'Ideals of Democracy', 1896, *PWW*, 10: 7.

no type of an experiment in advanced democracy … it was simply an adaptation of English constitutional government.'[45]

Public Intellectual: The Pre-Wilsonian Wilson

The ideas by which the educated American public first came to know Wilson were simply not Wilsonian ideas. He was not yet speaking as a prophetic nationalist, but as a professional Princeton historian offering a very different vision of America's history—and destiny—from that which he would later espouse as a politician.

Wilson made it quite clear in his popular 1891 lecture on democracy, for example, that he saw no teleological continuity between the American past, present and future. Democracy was a novel development in the life of the nation and would have disconcerted the founding fathers. 'Those who framed our federal government', he specified, 'planned no revolution, did not mean to invent an American government, but only to Americanize the English government'. The revolutionaries had felt that government 'ought to be guarded against the heats and hastes, the passions and the thoughtless impulses of the people, no less than against selfish dynasties and hurtful class intrigues'. A hundred years after the Revolution, Wilson argued, Americans 'have in a measure undone their work. A century has led us very far along the road of change. Year by year we have sought to bring government nearer to the people, despite the original plan'.[46] Though accepting of the new democracy, Wilson was careful to limit the possibility of its ultimate extension. 'Democratic nations are not made in a day', he cautioned, 'and they have never been made at all save in Switzerland, in England, and the United States'.[47]

Reacting xenophobically to the wave of non-Western European immigrants that was beginning to transform America in the 1890s, he suggested that democracy might be imparted 'to the best of those who come to us with other blood in their veins', yet considered it vital that the 'first blood … kept its advantage'.[48] Wilson feared deeply for the native democracy born of British custom in an urbanised America rapidly filling up with 'other' peoples. 'We have been steadily receiving into our midst and to full participation in our national life', he wrote, 'the very people whom their home politics have familiarized with revolution: our own equable blood we have suffered to receive into it the most feverish bloods of the old world'. Because of this destabilising presence, America now faced 'an ever-increasing difficulty of self-possession with ever-deteriorating materials: for your only reliable stuff in this strain of politics is Character.'[49] Wilson's emphasis on the primacy of race correlated with nationalist thinking in Europe and other modern European settler societies (such as Australia, New Zealand and South Africa). By defining the nation in exclusive racial terms, Wilson was expressing a vision that diverged significantly from the essence of the American national myth, namely, that Americans were not bound together

---

[45] Wilson, 'Nature of Democracy in the United States'.
[46] Wilson, 'A Lecture (Democracy)', 5 December 1891, *PWW*, 7: 351.
[47] Ibid., 358.
[48] Ibid.
[49] Wilson, 'Washington Centennial Address', 1889, *PWW*, 6: 181.

primarily by 'blood' but by common allegiance to the idea of America's democratic mission to the world.

While it is true that Wilson did exhibit some interest in the Frontier Thesis of Frederick Jackson Turner, this did not supplant his racial understanding both of America's origins and her place in the world. In an influential 1893 paper, Turner proposed that the American frontier experience had forged a distinctive political culture that set America apart. Environment rather than race, according to the essence of Turner's thesis, was the wellspring of American democracy. It was more in a spirit of academic engagement that Wilson lent sympathetic consideration to these ideas—and it is true that he produced some works (such as the 1895 address 'The Course of American History') which unmistakably bore Turner's influence. Fundamentally, however, Wilson remained convinced, as his 1902 *History of the American People* clearly shows, that everything in America worth preserving stemmed from its Anglo-Saxon heritage.[50] The environment may have produced some positive New World modifications in the American character, but only because of the inherent superiority of the Anglo-Saxon people who pushed the frontier west.

Wilson's increasing tendency to assert the supremacy of the Anglo-Saxon race also defined his emerging philosophy of international relations. During the 1895 Venezuelan boundary dispute with British Guiana, his old sense of kinship with the mother country's fundamental interests came instinctively to the fore. Unmoved by President Grover Cleveland's appeal to the Monroe Doctrine, Wilson urged the principle of Anglo-American cooperation above all else. 'Do we wish—ought we to dare', he asked, 'unless driven by imperative justice and necessity—to bring about a deadly war between the two branches of the Eng[lish] race, in whose hands lie, if they be united, the future destinies of the world … who, if divided, may be ousted of their supremacy?' Such a war, he concluded, would entail laying 'violent hands on civilization itself' and the 'disaster of it … no man can adequately imagine'.[51] Wilson was not alone in the voicing of such sentiments. Among the elites of both countries, the ideal of Anglo-American kinship and cooperation was becoming an important factor during the 1880s and 1890s. 'Toward Great Britain, alone of the major powers', according to one authority on the subject, 'the United States became more friendly in the two decades before Sarajevo.'[52] As evidenced by his response to the border crisis, this

---

[50] In that work, Wilson notoriously praised racial vigilante organisations like the Ku Klux Klan, arguing that: 'The white men of the South were aroused by the mere instinct of self-preservation to rid themselves … of governments sustained by … ignorant negroes … Year by year the organization spread … until at last there had sprung into existence a great Ku Klux Klan … to protect the southern country.' D. W. Griffith later drew heavily on these remarks when composing the intertitles of the 1915 silent racist classic, *Birth of a Nation*. See Wilson, *A History of the American People*, vol. 5, *Reunion and Nationalization*, cited in Melvyn Stokes, *D.W. Griffith's The Birth of a Nation: A History of 'The Most Controversial Motion Picture of all Time'* (Oxford: Oxford University Press, 2007), 199.

[51] Wilson, 'Memorandum for an Interview', 18 December 1895, *PWW*, 9: 365.

[52] Bradford Perkins, *The Great Rapprochement: England and the United States, 1895–1914* (New York: Atheneum, 1968), 8. Numerous other studies have dealt with this topic, including Charles S. Campbell, *Anglo-American Understanding. 1898–1903* (Baltimore: Johns Hopkins Press, 1957); Alexander E. Campbell, *Great Britain and the United States, 1895–1903* (London: Longmans,

divergent geopolitical paradigm appealed to Wilson's ingrained Anglophile sensibilities far more than the Bancroftian conception of America's role in the world.

By the turn of the twentieth century, Wilson found himself increasingly comfortable with this imagined fraternal association of the English-speaking countries. The Social Gospel was beginning to flourish in America, and Wilson saw a connection between its vision of self-sacrificing internationalism and the missionary, 'white-man's burden' role of the English-speaking world.[53] Social Gospel adherents drew on the theology of liberal Protestantism and applied its precepts to a specific social-reform program, one which ultimately entailed the establishment of a democratic and altruistic new world order.[54] Wilson's increasingly 'progressive' outlook on the general course of human affairs was expressed in the notion of a combined Anglo-American imperial mission. 'We know', he said in a live 1904 New York broadcast to London from a dinner gathering of The Pilgrims (an important Anglophile society), 'that our people stand for what you stand for'. Wilson then exhorted his fellow Americans to recognise the moral necessity of trans-Atlantic solidarity in the service of the world:

> We now have difficulties confronting us in international matters, and I take it that we are in a position to go to school to those who are more experienced than ourselves. And in the proper temper of men who know how to consult experts, we should forego our ancient Revolutionary attitude toward England and seek to know how she has managed her foreign affairs … In this way we shall show our mature wisdom. We should be partners with the nation that stands for the things for which we stand.[55]

In a 4 July speech from this turn-of-the-century period, Wilson sought to connect the ideal of applied Christianity to the theme of Anglo-American cooperation. 'That flag which we honor in this country', he opined, 'seems to me sometimes to be composed of stripes of parchment upon which are written the principles of the ancient liberty of the English speaking peoples. [Great Britain and the United States] stood together to represent … liberty'.[56] Accordingly, the two great nations had a 'responsibility laid upon us here which

---

1960); Bruce M. Russett, *Community and Contention: Britain and America in the Twentieth Century* (Cambridge, MA: MIT Press, 1963); and David Dimbleby and David Reynolds, *An Ocean Apart: The Relationship between Britain and America in the Twentieth Century* (London: Random House, 1988).

[53] Wilson's response to the Spanish-American War was particularly revealing of this increasingly millennial yet still pre-nationalist foreign policy views. See *PWW*, 10: 574–576 and 12: 215–216.

[54] See, for example, Robert T. Handy, ed., *The Social Gospel in America 1870–1920* (New York: Oxford University Press, 1966); William R. Hutchison, *The Modernist Impulse in American Protestantism* (Cambridge, MA: Harvard University Press, 1976); and Robert M. Crunden, *Ministers of Reform: The Progressives' Achievement in American Civilization, 1889–1920* (New York: Basic Books, 1982). In *Wilsonian Statecraft: Theory and Practice of Liberal Internationalism during World War I* (Wilmington, DL: Scholarly Resources Inc., 1991), Lloyd E. Ambrosius has correctly pointed to the influence of the Social Gospel on Wilson's understanding of the world.

[55] Wilson, speech in New York, 30 January 1904, *PWW*, 15: 149.

[56] Wilson, 'Religion and Patriotism', 4 July 1902, *PWW*, 12: 475.

is greater than the responsibility of individual salvation ... there is a duty to lift other men along ... in that great process of elevation; and that is the patriotic duty just as much as it is the religious duty.'[57] Here was 'idealism', yes, and a willingness to get involved in the internal affairs of other countries, but not yet was Wilson giving expression to Bancroftian nationalist ideas. Although Wilson did now envision a world reconstructed for the better, he still conceived of America and Great Britain as equal moral partners in the progressive project. In other words, the salvation of humanity did not depend on the fulfilment of America's own special destiny, but on the imperial destiny of the Anglo-Saxon people.

Even Wilson's 1902 speech 'The Ideals of America', which envisioned a missionary role for the US in the world, paid tribute to the English origins of American democracy. The 'American ideals' that Wilson spoke of were ancient English liberties that had been given new life in America and had in turn replenished the cause of freedom in England. 'Our Washington is become one of the heroes of the English race', he specified. 'We had begun the work of freeing England when we completed the work of freeing ourselves.' What this now meant for Puerto Rico and the Philippines, Wilson continued, was an extended period of tutelage in the ways of democratic self-governance. 'The spirit of English life has made comrades of us all to be a nation', he argued, and the United States had a moral duty to impart these lessons of Anglo-Saxon liberty to less advanced races. It was to be a long, slow process, for, '[t]hey are children and we are men in these deep matters of government and justice'.[58] The coming century, Wilson predicted, 'shall see us a great power in the world bent upon service and not mastery'. This was undoubtedly an important shift in Wilson's intellectual development, showing very clearly that he was starting to think in terms of a special American mission. However, it was a mission still conjoined with Britain's more established imperial role, a mission consistent with the general rubric of Anglo-Saxon benevolence and supremacy.

Wilson specified that the ideals America would offer the world were not uniquely American in origin; instead they were an extension of the ancient tradition of English liberty.[59] Thus, for all his millennial imperialist enthusiasm, Wilson had stopped short of subscribing to the essence of the Bancroftian vision, which viewed American democracy not as an outgrowth of British traditions but as a radical new departure from anything that had gone before. Hence, although Wilson was increasingly voicing proto-Wilsonian sentiments at the turn of the century, his ultimate conversion to American nationalism still lay some years in the future. Wilson's thinking still needed a final twist to create the Wilsonian vision in its final, mature form. That twist came when he entered politics.

---

[57] Ibid., 476.

[58] See Paul A. Kramer, *The Blood of Government: Race, Empire, the United States, & the Philippines* (Chapel Hill: University of North Carolina Press, 2006) for a comprehensive study of this issue, including aspects of Wilson's racial thinking.

[59] Wilson, 'The Ideals of America: An Address Delivered on the One Hundred and Twenty-Fifth Anniversary of the Battle of Trenton', 26 December 1901, *PWW*, 12: 215.

1910: Wilson Embraces American Nationalism

Throughout his long career as an academic historian, Wilson had never accepted the nationalist dogma that America's special destiny was to single-handedly redeem the world by bequeathing its democracy to all humanity. Indeed, as late as December 1909, Wilson had still been pointing to non-British immigrants as a threat to the health of American democracy. The country had achieved early success 'with the establishment of English sentiments' but the present 'mixture of bloods … brings about a social complexity very difficult to make compact'. From the British 'older order' had stemmed a cohesive respect for law. 'The sinews of law are what holds us together', he warned, 'and these sinews are being loosened by these newcomers'.[60]

It was only in 1910 that he gave his progressivism a Bancroftian dimension to create the Wilsonian vision. On accepting the Democratic Party's nomination for the New Jersey gubernatorial campaign, Wilson's rhetoric, as though responding to some silent, compelling cue, became distinctly nationalist in tone. He now referred to the American Revolution as '[t]he most extraordinary passage in history'.[61] America, he argued:

> has undertaken to be the haven of hope, the opportunity of all men … to hold the lamp of progress up to the nations, not only to guide her own feet with a little lamp of her own kindling, but to guide the feet of all men who seek that which is just.[62]

These and many other similar remarks made during the campaign signified Wilson's surrender to the national mythology that he had previously resisted. At this most crucial of junctures in his life, the 'Wilsonian' Wilson finally emerged. After 1910, the public Wilson regarded democracy in purely Bancroftian terms as pertaining equally to the deepest instincts of all peoples and awaiting its final victory in the form of an American-dominated world order:

> The manifest destiny of America is not to rule the world by physical force … The destiny of America and the leadership of America is that she shall do the thinking of the world … and that there will be throughout her great thought the pulse of the common man, of the average man, of all men—the thought of humanity itself.[63]

The United States was special among nations because, as Wilson now unhesitatingly put it:

> Men flock to America from many continents … They unite together in a single community and find themselves engrossed in that thing that we call the American spirit … America was built as a heart structure … it was meant to be an asylum for those who could not get their rights anywhere else … it was meant as a gathering place for [people] of all nations who wanted to have their principles, rights and equality recognized and applied in their case.[64]

---

[60] Wilson, 'To Make Men Unlike Sires', 10 December 1909, *PWW*, 19: 600.
[61] Wilson, 'A Campaign Address in Montclair, New Jersey', 29 September 1910, *PWW*, 21: 517.
[62] Wilson, 'A Campaign Address in Newton, New Jersey', 22 October 1910, *PWW*, 21: 404–05.
[63] Wilson, 'A Campaign Address in Atlantic City, New Jersey', 13 October 1910, *PWW*, 21: 318.
[64] Wilson, 'A Campaign Address in Perth Amboy', 4 November 1910, *PWW*, 21: 545.

Elsewhere, Wilson claimed that:

> America is not merely a body of towns … America is an idea, America is an ideal, America is a vision … America for the leadership of the world, America for the purification of the world, America for the example of the world.[65]

America alone had the moral prerogative, he now argued, and stood apart from the nations of the Old World—including Great Britain. Having incorporated the Bancroftian vision into his rhetoric, Wilson had become a true believer in the nationalist gospel. Expelled from his official worldview was the notion of Anglo-Saxon imperial cooperation: there was only one national mission that mattered now—America's own. This was a crucial distinction between the Wilson of 1910 and the Wilson who at the turn of the century had conceived of America's role in the world in terms of a morally equal partnership with Great Britain.

At the age of fifty-three, a great shift had taken place in Wilson's thinking. This naturally begs the question, what motivated such a remarkable transformation? Although the timing of the conversion experience may at first glance suggest that he was primarily motivated by political expediency, the consistency with which Wilson subsequently championed Bancroftian ideas indicates that a genuine revolution in outlook had taken place. Wilson had not merely paid lip service to the national myth; he had reinvented himself according to its fundamental precepts.

By the end of the nineteenth century, a collective hunger for national identity had secured the absolute predominance of the Bancroftian vision in American public life. According to William McKinley (president from 1897–1901), who helped usher the US into a new era of global influence with the Spanish–American War, the American flag represented 'more than any other banner in the world the best hopes and aspirations of mankind'.[66] American history, he claimed in language that directly anticipated the lofty timbre of Wilsonian rhetoric, had 'exalted mankind and advanced the cause of freedom throughout the world … we shall attain to our high destiny as the foremost of the enlightened nations of the world which, under Providence, we ought to achieve.'[67] After 'more than a hundred years of national existence', McKinley remarked on one occasion, the 'ship of state has sailed uninterruptedly in its mission of liberty, and … this nation … never raised its arm against humanity, never struck a blow against liberty, never struck a blow except for civilization and mankind'.[68] Wilson entered politics less than a decade after the McKinley era, and for him there was simply no other way of relating to the electorate other than to espouse the body of myths by which the US now defined itself. We have seen how, at different stages of his life, Wilson was capable of engaging with new ideas and incorporating them into his world view. In the 1880s, for example, he became a liberal Protestant democrat and, in a sense, a new man. Something similar occurred in 1910, when Wilson became an American nationalist and simultaneously became 'Wilsonian'.

---

[65] Wilson, 'A Campaign Address in Atlantic City'.
[66] William McKinley, *Speeches and Addresses of William McKinley* (New York: Doubleday & McClure, 1900), 370.
[67] Ibid., 10.
[68] Ibid., 309.

The ideas that Wilson took up in 1910 became the core of his presidential foreign policy vision, underpinning numerous interventions in the Caribbean and Central America during his first term in office. As a late convert to the Bancroftian world view, a sort of Pauline intensity characterised Wilson's appropriation of the national myth. Unlike Theodore Roosevelt and William Howard Taft who combined the concept of a national mission with more frankly mercenary considerations of geopolitical and material self-interest, Wilson went to extraordinary rhetorical lengths to emphasise the altruistic basis of his administration's foreign policy. He rejected Taft's 'Dollar Diplomacy' as a betrayal of America's true principles and promised the other nations of the Western Hemisphere that the US sought no advantage whatsoever in its dealings with them. In a keynote address in 1913 delivered in Mobile, Alabama, where many representatives of Latin American states were present at a commercial congress, Wilson argued:

> It is a very perilous thing to determine the foreign policy of a nation in the terms of material interest … We must show ourselves friends by comprehending their interest whether it squares with our own interest or not … our real relationship with the rest of America … is the relationship of a family of mankind devoted to the development of true constitutional liberty.[69]

Ironically, in spite of Wilson's idealistic professions of selflessness and service, he turned out to be more of a hectoring interventionist than any of his presidential predecessors. At the head of the 'family of mankind' stood the United States, and to defy its will brought rebuke and punishment. Inwardly convinced that the US had a providentially ordained right to administer lessons—harsh lessons if need be—in morality and politics to 'childish' peoples, Wilson used force to extend or establish direct US control over nations such as Nicaragua (1914), Haiti (1915) and the Dominican Republic (1916). His administration also went to war with Mexico in an attempt to establish indirect control over the internal affairs of that country, a development that had a significant ripple effect through the rest of the Western Hemisphere. Historians of US foreign policy have long debated Wilson's controversial record in Latin America, some national liberals extolling his efforts (in varying degrees of nuance), others (particularly on the left) denouncing his 'imperialist' policies. And although 'imperialism' is a problematic and somewhat loaded term, it is at the least understandable why Wilsonian attitudes have so often been equated with it. In presenting the quest for control and dominance as a benevolent enterprise, Wilson was conforming to a classic imperial conceit. Throughout human history, from ancient times to the modern age, justificatory creeds have inevitably accompanied the pursuit of strategic, commercial and territorial self-aggrandisement by great powers. Generally such dogmas have revolved around the concept of a civilising mission to the 'barbarous' or 'savage' subjects of expansionary policies. When the United States emerged as a great power with a global reach at the outset of the twentieth century, it too felt the urge to elevate and sanctify its pursuit of what may arguably be termed hegemony. 'Wilsonianism' emerged out of this need, not as a rigidly codified ideology like other 'isms' of the twentieth century, but more as

---

[69] Wilson, 'Address Before the Southern Commercial Congress in Mobile, Alabama', 27 October 1913, in *Selected Addresses and Public Papers of Woodrow Wilson*, ed. Albert Bushnell Hart (Honolulu: University Press of the Pacific, 2002), 19.

a set of underlying assumptions with an ideological bent, ideological in the sense that these assumptions were derived from the Bancroftian world view. At its heart, the Wilsonian vision sought to establish nothing less than a global US empire—not a traditional empire based on territorial acquisition, but an empire of the spirit, as it were. The consolidation of US military and strategic dominance and the creation of a liberal capitalist global economic order favourable to the profit-seeking needs of US capital were certainly an important part of the process, but in Wilson's mind these 'secular' goals were not ends in themselves but means, rather, to a 'spiritual' end.

Even as Wilson's marines enforced US rule at gunpoint, killing or wounding thousands of dissenting civilians (as occurred in Haiti), the president consistently depicted US intervention as a lofty mission consistent with the highest ideals of democratic, benevolent, altruistic America. Writ large, the same set of assumptions underpinned Wilson's entry into the First World War—which he depicted as an eschatological struggle between the forces of New World democracy and Old World autocracy—and the treaty negotiations of 1919. 'America is going to grow more and more powerful', he predicted in Helena during the 1919 Western Speaking Tour, 'and the more powerful she is, the more inevitable it is that she should be entrusted with the peace of the world'. This was a good thing, argued the politically embattled president, because '[America] is the only national idealistic force in the world, and idealism is going to save the world'.[70] The 'great tramp, tramp of the American people sounded in the ears of the whole world', he remarked in a Seattle address, 'and they knew that the armies of God were on their way.'[71] Employing impeccably phrased Bancroftian sentiments, Wilson drew on the powerful mythology of American nationalism to create a self-sustaining creed that allowed America to act not only with potential impunity on the world stage but with total confidence its own holiness—whoever the enemy should be. Wilsonianism remains a vital—and arguably hubristic—idée fixe of US foreign policy, with dramatic and sometimes very negative consequences for the peoples of the developing world. While it may be relatively easy to reconcile Wilson's depiction of US military might as the 'armies of God' with the 1940s struggle against fascism, it is surely less comforting to review the US record in Indochina or, in more recent times, the Middle East.

Conclusion

Fundamentally, the story of Wilson's intellectual development from the 1870s to 1910 is about much more than Wilson the individual. Wilson's intellectual development is a microcosmic illustration of America's nineteenth-century transition from the pre-modern to the modern, from conservative Calvinism and cautious Anglophile republicanism to optimistic liberal theology, democracy and the towering nationalist shibboleth. His 1910 conversion illustrates the vital role that national mythology had come to play in American society as an organic whole. As the French historian and political commentator Alexis de Toqueville observed after visiting America in the 1830s,

> it will always be very difficult [in a society like the United States] for a man to believe what the mass rejects and to profess what it condemns … When an

---

[70] Wilson, 'An Address in the Marlow Theater in Helena', 11 September, 1919, *PWW*, 63: 183, 189.

[71] Wilson, 'An Address in the Seattle Arena', 13 September 1919, *PWW*, 63: 264.

> opinion has taken root in a democracy and established itself in the minds of the majority, it afterward persists by itself, needing no effort to maintain it since no one can attack it [and those] who at first rejected it as false come in the end to adopt it as accepted.[72]

These important insights, which remain as relevant today as when they were first written, help to contextualise Wilson's evolving relationship with the myths of American nationalism. Having started life as exactly one of those who 'professed what the mass condemned', to paraphrase de Toqueville, Wilson eventually embraced what he had 'at first rejected'.

---

[72] Alexis de Toqueville, *Democracy in America* (New York: Collins, 1966), 834.

14

Recovering the Roots of Reinhold Niebuhr's Critique of American Nationalism

Michael G. Thompson

Karl Paul Reinhold Niebuhr (1892–1971) had no PhD, no training in international relations, and no formal education either in political science or history. As a pastor in the German Evangelical Church in America, he could boast a masters degree from Yale Divinity School—but even there he felt as if he were a 'mongrel among thoroughbreds'.[1] A midwesterner by birth, Niebuhr's meagre education made his appointment to an academic post an unlikely possibility. Indeed, if not for a wealthy Christian radical activist offering to pay Niebuhr's wage out of his own pocket, he might never have secured his first and only academic post, the one he held at New York City's Union Theological Seminary for over three decades.[2]

With such a background, it is remarkable that Niebuhr eventually left a mark on all of the above disciplines: a figure to be reckoned with not only in theology (where to many he was still a 'mongrel') but also in political thought, history and international relations. What was at work here? How could a scholar of US foreign relations such as Andrew Bacevich label Niebuhr's 1952 work *The Irony of American History* the 'most important book ever written on foreign policy'?[3] How was it that one of the country's most prominent international relations theorists, Hans Morgenthau, could label Niebuhr the 'greatest living political philosopher of America'?[4] How was it that Niebuhr, while employed in a theological seminary, could find himself at different times appointed to George Kennan's long-range strategic research centre, the Council on Foreign Relations, and US delegations to the United Nations Educational Scientific and Cultural Organization?[5]

Niebuhr's influence on American politics has, of course, been both periodic and varied. Despite the earlier respect for Niebuhr and his corpus—and notwithstanding President Jimmy Carter's noted interest in his work in the 1970s—the theologian was by the turn of the twenty-first century a relatively forgotten figure, relegated for the most part to something of a Cold War relic. Columnist David Brooks captured the scene in 2002 in the pages of the *Atlantic*: 'I'm amazed', he wrote,

---

[1] Richard Wightman Fox, *Reinhold Niebuhr: A Biography* (Ithaca: Cornell University Press, 1996), 28.

[2] The philanthropist was Sherwood Eddy. See ibid., 105–06.

[3] Andrew Bacevich, 'Introduction', in Reinhold Niebuhr, *The Irony of American History* (Chicago: University of Chicago Press, 2008), ix.

[4] Cited in Ronald H. Stone, *Prophetic Realism: Beyond Militarism and Pacifism in an Age of Terror* (New York: T & T Clark International, 2005), 60.

[5] Fox, *Reinhold Niebuhr*, 238–39.

> that Reinhold Niebuhr hasn't made a comeback since September 11 ... If there is going to be a hawkish left in America again, a left suspicious of power but willing to use it to defend freedom, it will have to be revived by a modern-day Reinhold Niebuhr.[6]

Yet, in noting its absence, Brooks predicted exactly the kind of comeback that Niebuhr's work would make in the next five years. What started as a trickle soon became a small flood: academics, commentators and politicians took to Niebuhr's writings during the presidency of George W. Bush in a way that had not been seen since the early Cold War. Niebuhr's penchant for unintended consequences—and the way his apparent trajectory from radicalism to realism mirrored theirs—made him a candidate for adoption by some neo-conservatives.[7] Others, seeking to build a theological rationale for supporting President Bush's so-called 'war on terror' saw in Niebuhr's tough approach to totalitarianism a precedent for their own program.[8] Niebuhr was also making a comeback in Democratic circles not seen since Jimmy Carter's election. Then a senator, Barack Obama endorsed the publication of a new edition of Niebuhr's *Irony of American History*, labelling Niebuhr as one of his 'favourite political philosophers'.[9] Indeed, the rapid outpouring of interest in Niebuhr was noted in another *Atlantic Monthly* article—only five years after Brooks had complained about the lack of interest in Niebuhr in the same magazine. In late 2007 it ran a multi-page feature on the various uses to which Niebuhr's legacy was being put; the title of the piece, authored by Paul Elie, identified the long-departed theologian as the 'man for all reasons'.[10]

What became clear in the Niebuhr revival, however, was just how flexible his legacy was. Niebuhr's realism could be pressed into service for a variety of ends: either 'tough' on the reality of evil, or a proponent of humility as opposed to hubris. Indeed, between Bush's first and second presidential terms—with the occupation of Iraq in apparent crisis—the tone of writings about Niebuhr swung subtly from the former to the latter. Niebuhr was found less to be a source for the hawkish realism needed to wage the war on terror (as in Brooks and Elshtain) and more a figurehead in an emerging call for a humble, or 'ethical' realism (as in the works of Andrew Bacevich and Anatol Lieven).[11] Yet this essay

---

[6] David Brooks, 'A Man on a Gray Horse', *The Atlantic Monthly*, 290 (2), September 2002, 24.

[7] Paul Elie points to the example of 'theocon' historian Wilfred McClay who claimed Niebuhr would have held it to be 'right and just for Christians to support this war [on terror]. Indeed, they have an obligation to do so'. See Paul Elie, 'A Man for All Reasons', *The Atlantic Monthly*, 300 (4), November 2007, 88.

[8] For example, see Jean Bethke Elshtain, *Just War Against Terror: The Burden of American Power in a Violent World* (New York: Basic Books, 2003), which contains a chapter entitled 'Where is the legacy of Niebuhr and Tillich?'.

[9] See the cover of the 2008 University of Chicago Press edition of *The Irony of American History*. The quote was actually given as Obama left the Senate floor to speak to journalists in 2007. See Elie, 'A Man for All Reasons', 84.

[10] Ibid., 82–84, 86, 88–90, 92, 94, 96.

[11] Andrew J. Bacevich, *The Limits of Power: The End of American Exceptionalism* (New York: Metropolitan Books, 2008); Anatol Lieven and John Hulsman, *Ethical Realism: A Vision for America's Role in the World* (New York: Pantheon Books, 2006).

suggests that both kinds of invocations of Niebuhr's legacy—those that interpret Niebuhr as wanting to inject some modesty and humility into US foreign policy, or those who see him as supporting a tough, hawkish realism—run the danger of missing what was arguably Niebuhr's deepest and most significant contribution, and one that coloured all his work: namely, his reflection on the nature of nationalism itself, and in particular, on the problems of American nationalism.

To invoke Niebuhr's legacy in the twenty-first century of course requires facing the general methodological problem of how to transplant a thinker's insights across time while maintaining the integrity of the original root structure of those ideas. The challenge is by no means restricted to those studying Niebuhr, but in Niebuhr's case it has tended to result in a particular omission. Efforts to transplant Niebuhr primarily as an American foreign policy realist have by and large missed the embeddedness of Niebuhr's critique of nationalism in the wider political-theological enterprises of the decades spanning the 1920s to the 1940s. As a result, not only is the transplanted Niebuhr all the poorer, but scholars and commentators, and those for whom they write, also miss the opportunity of encountering the wider world of which Niebuhr was a part—a world of historical interest and importance in itself.

Problems both of periodisation and disciplinary division make the task of transplanting Reinhold Niebuhr even more difficult. Temporally, transplanting Niebuhr the Cold War liberal and realist of the 1950s, means artificially severing him from his roots in the 1920s and 1930s, when he was a socialist, pacifist and anti-imperialist, rather than the robust liberal supporter of the 'Vital Center' as he became in the mid-1940s (though one with qualms, to be sure). Substantively, taking Niebuhr merely as a political realist artificially separates him from the world of transatlantic ecumenical theology in which he spoke and debated and worked. Working against both these tendencies, this essay explores aspects of the root structure of Niebuhr's thought by intentionally relocating him as one part of a broader, collective political-theological critique of nationalism from the 1920s to the 1940s—one that included, but was larger than, him. Placing Niebuhr in this broader context at once better serves to highlight his individual contribution (making it less unique, but no less important) while also arguably affording him an increased immunity against efforts to coopt his legacy into the very kinds of exceptionalist and nationalistic projects he—and his peers—once stood against.

This chapter, then, explores two key strands of the political-theological critique of nationalism from the 1920s to the 1940s in which Niebuhr played a leading part. The two strands have both a continuous and complementary quality to them; they overlapped and yet were distinguishable. They represent two enterprises that together shaped and constituted a new kind of Christian internationalism in the interwar years, a movement that needs to be understood as standing apart from both the Wilsonian liberal internationalism of the early 1920s and the Christian nationalism that emerged in American political culture in the 1950s, 1980s and early twenty-first century. The two strands are, firstly, the Social Gospel critique of nationalism as artificial, dangerous and functionally religious—a view that held nationalism to be a component of the wider 'war system' in which America as well as Europe was complicit; and secondly, the ecumenical theological critique in the mid-1930s of nationalism as idolatry, or as a form of self-deification, an approach forged in the crucible of the Nazi–Church struggle in Europe and brought home to America (even while being Americanised) by ecumenists such as Niebuhr. In each strand, Niebuhr was among the most innovative and influential of the networks' leaders and exponents; but equally so, he was as much shaped by those around him as he helped shape them.

Nationalism as Artificial, Dangerous and Falsely Religious: Niebuhr and Social Gospel Thought in the 1920s

The orientation of Niebuhr's views on American nationalism was set by the general wave of repugnance toward the war system that swept progressive Social Gospel circles in the 1920s. Historians have often been so preoccupied by the way religious figures have contributed to the force of nationalism, that they have missed—almost by definition—Christian critics of nationalism. Yet the 1920s enthusiasm for pacifism was, in many cases, combined with a new kind of Christian internationalism (a term coined and used in the period) that overtly opposed the complicity of religion in nationalism and war.[12] Popular campaigns for disarmament, the 'outlawry of war' and World Court arbitration are well-known features of 1920s internationalism; but less well known is the way that within Social Gospel circles such efforts were often couched as a deeper, deliberate effort to break the normative ties between Christianity and nationalism. Nationalism, in this period, became a conscious problem in Christian writing—an object of ethical scrutiny—in a way that it had not been earlier. According to New York preacher Harry Emerson Fosdick in 1928, himself a barometer for the climate of liberal Protestant thought, nationalism represented 'a competing religion … the most dangerous rival of Christian principles on earth.'[13]

Aspects of this anti-nationalism soaked into Niebuhr's pores, never to be dislodged. Much of the affective basis of the new critique of nationalism lay in what Niebuhr later identified as the 'moral nausea' felt by many liberal Protestant leaders after the First World War—revulsion that they had given religious endorsement to a war effort that no longer appeared redemptive so much as catastrophic. The moral nausea provoked among them a revisionist interpretation of the causes of the past war and a corresponding suspicion over anything that resembled those causes in the present. American responses to the widespread disillusionment of the 'Wilsonian moment' were, of course, many and varied, but two of the most notable positions were that of the mainstream liberal internationalists, who waited and lobbied for a second chance for America to join the League of Nations, and the nationalist-isolationists who insisted it was time to put America first.[14] But standing apart

---

[12] Some examples of the use of the term Christian internationalism include William Pierson Merrill, *Christian Internationalism* (New York: Macmillan, 1919); Jun Xing, *Baptized in the Fire of Revolution: The American Social Gospel and the YMCA in China, 1919-1937* (Bethlehem: Lehigh University Press, 1996), esp. ch. 5; and Heather A. Warren, *Theologians of a New World Order: Reinhold Niebuhr and the Christian Realists* (New York: Oxford University Press, 1997), 71.

[13] Cited in Kirby Page, *National Defense: A Study of the Origins, Results and Prevention of War* (New York: Farrar & Rinehart, 1931), 204.

[14] The term 'Wilsonian moment' is taken from Erez Manela, *The Wilsonian Moment: Self-Determination and the International Origins of Anticolonial Nationalism* (Oxford: Oxford University Press, 2007). On liberal internationalists waiting for a second chance, see Robert A. Divine, *Second*

from both these options, the new generation of radical Christian internationalists such as Niebuhr, Sherwood Eddy and Kirby Page focused instead on exposing the war-causing forces of nationalism, imperialism, and militarism in American life, and calling upon the nation to repent of such collective sins if it claimed indeed to be Christian.

Niebuhr's own suspicion of nationalism as something dangerous was rooted in this post-war moral nausea. His insistence on a gulf between God and nation was forged in these very revisionist projects. Indeed, he was a typical example of many among his liberal Protestant Social Gospel network—a network centred on periodicals such as *The Christian Century* and *The World Tomorrow*, and such organisations as the Young Men's Christian Association (YMCA), its sister unit, the Young Women's Christian Association (YWCA), and the Fellowship for a Christian Social Order—in announcing his conversion to pacifism in the early to mid-1920s. On a trip through the Ruhr with YMCA internationalist Sherwood Eddy's 'traveling seminar' in 1923, he wrote in his journal that he was finally 'done with the war business'.[15] Observing the French occupation of the area—in cities that were 'the closest thing to hell I have ever seen'—was enough to cure him of his illusions concerning the efficacy of the war. 'This, then, is the glorious issue for which the war was fought!', he concluded sarcastically.[16] Niebuhr returned to the US to work within an interlocking directorate of fellowships, leagues, Christian campus groups, and periodicals to crusade against the 'war system'.

Niebuhr, along with Sherwood Eddy (who announced his conversion to pacifism in 1924) and Kirby Page (a pacifist since 1917) began to appear at the forefront of a new kind of popular revisionist historical literature. Niebuhr, Eddy, Page and others argued at student conferences and on campuses, in books, pamphlets and journals of opinion such as *The World Tomorrow* and *The Christian Century*, that the war system, once seen to reside solely in the Old World, was in fact alive and well in the contemporary mid-1920s United States. Joining forces with the more radical pacifists of the Fellowship of Reconciliation, a group with Quaker influence formed during the war, they argued that the deeper war-making forces of nationalism, militarism and imperialism were present not only in pre-war Prussia but also among the Allies—and not only among the European allies, but also in the United States. Naturally, this stood in contrast with the account that held Germany solely responsible for the war, a claim inscribed into the war guilt clause of the Treaty of Versailles.[17] More significantly, it challenged the kind of exceptionalist narrative propounded by President Wilson and many other Americans that held war-making forces to be a European problem rather than an American one—albeit one into which Americans were mistakenly drawn from time to time, as in the First World War. Rather, if the deeper causes of the war system lay in the universal tendencies of humans toward collective sin

---

Chance: The Triumph of Internationalism in America During World War II (New York: Atheneum, 1967). For a helpful survey of inter-war isolationism, see George C. Herring, *From Colony to Superpower: U.S. Foreign Relations Since 1776* (New York: Oxford University Press, 2008), 436–537.

[15] Later published in Reinhold Niebuhr, *Leaves from the Notebook of a Tamed Cynic* (Cleveland: Meridian, 1964 [1929]), 67–68.

[16] Ibid.

[17] The Versailles Treaty, 28 June 1919, Part VIII: Reparation, Section 1, Article 231.

in the form of nationalism, imperialism and militarism, then America could neither be immune nor exceptional. Such was the level of suspicion, in fact, that Niebuhr and others tarred military training in American colleges with the same brush as they did Prussian militarism before the war: both were part of a universal war system that needed to be resisted. Writing in a 1926 special edition of *The World Tomorrow* on 'Militarism in the USA', Niebuhr warned that the American public suffered 'blindness' if they could not detect 'the war system' at work in the growing levels of compulsory Reserve Officer Training Corps (ROTC) programs on college campuses.[18]

Beneath the war system, according to these internationalists, lay the force of nationalism; it was the deeper cause that drove the secondary phenomena of militarism on school campuses and US imperialist ventures in Nicaragua and Haiti. Here Niebuhr's network of radical Christian internationalists were influenced by a new turn in historical scholarship that began to present nationalism as something historically contingent, as artificial rather than natural, though no less powerful for being so. Nationalism was formed, such scholarship argued, out of complex socio-psychological processes: it was instilled by the cultural environment, and thus could be checked and countered by similarly environmental means—the revision of history textbooks, for example. British scholars such as Alfred Zimmern, A. D. Lindsay and G. P. Gooch fed the view that nationalism was a psychological and emotional phenomenon, rather than a natural outworking of some empirical reality such as the biological or territorial basis of a people group.[19] Similarly, America's Carlton Hayes, a historian at Columbia University and later ambassador to Spain, essayed both on the artificiality of nationalism and its emotional significance in public life, anticipating Hans Kohn's depiction of nationalism in the 1940s as 'a state of mind' and Benedict Anderson's classic postulation of nations as 'imagined communities' in the 1980s.[20]

But the Christian internationalists of the 1920s went beyond the line of argument proffered by contemporary scholars such as Hayes in at least two ways. First, many of them, including Niebuhr, began historicising nationalism against the longer backdrop of the changes wrought by the Reformation. Nationalism was the fruit of a culture, they argued—appealing to a rather romanticised and sanitised narrative of medieval history—that had lost the sense of unity provided earlier by Christendom. Despite their overwhelmingly Protestant base, and with little sign of much rapprochement toward contemporary Catholics, these Christian internationalists were nostalgic for what they saw as the redemptive influence of the supranational Church of times past.[21] Protestant individualism, they argued, had aided

---

[18] Niebuhr, 'The Threat of the ROTC', *The World Tomorrow*, October 1926, 154–156.

[19] See, for example, Niebuhr's close colleague Kirby Page's reading of these forces in *Imperialism and Nationalism* (New York: George H. Doran, 1925), 23–24.

[20] Carlton J. H. Hayes, *Essays on Nationalism* (New York: The Macmillan Company, 1926). See also Hans Kohn, *The Idea of Nationalism: A Study in its Origins and Background* (New York: The Macmillian Company, 1958 [1944]) and Benedict Anderson, *Imagined Communities: Reflections on the Origin and Spread of Nationalism* (London: Verso, 1983).

[21] For example, see Conference on Christian Politics, Economics and Citizenship, *Being the Report presented to the Conference at Birmingham, April 5–12, 1924*, vol. VII, *International Relations* (London: Longmans Green & Co., 1924). Such a line of argument was also embedded in the emerging scholarship on medieval Christendom in the 1920s coming from neo-Catholic figures

and abetted the rise of post-Reformation nationalism. Although not unique to him—and although he never made much of the idea in comparison to his British contemporaries such as Christopher Dawson and J. H. Oldham—Niebuhr did briefly touch on the theme in his 1928 book, *Does Civilization Need Religion?*.[22] He regretted that historically 'Protestantism became the handmaiden of a budding nationalism which was impatient of the restraints of an international papacy, as it has since been impatient of every other type of international control'.[23] It was time for Protestantism to become conscious of this tendency and work out the implications of the faith for the new era of international interdependency. There were signs of positive growth. Niebuhr welcomed what he saw as a 'wholesome mood of repentance in the church for its easy connivance with an unethical nationalism in the past centuries'—a sense of repentance he and his colleagues were themselves doing their best to promote.[24]

Second, and going further, Niebuhr and others began arguing that the role nationalism played in modern culture was, despite the increasingly secular character of the age, functionally equivalent to religion. Although this idea was made prominent by Carlton Hayes in his *Essays on Nationalism*, Christian internationalists did not need Hayes to tell them that nationalism was a new kind of secular religion. Such an argument was already a well-developed part of their arsenal. Another colleague of Niebuhr's on the Christian student scene from the 1920s to the 1940s, Francis Pickens Miller, wrote in *The World Tomorrow* that he was concerned about President Calvin Coolidge's populist nationalism and he loathed hearing the US ambassador to the court of St James tell the British people in 1922 that it was a case of 'America first'. But looking at domestic culture, Miller was almost more concerned about the religion of nationalism taking hold through daily ritual in schools. Every day, he opined, 'hundreds of thousands of school children stand at attention … before the national emblem and hymn its spangled stars'. For Miller, this was 'the cult of the National Being'. Referring to Jesus' famous separation of that which is owed to Caesar and that which is owed to God, Miller offered a memorable quip that summed up the thinking of Christian internationalism at this time: 'It isn't any longer a question of God or Caesar, for in the schools Uncle Sam is two in one'.[25]

The three-pronged critique of nationalism as artificial, dangerous and falsely religious stayed with Reinhold Niebuhr for life. Although much has been made by scholars of Niebuhr (and, indeed, by Niebuhr himself) of his apparent departure from what he called liberalism and pacifism in the 1930s and 1940s, these contours of his critical outlook on

---

such as Christopher Dawson and J. H. Oldham. On the latter, see John Nurser, *For All Peoples and All Nations: Christian Churches and Human Rights* (Geneva: WCC Publications, 2005), 11–27.

[22] Compare, for example, Christopher Dawson, *The Making of Europe: An Introduction to the History of European Unity* (London: Sheed and Ward, 1932) and Joseph Houldsworth Oldham, *The Resurrection of Christendom* (London: Sheldon Press, 1940).

[23] Niebuhr, *Does Civilization Need Religion? A Study in the Social Resources and Limitations of Religion in Modern Life* (New York: The Macmillan Company, 1928), 65.

[24] Ibid., 229–30.

[25] Francis P. Miller, 'These Sovereign United States', *The World Tomorrow*, November 1926, 197–98.

nationalism remained. This basic continuity can be clearly seen when examining his major work of the period, *Moral Man and Immoral Society*, a text that signalled the beginning of his departure from pacifism, rationalism and liberalism.[26] Here Niebuhr took the 1920s Christian internationalist critique of nationalism and developed it even more systematically than those who had originated it.

Penned in the context of the financial and economic collapses of 1929–32, *Moral Man and Immoral Society* was an enraged lament that liberal thought and politics, whether Christian or secular, had failed to give an adequate account of the way power and interest shaped social life. According to Niebuhr, those who hoped to change the world by appealing to reason and education not only overestimated human rationality, they also neglected the vast difference between collective morality and individual morality.[27] Attempting a Christian reading of Marx (Niebuhr ran on the Socialist Party ticket in the New York state election, labelled himself a 'Christian Marxian' and founded a small 'Fellowship of Socialist Christians' at the time of writing), Niebuhr argued for the need for what he saw as a more realistic account of egoistic group behaviour. His thesis, expressed in the title, was that even if there were 'moral' individuals, their very morality could be compounded into a collective egoism, or social immorality. The virtue of a thrifty middle-class businessman, for example, might add to the weight of structural economic injustice wrought against the working class. A soldier dying self-sacrificially, a moral act, might do so serving in an unjust, imperialistic war.[28]

In its critique of some of the rationalist and pacifist strands of American liberalism the book did indeed signal Niebuhr's departure from aspects of his 1920s Social Gospel roots. But its critique of nationalism was clearly an elaboration of what had come before—not a departure but an extension. On one level, nationalism appeared in the book simply as another ideology in the Marxian sense—another means of deception that collective groups used to cloak their actual narrow self-interest (although he stopped short of accepting Marx's dictum on religion as 'the opiate of the people'). At the same time, Niebuhr did not succumb to some simple belief that this amounted to little more than the deception of the masses by a cynical elite; rather, the *self*-deception of the sophisticated 'men of culture' was just as much a feature of the way nationalism functioned as a religion. Under the influence of rationalism and religion (Niebuhr may have had Immanuel Kant in mind, although he did not name him), the educated elite understood that 'moral values must be universal, if they are to be real'. Thus they could not 'give themselves to national aspirations, unless they clothe them in the attributes of universality'.[29] In arguing this point, Niebuhr not only pointed to the 'Christentum and Deutschtum' cult of the First World War, but also to other pertinent examples of the nation appropriating religion for its own purposes: President William McKinley's 'heavenly vision' to keep and 'Christianise' the Philippines in the late

---

[26] Niebuhr, *Moral Man and Immoral Society* (London: Continuum, 2005 [1932]).

[27] Ibid., xii–xvii.

[28] See ibid., 58, for example, on patriotism's ability to transmute an individual's unselfish devotion to country into support for a collectively 'immoral' national action.

[29] Ibid., 65.

1890s and the efforts of the major European powers in 1815 to quell revolution by forming a so-called 'Holy Alliance'.[30]

Even more disturbing than this appropriation of religion to add moral force to nationalism's self-justifying myths was the particular propensity of the modern state to go further and make moralising, religious claims. Like religion, nationalistic claims tended to be universalistic claims. In matters of war and peace, nations faced the awkward dilemma of identifying themselves as especially unique on the one hand and the 'incarnation of universal values' on the other. They typically resolved the dissonance, Niebuhr argued, by resorting to false absolutes—so that 'in the mind of the simple patriot the nation is not a society but Society. Though its values are relative, they appear, from his naïve perspective, to be absolute'.[31] Nationalism both mimicked and absorbed religion:

> the nation is always endowed with an aura of the sacred, which is one reason why religions, which claim universality, are so easily captured and tamed by national sentiment, religion and patriotism merging in the process.[32]

In this sense, *Moral Man* revealed Niebuhr's indebtedness to the radical Christian internationalist critique of nationalism from the 1920s. As Niebuhr argued, nationalisms—including the American variety—were artificial, dangerous and made falsely religious and universalistic claims. As the next two sections will show, during the 1930s and 1940s Niebuhr took this basic orientation and developed it in more nuanced theological terms. Leaving behind his quasi-Marxian functionalism, Niebuhr, along with other ecumenical theologians, turned increasingly to Biblical and orthodox theological themes of pride, sin and self-deification in the 1930s. Attention to doctrines of the universality of sin—especially to what he saw as the quintessential sin of pride—was perhaps one reason Niebuhr's voice shifted in those same years; between *Moral Man* and *Irony of American History* Niebuhr's somewhat irate finger-pointing, which implicitly cast him as being outside nationalism, gave way to a warmer recognition of shared participation in the ironies of American nationalism. This corresponded, as the final section below shows, with a turn from looking at American nationalism in generic terms (as in *Moral Man*, where it was merely one class of ideologies found among all nations) to seeing its specific characteristics, born out of the historical experience of the American people. The next section, then, turns to the role played in this process by Niebuhr's engagement with ecumenical theology in the 1930s.

Nationalism as Idolatry: 1930s Trans-Atlantic Ecumenical Theology

Ecumenism in the 1920s and 1930s is often narrated today as simply a precursor to the formation of the World Council of Churches, which had its first general assembly in Amsterdam in 1948.[33] While the formation of the World Council was a prominent outcome

---

[30] Ibid., 68–69.

[31] Ibid., 64.

[32] Ibid.

[33] See for example, G. K. A. Bell, *The Kingship of Christ: The Story of the World Council of Churches* (Middlesex: Penguin, 1954); Ruth Rouse and Stephen Neill, *A History of the Ecumenical Movement,*

of ecumenical work in the interwar period, it cannot be seen as the only one, or indeed as a necessary or inevitable outworking of it. Such a teleological account, though, is common and tends to render interwar ecumenism as merely part of a sacred narrative of church unification—in the sphere of religion as opposed to the secular sphere of world politics. As a result, the rich contours of international thought that developed in certain parts of the ecumenical movement during these critical years (there were in fact plural movements) can be too easily overlooked. It is beyond the scope of this essay to fully develop this line of argument here, but one shorthand indicator of the importance of ecumenical theology in mid-century international thought is simply the names associated with the movement. Not only Reinhold Niebuhr, but also interwar scholars such as Oxford University's first professor of international relations, Alfred Zimmern, the Swiss international jurist Max Huber, and one of the most foundational thinkers of the English school of international relations, Martin Wight, were significant parts of the ecumenical conversation on the nature of world politics in the 1930s and 1940s. And this is not to mention John Foster Dulles (US secretary of state from 1953–59) who combined heavy involvement in ecumenical networks in the mid-1940s with simultaneous involvement in State Department and White House post-war planning efforts.[34]

From the mid-1930s to the mid-1940s, the sphere of Niebuhr's work expanded from the American Christian Socialist scene to include involvement overseas in the Life and Work movement—an ecumenical organisation formed in the early to mid-1920s under the influence of an older generation of British, European, American and Scandinavian Christians (Sweden's archbishop of Uppsala, Nathan Söderblom, is credited as the main architect of the movement). Life and Work, unlike its counterpart, the Faith and Order movement, defined its interests primarily as those associated with ecumenical cooperation specifically in areas of practical service, such as the promotion of international peace and social reform. 'Doctrine divides, service unites' was an early, well-known motto among the group.[35] Niebuhr's involvement in the movement from the mid-1930s was part of a generational shift in Life and Work and a concomitant interest in the theological assumptions on which ecumenical social and ethical endeavours could be built. What did it mean, many were asking, to promote the Kingdom of God on Earth now? Was it to

---

1517–1948 (Philadelphia: Westminster Press, 1954); Michael Kinnamon and Brian E. Cope, *The Ecumenical Movement: An Anthology of Key Texts and Voices* (Geneva: WCC Publications, 1997); and Willem Adolph Visser 't Hooft, *The Genesis and Formation of the World Council of Churches* (Geneva: World Council of Churches, 1982).

[34] In 1945, for example, John Foster Dulles was a Department of State consultant at the San Francisco conference that established the United Nations, and apart from a few weeks reprieve, maintained his leadership of the Federal Council of Churches' Commission on a Just and Durable Peace, arguably then the peak American body connected to the ecumenical movement. See correspondence files for United Nations and Federal Council of Churches of Christ in America for 1944–1946, John Foster Dulles Papers, Seeley G. Mudd Manuscript Library, Princeton: MC016, Series 1.

[35] Thomas E. Fitzgerald, *The Ecumenical Movement: An Introductory History* (Westport: Praeger, 2004), 90. For the views of a participant and major leader of the movement, see W. A. Visser 't Hooft, *Memoirs* (London: S. C. M. Press, 1973), 25.

strengthen the League of Nations as British and French ecumenists had once argued, or should church work be restricted to the proclamation of the Biblical gospel, as some of the Lutheran-influenced continental thinkers suggested?[36]

Niebuhr's involvement in ecumenical theology was also part of a conscious attempt on his part to ground his work in a more distinctly theological—as opposed to a merely reformist, muckraking—register. His work from the mid- to late-1930s engaged with more traditional and overtly theological sources and ideas than it had in the 1920s, or even in *Moral Man and Immoral Society*.[37] Signs of such a trajectory were seen in his 1935 work *An Interpretation of Christian Ethics*, which explored what he saw as the prophetic implications of a belief in God's transcendence over the historical process. Christianity's ethical potency, he argued, arose from not identifying the status quo with divine order (God needed to be seen as transcendent in this sense) while also not seeing religion as so other-worldly that it had nothing to say to the given order.[38] Yet the theological shifts were most apparent in his delivery of the Gifford lectures in Edinburgh in 1939—a pinnacle in trans-Atlantic academic theology—which he later published as his two-volume theological magnum opus, breezily titled *The Nature and Destiny of Man*. The character of Niebuhr's theological turn has been extensively examined by generations of scholars.[39] In attempting to distance himself from theological as well as political liberalism, Niebuhr turned to Augustinian and Reformation themes of human sin and divine grace—themes historically associated with theological conservatism rather than the Social Gospel—as starting points for ethical reflection. But less well known is the way that Niebuhr's theological turn was set within a trans-Atlantic ecumenical context that was devoted to the theological exploration of nationalism.

From the late 1930s through the late 1940s, Niebuhr gradually came to the fore of ecumenical dialogue on social, economic and political ethics. At the Oxford 1937 World Conference on Church, Community and State (convened by Life and Work, and the single most important event in 1930s ecumenical international thought), Niebuhr contributed 'like a volcano in perpetual eruption'.[40] The positive impressions were mutual; the conference exceeded all Niebuhr's expectations. While 'one does not expect too much of an ecumenical conference', he wrote soon afterwards, the Oxford reports achieved 'a remarkably high level of genuine Christian testimony'.[41] Surprisingly, given his later reputation as a foreign policy

---

[36] For details, see ibid.

[37] On the influence of German émigré and Union Seminary colleague Paul Tillich in this 'postliberal' theological turn, see Fox, *Reinhold Niebuhr*, 160–61.

[38] Niebuhr, *An Interpretation of Christian Ethics* (San Francisco: Harper San Francisco, 1963 [1935]).

[39] See for example, Charles W. Kegley and Robert W. Bretall, eds, *Reinhold Niebuhr: His Religious, Social, and Political Thought* (New York: Macmillan, 1956); Langdon Gilkey, *On Niebuhr: A Theological Study* (Chicago: University of Chicago Press, 2001); and Charles C. Brown, *Niebuhr and His Age: Reinhold Niebuhr's Prophetic Role and Legacy* (Harrisburg: Trinity Press International, 2002).

[40] Eric Fenn cited in Fox, *Reinhold Niebuhr*, 180.

[41] Niebuhr, 'The Oxford Conference on Church and State', *Radical Religion*, Autumn, 1937, reproduced in *Essays in Applied Christianity*, ed. D. B. Robertson (New York: Meridian Books, 1959), 295–97.

commentator, Niebuhr does not seem to have been given recognition as an expert on international affairs. He was not, for example, afforded a role in the special 'study section' examining international affairs at the conference. John Foster Dulles, Max Huber, the Marquess of Lothian (Phillip Kerr) and Alfred Zimmern, to name only a few, were assigned to that section, while Niebuhr was involved in the work of sections devoted to questions of social and economic order. Nonetheless in becoming immersed in the ecumenical movement's dialogues and publications, Niebuhr was drawn into, and contributed to, a long deliberation on the theme of nationhood and nationalism that would shape the way he wrote about US foreign relations well into the Cold War.

The character of the ecumenical critique of nationalism needs to be seen, of course, in the context of the colossal political-theological questions raised by the advent of Nazism in Germany. The ecumenical movement had always been sympathetic with internationalism more broadly, its British and French constituents having had a close relationship with the League of Nations from early on.[42] Ecumenists remained concerned with international organisation, most famously by later helping to generate widespread political support for the proposed United Nations organisation during the Second World War—especially under the direction of John Foster Dulles on the US political scene.[43] Yet, rather than any particular focus on international organisation, it was the deeper, more theological deliberations on the status and ethics of nationalism itself, deliberations given urgency by the crisis in Germany, that were intellectually significant in shaping Niebuhr's outlook. Among the Life and Work movement of the mid-1930s, debates about the respective roles, scope, and capacities of church and state in Germany, provoked by the Nazi policy of creating a *Volkskirche* (State Church), rolled into deeper debates about the spiritual status of nationalism, or rather, the nature of *Volkstum* (nationhood) itself.[44] The influential Scottish ecumenist, Joseph Oldham, who was known to Niebuhr personally, and his emerging network of realist theologians, spelt out the implications of Nazi nationalism for nationalism in general when he issued a call for what became the Oxford 1937 conference:

> What in the Christian view is the significance of national individuality? What place in God's purpose does the nation hold? What is the relation of the Church to the communal life with which its own life is inseparably intertwined? How is membership in the one body of the universal Church of Christ related to the fact that Christians become members of it through membership of national Churches united by a multitude of intimate ties to the distinctive historical life of the communities to which they belong?[45]

Incidentally, in setting these parameters for the impending conference, Oldham assigned Niebuhr's *Moral Man and Immoral Society* as part of the list of recommended reading,

---

[42] Darril Hudson, *The Ecumenical Movement in World Affairs* (London: Weidenfeld & Nicolson, 1969).

[43] Warren, *Theologians of a New World Order*. See also M. G. Thompson, 'For God and Globe: Christian Internationalism in the United States, 1919–1945', PhD thesis, University of Sydney, 2012.

[44] For an account of one formative meeting between Nazi church officials and ecumenical theologians, see 'Nazi Church Defies All World Critics', *New York Times*, 28 August 1934, 6.

[45] Joseph Houldsworth Oldham, *Church, Community and State, a World Issue* (New York: Harper, 1935), 29.

highlighting its critique of traditional individual-oriented Protestant ethics. Meanwhile he set about co-opting Niebuhr and his closest circle of theologian colleagues into attending and participating at the conference.[46]

In answering their broad, ambitious questions about nationalism, ecumenists at the Oxford 1937 conference (who were mainly from Europe, Britain, and the US, although some attendees were from other countries including China and Japan) developed a more nuanced treatment of nationalism than the post-First World War revisionists and radicals examined above. Whereas Niebuhr and the Social Gospel revisionists of the 1920s had been quick to dismiss all nationalism as artificial and dangerous, the ecumenists of the 1930s developed a more philosophically and theologically based approach that actually conceded some legitimacy, or at least sympathy, to nationalism. In part, this was due to the influence of the substantial continental contingent in the ecumenical movement. In the meeting of a continental Protestantism that was heavily imbued with Lutheran and Hegelian notions of the God-given-ness of the nation, and an Anglo-American social Christianity that tended to see nationalism as artificial, a new kind of synthesis emerged. Ecumenists sought to salvage what they saw as valuable in the German Romanticist critique of Anglo-American liberalism and rationalism, namely that there was indeed more to the nation, phenomenologically speaking, than liberal social contract theory allowed for: the nation had to be seen in part as a gift from God in his creative and providential capacities. Yet at the same time they also sought to articulate a critique of overgrown, or in their terms, 'demonic' nationalisms, the most threatening of which seemed to be growing out of that very German Romanticist culture.[47] Thus they gave more recognition to the positive status of the nation than the 1920s pacifists had while seeking to oppose nationalism as a false deification of the nation.

The essence, then, of the ecumenical response—to which Niebuhr, as explored below, was as much a contributor as an heir—was its dialectical structure. The relationship of God to the historical realm, to the state, to the nation, to all historical forms of community, had to be articulated in a constant and complex negotiation of yes and no. There could be no seamless identification of the Kingdom of God with the nation-state, nor indeed with the League of Nations. While the Christian response was to acknowledge a 'yes' to the 'given-ness' of nations as historical communities, it also always had to maintain a 'no', an expression of permanent protest implied in the transcendent judgement of God. According to the published statements from Oxford 1937 (which had been drafted and redrafted several times by groups of several dozen delegates), all social and political solidarities had a 'dual character': they were divine gifts on the one hand, and potentially 'demonic' on

---

[46] Keith Clements, *Faith on the Frontier: A Life of J. H. Oldham* (Edinburgh: T&T Clark, 1999), 317–18.

[47] This can be seen in comparing the preparatory volume on *Church and Community*, where individual contributors offered a spectrum of views, and the final synthetic reports generated collectively by the conference. For the preparatory volume, see Kenneth S. Latourette et al., *Church and Community: Church, Community, and State Series, Volume Five* (London: G. Allen & Unwin, 1938); for the final documents, see Federal Council of Churches, 'Church and Community', *Official Reports of the Oxford Conference*, in Box 14, Life and Work Collection, Ecumenical Library, Interchurch Center, New York City.

the other. National egotism, the conference report on 'Church and Community' argued, provided a clear example of where nationality, 'essentially a gift of God to mankind', was transformed into something evil because of its 'infection by human sinfulness'. They thus concluded that the Christian ought to find himself in

> perpetual tension and conflict. He accepts thankfully his community in order to live and to work in it and for it; yet if he would work in it and for it for Christ he must be in continuous protest against it.[48]

Indeed, the reports of the Oxford 1937 conference anticipated later scholarship on nationalism (such as that of Ernest Gellner and Anthony Giddens) in stressing the importance of modern social fragmentation as a prior cause.[49] Modern, secular, industrialised life, the Oxford delegates argued, had seen the disintegration of traditional modes of loyalties. With old loyalties gone, and no new ones to take their place, 'the community life of mankind has been thrown into confusion.' In the face of this disintegration, the world was now witnessing a range of new and desperate attempts to reintegrate communities particularly in, but not restricted to, Germany, Japan, Russia and Italy. People were seeking to meet their 'primal need' for community and fellowship by creating new solidarities, new centres of life. Yet in the effort to reintegrate social life the elevation of the nation to 'supreme good' resulted in the 'deification' or idolatry of the nation. This was dangerous, they argued, for 'a false sacred, a false God, merely adds demonic power to the unredeemed passions of men. Though bringing about temporary and local unity it prepares for mankind an even worse and wider conflict.'[50]

Such reports as these reveal the character of the political-theological world in which Niebuhr's own treatment of nationalism was developing in the mid- to late-1930s, another key part of his root structure. While the exact text of the reports may not have been written by him—he was merely one part of a wider, collective deliberation involving dozens of theologians and academics whose voices were reflected in the reports—the dialectical structure of the Oxford 1937 conference's 'yes-and-no' response to nationalism, its protest mixed with thanksgiving, was entirely congruent with the direction and tenor of Niebuhr's work. One can hear the parallels between the Oxford report of 1937, for example, and Niebuhr's own dialectical approach in a paper given to British students the same year. In the paper, published under the title *Do the State and Nation Belong to God or the Devil?*, Niebuhr critiqued the tendencies of the state and nation toward self-deification. The response he called for—permanent tension and criticism—was almost identical to that of the Oxford reports:

> Orthodox Christianity, both Catholic and Protestant, has consistently failed to maintain the prophetic criticism against both the nation and the state which inheres in a prophetic religion's faith in a God of transcendent majesty, who

---

[48] *Official Reports of the Oxford Conference*, 55–60.

[49] Compare, for example, Ernest Gellner, *Nations and Nationalism* (Ithaca: Cornell University Press, 1983) and Anthony Giddens, *A Contemporary Critique of Historical Materialism* (Berkeley: University of California Press, 1981), 13.

[50] *Official Reports of the Oxford Conference*, 55–56.

judges the pretensions of majesty, inevitably made by temporal rulers and particular human communities.[51]

To be sure, Niebuhr accepted that a measure of qualified reverence toward power was appropriate; but, equally so, the tendency of the state and nation to make pretensions to majesty 'requires an unrelenting critical attitude toward all government'.[52] The kind of prophetic religion he called for would be ready when necessary to 'speak a word of judgement against every ruler and every nation.'[53]

Niebuhr's great theological and political works of the 1940s also demonstrated the ongoing influence of the dialectical framework developed at Oxford. In his most widely celebrated theological work, the two-volume *The Nature and Destiny of Man*, nationalism appears on the one hand as collective egoism, a line of argument from the earlier *Moral Man and Immoral Society*. However, Niebuhr added to this older layer of argument a new layer of more explicitly theological language with clear parallels to the Oxford reports. There was a 'temptation to idolatry', Niebuhr argued, 'implicit in the state's majesty'.[54] Dangerous forms of 'self-deification' occurred when a social group made 'pretensions of itself as the source and end of existence'.[55] These could have been lines and phrases straight out of the Oxford 1937 reports. While it may be tempting to see the ecumenical movement as merely echoing Niebuhr's arguments, close reading of the sources lends that interpretation very little plausibility. It is far better to understand the influence as mutual and two-way. Niebuhr absorbed the ecumenical critique of nationalism even as he helped, among others, to shape its character.

Niebuhr's Critique of US Nationalism During the Second World War and the Early Cold War

It is well known that Niebuhr sided with the emerging American internationalist-interventionist consensus in the foreign policy debates of the 1940s. His support for the extension of American power beyond the Western Hemisphere in the Second World War and the early Cold War was a definitive element of his self-professed realism. Rather than following majority liberal Protestant opinion of the late 1930s, and holding to a combination of pacifism and neutralism that opposed *all* war, he made it his mission to delegitimise pacifism as the unquestioned commitment of liberal Protestants on matters of war, peace and international affairs. Thus, while his former radical Christian internationalist colleague Kirby Page (once a fellow editor at *The World Tomorrow*) toured as a speaker for the Keep America Out of War Committee, Niebuhr set to work for the opposing publicity group, the

---

[51] Niebuhr, *Do the State and Nation Belong to God or the Devil?* (London: SCM Press, London, 1937), 29–30.

[52] Ibid., 21–22.

[53] Ibid., 42.

[54] Niebuhr, *The Nature and Destiny of Man*, vol. I, *Human Nature* (New York: C. Scribner's Sons, 1941), 222.

[55] Ibid., 226.

Committee to Aid the Allies.[56] He and other realists started the influential new periodical *Christianity and Crisis* to oppose the pacifist commitments of the leading liberal Protestant periodical, *The Christian Century*.[57] The new journal became the site par excellence for the articulation of Niebuhrian Christian realism. In the opening edition Niebuhr called for congressional support for President Franklin D. Roosevelt's lend-lease plans, and argued that the risk of American entanglement in war was a lesser evil than allowing Hitler to hold Europe unchallenged.[58] To the objection, voiced by some Christian internationalists, that America was just as guilty of nationalism and imperialism as Germany was, Niebuhr responded by condemning what he saw as an unrealistic moralism that was unable to distinguish between greater and lesser evils. There was an alternative, he argued, between fanaticism, which claimed unqualified sanctity for the nation's cause, and inaction; making an historic judgment didn't constitute a 'holy war.'[59]

In the wake of the Second World War, as American foreign policy debate began to centre on the question of Russia, Niebuhr emerged once again as a public spokesman for a 'tough', interventionist foreign policy on the part of the United States. As an early proponent of the Munich analogue, from 1946 he began to argue that Russian 'tyranny' was equivalent to the Nazi threat of previous years. Attacking former vice-president Henry Wallace in *Life* magazine, he conceded, 'there were once more creative elements in Communism than in Nazism' but insisted that 'the actual tyranny which has emerged and the fanatic fury which has been generated by these illusions are, unfortunately, not distinguishable from the practices derived from the purer paganism and cynicism'.[60] In the pages of *Christianity and Crisis* he went on to applaud the Truman administration's containment policies, which he saw as having the right mix of deterrence toward Russia and positive economic implications for Europe. 'No decision of war-time was more fateful', Niebuhr urged, than seeing the Marshall Plan safely through Congress.[61]

How then did Niebuhr's ongoing critique of nationalism, grounded in the theological reflections of the 1920s and 1930s, feature in his new support of American interventionism? The question is important as his specific policy recommendations were for several years so entirely congruent with those of the Truman administration, one could be forgiven for seeing him—as several historians from Walter LaFeber to John Fousek and Mark Kleinman have done—as merely an articulate champion of the Cold War liberal consensus.[62] Yet

---

[56] Fox, *Reinhold Niebuhr*; Kirby Page, *Kirby Page, Social Evangelist: The Autobiography of a 20th Century Prophet for Peace,* ed. Harold E. Fey (Nyack, N.Y.: Fellowship Press, 1975), 106.

[57] See Mark Hulsether, *Building a Protestant Left:* Christianity and Crisis *Magazine, 1941–1993* (Knoxville: University of Tennessee Press, 1999), 26.

[58] Niebuhr, 'The Christian Faith and the World Crisis', *Christianity and Crisis*, 10 February 1941, 4–5.

[59] Ibid.

[60] Niebuhr, 'The Fight for Germany', *Life*, 21 October 1946, 72.

[61] Niebuhr, 'The Marshall Plan', *Christianity and Crisis*, 13 October 1947, 2.

[62] Walter LaFeber, *America, Russia, and the Cold War, 1945–66* (New York: John Wiley & Sons, 1967), 40–41; John Fousek, *To Lead the Free World: American Nationalism and the Cultural Roots of the Cold War* (Chapel Hill: University of North Carolina Press, 2000), 121; Mark L. Kleinman,

Niebuhr's critique of American nationalism did not recede in the Cold War but operated alongside of—in tension with—his support of interventionism. Indeed, such a tension, which was arguably the primary characteristic of his 1940s work, must also be seen as a factor in the divergent interpretations of Niebuhr's realism in the revival of his work today. As discussed above, for some twenty-first century writers, Niebuhr's efforts in naming German and Soviet 'tyranny' as a greater threat than war, and his demand that American Christians support the extension of American military might to check such tyrannical power, made him an ideal forefather for invocation in an age of terrorism. Such was Jean Bethke Elshtain's adaptation of Niebuhr in her *Just War on Terror*, for example.[63] Others have been attracted to what they see as Niebuhr's sense of the 'limits of power'. Niebuhr was a source of wisdom, they argued, at a moment when America had seemingly overreached its ambitions and power. For Anatol Lieven and John Hulsman, Niebuhr, together with Hans Morgenthau and George Kennan, bequeathed a legacy of what they term 'ethical realism'. The tradition of ethical realism revived today, they argue, would make a salutary basis for a new American strategy, being characterised by 'a mixture of profound American patriotism with an equally profound awareness of the limits on both American power and on American goodness'.[64] Yet many such framings of Niebuhr—whether of Niebuhr the Cold War liberal, Niebuhr the resister of evil, or Niebuhr the statesman alert to the limits of power—tend to fail on the same count: they overlook the way he applied the interwar Christian internationalist critique of nationalism to American nationalism.

The continuities, however, are clear. Elements of both strands of Christian internationalist critique were blended in Niebuhr's Cold War writings. While he dropped much of the Marxian rationalism of *Moral Man*, Niebuhr retained one of the main arguments he took from the radical Christian internationalist strand: namely, that nationalism was 'religious' in that it consisted in a partial entity falsely claiming universal, absolute status. From the ecumenical internationalism of the 1930s, he retained the critique of nationalism as self-deification and idolatry. The influence of both strands can be seen in the way Niebuhr wrote of what he saw as a particular temptation for Americans in the Cold War: the tendency to ascribe false universality to values they saw as implicated in their geopolitical standoff with Russia. In August 1947, for example, in *Christianity and Crisis*, Niebuhr ran a piece entitled 'Democracy as a Religion'. Americans, he complained, were tending to show they

> have only one religion: devotion to democracy. They extol its virtues, are apprehensive about the perils to which it is exposed, pour maledictions upon its foes, rededicate themselves to its purposes and claim unconditioned validity for its ideals.[65]

Niebuhr had argued in earlier works that democracy was the best available option for organising a government, in that freedom and order could be brought to support each

---

A World of Hope, a World of Fear: Henry A. Wallace, Reinhold Niebuhr, and American Liberalism (Columbus: Ohio State University Press, 2000).

[63] Jean Bethke Elshtain, *Just War on Terror? The Burden of American Power in a Violent World* (New York: Basic Books, 2003).

[64] Lieven and Hulsman, *Ethical Realism*, xvii.

[65] Niebuhr, 'Democracy as a Religion', *Christianity and Crisis*, 4 August 1947, 1.

other most successfully given human nature.⁶⁶ Nevertheless, democracy was more of a procedural necessity, and was not, for Niebuhr, the 'End of History'.⁶⁷ Certainly, he conceded, democracy was 'a worthy object of qualified loyalty'. But was it 'a proper object of unqualified loyalty?' The imbuing of the relative good with absolute status produced a dangerous 'religious' phenomenon, Niebuhr warned. 'It tempts us', he went on, 'to identify the final meaning of life with a virtue which we possess, and thus to give a false and idolatrous religious note to the conflict between democracy and communism'.⁶⁸ Similarly elsewhere, he castigated what he saw as the American tendency to transmute the necessities of Cold War geopolitics into an 'idolatry' of free enterprise and the American 'way of life'.⁶⁹ Later still, in 1951, he opposed calls for the US to invade China not merely on the strategic grounds of classical realism—nor yet merely out of recognition of the limits of power—but by arguing that such a strategy was premised on an 'idolatrous conception of the perfection of American democracy, and its appeal to other peoples'.⁷⁰

In such Cold War writings, then, Niebuhr took the general Christian internationalist critiques of nationalism that had been formed in the 1920s and 1930s (in which all nationalisms were basically the same) and applied them with more specificity to America. His focus increasingly came to rest on what later scholars have termed American 'exceptionalism'.⁷¹ He turned his attention to the prevailing idea that the US had been set apart from the ordinary, governing forces of history by merit of its unique birth, and as a result, was now placed to shape the rest of the world's history. Without using such terms, his critique revolved around the way the *particularism* of American nationalism (the belief that the nation was uniquely set apart) was yoked to a kind of *universalism* (the belief that the chosen nation was an instrument of world redemption); that is, Americans held democracy to be a particularly American value on one hand, and a potentially universal value on the other.

Niebuhr gave his most developed attention to this exceptionalist narrative in his major work of the early Cold War, *The Irony of American History*. Whereas in *Moral Man and Immoral Society* Niebuhr had cast American nationalism as no different from any other nationalism, in *The Irony of American History* he gave sustained attention to the particularities of American self-image. 'Every nation has its own form of spiritual

---

⁶⁶ Niebuhr, *The Children of Light and The Children of Darkness* (New York: Scribner's, 1945). On this point, the work contains one of Niebuhr's famous paradoxical formulations: 'Man's capacity for justice makes democracy possible. Man's tendency to injustice makes democracy necessary' (xi).

⁶⁷ The phrase is from Francis Fukuyama's *The End of History and the Last Man* (New York: Free Press, 1992).

⁶⁸ Niebuhr, 'Democracy as a Religion', 1.

⁶⁹ See, for example, Niebuhr, 'The Idolatry of America', *Christianity and Society*, Spring 1950, reprinted in *Love and Justice: Selections from the Shorter Writings of Reinhold Niebuhr*, ed. D. B. Robertson (Cleveland: Meridian Books, 1967), 94–97.

⁷⁰ Niebuhr, 'Ten Fateful Years', *Christianity and Crisis*, 5 February 1951, 2.

⁷¹ For an excellent survey of the history and provenance of the term 'exceptionalism', which although dating back to the late 1920s, Niebuhr did not personally use, see Daniel Rodgers, 'Exceptionalism', in *Imagined Histories: American Historians Interpret the Past*, eds Anthony Molho and Gordon S. Wood (Princeton: Princeton University Press, 1998), 21–40.

pride', he argued, in a concession absent from *Moral Man*. 'Our version is that our nation turned its back on the vices of Europe and made a new beginning.'[72] The myth of new beginnings, he argued—which had both Puritan and Jeffersonian origins—emerged not only from ideology but also from the actual historical experience of American people. This was no instrumental imposition of ideology; rather, the exceptionalist myth had an organic character. Yet the myth mattered also because it shaped American behaviour in the world: it led Americans, he argued (using the first-person plural 'we'), to overestimate their virtue and innocence, to falsely imagine—as the Soviets did—that they had the capacity to manage history, and to naively underestimate the hostility and suspicion of others. Americans are 'hurt', Niebuhr mused, 'when we discover that Asians ... regard us as imperialistic when we are "by definition" a non-imperialistic nation'.[73] The 'ironic' gap between American self-image and actual historical reality needed to be countered, he urged, with a 'religious sense of an ultimate judgement upon our individual and collective actions'. With such 'an awareness of our own pretensions of wisdom, virtue or power', Niebuhr projected, 'the irony would tend to dissolve into the experience of contrition and to an abatement of the pretensions which caused the irony'.[74]

Conclusion

Niebuhr's treatment of nationalism, then, was evolving, linear and continuous, unlike the many other changing aspects of his thought. While between the 1920s and 1940s Niebuhr moved dramatically from pacifism to anti-pacifism, from socialism to New Deal centrism, and from anti-militarism to advocating a 'tough' Democratic foreign policy against Russia, the posture and structure of his critique of American nationalism remained, and in fact deepened. Such a critical perspective needs to be seen as having its root structure in the discursive arenas and networks provided by the two strands of Christian internationalism examined in this essay—the radical pacifism and internationalism of Social Gospellers in the 1920s, and the dialectical political theology of the ecumenical movement of the 1930s and 1940s. In both strands—which overlapped in their own way at various points—Niebuhr played a major and influential role. But, importantly, as has been demonstrated, the influence was mutual; his was not the only voice and it cannot be properly heard in isolation.

Yet efforts to transplant Niebuhr from the Cold War to the twenty-first century have tended overwhelmingly to miss this wider root structure, and have thus relocated a 'flattened' Niebuhr into a foreign landscape. To appreciate the way Niebuhr balanced a note of 'permanent protest' with an endorsement of America taking up its international responsibilities in the 1940s requires that we do not separate him too quickly from his roots in the 1920s and 1930s, nor separate him as a political thinker from a theologian. To the extent, then, that Niebuhrian revivalists in the twenty-first century have used Niebuhr's legacy to call for a renewed sense of 'modesty' and an appreciation of the limits

---

[72] Niebuhr, *The Irony of American History*, 28.
[73] Ibid., 34.
[74] Ibid., 169.

of power in foreign policymaking, they are right. But only half right. Recovering Niebuhr's critique of American nationalism in the context of its original discursive and intellectual root structures speaks to a problem bigger than the Bush administration or the nature of foreign policy and statecraft: it brings into stark relief the character of twenty-first century American religio-political culture itself.

15

An Ideological Odyssey: Nixon, China and the Decline of American Nationalism[1]

Tom Switzer

On 10 August 1966, America decided to take a closer look at the Earth's nearest neighbour by launching the first lunar orbiter. That same day, Richard M. Nixon, then on a visit to Hong Kong, decided to take a tentative look at the alien world of the People's Republic of China (PRC). On a stroll through the backstreets of the city he spied an exhibition of photographs in a public gallery and went in, later unconvincingly claiming not to have realised that it was a communist display of the regime's claimed achievements. The next day, for whatever reason, Nixon cancelled his proposed sixth trip to Taiwan, the renegade province whose rulers Washington had recognised as the legitimate government of China since the communist revolution in 1949.[2] In the same way that Americans' fascination with landing on the lunar surface had been sparked that day, so too had Nixon's desire to set foot on Chinese mainland soil been activated. The following month, the Taiwanese ambassador to the US wrote to Nixon, praising him as a 'statesman of principle and vision' who championed 'the cause of freedom in general and the Republic of China in particular'.[3] Little did he, or virtually anyone else, know that the aspiring presidential candidate had begun the process of rethinking US relations with both the PRC and with Taiwan, a shift that would lead to one of the most dramatic realignments of Cold War foreign policy.

For the next twelve months Nixon did not comment publicly on Sino–American relations. To say his silence was significant would be an understatement. For more than fifteen years, Nixon had been a relentless proponent of US policy to isolate mainland China and a fierce critic of any proposal to accommodate the communist regime. In speeches, committee hearings, interviews and articles, the congressman (1947–51), senator (1951–53), vice-president (1953–61) and private citizen (1961–67) had consistently argued that 'Red China' was an 'outlaw nation' while the Nationalists in 'Free China'—Formosa, later known as Taiwan—were the true representatives of the Chinese people. Trade, US recognition or admission to the United Nations (UN) would amount to 'appeasement'. From the early 1950s, when he endorsed Senator Joe McCarthy's charge that treasonous

---

[1] This chapter is drawn from the author's fourth-year Sydney University honours thesis, which was supervised by Neville Meaney in 1993. Short extracts have subsequently appeared elsewhere, including in Switzer, 'The World Today, Foretold by Nixon', *New York Times*, 6 July 2011; Switzer, 'Avowed Anti-Communist Opened China to the World', *Australian*, 18 February 2011; and Switzer, 'Not Only Nixon Could go to China', *National Review*, 23 February 2012.

[2] 'Nixon Pays Visit to Wrong Centre', *Hongkong,* 11 August 1966.

[3] Letter, Chow Shu-kai to Richard M. Nixon, 9 September 1966, Richard Nixon Presidential Library (RNPL): Wilderness Years Series II (WYS II), Trip Files 1963–67, PPS 347, Box 9.

US diplomats 'lost China', to the mid-1960s when he goaded President Lyndon B. Johnson to escalate the Vietnam War (ostensibly to fight the spread of Chinese communism) Nixon earned his reputation as an arch Cold Warrior.

However, shortly after his Hong Kong odyssey in August 1966, Nixon had jettisoned both his strident anti-communism rhetoric and strong support for a Pax Americana—the idea that the US, as predominant power, should impose its will and leadership to secure freedom across the globe. By September 1967, he had provided the first public signs of a new Nixon. Arguing on behalf of the 'long view', the old Red-baiter wrote that Washington could not afford to leave mainland China 'forever outside the family of nations'.[4] He also questioned whether America could play the role of world policeman in the post-Vietnam era and whether democracy could be treated as an export commodity to be sold across East Asia.

The Historiography

Nixon's overtures to the PRC have been the subject of a large and rapidly growing scholarly literature. Yet in their treatment of his long intellectual march, historians and biographers have intriguingly failed to devote close attention to the question of how Nixon during his years out of office came to terms with the very Chinese communists he had made a political career out of denouncing.[5] When scholars have attempted to account for President Nixon's reversal, more often than not they have pointed to his belief that Washington should exploit the Sino–Soviet split and use the China card to counter the USSR.[6] Other schools of thought have highlighted the desire for the Chinese communists to reduce aid to North Vietnam and to urge a political settlement upon Hanoi, the economic benefits of opening the potentially lucrative China market to US trade, the need for Peking to accept international anti-proliferation nuclear agreements, and Washington's attempts to keep pace with political developments in the world and the UN.[7]

---

[4] Nixon, 'Asia after Vietnam', *Foreign Affairs*, 46 (1), 1967, 113–25.

[5] For the best accounts of Nixon's wilderness years, see Gary Wills, *Nixon Agonistes: The Crisis of the Self-Made Man* (Boston: Houghton Mifflin, 1970); Jules Witcover, *The Resurrection of Richard Nixon* (New York: G. P. Putnam's Sons, 1970); Stephen E. Ambrose, *Nixon: The Triumph of a Politician 1962–1972* (New York: Simon & Schuster, 1989); Herbert S. Parmet, *Richard Nixon and His America* (Boston: Little, Brown & Company, 1990); Tom Wicker, *One of Us: Richard Nixon and the American Dream* (New York: Random House, 1991); Jonathan Aitken, *Nixon: A Life* (London: Weidenfeld and Nicolson, 1993); and Conrad Black, *Richard Milhous Nixon: The Invincible Quest* (London: Quercus, 2007). See also Nixon's treatment of this period in his own writings: Nixon, *RN: The Memoirs of Richard Nixon* (New York: Grosset & Dunlap, 1978); Nixon, *In the Arena: A Memoir of Victory, Defeat, and Renewal* (New York: Simon & Schuster, 1990).

[6] See, for instance, Bruce Mazlish, *Kissinger: The European Mind in American Policy* (New York: Basic Books, 1976); Tad Szulc, *The Illusion of Peace: Foreign Policy in the Nixon Years* (New York: Viking, 1978); Franz Schurman, *The Foreign Politics of Richard Nixon* (Berkley, CA: Institute of International Studies, 1987); Cyrus L. Sulzberger, *The World and Richard Nixon* (New York: Prentice Hall, 1987); and Walter Isaacson, *Kissinger: A Biography* (New York: Simon & Schuster, 1992).

[7] For ending the Vietnam War, see for instance, Raymond Garthoff, *Détente and Confrontation:*

Several scholars have also interpreted Nixon's turnaround toward China not because of a change in his ideological world view but because of a realistic reassessment of American national interests and changing international circumstances. In this interpretation, Nixon's basic world view and his strategic goals did not greatly alter during his long public life: he was a committed Cold Warrior.[8] In making this argument, scholars and journalists accept the widespread belief that only Nixon could go to China without causing a domestic backlash. They argue that only an anti-Red China right-winger could do something that would have been totally out of reach for a Democrat politician; and only an anti-communist Cold Warrior, whose credibility with conservatives and Republican hawks would shield him from any domestic attack, could sup with the devil. Prominent liberals and Democrats themselves have acknowledged this argument. Following Nixon's announcement that he would visit China, liberal columnist Walter Lippmann remarked:

> Only Nixon, among the available public men, could have made such a reversal. The reason there was no outcry about the reversal was that it was made under the auspices of a certified anti-Communist like Nixon.[9]

The Senate Democratic Majority Leader Mike Mansfield declared: 'Only a Republican, perhaps only a Nixon, could have made this break and gotten away with it.'[10] Subsequently, the phrase 'only Nixon could go to China' has become political folklore to describe a moment when a political leader defies expectations by taking actions that would anger their supporters if taken by someone on the opposite side of the ideological spectrum.[11]

This interpretation, however, begs several questions. If the Sino–Soviet split played a decisive role in shaping Nixon's new thinking, why did he refrain from advocating a China opening during the first half of the 1960s when the cracks in the Peking–Moscow alliance became increasingly evident? In 1963 and 1964, French president Charles de Gaulle, West German chancellor Konrad Adenauer and Pakistani president Ayub Khan had told Nixon, as a globe-trotting private citizen, that the Sino–Soviet split was 'real', that nationalism more than any ideological differences was the driving force in the rift, and that Washington

---

American–Soviet Relations from Nixon to Reagan (Washington: Brookings, 1985). For trade benefits, see for instance, Thomas Paterson, *Meeting the Communist Threat: Truman to Reagan* (New York: Oxford University Press, 1988). For China's nuclear concerns, see for instance, Robert Sutter, *Chinese Nuclear Weapons and American Interests: Conflicting Policy Choices* (Washington: Congressional Research Service, 1983). For international developments, see for instance, Arnold Xiangze Jiang, *The United States and China* (Chicago: University of Chicago Press, 1988).

[8] See Michael Handel, *The Diplomacy of Surprise: Hitler, Nixon, Sadat* (Cambridge, MA: Center for International Affairs, 1981); James Reichley, *Conservatives in an Age of Change: The Nixon and Ford Administrations* (Washington: Brookings, 1981); John Lewis Gaddis, *Strategies of Containment: A Critical Appraisal of Postwar American National Security Policy* (New York: Oxford University Press, 1982).

[9] Ronald Steel, 'The World We're In: An Interview with Walter Lippmann', *The New Republic*, 13 November 1971, 18.

[10] 'A Size-up of President Nixon: Interview with Mike Mansfield', *US News & World Report*, 6 December 1971, 61.

[11] David Ignatius, 'The Greatest Flip-Flop: Nixon in China', *Washington Post*, 12 February 2012, A21.

would be wise to exploit the tensions and play off Peking against Moscow.[12] Yet although Nixon privately noted their advice during his foreign trips, he publicly repudiated such arguments when they were made by Democrats at home. It was not until his meetings with de Gaulle, Adenauer and Ayub in March and April 1967 that it became clear that Nixon had changed. Not only was he by then heeding their counsel that Washington ought to normalise relations with Peking, but he was also advocating the use of the China card to balance the Soviet Union.

Other questions are worth pondering. If Nixon argued during the fifteen years following the communist victory that any US accommodation was conditional on China changing and turning away from its aggressive stance, why did he eventually support an opening with the same 'outlaw nation' that continued to support violent revolution at home and abroad? If his policy turnaround was not driven by a change in his ideological world view, why did Nixon, from the second half of 1967 onwards, increasingly advocate a foreign policy sharply at variance with the dominant US post-war world view, an agenda which he once shared? If 'only Nixon' could go to China in the early 1970s, how does one explain the softening public attitudes towards US policy regarding China and the cracking of the Cold War domestic consensus five years earlier? And if only a political figure with impeccable anti-communist credentials could pacify the right wing of the Republican Party, how does one account for the conservative backlash against his landmark initiative?

Cold War Consensus

This article contends that Nixon's about-face can only be understood in the context of American nationalism and its impact on the national psychology. For two decades following the defeat of Nazism and Japanese militarism, America had continued to achieve an unprecedented level of material wealth and moral self-assurance. Its economic and military predominance in the world had reinforced the widespread belief among both liberals and conservatives that the US was an 'exceptional' nation and that Americans were a 'chosen people' who had a special mission to redeem the world and build what *Time* magazine founder Henry Luce referred to as the 'American Century'. This vision had deep roots in American history, from George Bancroft's 1826 reinterpretation of America's founders as liberal idealists bent on remaking the world, to Abraham Lincoln's conception of America as 'the last best hope of Earth', to Woodrow Wilson's sense of America's mission as 'the liberation and salvation of the world'. After the Second World War, this understanding of America's mission was transposed to a battle to transform the world according to the American image of democracy. In this apocalyptic struggle between good and evil, few important public figures openly raised doubts about the limitations of US power, nor did they suggest any position toward the communist bloc other than unrelieved hostility. If communism was bad for Europe, a point on which there was broad agreement, it was bad

---

[12] Private notes of Nixon's meetings with Charles de Gaulle and Konrad Adenauer, 23 July, 2 August 1963; private notes of Nixon's meeting with Ayub Khan, 25 March 1964, all in RNPL: WYS II, Trip Files 1963–67, PPS 347, Box 3.

for Asia—and the world generally—and victory in the Cold War would represent a triumph of America's mission.[13]

In 1949, with the communists poised to achieve victory over the US-backed Nationalist government of Chiang Kai-shek, the Truman administration had declared that Chinese communism was not a genuinely Chinese movement. The US State Department, reflecting the thoughts and attitudes of Congress and the American people, declared that China's communist leaders had 'foresworn their Chinese heritage' and had 'publicly announced subservience to a foreign power Russia'. They had become tools of the Soviets. But the Chinese people, who historically had enjoyed a special relationship with the US, could not tolerate the intrusion of this monolithic communism forever, and would ultimately cast off the tyranny of the Kremlin-controlled puppets. The task of the US, the State Department recommended, was 'to encourage all developments in China which now and in the future work toward this end'.[14] Consequently, unlike other Western governments, Washington refused to deal with the communist regime. It imposed and maintained an embargo on trade with, and travel to, the Chinese mainland; recognised Chiang's Nationalist regime as the legitimate government for all of China; and supported Taiwan as one of the five permanent members of the Security Council at the same time that it excluded the Peking government from the UN. As leader of the Free World, the US created an arsenal of nuclear deterrents and worked to 'contain' communist China with a network of military bases and defence pacts with non-communist states in the region, including Taiwan, Japan, South Korea, Thailand, the Philippines, Australia and New Zealand.

Sino–American relations were thus frozen for more than two decades. No doubt the communist leaders in Peking showed little interest in negotiating with the US; and with the Great Leap Forward in the late 1950s and the Cultural Revolution a decade later, the country was plunged into mass terror and famine, thereby precluding any substantive review of US policy towards China. But it was the teleological nature of American nationalism that had shaped the US response to the communist threat in Asia during the crucial period of 1949–50. Moreover, it was this Manichean world view—that the Free World was engaged in a battle against the tyrannical forces of monolithic communism—that dominated US politics and foreign policy throughout the rest of the 1950s before reaching its apogee in the first half of the following decade.

No political figure better reflected the prevailing mindset than Nixon. Like most Americans, conscious of the 'lessons of Munich' and jolted by the spread of 'Red Fascism' in the aftermath of the Second World War, Nixon saw the emergence of the communist regime in China in 1949 as evidence that the Free World had 'lost' an ally and acquired a dangerous enemy that belonged to the centralised bloc led by the Soviet Union. A few foreign policy experts took issue with this consensus. Although they expressed themselves

---

[13] See Neville Meaney, 'Introduction: The American Revolution in Search of a Future', in *Studies on the American Revolution*, ed. Meaney (Melbourne: Macmillan, 1977), 1–32; Michael H. Hunt, *Ideology and U.S. Foreign Policy* (New Haven: Yale University Press, 1987); and Meaney, 'American Decline and American Nationalism', *Australian Journal of International Affairs*, 45 (1), 1991, 89–97.

[14] See David McLean, 'American Nationalism, the China Myth, and the Truman Doctrine: The Question of Accommodation with Peking, 1949–50', *Diplomatic History*, 10 (1), 1986, 25–42.

in different ways, leading academics such as the self-professed realist Hans J. Morgenthau and Sinologist John Fairbanks were sharply critical of the universal and ideological tone of the Truman Doctrine, suggesting that the Chinese communists, as authentic nationalists, might eventually resist Soviet intrusion upon Chinese sovereignty. Mao, they argued, could become an Asian Tito and practice an independent brand of communism like that of Yugoslavia. Hostile US policy would only drive Mao closer to Moscow.[15] Such views were widely dismissed. As an ambitious Republican congressman, Nixon reflected the public mood in arguing that it was a 'fallacious theory' to suggest that the Chinese communists were any different from communists in other countries.[16] For the next fifteen years, as senator, vice-president and private citizen, Nixon fiercely opposed trade with China, US recognition of the PRC or admission of the regime to the United Nations, lest these overtures spur China to pursue its plan for 'world revolution'. America was 'on the side of freedom and justice', he proclaimed, and 'against the forces of slavery and totalitarianism'.[17]

The 'Wilderness Years'

Nixon's change of heart took place during his years out of office. Despite his defeat in both the 1960 presidential and 1962 Californian gubernatorial elections, Nixon remained in the public arena. During the so-called 'Wilderness Years', from 1963, when he moved to New York to practice law and represent the Pepsi Cola company's interests around the world, to 1968, when he ran for president again, Nixon frequently wrote magazine and newspaper articles and made wildely publicised speeches on foreign policy before partisan Republican crowds and highly influential audiences. He also travelled extensively around the world, including making four trips across Asia in March–April 1964, August–September 1965, August 1966 and April 1967.[18] These excursions abroad were not simply exchanges of courtesies; they included various meetings with leading political figures that ranged across serious and substantial discussions about regional politics and international relations. The scholarly scrutiny of Nixon's foreign trips from 1963 to 1967 is limited. The only travelling that has attracted much attention is his final pre-presidential trip in April 1967. A study of the private notes of Nixon's numerous meetings with world leaders, taken together with his public statements during these years, is revealing. Hand written on his yellow legal pads, the notes highlight Nixon's keen, analytical mind and reveal his command of contemporary strategic issues and key political figures. They also provide a glimpse into Nixon's evolving views on US policy towards China.

---

[15] See, for instance, John K. Fairbank, *The United States and China* (Cambridge, MA: Harvard University Press, 1949); and Hans Morgenthau, *In Defence of the National Interest: A Critical Examination of American Foreign Policy* (New York: Alfred A. Knopf, 1951).

[16] Nixon, 'Mao no Tito: US Must Act', *Appendix to the Congressional Record*, 81st congress, 1st session (1949), (14), 2871.

[17] 'Mr Nixon Attacks Communist Conspirators', *US News & World Report*, 11 September 1953, 31.

[18] Nixon also made numerous brief visits to Asian countries during this period, including to Taiwan for a speaking engagement in November 1964 and to Japan for business purposes on ten occasions.

An Ideological Odyssey

While Americans were locked in a Cold War mindset at home, the subject of an accommodation with mainland China kept coming up during Nixon's travels. In July 1963, West German chancellor Konrad Adenauer told Nixon privately that the US should move towards an opening to communist China as a buffer to Soviet expansionism.[19] A few days later in Paris, French president Charles de Gaulle, who was in the process of recognising the PRC, gave similar advice, suggesting to Nixon that although he had no illusions about China's ideology, Washington should not leave them isolated in their rage.[20] Pakistani president Muhammad Ayub Khan, who would become a White House secret emissary to China, told Nixon that the Sino–Soviet split was 'real' and 'driven by nationalism', which 'was the greatest guarantee against Communism'. Ayub's assessment, provoked by Pakistan's tensions with India and the desire not to face three fronts of potential enemies, was that Washington should 'exploit the split by playing China off against Moscow'.[21]

However sound such advice would later appear, Nixon was in no mood to accept it in the early to mid-1960s. For the former vice-president, the disintegration of the Moscow–Peking alliance had more to do with ideological disputes about whose brand of communism was purest. 'Red China and Russia', he argued, altogether avoiding the logical implications of the Sino–Soviet split for US views on monolithic communism, 'are simply arguing about what kind of shovel they should use to dig the grave of the United States'.[22] Consequently, the role of US foreign policy 'must be nothing less than to bring freedom to the communist world'.[23]

Such views not surprisingly resonated with Chiang Kai-shek and his wife Madame Chiang. As vice-president during the 1950s, Nixon had twice met the Taiwanese president, and he kept in touch with him in the 1960s, visiting him in 1964 (twice), 1965 and 1967. According to the Chiangs' staff, Nixon was so close to Taiwan's first couple that they treated him as though he were their son.[24] For Chiang, the Sino–Soviet split was a 'personal' rift between Mao and Khrushchev over who should be 'top dog'. It was 'ridiculous to think it would change China to admit to UN'. He told Nixon that the Chinese were then weaker than a decade earlier, that there was 'great unrest' in the army and that 'ten years from now, China will be more dangerous than Russia'. Chiang warned: 'They [China] will have all of South-east Asia, Japan, India and you will be lost.' Baffled by American 'uncertainty' on whether to support Taiwan's return to the mainland, Chiang called for 'complete opposition

---

[19] Nixon, *Leaders* (New York: Simon and Schuster, 1990), 160; see also RNPL, WYS II, Trip Files 1963, PPS 347, Box 3.

[20] Aitken, *Nixon: A Life*, 318; Nixon, *Leaders*, 74.

[21] Private notes of Nixon's meeting with Ayub Khan, 25 March 1964, RNPL: WYS II, Trip Files 1963–67, PPS 347, Box 4; Private notes of 1965–66 Asian trip, RNPL: WYS II, Far East Trip 1965, PPS, Box 7.

[22] 'Excerpts from Address by Nixon Calling for a Stronger US Foreign Policy', *New York Times*, 21 April 1963, A62.

[23] Nixon, 'Khrushchev's Hidden Weakness', *Saturday Evening Post*, 12 October 1963, 25.

[24] Laura Tyson Li, *Madame Chiang Kai-Shek: China's Eternal First Lady* (New York: Grove Press, 2006), 398.

on all fronts and eventual overthrow' of the communist regime. Nixon drew the following conclusions for US policy: 'Must have absolute policy of no compromise. Must strengthen alliances—free nations.'[25]

In Taiwan, Nixon was widely seen as a champion of its cause. Madame Chiang, who interpreted and occasionally participated in the discussions, told Nixon: 'We heartily concur with your views that the Free World should strengthen its policy rather than weaken them in the struggle against Communism.' The Chiangs saw Senator Fulbright's 1964 proposal to review China policy as a sign of weakness. 'I think that you will agree too', Madame Chiang told Nixon, that 'unless vacillation is stopped the Free World will lose by default in the foreseeable future.'[26] After a brief visit to Taiwan later that year, Nixon wrote to Chiang: 'Your continued strong leadership of the forces for freedom in Asia has never been more necessary than now.'[27]

According to one interpretation, Nixon's Asian tour in August and September 1965 witnessed early signs of the former vice-president's changing views. Nancy Tucker and James Mann have traced Nixon's interest in improving relations with China to two US diplomats who hosted the former vice-president at this time. According to Tucker, Nixon told a surprised Arthur W. Hummel, deputy chief of mission at the American Embassy in Taiwan and, later, US ambassador to the PRC, that Chiang's Nationalists would never achieve their dream of returning to the mainland. Therefore, Nixon suggested, US relations with communist China would need to be improved. 'He said that in the hotel room [at Taipei's Grand Hotel], with all the microphones in it', Hummel told Tucker in an interview in 1992, inferring that Taiwan's intelligence was probably monitoring the conversation and reporting it back to Chiang.[28] According to Mann, Nixon went on to sketch for Roger Sullivan, head of the political section of the US Embassy in Singapore and later a leading State Department specialist on China, the rough outlines of his later path to normalisation with Peking. Sullivan recalled in 1996 having a long conversation with Nixon in 1965. 'He pretty well spelled out how we could reach a normal relationship with China, and said that was what we ought to do.'[29]

These accounts are unconvincing. For one thing, as Mann concedes, the former diplomats' reminiscences in the 1990s may have been clouded by an awareness of subsequent events. There is no evidence in Nixon's handwritten notes from his Asian trip in 1965 to demonstrate he was contemplating a change of heart. Nor is there anything in Nixon's public comments after his meeting with Chiang in Taipei to suggest that he was flirting with

---

[25] Private notes of Nixon's meeting with General Chiang, 8 April 1964, RNPL: WYS II, Trip Files 1963–67, PPS 347, Box 4.

[26] Letter, Madame Chiang to Nixon, 15 May 1964, RNPL: WYS II, Trip Files 1963–67, PPS 347, Box 6.

[27] Letter, Nixon to Chiang, December 8, 1964, RNPL: WYS II, Trip Files 1963–67, PPS 347, Box 6.

[28] Nancy Bernkopf Tucker, *Taiwan, Hong Kong and the United States, 1945–1992* (New York: Tawyne Publishers, 1994), 272; Nancy Bernkopf Tucker, *Strait Talk: United States–Taiwan Relations and the Crisis with China* (Cambridge: Harvard University Press, 2009), 35–36.

[29] James Mann, *About Face: A History of America's Curious Relationship with China, From Nixon to Clinton* (New York: Vintage, 1999), 17.

a rapprochement. On 28 August, Nixon warned that if 'Red China' intervened in Vietnam, 'there would certainly be justification for the Chinese nationalists to counterattack the Chinese Communists'.[30] Moreover, if the September 1965 conversation were bugged, as Hummel suspected, knowledge of Nixon's alleged apostasy in 1965 apparently never reached the highest level of Taiwan's leadership. While Chiang was tetchy during his meeting in late August 1965, telling Nixon that 'there'll be no settlement [in Vietnam] because it's not in China's interest' and urging that Washington 'must not recognize or do anything which brings [the Chinese communists] respectability', there was no sense that he was angry with Nixon because of a supposed change of heart.[31] Sullivan's testimony is also not persuasive, given that Nixon did not visit Singapore in 1965. When he did go there two years later, in April 1967, Singapore's prime minister Lee Kuan Yew found himself in a serious and sustained discussion with Nixon about a China opening, 'his main interest', according to Lee Kuan Yew, and obviously a topic more engaging to him than Vietnam.[32]

The Sullivan recollection, like that of Hummel's, is more likely off by a couple of years. The year is important: if Nixon's ideological odyssey took place in 1965, as Tucker and Mann suggest, it preceded the collapse of the Cold War consensus to isolate 'Red China'. However, if Nixon changed his thinking about US policy towards China some time from August 1966, when he visited Hong Kong, and March–April 1967, when he visited European and Asian capitals, it reinforces this paper's central thesis; namely, that Nixon's volte-face reflected the dramatically shifting American public opinion on the China question in 1966–67.

At home, polls showed weakening American support for Taiwan and a more favourable attitude to China's recognition and admission to the UN.[33] Still, in December 1965, about two thirds of Americans considered it essential to support the Vietnam War, in which China was supporting and supplying US enemies. There was a genuine fear that appeasing the communists in Indochina might be the prelude to bolder actions leading to a Sino-American confrontation that could result in nuclear war. Further, the 'loss' of Vietnam could mean the start of a chain reaction in South-East Asia that would put anti-communist countries on the defensive around the region. In late November 1965, Nixon went so far as to warn that if North Vietnam won, 'the Pacific will become a Red Sea'. The dominoes were falling again, including Indonesia; 'China would be only fourteen miles from the Philippines and less than a hundred miles from Australia.'[34]

A month later, Nixon, while believing that the PRC was incapable of committing overwhelming economic resources to its military machine, nevertheless still identified

---

[30] Nixon, remarks at press conference in Taipei, Taiwan, 28 August, 1965, RNPL: WYS II, Trip Files 1963–67, PPS 347, Box 7.

[31] Private notes of Nixon's meeting with Chiang, August–September, 1965, RNPL: WYS II, Trip Files 1963–67, PPS 347, Box 7.

[32] Lee Kuan Yew, 'How the United States Should Engage Asia in the Post-Cold War Period', acceptance speech on receiving the Architect of the New Century Award, Nixon Center for Peace and Freedom, Washington, DC, 11 November 1996. Reprinted in *Straits Times*, 13 November 1996.

[33] See details in Leonard A. Kusnitz, *Public Opinion and Foreign Policy: America's China Policy, 1949–1979* (Westport: Greenwood Press, 1984), 112–14.

[34] Nixon, 'Why Not Negotiate in Vietnam?', *Reader's Digest*, 21 December 1965, 52

communist China as the main threat to the world peace. 'The reason was not a lack of will', he explained, 'but rather a lack of power'.[35] 'The threat of the Chinese Communists to the peace of the world is the major question confronting the nation', he argued in stump speeches at Republican rallies across the nation. Vietnam was 'about the monolithic power of Communist China'—which meant the US needed to stop 'aggression now when risks are minimal' instead of later 'being blackmailed out of the Pacific' by China's nuclear bomb. That was why proponents of a rapprochement with China were wrong and dangerous. 'Those who advocate appeasement and peace at any price actually are the war mongers', he warned. 'Appeasement would lead to World War III.'[36]

And yet, even as he uttered these Cold War shibboleths in 1966, Nixon was privately taking his first tentative steps towards a new way of understanding US–China relations. Two days before he dropped in at the wrong Chinese exhibition centre in Hong Kong's backstreets, he privately acknowledged what Adenauer, de Gaulle, Ayub, as well as several prominent Sinologists and realist intellectuals in the US, had long believed: that the 'cement of communism can't hold against nationalism'.[37] During his last European pre-presidential trip several months later in March 1967, it was Nixon himself who was enthusiastically promoting the idea of a China opening. Nixon told de Gaulle: 'In ten years, when China has made significant nuclear progress, we will have no choice [but to engage Peking]. It is vital that we have more communications with them than we have today.'[38] Nixon was asking the rhetorical question: 'Why not play China off Russia?'[39] De Gaulle agreed, suggesting that 'it would be better for you to recognise China before you are obliged to do so by the growth of China'.[40] In West Germany, the ninety-one-year-old Adenauer suggested, as he did in 1963, that the US should tilt toward the Chinese as long as the Soviets presented the greater military threat.[41] In contrast to his attitude in 1963, Nixon agreed, jotting down the following notes:

> RN pointed up the danger of isolating China … Accommodation with China would be welcomed (by China) … Chinese are cautious in foreign policy acts … China: need for a breakthrough. Can't have all eggs in one basket.[42]

The days of the relentless and strikingly combative Cold Warrior were fading fast.

---

[35] Ibid.

[36] See, for instance, Nixon, remarks at Vanderbilt University, Nashville, 4 February 1966; Nixon, remarks at the Republican state convention, New Orleans, 16 April 1966; Nixon, remarks at Robert Finch fundraiser, San Diego, 10 May, 1966; and Nixon, remarks at General Federation of Women's Clubs, Chicago, 10 June 1966, all in RNPL, WYS V, Appearance Files 1962–68, PPS 214, Boxes 19, 20 and 24 (respectively).

[37] Private notes of Nixon's meeting with Harold B. Lee in Hong Kong, 8 August 1966, RNPL: WYS II, Trip Files 1963–67, PPS 347, Box 8.

[38] Nixon, *1999: Victory without War* (London: Sidgewick & Jackson, 1988), 244–5.

[39] Private notes of Nixon, 5 March–25 March 1967, RNPL: WYS II, Trip Files 1963–67, PPS 347, Box 9.

[40] Nixon, *Leaders*, 74.

[41] Ibid., 163; Nixon, *RN*, 281.

[42] Private notes of Nixon, 5 March–25 March 1967, RNPL: WYS II, Trip Files 1963–67, PPS 347, Box 9.

The extent of Nixon's transformation was evident when on 22 March he met communist dictator Nicolae Ceaușescu. During their meeting, he told the Romanian leader that the US should take important steps towards normalising Sino–American relations. Reading the State Department's cable summary of the two-hour conversation, it is clear Nixon was strongly driving the China issue.[43] If anything, Ceaușescu appeared perplexed. In Nixon's view, it would be necessary for the Americans or Soviets to have the Chinese to commit arms control in order to improve prospects for genuine nuclear disarmament.

Nixon travelled to Asia the following month for his final regional trip before the presidential primary season. In his memoirs, Nixon recalled that during his three-hour meeting with Chiang he 'listened sceptically' to the Taiwanese president's confident talk of returning to the mainland. 'It was unthinkable that the US could underwrite support for a Nationalist strike', Nixon told Chiang, pointing to the danger of the US becoming involved in a 'long and inconclusive war on the mainland' that the American people would never support. Such actions 'might cause Peiping and Moscow to close ranks' against Taiwan and the US.[44] Yet it is worth noting that Chiang was putting to the aspiring presidential candidate some of the very points Nixon himself had raised on earlier occasions: that US–Nationalist resistance to Peking would end not only China's support for North Vietnam, but the threat of a Red Chinese atomic bomb explosion, as well as prospects of a Sino–Soviet rapprochement. In any case, the Taiwanese championed Nixon. 'Your periodical visits to Taiwan throughout the years', wrote one leading Taiwanese political figure:

> have always been interpreted as an encouragement from a distinguished American, who knows well where the common interests of our two countries lie, to us Free Chinese who have been struggling for peace and justice and for the recovery of our mainland now under the Communist domination.[45]

But the Taiwanese would have been perplexed, not to mention outraged, if they heard about Nixon's other meetings. Just as with his meetings with de Gaulle, Adenauer and Ceaușescu in Europe, Nixon was privately supporting the idea of engaging China during the rest of his Asian trip. For instance, during a two-hour discussion with Lee Kuan Yew on 18 April, Nixon kept asking: What should US policy towards China be? The Singaporean prime minister's answer was a familiar one: there was much to be gained by exploiting unresolved border tensions between Moscow and Peking and engaging China.[46] A few days later, Nixon told Chester Bowles, the US ambassador to India, that good relations with the PRC were more important than good relations with the Soviets. An incredulous Bowles promptly reported to Secretary of State Dean Rusk that he 'disagreed with [Nixon] strongly on this point, pointing out that the door to Moscow was ajar while the door to Peking was locked and bolted'.[47]

---

[43] State Department cable A-283, 'Memorandum of Conversation between Richard Nixon and Nicolae Ceaușescu', 22 March 1967, RNPL: WYS II, Trip Files 1963–67, PPS 347, Box 9.

[44] Cited in Hannah Pakula, *The Last Empress: Madame Chiang Kai-Shek and the Birth of Modern China* (London: Weidenfeld & Nicolson, 2009), 638.

[45] Letter, H. K. Yang to Nixon, 11 May 1967, RNPL: WYS II, Trip Files 1963–67, PPS 347, Box 10.

[46] Exchange reported in *Straits Times*, 13 November 1996.

[47] Cited in Gordon H. Chang, *Friends and Enemies: The United States, China, and the Soviet Union, 1948–1972* (Stanford: Stanford University Press, 1990), 283.

Tom Switzer

Winds of Change

A few weeks later, Nixon noted that his recent tours to Asia and Europe had shown a 'desire that US leaders reappraise our policies around the world'. With very different tone and emphasis, he declared: 'The US must lead, but the way to lead is by example and not by dictation.'[48] This new Nixon was being detected by leading journalists at *Time*, *Newsweek* and *Foreign Affairs*, scribes not known for holding any sympathies for the Republican firebrand. Harry Baehr, editorial writer for the *International Herald Tribune* in Paris, reflected the consensus of the other distinguished media guests who heard Nixon's tour d'horizon at a private dinner in May 1967. He expressed himself to be 'very favourably impressed' with Nixon's command of Asia and the world, 'especially struck by a greater maturity, greater assurance, greater authority' on Nixon's part, and he thought the old Cold Warrior showed himself 'both quite frank and well-informed'.[49]

During July–September 1967, Nixon delivered two landmark statements: an off-the-record address at the Bohemian Grove, an annual gathering of the nation's business elite in northern California; and an article in *Foreign Affairs*, the prestigious journal published by the Council on Foreign Relations (CFR). In his Bohemian Grove address, which marked the first milestone on his road to the presidency, he noted among other things that the communist world was no longer 'monolithic' and that it was 'time for us to recognize that … American style democracy is not necessarily the best form of government for people in Asia'. By all accounts, he dazzled the immensely wealthy and politically savvy audience with an overview of his world tour.[50]

In the *Foreign Affairs* piece, containing the first public manifestation of his new-look China policy, Nixon began by noting that 'bitter dissension has torn the fabric of American intellectual life and whatever the outcome of the [Vietnam] war the tear may be a long time mending'. Because the war would impose severe military, economic, political and social strains on the American psyche, the legacy of Vietnam would deprive America's leaders of the option of deploying US troops in protracted areas designed to meet a foreign threat. 'The role of the United States as world policeman', he wrote, anticipating the promulgation of the so-called Nixon Doctrine two years later, 'is likely to be limited in the future'. Along with this sober acknowledgment of the limitations of US power—or perhaps because of it—Nixon also called for the US to come 'urgently to grips with the reality of China' by pulling her 'back into the world community'. Taking the long view, he wrote:

> we simply cannot afford to leave China forever outside the family of nations, there to nurture its fantasies, cherish its hates and threaten its neighbours …

---

[48] Nixon, remarks to American Feed Manufacturers Association, Chicago, 23 May 1967, RNPL: WYS V, Appearance Files 1962–68, PPS 214, Box 28.

[49] Memorandum, Ray Price to Nixon, 4 May 1967, RNPL: WYS V, Appearance Files 1962–68, PPS 214, Box 27.

[50] Nixon, address to Bohemian Club, San Francisco, 29 July 1967, RNPL: White House Special Files Collection, Box 1, File 5. See also Aitken, *Nixon: A Life*, 330; Louis J. Smith and David H. Herschler, eds, *Foreign Relations of the United States, 1969–1976*, vol. 1, *Foundations of Foreign Policy, 1969–1972* (Washington: US Government Printing Office, 2003), 4–6.

> There is no place on this small planet for a billion of its potentially most able people to live in angry isolation.[51]

If a Democrat had made this argument twelve months earlier, Nixon would have denounced him as 'soft', 'naïve', 'woolly headed' and an 'appeaser'.

Yet a careful reading of the article revealed that Nixon had not completely jettisoned his previous thinking. He spoke of the need to 'recognise a common danger, and see its source as Peking'. He labelled China as the 'epicentre of world revolution,' referred to the 'poison from the Thoughts of Mao', and decried Peking's 'imperial ambitions' and its 'expansionist goals towards India, Thailand and Malaysia'. Nixon also urged Washington to give even greater assistance to its South-East Asian allies to contain China militarily. Moreover, he suggested that any accommodation was conditional on Peking altering its attitude to the rest of the world. Still, for Nixon, 'containment' no longer meant isolating and eventually destroying the PRC; it had now come to mean 'pulling China back into the world community … as a great and progressing nation'.

1966: The Emergence of a New China Consensus

Why then was Nixon changing his position on China in 1967? The answer lies in understanding the broader reconsideration of US China policy taking place at this time among both the political elite and the American public. By 1966–67 it had become increasingly evident that the North Vietnamese and Viet Cong would not easily succumb to American power. Domestic discontent climbed as American casualties rose and US involvement escalated. Meanwhile, in May 1966, China's Great Proletarian Cultural Revolution had commenced. The infamous Red Guards took to the streets and randomly punished anyone who was identified as inimical to Mao Zedong's world view. It sparked a political crisis, further plunging the Chinese mainland into a morass of chaos and zealous fanaticism.

All of this prompted a great debate over policies towards China in 1966. Opinion leaders—politicians, journalists and businessmen—began to reassess the longstanding policy of isolating Peking. Suddenly, the Sinophiles and realist intellectuals who had been widely dismissed as academic fringe-dwellers in the 1950s and early 1960s—most notably Harvard's John Fairbanks, Columbia's A. Doak Barnett and Chicago's Hans J. Morgenthau—gained a new legitimacy in Congress.[52] In March, Senator William Fulbright, the Democratic chairman of the Senate Committee on Foreign Relations (CFR), presided over three weeks of televised hearings on America's China policy. Most of the leading scholars and experts who testified before the committee echoed what Adenauer, de Gaulle and Ayub had been telling Nixon since 1963: namely, that China, far from being a reckless dragon bent on world revolution, had been more moderate and cautious in practice. These academics had developed the theme of 'containment without isolation': trade in non-strategic goods, an end to the travel embargo and recognition in the UN.

---

[51] Nixon, 'Asia after Vietnam', 111–25.

[52] Senate Committee on Foreign Relations, *Hearing on China, Hearings before the Senate Foreign Relations Committee,* 89th Congress, 2nd Session (Washington, DC: Government Printing Office, March 1966).

That month, 198 Asian scholars—opposed by only nineteen members of the Association for Asian Studies—published a statement declaring that Peking's continued isolation was not in the interest of the US or world peace.[53] The CFR spent more than a million dollars on a massive eight-volume study, *The United States and China in World Affairs*, probably the most ambitious scholarly project on China ever undertaken in the US.[54] The proposals were familiar: support Peking's admission into the UN, offer negotiations for diplomatic recognition, attempt to bring the communist leaders into disarmament talks and rescind the trade embargo on non-strategic goods.

In 1966, the *New York Times* published more than a dozen editorials favouring Peking's inclusion in the UN on some form of 'two China' basis.[55] Even the editorial page of the *Wall Street Journal*, although uneasy about softening US policy, recognised that attitudes towards China were changing rapidly.[56] *Commentary*, the hawkish liberal magazine, published a symposium of views on the subject. In it, Senator George McGovern, the Democratic presidential candidate whom Nixon would defeat in 1972, reflected the emerging consensus among lawmakers on Capitol Hill when declaring: 'The more diplomatic and economic contact there is between China and the outside world, the more likely it is that China will move in a less belligerent course.'[57] Opinion polls, meanwhile, showed increasing public support for negotiating with Peking, easing the travel ban and supporting China's admission into the UN. In June 1966, a Gallup poll showed that fifty-six per cent favoured admitting mainland China into the UN while only twenty-eight per cent opposed it.[58]

Even the Johnson administration was floating the idea of a rapprochement.[59] In July, President Lyndon Baines Johnson gave a nationally televised address to advocate 'reconciliation' with the mainland.[60] He repeated this message in his State of the Union address six months later.[61] But prospects for a diplomatic breakthrough in Sino–American relations remained on hold. The Vietnam War was increasingly sapping Washington's

---

[53] See 'The China Debate', *New York Times*, 23 March 1966, 46.

[54] Doak A. Barnett, ed., *The United States and China in World Affairs* (New York: McGraw-Hill, 1966).

[55] See, for instance, 'Ending China's Isolation', *New York Times*, 1 June 1966, 46.

[56] See, for instance, 'The Inevitable Can Wait', *Wall Street Journal*, 9 November 1966, 20.

[57] George S. McGovern, 'Containing China: A Round Table Conservation', *Commentary*, May 1966, 25–26.

[58] Kusnitz, *Public Opinion and Foreign Policy*, 115. See also A. T. Steele, *The American People and China* (New York: McGraw Hill, 1966).

[59] See Robert Garson, 'Lyndon B. Johnson and the China Enigma', *Journal of Contemporary History*, 32 (1), 1997, 63–80; and Michael Lumbers, 'Staying out of this Chinese Muddle: The Johnson Administration's Response to the Cultural Revolution', *Diplomatic History*, 31 (2), 2007, 259–94.

[60] Johnson remarks, 12 July 1966, in *Public Papers of the Presidents, Lyndon B. Johnson: Containing the Public Messages, Speeches, and Statements of the President* (hereafter *PPP: LBJ*), vol. 3, bk 2, *July 1–December 31 1966* (Washington: Government Publishing Office, 1967), 721–22.

[61] Johnson, State of the Union address, 10 January 1967, in *PPP: LBJ*, vol. 4, bk 1, *January 1–June 30 1967* (Washington: Government Publishing Office, 1968), 13.

energy and attention span, while the Cultural Revolution meant that China's leaders were increasingly xenophobic and irrational.

As the China expert Lucian Pye noted, all the evidence suggests that 1966 was 'a year of significant albeit gradual change in American policy toward Communist China'.[62] The CFR's annual appraisal of US activities in the world described the year as one in which there was a 'gradual but highly significant modification of American attitudes on the whole China question'.[63] In June the following year, a State Department-instigated China Advisory Panel that included many of the leading China experts reiterated the emerging consensus of opinion: that China's Cultural Revolution should not be considered a barrier to a reassessment of the US policy towards China.[64] In this environment, Nixon's changing views hardly qualified as thinking the unthinkable; he was merely reflecting an emerging US consensus.

All of this may explain Nixon's uncharacteristic refusal to address publicly the US policy towards China policy between his Hong Kong odyssey in August 1966 and the publication of his *Foreign Affairs* article in September 1967. During this period, there is hardly any evidence to indicate he had said anything publicly about China policy. Actions speak louder than words, according to the adage, but there are times when silence speaks louder still, a point Nixon himself once made in a different context.[65] From 1949 to 1966, Nixon had relentlessly condemned any proposal to accommodate the Chinese communists. But here he was in 1966–67, with a wet finger to the political wind, catching the significance of the changing intellectual climate and emerging national consensus and flirting with new policy proposals to bring China in from the cold. According to Elmer Bobst—an eighty-one-year-old mentor, wealthy businessman and son of an American missionary to China—the PRC was one of the subjects he had most frequently discussed with Nixon in 1966. They agreed that 'the most important thing' done in world affairs was 'bringing China into the world'—whether communist or not:[66] no more Red-baiting for Nixon. Nor was his changing mindset limited to the China issue. During the mid-term election campaigns, Nixon also softened his rhetoric on the increasingly unpopular Vietnam War.[67]

Nixon's long period of silence on China policy was symptomatic of someone on the verge of jettisoning longstanding and forthright views. Such a trait had been observed by veteran Nixon watchers. For example, a *National Review* editorial once observed: 'It is characteristic of Richard Nixon that before one of his famous spectacular moves he goes into a period of seclusion, meditating, it is said, over his yellow legal pads.'[68] According

---

[62] Lucian W. Pye, 'China in Context', *Foreign Affairs*, 45 (2), 1967, 229.

[63] Richard P. Stebbins, *The United States in World Affairs, 1966* (New York: Harper & Row, 1967), 267.

[64] Garson, 'Lyndon B. Johnson and the China Enigma', 71.

[65] Nixon, *In the Arena*, 292.

[66] Parmet, *Richard Nixon and his America*, 495; Wicker, *One of Us*, 17–18.

[67] Andrew L. Johns, 'A Voice from the Wilderness: Richard Nixon and the Vietnam War, 1964–66', *Presidential Studies Quarterly*, 29 (2), 1999, 325–26; Johns, 'Doves Among Hawks: Republican opposition to the Vietnam War, 1964–1968', *Peace & Change*, 31 (4), 2006, 594.

[68] Editorial, *National Review*, 8 June 1973, 618.

to his biographer: 'No account of Nixon the public politician is complete without an understanding of Nixon the private intellectual, and no perception of the private Nixon is possible without some glimpses of the personal changes that came about in him during his wilderness years.' Jonathan Aitken, to whom Nixon granted sixty hours of interviews in the early 1990s, further asserted: 'Although his wilderness years were busy ones, he remained a loner who relished his solitude. He did his best work, and had his greatest enjoyment, in his mind.'[69] Given that this 'self-described egghead' read omnivorously—in March 1966, with the China debate well underway, Nixon, according to one report, read 'three hours a night—magazines, newspapers, books—to keep informed'—it is highly likely that this man who yearned to lead the contemplative life caught the significance of the emerging China policy consensus.[70]

Nixon's Betrayal of Conservatives

Clearly, then, Nixon was changing his views in 1966 and 1967. Why, though, was his case for engagement towards China in *Foreign Affairs* so nuanced? After all, public opinion had changed rapidly and the political consensus to isolate the mainland had begun to collapse. Numerous foreign governments were increasingly recognising the Peking regime. Privately, Nixon supported an opening; publicly he was more qualified. Why?

Nixon's political priorities during the second half of 1967 provide an explanation. When Nixon started looking seriously at the 1968 presidential primaries, he feared that Ronald Reagan, the darling of conservatives who was popular in the western and southern states, could hurt him. This was especially the case given that since 1960, the Nelson Rockefeller liberal wing of the Republican Party had been losing its influence to the more conservative forces led by Barry Goldwater. Given these circumstances, Nixon made great efforts to court the conservative faithful, including those he called Buckleyites at the *National Review*, so named for its founding editor and the widely recognised patron saint of American conservatives, Bill Buckley.[71] As Nixon once advised Robert Dole: 'You run as fast as hell to the right during the primaries; then you move fast as hell to the centre in the general election.'[72] Therefore, as a shrewd politician, he was careful not to commit himself too firmly to the new consensus of revisionism on China policy, lest a 'soft' stance evoke a negative response from conservatives who were unashamed supporters of Taiwan.

Once he secured the Republican nomination, the previously staunch anti-communist could move closer to the centre of the political spectrum and start to send subtle messages about a China opening. And when Nixon eventually announced his decision on 15 July 1971 to visit Peking—done in the absence of any public concessions by the communist leaders bogged down in their Cultural Revolution—conservatives, with rare exceptions,

---

[69] Aitken, *Nixon: A Life*, 335–6.

[70] 'Amazing Mr Nixon hasn't won race since 1950', *Clearwater Sun*, 13 March 1966; Witcover, *The Resurrection of Richard Nixon*, 150.

[71] See John B. Judis, *William F. Buckley Jr.: Patron Saint of Conservatives* (New York: Simon & Schuster, 1988), 278–81.

[72] Doyle McManus, 'Rightward Ho!: This Year's GOP is Pulling all of its Candidates Away from the Center', *Los Angeles Times*, 25 September 2011, A34.

responded angrily. They had never forgiven Harry Truman and Dean Acheson for allegedly betraying Chiang Kai-shek in 1949 and two decades later they were in no mood to tolerate what publisher William Rusher called 'one of the greatest double crosses of all time'.[73] The episode further challenges the conventional wisdom that only someone with such authority and credibility on the Republican right would meet little resistance from his own side. Indeed, Nixon's rapprochement was the tipping point in a fractious relationship that included several betrayals including on the issues of price and wage controls, détente with the Soviets and ending the gold standard.

After Nixon's announcement on 15 July 1971, several Republican lawmakers—from congressmen Walter Judd and John Ashbrook to senators John Tower and Strom Thurmond—broke off relations with the White House. William Loeb, publisher of New Hampshire's *Union Leader*, warned that Nixon's shift of attitude was 'immoral, indecent, insane and fraught with danger for the survival of the United States'.[74] The Reverend Carl McIntire of the Vietnam 'March for Victory' committee charged that Nixon had 'abandoned all moral principles: it is like God and the devil having a high-level meeting'.[75] Bill Buckley, who had said in April 1968 that Nixon's 'anti-communist resolution is as firm as just about anything in national politics', complained during Nixon's rapprochement that the US had 'lost—irretrievably—any remaining sense of moral mission in the world'.[76] The accepted wisdom posits that if Nixon had been a Democrat then the Republican right would have been outraged. Yet it was outraged anyway. On this issue, Nixon had shown himself to be fiercely calculating.

An Ideological Odyssey

What then explains Nixon's change of heart? Perhaps the cynical response is to understand Nixon as a talented opportunist, not burdened with any deep convictions. In the late 1940s and early 1950s, he exploited strong anti-communist feelings in the community because it was the right career move for an ambitious young politician at the time. Even as he assumed the role of arch Cold Warrior in the 1950s and early to mid-1960s, there was an air of detached calculation about his public performances, a sense that in different circumstances he could just as easily have made the opposing case.

By the mid- to late-1960s, the circumstances had indeed changed. Vietnam had broken Americans' faith in the ability of massive military and economic power to remake the world in their own image. Aware that the country was increasingly tired of two decades of moral and military confrontation, he set out to redefine the Cold War as a traditional great-power rivalry rather than a war to the death with a revolutionary totalitarian force bent on world domination. The Sino–Soviet quarrel, including border disputes in 1969, suddenly lent

---

[73] William A. Rusher cited in Gerald S. and Deborah H. Strober, *Nixon: An Oral History of his Presidency* (New York: HarperCollins, 1994), 131.

[74] David W. Reinhard, *The Republican Right Since 1945* (Lexington: University Press of Kentucky, 1983), 224.

[75] 'Nixon's Coup: To Peking for Peace', *Time*, 26 July 1971, 10.

[76] Cited in Judis, *William F. Buckley Jr.*, 281; William F. Buckley Jr, 'Veni, Vidi, Victus', *National Review*, 17 March 1972, 258.

itself to this interpretation. Accepting that view, it made sense to exploit tensions between Peking and Moscow by reaching an accommodation with the weaker Communist state against the stronger one. The influence of self-described realist Henry Kissinger would have reinforced this line of thought, but one should not overstate the national security adviser's role. As Kissinger aide Roger Morris has observed: 'The initiative to China loomed very much as the work of one man', and furthermore, 'the China policy reflected the abiding style as well as intellectual substance of the lonely, controlling politician in Nixon'.[77] The point here is that an opportunistic realism fitted Nixon's character and temperament.

But even if it is the case that he was not taking serious political risks in opening windows to the PRC, it is still worth asking: why did Nixon bother? He could have left the Sino–American relationship as he had inherited it; few American voters would have punished him for not taking such an initiative and his party's base may have rallied around his presidency. Having been such a rabid, almost pathological anti-Red China spokesman during the preceding two decades, why did he, unlike other Cold Warriors, accept the need for a change of policy?

Perhaps the answer lies in understanding that Nixon, a student of European history who greatly valued his relationships with Adenaur and de Gaulle, abandoned the myth of American exceptionalism and embraced a Realpolitik view of power politics. After all, it was one thing for President Nixon to recognise that the forces of nationalism more than any ideological differences were responsible for dissolving communist unity; that the US must deal with nations on the basis of their actions, not an abstract ideological formula; that Chinese foreign policy more than anything else reflected the complexity of China's historical relationships with the outside world and not an abiding commitment to 'world revolution'; and that the US had a strategic interest in the survival of a major communist country in order to keep in check another communist power—all ideas that Nixon himself had repudiated as late in his career as August 1966. It was something else altogether for Nixon to talk a different language about America's destiny and enunciate a European world view. At a time of deep doubts and widespread uncertainty about America's place in the world, taken together with the violence on the streets and the widespread adoption of a permissive ethic at home, Nixon prepared his fellow citizens to adapt to decline in a more plural world and to adopt policies which would smooth the path to a new, more limited role in international relations. In short, Nixon was no true believer in the American mission.

On 6 July 1971, as Kissinger was secretly on route to Peking to complete plans for the first presidential visit, Nixon acknowledged that the American Century was drawing to a close. 'In five years, ten years, perhaps it is 15, but in any event within our time', America's global hegemony would be replaced by a multipolar world, in which the United States, the Soviet Union, Western Europe, Japan and China would be leading powers. 'The United States no longer is in the position of complete pre-eminence or predominance [and] that is not a bad thing. As a matter of fact, it can be a constructive thing.'[78] A man who had earlier

---

[77] Roger Morris, *Uncertain Greatness: Henry Kissinger and American Foreign Policy* (London: Harper & Row, 1977), 203–5.

[78] Nixon, 'Remarks to Midwestern News Media Executives Attending a Briefing on Domestic Policy in Kansas City, Missouri', 6 July 1971, *Public Papers of the Presidents, Richard Nixon:*

championed a Pax Americana now acknowledged that Americans had to learn to adapt themselves to their new status as only one power in a five-centred multipolar international system.

> I think of what happened to Greece and Rome, and you see what is left—only the pillars. What has happened, of course, is that the great civilisations of the past, as they have become wealthy, as they have lost their will to live, to improve, they then have become subject to decadence that eventually destroys the civilisation.'

He concluded sombrely: 'The US is now reaching that period.'[79]

'I think it will be a safer world and a better world', Nixon argued before his February 1972 visit to China, 'if we have a strong, healthy United States, Europe, Soviet Union, China, Japan, each balancing the other, an even balance'. Instead of looking at the post-Vietnam world through the prism of American exceptionalism, Nixon and Kissinger envisaged it as an emerging multipolar system to be structured and regulated by a balance of power à la the 1815 Congress of Vienna, the subject of the latter's doctoral dissertation. 'It is when one nation becomes infinitely more powerful in relation to its potential competitor that the danger of war arises', Nixon declared in language more reminiscent of von Metternich, von Bismarck and de Gaulle than Truman, Kennedy and Reagan.[80] Walter Lippmann had spent much of the 1950s and 1960s railing against Nixon's strident anti-communist views, but he caught the significance of the new Nixon. 'His role', Lippmann conceded in 1973:

> has been that of a man who had to liquidate, defuse, deflate the exaggerations of the romantic period of American imperialism and American inflation. Inflation of promises, inflation of hopes, the Great Society, American supremacy—all that had to be deflated because it was all beyond our power.[81]

Reading the article in his White House daily briefing, Nixon noted: 'Wise observation.'[82]

But Nixon's task of building a Realpolitik world order was complicated by the fact that the historical experience of Europe bore little resemblance to how the American people in the post-war era had viewed international affairs. Deriving from the nation's history, according to the national myth, Americans had grown to feel comfortable with their own idealistic sense of exceptionalism. Based on a distinction between the founding moral principles of America and the corruption of the Old World of Europe, exceptionalism for them explained the international predominance of America in terms of its moral and material uniqueness. Americans had come to believe that the US had been deliberately founded as a nation unlike any other and had a mission to regenerate the world and international relations in their own image. Nixon's new-found realism was ultimately incompatible with this culture and it met a backlash from both the left and the right. According to Eugene Genovese,

---

Containing the Public Messages, Speeches, and Statements of the President, 1971 (Washington: Government Publishing Office, 1972), 806–07.

[79] Nixon wrote two drafts of his 6 July, 1971 speech; see RNPL: President's Speech File, 1969–74, SFSM PPF067, Box 67, Folder 18.

[80] 'An Interview with the President: The Jury is Out', *Time*, 3 January 1971, 9.

[81] 'Walter Lippmann at 83: An Interview with Ronald Steel', *Washington Post*, 25 March 1973, C1.

[82] John B. Judis, *Grand Illusion: Critics and Champions of the American Century* (New York: Farrar Straus and Giroux, 1992): 210.

liberal academic and nemesis of Nixon: 'Even those who speak for Realpolitik, including the most cynical and opportunist, have unwittingly contributed to the breakdown of an increasingly brittle and shoddy spiritual façade.'[83] And as conservative pundit Richard Whalen argued: 'Neither Nixon nor Kissinger, for all their undoubted qualities of intellect, has a sure intuitive sense of this country, its people and their guiding sentiments.'[84]

Nixon's realist rhetoric was not the language of his Cold Warrior predecessors, who articulated a vision of America rooted in this idea of US exceptionalism. Nor was it the language of his successors, who had been periodically affected by bouts of evangelical idealism, even though in practice they retreated before the complex realities of a messy world. For many Americans, Nixon's European-style solution to the crisis of American nationalism was a dry, tasteless meal for the soul, and it sorely lacked any exceptional redeeming qualities for the national experience. In adopting a position of Realpolitik towards foreign relations, exemplified in the opening of China, Nixon was not a true believer in the American national mission.

Conclusion

No proper account of Nixon's long intellectual march on China is satisfactory without an understanding of American nationalism and its dwindling impact on the nation's social psychology during the mid- to late-1960s. From the communist revolution of 1949 to the great China debate in 1966–67, the ideology of American nationalism had profoundly shaped the community's view of China policy and America's role in the world. Peking was simply a tool of the Soviet Union bent on world revolution; any Sino–Soviet rifts were driven by ideology, not nationalism and age-old strategic rivalry; and the US had a special mission to redeem the world. That is why even as Konrad Adenauer, Charles de Gaulle and Ayub Khan voiced misgivings with US policy and expressed support for an opening to China, Nixon, like most Americans, steadfastly opposed any rapprochement. It was a politically astute strategy, but it was also in accordance with the national psyche. For history, it was widely assumed, was on America's side.

Yet the events of the mid- to late-1960s undermined this historic sense of national destiny. The Vietnam War and the domestic economic and social crises that accompanied it threw into question American's omnipotence and shattered their hopes for an American Century without leading to a new millennial vision. In 1966–67, the Truman Doctrine in Asia had been lost in the flames of Vietnam and a new era in US understanding of China had begun. It became clear that Washington would need to learn to live with rather than convert or crusade against the communist regime. And so the ideology of American nationalism became less central for policymakers in their dealings with Peking.

Aware of these shifting winds, the pliant Richard Nixon began to embark on an ideological odyssey. Shortly after his Hong Kong trip in August 1966, the erstwhile anti-PRC hawk had been uncharacteristically silent as a wide range of opinion leaders called for the normalisation of relations with Peking. By early 1967, he privately urged such a policy

---

[83] Eugene Genovese, 'A Massive Breakdown,' *Newsweek*, 6 July, 1970, 18.
[84] Richard Whalen, 'A Foreign Policy Without a Country', *National Review*, 14 September 1973, 1005.

with the foreign leaders who had only a few years earlier given him the same advice. In September 1967, he broke his year-long silence and argued that American-style democracy was not an export commodity to Asia and mainland China should be welcomed back into the world community. This was a shift in thinking that would finally force America to come to terms with the communist revolution of 1949. Such views were a far cry from a year earlier when Nixon warned that appeasement of Red China would lead to 'World War III with nuclear weapons'.

In July 1971, when President Nixon announced his decision to visit China, the amazing thing is that America and the world were amazed. Long gone were the days when mainstream US politicians, most notably Nixon, felt compelled to outlaw and blacklist anything Chinese. Indeed, Nixon's reversal of two decades of isolating China met with overwhelming majority approval, which confirms that government policy had fallen behind public opinion. After all, the national consensus to ostracise China had started to crack dramatically five years before Nixon announced that he would go to China. But although the American people supported Nixon's about-face on China policy, they could not countenance the idea that the US was an ordinary nation, bound by limits in a plural world that would not conform to American expectations. Not surprisingly, they refused to be born again as a new people and to replace the idealism of Jefferson and Wilson with the Realpolitik of Metternich and Bismarck. By surrendering the American nationalist tradition abroad, Richard Nixon perhaps only made his failure at home more likely.

Select List of Publications by Neville Meaney

Books

ed., *Studies on the American Revolution* (Melbourne: Macmillan, 1976).

A History of Australian Defence and Foreign Policy, 1901–23, vol. 1, *The Search for Security in the Pacific, 1901–14* (Sydney: Sydney University Press, 1976).

ed., *Australia and the World: A Documentary History from the 1870s to the 1970s* (Melbourne: Longman Cheshire, 1985).

with Sol Encel and Trevor Matthews, *The Japanese Connection: A Survey of Australian Leaders' Attitudes Towards Japan and the Australia–Japan Relationship* (Melbourne: Longman Cheshire, 1988).

ed., *Under New Heavens: Cultural Transmission and the Making of Australia* (Port Melbourne: Heinemann Educational, 1989).

Fears and Phobias: E. L. Piesse and the Problem of Japan, 1909–1939 (Canberra: National Library of Australia, 1996).

Towards a New Vision: Australia and Japan through 100 Years (Sydney: Kangaroo Press, 1999).

Japan and Australia's Foreign Policy, 1945–1952 (London: Suntory Centre, London School of Economics and Politics, 2000).

The Making of the Commonwealth and the Defence of Australia (Armidale: University of New England, 2001).

Towards a New Vision: Australia and Japan Across Time (Kensington: University of New South Wales Press, 2007).

A History of Australian Defence and Foreign Policy, 1901–23, vol. 2, *Australia and World Crisis, 1914–23* (Sydney: Sydney University Press, 2009).

Book Chapters

'Introduction: The American Revolution in Search of a Future', in *Studies on the American Revolution*, ed. Neville Meaney (Melbourne: Macmillan, 1976), 1–32.

'The Trial of Popular Sovereignty in America: The Case of Shays' Rebellion', in *Studies on the American Revolution*, ed. Neville Meaney (Melbourne: Macmillan, 1976), 151–75.

'The United States', in *Australia in World Affairs, 1971–1975*, ed. W. J. Hudson (Sydney: George Allen and Unwin, 1979), 163–208.

'Introduction: The Meaning of the Past', in *Australia and the World: A Documentary History from the 1870s to the 1970s*, ed. Neville Meaney (Melbourne: Longman Cheshire, 1985), 1–29.

with Paul Bourke, 'The Development of Teaching and Research on United States History in Australia', in *Guide to the Study of United States History outside the US, 1945–1980*, vol.1, ed. Lewis Hanke (White Plains, New York: Kraus International Publications, 1985), 137–59.

Select List of Publications by Neville Meaney

'Introduction: "Sidere Mens Eadem Mutato"', in *Under New Heavens: Cultural Transmission and the Making of Australia*, ed. Neville Meaney (Port Melbourne: Heinemann Educational, 1989), 1–20.

'Australia and the World', in *Under New Heavens: Cultural Transmission and the Making of Australia*, ed. Neville Meaney (Port Melbourne: Heinemann Educational, 1989), 379–450.

'American Nationalism, the Monroe Doctrine and Woodrow Wilson's New World Order', in *Relacoes Internacionais Dos Paises Americanos: Vertentes da Historia*, eds Amado Luiz Cervo and Wolfgang Dopcke (Brasilia, Linha Gráfica: 1994), 230–48.

with James Cotton, Takeshi Ishida, Ben Kerkvliet, et. al, 'Government', in *Australia in Asia: Comparing Cultures*, eds Anthony Milner and Mary Quilty (Melbourne: Oxford University Press, 1996), 253–83.

'"The Yellow Peril", Invasion Scare Novels and Australian Political Culture', in *The 1890s: Australian Literature and Literary Culture*, ed. Ken Stewart (St. Lucia: University of Queensland Press, 1996), 228–63.

'"In History's Page": Myth and Identity', in *Australia's Empire*, eds Deryck Schreuder and Stuart Ward (Oxford History of the British Empire Companion Series) (Oxford: Oxford University Press, 2008), 363–87.

'The First Australian High Commissioners: George Houston Reid and Andrew Fisher', in *The High Commissioners: Australia's Representatives in the United Kingdom, 1910–2010*, eds Carl Bridge, Frank Bongiorno and David Lee (Canberra: DFAT, 2010), 36–55.

'The Problem of "Greater Britain" and Australia's Strategic Crisis, 1905–1914', in *1911: Preliminary Moves. The 2011 Chief of Army History Conference*, eds Peter Dennis and Jeffrey Grey (Canberra: Army History Unit, 2011), 42–55.

'Dr H. V. Evatt and the United Nations: The Problem of Collective Security and Liberal Internationalism', in *Australia and the United Nations*, eds James Cotton and David Lee (Sydney: Longueville Media, 2012), 34–65.

Articles in Scholarly Journals

'The British Empire in the American Rejection of the Treaty of Versailles', *Australian Journal of Politics and History*, IX (2), 1963: 213–34.

'Woodrow Wilson as Machiavelli's Prince of Peace: A New Point of Departure for the Study of President Wilson's Foreign Policy', *Proceedings of the First Biennial Conference of the Australian–New Zealand American Studies Association*, ed. Norman Harper (August 1964): 108–20.

'Arthur S. Link and Thomas Woodrow Wilson', *Journal of American Studies*, 1 (1), 1967.

'"A Proposition of the Highest International Importance": Alfred Deakin's Pacific Agreement Proposal and its Significance for Australia–Imperial Relations', *Journal of Commonwealth Political Studies*, V (3), 1967: 200–14.

'Australian Defence and Foreign Policy: History and Myth', *Australian Outlook*, XXIII (2), 1969: 173–81.

'American Studies in Australia and New Zealand', *American Studies: An International Newsletter*, IX (2), 1970: 9–16.

'From the Pentagon Papers: Reflections on the Making of America's Vietnam Policy', *Australian Outlook*, XXVI (2), 1972: 163–92.

'Australia's Secret Service in World War I: Security, Loyalty and the Abuse of Power', *Quadrant*, XXIII (7), 1979: 19–23.

'"The Yellow Peril" and the "Australian Crisis": The Japanese Phase in the History of Australian Foreign Policy, 1905–1941', *Kokusai Seiji* (Journal of the Japanese International Relations Association), 2 (1981).

'Reflections on Hancock's Australia', *Australian Historical Association Bulletin*, 43, June 1987: 8–13.

'American Decline and American Nationalism', *Australian Journal of International Affairs*, 45 (1), 1991: 89–98.

'Australia, the Great Powers and the Coming of the Cold War', *Australian Journal of Politics and History*, 38 (3), 1992: 316–33.

'The End of "White Australia" and Australia's Changing Perceptions of Asia, 1945–1990', *Australian Journal of International Affairs*, 49 (2), 1995: 171–90.

'The Commonwealth and the Republic: An Historical Perspective', *Papers on Parliament No. 27: Reinventing Political Institutions*, ed. Kathleen Dermody (Canberra: Department of the Senate, 1996), 15–30.

'Britishness and Australian Identity: The Problem of Nationalism in Australian History and Historiography', *Australian Historical Studies*, 32 (116), 2001: 76–90.

'Britishness and Australia: Some Reflections', *Journal of Imperial and Commonwealth History*, 31 (2), 2003: 121–35.

'Look Back in Fear: Percy Spender, the Japanese Peace Treaty and the ANZUS Pact', *Japan Forum*, 15 (3), 2003: 399–410.

'Frederic Eggleston on International Relations and Australia's Role in the World', *Australian Journal of Politics and History*, 51 (3), 2005: 359–71.

'The Problem of Nationalism and Race: Australia and Japan in World War I and World War II', *Journal of the Oriental Society of Australia*, 42, 2010: 1–30.

'Australian Irish Catholics and Britishness: The Problem of British "Loyalty" and "Identity" from the Conscription Crisis to the End of the Anglo-Irish War', *Journal of the Australian Catholic Historical Society*, 34, 2014 (forthcoming).

Contributors

Joan Beaumont is a professor in the Strategic and Defence Studies Centre at the Australian National University.

Hugh Clarke is an emeritus professor in the Department of Japanese Studies at the University of Sydney.

James Cotton is an emeritus professor of politics in the School of Humanities and Social Sciences, Australian Defence Force Academy (University of New South Wales).

Dr James Curran is an associate professor at the University of Sydney and Keith Cameron Professor of Australian History at University College, Dublin.

Dr Matthew Jordan is a historian in the Historical Publications and Information section of the Department of Foreign Affairs and Trade.

Dr Richard Lehane is an archivist with the State Records Authority of New South Wales.

Dr Ross McKibbin is an emeritus research fellow at St John's College, Oxford.

Dr David McLean is an honorary fellow of the School of Humanities and Social Sciences at Charles Sturt University.

Eric Meadows is a visitor at Deakin University, Melbourne.

Colin Milner is a founding member of the steering committee for the Historians of Australia's Foreign Relations.

Dr David Rowlands is a history teacher in New South Wales.

Tom Switzer is a research associate in the United States Studies Centre at the University of Sydney.

Dr Michael Thompson is a lecturer in US Studies in the United States Studies Centre at the University of Sydney.

Stuart Ward is a professor in the Centre for Australian Studies at the University of Copenhagen.

Index

A

Abe, Shirzō 22
abolitionists 268–269
Acheson, Dean 316
Adams, Charles Francis 268
Adams, John 263, 268
Adenauer, Konrad 303–304, 307, 310–311, 313, 318
Advance Australia Fair 207–208
Afghanistan War (2001–) 237, 240, 245, 247, 250, 252, 253, 256
Aitken, Jonathan 316
Aldershot Military Society 105, 106, 110–111
Aliens Act 1905 (UK) 179
Aliens Order 1920 (UK) 179
Aliens Registration Act 1914 (UK) 179
Aliens Restriction (Amendment) Act 1919 (UK) 179
Altman, Dennis 243, 248
American Century 304, 318, 320
American Civil War 28, 32, 133
American Revolution 26, 28, 135–136, 141, 262, 272, 276
Anderson, Benedict 103, 286
Andrews, Eric 8, 11
Angel, J. R. 7
Animania Festival 20
anime 20
anti-communism 4, 91–93, 183–186, 243, 301, 304–305, 316–317. *See also* communism, containment of
anti-militarism 299
anti-proliferation of nuclear weapons 302
ANZAC Agreement 45
Anzac Day 44, 210
Anzac legend 3, 49, 187, 238, 254
ANZUS Treaty 7, 47–48, 52, 218, 221, 227, 239, 240, 245, 246, 256–257
apartheid 94–96, 98
appeasement 145–146, 159–166, 301, 310
Armitage, Richard 248

Ashbrook, John 317
Asian Relations Conference (1947) 86
Asia-Pacific region
    Australia's position within 4–5, 37–38, 51, 145, 149, 160, 217, 219–220, 225–228, 233–234, 239, 242–243, 244, 247, 249, 253
    British power in 4, 11, 222
    US power in. *See* Vietnam War
Asquith, Henry Herbert 187
assimilation 59, 70, 72, 74–78, 82–83, 91
asylum seekers 186
Atkinson, Alan 136
Attlee, Clement 171, 174
Auckland Anniversary Day 208
Auckland Historical Society 210
Australasian Federation League 130
Austral-Asiatic Bulletin 6
Australia as a constitutional monarchy 174, 231
Australia as a US satellite, perceptions of 229, 238, 240, 242, 251
Australia Council for the Arts 195, 204
Australia Day 195, 204
Australia, independence of 148
Australia in World Affairs 6, 11
Australian Broadcasting Corporation (ABC) 94–95
Australian culture and cultural identity 9, 32–35, 49, 60, 137–143, 169–189, 253. *See also* Australian national identity
    American influence on 170–171, 218, 220, 242, 253
    Australian Britishness 32, 169–170, 175, 193, 195–196, 200, 207, 230. *See also* Australian national identity; Australian nationalism; British race patriotism
Australian Defence Force Academy 13
Australian expatriate communities in Britain 169

329

Index

Australian Federal Defence Agreement 107–109
Australian Federal Defence Scheme 112
Australian Federation League 130
Australian foreign policy. *See also* defence of Australia
  during the Cold War. *See* Cold War: Japan–Australia relations during; Cold War: US–Australia relations during
  during the First World War. *See* First World War: Australia's involvement
  during the Second World War. *See* Second World War: Australia's involvement; Second World War: Great Britain–Australia relations; Second World War: US–Australia relations
  Holt years 217–235
  Howard years 237–257
  Menzies years 238–249
  S. M. Bruce years 160
  study of 3–12
Australian Institute of International Affairs (AIIA) 6–7, 11, 140, 150, 163–164
Australian Journal of International Affairs (*AJIA*) 6, 11. *See also Australian Outlook*
Australian Labor Party (ALP) 39, 124, 184–185, 186, 187, 238
Australian national anthem 199, 203–207, 212, 232. *See also Advance Australia Fair*
Australian national identity 185, 194, 196, 197–199, 203–207, 213, 238. *See also* Australian culture and cultural identity; British race patriotism
  identity crisis 20–21
Australian nationalism 32, 34–35, 48, 51, 137–143, 146, 148–149, 165, 169, 250. *See also* new nationalism: in Australia
Australian National University 8, 13, 18, 91, 125, 143
Australian Natives Association 87
Australian Outlook 6. *See also Australian Journal of International Affairs* (*AJIA*)
Australian republicanism 142, 174, 231
Australian universities, expansion of 4
Australian War Memorial 20

Australia's immigration policies 19, 134. *See also* White Australia policy
  British immigrants to Australia 169
  Irish immigrants to Australia 169
  restriction or exclusion of Chinese immigrants 57–80, 149
  restriction or exclusion of Indian immigrants 83–98
autonomy of British colonies 103

B

Bacevich, Andrew 281–282
Baehr, Harry 312
Bailey, Kenneth 122
Bajpai, Girija 89
Balfour Declaration 139–140, 142
Bancroft, George 28, 263, 304
Bancroftian typology 264, 268, 275–276, 276
Banerjee, R. N. 86
Barclay, Glen 218, 225
Barnett, A. Doak 313
Barton, Edmund 71, 115, 116, 123–124, 130, 143
Bassett, Jan 219
Bastian, Peter 6
Beale, Howard 7
Bean, C. E. W. 43
Bedi, Daya Singh 88
Belich, James 193
Belloc, Hilaire 185
Bell, Roger 6
Bevan Edwards, J. 129
bicameralism 173–174
Biddle, Francis 133
Bird, David 146, 155, 157, 159
von Bismarck, Otto 319
Blainey, Geoffrey 20
Blair, Tony 248
Blyton, Enid 170
Bobst, Elmer 315
Boer War 34, 104, 114, 117
Bolton, Geoffrey 146
Borden, Frederick 113–114
Bourne, Francis 182
Bowker, Richard 63
Bowles, Chester 311
Boyce, Peter 7

Boyd, Robin 197
Brenan, John 162
Britannia 102
British Australianness 171, 175
British imperial sentiment 194
British Labour Party 184
British Legion 188
British nationalism 194
Britishness. *See* Australian culture and cultural identity: Australian Britishness
British parliamentary form 132
British perceptions of Australia 172. *See also* British Australianness
British race patriotism. *See also* Great Britain, Australia's relationship with: cultural ties to; Australian national identity; Australian Britishness; Australian culture and cultural identity; Australian nationalism
   in Australia 4, 34–35, 36–39, 43, 48–49, 51, 74, 134–135, 137–143, 169, 187, 198
   in Canada 192–196
   in New Zealand 192–193
   in the British colonies 101–102, 107
Brodrick, St John 117–118
Broinowski, Alison 241, 242, 250
Brooks, David 281–282
Brownrigg, Jeff 126–127, 129
Bruce, S. M. 9, 44, 138, 160–162, 164–165
Buckley, Bill 316
Buckner, Phillip 194, 196
Bundy, William 225, 233
Burke, Anthony 241, 242, 250
Burton, John 86
Bush, George H. W. 232
Bush, George W. 240, 248, 254–255, 282
Butler, R. A. 164

C

Califano, Joseph A. 221
Calvinism 266–267, 271
Calwell, Arthur 86, 87–88, 93
Cambodia, restoration of 21
Camilleri, Joseph 238, 250, 252–253
Campbell, Alistair 199
Canada Council for the Arts 195
Canada Day / Dominion Day 195–197

Canada, immigrantion to 194
Canada, immigration policy of 90–91
Canada, India's relationship with 90–91
Canadian flag 195, 200–203
Canadian national identity 194, 196–197, 200–203, 213
Canadian parliamentary form 132
Canberra as the capital of Australia 125–126
Cariappa, H. M. 84, 92–94
Carnegie Corporation 157
Caro, Robert A. 222
Carrington, Peter 230–231
Carter, Jimmy 232
Cartwright, Richard 114
Casey, R. G. 9, 96–97, 139, 154, 160–162
Catholicism 182, 185–186
Catholic Rural Movement 185
Cawte, Alice 6
Ceauşescu, Nicolae 311
Chamberlain, Joseph 101–102, 113, 117–118, 164, 177–178
Channon, Henry 172
Chesterton, G. K. 185
Chiang Kai-shek 307–309, 311, 316
Chifley, J. B. (Ben) 45–46, 170, 174, 186
China, Australia's relationship with 150–153, 162, 239, 252
China's imperialistic ambitions 21–22, 145, 234–235, 243, 244, 304, 314
China, Soviet Union's relationship with. *See* Sino–Soviet split
Chinese foreign policy 318
Chinese immigration crisis (1888) 51
Chinese labour in South Africa 180
Chinese Restriction and Regulation Act 1888 67
The Christian Century 285, 296
Christianity and Crisis 296, 297
Churchill, Gordon 202
Churchill, Winston 37, 132, 181, 230
Churchward, L. G. 238, 250
civil rights movement in the US 208
Clark, Andrew Inglis 77–78
Clark, Ed 217, 224
Clarke, Sydenham 114
Clark, Manning 204
Cleveland, Grover 273
Clive, John 105

Cobbett, Pitt 125
Cold War
  Australia during 251
  China–Soviet relations during 317
  coming of 5, 281–283
  end of 20
  historiography of 11
  Japan–Australia relations during 46, 81
  US–Australia relations during 98, 218–220, 232, 240
  US–China relations during 301, 309–310, 312
  US during 254, 292, 297–300, 307, 320
  US–Soviet relations during 30–31, 303–304
  US–Vietnam relations during. *See* Vietnam War
Cole, Douglas 192–194, 213
collective bargaining 178–180, 185
Colombo Plan 7, 82
Colonial Conference (1887) 129
Colonial Defence Committee 102, 108
colonial nationalism 192–196
Columbia University 286
Commentary 314
Committee to Aid the Allies 296
communism, containment of 46, 152, 219, 222, 234–235, 305, 307, 309, 313–314. *See also* anti-communism
communist revolution (China, 1949) 301
comparative history 18, 20
Conference on Eastern Trade (1933) 151
Confrontation 256
Congress of Vienna (1815) 319
conscription 4, 41–42, 106, 124
Conservative Party (UK) 177, 183, 185, 187
constitutional monarchy 132. *See also* Australia as a constitutional monarchy
constitutional transgressions 63
Constitution of Australia 173
  the making of a 130, 134
Cooke, N. M. 206
Coolidge, Calvin 287
cooperative system for defence 101–118, 129–130. *See also* Hutton, E. T. H.
Corowa Conference (1893) 130–131
Cotton, James 7

Council on Foreign Relations (US) 140, 281, 312, 314
cricket 172
Crocker, Walter 7, 91, 94, 97
cross-cultural understanding 17
C Series Index 188
Cultural Revolution 305, 313, 315, 316
Curran, James 6, 126, 196, 204, 254
Curtin, John 5, 45, 170, 174
Curtis, Lionel 140

D

Dalley, William Bede 63
Dalton, Hugh 171–172
data analysis 3
Dauth, John 6
Davidson, Graeme 59
Davies, John 71
Dawson, Christopher 287
Deakin, Alfred 5, 35–36, 44, 59, 66, 123, 127, 233
  The Federal Story 130
decolonisation 11
defence of Australia 36, 107–112, 115–119, 154, 220, 222, 239, 245–250, 252, 253–256. *See also* cooperative system for defence; Asia-Pacific region: Australia's position within; Australian foreign policy
defence of British colonies 101, 105–108, 111, 113, 129–130
defence of Canada 112–114
defence of Great Britain 111. *See also* cooperative system for defence
Defence of the Realm Act 1914 (UK) 187
defence of the US 220
democracy 28, 131, 176, 248, 263, 269–270, 272, 302
Democratic Party (US) 276
Department of External Affairs (DEA) 7, 86, 89
Department of Foreign Affairs and Trade (DFAT) 5, 9
  Historical Publications and Information Section 4, 10–11
Department of Immigration 89
Dibbs, George 61, 107

Diefenbaker, John 202–203
Dilke, Charles 101
Disraeli, Benjamin 102
Dole, Robert 316
Dominican Republic 278
Dominion Day (NZ) 210
Downer, Alexander 245–246
Drakeford, Arthur 186
Duke University 25
Dulles, John Foster 290, 292
Dutton, David 10
Dutton, Geoffrey 232

E

Eastern Mission (1934) 161
East Timor 255
ecumenism 289
Eddy, Sherwood 285
Education Act 1902 (UK) 183
education, value of 111
Edwards, Bevan 108, 114
Edwards, P. G. (Peter) 10–11, 218, 224
Eggleston, Frederic 122, 140
Elie, Paul 282
Ellis, Bob 205
Elshtain, Jean Bethke 297
Ely, Richard T. 270–271
Empire Day (NZ) 208
empiricism 4
Endō, Masako 17
European Economic Community 220
evangelicalism 270
Evatt, H. V. 5, 45–46, 87–88, 121

F

Fairbanks, John 306, 313
Faith and Order movement 290
Fanning, Len 199
Faulkner, A. J. 209
Federal Advisory Committee on Eastern Trade 147–148
Federal Council of Australasia 33
federation of Australia 18, 107–108, 121–144
Fellowship for a Christian Social Order 285
Finn, Mary 124
First World War
  aftermath of 121, 181, 186–189, 293
  Australia's involvement 35–36, 38–39, 43, 124–125, 148, 170, 176, 179, 238
  conscription 41–42
  Great Britain–US relations 25
  Japan during 19–20
  pacifism 284
  peace negotiations 29, 140, 261
  US involvement 279, 285
Fisher, Andrew 38–39, 45, 124, 170
Fletcher, James 61
Foreign Affairs 312, 315–316
Forrest, John 115, 116
Fosdick, Harry Emerson 284
Foster, Leonie 140
Fourteen Points 42
Fousek, John 296
Francis, Noel 128
Franco-Prussian War 106
Fraser, Malcolm 50, 67
free trade 22, 176–182, 184
Frontier Thesis 273–274
Froude, James 101
Fry, T. P. 150
Fulbright, J. William 226, 308, 313
Fysh, Philip Oakley 77

G

Garran, Andrew 63, 73–74, 136
Garran, Mary 136
Garran, Robert Randolph
  as a proponent of federation 129–131
  career 51, 123–126
  family history 131–132
  historians' perspectives on the work of 126–129
  influences on 121–123
  publications 122, 126, 128, 131
de Gaulle, Charles 303–304, 307, 310–311, 313, 318–319
Gellner, Ernest 103, 294
general strike (UK, 1926) 182, 184–185, 187
Genovese, Eugene 319
Gepp, Herbert 147
Germany, Australia's relationship with 35, 40, 41–42, 124, 252
Germany's imperialistic ambitions 286, 296–297

Gerster, Robin 219
Giddens, Anthony 294
Gillies, Duncan 66–68, 76
Gilroy, Norman Thomas 185
Girouard, Marc 136
Glover, Denis 199
God Defend New Zealand 199
God Save the Queen 199, 204, 205–206, 232
Goldsworthy, David 196
von der Goltz, Colmar 106–107
Gooch, G. P. 286
Gordon, Charles 102
Gordon-Reed, Annette 143
Gorton, John 191, 198, 199, 227
Grant, Bruce 243–244, 248
Grattan, C. Hartley 181
Great Britain as a great power 177–178, 187, 240, 242
Great Britain, Australia's relationship with 9, 33–34, 36, 44, 48, 111–112, 115–119, 129–130, 137–143, 147–148, 153–156, 165, 169–189, 203–207, 219–220, 228–229, 230–236, 251. *See also* Australian culture and cultural identity: Australian Britishness; British Australianness
Great Britain, British colonies' relationship with 110
Great Britain, Canada's relationship with 114–115, 189, 200–203
Great Britain, China's relationship with 159
Great Britain, Germany's relationship with 179, 189
Great Britain, immigration to 179–180, 182
Great Britain, India's relationship with 105
Great Britain, Japan's relationship with 159
Great Britain, New Zealand's relationship with 208–213
Great Britain, Russia's relationship with 179
Great Depression 147, 288
Greater Britain 49, 102–103, 105, 109–110, 118, 212
Great Leap Forward 305
Great White Fleet 220, 232
Greenwood, Gordon 6
Griffith, Samuel Walker 76
Griffith University 8

Guam Doctrine 49, 228, 235, 312
Gullett, Henry 153–154, 155, 165

H

Haiti 278, 286
Hamilton, Alexander 263
Hancock, W. K. 138, 179, 181, 193
Harper, Norman 7, 239
Harries, Owen 243–244, 248
Harvester case (Australia, 1907) 176–177
Hasluck, Paul 8, 198
Hawker, Charles 157
Hayes, Carlton 286–287
Healey, Dennis 228
Henderson, Arthur 177
Heydon, Peter 82, 97
Heyes, Tasman 86
Higgins, Henry Bournes 176
Higgins, James 17
Hirst, John 194
Historians of Australian Foreign and Defence Policy (HAFDP) 13
historiography of Australian foreign policy 3–12, 126–129, 218, 237–240, 256, 266, 302–304
history wars 20
Hitler, Adolf 162, 296
Hodgson, W. R. 161
Holocaust 13
Holt, Harold 5, 89, 91, 217, 220, 226–227, 229, 233, 235
    visit to the US 218, 225
honours systems 174, 204, 232
Hope, A. D. 205
Horne, Donald 142, 191, 198, 219
Horner, David 128–129
Howard Doctrine 240
Howard, John 52, 237, 242, 245–247, 248, 250–251, 254–255
Howe, John 176
Howson, Peter 220, 235
Huber, Max 290, 292
Hudson, W. J. (Bill) 7–11
Hughes, W. M. (Billy) 5, 19, 38, 40–44, 124–125, 161, 246, 249
Hulsman, John 297
Hummel, Arthur W. 308

Hunt, Atlee 124
Hussein, Saddam 248, 254
Hutton, E. T. H.. *See also* cooperative system for defence
   Australian command 51, 115–119
   Canadian command 112–115
   cooperative system of defence. *See* cooperative system for defence
   Greater Britain, idea of 101–104
   influences on 104–107
   'Minute upon the Defence of Australia' 116
   New South Wales command 107–110
   Primrose Day speech 101, 104

I

idealism 265, 275
identity crisis in Australia. *See* Australian national identity: identity crisis
identity crisis in Japan 20
idioms 171
Igartua, Jose 196
imagined communities 103, 200, 262–263, 286
Immigration Restriction Act 1901 86, 134
Imperial Conference (1923) 125, 138
Imperial Conference (1926) 139, 142
Imperial Conference (1930) 125, 138
Imperial Conference (1937) 159, 161
Imperial Defence Conference (1909) 37
Imperial Federation League 101, 105
India, Australia's relationship with 81
India becoming a republic 143
Indigenous Australians, treatment of 20, 134–135
indigenous New Zealanders, treatment of 208–209
Indonesian imperialist ambitions 244
Influx of Chinese Restriction Act 1881 60
Inglis Moore, Tom 122
Innis, Harold 201, 203
Institute of Pacific Relations 151
International Court of Justice 22
International Herald Tribune 312
internationalism 262, 284
International Research Center for Japanese Studies 15
Iraq War (2003–2011) 31, 52–53, 237–238, 240, 243, 248, 250–251, 253–255, 282

Ireland, population of 169
Irish community in Australia 38
Irish Free State, creation of the 180, 182
Irish Republic, creation of the 180
Irving, Helen 127

J

Japan–Australia Society 153
Japan, Australia's relationship with 15–22, 125, 145–165, 252
   Acquisition and Cross Servicing Agreement 22
   Australia–Japan Agreement on Commerce 16
   Basic Treaty of Friendship and Co-operation 16
Japanese imperialistic ambitions 18, 36, 39–41, 43–44, 46–47, 145–146, 153–156, 159–165
   militarism 304
Japanese language 19, 157
Japanese ultranationalism 15
Jebb, Richard 140
Jefferson Memorial 133
Jefferson, Thomas 133–134, 141–142, 299
Johns Hopkins University 270–271
Johnson, Lyndon B. 52, 302
   first visit to Australia 222
   presidential visit to Australia 217–235
   presidential visit to New Zealand 230
   State of the Union address 314
   White Sulphur Springs speech 234
Johnston, Charles 229, 232
Jones, Noreen 17
Jordan, Matthew 6, 10
Judd, Walter 317
Judt, Tony 238

K

Kai-shek, Chiang 305
Kant, Immanuel 288
Keep America Out of War Committee 295
Kelly, Paul 238, 245, 246–249, 252
Kelton, Maryanne 251–252
Kennan, George 281, 297
Kennedy, John F. 221, 319
Kennedy, Paul 30

Index

Kerr, Phillip 292
Keynes, John Maynard 132–133, 181, 187
Khan, Muhammad Ayub 303–304, 307, 310, 313
Khare, N. B. 83
Khrushchev, Nikita 307
King George III 141
Kingston, Beverley 175
Kingston, Charles Cameron 66
Kirk, Neville 173, 175, 186
Kirk, Norman 199, 209–210
Kissinger, Henry 318–320
Kleinman, Mark 296
Knowland, William 237
Kohn, Hans 102
Kōki Hirota 161
Konoe, Fumimaro 162
Korean War 239, 245, 256
Kristensen, Jeppe 233

L

Labour Party (UK) 182, 183
LaFeber, Walter 296
Lake, Marilyn 179
Lang, J. T. 184
Latham, J. G. 139, 148, 153, 161
Laurier, Wilfred 103, 114–115
League of Nations 9, 19, 25, 29–30, 42, 125, 161, 264, 284, 291–292, 293
Lee, David 8, 10
Lee Kuan Yew 309, 311
Liberal–Country Party coalition 217
Liberal Party of Australia 218
Liberal Party (UK) 187
liberty 269
Lieven, Anatol 282, 297
Life 296
Life and Work movement 290–292
Lincoln, Abraham 31, 304
Lindsay, A. D. 286
Link, Arthur S. 261, 265
Lippmann, Walter 303, 319
Lloyd, Longfield 148, 156–157
Loeb, William 317
Lost Decades (Japan) 15
Louis, William Roger 161
Lovitt, William 17

Loyalists 135–137
Lucas, Rachael 21
Luce, Henry 304
Lutheranism 291, 293
Lyons, Joseph 145, 150, 153–154, 155, 159–161, 162, 165, 181
   The Truth About the Japanese Trade Position 154

M

Macarthur, James 137
MacDonald, Malcolm 162–163
MacDonald, Ramsay 183
Macintosh, John 73–74
Macintyre, Stuart 219
Mackay, Iven 85
MacKellar, Michael 206
Macmahon Ball, W. 88, 89
Macpherson, Harry 226
Macrossan, James Murtagh 66
Madison, James 263
Magna Carta 132
Mahon, Hugh 183
Malan, D. F. 95
manga 20
Manila Security Conference 217–218, 233
Manne, Robert 245, 252–253
Manning, William 63, 73–74
Mannix, Daniel 41, 182, 185
Mann, James 308
Mansfield, Mike 303
Maori Women's Welfare League 210
Mao Zedong 306–307, 313
Markus, Andrew 58
Marshall, John 133
Marshall Plan 296
Martens, Jeremy 58
Marxism 288, 297
Matheson, John 200, 203
Mathews, John 252–253
May, Henry 209, 211
McAuley, James 205
McBride, Phillip 93
McCarthy, Joe 301
McCormick, Peter Dodd 207
McGovern, George 314
McIntire, Carl 317

336

McKell, William 174
McKinley, William 277, 288
McLean, David 6, 219, 232
McNamara, Robert 225
McQueen, Humphrey 220
Meale, Richard 205
Meaney, Neville
  Australia and the World 52
  Australia and World Crisis 38
  Australia's foreign policy, research on 5, 8, 11, 20–23
  Fears and Phobias 18
  Great Britain–Australia relations 140–142
  Historians of Australian Foreign and Defence Policy (HAFDP) 13–14
  Japan–Australia relations 16
  on Australian identity 136, 137
  on Britishness 43–53, 101, 169–170, 193–194
  on multiculturalism 82
  on the American national myth 262
  teaching 20–23, 25–41, 121–122
  Towards a New Vision first edition 16, 20
  Towards a New Vision second edition 16, 19, 21
Melbourne, A. C. V. 51, 145–165
Melville, Ninian 61
memory 254, 256
Menzies, R. G.
  British race patriotism 44, 172, 198, 253
  Great Britain–Australia relations 9, 159, 170, 174, 242
  India–Australia relations 81, 88, 91, 95–96
  Second World War 161, 170, 172
  US–Australia relations 4–5, 47–48, 238–239, 242, 244, 246, 249–251
Métin, Albert 176
von Metternich, Klemens 319
Mexico 278
Millar, T. B. 8, 239
Miller, Francis Pickens 287
Miller, J. D. B. 8
Minogue, Kylie 171
Mitchell Library 17
modernisation of Australia (1870s–1880s) 73, 102
Monroe Doctrine 28, 33, 233, 273
Moodie, Colin 86, 89–90

moralism 296
Morgenthau, Hans J. 281, 297, 306, 313
Mosley, Oswald 181
Muldoon, Robert 212
multiculturalism 20, 50, 209
Murai Kuramatsu 154–157
Murdoch, James 19

N

Nash, Walter 208
Nathan, Matthew 108
national anthems 195, 199–200, 203
National Australasian Convention (1891) 129
nationalism 74, 102–103, 194, 237, 251, 262–263, 303. *See also* radical nationalism; Australian nationalism; colonial nationalism; new nationalism; US nationalism
National Library of Australia 18, 130
National Review 316
Nazism 44, 162, 304
  struggle with the Church 284
  Volkskirche 292
Nazi–Soviet Pact 163
Neale, R. G. 9
Nehru, Jawaharlal 81, 87, 96–97
New Deal centrism 299
New Guinea 33
new nationalism
  definition of 191–192
  in Australia 51, 191, 197–199, 203–207, 227
  in British colonies 192–196
  in Canada 191, 192, 196–197, 200–203
  in New Zealand 191, 198–199, 208–213
  symbols of nationhood 200–213
Newsweek 312
Newton, A. P. 146
New York Times 314
New Zealand Day 195, 199, 208–213
New Zealand Labour Party 209, 210
New Zealand national anthem 199
New Zealand national identity 194, 196, 198–199, 208–213, 213
Nicaragua 278, 286
Nicolaidi, Mike 199
Nicolson, Harold 181

Index

Niebuhrian Christian realism 296
Niebuhr, Reinhold 52, 281–299
 An Interpretation of Christian Ethics 291
 'Democracy as a Religion' 297
 Does Civilization Need Religion? 287
 Do the State and Nation Belong to God or the Devil? 294
 The Irony of American History 281–282, 289, 298
 Moral Man and Immoral Society 288–289, 291, 293, 295, 297, 298
 The Nature and Destiny of Man 291, 295
Nine-Power Treaty 162–163
Nixon Doctrine. *See* Guam Doctrine
Nixon, Richard M. 49, 52, 232, 301–320
 visits to Taiwan 301, 307–308
 visit to China 301, 321
 visit to Hong Kong 302
North Korea, threats by 22, 255
nuclear war, fear of 309, 321
 disarmament 311
nuclear weapons capability of Australia 48
Nuremberg war crimes trials 133

O

Obama, Barack 31, 282
O'Connor, Dick 63
O'Donoghue, Lowitja (Lois) 134–135
Officer, Keith 161
O'Keefe, Annie 87, 89
Oldham, J. H. 287, 292–293
Olney, Richard 28
Olympics 172
Ommanney, Montagu 112
oral history 3
oriental studies 19
Ottawa Agreement 148, 150
Oxford University 290

P

Pacific pact 159
Pacific War 15, 158, 160, 222
pacifism 284, 288, 299
Page, Kirby 285, 295
Paine, Thomas 142
Pakistan, India's relationship with 307
Paranjpye, Raghunath 83, 84, 95

Paris Peace Conference (1919) 9, 19, 125, 261
Parkes, Henry 34, 48, 57, 60–62, 65–66, 69, 70, 75–76, 78, 129, 137–138, 143
 Tenterfield Address 129
Parkin, George 113
Parliament Act 1911 (UK) 173
Parliamentary War Committee 40
patriotism 27, 105–106, 192–194, 198
Paul, Erik 241, 242, 250
Pax Americana 302, 318
Paxman, Jeremy 213
peace 290, 310, 314
Pearce, George 19
Pearson, C. H. 59
Pearson, Lester B. 191, 200–204
Pemberton, Greg 220
People's Federal Convention (1896) 130
Philippines 275, 288
pictorial histories 16–19, 21
Piesse, E. L. 18–19, 43–45, 121–122
The Pilgrims 274
Plantagenet dynasty 131
Playford, Thomas 65
Pocahontas 134, 135
poll tax 60, 63, 66–68
popular music 170–171
Porritt, Arthur 191
postcolonial studies 15
postmodernism 3
post-nationalism 261
Potter, David 32
Poynter, John R. 14
Presbyterianism 265, 267
president, function of the US 224
Price, Charles 59
protectionism 114, 176–182
Protestantism 182, 263, 266–267, 271, 274, 277, 284, 286–287, 293, 296
Psihoyos, Louie 22
Puerto Rico 275
Pye, Lucian 315

Q

QEII Council for the Arts (New Zealand) 195, 199
Quebec separatism 196, 201

338

Queen Elizabeth II's visit to Australia 48, 142, 229
Queensland Advisory Committee on Eastern Trade 147
Queen Victoria 102
Quick, John 122, 130–131, 143
Quong Tart 70

R

racial supremacism and racial discrimination 58–61, 65, 71–73, 77–78, 82, 85–87, 91, 134–135, 150, 179–180, 272–273, 278–279
radical nationalism 49
Ramsey, Alan 222, 229
Randolph, Edmund 132
Randolph, John 133–134
Rata, Matiu 209
Ratnam, Perelal 93
Ravenhill, John 7
Reagan, Ronald 232, 316, 319
realism 282–283, 295–297
Realpolitik 318, 319
Reconstruction 268
reconstruction after the First World War 187–188
Reformation 286, 291
Reid, George 103–104, 127
Renouf, Alan 121–122
republicanism 262
responsible government 131
Returned Services League (RSL) 187
Reus-Smit, Chris 251
Reynolds, Henry 179
Richardson, James L. 249
Rickard, John 193
Robson, Hilda 134
Roosevelt, Franklin D. 133, 296
Roosevelt, Theodore 220, 232, 278
Ross, Ian Clunies 151, 157
Rostow, Walt 218
Royal Colonial Institute 101
Royal Institute of International Affairs (Chatham House) 6, 140, 163
Royal Style and Titles Act 1973 142
royal visits to Australia 232. *See also* Queen Elizabeth II's visit to Australia
Ruhr 285
Rusher, William 317
Rusk, Dean 225, 311
Russell, Bourn 17
Russo-Japanese War 20, 35, 43
Russo, Peter 149
Ryan, Claude 191
Ryan, T. J. 41
Ryonosuke, Seita 149

S

Sakatani, Baron 153, 154
Santamaria, B. A. 185
Sarajevo 273
Sawer, Geoffrey 125
Scott, Andrew 175
Scott, Walter 136–137
Sculthorpe, Peter 205
Second World War
    aftermath of 51, 175, 243, 296, 304–305
    Australia during 186
    Australia's involvement 12, 241
    Britishness 196
    coming of 4, 44–46
    communism 184
    creation of the United Nations 292
    Great Britain–Australia relations 35, 141, 170–171
    US–Australia relations 170–171, 233, 255
    US involvement 30, 220, 222–223
sectarianism in Australia 182–183, 186
sectarianism in Britain 182–183
Seeley, John 101–102, 104–105, 109–111, 118
September 11 240, 246–248, 282
Serle, Geoffrey 228
sex slavery 22
Shai, Aron 164
Shedden, Frederick 128
Sheridan, Greg 245, 247–250, 252
Sinclair, Keith 193
Sino-Japanese War 151, 159–160
Sino–Soviet split 302–303, 307, 311, 317, 320
Sissons, David 18
sister-city relationships 18
Skidelsky, Robert 132–133
slavery 268–269
soccer 172

339

Index

Social Christianity 270
social Darwinism 59, 71–73
social democracy 170
Social Gospel 270, 274–275, 283–289, 291, 293, 299
socialism 271, 288, 299
social reform 290
Society of Friends 285
Söderblom, Nathan 290
South-East Asian conflicts (1950s, 1960s) 10
South-East Asia Treaty Organisation (SEATO) 221, 225
South Manchuria Railway Company 151
Soviet Union's imperialistic ambitions 297, 310
space exploration 301
Spanish–American War 277
Spanish Civil War 182
Spender, Percy 7, 47, 249
sporting rivalries 172–173
Stanhope, Edward 107
Stanner, W. E. H. 135
Starr, Michael 202
state aid to Catholic education 183
Statute of Westminster (1931) 4, 140, 142
Stewart, Frederick 151
Stuart, Francis 89
Sudan War (1885) 34
Suez Crisis 9, 48, 196, 201
suffrage 269
Sullivan, Roger 308–309
Sutch, W. B. 199
Switzerland 272

T

Taft, William Howard 278
Taiwan 301, 305
Tange, Arthur 11
Taylor, A. J. P. 13
terrorist threats 240, 243, 245, 248–249, 253, 255, 282, 297
theology 281
Thorpe, Ian 21
Thurbon, Elizabeth 252–253
Thurmond, Strom 317
Tillett, Ben 177
Time 312

de Toqueville, Alexis 280
total war 106–107
tourism 15
Tower, John 317
trade, Australian 21, 82, 85, 105–106, 145, 165, 176–182, 247
  within Asia 147–151
  with Japan 48, 150–159
trade, Canadian 114
trade tariffs 148–149, 176–182
trade unions 177–178, 184–186, 238
trade, US 301–302, 305, 314
Treaty of Versailles 42, 285
Treaty of Waitangi 208
Truman Doctrine 306, 320
Truman, Harry S. 296–297, 305, 316, 319
Tucker, Nancy 308
Tulloch, Alexander 108
Turner, Frederick Jackson 273–274
Turner, Harry 207

U

ultranationalism 262
unemployment 181
Union Leader 317
Union Theological Seminary 281
United Nations 5–6, 22, 30, 47, 90, 240, 243, 292, 301–302, 306–307, 313
  admission of China to 309
  Educational Scientific and Cultural Organization 281
  Security Council 305
universal suffrage 176
University of Adelaide 25
University of Göttingen 263
University of Melbourne 7
University of Newcastle 8
University of New South Wales 8, 25
University of Queensland 146–147, 149, 151–152
University of Sydney 5, 18, 19, 25, 131, 157
University of Tokyo 152
US as a great power 28, 46, 228, 239–240, 242, 250, 261, 279, 295, 302
US as a hyperpower 252
US, Australia's relationship with 9, 12, 45–46, 52, 132, 146, 151, 170, 237–256

Bush–Howard years 240–241, 244, 247–248, 251–252, 254–256
Johnson–Holt years 217–235
US, Canada's relationship with 114, 201
US, China's relationship with 52, 234, 235, 239, 301–320
US recognition of China 306
US Civil War 268
US culture 31
US Declaration of Independence 28, 141, 263, 268
US foreign policies 25–32
under Woodrow Wilson 261–279
US, Germany's relationship with 263
US, Great Britain's relationship with 26–28, 105, 159, 171, 189, 217, 269, 271–272, 274–277, 287
US history 25–26
US imperialistic ambitions 261, 279–280, 295, 299
US interventionism 296. *See also* US perceived superiority
US military spending 261
US nationalism 26, 52, 261–279, 277
decline of 301–320
during the Second World War and early Cold War 295–298
Niebur's critique of 283–294
US national myth 25–27, 29–31
US, New Zealand's relationship with 226
US parliamentary form 132
US perceived superiority 298–299, 302, 304, 312
US, Taiwan's relationship with 307–308, 311

V

Vietnam War
anti-war demonstrations 223–224
Australia's involvement 4, 49, 217–218, 228–229, 237, 256
US–Australia relations 224–225, 231–232, 234–235, 240, 243, 251, 253
US defeat 20, 30, 82, 320
US involvement 219, 302, 309–310, 312–313, 314–318

W

wage determination 176, 179
Waitangi Day 208–211
Walker, David 147, 210
Walker, Kath 205
Wallace, Henry 296
Wall Street Journal 314
Waltzing Matilda 207
Want, John 71
Ward, Stuart 6, 126, 135, 235
war guilt clause 285
War Precautions Act 1914 124, 187
Waseda University 15
Washington, George 27, 133, 263
Washington Treaties 159
Watt, Alan 7, 8
Watt, William 43
Way, Wendy 10
weapons of mass destruction (WMDs) 248
Webb, Beatrice 177
Webb, Sidney 177
Weiss, Linda 252–253
Werder, Felix 205
Wesley, Michael 242, 245, 246, 249, 252
Whalen, Richard 320
whaling 22
White Australia policy 4, 15, 35, 44, 51, 59, 81–98, 134, 149–150, 179, 180
Whitlam, Gough 142, 175, 203, 206–207, 212, 227, 232
Wight, Martin 290
Willard, Myra 59, 134
Williams, E. E. 177
Williamson, David 204–205
Wilson, Harold 229, 233
Wilsonianism 261–279
Wilson, Joseph Ruggles 266–268
Wilson, Woodrow 28, 42, 52, 261–279, 285, 304
background 266–271
'The Ideals of America' 275–276
Windschuttle, Keith 58
Wolseley, Garnet 101, 106–107, 112, 118
working classes
perceived threats to the 69, 75, 83
political activism of the 177–178

World Conference on Church, Community and State (1937) 291–295
World Council of Churches 289
The World Tomorrow 285–287, 295
World War I. *See* First World War
World War II. *See* Second World War
Wright, Judith 205

Y

Yale Divinity School 281
Yasukuni Shrine 20
Yellow Peril 37
Young Men's Christian Association (YMCA) 285
Young Women's Christian Association (YWCA) 285

Z

Zimmern, Alfred 286, 290, 292
Zines, Leslie 127, 128

www.ingramcontent.com/pod-product-compliance
Lightning Source LLC
Chambersburg PA
CBHW081202170426
43197CB00018B/2898